Lecture Notes of the Institute for Computer Sciences, Social Informatics and Telecommunications Engineering 302

More information about this series at http://www.springer.com/series/8197

Guan Gui · Lin Yun (Eds.)

Advanced Hybrid Information Processing

Third EAI International Conference, ADHIP 2019
Nanjing, China, September 21–22, 2019
Proceedings, Part II

 Springer

Editors
Guan Gui 🆔
Nanjing University
Nanjing, China

Lin Yun
Harbin Engineering University
Harbin, China

ISSN 1867-8211   ISSN 1867-822X (electronic)
Lecture Notes of the Institute for Computer Sciences, Social Informatics
and Telecommunications Engineering
ISBN 978-3-030-36404-5   ISBN 978-3-030-36405-2   (eBook)
https://doi.org/10.1007/978-3-030-36405-2

This Springer imprint is published by the registered company Springer Nature Switzerland AG
The registered company address is: Gewerbestrasse 11, 6330 Cham, Switzerland

Preface

We are delighted to introduce the proceedings of the Third European Alliance for Innovation (EAI) International Conference on Advanced Hybrid Information Processing (ADHIP 2019). This conference has brought together researchers, developers, and practitioners from around the world who are leveraging and developing information processing technology for a deeper and wider use of hybrid information.

The technical program of ADHIP 2019 consisted of 104 full papers in oral presentation sessions at the main conference tracks. The conference topics were: Topic 1 – Big Data Processing; Topic 2 – Real Applications of Aspects with Big Data; and Topic 3 – Huge Signal Data Processing.

Coordination with the Steering Committee members, Imrich Chlamtac, Yun Lin, Shuai Liu, and Guanglu Sun, was essential for the success of the conference. We sincerely appreciate their constant support and guidance. It was also a great pleasure to work with such an excellent Organizing Committee team, and we thank them for their hard work in organizing and supporting the conference. In particular we thank the Technical Program Committee (TPC), led by our TPC co-chairs, Prof. Shuai Liu, Prof. Zhen Yang, Prof. Liang Zhou, Prof. Fumiyuki Adachi, Prof. Hikmet Sari, and Prof. Xiaodong Xiong, who completed the peer-review process of technical papers and made a high-quality technical program. We are also grateful to conference managers and all the authors who submitted their papers to the ADHIP 2019 conference and workshop.

We strongly believe that the ADHIP 2019 conference provides a good forum for all researcher, developers, and practitioners to discuss all science and technology aspects that are relevant to hybrid information processing. We also expect that the future ADHIP conferences will be as successful and stimulating, as indicated by the contributions presented in this volume.

September 2019

Miao Liu
Jinlong Sun
Wei Zhao

Organization

Steering Committee

Imrich Chlamtac   Bruno Kessler Professor, University of Trento, Italy
Yun Lin   Harbin Engineering University, China
Shuai Liu   Inner Mongolia University, China
Guanglu Sun   Harbin Engineering University, China

Organizing Committee

General Chairs

Shuai Liu   Inner Mongolia University, China
Zhen Yang   Nanjing University of Posts and Telecommunications, China

General Co-chairs

Liang Zhou   Nanjing University of Posts and Telecommunications, China
Fumiyuki Adachi   Tohoku University, Japan
Hikmet Sari   Nanjing University of Posts and Telecommunications, China
Xiaodong Xiong   Yangtze University, China

TPC Chair and Co-chairs

Zhiping Lin   Nanyang Technological University, Singapore
Tomohiko Taniguchi   Fujitsu Laboratories Limited, Japan
Qun Wan   University of Electronic Science and Technology of China, China
Mingwu Zhang   Hubei University of Technology, China
Yun Lin   Harbin Engineering University, China
Li Xu   Akita Prefectural University, Japan
Guangjie Han   Hohai University, China
Bo Gu   Kogakuin University, Japan
Guan Gui   Nanjing University of Posts and Telecommunications, China

Sponsorship and Exhibit on Chairs

Local Chairs

Ying Lu	Nanjing Sari Intelligent Technology Co., Ltd, China
Shujie Lu	NARI Group Corporations/State Grid Electric Power Research Institute, China

Workshops Chairs

Xin Liu	Dalian University of Technology, China
Xi Shao	Nanjing University of Posts and Telecommunications, China
Xingguo Zhang	Tokyo University of Agriculture and Technology, Japan
Wenmei Li	Nanjing University of Posts and Telecommunications, China
Zhiyi Lu	Nanjing Sari Intelligent Technology Co., Ltd, China

Publicity and Social Media Chairs

Lei Chen	Georgia Southern University, USA
Sheng Zhou	Tsinghua University, China
Yue Cao	Northumbria University, UK
Lin Bai	Beihang University, China
Haibo Zhou	Nanjing University, China
Xianpeng Wang	Hainan University, China
Shuai Han	Harbin Institute of Technology, China
Ying Cui	Shanghai Jiaotong University, China
Wei Peng	Huazhong University of Science and Technology, China
Zheng Wang	Nanjing University of Aeronautics and Astronautics, China
Yimu Ji	Nanjing University of Posts and Telecommunications, China
Yongjun Xu	Chongqing University of Posts and Telecommunications, China
Yingsong Li	Harbin Engineering University, China
Tingting Yang	Dalian Maritime University, China
Yu Gu	Hefei University of Technology, China
Xiao Zheng	Anhui University of Technology, China
Yuan Wu	Zhejiang University of Technology, China
Jumin Zhao	Taiyuan University of Technology, China

Publications Chairs

Miao Liu	Nanjing University of Posts and Telecommunications, China
Jinlong Sun	Nanjing University of Posts and Telecommunications, China
Wei Zhao	Anhui University of Technology, China

Web Chairs

Jian Xiong	Nanjing University of Posts and Telecommunications, China
Hao Jiang	Southeast University, China
Jie Yang	Nanjing University of Posts and Telecommunications, China

Posters and PhD Track Chairs

Panels Chairs

Guohua Zhang	BOCO Intel-Telecom Co., Ltd, China
Yunjian Jia	Chongqing University, China
Lin Shan	National Institute of Information and Communications Technology, Japan
Wang Luo	NARI Group Corporations/State Grid Electric Power Research Institute, China
Zhaoyue Zhang	Civil Aviation University of China, China

Demos Chairs

Tutorials Chairs

Nan Zhao	Dalian University of Technology, China
Guoyue Chen	Akita Prefectural University, Japan
Wei Xu	South University, China
Xuangou Wu	Anhui University of Technology, China

Technical Program Committee

Fang-Qing Wen	Yangtze University, China
Zheng Wang	Nanjing University of Aeronautics and Astronautics, China
Jinlong Sun	Nanjing University of Posts and Telecommunications, China
Wenmei Li	Nanjing University of Posts and Telecommunications, China
Miao Liu	Nanjing University of Posts and Telecommunications, China
Yue Cao	Northumbria University, UK
Yun Lin	Harbin Engineering University, China

Contents – Part II

Contents – Part I

Research on the Large Data Intelligent Classification Method for Long-Term Health Monitoring of Bridge

Xiaojiang Hong[✉] and Mingdong Yu

Department of Civil and Hydraulic Engineering Institute, Xichang University, Xichang, China
xcxyymd@163.com

Abstract. In order to improve the intelligent management and information scheduling ability of bridge long-term health monitoring, the real-time data monitoring and automatic collection design of bridge long-term health monitoring are carried out with big data analysis method. A classification method of bridge long-term health monitoring data based on fuzzy correlation feature detection and grid area clustering is proposed. The information fusion and fuzzy chromatography analysis method are used to realize the information fusion of the real-time data of bridge long-term health monitoring, and the adaptive feature extraction of related data is carried out. Excavate the positive correlation characteristic quantity of bridge long-term health monitoring real-time monitoring data flow, carry on the fuzzy clustering and information prediction of bridge long-term health monitoring data flow, and improve the accuracy of bridge long-term health monitoring real-time data monitoring. The simulation results show that the intelligent classification of bridge long-term health monitoring based on this method has high accuracy and low error rate, which improves the real-time performance of bridge monitoring.

Keywords: Bridge · Long-term health monitoring · Big data classification

1 Introduction

With the development of big data's information processing technology, artificial intelligent information management technology is used to carry out bridge long-term health monitoring information management, and pattern recognition technology is used to carry out bridge health monitoring functional information monitoring. Improve the initiative of bridge health monitoring, study the information management technology of bridge long-term health monitoring, construct the bridge long-term health monitoring under the information construction environment, and improve the bridge health quality [1]. The intelligent information construction of bridge long-term health monitoring is based on the automatic monitoring of bridge long-term health monitoring data stream, and the automatic real-time data flow monitoring design is carried out by using artificial intelligence scheduling technology in all kinds of bridge long-term health monitoring. To improve the operation efficiency of bridge long-term health monitoring, the real-time data flow monitoring of bridge long-term health monitoring has attracted great attention [2].

G. Gui and L. Yun (Eds.): ADHIP 2019, LNICST 302, pp. 1–10, 2019.
https://doi.org/10.1007/978-3-030-36405-2_1

At present, the research on intelligent real-time data flow monitoring and scheduling method for bridge long-term health monitoring mainly adopts traffic statistics method, and the main data mining methods are fuzzy mining method. C-means mining method and dynamic ARMA model mining method [3]. The information flow of intelligent real-time data flow monitoring for bridge long-term health monitoring is used for balanced scheduling and global equilibrium design. Improve the real-time data flow monitoring ability of bridge health monitoring center. In reference [4], an intelligent real-time data flow monitoring and equilibrium control method for bridge long-term health monitoring based on artificial intelligence control technology is proposed. The intelligent real-time data flow monitoring information transmission model of bridge long-term health monitoring is constructed by using fuzzy constraint control method, and the intelligent real-time data flow monitoring and classification scheduling of bridge long-term health monitoring is carried out by using Gaussian aggregation classification method. It has good data recall performance, but the online scheduling ability of this method in bridge long-term health monitoring real-time data monitoring is not good [5].

In view of the above problems, a long-term health monitoring data classification method based on fuzzy correlation feature detection and mesh region clustering is presented in this paper. establishing a grid distribution structure model of long-term health monitoring of the bridge and carrying out long-term health monitoring data flow monitoring statistical analysis of the bridge, and realizing the information fusion by adopting the information fusion and the fuzzy chromatography analysis method on the long-term health monitoring real-time data of the bridge, And the positive correlation characteristic quantity of the information flow of the real-time monitoring data of the long-term health monitoring of the bridge is excavated. Based on the hierarchical clustering algorithm, the fuzzy clustering and information prediction of long-term health monitoring data flow of the bridge are carried out by self-regression analysis, and finally, the simulation experiment analysis is carried out, and the superiority of the method in improving the automatic monitoring capability of the long-term health monitoring data flow of the bridge is shown.

2 Real-Time Data Flow Monitoring Information Flow Model and Preprocessing for Long-Term Health Monitoring of Bridges

2.1 Bridge Long-Term Health Monitoring Real-Time Data Flow Monitoring Information Flow Model

In order to realize real-time data monitoring and balanced management control for long-term health monitoring of bridges, fuzzy correlation feature detection and analytic hierarchy process (AHP) are used for data monitoring. Firstly, the grid distribution structure model of bridge long-term health monitoring is established and the statistical characteristics of bridge long-term health monitoring data flow monitoring are analyzed. In the distributed structure model of bridge long-term health monitoring real-time monitoring data, if directed graph $G_1 = \left(M_1^\alpha, M_1^\beta, Y_1 \right)$, $G_2 = \left(M_2^\alpha, M_2^\beta, Y_2 \right)$ are used as the candidate set of bridge long-term health monitoring real-time monitoring data, then $G_1 \subseteq G_2 \Leftrightarrow Y_1 \subseteq Y_2$, so that $A = \{a_1, a_2, \ldots a_n\}$ can generate candidate set for the model of bridge long-term health monitoring real-time monitoring data acquisition model, and the edge $(u, v) \in E$, of directed graph of bridge long-term health monitoring real-time monitoring data distribution [6]. Under the information management environment, the statistical feature analysis model of bridge long-term health monitoring real-time monitoring is constructed, which is represented by five-tuple $O = (C, I, P, Hc, R, A^0)$, in which C is the utility threshold item set of real-time monitoring data sampling time series of bridge long-term health monitoring. S is an example set of data flow, so the efficient item set for bridge long-term health monitoring is:

$$x(t) = \sum_{i=0}^{p} a(\theta_i) s_i(t) + n(t) \tag{1}$$

Wherein, p is the number of the minimum utility threshold, the $n(t)$ is the output characteristic item which is directly mined, the $s_i(t)$ is the data fuzzy clustering measure value of the relative utility threshold value, and the $a(\theta_i)$ is the long-term health monitoring real-time monitoring data for each transaction set, The data update rules for long-term health monitoring of the bridge are as follows:

$$R_s^{(0)} = \sum_{n=0}^{k} \left\langle R_s^{(n)}, d_{\gamma n} \right\rangle d_{\gamma n} + R_s^{(k+1)} \tag{2}$$

Where, $R_s^{(n)}$ represents the structural scale characteristics of bridge long-term health monitoring real-time monitoring data, $d_{\gamma n}$ is the variation operation of bridge long-term health monitoring real-time monitoring data, and $R_s^{(k+1)}$ is the joint distribution coefficient of internal utility and external utility. According to the above analysis, the grid distribution structure model of bridge long-term health monitoring is constructed, and the minimum relative utility threshold analysis method and analytic hierarchy process (AHP) are used for data information fusion and adaptive feature extraction preprocessing [7].

2.2 Analysis of Real-Time Data Attribute Set for Long-Term Health Monitoring of Bridges

The long-term health monitoring real-time data of the bridge is fused with the information fusion and the association mining method information, a grid distribution structure model of the long-term health monitoring of the bridge is established, and the statistical characteristics of the long-term health monitoring data flow of the bridge are carried out, the vector quantization characteristic decomposition of the real-time data attribute set of long-term health monitoring of the bridge is carried out, the relevant data self-adaptive feature extraction is realized, the utility information is divided into the internal utility and the external utility in the long-term health monitoring real-time data clustering space of the bridge, and the main frequency characteristic quantity is obtained as follows:

$$X_p(u) = s_c(t)e^{j2\pi f_0 t} = \frac{1}{\sqrt{T}} rect(\frac{t}{T})e^{j2\pi(f_0 t + Kt^2)/2} \tag{3}$$

Where, $s_c(t)$ represents the feature attribute, $e^{j2\pi f_0 t}$ represents the structural similarity measure of the finite data set, f_0 is the main frequency of the feature, and T represents the time delay of the global feature extraction. After extracting the global time feature, the finite dataset is obtained:

$$X = \{x_1, x_2, \cdots, x_n\} \subset R^s \tag{4}$$

Wherein, the real-time data set of bridge long-term health monitoring contains n samples, sample x_i, $i = 1, 2, \cdots, n$. The relationship between other related parameters extracted from real-time information is expressed as follows:

$$h(t) = \sum_i a_i(t)e^{j\theta_i(t)}\delta(t - iT_S) \tag{5}$$

Through the mining of association rules by the upper bound of itemset utility, the fuzzy index set of real-time data of bridge long-term health monitoring is obtained by using the basis function d_{γ_0} for feature transformation and template matching.

$$\Lambda_0 = \left\{ \beta \in \Gamma : |\langle f, d_{\gamma_0}\rangle| \geq a.\sup_{\gamma \in \Gamma}|\langle f, d_\gamma\rangle| \right\} \tag{6}$$

The fuzzy hierarchical matching of bridge long-term health monitoring real-time data transmission is used for adaptive optimization, and the decentralized subspace method is used to obtain the statistical characteristic information flow of bridge long-term health monitoring real-time data:

$$X = F_\alpha \cdot x \tag{7}$$

The N subspace is searched, and the data clustering results of N subspace mining are fuzzy predictive control, and the output subsequence is obtained as:

$$X = [X_\alpha(0), X_\alpha(1), \cdots, X_\alpha(N-1)]^T \tag{8}$$

With the above feature extraction and processing of associated data, big data fusion of real-time data flow monitoring sequence is carried out by cloud computing, which reduces the overhead of data prediction and improves the accuracy of data monitoring and fuzzy clustering [8].

3 Automatic Detection and Optimization of Data Flow

3.1 Feature Extraction and Grid Region Clustering

On the basis of the above-mentioned grid distribution structure model for establishing the long-term health monitoring of the bridge and carrying out long-term health monitoring data flow monitoring statistical analysis of the bridge, an automatic monitoring and optimization design of the long-term health monitoring data flow of the bridge is carried out [9], a long-term health monitoring data classification method based on fuzzy correlation feature detection and mesh region clustering is presented in this paper. when the type of the interference vector r_j in the long-term health monitoring intelligent real-time data flow monitoring system of the bridge is H, the maximum independent set $P(n_i) = \{p_k | pr_{kj} = 1, k = 1, 2, \cdots, m\}$ exists for all the node sets, the fuzzy correlation characteristic detection and the grid region clustering design are carried out, and the fuzzy membership function of the extracted data is as follows:

$$P_F = \sum_{j=k}^{N} \sum_{\sum u_i = j} \prod_{i=1}^{N} (P_{fi})^{u_i} (1 - P_{fi})^{1-u_i} \tag{9}$$

$$P_D = \sum_{j=k}^{N} \sum_{\sum u_i = j} \prod_{i=1}^{N} (P_{di})^{u_i} (1 - P_{di})^{1-u_i} \tag{10}$$

Wherein, P_{fi} represents the clustering center of bridge long-term health monitoring real-time data fusion. P_{di} is the sampling frequency of bridge long-term health monitoring real-time data. The average value of positive correlation characteristic components of bridge long-term health monitoring real-time data is obtained as:

$$\bar{x} = \frac{1}{N} \sum_{i=1}^{N} |x_i| \tag{11}$$

The real-time data matching detection of bridge long-term health monitoring is carried out in the decentralized subspace, and the variance of the relevant statistical features of the data monitoring output in the subspace is obtained:

$$\sigma^2 = \frac{1}{N} \sum_{i=1}^{N} |x_i - \bar{x}|^2 \tag{12}$$

The variance reflects the oscillatory amplitude of the real-time data of bridge long-term health monitoring, and the information fusion and fuzzy chromatography analysis method are used to realize the information fusion of the real-time data of bridge long-term health monitoring [10]. The dynamic copy of the real-time data of bridge long-term health monitoring is obtained, and the results of AHP mining are as follows:

$$x_i' = \frac{x_i}{\|x_i\|} = \left(\frac{x_{i1}}{\|x_i\|}, \frac{x_{i2}}{\|x_i\|}, \cdots, \frac{x_{iN}}{\|x_i\|}\right) \tag{13}$$

Wherein, the end value of real-time data of bridge long-term health monitoring x_N, is fuzzy scheduling according to prior knowledge and itemsets, which improves the accuracy and real-time performance of data monitoring [11].

3.2   Data Mining and Monitoring Output

The real-time data of long-term health monitoring of the bridge needs to be fused with the information fusion and the association mining method information, so that the relevant data self-adaptive feature extraction can be realized, and the prediction cost and the calculation complexity are reduced. the fuzzy clustering and information prediction of long-term health monitoring data flow of the bridge are carried out on the basis of the hierarchical clustering algorithm, and the fuzzy set quality of the real-time data attribute set of the long-term health monitoring of the bridge is adopted, $R_{u,v}$ is a cross-correlation function, the optimization index of the long-term health monitoring data flow monitoring of the bridge is (RT_1, RT_2), the degree of fuzzy clustering is RW, the convergence constraint function of the long-term health monitoring data flow monitoring process of the bridge is as follows:

$$F_j = \sum_{k=1}^{n} X_{kj}, Q_j = \sum_{k=1}^{n} (X_{kj})^2 \tag{14}$$

By adjusting the total utility ratio for many times, the time series of data flow for bridge long-term health monitoring is $\{x(t_0 + i\Delta t)\}$, $i = 0, 1, \cdots, N - 1$. The length of sample set output from the automatic monitoring system of bridge long-term health monitoring is N. The fuzzy convergence control function of bridge long-term health monitoring is given as follows:

$$M_v = w_1 \sum_{i=1}^{m \times n} (H_i - S_i) + M_h w_2 \sum_{i=1}^{m \times n} (S_i - V_i) + w_3 \sum_{i=1}^{m \times n} (V_i - H_i) \tag{15}$$

In the above formula, the load of the long-term health monitoring real-time data prediction of the bridge is V, and after a group of cluster attribute characteristics M_h is generated, the long-term health monitoring real-time data attribute set dispatching of the bridge is carried out, and the main component characteristic quantity of the long-term health monitoring data flow monitoring of the bridge is as follows:

$$s(t) = s_c(t)e^{j2\pi f_0 t} = \frac{1}{\sqrt{T}} rect(\frac{t}{T})e^{j2\pi(f_0 t + Kt^2)/2} \tag{16}$$

The vector quantitative feature decomposition function of the real-time data attribute set of bridge long-term health monitoring is as follows:

$$f(k) = \begin{cases} f(k-1) - \frac{1}{n}, 1 \le k < n \\ 1, k = n \end{cases} \tag{17}$$

Wherein, k represents the feature fusion center of real-time data for long-term health monitoring of distributed bridges, and the data queue is used as a Chunk to reorganize the time area. The information fusion set of predicting spatial vector in real-time data of bridge long-term health monitoring is expressed as follows:

$$P = \{p_1, p_2, \cdots p_m\}, m \in N \tag{18}$$

Wherein, m is the embedded dimension of the automatic monitoring system of bridge long-term health monitoring data stream. In the statistical regression analysis model, the training sample set of vector quantification feature decomposition of the attribute set of bridge long-term health monitoring real-time data is $X = [X_1, X_2, \cdots, X_k, \cdots, X_N]^T$. One of the training samples is $X_k = [x_{k1}, x_{k2}, \cdots, x_{km}, \cdots, x_{kM}]$, from the above feature decomposition results, it is known that the real-time data output of bridge long-term health monitoring meets the convergence condition, according to the above analysis, On the basis of hierarchical clustering algorithm, autoregression analysis is used to monitor bridge long-term health monitoring real-time data monitoring fuzzy clustering and information scheduling, so as to improve the accuracy of bridge long-term health monitoring real-time data monitoring. At the same time, the risk of long-term health monitoring data flow monitoring is reduced [9].

4 Analysis of Simulation Experiment

In order to test the application performance of this algorithm in realizing long-term health monitoring data flow monitoring of bridges, simulation experiments are carried out. Big data hierarchical cluster analysis of bridge long-term health monitoring real-time data monitoring is carried out by using C and Matlab 7 mixed programming. The sampling length of single group bridge long-term health monitoring real-time data time series is 800. The time interval of real-time data packet collection for bridge long-term health monitoring is 0.28 s, and characteristic sampling frequency $f_s = 4f_0 = 20\,kHz$, the maximum iteration number is 2000. According to the above simulation environment and parameters, the automatic monitoring and simulation analysis of bridge long-term health monitoring data flow is carried out, and the time-domain output of bridge long-term health monitoring data flow monitoring is shown in Fig. 1.

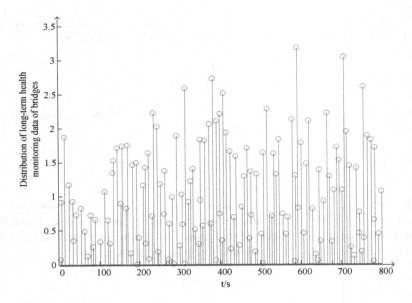

Fig. 1. Monitoring and output of long-term health monitoring data flow of bridge

Analysis Fig. 1 shows that the method can effectively realize the monitoring of long-term health monitoring data flow of the bridge, and analyze the convergence curve of the test data monitoring level, and the result is shown in Fig. 2.

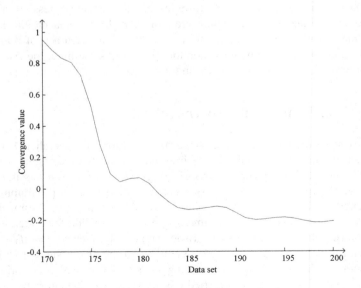

Fig. 2. Convergence test of data monitoring

Figure 2 shows that the convergence of this method for automatic monitoring of long-term health monitoring data flow of bridges is better, and the recall rate of data monitoring by different methods is tested. The comparative results are shown in Table 1, and Table 1 of the analysis shows that the method in this paper has good convergence for automatic monitoring of long-term health monitoring data streams of bridges. In this paper, the recall rate of bridge long-term health monitoring data flow automatic monitoring is high.

Table 1. Comparison of recall of data flow monitoring

Data sample set	Proposed method	Reference [3]	Reference [4]
100	0.943	0.843	0.887
200	0.987	0.889	0.954
300	0.997	0.921	0.969

5 Conclusions

In this paper, a classification method of bridge long-term health monitoring data based on fuzzy correlation feature detection and grid area clustering is proposed. The information fusion and fuzzy chromatography analysis method are used to realize the information fusion of the real-time data of bridge long-term health monitoring, and the adaptive feature extraction of related data is carried out. Excavate the positive correlation characteristic quantity of bridge long-term health monitoring real-time monitoring data flow, carry on the fuzzy clustering and information prediction of bridge long-term health monitoring data flow, and improve the accuracy of bridge long-term health monitoring real-time data monitoring. The simulation results show that the intelligent classification of bridge long-term health monitoring based on this method has high accuracy and low error rate, which improves the real-time performance of bridge monitoring. This method has important application value in improving the health monitoring ability of bridges.

Acknowledgement. Two heights "project of xichang university (LGLZ201824): settlement characteristics analysis and deformation prediction research of xigeda high-rise building with soil layer in xichang.

References

1. Liu, Y., Yang, H., Cai, S., Zhang, C.: Single image super-resolution reconstruction method based on improved convolutional neural network. J. Comput. Appl. **39**(5), 1440–1447 (2019)
2. Xu, R., Zhang, J.G., Huang, K.Q.: Image super-resolution using two-channel convolutional neural networks. J. Image Graphic **21**(5), 556–564 (2016)

3. Megha, G., Yashpal, L., Vivek, L.: Analytical relation & comparison of PSNR and SSIM on babbon image and human eye perception using Matlab. Int. J. Adv. Res. Eng. Appl. Sci. **4** (5), 108–119 (2015)
4. Li, Y.F., Fu, R.D., Jin, W., et al.: Image super-resolution using multi-channel convolution. J. Image Graphics **22**(12), 1690–1700 (2017)
5. Dong, X.W., Yao, S.M., Wang, Y.W., et al.: Virtual sample image set based multi manifold discriminant learning algorithm. Appl. Res. Comput. **35**(6), 1871–1878 (2018)
6. Zhu, Y., Zhu, X., Wang, J.: Time series motif discovery algorithm based on subsequence full join and maximum clique. J. Comput. Appl. **39**(2), 414–420 (2019)
7. Wang, Z., Huang, M., et al.: Integrated algorithm based on density peaks and density-based clustering. J. Comput. Appl. **39**(2), 398–402 (2019)
8. Gui, J., Sun, Z.N., Jia, W., et al.: Discriminant sparse neighborhood preserving embedding for face recognition. Pattern Recogn. **45**(8), 2884–2893 (2012)
9. Dong, B., Chen, D., Jing, W.: Salient region detection method based on symmetric region filtering. Comput. Eng. **45**(5), 216–221 (2019)
10. Zhou, S.B., Xu, W.X.: A novel clustering algorithm based on relative density and decision graph. Control Decis. **33**(11), 1921–1930 (2018)
11. Tu, B., Chuai, R., Xu, H.: Outlier detection based on K-mean distance outlier factor for gait signal. Inf. Control **48**(1), 16–21 (2019)

Construction Quality Inspection Method of Building Concrete Based on Big Data

Mingdong Yu[✉] and Xiaojiang Hong

Department of Civil and Hydraulic Engineering Institute,
Xichang University, Xichang 615013, China
xcxyymd@163.com

Abstract. In order to improve the construction quality detection ability of building concrete, the construction quality detection method of building concrete based on big data is put forward, and a construction quality detection model of building concrete based on feature extraction of association rules is proposed. The nonlinear time series analysis method is used to model the construction quality information flow of building concrete, and the quantitative feature information flow of construction quality of building concrete is reconstructed by quantitative regression analysis. The statistical characteristic quantity of quantitative characteristics of construction quality of building concrete is extracted by statistical feature analysis method, and the spectral density analysis and feature detection of quantitative characteristics of construction quality of building concrete are carried out in the moving average window. According to the abnormal spectrum distribution of high-order statistics, the construction quality inspection of big data building concrete is realized. The simulation results show that the accuracy of using this method to detect the construction quality of building concrete is high.

Keywords: Big data · Building concrete · Construction quality · Inspection

1   Introduction

The quality and fluctuation of concrete raw materials will have a great impact on its quality and construction technology. For example, the fluctuation of cement strength will directly affect the strength of concrete, and the change of super-particle size particle content of stone at all levels will lead to the change of concrete gradation, and will affect the workability of fresh concrete. The change of aggregate water content has a great influence on the water-cement ratio of concrete. Therefore, in the process of concrete production, the quality control of raw materials, in addition to regular testing, but also requires the quality control personnel to master the change law of its content at any time, and draw up the corresponding countermeasures. The quality of concrete engineering is the result of the joint efforts of designers, supervisors and constructors. The quality of concrete, in addition to the appearance of honeycomb, hemp surface defects, is mainly whether the concrete strength can meet the requirements, when the concrete strength cannot meet the engineering requirements, the supervisor can only require demolition rework. The strength of concrete is usually determined 28 days after

G. Gui and L. Yun (Eds.): ADHIP 2019, LNICST 302, pp. 11–21, 2019.
https://doi.org/10.1007/978-3-030-36405-2_2

concrete pouring, and the conclusion is drawn [1]. During this period, a large number of inferior concrete may also be poured, so that the amount of demolition works will be large. Therefore, every person responsible for quality must pay attention to preventing the occurrence of quality defects or discovering possible defects in construction as soon as possible, so as to take remedial measures without losing time, all construction personnel, Supervisors should monitor the preparation, mixing, pouring and mainte- nance of concrete at any time [2]. At the same time, it is necessary to check whether to do the concrete slump experiment on time, etc., the slump is the simplest, the fastest index to judge the quality of concrete, the collapse is too large, too small will produce vibration false, there will be honeycomb, holes, segregation, Whether the delamination or strength is tested according to the requirements of the technical specification, and the test results are checked. When the strength of the 7-day-old period may be lower than the strength required by the project site, the cause should be found out in time and the concrete construction should be stopped in the unqualified strength project site, and the concrete construction should be determined until 28 days after the specimen test is available [3].

The research on the construction quality detection model of building concrete is based on the channel equilibrium configuration and feature extraction of building concrete construction quality, and the load abnormal characteristic quantity of big data is extracted from the balanced construction quality transmission channel of building concrete. The correlation statistical analysis method is used to realize the construction quality detection of building concrete. The typical algorithms are association rule mining method, closed frequent itemset mining method, particle swarm optimization algorithm, etc., combined with the corresponding learning algorithm. Realize the construction quality inspection of building concrete and improve the detection per- formance. In reference [4], a construction quality detection algorithm based on fuzzy constrained adaptive beamforming is proposed. Firstly, the construction quality signal model of building concrete is constructed, and the quantitative characteristic signal of construction quality of big data construction is treated by anti-interference filtering with cascade subsidence filter, so as to realize the detection and location of load anomaly. The calculation cost of this method is large and the real-time performance is not good. In reference [5], a construction quality detection model of big data building concrete based on autocorrelation matching filter is proposed. When the construction quality data of building concrete are interfered by the background of construction quality of building concrete, the detection accuracy is not high. In reference [6], a construction quality detection algorithm of building concrete based on IMF component decompo- sition of multiple narrowband signals is proposed. The instantaneous frequency filter is used to purify the signal, which improves the detection probability of construction quality of building concrete. There are some problems in this method, such as poor global convergence and weak anti-interference ability.

In order to solve the above problems, a construction quality detection model of building concrete based on feature extraction of association rules is proposed in this paper. Firstly, the time series distribution model and information flow model of quantitative characteristics of building concrete construction quality are constructed, and the balanced allocation of big data transmission channel for construction quality of building concrete is carried out. Then the quantitative characteristics of construction quality of building concrete are extracted by high-order statistics, and the quantitative features of construction quality of building concrete are extracted. Finally, the simulation analysis is carried out. The superior performance of this method in improving the accuracy of construction quality inspection of building concrete is verified.

2 Modeling and Data Structure Analysis of Quantitative Characteristic Information Flow of Building Concrete Construction Quality

2.1 Modeling of Quantitative Characteristic Information Flow of Building Concrete Construction Quality

In order to realize the construction quality inspection of building concrete, it is necessary to analyze the data structure and construct the quantitative characteristic information flow model of building concrete construction quality. The statistical feature analysis method is used to calculate the characteristic quantity of quantitative characteristic data of construction quality of building concrete. According to the distribution attribute of characteristic quantity, the detection model of quantitative characteristic data of construction quality of building concrete is designed. The output link model of construction quality of building concrete is established, and the channel equilibrium control model of construction quality of building concrete under cloud computing environment is designed [7]. The distribution model of big data sampling nodes for construction quality of building concrete is constructed by using irregular triangulation model, as shown in Fig. 1.

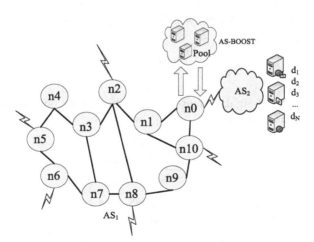

Fig. 1. Distributed structural model of construction quality data of building concrete

In the building concrete construction quality data distribution structure model shown in Fig. 1, the large data anomaly detection model is composed of a link layer, a backbone node and a Sink node, and the sampling data rule vector set of the cluster head node of the building concrete construction quality data is distributed as follows:

$$SLi' = \begin{cases} Li & if \ i = 1 \\ New i' & otherwise \end{cases} \tag{1}$$

The iterative equation of link offset correction for construction quality channel of building concrete is expressed as follows:

$$f_{ij}(n+1) = f_{ij}(n) + \mu_{MCMA} \frac{\partial J_{MCMA}(n)}{\partial f_{ij}(n)} \tag{2}$$

Where, μ_{MCMA} represents the initial route positioning of building concrete construction quality, $f_{ij}(n) = [f_{ij}^{(0)}(n), f_{ij}^{(1)}(n), \cdots, f_{ij}^{(L-1)}(n)]^T$, represents the initial sampling value of quantitative characteristic information flow of building concrete construction quality, combined with quantitative regression analysis method. The quantitative characteristic information flow model of building concrete construction quality is constructed.

2.2   Analysis of Quantitative Characteristic Distribution Data Structure of Building Concrete Construction Quality

The building concrete construction quality information flow modeling is carried out by adopting a non-linear time series analysis method [8], and the output of the offset load in the obtained channel is expressed as follows:

$$x_i(n) = \sum_{j=1}^{M} h_{ij}(n)^T s_j(n) + v_i(n) \tag{3}$$

The channel model of big data transmission in the construction quality of building concrete is expressed as follows:

$$y_j(n) = \sum_{i=1}^{P} f_{ij}(n)^T x_i(n) \tag{4}$$

Among them, f_{ij} represents big data's DNS load frequency. If the number of accurate data categories satisfying the data classification in the current snapshot window B_i is DB_{ij}, the weight coefficient $W_c < \delta(t_c, t_a)$, and t $\delta(t_c, t_a) = \frac{2^{-\lambda(t_c - t_a + T_d) - 1}}{2^{-\lambda T_d} - 1}$, building concrete will be deleted and $A[j] = A[j+1]$, in the phase space supported by finite data set, the vector quantitative decomposition of construction quality of building concrete can be described as follows:

$$
\begin{aligned}
\min_{\beta}\|\mathbf{Y} - \mathbf{X}\boldsymbol{\beta}\| &= \min_{\beta}\|\mathbf{U}^T\mathbf{Y} - \boldsymbol{\Sigma}\mathbf{V}^T\boldsymbol{\beta}\| \\
&= \min_{\beta}\left\|\begin{bmatrix} \mathbf{U}_1^T \\ \mathbf{U}_2^T \end{bmatrix}\mathbf{Y} - \begin{bmatrix} \boldsymbol{\Sigma}_1 & 0 \\ 0 & 0 \end{bmatrix}\begin{bmatrix} \mathbf{V}_1^T \\ \mathbf{V}_2^T \end{bmatrix}\boldsymbol{\beta}\right\| \\
&= \min_{\beta}\left\|\begin{bmatrix} \mathbf{U}_1^T\mathbf{Y} - \boldsymbol{\Sigma}_1\mathbf{V}_1^T\boldsymbol{\beta} \\ \mathbf{U}_2^T\mathbf{Y} \end{bmatrix}\right\| \\
&= \min_{\beta}\{\|\mathbf{U}_1^T\mathbf{Y} - \boldsymbol{\Sigma}_1\mathbf{V}_1^T\boldsymbol{\beta}\| + C\}
\end{aligned}
\tag{5}
$$

Which represents the correlation coefficient and aggregation coefficient of big data abnormal data of construction quality of building concrete. The quantitative feature information flow of construction quality of building concrete is reconstructed by quantitative regression analysis. When the construction quality scale set of building concrete tends to infinity. You can give up, that is:

$$
\min_{\beta}\|\mathbf{Y} - \mathbf{X}\boldsymbol{\beta}\| = \min_{\beta}\|\mathbf{U}_1^T\mathbf{Y} - \boldsymbol{\Sigma}_1\mathbf{V}_1^T\boldsymbol{\beta}\|
\tag{6}
$$

In the link model of big data transmission of construction quality of building concrete, the spatial distribution cluster of K load sampling node in m dimensional space is obtained by N iteration calculation, then the spatial distribution cluster of K load sampling node in m dimensional space is S, then the spatial distribution of K load sampling node in m dimensional space is $d_{ij}(t)$:

$$
d_{ij}(t) = \left|x_{ij}(t) - g_{best}(t)\right|
\tag{7}
$$

Where, $x_{ij}(t)$ represents the load time series, $g_{best}(t)$ represents the fitness function, and adopts the adaptive random link configuration method to carry on the construction quality inspection and data structure reorganization of big data's construction concrete in the construction quality of building concrete. Improve the channel balance and the positioning ability of quantitative characteristics of construction quality of building concrete.

3   Optimization of Construction Concrete Construction Quality Testing Model

3.1   Feature Extraction of Association Rules

On the basis of the above nonlinear time series analysis method for building concrete construction quality information flow modeling and data distributed structure analysis, the optimal design of building concrete construction quality detection model is carried out. In this paper, a construction quality detection model of building concrete based on association rule feature extraction is proposed. If the scale of big data difference in the construction quality of building concrete is $X_i = \{x_{i1}, x_{i2}, \ldots, x_{iD}\}$, space dimension D, then the quantitative feature distribution set of construction quality of the i load joint in m dimensional space is $V_i = \{v_{i1}, v_{i2}, \ldots, v_{iD}\}$. The load gain set transmitted by big data is the optimal position set of $P_i = \{p_{i1}, p_{i2}, \ldots, p_{iD}\}$, individual for $P_g = \{p_{g1}, p_{g2}, \ldots, p_{gD}\}$, mining limit learning method for load balancing scheduling, and the global optimal position set of big data for construction quality of building concrete is GSS. Then the anomaly detection update strategy of data sampling node i at $(t+1)$ time is as follows:

$$\begin{cases} v_{id}^{(t+1)} = v_{id}^t + c_1 * r_1 \left(p_{id}^t - x_{id}^t\right) + c_2 * r_2 \left(p_{gd}^t - x_{id}^t\right) \\ x_{id}^{(t+1)} = x_{id}^t + v_{id}^{(t+1)} \end{cases} \tag{8}$$

Where, $\{c_1, c_2\}$ represents the acceleration coefficient of univariable load detection, $\{r_1, r_2\}$ is the random number between $[0, 1]$, and w is the lag detection coefficient of quantitative characteristics of construction quality of building concrete [9]. The statistical characteristic quantity of quantitative characteristics of construction quality of building concrete is extracted by statistical feature analysis method. According to the residual error of detection model, the regression analysis model of construction quality of building concrete is constructed. According to the regression residual, the low inertia coefficient is adjusted adaptively, and there are:

$$\begin{cases} d_{mean}(t) = \dfrac{\left| \sum\limits_{j=1}^{n} \sum\limits_{i=1}^{d} d_{ij}(t) \right|}{n*d} \\ d_{\max}(t) = \left| \max\left[d_{ij}(t)\right] \right| \\ k = \dfrac{|d_{\max}(t) - d_{mean}(t)|}{d_{\max}(t)} \end{cases} \tag{9}$$

Where, $d_{mean}(t)$ is the average grain distance to detect the construction quality of big data building concrete, $d_{\max}(t)$ is the maximum grain moment, k is the clustering degree of big data distribution of construction quality of construction concrete, and its range is $[0, 1]$. From this, the statistical characteristics of quantitative characteristics of construction quality of building concrete are extracted, and the construction quality of building concrete is tested according to the results of feature extraction.

3.2   Implementation of Construction Quality of Construction Concrete

On the basis of using statistical characteristic quantity analysis method to extract the statistical characteristic quantity of quantitative feature of building concrete construction quality, combined with limit learning method, the adaptive correction of construction quality detection of building concrete is carried out. The mapping strategy for getting limit learning is as follows:

$$\begin{cases} w = w(t) * w_{start} & k \geq \alpha \\ w = w(t) * \frac{1}{w_{end}} & k < \beta \end{cases} \tag{10}$$

For the quantitative characteristic data of building concrete construction quality with three different attribute categories, the individual $\{x_{r1}, x_{r2}, x_{r3}\}$, takes x_{r1} as the base vector and $\{x_{r2}, x_{r3}\}$ as the difference vector, and carries on the multiple collinear scheduling according to the modified result of limit learning. According to a certain proportion, it is superimposed on the base vector, and the statistical characteristic quantity of the quantitative characteristics of the construction quality of the building concrete is calculated as follows:

$$z_{(i,d)} = x_{r1} + F * (x_{r2} - x_{r3}) \tag{11}$$

Where, F is the scaling factor. The spectral density analysis and feature detection of quantitative characteristics of construction quality of building concrete are carried out in the moving average window, and the binary collinear analysis method is adopted. The variation vector z_i of quantitative characteristics of construction quality of building concrete and the corresponding original vector x_i are crossed, and the load balance test is carried out by means of mean test method, which is described as follows:

$$u_{(i,d)} = \begin{cases} z_{(i,d)} & rand \leq C_R, d = rn_i \\ x_{(i,d)} & other \end{cases} \tag{12}$$

Where, $\{x_{(i,d)}, z_{(i,d)}, u_{(i,d)}\}$ is the d dimensional component of solution vector $\{x_i, z_i, u_i\}$, C_R is the balance control coefficient of big data, and rn_i is a random integer. According to the detection results of quantitative characteristics of construction quality of construction concrete, the distribution of characteristic vectors and data information of data sets in the construction quality of building concrete is expressed as follows:

$$\begin{cases} v_{id}^{(t+1)} = w * v_{id}^t + c_1 * r_1 \left(p_{id}^t - x_{id}^t \right) + c_2 * r_2 \left(p_{gd}^t - x_{id}^t \right) \\ x_{id}^{(t+1)} = x_{id}^t + v_{id}^{(t+1)} \end{cases} \tag{13}$$

$$u_{(i,d)}^{k+1} = \begin{cases} x_{id}^{(t+1)} & f_{fitness}^t < f_{fitness}^* \\ z_{(i,d)}^{(k+1)} & f_{fitness}^t \geq f_{fitness}^* \end{cases} \tag{14}$$

Where, the candidate solution is $u_i^{(k+1)} = \{u_{i1}^{(k+1)}, u_{i2}^{(k+1)}, \ldots, u_{iD}^{(k+1)}\}$ and the optimal solution is $x_i^k = \{x_{i1}^k, x_{i2}^k, \ldots, x_{iD}^k\}$, to compare the fitness value of the solution vector, and the optimal value is selected to save to the channel model to improve the accurate positioning ability of the quantitative characteristics of the construction quality of the building concrete [10].

4 Simulation Experiment and Performance Analysis

In order to test the application performance of this method in the construction quality detection of building concrete, the simulation experiment is carried out, and Matlab 7 is used to design the load detection algorithm. SPSS 1.4 statistical software is used to analyze the quantitative characteristics of building concrete construction quality of big data. The sampling interval of big data is $\Delta t = 2.4$ ms, the symbol interval is 1.2 Kbps, and the length of data sample is 1024. The symbol rate of quantitative characteristic distribution of construction quality is 1kBaud. the equalizer order of construction quality transmission channel is 24, the frequency of baud interval sampling is 200 kHz, and the iterative step size is 0.01. According to the above simulation environment and parameter setting, the construction quality of building concrete is tested, and the sequence of big data samples to be tested is shown in Fig. 1.

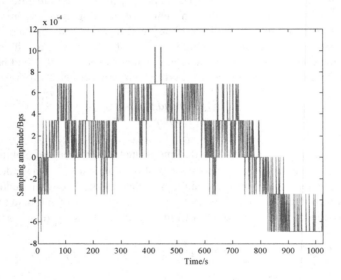

Fig. 2. Big data sample sequence of construction quality of building concrete

Taking the sampling data of Fig. 2 as the research object, the construction quality of building concrete is detected, and the statistical characteristic quantity of quantitative characteristics of construction quality of building concrete is extracted by using the method of statistical characteristic quantity analysis, combined with the method of spectral analysis. The output timing waveform of building concrete construction quality is shown in Fig. 3.

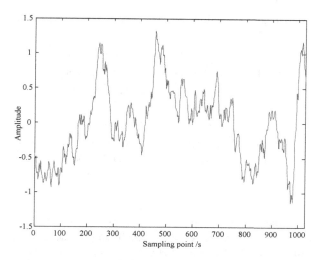

Fig. 3. Timing waveform of construction quality inspection of building concrete

Figure 3 shows that the characteristic resolution of the output sample sequence is good and the overlapping interference is effectively suppressed by using this method to detect the construction quality of building concrete. The accurate transmission ability of big data in the construction quality of building concrete is improved. In order to compare the performance, the load anomaly detection is carried out by different methods in this paper, and the accurate probability comparison is shown in Fig. 4.

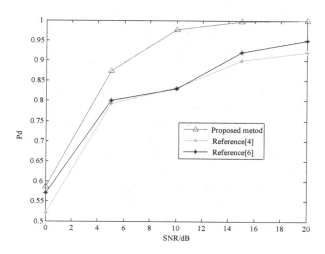

Fig. 4. Comparison of detection accuracy

The comparison of false detection rate of construction quality output of building concrete is shown in Table 1.

Table 1. Comparison of output error detection rates

SNR/dB	Proposed method	PCA	PSO
0	0.097	0.233	0.125
5	0.076	0.122	0.097
10	0.053	0.065	0.087
15	0.004	0.043	0.065
20	0	0.023	0.021

The analysis of the above simulation results shows that with the increase of interference SNR, the interference intensity is small, and the accuracy of construction quality detection of big data building concrete is gradually improved, and the detection accuracy of this method is 21.7% higher than that of the traditional method on average. Because this method can effectively detect the quantitative characteristics of building concrete construction quality in big data, thus reducing the output error detection rate of building concrete construction quality, the comparison Table 1 shows, the output error detection rate of this method is obviously lower than that of the traditional method.

5 Conclusions

In this paper, a construction quality detection model of building concrete based on feature extraction of association rules is proposed. The nonlinear time series analysis method is used to model the construction quality information flow of building concrete, and the quantitative feature information flow of construction quality of building concrete is reconstructed by quantitative regression analysis. The statistical characteristic quantity of quantitative characteristics of construction quality of building concrete is extracted by statistical feature analysis method, and the spectral density analysis and feature detection of quantitative characteristics of construction quality of building concrete are carried out in the moving average window. According to the abnormal spectrum distribution of high-order statistics, the construction quality inspection of big data building concrete is realized. The simulation results show that the accuracy of using this method to detect the construction quality of building concrete is high. This method has important application value in improving the construction quality of building concrete.

References

1. Zhou, S.B., Xu, W.X.: A novel clustering algorithm based on relative density and decision graph. Control Decis. **33**(11), 1921–1930 (2018)
2. He, H., Tan, Y.: Automatic pattern recognition of ECG signals using entropy-based adaptive dimensionality reduction and clustering. Appl. Soft Comput. **55**, 238–252 (2017)
3. Zhu, Y., Zhu, X., Wang, J.: Time series motif discovery algorithm based on subsequence full join and maximum clique. J. Comput. Appl. **39**(2), 414–420 (2019)
4. Sun, X., Li, X.G., Li, J.F., et al.: Review on deep learning based image super-resolution restoration algorithms. Acta Automatica Sinica **43**(5), 697–709 (2017)
5. Yan, S., Xu, D., Zhang, B., et al.: Graph embedding and extensions: a general framework for dimensionality reduction. IEEE Trans. Pattern Anal. Mach. Intell. **29**(1), 40–51 (2007)
6. Li, B., Wang, C., Huang, D.S.: Supervised feature extraction based on orthogonal discriminant projection. Neurocomputing **73**(1), 191–196 (2009)
7. Hou, C., Nie, F., Li, X., et al.: Joint embedding learning and sparse regression: a framework for unsupervised feature selection. IEEE Trans. Cybern. **44**(6), 793–804 (2014)
8. Liu, Q., Guan, W., Li, S., Wang, F.: Indoor WiFi-PDR fusion location algorithm based on extended Kalman filter. Comput. Eng. **45**(4), 66–71, 77 (2019)
9. Wang, Z., Huang, M., et al.: Integrated algorithm based on density peaks and density-based clustering. J. Comput. Appl. **39**(2), 398–402 (2019)
10. Liu, Y., Yang, H., Cai, S., Zhang, C.: Single image super-resolution reconstruction method based on improved convolutional neural network. J. Comput. Appl. **39**(5), 1440–1447 (2019)

Research on Visual Display Method of Virtual Experimental Elements Based on Big Data Technology

Wei-wei Xu[1($\boxtimes$)] and Chen-guang Bai[2]

[1] Teaching Equipment Department, Xuzhou Institute of Technology,
Xuzhou, China
Krityfeier@163.com
[2] Lianyungang Jari Electronics Co., Lianyungang, China
tcbai0528@163.com

Abstract. In order to solve the problem that the visual simulation image of virtual experimental element is missing in the reconstruction module of virtual experimental element, and the reconstruction accuracy of virtual experimental element is not good. A visual display method of virtual experimental element visual simulation image based on big data technology and virtual visual reconstruction is proposed. Firstly, the information transmission model of virtual experimental element visual simulation image is constructed. Then the 5-level wavelet decomposition method is used to decompose and fuse the visual simulation images of virtual experimental elements, and big data fusion technology is used to reconstruct the visual information of virtual experimental elements. The visual simulation image visualization of virtual experimental elements is realized. The simulation results show that this method has good visual display performance and high feature fusion degree in the reconstruction and modeling of virtual experimental element visual simulation image, and has high value in the application of virtual experimental element visual display and digital reconstruction.

Keywords: Big data technology · Virtual experimental elements · Visual display

1 Introduction

With the development of image processing technology, the visual display of virtual experimental elements by using big data technology can improve the visual reconstruction and recognition ability of virtual experimental elements. The application of virtual visual simulation imaging has a broad application prospect in the scientific and technological fields such as visual display and display of virtual experimental elements [1]. The virtual experimental element visual simulation image is used to reconstruct and model the virtual experimental element, and the digital reproduction and visual display of the virtual experimental element are realized. The research on visual display method of virtual experimental elements based on big data technology and virtual scene reconstruction has been paid more and more attention [3].

© ICST Institute for Computer Sciences, Social Informatics and Telecommunications Engineering 2019
Published by Springer Nature Switzerland AG 2019. All Rights Reserved
G. Gui and L. Yun (Eds.): ADHIP 2019, LNICST 302, pp. 22–31, 2019.
https://doi.org/10.1007/978-3-030-36405-2_3

The visual display of the virtual experiment element by using the virtual scene simulation method is mainly to carry out three-dimensional scattered point recombination and visual display through the three-dimensional organization model, and the template matching is carried out in combination with the statistical shape model (SSM) method, the visual display and reconstruction of the pixel information points of the visual simulation image of the virtual experimental element are realized, a point distribution model (PDM), The LWT wavelet decomposition reconstruction method and the irregular triangular network modeling method and the like, the method uses the laser beam to scan the object to carry out three-dimensional characteristic reconstruction and information modeling of the image, improves the texture information and the pixel point characterization ability of the image, in which, the reference [3] proposes an image modeling method based on a transmission space and a color texture correlation image segmentation, the reconstruction precision of the image is improved, the signal-to-noise ratio of the digital image output is high, but the calculation cost of the virtual experimental element visual simulation image processing algorithm is large, and the modeling real-time of the laser imaging is not good [4]. A three-dimensional reconstruction and modeling method of an ultrasonic image based on a multi-scale Retinx image denoising and enhancement processing is adopted to realize the visual display of the three-dimensional ultrasound image [5], by denoising and enhancing the ultrasonic image, the feature point tracking and calibration capability of the three-dimensional scanning image is highlighted, but the method is easy to be interfered by the external disturbance information in the modeling of the three-dimensional image, and the modeling effect of the output image is not good when the interference intensity is large, The accuracy is not high.

In view of the above problems, a visual simulation image display method based on large data technology and virtual scene reconstruction is presented in this paper. Firstly, the information conduction model of the virtual experiment element visual simulation image is constructed, and the priority judgment of the sub-space structure block matching and the visual display of the virtual experimental element information missing area is carried out. Then the feature decomposition and information fusion of the visual simulation image of the virtual experimental element are carried out by adopting the wavelet decomposition method, and the visual information reconstruction of the virtual experimental element is carried out to realize the visual display of the visual simulation image of the virtual experimental element. Finally, the performance test is carried out by the simulation experiment, and the superiority of the algorithm in the information reconstruction and modeling of the visual simulation image of the virtual experimental element is shown.

2   Information Conduction Model and Image Preprocessing

2.1   Visual Simulation Image Information Transmission Model of Virtual Experimental Elements

By constructing the information transmission model of the visual simulation image of the virtual experimental element, the information acquisition and feature extraction of the visual simulation image of the virtual experimental element are carried out. in the acquisition of the visual simulation image of the virtual experimental element, the reflected beam is reflected to the laser output port by using the virtual experimental element of laser beam scanning [6]. The pixel feature arrangement sequence is different and the three-dimensional laser imaging is obtained. In the information reconstruction of the visual simulation image of the virtual experimental element, the size of the sub-block of the modeling feature area is selected. The visual simulation image of each M < N virtual experimental element is divided into rectangular blocks of ((M/16) + 1) * ((N/16) + 1), as shown in Fig. 1.

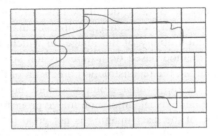

Fig. 1. Visual simulation image rectangular block of virtual experimental element

Selecting the most similar matching block to perform three-dimensional feature reconstruction on the image to be visualized display area to obtain the information conducting pixel set of the internal points of each sub-block, the point on the boundary is determined by the similarity degree of the dark primary color current block in the visual simulation image of the virtual experimental element and the display block to be visualized, the information conducting priority characteristic matching is carried out, and when the information conduction iteration is carried out, The related elements of the adjacent blocks of the visual simulation image of the virtual experimental element need to be gradient-smoothed [7]. The affine invariant moment feature extraction is carried out with the affine invariant kernel function of 3 * 3, and the affine invariant moment has the invariance of the rotation translation and the scale, so that the feature mining can be carried out through the template matching of the image, and the template size m * n determines the image processing template. The visual simulation image texture information of the virtual experimental element in the unit time is $G(x, y; t)$, and the intuitionistic fuzzy set of the visual simulation image texture sub-space of the virtual experimental element is defined as the conduction function as follows:

$$p(x, t) = \lim_{\Delta x \to 0} [\sigma \frac{u - (u + \Delta u)}{\Delta x}] = -\sigma \frac{\partial u(x, t)}{\partial x} \tag{1}$$

The ergodic characteristics of the image features in the scene are obtained, and the information flow density vector of the virtual experimental element visual simulation image texture structure is obtained as follows:

$$p(x, y; t) = -\sigma \nabla u(x, y; t) = -\sigma G(x, y; t) = -\sigma [G_x(x, y; t)i + G_y(x, y; t)j] \tag{2}$$

In which, i, j is a unit direction vector, and based on the visual significance of the target in the visual display process of the virtual experimental element, the visual simulation image structure texture information conduction model of the virtual experimental element is constructed, and the rare degree in the whole scene is obtained, And the global rare degree of the visual simulation image of the virtual experimental element is obtained by adopting the zero-uniform traversal [8]. On the basis of the analysis, the state equation of the texture information conduction model of the visual simulation image of the virtual experimental element is described as:

$$\begin{cases} f(x_1, x_2) = r_1 x_1 (1 - \frac{x_1}{N_1} - \sigma_1 \frac{x_2}{N_2}) = 0 \\ g(x_1, x_2) = r_2 x_2 (1 - \sigma_2 \frac{x_1}{N_1} - \frac{x_2}{N_2}) = 0 \end{cases} \tag{3}$$

In the above formula, r_1 and r_2 represent the local and global salient feature sets of the virtual experimental element visual simulation image, σ_1 represents the mean value of the image feature, and N_1, N_2 are the noise component.

On the basis of constructing the information transmission model of the virtual experimental element visual simulation image, the information collection and feature analysis of the virtual experimental element visual simulation image are realized, which provides an accurate data basis for the virtual experimental element modeling [9].

2.2 Priority Determination of Visual Simulation Image Reconstruction of Virtual Experimental Elements

In the information transmission model, the priority of visual display of the information missing area of the virtual experimental element visual simulation image is determined by using the sub-spatial structure block matching method [10]. The subspatial structure model of visual simulation image of virtual experimental element is designed as shown in Fig. 2.

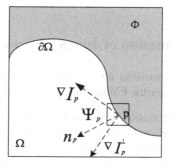

Fig. 2. Subspatial structure model of image

In Fig. 2, Ω represents the absence of information from the visual simulation image of the virtual experimental element (the white area), ϕ represents the information intact area (gray area) of the virtual experimental element graph, $\partial\Omega$ represents the edge line of the information intact area and the information missing area, p represents the pixel point of the virtual visual simulation of the virtual experimental element on $\partial\Omega$, and Ψ_p represents the fuzzy membership degree set of the visual pixel point of the virtual experimental element visual simulation image centered on the SF point. The priority of 3D image reconstruction in the subspatial structure of the image [11].

Firstly, the priority coefficient of the block to be rebuilt is calculated, the edge pixel points of the virtual experimental element visual simulation image are updated, and the multi-dimensional search method of subspace feature information is adopted. The information points of the virtual experimental element visual simulation image are searched by gray level until there are no edge pixels. The mean value of the features is used as the pheromone in the sub-spatial structure block, and the global rarity feature decomposition of the virtual visual simulation imaging is carried out. The iterative equation of feature decomposition is described as follows:

$$u^{(n+1)}(x, y) = u^{(n)}(x, y) + \delta u_1^{(n)}(x, y) \tag{4}$$

$$u_1^{(n)}(x, y) = M\Delta_s u^{(n)}(x, y) + N\Delta_t u^{(n)}(x, y; d) \tag{5}$$

It is assumed that the size of the visual simulation image of the virtual experimental element to be rebuilt is that the size of the $m \times n$, feature scale block Ψ_p is $s \times s$. Through the matching of the sub-spatial structure blocks, the priority determination of the unknown pixel points of the virtual experimental element visual simulation image is realized. The priority ranking of pixel points satisfies:

$$P(|\overline{x_T} - K| < \frac{\lambda_\chi \sigma}{\sqrt{N}}) \approx \frac{2}{\sqrt{2\pi}} \int_0^{\lambda_\chi} e^{-\frac{1}{2}t^2} dt = 1 - \chi \tag{6}$$

Wherein, $\overline{x_T}$ is the mean value of local contrast window of virtual experimental element visual simulation image, χ is significance weight, K is global rarity coefficient, σ is threshold.

3   Improved Implementation of Image Processing Algorithm

3.1   Image Feature Decomposition and Information Fusion of Visual Simulation of Experimental Elements

On the basis of the above information transmission model construction and the priority determination of virtual experimental element visual simulation image reconstruction, the visual display design of virtual experimental element is carried out. In this paper, a visual display method of virtual experimental element visual simulation image based on big data technology and virtual visual reconstruction is proposed [12]. The 5-level wavelet decomposition method is used to decompose and fuse the visual simulation images of virtual experimental elements. For the visual simulation images X and Y of two virtual experimental elements in the information transmission model, The SSIM value of the similarity between the visual simulation images of the two virtual experimental elements is defined as follows:

$$SSIM = [l(X,Y)]^\alpha [c(X,Y)]^\beta [s(X,Y)]^\gamma \tag{7}$$

The 5-level wavelet decomposition is used, the whole frequency band of the virtual experimental element visual simulation image can be divided into six. According to the wavelet decomposition CSF characteristic curve, the grid vertexes of the virtual experimental element visual simulation image reconstruction are determined. Six weights are taken for the scattered three-dimensional sampling points. Through the 5-level wavelet decomposition of the visual simulation image of the virtual experimental element, the structure similarity characteristics of the wavelet of the visual display image of the virtual experimental element are obtained as follows:

$$ws(X,Y) = \frac{2|\sum_{i=1}^{N} c_{x,i} c_{y,i}| + K}{\sum_{i=1}^{N} |c_{x,i}|^2 + \sum_{i=1}^{N} |c_{y,i}|^2 + K} \tag{8}$$

The gray information contrast of $l(X,Y)$, virtual experimental elements visually displayed by virtual experimental elements is characterized by the feature structure of $c(X,Y)$, virtual experimental elements. The results of feature decomposition and information fusion of images obtained by wavelet decomposition of $s(X,Y)$, are as follows:

$$l(X,Y) = (2u_x u_y + C_1)/(u_x^2 + u_y^2 + C_1) \tag{9}$$

$$c(X,Y) = (2\sigma_x \sigma_y + C_2)/(\sigma_x^2 + \sigma_y^2 + C_2) \tag{10}$$

$$s(X,Y) = (\sigma_{xy} + C_3)/(\sigma_x \sigma_y + C_3) \tag{11}$$

Wherein, u_x, u_y are the pixel intensity mean of image X, Y, σ_x, σ_y are the standard deviation of local contrast window of X, Y, σ_{xy} is edge information covariance, and C_1, C_2, C_3 are global rarity constants.

3.2 Realization of 3D Reconstruction of Visual Simulation Image of Virtual Experimental Element

On the basis of the above five-level wavelet decomposition method for the feature decomposition and information fusion of the visual simulation image of the virtual experimental element, the visual information reconstruction of the virtual experimental element is carried out. The visual simulation image visualization of virtual experimental elements is realized, and the parameters of wavelet structure similarity WSSIM of visual simulation images of two virtual experimental elements are calculated.

$$WSSIM = [l(X,Y)]^{\alpha}[c(X,Y)]^{\beta}[ws(X,Y)]^{\gamma} \tag{12}$$

and through the multi-scale decomposition of the global rare degree, the energy of the two direction sub-bands in the information conduction model of the visual display imaging of the virtual experimental element is respectively:

$$E_{HL_i} = \sum_j (c_j^{HL_i})^2, E_{LH_i} = \sum_j (c_j^{LH_i})^2 \tag{13}$$

The weight of the global and local operations is updated by the fusion of the similarity of the SSIM, and the image is subjected to convolution with a Gaussian kernel function of different scales, so that the reconstruction output of the visual simulation image of the virtual experimental element is obtained as follows:

$$\omega_{HL_i} = \frac{E_{HL_i}}{E_{HL_i} + E_{LH_i} + E_{HH_i}} \tag{14}$$

$$\omega_{LH_i} = \frac{E_{LH_i}}{E_{HL_i} + E_{LH_i} + E_{HH_i}} \tag{15}$$

$$\omega_{HH_i} = \frac{E_{HH_i}}{E_{HL_i} + E_{LH_i} + E_{HH_i}} \tag{16}$$

The probability of each pixel variance in the whole diagram is calculated, the significance of the characteristic points of virtual experimental elements is measured, and the structural similarity characteristics of the images in the high-frequency subband of the wavelet is calculated as:

$$WSSIM_{H_i} = \omega_{HL_i} \cdot WSSIM_{HL_i} + \omega_{LH_i} \cdot WSSIM_{LH_i} + \omega_{HH_i} \cdot WSSIM_{HH_i} \tag{17}$$

Thus, the wavelet structure similarity of the visual simulation image of the virtual experimental element is calculated, which is recorded as FWSSIM:.

$$FWSSIM(X,Y) = \frac{\omega_{LL} \cdot WSSIM_{LL} + \sum_{i=1}^{5} (\omega_{H_i} \cdot WSSIM_{H_i})}{\omega_{LL} + \sum_{i=1}^{5} \omega_{H_i}} \tag{18}$$

Based on the above processing, the visual display of virtual experimental elements is realized.

3.3   Simulation Experiment and Result Analysis

In order to verify the effectiveness of the algorithm, the visual simulation images of different types of virtual experimental elements are used for reconstruction simulation. The test platform is, Pentium (R) 4 CPU 3.00 GHz and 1 G memory of windows 10

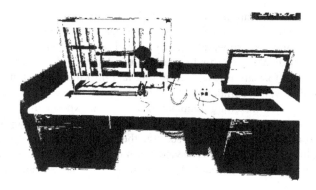

(a) Original experimental element image

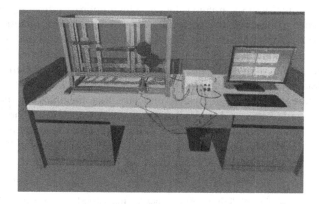

(b) Reconstruction with traditional method

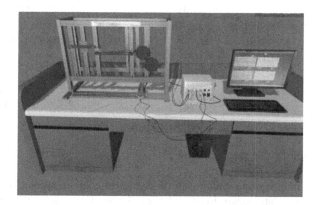

(c) Reconstruction with proposed method

Fig. 3. Virtual scene simulation modeling and simulation of virtual experimental elements

system. Using Matlab simulation software, the algorithm is programmed and designed. The experimental samples are taken from the visual simulation image database of Criminisi large virtual experimental elements, and the sub-spatial structure block matching and visual display of virtual experimental element information missing area are carried out. The information feature sampling and information fusion of the virtual experimental element visual simulation image are realized, the search step size N = 4 is set, and the sample block matching template of the virtual experimental element image is 9 × 9. The window sizes are 3 * 3, 5 * 5, 9 * 9, 17 * 17. According to the above simulation environment and parameter setting, the original virtual experimental element image is obtained, and the virtual visual simulation reconstruction results of the virtual experimental element are carried out by using this method and the traditional method, as shown in Fig. 3.

It can be seen from the diagram that the virtual visual scene reconstruction of virtual experimental elements is carried out by using this method, and the visual display and reconstruction quality of the image is better, which improves the imaging quality of the image, in order to describe the performance of the algorithm quantitatively. The root mean square error (RMSE) and execution time of peak signal-to-noise ratio (PSNR), reconstruction are used as test indexes, and the comparative results are shown in Table 1. The results show that the virtual scene simulation modeling of virtual experimental elements is carried out by using this method, and the peak signal-to-noise ratio of the output image is high, which indicates that the imaging quality of the reconstructed image is better and the root mean square error is low. The results show that the feature extraction accuracy of virtual visual simulation imaging is high and the execution time is short, which shows that the real-time performance of this method is better and the performance index is superior to the traditional method.

Table 1. Comparison of the modeling performance of the virtual experimental element of the virtual scene simulation.

Test pattern	PSNR/dB		RMSE		E-time/ms	
	Proposed method	Traditional method	Proposed method	Traditional method	Proposed method	Traditional method
1	55.6	32.1	0.025	0.168	3.1	43.7
2	73.4	44.2	0.046	0.114	3.4	32.5
3	48.6	42.4	0.058	0.254	2.7	12.4
4	66.4	51.6	0.028	0.318	2.3	18.6

4   Conclusions

In this paper, a visual display method of virtual experimental element visual simulation image based on big data technology and virtual visual reconstruction is proposed. Firstly, the information transmission model of virtual experimental element visual simulation image is constructed, and then the feature decomposition and information fusion of virtual experimental element visual simulation image are carried out by using wavelet decomposition method, and the visual information reconstruction of virtual experimental element is carried out. The visual simulation image visualization of virtual experimental elements is realized. The results show that the visual display performance of virtual experimental element scene simulation image reconstruction modeling is better, the PSNR of the output image is improved, the reconstruction error is reduced, and the image quality is improved. The method in this paper has a good application value in the visual display and reconstruction of experimental elements.

References

1. Tu, B., Chuai, R., Xu, H.: Outlier detection based on K-mean distance outlier factor for gait signal. Inf. Control **48**(1), 16–21 (2019)
2. Wei, X.S., Luo, J.H., Wu, J.: Selective convolutional descriptor aggregation for fine-grained image retrieval. IEEE Trans. Image Process. **26**(6), 2868–2881 (2017)
3. Liu, Q., Guan, W., Li, S., Wang, F.: Indoor WiFi-PDR fusion location algorithm based on extended Kalman filter. Comput. Eng. **45**(4), 66–71, 77 (2019)
4. Wang, Z., Huang, M., et al.: Integrated algorithm based on density peaks and density-based clustering. J. Comput. Appl. **39**(2), 398–402 (2019)
5. Liu, Y., Yang, H., Cai, S., Zhang, C.: Single image super-resolution reconstruction method based on improved convolutional neural network. J. Comput. Appl. **39**(5), 1440–1447 (2019)
6. Xu, R., Zhang, J.G., Huang, K.Q.: Image super-resolution using two-channel convolutional neural networks. J. Image Graphic **21**(5), 556–564 (2016)
7. Megha, G., Yashpal, L., Vivek, L.: Analytical relation & comparison of PSNR and SSIM on babbon image and human eye perception using Matlab. Int. J. Adv. Res. Eng. Appl. Sci. **4**(5), 108–119 (2015)
8. Li, Y.F., Fu, R.D., Jin, W., et al.: Image super-resolution using multi-channel convolution. J. Image Graphics **22**(12), 1690–1700 (2017)
9. Sun, X., Li, X.G., Li, J.F., et al.: Review on deep learning based image super-resolution restoration algorithms. Acta Automatica Sinica **43**(5), 697–709 (2017)
10. Yan, S., Xu, D., Zhang, B., et al.: Graph embedding and extensions: a general framework for dimensionality reduction. IEEE Trans. Pattern Anal. Mach. Intell. **29**(1), 40–51 (2007)
11. Li, B., Wang, C., Huang, D.S.: Supervised feature extraction based on orthogonal discriminant projection. Neurocomputing **73**(1), 191–196 (2009)
12. Hou, C., Nie, F., Li, X., et al.: Joint embedding learning and sparse regression: a framework for unsupervised feature selection. IEEE Trans. Cybern. **44**(6), 793–804 (2014)

Research on Distributed Power Energy Grid-Connected Control Method Based on Big Data

Chen-guang Bai[(✉)]

Lianyungang Jari Electronics Co., Lianyungang, China
tcbai0528@163.com

Abstract. In the process of modeling distributed power grid connection, the parameter control effect is not good, and the modeling is not stable. A distributed power energy grid-connected control method based on large data is put forward. Distributed power energy-energy grid-connected model is established, a DC/AC inverter model and a current inner-loop controller model are analyzed. And an equivalent circuit model analysis of the terminal voltage of the grid-connected inverter of the controller is analyzed. The fuzzy PID control algorithm is introduced to identify the unknown parameters in the distributed power energy grid-connected control, the fitness function of the inner ring controller and the fitness function of the outer ring controller are obtained. Expert database is initialized and updated, Until the maximum number of iterations or convergence accuracy is reached. The simulation results show that the proposed method can effectively improve the performance of the distributed power grid-connected control.

Keywords: Big data · Distributed power energy · Grid-connected control · Fuzzy PID

1 Introduction

With the gradual increase of the scale of grid-connected photovoltaic system, its effect on power grid is becoming more and more obvious, and the safety and reliability of grid-connected photovoltaic power generation have been paid more and more attention. Among them, distributed power energy grid-connected is the basis of simulation research on photovoltaic power supply system, and whether it can effectively reflect the dynamic characteristics of photovoltaic power generation system mainly depends on its reasonable model structure and accurate model parameters [1]. Therefore, it has great significance to study distributed power energy grid-connected control.

At present, many algorithms have been applied to distributed power energy grid-connected control. The commonly used algorithms include genetic algorithm, particle swarm optimization algorithm, ant colony algorithm and imitating electromagnetics algorithm [2, 3]. In reference [4], the proportional integral control algorithm is applied to the distributed power energy grid-connected control. The current is decomposed into positive and negative sequence by two current controllers in synchronous reference

G. Gui and L. Yun (Eds.): ADHIP 2019, LNICST 302, pp. 32–40, 2019.
https://doi.org/10.1007/978-3-030-36405-2_4

coordinate system. The PI control in synchronous coordinate system is carried out respectively, but this method has the disadvantage of complicated calculation process. In reference [5], the proportional resonance control algorithm is applied to the distributed power energy grid-connected control. The current can directly control the output current in two-phase static coordinates, but to some extent, this method is difficult to achieve. In reference [6], genetic algorithm is applied to distributed power energy grid-connected control. The performance of the system is degraded by eliminating positive and negative sequence decomposition by genetic algorithm. This method takes a long time and the efficiency is very low.

In order to solve the above problems, a distributed power energy grid-connected control method based on big data is proposed, the distributed power energy grid-connected model is established, and the DC/AC inverter model is analyzed. In the process of establishing the current inner loop controller model and the voltage outer loop controller model, the fuzzy PID control algorithm is introduced to identify the unknown parameters of the modeling of the grid photovoltaic power generation unit. The experimental results show that the proposed method can effectively improve the performance of distributed power energy grid-connected control.

2 Parameter Optimization Identification in Distributed Power Energy Grid-Connected Control

2.1 Establishment of a Distributed Power Grid-Connected Model

The distributed power energy grid-connected model is mainly composed of DC/AC inverter model, current inner loop controller model and voltage outer loop controller model. Below, the establishment of each model is analyzed in detail. The equivalent circuit diagram is shown in Fig. 1.

The establishment of DC/AC inverter model is the foundation of distributed power energy grid-connected model. Its model can be simulated by inertia link. Because the frequency of modulation wave is obviously higher than that of power grid frequency, the inertia delay time constant is very small. Then the DC/AC inverter model can be described as:

$$G_1(s) = \frac{1}{1 + 0.5sT_{SW}} \tag{1}$$

Wherein, S is used to describe the control signal, T_{SW} is used to describe the inertia delay time constant, and $T_{SW} = 1/f_{SW}, f_{SW}$ is used to describe the switching frequency of the inverter.

Based on the DC/AC inverter model, the current inner loop controller model is established, which provides the basis for the establishment of the voltage outer loop controller model. The inner loop must follow the transient change of the reference current quickly, and its response speed is much higher than that of the voltage outer loop controller [7]. The current formed by the outer loop control loop is regarded as the reference I_{sd_ref}, passing through a series of control stages. The grid-connected current

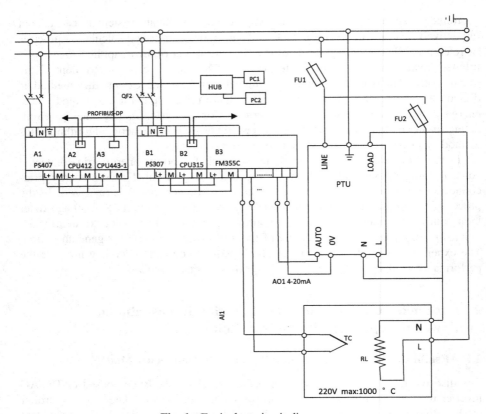

Fig. 1. Equivalent circuit diagram

of the converter is controlled, that is, the reference voltage U_{dq_ref}. The reference voltage U_{abc_ref} is transformed into the reference voltage U_{dq_ref}, needed by the inverter through the conversion of dp coordinates to form a trigger pulse. Therefore, the models of inner loop controller and outer loop controller can be established respectively.

T_s is used to describe the measurement sampling time, $\frac{1}{1+sT_s}$ is used to describe the control delay link, $\frac{1}{1+0.5sT_s}$ is used to describe the measurement sampling link, i_{d_ref} is used to describe the reference values of active current and reactive current, and Ls is used to describe inductance. i_d, i_q is used to describe the d, q axis component of the three-phase current fundamental wave on the grid-connected side; $G_{cuur\_d}(s)$, $G_{cuur\_q}(s)$ are used to describe the resistance of the grid-connected side line; it is used to describe the inner ring $d - axis$ and $q - axis$ current PI controllers, respectively. The formula is described as follows:

$$G_{cuur\_d}(s) = \frac{K_{P1}s + K_{11}}{sG_1(s)} \tag{2}$$

$$G_{cuur\_q}(s) = \frac{K_{P2}s + K_{12}}{sG_1(s)} \tag{3}$$

Wherein, K_{P1}, K_{11}, K_{P2}, K_{12} are used to describe the parameters of the axis PI controller of the inner ring d axis and Q, respectively.

In that model, the influence of the capacitance H on the current loop in the LC low-pass filter cannot be taken into account due to the influence of the power factor of the unit when the inverter is in operation, the expression of the inner ring current control model is as follows:

$$G(s) = \int \frac{T_s.G_{cuur\_d}(s)i_{d\_ref} * i_d}{T_{SW}.G_{cuur\_q}(s)i_{q\_ref} * i_q} \tag{4}$$

Both of them can be obtained by measurement, and the controller parameters are unknown and need to be identified [8].

2.2   Establishment of Voltage Outer Loop Controller Model

After the current inner loop controller model is established, the voltage outer loop controller model is established. Because the response speed of the outer loop controller is slow, in the process of modeling the voltage outer loop controller, it is necessary to complete the non-mechanism modeling equivalence of the current inner loop controller model [9]. According to the characteristics of the equivalent inner loop controller of the first order inertia link, it is called the equivalent inner loop control model, and the transfer function SF is the equivalent model of the current inner loop, which is mainly used in the control loop of the voltage outer loop. The equivalent $G_{eq}(s)$ voltage outer loop controller model can be described in Fig. 2.

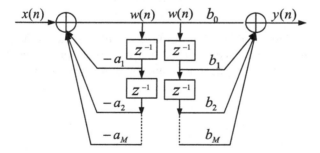

Fig. 2. Equivalent DC voltage outer loop controller model

After completing the equivalence of the inner loop current controller, it is necessary to identify the parameters K_{eq} and T_{eq}, so as to establish the voltage outer loop controller model more accurately. DC voltage control method is usually selected for outer loop control, which operates with a unit power factor. Therefore, suppose the reference value of $Q - axis$ current $i_{q\_ref} = 0$, is mainly responsible for providing $d - axis$

reference current i_{d_ref}. Therefore, the outer loop controller model is mainly affected by the d-axis current inner loop model. The model expression is as follows:

$$G_{eq}(s) = \frac{K_{eq}G(s)}{1 + T_{eq}s} \tag{5}$$

In the outer loop voltage control model, U_{dc_ref} and U_{dc} can be obtained by measurement, and the parameters K_{eq} and T_{eq} need to be obtained by identification. Above, the establishment of distributed power energy grid-connected model is analyzed, but the model parameters cannot be determined. The fuzzy PID control algorithm is applied to distributed power energy grid-connected control to obtain unknown model parameters in each stage.

3 Distributed Energy Grid-Connected Control Based on Big Data

After the distributed power energy grid-connected model is established, the parameters of the model need to be identified. Because the fuzzy PID control (HS) algorithm is a heuristic global optimization algorithm, when performing music, musicians through their own memory, by constantly changing the music of each musical instrument in the band. Finally, a process simulation of the optimal harmony state is obtained [10]. Therefore, in this paper, the fuzzy PID control algorithm is used as the parameter optimization method to identify the unknown parameters in the previous analysis model, and the best fitting process can be achieved according to some principles. Then the objective function can be described as:

$$F = \sum_{k=1}^{M} |e(k)| G_{eq}(s) \tag{6}$$

Where, F is used to describe the fitness function, $e(k)$ is used to describe the error between the measured value and the identified calculated value, and M is used to describe the length of the data. The fitness function of the inner loop controller may be described as:

$$F_{inner\_dq} = \sum_{k=1}^{M} F|i_{dq}(k) - i_{dq\_cal}(k)| \tag{7}$$

Similarly, the fitness function of the outer loop controller can be described as follows:

$$F_{outer\_dq} = \sum_{k=1}^{M} F|i_d(k) - i_{d\_cal}(k)| \tag{8}$$

Where, i_{dq} is used to describe the dq axis component of the measured inverter output current, and i_{dq_cal} is used to describe the calculated value of the dq axis component of the inverter output side current identified by the fuzzy PID control algorithm. i_{d_cal} is used to describe the d-axis component of the measured three-phase current fundamental wave on the grid-connected side, and i_{d_cal} is used to describe the $d - axis$ component of the identified three-phase current fundamental wave on the grid-connected side.

The detailed process of identifying unknown parameters in distributed power energy grid connection model by PID algorithm is as follows:

(1) Problem and algorithm parameter initialization: the parameters of the optimization problem are mainly the target function F_{inner_dq} and F_{outer_dq}, the variable set $x = \{K_{P1}, K_{11}, K_{P2}, K_{12}, R, L, K_{eq}, T_{eq}\}$, the lower limit L_{x_i} of each variable value and the upper limit U_{x_i}; the parameters of the HS algorithm are mainly the expert database size (HMS), the expert database consideration probability (HMCR), a fine-tuning probability (PAR), a maximum number of iterations (NI), and a termination condition;

(2) Initializing the expert database: randomly generating HMS initial solutions are stored in the expert database, and the objective function values of each solution are obtained at the same time.

(3) A new solution is generated: any random number $R1$ is selected, and if $R1 < HMCR$, a variable is selected in the expert database; on the contrary, the value is randomly selected outside the expert database. If you select a value in the expert database, you need to select another random number $R2$, if $R2 < PAR$, you need to complete the disturbance processing of the value. A new solution can be formed by using the above rules for all variables.

(4) If that new solution is better than the optimal solution in the expert database, replace the worst solution to the expert database;

(5) The above process is carried out continuously until the maximum number of iterations or convergence accuracy is reached.

4 Simulation Experiment Analysis

In order to verify the effectiveness of the fuzzy PID control algorithm applied to distributed power energy grid-connected control, it is necessary to carry out relevant experimental analysis. In the experiment, the genetic method is compared and analyzed. The experimental software platform is based on the simulation software of MATLAB 7.0. the hardware system platform of the simulation experiment is as follows: model Dell 2210b, processor is Intel Core2 Duo1.80 GHz, 1 G memory, the hardware system platform of the simulation experiment is model Dell 2210b, the processor is Intel Core2 Duo1.80 GHz, 1 G memory, the main frequency is DDR2 667.

50 simulations are carried out by using this method and the traditional genetic method, and the number of iterations, the time consuming and the statistical results of the model simulation accuracy are counted and described in Table 1.

Table 1. Simulation results of two methods.

	Number of iterations			Time/s			Accuracy/%
	Minimum number of iterations	Average number of iterations	Maximum number of iterations	Minimum number of iterations	Average number of iterations	Maximum number of iterations	
Method of this paper	5	21	68	0.004	0.021	0.042	97
Genetic method	12	45	100	0.032	0.065	0.098	89

It can be seen from the analysis of Table 1 that the number of iterations of this method is lower than that of the genetic method. In addition, the time consuming of this method is obviously less than that of the genetic method, and the accuracy is much higher than that of the genetic method.

In order to further verify the effectiveness of the proposed method, the performance indexes of the two methods are compared and analyzed, and the results are shown in Table 2.

Table 2. Comparison results of performance indicators of the two methods.

Number of experiments	Proposed method		Genetic method	
	Time delay/s	Overshoot/%	Time delay/s	Overshoot/%
1	8	0	16	2.3
2	12	0.3	18	1.8
3	14	0.8	22	2.9
4	12	0.5	24	1.5
5	8	0.3	18	2.1

The analysis of Table 2 shows that compared with the genetic method, the overshoot produced by this method is smaller and the time required for the whole simulation process is shorter, which shows that the energy saving control performance of this method is much better than that of genetic method. The effectiveness of the proposed method is further verified.

Figures 3 and 4 respectively illustrate the comparison between the fitness value of the target function of the inner ring and the outer ring controller model and the optimal fitness curve obtained by the method and the genetic method of the present invention with the increase of the number of iterations.

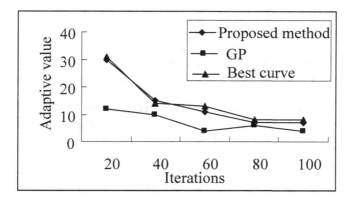

Fig. 3. Comparison of fitness of two methods of inner loop controller model

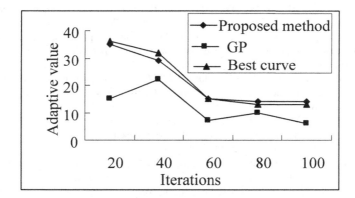

Fig. 4. Comparison of fitness of two methods of outer loop controller model

Figures 3 and 4 show that the fitness curve of this method is closer to the optimal fitness curve than the genetic method for both the inner loop controller model and the outer loop controller model. It is shown that the distributed power energy grid-connected model under this method has higher fitting accuracy. The output dynamic response of the inner ring and the outer ring is closer to the output curve of the detailed model than the genetic method, which shows that it is reasonable and effective, and the structure of the model is greatly simplified by using the method in this paper, which is beneficial to the identification of the model parameters.

5 Conclusions

In this paper, a method of applying fuzzy PID control algorithm to distributed power energy grid-connected control is proposed, the distributed power energy grid-connected model is established, and the DC/AC inverter model is analyzed. In the process of establishing the current inner loop controller model and the voltage outer loop controller model, the fuzzy PID control algorithm is applied to the identification of unknown parameters in distributed power energy grid-connected control. The fitness function of the inner loop controller and the fitness function of the outer loop controller are given, and the expert database is initialized. According to the objective function, a new solution is generated and the expert database is updated. Until the maximum number of iterations or convergence accuracy is reached. The simulation results show that the proposed method can effectively improve the performance of distributed power energy grid-connected control.

References

1. Ding, Q.-Q., Lu, W., Xu, C.-B., et al.: Passivity-based control of a three-phase shunt hybrid active power filter. J. Electr. Mach. Control **18**(05), 1–6 (2014)
2. Liang, S., Hu, X., Zhang, D., et al.: Probabilistic models based evaluation method for capacity credit of photovoltaic generation. Autom. Electr. Power Syst. **36**(13), 32–37 (2012)
3. Wang, Q., Dong, W., Yang, L.: A wind power/photovoltaic typical scenario set generation algorithm based on wasserstein distance metric and revised K-medoids cluster. Proc. CSEE **35**(11), 2654–2661 (2015)
4. Alfaro, V.M., Vilanovab, R.: Robust tuning of 2DoF five-parameter PID controllers for inverse response controlled processes. J. Process Control **23**(4), 453–462 (2013)
5. Ma, Z., Chen, W.: Friction torque calculation method of ball bearings based on rolling creepage theory. J. Mech. Eng. **53**(22), 219–224 (2017)
6. Zhou, S.B., Xu, W.X.: A novel clustering algorithm based on relative density and decision graph. Control Decis. **33**(11), 1921–1930 (2018)
7. He, H., Tan, Y.: Automatic pattern recognition of ECG signals using entropy-based adaptive dimensionality reduction and clustering. Appl. Soft Comput. **55**, 238–252 (2017)
8. Zhu, Y., Zhu, X., Wang, J.: Time series motif discovery algorithm based on subsequence full join and maximum clique. J. Comput. Appl. **39**(2), 414–420 (2019)
9. Wang, Y., Zhou, J., Mo, L., et al.: Precise scheduling method for daily generation plan of large-scale hydropower station based on comprehensive state evaluation strategy for generating units. Power Syst. Technol. **36**(7), 94–99 (2012)
10. Chen, Z., Wang, K., Sun, M., Sun, Q.: Sensorless control of flux-switching permanent magnet motor based on extended state observer. Inf. Control **48**(2), 194–201 (2019)

Blind Identification of Sparse Multipath Channels Under the Background of Internet of Things

Ying Li, Feng Jin$^{(\boxtimes)}$, and Qi Liu

Information and Communication College,
National University of Defense Technology, Xi'an 710106, China
jf_phoenix@163.com

Abstract. To improve the ability of blind identification and scheduling of sparse multipath channels in wireless communication networks under the background of Internet of things, a blind identification algorithm for sparse multipath wireless communication based on random sampling interval equalization and BPSK modulation is proposed. The sparse multipath channel model of wireless communication network under the background of Internet of things is constructed, and the multipath characteristics of sparse multipath channel of wireless communication network are analyzed. The BPSK modulation method is used to filter the inter-symbol interference of sparse multipath channel of wireless communication network. Based on the adaptive random sampling interval equalization technique, blind channel identification is designed, and the tap delay line model is used to suppress the multi-path of sparse multipath channel in wireless communication network. The simulation results show that the blind identification of sparse multipath channels in wireless communication networks is well balanced and the bit error rate (BER) is reduced.

Keywords: Internet of things · Sparse multipath channel · Blind identification · Communication

1 Introduction

The Internet of things is a smart object with the ability of online real-time, comprehensive and accurate positioning perception, the ability of "unobstructed" large data comparison and query, and the ability of daily management and emergency response with super intelligence beyond the individual's brain. Therefore, wireless communication networks can use the advantages of the Internet of things to blindly identify and schedule sparse multipath channels. Under the background of Internet of things, the sparse multipath channel of wireless communication network is easy to be interfered by the spectrum of the network, it is easy to appear multi-path effect. The attenuation of signal energy is large, so it is necessary to develop and store reasonable information resources in the spectrum. Transmission and utilization can realize blind identification scheduling of sparse multipath channel in wireless communication network, improve the fidelity of big data communication transmission. And study the blind identification scheduling model of sparse multipath channel in wireless communication network

© ICST Institute for Computer Sciences, Social Informatics and Telecommunications Engineering 2019
Published by Springer Nature Switzerland AG 2019. All Rights Reserved
G. Gui and L. Yun (Eds.): ADHIP 2019, LNICST 302, pp. 41–51, 2019.
https://doi.org/10.1007/978-3-030-36405-2_5

under the background of Internet of things [1]. The sparse multipath channel and spectrum of the wireless communication network are effectively managed and controlled, and the error-free control of the sparse multipath channel of the Internet of things is carried out with joint feature recognition and blind channel identification design, so as to improve the efficiency and intelligence of Internet of things communication and resource transmission control [2].

The invention relates to a sparse multi-path channel blind identification and scheduling technique of a wireless communication network under the background of internet of things. In the background of internet of things, the sparse multi-path channel of the wireless communication network is affected by the interference of the electromagnetic medium. The multi-path effect of the channel output, the inter-code interference is easily generated, the communication channel is unbalanced, the channel blind identification design and the scheduling are needed, and the fidelity of the large-data output is improved [3]. Conventionally, a blind identification algorithm for a sparse multi-path channel of a wireless communication network mainly comprises a decision feedback blind identification algorithm, an LMS blind identification algorithm, a diversity blind identification algorithm and the like, the output symbol modulation is carried out in combination with the adaptive modulation and demodulation technology. The channel spread spectrum scheduling is carried out by adopting a spread spectrum technology, the anti-interference and the robustness of the channel scheduling are improved, a certain research result is obtained. The invention provides a blind identification algorithm based on a judgment feedback self-coherent matching object-to-internet communication blind identification algorithm, which consists of a feed-forward filter and a feedback filter, But the method cannot effectively inhibit the impulse response interference in the background of the electromagnetic radiation and the internet of things, so that the anti-interference capability of the channel blind identification and scheduling is not strong; the channel blind identification algorithm based on the combination of the PTRM and the DS is proposed in the reference [4], the blind identification design of the internet of things communication in the background of internet of things is carried out, the inter-code interference suppression model is adopted for multi-path filtering and channel anti-interference processing, the PTRM direct-expanding simulation communication system is constructed. In the three cases of PTRM, the Internet of Things communication system is studied, the error rate of three blind identification scheduling models under different signal-to-noise ratios and different processing gains is analyzed, and the blind identification and scheduling capability of the sparse multi-path channel of the wireless communication network is improved. But the method has the problem that the computational expense is too large and the complexity is high; in the reference [5], a sparse multi-path channel blind identification algorithm based on a wireless communication network under the object of networking background based on a direct sequence spread spectrum is proposed, and a self-correlation matched filter is designed. By direct sequence spread spectrum method, the channel blind identification of the Internet of things communication in the Internet of things is realized, the blind identification effect of the communication channel is good, and the error bit rate of the communication is low. But with the increase of the impact strength of the large data, the impact resistance of the channel is not good, and it needs to be improved [6].

In order to solve these problems, this paper proposes a blind identification algorithm for sparse multipath wireless communication based on random sampling interval equalization and BPSK modulation. Firstly, the sparse multipath channel model of wireless communication network under the background of Internet of things is constructed. The blind identification scheduling of sparse multipath channel in wireless communication network is realized by combining BPSK modulation and demodulation technology, and the blind identification of channel is improved. Finally, the simulation results show that the proposed method can improve the performance of blind channel identification scheduling and improve the transmission quality of Internet of things (IoT) communication.

2 Network Multipath Channel Model and Channel Characteristic Analysis Under the Background of Internet of Things

2.1 Network Multipath Channel Model Description Under the Background of Internet of Things

In order to realize blind identification scheduling of sparse multipath channel in wireless communication network under the background of Internet of things, it is necessary to construct sparse multipath channel model of wireless communication network under the background of Internet of things, and analyze the input and output characteristics of communication signal. The sparse multipath channel of wireless communication network in the context of Internet of things is an extended channel, which is modelled and demodulated by multi-input multi-output MIMO multi-path channel model [7]. The sparse multipath channel of wireless communication network has two main characteristics: one is that it is easy to appear channel distortion in the background of Internet of things, and the sparse multipath channel of wireless communication network is bandwidth-limited channel. Blind identification technology can be used for blind channel identification scheduling to suppress distortion and improve the blind identification of the channel. Second, the sparse multipath channel of wireless communication network under the background of Internet of things has a larger absorption coefficient for higher frequency signals, which can compensate for the inherent channel distortion in the received signal, and the channel characteristics change with time. Under the condition of limited space, the blind identification scheduling of symbol interval and fractional interval has the adaptability under the condition of strong micro-multipath and strong micro-multipath. Under the background of Internet of things, doppler frequency shift affects carrier tracking and symbol synchronization of IoT communication. A coherent multi-path channel model is used to optimize the sparse multipath channel model of wireless communication network under the background of Internet of things. The channel model is constructed by using a digital communication system with blind identifier [8]. The impulse response of the channel after sampling decision can be expressed as follows:

$$h(t) = \sum_i a_i(t)e^{j\theta_i(t)}\delta(t - iT_S) \tag{1}$$

Where, $\theta_i(t)$ is the phase offset of each path. The blind identifier parameters weights are installed for blind channel identification scheduling, and the modified filter coefficients are used to compensate $\theta_i(t)$ and symbol rate H adaptively. The dynamic compensation technique is used to process the symbol sampling of sparse multipath channel in wireless communication network under the background of Internet of things [9]. The output signal model is reconstructed by using positive and negative signal flipping method:

$$\tilde{y}_k^+ = \begin{cases} y_k^+, & y_k^+ \geq 0 \\ 0, & y_k^+ < 0 \end{cases} \tag{2}$$

$$\tilde{y}_k^- = \begin{cases} y_k^-, & y_k^- \geq 0 \\ 0, & y_k^- < 0 \end{cases} \tag{3}$$

The transverse time domain filter shown in Fig. 1 is used to modulate the communication channel, so that the output time delay of the Internet of things communication system is equal to the slope of the phase-frequency characteristic curve, and the tap weighted control is combined [10]. Each multipath signal is added to the output, and the blind identified communication signal is outputted.

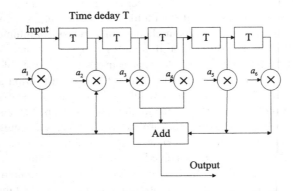

Fig. 1. Structure diagram of transverse time domain filter

In Fig. 1, the big data impact signal is outputted in the multipath channel as follows:

$$x_k = \sum_{n=0}^{N-1} C_n \cdot e^{j2\pi kn/N} \quad k = 0, 1, \cdots, N - 1 \tag{4}$$

According to the channel difference value of channel impulse between receiving and sending nodes, the complex coefficient is used to simulate the impulse response of the channel accurately. And the instantaneous quantity is used instead of the statistical average to obtain the network multipath channel model under the background of the Internet of things:

$$x_k = \sum_{n=0}^{N/2-1} 2\left(a_n \cos\frac{2\pi kn}{N} - b_n \sin\frac{2\pi kn}{N}\right) \quad k = 0, 1, \ldots N - 1 \quad (5)$$

In the above formula, a_n denotes the tap interval, and b_n is the time-varying tap coefficient of the blind identifier.

2.2 Inter-symbol Interference Filtering for Sparse Multipath Channels in Wireless Communication Networks

The BPSK modulation method is used to filter the inter-symbol interference (ISI) in sparse multipath channels of wireless communication networks, and the blind channel identification design is carried out with adaptive random sampling interval equalization technique [11]. The channel bandwidth of IoT communication network is obtained under the background of Internet of things:

$$T_s = N_f T_f \quad (6)$$

After the multipath propagation of the channel, the time delay of the sparse multipath channel receiver of the wireless communication network under the background of the Internet of things is obtained as follows:

$$x(t) = \sum_{m=1}^{M} \sum_{k=1}^{K(m)} w_{nk} s(t - T_m - \tau_{mk}) + v(t) \quad (7)$$

In the equation, w_{mk} is the superposition of multiple components with phase offset, and $v(t)$ is noise. According to the channel characteristic range, the interference filtering is carried out, and the adaptive cascade filtering model is used to suppress the interference. The filtering function is expressed as follows:

$$x(t) = \sum_{j=1}^{N_S} \sum_{m=1}^{M} \sum_{k=1}^{K(m)} q_j w_{mk} p(t - jT_s - T_m - \tau_{mk}) + v(t) \quad (8)$$

Where, q_j is the instantaneous impulse response of the channel in a short time, the data training sequence is represented as a_j, and the tap delay model of blind identifier is c_j. The channel output code stream after inter-symbol interference filtering is obtained by suppressing the inter-level interference:

$$T(n) = \sum_i R(n, i) + T(n+1) \qquad (9)$$

While n = 0, T(0) = T(1), while n = N, T(n) = $\sum\limits_i$ R(n, i), according to the above analysis, the proposed method is used to filter the inter-symbol interference of the sparse multipath channel in the wireless communication network, which can effectively suppress the interference term and improve the effective transmission ability of the signal in the channel.

3 Optimal Implementation of Blind Channel Identification Algorithm

3.1 Multipath Suppression in Sparse Multipath Channels

In this paper, a blind identification algorithm for sparse multipath wireless communication based on random sampling interval equalization and BPSK modulation is proposed. The BPSK modulation method is used to filter the inter-symbol interference of sparse multipath channels in wireless communication networks. The fading signal $Y(n)$ is determined by the output signal $d(n)$ of coherent multi-path channel, the tap coefficient of blind identifier is adjusted. And the adaptive weighting is carried out to construct the channel model of Internet of things communication under the background of Internet of things. The blind channel identification design is also carried out [12]. The satisfaction function for the throughput of the Internet of things communication nodes is shown in the following formula:

$$U_{v_i} = \beta_{v_i} \times \log\left(1 + \partial_{v_i} \times \sum_{j=1}^{K} S_{v_i} e_j^T \frac{R_{C_j}}{n_{C_j}}\right), \ v_i \in v, \ C_j \in C \qquad (10)$$

Under the constraint of network utility maximization, the probability formula for obtaining optimal channel matching using channel allocation strategy is expressed as follows:

$$p(i, j) = p(i)p(j) = \frac{\frac{\rho^i}{i!} \cdot \frac{\rho^i}{j!}}{\sum\limits_{i=0}^{n} \frac{\rho^i}{i!} \sum\limits_{j=0}^{n} \frac{\rho^i}{j!}}, \ i, j = 0, 1, \ldots, n \qquad (11)$$

Taking the throughput maximization of node interface receiving data as the objective function, the multipath characteristic parameters of sparse multipath channel transmission in wireless communication network are constructed under the background of Internet of things. The $C_0 = C_{N/2} = 0$, $C_{N-n} = C_n^*$, $n = 0, 1, 2 \cdots N/2 - 1$, tap delay linear model for blind identification scheduling is adopted, the tap delay function is:

$$s_{PPM}(t) = \sum_{i=-\infty}^{\infty} \sum_{j=0}^{N_p-1} p(t - iT_s - jT_p - c_j T_c - a_i \varepsilon) \tag{12}$$

$$s_{PAM}(t) = \sum_{j=-\infty}^{\infty} d_j p(t - jT_s) \tag{13}$$

Assuming that the step-size transformation factor is $\mu \big/ 1 + \mu \|e(n)\|^2$, the steady-state error of blind identification scheduling of sparse multipath channels in wireless communication networks satisfies $T_p = N_p T_c$. a_i is the channel system parameter and ε is the modulation time offset constant under the tap linear blind identification model. The time function of multipath suppression for sparse multipath channels in wireless communication networks is T_c. The sparse multipath channel multipath suppression in wireless communication network is designed by tap delay linear model, and the modulation function of output channel is obtained as follows:

$$U_{v_i} = \beta_{v_i} \times \log(1 + \partial_{v_i} \times \sum_{j=1}^{K} S_{v_i} e_j^T \frac{R_{C_j}}{n_{C_j}}), \; v_i \in v, \; C_j \in C \tag{14}$$

Where $n_{C_j} = \sum_{j=1}^{K} S_{v_i} e_j^T$, $e_j^T = (0, \ldots, 1, \ldots, 0)$ denotes the error correction feedback coefficient of the multipath vector v_i given different initial μ values, and $\sum_{j=1}^{K} S_{v_i} e_j^T \frac{R_{C_j}}{n_{C_j}}$ denotes the energy decay term.

3.2   Random Sampling Interval Equalization Channel Scheduling Algorithm

In order to eliminate crosstalk caused by the preceding symbol, the optimal solution of sparse multipath channel sparse table matrix W in wireless communication network under the background of Internet of things is solved as:

$$W_{opt} = \arg \min_{W} \lambda \|(X - DW)G\|_F^2 \; s.t \; \|w_i\|_0 \le k \; \forall i \tag{15}$$

A transverse filter is used for forward filtering, and the optimal estimation of output nonlinear filtering is expressed as follows:

$$D_{opt} = \lambda X V^{-1} W^T (W V^{-1} W^T)^{-1} \tag{16}$$

By adaptive spectrum spread, the channel phase shift under the background of Internet of things is obtained as follows:

$$S_{v_i} = \{k(v_1, 1), \ldots, k(v_1, i), \ldots, k(v_1, K)\}, \ K \leq M, j \in M \qquad (17)$$

According to the spectrum of sampled communication signals, the diversity blind identification scheduling is carried out. The competition model for blind identification scheduling of sparse multipath channels in wireless communication networks under the background of Internet of things is shown as follows:

$$\alpha(i, j) = \begin{cases} 0, \ i = 0 \ or \ j = 0 \\ 1, \ n - j < i, \ i \geq j \\ 1, \ n - i < j, \ j \geq i \\ 1 - {}_{n-j}C_i/{}_nC_i, \ n - j \geq i, \ i \geq j \\ 1 - {}_{n-i}C_j/{}_nC_j, \ n - i \geq j, \ j \geq i \end{cases} \qquad (18)$$

$\alpha(i, j)$ is used to represent the transmission state of a node in (i, j) state, and the formula $P_C = \sum_{i=0}^{n} \sum_{j=0}^{n} \alpha(i, j)P(i, j)$ is obtained, which is used as the allocation strategy for blind identification scheduling of sparse multipath channels in wireless communication networks under the background of the Internet of things.

4 Simulation Experiment and Performance Analysis

In order to test the blind identification scheduling of sparse multipath channel in wireless communication network under the background of Internet of things, and to improve the transmission quality of Internet of things, the simulation experiment is carried out. The experiment is based on Matlab simulation software. In order to facilitate the simulation, the transmitted data from the Internet of things communication system under the background of the Internet of things in the experiment is simulated by BPSK modulation carrier signal. In order to make it easy to simulate the transmitted data through the simulation environment VisualDSP. In the background of Internet of things, the frequency of communication signal is 14.5 kHz, the carrier signal is a set of sine signals with 24 kHz frequency, the sampling rate of Porter interval is 50 kHz, and the sensitivity of communication signal collector is about −265.7 dB (8 kHz–20 kHz). The LFM signal and BPSK signal are transmitted at the transmitting end of the signal, in which the LFM signal is used to test the multipath of the channel, and the BPSK signal is used to verify the blind identification effect. The bandwidth of the signal is 8 kHz–15 kHz, the frequency interval is $\Delta f = 10 \, Hz$, and the cut-off frequency of the pass band is 5 kHz. According to the above simulation environment and parameter setting, the blind identification scheduling experiment of sparse multipath channel in wireless communication network is carried out. In the experiment, the LFM signal is transmitted at the score transmitter of the Internet of things communication system, as shown in Fig. 2.

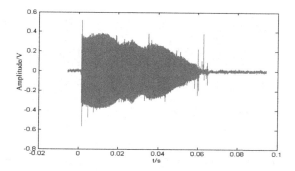

Fig. 2. Output multipath LFM signal from Internet of things communication system

Figure 2 the multipath interference of the transmitted LFM signal leads to poor symbol reception. Therefore, the tap delay line model of the channel is used to suppress the multipath of the sparse multipath channel in the wireless communication network. The blind identification scheduling of sparse multipath channel in wireless communication network is realized by combining BPSK modulation and demodulation technology. The impulse response and cross-correlation of sparse multipath channel of output wireless communication network after multipath suppression are obtained as shown in Fig. 3.

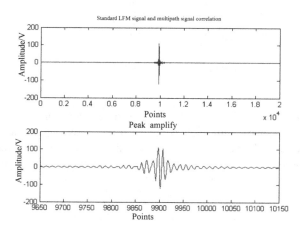

Fig. 3. Channel impulse response and cross-correlation after multipath interference suppression

The results of Fig. 3 show that the blind identification scheduling of sparse multipath channel in wireless communication network using this method has a good impulse response and improves the anti-jamming ability of the channel. As a result, the symbol receiving ability of sparse multipath channel in wireless communication network is improved. Finally, the signals before and after blind channel identification scheduling are compared as shown in Fig. 4.

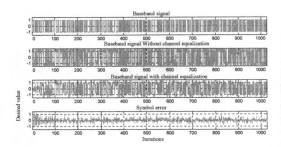

Fig. 4. Baseband signal transmission waveform before and after blind channel identification scheduling

The results of Fig. 4 show that the signal output performance of blind channel identification scheduling using this method is better and the fidelity of symbols is higher. Finally, the method is compared with the traditional method. The interference signal-to-noise ratio of big data is −10–10 dB. Under the same other conditions, the error bit rate of output is tested, and the comparison results are shown in Table 1.

Table 1. Comparison of bit error rates for output streams.

SNR	Proposed method	Traditional method
−10	0.0572	0.1644
−5	0.0431	0.0934
0	0.0312	0.0632
5	0.0006	0.0546
10	0.0001	0.0087

The results of Table 1 show that the proposed method is used for blind identification scheduling of sparse multipath channels in wireless communication networks under the background of Internet of things, and the output bit error rate is low. The robustness and anti-jamming ability of the sparse multipath channel in the wireless communication network are improved, and the robustness of the communication channel is better.

5 Conclusions

In this paper, a blind identification algorithm for sparse multipath wireless communication based on random sampling interval equalization and BPSK modulation is proposed. The sparse multipath channel model of wireless communication network under the background of Internet of things is constructed, and the multipath characteristics of sparse multipath channels in wireless communication networks are analyzed. The BPSK modulation method is used to filter the inter-symbol interference of sparse multipath channel of wireless communication network. Based on the adaptive random sampling interval equalization technique, blind channel identification is designed, and the tap delay line model is used to suppress the multi-path of sparse multipath channel in wireless communication network. The simulation results show that the blind identification of sparse multipath channels in wireless communication networks is well balanced and the BER is reduced. This method has important application value in improving the communication quality of Internet of things.

References

1. Hu, S., Ding, Z., Ni, Q.: Beamforming optimisation in energy harvesting cooperative full-duplex networks with self-energy recycling protocol. IET Commun. **10**(7), 848–853 (2016)
2. Tang, L., Yang, X., Shi, Y.J., Chen, Q.B.: ARMA-prediction based online adaptive dynamic resource allocation in wireless virtualized networks. J. Electron. Inf. **41**(1), 16–23 (2019)
3. Zhang, M., Jin, L.X., Li, G.N., Wu, Y.N., et al.: Design of image simulation system of TDICCD space camera. Chin. J. Liq. Cryst. Displays **31**(2), 208–214 (2016)
4. Li, Y.B., Wang, D., et al.: Distributive beamforming design in multicell downlinks using interference and power control. Acta Electronica Sin. **43**(3), 597–600 (2015)
5. Li, H., Huang, C., Cui, S.: Multiuser gain in energy harvesting wireless communications. IEEE Access **34**(5), 10052–10061 (2017)
6. Wang, Y., Sun, R., Wang, X.: Transceiver design to maximize the weighted sum secrecy rate in full-duplex SWIPT systems. IEEE Signal Process. Lett. **23**(6), 883–887 (2016)
7. Eo, D.W., Lee, J.H., Lee, H.S.: Optimal coupling to achieve maximum output power in a WPT system. IEEE Trans. Power Electron. **31**(6), 3994–3998 (2016)
8. Dai, H., Huang, Y., Li, C., et al.: Energy-efficient resource allocation for device-to-device communication with WPT. IET Commun. **11**(3), 326–334 (2017)
9. Helmy, A., Hedayat, A., Al-Dhahir, N.: Robust weighted sum-rate maximization for the multi-stream MIMO interference channel with sparse equalization. IEEE Trans. Commun. **60**(10), 3645–3659 (2015)
10. Alfaro, V.M., Vilanovab, R.: Robust tuning of 2DoF five-parameter PID controllers for inverse response controlled processes. J. Process Control **23**(4), 453–462 (2013)
11. Han, D.Z., Chen, X.G., Lei, Y.X., et al.: Real-time data analysis system based on spark streaming and its application. J. Comput. Appl. **37**(5), 1263–1269 (2017)
12. Feng, W., Wang, Y., Lin, D., et al.: When mm wave communications meet network densification, a scalable interference coordination perspective. IEEE J. Sel. Areas Commun. **35**(7), 1459–1471 (2017)

Design of Anti-Co-Frequency Interference System for Wireless Spread Spectrum Communication Based on Internet of Things Technology

Feng Jin[✉], Ying Li, and Wu-lin Liu

Information and Communication College,
National University of Defense Technology, Xi'an 710106, China
jf_phoenix@163.com

Abstract. An anti-co-frequency interference suppression method for wireless spread spectrum communication based on equivalent low-pass time-varying pulse modulation technology is proposed. The anti-co-frequency interference system for wireless spread spectrum communication is designed based on Internet of things technology, and the multi-path channel model for wireless spread spectrum communication is constructed. The Doppler spread technique is used to design the channel equalization of wireless spread spectrum communication system. The equivalent low-pass time-varying pulse modulation method is used to suppress the same-frequency interference and blind source separation. Improve the lossless transmission ability of the Internet of things (IoT) transmission signal in the wireless spread spectrum communication system. The simulation results show that this method is used to design the wireless spread spectrum communication system and the co-frequency interference is effectively suppressed and the bit error rate of communication is lower than that of the traditional method.

Keywords: Wireless spread spectrum communication · Internet of things · Co-frequency interference · Channel equalization · Blind source separation

1 Introduction

With the rapid development of the wireless communication technology, the accuracy and the high-capacity of the wireless communication are required to be higher, and the wireless spread spectrum communication is a new communication technology, which has the advantages of large transmission bandwidth, strong confidentiality and the like, and has the advantages of large data wireless transmission field. by adopting the wireless spread spectrum communication technology [1], the communication system is designed in combination with the radio principle, the long-distance transmission of the non-stationary signal is realized, the modulation and the demodulation of the signal are realized, The information such as an image is converted into an electric signal and an optical signal, and the like, and the spread spectrum communication is realized by using a wireless communication signal. It can be seen that the wireless spread spectrum communication has a wide application in the field of communication [2].

© ICST Institute for Computer Sciences, Social Informatics and Telecommunications Engineering 2019
Published by Springer Nature Switzerland AG 2019. All Rights Reserved
G. Gui and L. Yun (Eds.): ADHIP 2019, LNICST 302, pp. 52–61, 2019.
https://doi.org/10.1007/978-3-030-36405-2_6

In wireless spread spectrum communication, Internet of things transmission signal transmission is easy to be affected by initial frequency and initial phase co-frequency disturbance, resulting in increased error code and signal transmission distortion, so, it is necessary to optimize the lossless transmission of the IoT transmission signal in wireless spread spectrum communication system [3], so as to reduce the BER of communication. In the traditional method, the lossless transmission of the signal transmitted by the Internet of things in wireless spread spectrum communication is designed mainly through signal interference filtering and modulation and demodulation, such as keying phase shift algorithm, the vertical linear array spatial beamforming method and the interference suppression method based on BPSK modulation are used to optimize the transmission of communication signals using channel equalization design to reduce the bit error rate of wireless spread spectrum communication, and some research results have been achieved [4]. In reference [5], a frequency domain equalization technique for wireless spread spectrum communication channel based on vertical linear array spatial gain modulation is proposed to achieve error suppression and modulation and demodulation [6]. The multi-path interference separation of the wireless spread spectrum communication system is realized by BPSK modulation, and the multipath effect in the communication process is suppressed. However, in this method, there is drift distortion of the received signal. With the increase of the interference intensity, the distortion of communication transmission increases. In view of the disadvantages of traditional methods, this paper proposes an anti-co-frequency interference suppression method for wireless spread spectrum communication based on equivalent low-pass time-varying pulse modulation technology, which can realize the lossless transmission of communication signals in the Internet of things environment. Firstly, the multipath channel model of wireless spread spectrum communication is constructed, then channel equalization design and co-frequency interference suppression design are carried out. Finally, the performance of wireless spread spectrum communication is tested and the validity conclusion is drawn.

2   Channel Model and Analysis of Internet of Things Transmission Signal

2.1   Channel Model of Wireless Spread Spectrum Communication System

In order to realize lossless transmission and channel equalization design of Internet of things transmission signal in wireless spread spectrum communication system, the channel model of wireless spread spectrum communication system needs to be constructed firstly [7], and the impact response in wireless spread spectrum communication channel is assumed to be $n(n)$. The statistical average of time delay spread is $y(n)$, the signal of Internet of things transmission is $\tilde{x}(n)$ channel equalization system output signal is $n(n)$. Taking the discrete multipath case as an example, the signals received by the spread spectrum communication channel are as follows:

$$x(t) = \text{Re}\{a_n(t)e^{-j2\pi f_c \tau_n(t)} s_l(t - \tau_n(t))e^{-j2\pi f_c t}\} \tag{1}$$

It can be seen that the received signal is a time-varying signal and the time-reversal mirror (TRM) recombination of the multipath signal transmitted in the wireless spread spectrum communication channel is carried out. The frequency domain characteristics of the communication channel can be described as follows:

$$c(\tau, t) = \sum_n a_n(t)e^{-j2\pi f_c \tau_n(t)} \delta(t - \tau_n(t)) \tag{2}$$

Where, $a_n(t)$ is the propagation loss of the nth path, $\tau_n(t)$ is the channel attenuation coefficient of the nth path, $s_l(t)$ is the modulation frequency, and f_c is the noise component of the signal transmitted by the Internet of things. Because the bandwidth of the spread spectrum code sequence is much larger than the minimum bandwidth of the transmitted information, the pulse response of the multipath channel in the wireless spread spectrum communication system is obtained by adaptive equalization of the instantaneous frequency and time of the signal:

$$R(t) = \frac{\sqrt{WT}}{WT} \sin[\pi WT(1 - \frac{|\tau|}{T})] \cos(2\pi f_0 \tau) \tag{3}$$

In this case, WT is the channel output gain with a fixed initial frequency. If the extended sweep bandwidth of the frequency band is W and the time length of the LFM signal is T, there are:

$$\beta = \frac{W}{T} \tag{4}$$

On the basis of the above-mentioned communication channel model, narrow band filter is used to filter the signal of the input spread spectrum communication system and blind source separation is carried out, and the adaptive algorithm is used to suppress the same frequency interference to realize the optimization of the spread spectrum communication. The block diagram of the overall design is shown in Fig. 1.

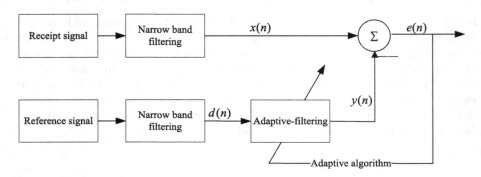

Fig. 1. Structure model of spread spectrum communication system

2.2   Multi-path Characteristic Measurement and Signal Analysis of the Signal Transmitted by the Internet of Things

The wireless spread spectrum communication channel model is constructed, the signal analysis is carried out to realize the lossless transmission design of the Internet of things transmission signal [8], and the multi-path characteristic measurement method is used to analyze the Internet of things transmission signal. Suppose the impulse response expression for the Internet of things transmission signal transmission for each multipath channel is:

$$h(\tau_{i,}t) = \sum_{i=1}^{N_m} a_i(t)e^{j\theta_i(t)}\delta(t - \tau_i(t)) \qquad (5)$$

In the above formula, $a_i(t)$ is the normalized amplitude of each path of wireless spread spectrum communication, $\tau_i(t)$ is the time delay of multi-channel components, and the number of paths of H communication channel. The transmitted signals of the Internet of things are spread and blindly separated by pseudo-random (PN) sequence coding. The fast frequency hopping method is used to spread the time delay between each path and the direct path. The multipath component of the channel expansion is obtained as follows:

$$x_k = \sum_{n=0}^{N/2-1} 2(a_n \cos\frac{2\pi kn}{N} - b_n \sin\frac{2\pi kn}{N}) \quad k = 0, 1, \ldots N - 1 \qquad (6)$$

When $S_0(t) = a_0\delta(t)$ to receiver, the Internet of things transmission signal $S(t)$, which is obtained by adaptive equalization modulation, is composed of multi-pulse of transmission signal, which is expressed as:

$$S(t) = a_0 \sum_{i=1}^{N} a_i\delta(t - \tau_i)e^{jw_ct} \qquad (7)$$

$$e(n) = d(n) - u^T(n)w(n) \qquad (8)$$

The channel modulation is carried out by keying phase shift technique (PSK), and the frequency domain data signal is obtained [9]. The iterative formula of coded amplitude modulation for spread spectrum communication is expressed as follows:

$$f(k+1) = f(k) - \mu \cdot \rho \cdot e_{MDMMA}(k)y^*(k) \qquad (9)$$

Wherein:

$$e_{MDMMA}(k) = z(k)[|z(k)|^2 - R_{MDMMA}(k)] \qquad (10)$$

Where, ρ is the symbol width and complex coefficient is used to simulate the pulse response of the channel accurately. The information code signal $S_r(t)$ received by the wireless spread spectrum communication system is as follows:

$$S_r(t) = S(t) * h(t) + n_s(t) \tag{11}$$

According to the above-mentioned design principle, the optimization design of wireless spread spectrum communication system is carried out.

3   Improved Algorithm Implementation

3.1   Channel Equalization

On the basis of the channel model construction and signal analysis of the wireless spread spectrum communication system mentioned above, the communication optimization design is carried out. Under the influence of the multi-path effect, the communication channel produces the same frequency interference, which leads to the increase of the error code and the distortion of the signal transmission [10]. In this paper, an anti-co-frequency interference suppression method for wireless spread spectrum communication based on equivalent low-pass time-varying pulse modulation technique is proposed. The channel equalization is designed by Doppler spread technique. It is assumed that the transmission signal of the wireless spread spectrum communication system under the multi-path effect is expressed as follows:

$$x_k = \sum_{n=0}^{N-1} C_n \cdot e^{j2\pi kn/N} \ k = 0, 1, \cdots, N-1 \tag{12}$$

The channel has the characteristic of fast time-varying fading. The time-frequency decomposition method is used to decompose the Internet of things transmission signal into positive signal and negative signal:

$$x_k^+ = \begin{cases} x_k & x_k \geq 0 \\ 0 & x_k < 0 \end{cases} \qquad x_k^- = \begin{cases} x_k & x_k < 0 \\ 0 & x_k \geq 0 \end{cases} \tag{13}$$

Signal superposition is generated between received pulses and fractional interval equalization is designed by introducing limiting noise [11]. The transmission model of independent fading channel is obtained by using adaptive equalization technique:

$$\{b_1', b_2', \cdots, b_v'\} = \underset{\{b_1, b_2, \cdots, b_v\}}{\operatorname{argmin}} \left(\underset{\sum_{v=1}^{v} b_v \bullet x_v < 0, 1 \leq n \leq N}{\max} |\sum_{v=1}^{V} b_v \bullet x_v|^2 \right) \tag{14}$$

By combining the total received signals properly, the $x' = \sum\limits_{v=1}^{V} b'_v x_v$ is designed for fractional interval equalization through multiple independent fading channels, and the sampling amplitude of fractional interval equalization is satisfied:

$$\tilde{y}_k^+ = \begin{cases} y_k^+, & y_k^+ \geq 0 \\ 0, & y_k^+ < 0 \end{cases}, \quad \tilde{y}_k^- = \begin{cases} y_k^-, & y_k^- \geq 0 \\ 0 & y_k^- < 0 \end{cases} \tag{15}$$

The equalizer detects the data in a channel with co-frequency interference. The equalizer detects the signal model is expressed as follows:

$$y_k = \begin{cases} -y_k^- & y_k^- > y_k^+ \\ y_k^+ & y_k^+ \geq y_k^- \& y_k^- < \gamma \\ y_k^+ + y_k^- & y_k^+ \geq y_k^- \& y_k^- \geq \gamma \end{cases} \tag{16}$$

When $\tilde{y}_k^- < \gamma$, it is regarded as the number of information symbols covered by channel co-frequency interference. The frequency spectrum of the received signal is equalized by the equalizer with D tap interval, and the channel information power of the wireless spread spectrum communication channel is expressed as follows:

$$P_r = \frac{P_t}{(4\pi)^2 \left(\frac{d}{\lambda}\right)^\gamma} \left[1 + \alpha^2 + 2\alpha \cos\left(\frac{4\pi h^2}{d\lambda}\right)\right] \tag{17}$$

According to the above analysis, the Doppler spread technique is used for channel equalization, which reduces the channel attenuation loss and avoids the channel distortion caused by aliasing effect.

3.2 Co-frequency Interference Suppression and Blind Source Separation

On the basis of channel equalization design, in order to improve the lossless transmission ability of communication signals, the equivalent low-pass time-varying pulse modulation method is used to suppress the same-frequency interference and blind source separation. The process of equivalent low-pass time-varying pulse modulation in wireless spread spectrum communication systems can be expressed as follows:

$$p_{ri}(t) = p(t) * h_i(t) + n_{pi}(t) \tag{18}$$

The $h_i(t)$ indicates the impulse response of the received signal spectrum $p(t)$ during transmission. The interference information beyond Nyquist frequency is suppressed by time mirror inversion. The transfer function of time mirror inversion is as follows:

$$S_{ri}(t) = S(t) * h'_i(t) + n_{si}(t) \tag{19}$$

The $h_i'(t)$ in the communication system is the multi-path spread impulse response between the I elements of the receiving array of the Internet of things transmission signal in the communication system, from which the following can be obtained:

$$r_i'(t) = S_{ri}(t) * p_{ri}(-t) = S(t) * p(-t) * h_i'(t) * h_i(-t) + n_{1i}(t) \qquad (20)$$

Where

$$n_{1i}(t) = S(t) * h_i'(t) * n_{pi}(-t) + n_{si}(t) * p(-t) * h_i(-t) + n_{si}(t) * n_{pi}(-t) \qquad (21)$$

Because of the complexity of multipath structure, the blind source separation of signal is carried out by interference suppression method, the received signal is copied and correlated [12], and the channel impulse response function between receiving and sending nodes of wireless spread spectrum communication system is processed by adaptive weighting, and the results are as follows:

$$r(t) \cong S(t) * \delta(t) * \sum_{i=1}^{M} \delta(t) + \sum_{i=1}^{M} n_i(t) = MS(t) + \sum_{i=1}^{M} n_i(t) \qquad (22)$$

By estimating the autocorrelation function of the channel impulse response function in frequency domain, it is found that the impulse response $S(t)$ output by the time-backchannel modulation of the signal $\hat{h}(t) = \sum_{i=1}^{M} h_i'(t) * h_i(-t)$ is isomerism with $p(t)$, and its equivalent backimpulse response function should be as follows:

$$H(t) = \hat{h}(t) * p(t) * p(-t) = (\sum_{i=1}^{M} h_i'(t) * h_i(-t)) * p(t) * p(-t) \qquad (23)$$

Because $\hat{h}(t)$ and $p(t) * p(-t)$ are similar to $\delta(t)$ coherent multi-path channel, the equivalent low-pass time-varying pulse modulation method is used to suppress co-frequency interference and blind source separation, which can effectively achieve lossless transmission of the signal transmitted by Internet of things and reduce the bit error rate (BER) of communication.

4   Analysis of Simulation Experiment

The application performance of this method in improving the communication quality of wireless spread spectrum communication network is analyzed by simulation experiment, and the wireless spread spectrum communication network communication system is constructed. The input communication signal is LFM signal with the frequency band of 23 kHz–25 kHz and the time width of 5 ms. BPSK modulation carrier uses sine signal with frequency 10 kHz, multipath spread time of 34 ms, Internet of things transmission signal S, sampling frequency band of 2 kHz–10 kHz, time width of 4 ms

LFM signal, and signal-to-noise ratio of-10 dB of the same frequency interference, and the signal-to-noise ratio of the same frequency interference is-10 dB. The signal-to-noise ratio is-10 dB. The similarity between $H(t)$ and $\delta(t)$ is 0.23, and the signal autocorrelation spectral density is 3.23 dB. According to the above simulation environment and parameter setting, the time domain waveform of the Internet of things signal input from the wireless spread spectrum communication system is obtained as shown in Fig. 2.

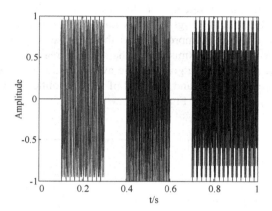

Fig. 2. Time-domain waveform of Internet of things transmission signal input from spread spectrum communication system

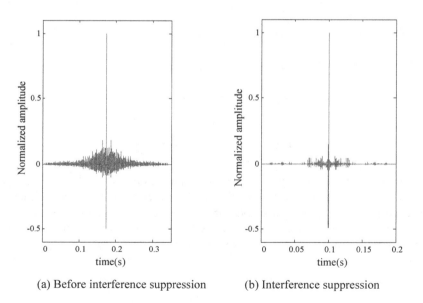

(a) Before interference suppression   (b) Interference suppression

Fig. 3. Impulse response pulses of communication channels

As can be seen from Fig. 2, the input signal of the spread spectrum communication system is affected by the initial frequency and the initial phase co-frequency disturbance, which causes the frequency domain aliasing and affects the equalization of the communication channel. The channel equalization design and interference suppression are carried out in this paper, and the impulse response signal of the communication channel before and after the same frequency interference suppression is obtained as shown in Fig. 3.

From the analysis of the simulation results in Fig. 3, it can be seen that this method is used to suppress the same frequency interference, and the blind source separation of the communication Internet of things transmission signal is realized. The equalization performance of the channel is improved, and the impulse response pulse output is relatively clean. The lossless transmission of the signal is realized. Finally, in order to compare the performance of the algorithm, the average value of 1000 experiments is carried out by different methods, and the BER of the transmitted signal of the Internet of things is obtained as shown in Fig. 4.

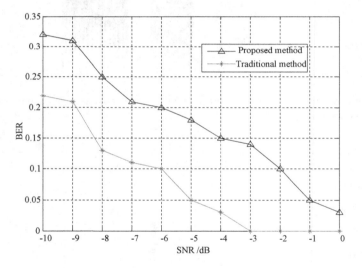

Fig. 4. BER comparison results

According to the data analysis of the above simulation results, the wireless spread spectrum communication system design using this method can eliminate the multipath channel co-frequency interference under the influence of multi-path effect, and make the channel equalization effect approximate to the ideal level. Reduce the bit error rate of communication and realize the lossless transmission of signal.

5 Conclusions

In this paper, an anti-co-frequency interference suppression method for wireless spread spectrum communication based on equivalent low-pass time-varying pulse modulation technology is proposed. The anti-co-frequency interference system for wireless spread spectrum communication is designed based on Internet of things technology, and the multi-path channel model for wireless spread spectrum communication is constructed. The Doppler spread technique is used to design the channel equalization of wireless spread spectrum communication system. The equivalent low-pass time-varying pulse modulation method is used to suppress the same-frequency interference and blind source separation. Improve the lossless transmission ability of the Internet of things transmission signal in the wireless spread spectrum communication system. The simulation results show that this method is used to design the wireless spread spectrum communication system and the co-frequency interference is effectively suppressed and the bit error rate of communication is lower than that of the traditional method. This method has good application value in wireless spread spectrum communication optimization.

References

1. Hu, S., Ding, Z., Ni, Q.: Beamforming optimization in energy harvesting cooperative full-duplex networks with self-energy recycling protocol. IET Commun. **10**(7), 848–853 (2016)
2. Seo, D.W., Lee, J.H., Lee, H.S.: Optimal coupling to achieve maximum output power in a WPT system. IEEE Trans. Power Electron. **31**(6), 3994–3998 (2016)
3. Han, D., Chen, X., Lei, Y., et al.: Real-time data analysis system based on Spark Streaming and its application. J. Comput. Appl. **37**(5), 1263–1269 (2017)
4. Sun, D.W., Zhang, G.Y., Zheng, W.M.: Big data stream computing, technologies and instances. J. Software **25**(4), 839–862 (2014)
5. Hao, S.G., Zhang, L., Muhammad, G.: A union authentication protocol of cross-domain based on bilinear pairing. J. Software **8**(5), 1094–1100 (2013)
6. Ma, Z., Chen, W.: Friction torque calculation method of ball bearings based on rolling creepage theory. J. Mech. Eng. **53**(22), 219–224 (2017)
7. Tu, G., Yang, X., Zhou, T.: Efficient identity-based multi-identity fully homomorphic encryption scheme. J. Comput. Appl. **39**(3), 750–755 (2019)
8. Wang, Z., Huang, M., et al.: Integrated algorithm based on density peaks and density-based clustering. J. Comput. Appl. **39**(2), 398–402 (2019)
9. Farnadi, G., Bach, S.H., Moens, M.F., et al.: Soft quantification in statistical relational learning. Mach. Learn. **106**(12), 1971–1991 (2017)
10. Tu, B., Chuai, R., Xu, H.: Outlier detection based on k-mean distance outlier factor for gait signal. Inf. Control **48**(1), 16–21 (2019)
11. Wei, X.S., Luo, J.H., Wu, J.: Selective convolutional descriptor aggregation for fine-grained image retrieval. IEEE Trans. Image Process. **26**(6), 2868–2881 (2017)
12. Huang, X., You, R., Zhou, C.: Study on optical properties of equivalent film constructed of metal nanoparticle arrays. J. Optoelectron. Laser **24**(7), 1434–1438 (2013)

Optimal Method of Load Signal Control of Power Based on State Difference Clustering

Yan Zhao[1(✉)] and Pengfei Lang[2]

[1] School of Power Engineering,
Nanjing Institute of Technology, Nanjing 211167, China
langpf1988@163.com
[2] China Academy of Launch Vehicle Technology, Beijing 100076, China

Abstract. In order to improve the power grid load detection ability, an optimal method of load signal control of power based on state difference clustering is proposed, and the big data statistical analysis model of the power grid load is constructed. The clustering analysis and state mining of grid load are carried out by using the distributed detection method of association features, and the regression analysis model of grid load state difference is constructed to realize the state differential clustering of power grid load signal in high-dimensional phase space. Based on the classification and fusion of the extracted characteristic sets of grid load, big data analysis method is used to optimize the intelligent control of power grid load signal. The simulation results show that the proposed method has better accurate classification performance and lower misdivision rate, which improves the output stability of power grid load.

Keywords: Power grid · Load · State difference clustering · Intelligent control

1 Introduction

Power grid load is the infrastructure to realize terminal high voltage power supply. In carrying out power grid load supply, it is necessary to accurately forecast the power load, analyze the trend of the grid load, and realize the optimal management and dispatching of the grid load [1]. To improve the power grid load application ability, reduce the unreasonable overhead of the power load, guarantee the safe and stable operation of the power equipment infrastructure, the foundation of studying the power grid load forecast is to carry on the load classification cluster processing. According to the classification clustering analysis of power grid load, the adaptive dispatching of power load is carried out to improve the optimal management ability of power grid load. The relevant cluster analysis methods of power grid load classification are of great concern [2].

At present, expert system forecasting method and fuzzy K-means clustering method are used to classify and cluster the load of power grid, and statistical sequence analysis method is used to reconstruct and analyze the characteristic signal of power grid load. The power grid load forecasting and characteristic reorganization are realized, and the load forecasting is carried out with fuzzy clustering method. However, the intelligent control of the power grid load signal is not good and the ambiguity is large [3].

G. Gui and L. Yun (Eds.): ADHIP 2019, LNICST 302, pp. 62–71, 2019.
https://doi.org/10.1007/978-3-030-36405-2_7

A power feedforward method combining inductance and capacitor power dynamics with load power static, dynamic feedforward feeds the energy consumed by the inductor and capacitor into the rectifier in stages, and the static feedforward feeds the output power of the PI controller to the rectifier. Stabilize the current on the grid side and reduce DC bus voltage fluctuations [4]. However, only OADs with low dimensional phase space are implemented. The compensation method based on the direct injection of the high-frequency component of the pre-inductor current can not only reduce the size of the bus filter capacitor in the power supply system, but also suppress the instability caused by the constant power load, and improve the stable operating range of the system [5]. However, the convergence of this method is poor, and the error rate of short-term power load classification is high.

In view of the above problems, the fuzzy clustering method is used to carry out the load forecasting. In this paper, an intelligent load control optimization method based on state difference clustering is proposed. The big data statistical analysis model of power grid load is constructed, and the distributed detection method of correlation features is used for the fusion clustering analysis and state mining of power grid load signal. Quantitative recursive analysis and subspace reengineering are used to analyze the structural characteristics of power grid load signal difference, and the state difference clustering of power grid load in high dimensional phase space is realized. Finally, the experimental analysis is carried out. The advantages of the proposed method in power load classification clustering and forecasting are demonstrated.

2   Model Construction and Pre-processing of Load Time Series in Power Grid

2.1   Construction of Power Load Time Series Model

In this paper, the load forecasting algorithm of power grid is studied. Firstly, the time domain signal model of power grid load is given, and the method of signal processing is used to forecast the power grid load. In the construction of network load time series information flow forecasting model, the dispatching model of power grid load is analyzed firstly, and the load data to be analyzed are classified according to five tuples, and the dispatching model of power grid load signal is obtained as shown in Fig. 1.

In the dispatching model shown in Fig. 1, the load sequence is divided into uplink load and downlink load inequality. The statistical characteristic sequence of grid load sequence is obtained as follows:

$$\sum_{i=1}^{c} \mu_{ik} = 1, k = 1, 2, \cdots, n \tag{1}$$

Where, k is the gray sequence of grid load. The characteristic matching model of power grid load is constructed. According to the fusion results of multiple classifiers, the

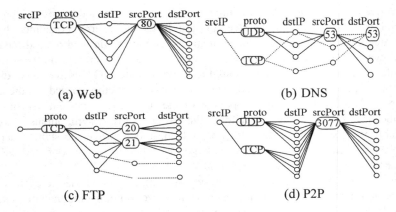

Fig. 1. Sampling and dispatching model of power grid load signal

information classification is carried out to realize the optimal detection of power grid load. The detection statistics are as follows:

$$V(a_1, \cdots, a_m) = \left(d_i^{j-1}\right)_{i,j=1}^m = \begin{pmatrix} 1 & a_1 & \cdots & a_1^{m-1} \\ 1 & a_2 & \cdots & a_2^{m-1} \\ \vdots & \vdots & \ddots & \vdots \\ 1 & a_m & \cdots & a_m^{m-1} \end{pmatrix} \tag{2}$$

$$A = (a_{i,j})_{i,j=1}^m = \begin{pmatrix} a_{1,1} & \cdots & a_{1,m} \\ \vdots & \ddots & \vdots \\ a_{m,1} & \cdots & a_{m,m} \end{pmatrix} \tag{3}$$

The finite data set model of power grid load signal distribution is constructed, and the energy consumption of power load is as follows:

$$\begin{vmatrix} t_{i_1 j_1} & t_{i_1 j_2} & \cdots & t_{i_1 j_k} \\ t_{i_2 j_1} & t_{i_2 j_2} & \cdots & t_{i_2 j_k} \\ \vdots & \vdots & \ddots & \vdots \\ t_{i_k j_1} & t_{i_k j_2} & \cdots & t_{i_k j_k} \end{vmatrix} \neq 0 \tag{4}$$

The big data statistical analysis model of power grid load is constructed. The clustering analysis and state mining of grid load fusion are carried out by using the distributed detection method of association features. The load operation and maintenance characteristics satisfy the $V(a_1, \cdots, a_m)^{-1} V(b_1, \cdots, b_m)$, covariance matrix satisfies:

$$(V(a_1, \cdots, a_m)^{(\alpha_1, \cdots, \alpha_m)})^{-1} V(b_1, \cdots, b_m)^{(\beta_1, \cdots, \beta_m)} \tag{5}$$

According to the above analysis, the power grid load time series sampling model is constructed, and the load classification and clustering processing is carried out according to the information sampling results.

2.2 Characteristic Analysis of Power Load

The fusion clustering analysis and state mining of power grid load signal are carried out by using the distributed detection method of association features. The transmission model of power grid load data can be described according to the state characteristics of time series [6]. If the time window function for short-term power load data transmission is $R_2^T R_2 = V_2 \sum_2 V_2^T$, and:

$$w(t) = w_{max} - \frac{\Delta w * t}{t_{max}} \tag{6}$$

While $R_2^T R_2 = \{X_{d+1}, X_{d+2}, \cdots X_{d+m}\}\{X_{d+1}, X_{d+2}, \cdots X_{d+m}\}^T$, the iterations of the Eigenvectors in the power grid load signal state space $V = [V_1, V_2, \cdots, V_m] \in R^{m \times m}$ are minimized. When $V \in R^{m \times m}$, $VV^T = I_M$ has a minimum value, the correlation dimension eigenvalue function of grid load is obtained as follows:

$$y(t) = \frac{1}{\pi} P \int \frac{x(\tau)}{t - \tau} d\tau = x(t) * \frac{1}{\pi t} \tag{7}$$

The linear superposition of power load series is carried out by using autocorrelation characteristic decomposition, and the time measure information of power grid load is obtained as follows:

$$S_{C/A}(f) = \frac{T_B}{(NT_C)^2} |X(f)|^2 + \sum_{l=-\infty}^{\infty} \sin c^2 \left(\pi T_B \left(f - \frac{l}{NT_C} \right) \right) \tag{8}$$

Where in:

$$|X(f)|^2 = T_C^2 N \sin c^2 (\pi f T_C) |X_{code}(f)|^2 \tag{9}$$

$$X_{code}(f) = \frac{1}{\sqrt{N}} \sum_{n=0}^{N-1} x_n \exp(-j2\pi f n T_c) \tag{10}$$

According to the above analysis, the association rules mining and feature analysis of short-term power load in distribution network are realized.

3 Optimization of Power Load Classification Clustering Model

3.1 Analysis of Structural Characteristics of Power Grid Load Difference

On the basis of the above-mentioned big data statistical analysis model of power load and the characteristic analysis, the power load classification clustering algorithm is designed. In this paper, the intelligent control optimization method of power load based on state difference clustering is put forward. The fractional Fourier transform matrix of grid load is constructed [7]. By setting the short-term load density parameters (MP and ε) of distribution network first, the discrete data analysis of the forecast value of power grid load is carried out, and it is known that $\alpha_k \geq 0$, $\sum_{k=1}^{K} \alpha_k = 1$, and:

$$G(U|\mu_k, \sum_k) = (2\pi)^{-d/2} \left|\sum_k\right|^{-1/2} \times \exp\left[-\frac{1}{2}(U - u_k)^T \sum_k^{-1} (U - u_k)\right] \quad (11)$$

Where, $G(U|\mu_k, \sum_k)$ is the statistical probability density characteristic of short-term power load in distribution network, and the random distribution sequence model of power load time series information flow is as follows:

$$E(e^{-sX}) = \exp(-\frac{\sigma^\alpha s^\alpha}{\cos(\pi\alpha/2)}) \quad (12)$$

Based on the energy conservation theorem, the acceleration energy function E_n in the dominant oscillation mode is calculated based on the fuzzy characteristic matching based on the extracted coherent distribution eigenvalues under variable load conditions:

$$E_n = \sum_{m=-\infty}^{\infty} [x(m)w(n - m)]^2 \quad (13)$$

The adjacent sub-module complementary switching modulation search algorithm is used to mine and reconstruct the information characteristics of power grid load [8]. The controlled source USD with AC port is controlled as follows:

$$T_j = \begin{cases} \sigma\sqrt{2\ln(N)}(1 - \frac{J}{2} \times \frac{E_j}{\sum_{j=1}^{J+1} E_j}), j = 1, 2, \ldots, J \\ \sigma\sqrt{2\ln(N)} \times \frac{E_j}{\sum_{j=1}^{J+1} E_j}, j = J + 1 \end{cases} \quad (14)$$

Where, N denotes the length of three-dimensional characteristic sequence of power load and J is the statistical frequency of power load. The quasi-harmonic oscillator module is equivalent to RC series circuit [9]. The three-dimensional reconstruction results of power grid load are as follows:

$$\hat{w}_j^k = \begin{cases} sign(w_j^k)\left(|w_j^k| - \beta \cdot T_j\right), & if|w_j^k| \geq T_j \\ 0, & else \end{cases}, j = 1, 2, \ldots, J+1 \quad (15)$$

Where, $\beta = e^{-m \times \frac{|w_j^k|^2 - T_j^2}{T_j}}$, $m > 0$, according to the above analysis, the structural characteristics of power grid load difference are analyzed, and the power load classification fusion and cluster processing are carried out according to the reconstruction results.

3.2 State Difference Clustering and Intelligent Control of Power Load

In the high-dimensional phase space, the probability that the correlation dimension index of the information flow time series $x(t)$ of the power grid load appears in the distributed interval i is statistically analyzed by clustering the state difference of the power grid load. When the correlation dimension exponential random variable satisfies the discriminant function $\alpha_k \geq 0$, $\sum_{k=1}^{K} \alpha_k = 1$, the output system state function of power grid load signal forecasting is as follows:

$$\begin{cases} x(k+1) = \left(\begin{bmatrix} 1 & 0.6 \\ -0.4 & 0.5 \end{bmatrix} + \begin{bmatrix} 0.02 & 0.01 \\ -0.2 & 0.12 \end{bmatrix} \right) x(k) \\ \quad + \begin{bmatrix} 1 \\ 1 \end{bmatrix} kx(k - \tau_k) + \begin{bmatrix} 0.1 \\ 0.1 \end{bmatrix} w(k) \\ z(k) = [1 \quad 1]x(k) + 0.1\,u(k) + 0.1w(k) \end{cases} \quad (16)$$

Feature mining and attribute clustering of power grid loads signal are described as:

$$\begin{cases} \dot{x}_1 = x_3 \\ \dot{x}_3 = f_\theta(X, t) + g_\theta(X, t)u(t) + d_\theta(t) \\ \dot{x}_2 = x_4 \\ \dot{x}_4 = f_x(X, t) + g_x(X, t)u(t) + d_x(t) \end{cases} \quad (17)$$

Where, $X = [\theta, x, \dot{\theta}, \dot{x}]^T$, based on the fuzzy grid clustering analysis of the association rule set of grid load, the characteristic quantity of grid load is extracted in the phase space [10]. In the finite universe, the distribution of grid area is obtained as follows:

$$T_j = \sigma_j \sqrt{2 \ln(N)}, j = 1, 2, \ldots, J+1 \quad (18)$$

$$\sigma_j = \frac{median(d_j(k))}{0.6745} \quad (19)$$

Where, $d_j(k)$ denotes the finite characteristic distribution set of grid load, extracts the coherent distribution source feature of grid load, and obtains the fuzzy spread function:

$$\hat{w}_j^k = \begin{cases} w_j^k, & \text{if } |w_j^k| \geq T_j \\ 0, & \text{else} \end{cases}, \; j = 1, 2, \ldots, J+1, \tag{20}$$

Big data analysis method is used to realize the intelligent control optimization of power grid load [11]. The optimal solution of clustering is as follows:

$$\hat{w}_j^k = \begin{cases} sign(w_j^k)(|w_j^k| - T_j), & \text{if } |w_j^k| \geq T_j \\ 0, & \text{else} \end{cases} \; j = 1, 2, \ldots, J+1 \tag{21}$$

According to the above analysis, the intelligent control optimization of power grid load is realized [12].

4   Simulation Experiment and Result Analysis

The intelligent control of power grid load is carried out in Matlab. Assuming the sampling length of data link of power grid load sampling is 2 600, the distribution dimension of load big data is 5, and the spatial sampling delay is 0.12 s. The characteristic distribution of power load dissimilarity in distribution network satisfies the

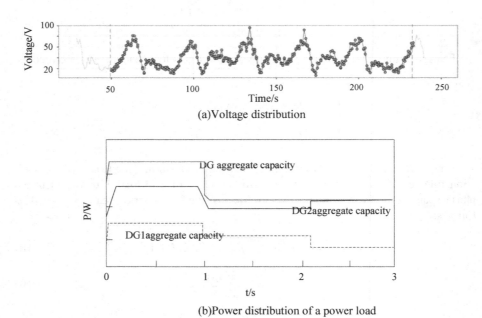

(a) Voltage distribution

(b) Power distribution of a power load

Fig. 2. Sampling results of power load by big data

average value of 0 and the variance of 0.25 is uniform normal distribution. The sampling frequency of power load is $f_1 = 0.3, f_2 = 0.05$, to classify and cluster the load according to the above simulation parameters. The power and voltage amplitudes of the power load are measured and the results are shown in Fig. 2.

Figure 2 shows the load power distribution between different DG units. It can be seen from the figure that the DG system can automatically adjust the power generation according to the load power from 0 to 2.0 s, and different DG units can automatically distribute the load power according to their maximum power. At 2.0 s, the DG2 unit fails, and the normally operating DG unit quickly adjusts the power generation to ensure normal power supply for critical loads. It is worth noting that if the normal power supply of the load cannot be satisfied at this time, the control can be taken after the load shedding operation is performed according to the priority of the load.

Taking big data of power grid load in Fig. 2 as the test object, the clustering results are obtained as shown in Fig. 3.

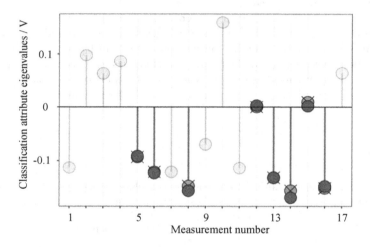

Fig. 3. Classification and clustering output of short-term Power load in distribution network

The analysis of Fig. 3 shows that the clustering method of short-term power load in this paper has a good characteristic convergence, and the error rate of classification of short-term power load in distribution network is tested by different methods. The comparison results are shown in Table 1, from which we can see that the classification of short-term power load in distribution network can be classified by different methods. In this paper, the classification of short-term power load in distribution network is classified by this method, and the misdivision rate is low.

Table 1. Comparison of error rates.

Iterations	Proposed method	Reference [4]	Reference [5]
100	0.113	0.198	0.242
200	0.023	0.145	0.211
300	0.015	0.089	0.178
400	0	0.045	0.102

5 Conclusions

In this paper, an intelligent control optimization method based on the state difference clustering is proposed, and the big data statistical analysis model of the power grid load is constructed. The clustering analysis and state mining of grid load are carried out by using the distributed detection method of association features, and the regression analysis model of grid load state difference is constructed to realize the state differential clustering of power grid load signal in high-dimensional phase space. Based on the classification and fusion of the extracted characteristic sets of grid load, big data analysis method is used to optimize the intelligent control of power grid load signal. The simulation results show that the proposed method has better accurate classification performance and lower misdivision rate, which improves the output stability of power grid load. This method has a good application value in the intelligent control of power grid load.

References

1. Wang, Y.Q., Zhou, J.Z., Mo, L., et al.: Precise scheduling method for daily generation plan of large-scale hydropower station based on comprehensive state evaluation strategy for generating units. Power Syst. Technol. **36**(7), 94–99 (2012)
2. Guney, M.S., Tepe, Y.: Classification and assessment of energy storage systems. Renew. Sustain. Energy Rev. **75**, 1187–1197 (2017)
3. Liang, S., Hu, X.H., Zhang, D.X., et al.: Probabilistic models based evaluation method for capacity credit of photovoltaic generation. Autom. Electric Power Syst. **36**(13), 32–37 (2012)
4. Wang, K., Fan, B., Zhang, F., et al.: Simulation of power optimization control of power supply load rectifier in power grid. Comput. Simul. **34**(3), 100–104 (2017)
5. Pang, S.Z., Huangpu, Q.Y., Guo, L., et al.: Wide stability control strategy of constant power load power supply converter based on Lyapunov indirect method. J. Electr. Technol. **32**(14), 146–154 (2017)
6. Sun, D.W., Zhang, G.Y., Zheng, W.M.: Big data stream computing, technologies and instances. J. Softw. **25**(4), 839–862 (2014)
7. Hao, S.G., Zhang, L., Muhammad, G.: A union authentication protocol of cross-domain based on bilinear pairing. J. Softw. **8**(5), 1094–1100 (2013)

8. Hu, S., Ding, Z., Ni, Q.: Beamforming optimisation in energy harvesting cooperative full-duplex networks with self-energy recycling protocol. IET Commun. **10**(7), 848–853 (2016)
9. Seo, D.W., Lee, J.H., Lee, H.S.: Optimal coupling to achieve maximum output power in a WPT system. IEEE Trans. Power Electron. **31**(6), 3994–3998 (2016)
10. Dai, H., Huang, Y., Li, C., et al.: Energy-efficient resource allocation for device-to-device communication with WPT. IET Commun. **11**(3), 326–334 (2017)
11. Hu, R.N., Guo, A.H.: Transmission reliability algorithm based on power control in Internet of vehicles. J. Comput. Appl. **35**(6), 1523–1526 (2015)
12. Ding, Q.Q., Lu, W., Xu, C.B., et al.: Passivity-based control of a three-phase shunt hybrid active power filter. J. Electr. Mach. Control **18**(05), 1–6 (2014)

Research on Intelligent Estimation Model of BER for High-Speed Image Transmission Based on LVDS Interface

Pengfei Lang[1($\boxtimes$)], Qingfeng Shi[1], Zebing Xie[1], Hongtao Zheng[1], and Yan Zhao[2]

[1] China Academy of Launch Vehicle Technology, Beijing 100076, China
langpf1988@163.com
[2] School of Power Engineering, Nanjing Institute of Technology, Nanjing 211167, China

Abstract. The high-speed image signal of LVDS interface is easy to be interfered by the outside world in the process of transmission, which results in packet loss and distortion of high-speed image communication, and the output error is high. Therefore, the lossless coding of high-speed image signal is needed. Intelligent estimation of bit error rate (BER) for high-speed image transmission is needed. The intelligent estimation model of high-speed image transmission bit error rate based on LVDS interface is proposed. The network structure model of high-speed image signal transmission is constructed to estimate the error code distortion of image transmission and the key frame feature extraction method is used to estimate the error rate of image transmission. The intelligent estimation of bit error rate (BER) of high-speed image transmission is realized in LVDS interface. The simulation results show that the proposed method has low bit error rate (BER) for high-speed image transmission and achieves lossless transmission of images.

Keywords: LVDS interface · High speed image · Transmission · Bit error rate · Intelligent estimation

1 Introduction

The phenomenon of high-speed image tampering and malicious compression is common in the process of network transmission. The user's easy processing and editing of high-speed image results in the distortion and packet loss of high-speed image information [1]. Especially in the process of transmission of high-speed image signal on LVDS interface, it is easy to be interfered by the outside world, which leads to packet loss and distortion in high-speed image communication. Therefore, lossless coding of high-speed image signal is needed. It has great significance to study the lossless coding algorithm for high-speed images [2].

In the process of high-speed image transmission and communication in LVDS interface, the packet loss and network delay of high-speed image communication lead to high-speed image transmission errors, which fundamentally affect the timeliness and authenticity of high-speed image transmission. The traditional coding algorithm uses

G. Gui and L. Yun (Eds.): ADHIP 2019, LNICST 302, pp. 72–81, 2019.
https://doi.org/10.1007/978-3-030-36405-2_8

fractional Fourier transform algorithm, which is constrained by the nonlinear characteristics of higher order, which affects the quality of service of the application layer. LVDS interface is an environmental factor which must be taken into account in complex scenes, and it is difficult to transmit lossless coding by large interference factors. In this paper, a high-speed image lossless coding algorithm with LVDS interface based on empirical moment estimation is proposed. Firstly, the network structure model of high-speed image signal transmission is constructed, and the key frame feature extraction is carried out [3]. By calculating the empirical moment estimation feature of the high-speed image transmission signal, the improvement of the high-speed image coding algorithm is realized. The performance test of the simulation experiment shows the superior performance of the proposed algorithm.

2 Design of Network Structure Model for High-Speed Image Communication Based on LVDS Interface

2.1 Design of High-Speed Image Transmission Network Structure Model Based on LVCDS Interface

In high-speed image coding, the packet loss rate is predicted by LVCDS interface (HMM) because of external interference. Firstly, the original CIF format YUV high-speed image is transformed from parent-child band to sub-band, and the hidden Markov information is obtained from each frame of GOP image [4]. This part of information is encoded by odd-even interlaced arrangement. The characteristic analysis of high-speed image information is realized. The network structure model of high-speed image transmission based on LVCDS interface is shown in Fig. 1.

Considering that packet loss rate Q in the network is a continuous variable and suitable for HMM modeling, this paper first designs a network structure model of high-speed image transmission based on LVCDS interface [5]. In the model structure shown in Fig. 1, C is initialized to 15. In order to ensure the real-time prediction and obtain a higher quantization accuracy. Therefore, using the time-domain luminance mean hash method to generate the block matrix on the screen, the high-speed image sequence of the high-speed image length 1 is obtained as follows:

$$\begin{cases} h(i,2j) = \frac{h(i,2j-1)+h(i,2j+1)}{2} \\ v(2i,j) = \frac{v(2i-1,j)+v(2i+1,j)}{2} \\ d(i,2j) = \frac{d(i,2j-1)+d(i,2j+1)}{2} \end{cases} \tag{1}$$

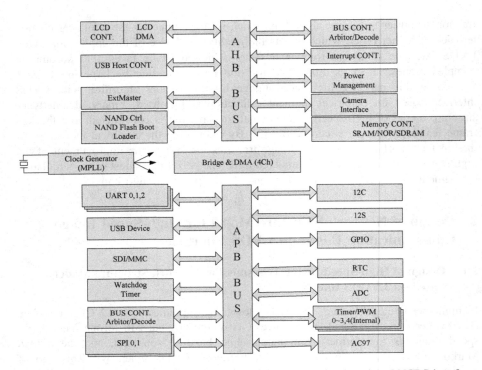

Fig. 1. Network structure model of high-speed image transmission based on LVCDS interface

The inter-frame prediction and inter-layer prediction under the network structure model of high-speed image transmission based on LVCDS interface are obtained:

$$
\begin{aligned}
E_{Tx}(l, d) &= E_{(Tx-elec)}(l) + E_{(Tx-amp)}(l, d) \\
&= lE_{elec} + l\varepsilon d^{\alpha} \\
&= \begin{cases} lE_{elec} + l\varepsilon_{fs}d^2, \ d < d_0 \\ lE_{elec} + l\varepsilon_{mp}d^4, \ d \geq d_0 \end{cases}
\end{aligned}
\tag{2}
$$

In the above formula, E_{elec} is the transmission energy consumed by the unit data of each frame of the high-speed image, X is the implicit state in the LVCDS interface, and $X = \{x_i, i = 1, 2, 3 \cdots, N\}$. Through the above analysis, it can be seen that because the LVDS interface high-speed image in the network transmission process, the coded scanning sequence from top to bottom leads to inter-frame redundancy, through complex motion estimation and motion compensation. In order to avoid the loss of coding information, 16 frames of GOP are used to encode odd signals alternately in time and space [6].

2.2   Key Frame Extraction of High-Speed Image Information

In the above-mentioned high-speed image transmission network model based on LVCDS interface, key frame extraction is needed in order to realize lossless coding for high-speed image transmission [7]. The separation and non-separation evaluation of the feature points in the frequency domain are carried out according to the correlation characteristics of the characteristic points and the correlation factors in the frequency domain. By analyzing the domain feature characteristics of domain feature points, we can get the correlation characteristics of domain feature points [8], which provides guidance for the separation analysis of domain feature points in high-speed images. The iterative updating of HMM parameters for lossless transmission of high-speed image coding is obtained by using maximum likelihood estimation (MLE):

$$\pi_i = \varepsilon_1(i) \tag{3}$$

$$a_{ij} = \frac{\sum_{i=1}^{U-1} \varepsilon_t(i,j)}{\sum_{i=1}^{U-1} \varepsilon_t(i)} \tag{4}$$

$$b_j(k) = \frac{\sum_{\substack{t=1 \\ s.t.o_t = v_k}}^{U} \varepsilon_t(j)}{\sum_{t=1}^{U} \varepsilon_t(j)} \tag{5}$$

It is assumed that in the domain characteristic point, the state equation and the domain characteristic point separation measurement equation of the domain characteristic point separation are respectively as follows:

$$\begin{aligned} x(k+1) &= f(x(k)) + v(k) \\ y(k+1) &= h(x(k+1)) + w(k+1) \end{aligned} \tag{6}$$

When the domain feature points are separated, the following formula holds:

$$x(n) = \frac{1}{\sqrt{N}} \sum_{k=0}^{N-1} X(k) \exp(j2\pi kn/N), n = 0, 1 \ldots N - 1 \tag{7}$$

Where in, $X(k)$ is the characteristic of domain characteristic point separation amplitude, and $\exp(j2\pi kn/N)$ is domain characteristic point separation phase characteristic.

In the key frame feature extraction, we need to separate the domain feature points, and expand the separation series of this separation function [9]. The results are expressed as follows:

$$x(k+1) = f(x(k|k)) + O + V(k) \tag{8}$$

Then the separation correlation degree from domain feature point separation point to domain feature point separation point is expressed as follows:

$$r(n) = y(n - m) \exp(j2\pi\varepsilon n/N) + w(n) \tag{9}$$

Through the above-mentioned processing, the key frame feature extraction of high-speed image information on LVDS interface is realized immediately, which provides an accurate data base for lossless coding of high-speed image [10].

3 Improved Implementation of High Speed Image Lossless Coding Algorithm Based on LVDS Interface

It can be seen from the above analysis that the traditional coding algorithm uses fractional Fourier transform algorithm, which is constrained by the nonlinearity of higher-order features, resulting in poor performance of high-speed image coding. In order to overcome the disadvantages of traditional algorithms, this paper proposes a high-speed image lossless coding algorithm with LVDS interface based on empirical moment estimation [11]. The frequency of high-speed image transmission is obtained from the quotient between each component and a response constant in the frequency domain:

$$\omega_0 = \theta_1 + \frac{\pi}{2}, \quad |\theta_1| < \frac{\pi}{2} \tag{10}$$

Firstly, on the basis of the correlation analysis of domain feature points, the high-speed image domain feature points are separated to form the original domain feature point library, which can be obtained as:

$$y(n) = \sum_{i=0}^{L-1} h_i x(n - \tau_i) \tag{11}$$

The empirical moment estimation algorithm is used to pre-scramble the original domain feature point database [12]. The next step correlation degree of domain feature point separation is as follows:

$$M_{SC}(d) = \frac{|P_{SC}(d)|^2}{(R_{SC}(d))^2} \tag{12}$$

For high-speed image sequences, the empirical matrix for X is:

$$M^X \overset{\Delta}{=} \{ m_{i_1, i_2, \cdots, i_{n+1}} = \frac{\theta_{i_1, i_2, \cdots, i_{n+1}}(x)}{L - n}, i_k \in B \} \tag{13}$$

Where in, $\frac{\theta_{i_1, i_2, \cdots, i_{n+1}}(x)}{L-n}$ is the gray value in X passing from i_1 to i_2, and the element X in x_t is defined to satisfy $P(x_t|x_{t-1}, x_{t-2}, \cdots, x_1) = P(x_t|x_{t-1}, x_{t-2}, \cdots, x_{t-n})$, to get the proportion of pixel transformation of high-speed image sequence i_3 state reaching i_{n+1} in the total pixel transformation. By using the method of domain feature point separation association, we can obtain the domain feature point separation state association estimation and domain feature point separation next-step correlation covariance:

$$x(k+1|k) = E[x(k+1)|z^k] \tag{14}$$

Because the correlation degree of domain feature point association is the correlation characteristic of feature point, the output feature of high speed image lossless coding in LVDS interface based on empirical moment estimation is as follows:

$$\hat{d} = \arg \max_d (M_{Minn}(d)) \tag{15}$$

Based on the above processing, the absolute values of H component and V component difference of each frame are calculated, the pixel difference of LVDS interface is obtained by amplitude-frequency transformation, and the number of bits used to store each pixel is defined as pixel depth [13], and the number of bits used to store each pixel is defined as pixel depth. As the parameters increase appropriately, the period of data pixels increases by multiple. The moving foreground image is obtained by bilinear transform method according to the initial threshold, and the lossless coding algorithm for high-speed image with LVDS interface is designed [14].

4 Analysis of Simulation Experiment

In order to test the performance of the algorithm in this paper, simulation experiments are carried out. The performance analysis of real-time transmission of high-speed image with LVDS interface is compared with the following performance indexes: CPU occupancy, delay, packet loss and frame queue length to be sent. The OpenCV technology is used to process the high-speed image information of LVDS interface. OpenCV is an open source computer visual library. In this paper, the sampling high-speed image set length is 300 frames, and the GOP structure is 320 frames image of IBBPBBPBBP. Taking the recorded high-speed image information of the monitoring camera as the research object, the high-speed image sequence of LVDS interface is acquired as shown in Fig. 2.

Fig. 2. Monitoring image information recorded by camera

Based on the above simulation environment and the model design of this paper, the lossless coding simulation of the two groups of dynamic images is carried out, and the codebook coding results of the high-speed image coding with the proposed algorithm are obtained as shown in Fig. 3. As can be seen from the graph, this algorithm can be used for high-speed image communication coding, which can effectively extract the static and dynamic features of the high-speed image frame sequence, especially for the high-speed image signal with LVDS interface, and the extraction result of foreground points is more accurate. The lossless coding transmission of high-speed image with LVDS interface is realized.

Fig. 3. High Speed Image coding results of LVDS interface

In order to quantitatively analyze the performance of the algorithm, the error foreground point rate (FP rate) of high-speed image transmission is taken as the test index, and the correct foreground point rate (TP rate) is used as the test index:

$$FP \ \ rate = \frac{fp}{fp + tn} \tag{16}$$

$$TP \ \ rate = \frac{tp}{tp + fn} \tag{17}$$

Using this algorithm and the traditional algorithm, the above two indexes are compared and analyzed, and the simulation results are shown in Fig. 4. Among them, the number of bit errors is the number of received bits of the data stream on the communication channel that is changed due to noise, interference, distortion or bit synchronization errors.

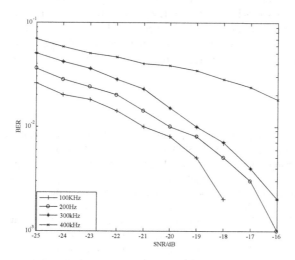

Fig. 4. Performance comparison

As can be seen from Fig. 4, at different signal-to-noise ratios, the bit error probability of different Hz image transmission exhibits a decreasing trend, and in the case of 400 kHz, with the change of the signal-to-noise ratio, the bit error probability change speed is most obvious, and the initial bit error probability is the lowest. It is obtained that the proposed algorithm can effectively improve the correct foreground point rate of high-speed image transmission with LVDS interface, improve the fidelity of high-speed image transmission, and realize the lossless coding high-speed image transmission. The BER of different image transmission methods is tested and the comparison results are shown in Table 1. The analysis shows that the BER of the proposed method for high-speed image transmission is low.

Table 1. BER comparison.

SNR/dB	Improved method	Reference [3]	Reference [4]
−10	0.0765	0.145	0.254
−8	0.0463	0.125	0.167
−6	0.0221	0.115	0.154
−4	0	0.102	0.132

5 Conclusions

In this paper, the intelligent estimation model of high-speed image transmission bit error rate based on LVDS interface is proposed. The network structure model of high-speed image signal transmission is constructed to estimate the error code distortion of image transmission and the key frame feature extraction method is used to estimate the error rate of image transmission. The intelligent estimation of bit error rate of high-speed image transmission is realized in LVDS interface. The simulation results show that the proposed method has low bit error rate for high-speed image transmission and achieves lossless transmission of images. This method has important application value in BER control of high-speed image transmission.

References

1. Han, D., Chen, X., Lei, Y., et al.: Real-time data analysis system based on Spark Streaming and its application. J. Comput. Appl. **37**(5), 1263–1269 (2017)
2. Sun, D.W., Zhang, G.Y., Zheng, W.M.: Big data stream computing, technologies and instances. J. Software **25**(4), 839–862 (2014)
3. Hao, S.G., Zhang, L., Muhammad, G.: A union authentication protocol of cross-domain based on bilinear pairing. J. Software **8**(5), 1094–1100 (2013)
4. Hu, S., Ding, Z., Ni, Q.: Beamforming optimisation in energy harvesting cooperative full-duplex networks with self-energy recycling protocol. IET Commun. **10**(7), 848–853 (2016)
5. Seo, D.W., Lee, J.H., Lee, H.S.: Optimal coupling to achieve maximum output power in a WPT system. IEEE Trans. Power Electron. **31**(6), 3994–3998 (2016)
6. Ma, Z., Chen, W.: Friction torque calculation method of ball bearings based on rolling creepage theory. J. Mech. Eng. **53**(22), 219–224 (2017)
7. Zhou, S.B., Xu, W.X.: A novel clustering algorithm based on relative density and decision graph. Control Dec. **33**(11), 1921–1930 (2018)
8. He, H., Tan, Y.: Automatic pattern recognition of ECG signals using entropy-based adaptive dimensionality reduction and clustering. Appl. Soft Comput. **55**, 238–252 (2017)
9. Zhu, Y., Zhu, X., Wang, J.: Time series motif discovery algorithm based on subsequence full join and maximum clique. J. Comput. Appl. **39**(2), 414–420 (2019)
10. Dai, H., Huang, Y., Li, C., et al.: Energy-efficient resource allocation for device-to-device communication with WPT. IET Commun. **11**(3), 326–334 (2017)

11. Helmy, A., Hedayat, A., Al-Dhahir, N.: Robust weighted sum-rate maximization for the multi-stream MIMO interference channel with sparse equalization. IEEE Trans. Commun. **60**(10), 3645–3659 (2015)
12. Alfaro, V.M., Vilanoab, R.: Robust tuning of 2DoF five-parameter PID controllers for inverse response controlled processes. J. Process Control **23**(4), 453–462 (2013)
13. Zhang, R., Zhao, F.: Foggy image enhancement algorithm based on bidirectional diffusion and shock filtering. Comput. Eng. **44**(10), 221–227 (2018)
14. Liu, D., Zhou, D., Nie, R., Hou, R.: Multi-focus image fusion based on phase congruency motivate pulse coupled neural network-based in NSCT domain. J. Comput. Appl. **38**(10), 3006–3012 (2018)

Anti-tampering Monitoring Method of Network Sensitive Information Based on Big Data Analysis

Yi Shen[✉] and Lu Zhang

Anyang Vocational and Technical College, Anyang 455000, China
zhanglu789111@163.com

Abstract. To improve the security of network sensitive information transmission and storage, it is necessary to design the anti-tampering monitoring of network sensitive information, and a tamper-proof monitoring technology of network sensitive information in big data environment based on big data dimension feature block is proposed. Big data feature space reconstruction method is used to calculate the grid density of network sensitive information distribution, and the network sensitive information to be tampered-proof monitoring is mapped to the divided high-dimensional phase space through the density threshold. The high dimensional phase space of information distribution is divided into dense unit and sparse unit. The coded key is matched to the corresponding network sensitive information block to realize information encryption and covert communication. The simulation results show that the information steganography performance of network sensitive information transmission and storage using this information tampering monitoring technology is better, and the information security transmission ability is improved.

Keywords: Big data · Network sensitive information · Tamper-proof monitoring · Information security

1 Introduction

With the development of big data information storage and transmission technology, the transmission and storage of network sensitive information has attracted more and more attention. The transmission of network sensitive information is to collect information through sensors [1]. Combined with big data network design, the transmission channel model is constructed to realize the communication system of information output and reception. The transmission and storage of network sensitive information has the advantages of simple networking design and large bandwidth. Under the environment of big data, the network sensitive information transmission and storage network can be constructed, which can realize the secure transmission of large-scale information data. The design of tamper-proof monitoring of network sensitive information in big data environment is the key to realize information secure communication and secure communication. It has great significance to study information tamper-proof monitoring technology to improve the security performance of communication [2].

© ICST Institute for Computer Sciences, Social Informatics and Telecommunications Engineering 2019
Published by Springer Nature Switzerland AG 2019. All Rights Reserved
G. Gui and L. Yun (Eds.): ADHIP 2019, LNICST 302, pp. 82–89, 2019.
https://doi.org/10.1007/978-3-030-36405-2_9

In order to achieve encrypted communication on the surface layer, the previously proposed tamper-proof monitoring algorithm for network sensitive information in a big data environment [3]. With the upgrade of hacker attack technology and the improvement of information security communication level, it cannot effectively meet the requirements of digital encryption transmission and communication. In this paper, a tamper-proof monitoring technology of network sensitive information in big data environment based on big data dimension feature block is proposed. Big data feature space reconstruction method is used to calculate the grid density of network sensitive information distribution, and the network sensitive information to be tampered-proof monitoring is mapped to the divided high-dimensional phase space through the density threshold. The coding key of the information tamper-proof monitoring algorithm is obtained, and the coding key is matched to the corresponding network sensitive information block to realize information encryption and covert communication. Finally, the simulation test and analysis are carried out, and the conclusion of effectiveness is obtained.

2 Data Coding and Tamper Proof Monitoring Key Construction

2.1 Network Sensitive Information Coding Based on Spatial Geometry Method

In order to realize the optimal design of anti-tampering monitoring technology of network sensitive information in big data environment, it is necessary to design the coding and encryption of tamper-proof monitoring data at first [4]. The grid density of network sensitive information distribution is calculated by big data feature space reconstruction method. It is assumed that the test sequence of network sensitive information coding pair is X and the training sequence is $P(r_i)$, which are G-dimensional randomly distributed binary data strings. Let $\sum_{i=1}^{n} P(r_i) = 0$ be a discrete distribution map model of order r. the coded linear mapping of network sensitive information transmission is represented as a bit sequence of c generated by X. Through spatial geometry segmentation, according to the principle of breadth first traversing, the probability distribution function of the source can be recorded as:

$$\begin{bmatrix} X \\ P \end{bmatrix} = \begin{bmatrix} r_1 & r_2 & \cdots & r_n \\ P(r_1) & P(r_2) & \cdots & P(r_n) \end{bmatrix} \tag{1}$$

The data point set $X = \{x_1, x_2, \cdots, x_N\}$ is mapped into geometric space, and the membership function relationship between $P(r_i)$ and r_i is obtained according to the input R_n value:

$$I(r_i) = -logP(r_i) \tag{2}$$

Where, the log base number is set to 2, and the entropy value of network sensitive information $I(r_i)$, which represents the coding of network sensitive information in high dimensional phase space, is calculated to be $H(X)$, entropy value, which reflects the average amount of data transmitted by network sensitive information:

$$H(X) = - \sum_{i=1}^{n} P(r_i) \times logP(r_i) \tag{3}$$

According to the above description, the operation of obtaining network sensitive information coding based on spatial geometry is as follows:

(a) Select the initial cell and randomly select: $r_1, r_2 \in Z_q^*$;
(b) The spatial geometric density difference between the high dimensional phase space and the initial element is calculated, and when the $R = g^{r_1}$, coding output is satisfied, the spatial geometric density difference between the high dimensional phase space w_b and the initial element h_l is calculated:

$$h_1 = \{X, w_b\} \tag{4}$$

$$wb = \{X, u_a, r_2\} \tag{5}$$

In the formula, u_a is the set density difference.

2.2 Construction of Information Tamper Proof Monitoring Key

The network sensitive information to be tampered-proof monitoring is mapped to the divided high-dimensional phase space through the density threshold, and the tamper-proof monitoring key of the network sensitive information is constructed. In the d-dimensional space, according to the grid relative density difference, the tamper resistant monitoring data are traversed deeply [5]. The grid cell sequence $g_0, g_1, \cdots, g_p$, is selected, where G is the relative density difference and g_1 is the initial key. $g_i \in NB(g_{i-1})(i = 2, 3, \cdots, p)$, represents the grid relative density difference between the channel g_1, g_0 transmitted and stored by the network sensitive information. For each i, the construction information tamper proof monitoring key satisfies:

(1) $rgdd(g_0, g_i) \leq \varepsilon$;
(2) For the dense distribution of data points in G, there is an average entropy value $j(1 < j \leq i)$, $rgdd(g_0, g_j) \leq \varepsilon$.

Then $g_i(i = 2, 3, \cdots, p)$ is called the classification key of information tampering monitoring algorithm. Through the above-mentioned design, the signcryption design of the network sensitive information is realized. According to the constructed key, the information encryption and the encrypted communication are carried out [6].

3 Improved Design of Information Tampering Monitoring Algorithm

Based on the technology of network sensitive information coding and key construction based on spatial geometry method, the anti-tampering monitoring technology of network sensitive information is improved. This paper proposes a tamper-proof monitoring technology for sensitive information in big data environment based on big data dimension features [7].

3.1 Sensitive Information Representation Processing

The sensitive information of the network for tamper-proof monitoring is mapped to the divided high-dimensional phase space through the density threshold, and the density threshold is calculated. In the discrete big data network sensitive information transmission system, the indicator function $i(n)$ is defined as:

$$i(n) = a(n)I_{1\{u(n)=1\}} = \begin{cases} 1 & if \ u(n) = 1 \,, a(n) = 1 \\ 0 & others \end{cases} \tag{6}$$

In the initial adjacent internal unit, the symmetric key S is randomly selected to encrypt k_A to obtain $item_A$, and in the divided high dimensional phase space, the output tamper proof monitoring data is obtained by the sensitive information representation coding.

$$\frac{B \lhd \{\{dsc_A, \{item_A\}_k, w(k)\}_{k_a^{-1}}\}_{k_b}, B| \equiv \stackrel{k_b}{\longmapsto} B}{B \lhd \{dsc_A, \{item_A\}_k, w(k)\}_{k_a^{-1}}} \tag{7}$$

The high-dimensional phase space of information distribution is divided into dense units and sparse units [8]. Data tamper-proof monitoring is performed according to the sensitive information representation model shown in Fig. 1.

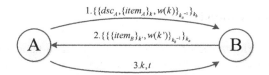

Fig. 1. Representation model of sensitive information

3.2 Code Key Matching for Information Tamper-Proof Monitoring

Because tamper-proof monitoring algorithms usually only change high-frequency data in network-sensitive information. The information classification features are screened based on the spatial geometry method [9]. The normalization of the low frequency vector of tamper proof monitoring information is obtained by using the coding key matching strategy:

$$\frac{A \lhd \{\{\{item_B\}_{k'}, w(k')\}_{k_b^{-1}}\}_{k_a}, A| \equiv \overset{k_a}{\mapsto} A}{A \lhd \{\{item_B\}_{k'}, w(k')\}_{k_b^{-1}}} \tag{8}$$

The coding key is matched to the corresponding network sensitive information block [10], and the average entropy value of information tampering prevention monitoring is obtained:

$$H_N(X) = \frac{-\sum_{i=1}^{n} P(x_i) \times \log P(x_i)}{N} \tag{9}$$

After the $H_N(x_i)$ is calculated, and then the calculated result is divided by N, the variance can be expressed as follows:

$$D(X) = \sum_{i=1}^{N} [H_N(x_i) - H_N(X)]^2 \tag{10}$$

Information tamper-resistant monitoring sequence for binary sequence [11], data tamper-proof monitoring transformation $c_i = E(z_i, m_i)(i = 1, 2, 3, \cdots)$, output plaintext:

$$m_i = D(z_i, E(z_i, m_i)) = m_1 m_2 m_3 \cdots (i = 1, 2, 3, \cdots) \tag{11}$$

The coding key of the network sensitive information tamper-proof monitoring algorithm determined by the classification feature selection method corresponds to the in-place plane data block, and the tamper-proof monitoring can be realized directly on the data block [12].

4   Experimental Analysis

In order to test the performance of the algorithm in the anti-tampering monitoring of network sensitive information in big data environment, the simulation experiment is carried out. The experiment is simulated with Matlab7 software. The test data set is recorded as DS1 and DS2, parameters as follows: $Rn = 56, \varepsilon = 0.53, \mu_\lambda = 0.71$, the sampling frequency of the data is 1.43 Hz, and the interval of the data coding code is 100 dB. The distribution of the original data is shown in Fig. 2.

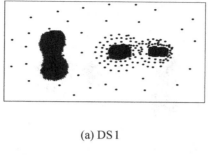

(a) DS 1

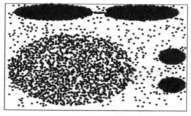

(b) DS2

Fig. 2. Original dataset

Taking the above test data as the research object, the high dimensional phase space of information distribution is divided into dense unit and sparse unit, and the data fusion and tamper proof monitoring and processing are carried out combined with similarity feature extraction method. The output results of tamper proof monitoring are shown in Fig. 3.

The results of Fig. 3 show that the data tampering monitoring is carried out by using this method, which hides the characteristics of the original data distribution and realizes the data encryption and encryption transmission. Table 1 gives the statistical performance analysis results of data tamper-proof monitoring of two groups of data by different methods. The results show that the accuracy of this method is high and the throughput of tamper-proof monitoring data is high. The distribution performance of information sparsity is good.

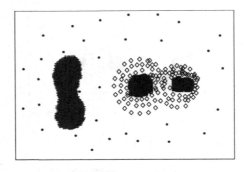

(a) DS 1

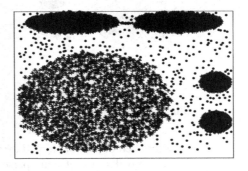

(b) DS 2

Fig. 3. Data tamper proof monitoring output

Table 1. Statistical table of performance verification results under different algorithms.

Algorithm	Size of sparse distribution of information/MBit	Tamper proof monitoring accuracy/%	Tamper proof monitoring data throughput/kMB
Algorithm in this paper	60 × 60	89	93.54
	120 × 120	90	94.45
Generalized tamper proof monitoring algorithm	60 × 60	82	66.67
	120 × 120	83	72.87
Bohzmann	60 × 60	69	87.34
	120 × 120	74	80.98

5 Conclusions

In this paper, a tamper-proof monitoring technology of network sensitive information in big data environment based on big data dimension feature block is proposed. Big data feature space reconstruction method is used to calculate the grid density of network sensitive information distribution, and the network sensitive information to be tampered-proof monitoring is mapped to the divided high-dimensional phase space through the density threshold. The high dimensional phase space of information distribution is divided into dense unit and sparse unit. The coded key is matched to the corresponding network sensitive information block to realize information encryption and covert communication. The simulation results show that the information steganography performance of network sensitive information transmission and storage using this information tampering monitoring technology is better, and the information security transmission ability is improved. This method has good application value in tampering prevention and monitoring of data information.

References

1. Han, D., Chen, X., Lei, Y., et al.: Real-time data analysis system based on Spark Streaming and its application. J. Comput. Appl. **37**(5), 1263–1269 (2017)
2. Zhu, Y., Zhu, X., Wang, J.: Time series motif discovery algorithm based on subsequence full join and maximum clique. J. Comput. Appl. **39**(2), 414–420 (2019)
3. Ma, Y., Zhang, Z., Lin, C.: Research progress in similarity join query of big data. J. Comput. Appl. **38**(4), 978–986 (2018)
4. Zheng, N., Wang, J.: Evidence characteristics and attribute reduction of incomplete ordered information system. Comput. Eng. Appl. **54**(21), 43–47 (2018)
5. Yang, L., Kong, Z., Shi, H.: Multi-controller dynamic deployment strategy of software defined spatial information network. Comput. Eng. **44**(10), 58–63 (2018)
6. Luo, H., Wan, C., Kong, F.: Salient region detection algorithm via KL divergence and multi-scale merging. J. Electron. Inf. **38**(7), 1594–1601 (2016)
7. Stoean, C., Preuss, M., Stoean, R., et al.: Multimodal optimization by means of a topological species conservation algorithm. IEEE Trans. Evol. Comput. **14**(6), 842–864 (2010)
8. Liang, J.J., Qu, B.Y., Mao, X.B., et al.: Differential evolution based on fitness Euclidean-distance ratio for multimodal optimization. Neurocomputing **137**(8), 252–260 (2014)
9. Xu, G., Cheng, X.J.: Adaptive reduction algorithm of scattered point clouds based on wavelet technology. J. Tongji Univ. (Nat. Sci.) **41**(11), 1738–1743 (2013)
10. Bi, A., Wang, S.: Transfer affinity propagation clustering algorithm based on Kullback-Leiber distance. J. Electron. Inf. **38**(8), 2076–2084 (2016)
11. Long, M., Wang, J., Ding, G., et al.: Adaptation regularization, a general framework for transfer learning. IEEE Trans. Knowl. Data Eng. **26**(5), 1076–1089 (2014)
12. Bi, A., Dong, A., Wang, S.: A dynamic data stream clustering algorithm based on probability and exemplar. J. Comput. Res. Dev. **53**(5), 1029–1042 (2016)

Research on Intelligent Detection Method of Weak Sensing Signal Based on Artificial Intelligence

Shuang-cheng Jia$^{(\boxtimes)}$ and Feng-ping Yang

Alibaba Network Technology Co., Ltd., Beijing, China
tomjia1980@126.com

Abstract. In order to improve the detection and recognition ability of weak sensing signal, an intelligent detection algorithm of weak sensing signal based on artificial intelligence algorithm is proposed. The weak sensing signal model is constructed, the weak sensing signal is separated and processed adaptively, the scale and delay of the weak sensing signal are estimated adaptively, and the high resolution spectral features are extracted. The extracted spectral feature is studied adaptively and detected intelligently by artificial intelligence algorithm, and the spectral peak search of weak sensing signal is realized. The spectral feature component method is used to realize the interference suppression of weak sensing signals, thereby improving the detection of the method. The simulation results show that the algorithm has high accuracy and anti-interference ability, and improves the detection and recognition ability of weak sensing signal.

Keywords: Artificial intelligence method · Wireless sensor network · Weak sensing signal · Intelligent detection

1 Introduction

The research on weak sensing signal detection method of wireless sensor network have important application value in the field of wireless sensor network communication optimization and signal recognition. The research of related signal detection method have paid great attention to [1]. In the detection and recognition of weak sensing signal, it is necessary to detect weak sensing signal, detect and estimate the weak sensing signal emitted by wireless sensor network, and detect the weak sensing signal through weak sensing signal. Realize weak sensing signal detection and weak sensing signal recognition, improve the accuracy and automation level of weak sensing signal detection and recognition. In the traditional method, the time-frequency coupling algorithm is used for the detection of weak sensing signal, and the time-frequency feature decomposition method is used to separate the signal to improve the fault detection performance [2]. If the weak sensing signal and interference noise have strong coupling, the detection performance is not good. In reference [4], a weak sensing signal detection algorithm based on fractional Fourier time-frequency coupling is proposed to solve the optimal solution of phase fuzzy number search for signal

© ICST Institute for Computer Sciences, Social Informatics and Telecommunications Engineering 2019
Published by Springer Nature Switzerland AG 2019. All Rights Reserved
G. Gui and L. Yun (Eds.): ADHIP 2019, LNICST 302, pp. 90–98, 2019.
https://doi.org/10.1007/978-3-030-36405-2_10

characteristics of wireless sensor networks, and the phase compensation results of weak sensing signal parameters are obtained [3]. The ability of fault detection is improved, but the anti-interference ability of this method is not good and the computational complexity is high. In order to solve the above problems, an intelligent detection algorithm of weak sensing signal based on artificial intelligence algorithm is proposed in this paper. The weak sensing signal model is constructed, the spectrum decomposition of the multi-carrier weak sensing signal is carried out, the weak sensing signal is separated and processed adaptively, and the parameters such as the scale and delay of the weak sensing signal are estimated adaptively. According to the spectrum offset characteristics of weak sensing signal, high resolution spectral feature extraction is carried out, and artificial intelligence algorithm is used for adaptive learning and intelligent detection of weak sensing signal, and the intelligent detection of weak sensing signal is realized. Finally, the simulation results show the superior performance of this method in improving the fault detection ability of wireless sensor networks.

2   Analysis of Weak Sensing Signal Model and Characteristic Parameters

2.1   Preliminary Knowledge of Model Construction of Weak Sensing Signal

Before studying the phase characteristics of weak sensing signal, it is necessary to construct the signal model of weak sensing signal and construct the model of signal output source. Pattern recognition of weak sensing signal is carried out, combined with sensing information processing method, the feature sampling of weak sensing signal is carried out, and the following three characteristics of weak sensing signal are given [4].

(1) Length of weak sensing signal
Because the length of the weak sensing signal interferes with the amplitude of the signal, the length of the signal can effectively feedback the fault category by taking the length of the signal as the characteristic quantity. Firstly, the length fl, between the optimal sampling points of the weak sensing signal n_b is obtained. Then with the parameter estimation results of fl, the weak sensing signal length l is obtained as:

$$fl = x(\max z_{xn_b}) - x(\min z_{xn_b}) \tag{1}$$

$$l = a \cdot fl + b \tag{2}$$

Where, a, b represent the characteristic decomposition coefficient, for the given broadband high resolution weak sensing signal $x(n)$ and scale d, $\bar{E}(n_i, d)$ F is used to represent the energy of the weak sensing signal, the maximum energy of the weak sensing signal is expressed by $max\{E(n_i, d)\}$, and λ is used as the correlation coefficient. Used to describe the signal to improve the resolution and sensitivity of weak sensing signal [5].

(2) Amplitude is the effective characteristic quantity of weak sensing signal, which represents the maximum wave peak and wave valley difference of weak sensing signal:

$$z_{max} = \max_{y=n_1}^{n_2}\left\{ \max_{x=m_1}^{m_2}\{z_{xy}\} - \min_{x=m_1}^{m_2}\{z_{xy}\} \right\} \tag{3}$$

The depth of weak sensing signal directly affects the amplitude of the signal, which is the characteristic of depth, and is related to the length and width of weak sensing signal [6].

(3) Energy distribution characteristics of weak sensing signals:

$$E = \sum_{x=n_1}^{n_2} \sum_{y=m_1}^{m_2} z_{xy}^2 \tag{4}$$

After analyzing the three main feature quantities of weak sensing signal, the correlation relationship of each feature quantity of weak sensing signal is analyzed and compared [7]. Combined with association rule mining and spectrum feature extraction method, the aggregation degree of weak sensing signal in each feature quantity is obtained [8]. According to the estimation results of signal characteristic quantity E, the 3D size of weak sensing signal is comprehensively reflected, and the fault detection of wireless sensor network is realized by combining artificial intelligence algorithm method.

2.2   Analysis of Characteristic Parameters of Weak Sensing Signal

Let the broadband high resolution weak sensing signal be a set of stationary random signals, which is represented by the power spectrum characteristic decomposition of the signal by $x(t)$, the joint parameter estimation of time and frequency of $x(t)$, and the acquisition of discrete signal $x(n)$. The short time Fourier transform is used to windowed the signal, and the output window function is $h(t)$. The spectrum width of the weak sensing signal is $T = (2d+1)T_s$, $F_s = 1/T_s$. Artificial intelligence algorithm is used to decompose the spectrum of weak sensing signal:

$$X_p(u) = F^p x(t) = F^{\alpha}[x(t)] = \int_{-\infty}^{+\infty} K_p(t,u)x(t)dt \tag{5}$$

Combined with the high-order statistic analysis method, the high-order cumulant special decomposition of $X_p(u)$ can be expressed as follows:

$$X_p(u) = \begin{cases} \sqrt{\frac{1-j\cot\alpha}{2\pi}}e^{j\frac{u^2}{2}\cot a}\int_{-\infty}^{+\infty} x(t)e^{j\frac{t^2}{2}\cot\alpha - jtu\csc\alpha}dt \\ \alpha \neq n\pi \\ x(u),\ \alpha = 2n\pi \\ x(-u),\ \alpha = (2n\pm 1)\pi \end{cases} \tag{6}$$

Adaptive blind separation is performed for weak sensing signal, and parameters such as scale and delay of weak sensing signal are estimated by adaptive estimation of parameters of weak sensing signal:

$$X_1(k) = FFT[x_1(k), x_1(k+1), \ldots \ldots, x_1(k+N-1)]^T \tag{7}$$

The wavelet detector is used to combine the time domain characteristic quantity and the frequency domain feature quantity of the signal to estimate the joint parameters [9]. The estimation model of the characteristic parameters of the weak sensing signal is obtained as shown in Fig. 1.

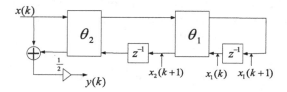

Fig. 1. Estimation model of characteristic parameters of weak sensing signal

3 Optimization of Intelligent Detection Algorithm for Weak Sensing Signal

On the basis of constructing the weak sensing signal model, the spectrum decomposition of the multi-carrier weak sensing signal is carried out, and the weak sensing signal is separated adaptively and blindly [10]. The order of the spectrum decomposition of the weak sensing signal is order 2. The parameters $a_1(t)$ and $a_2(t)$ of the time-frequency joint of the weak sensing signal are determined by the following formula:

$$\begin{cases} a_1(t) = -2m(t)\cos(\theta(t)) \\ a_2(t) = m^2(t) \end{cases} \tag{8}$$

According to the spectrum offset characteristics of the weak sensing signal, the high resolution spectral feature extraction is carried out [11], and the sampling signal of the m element of the signal acquisition array is obtained as follows:

$$s_m(t) = \cos\{2\pi f_0[t + \tau_m(\theta)]\} \tag{9}$$

The left beam output of weak sensing signal windowing using narrow time domain window is expressed as follows:

$$l(t) = \left(\sum_{m=1}^{M} u_m\right)\cos(2\pi f_0 t) - \left(\sum_{m-1}^{M} v_m\right)\sin(2\pi f_0 t) \tag{10}$$

Where, the high resolution spectral feature extraction of weak sensing signal is as follows:

$$u_m = \cos[2\pi f_0 \tau_m(\theta)]; v_m = \sin[2\pi f_0 \tau_m(\theta)] \tag{11}$$

For weak sensing signals, artificial intelligence algorithm is used for adaptive learning and intelligent detection of the extracted spectral features [12]. The modulation pulse parameters of the two array outputs are obtained as follows:

$$l(t) = A_l \cos(2\pi f_0 t + \alpha_l) \tag{12}$$

According to the characteristic aggregation point of weak sensing signal, the time frequency localization of weak sensing signal is carried out, and the output sample of window function is recorded as follows:

$$x_k = \sum_{n=0}^{N/2-1} 2(a_n \cos\frac{2\pi kn}{N} - b_n \sin\frac{2\pi kn}{N}) \quad k = 0, 1, \ldots N - 1 \tag{13}$$

Where, a_n represents the variable scale offset, from which the spectral peak of the weak sensing signal is obtained as follows:

$$f_{Env}(s) = \begin{cases} \sqrt{\frac{2}{\pi}}e^{-s^2/2}, & s \geq 0 \\ 0, & y < 0 \end{cases} \tag{14}$$

$$f_{power}(p) = \begin{cases} \frac{1}{\sqrt{2\pi}}p^{-1/2}e^{-p/2}, & p \geq 0 \\ 0, & p < 0 \end{cases} \tag{15}$$

Artificial intelligence algorithm is used, the minimum convergence error iteration of spectral peak search for weak sensing signal is expressed as follows:

$$\begin{aligned} e(n) &= d(n) - \hat{\mathbf{w}}^H(n) \cdot \mathbf{x}(n) \\ \hat{\mathbf{w}}(n+1) &= \hat{\mathbf{w}}(n) + \mu \cdot \mathbf{x}(n) \cdot e(n) \end{aligned} \tag{16}$$

Combined with beamforming method to suppress sidelobe interference, if $x = 0$, the gain vector is updated:

$$\begin{aligned} \mu(n) &= \mathbf{x}^T(n)\mathbf{P}(n-1)\mathbf{x}(n) \\ \mathbf{k}(n) &= \frac{\mathbf{P}(n-1)\mathbf{x}(n)}{\lambda + \mu(n)} \end{aligned} \tag{17}$$

According to the results of artificial intelligence algorithm, the output signal model of weak sensing signal intelligent detection is obtained [13–15]. The structure model of weak sensing signal intelligent detector is shown in Fig. 2.

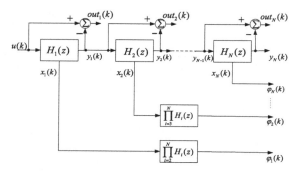

Fig. 2. Structure model of intelligent detector for weak sensing signal

4 Simulation Experiment and Result Analysis

In order to test the performance of this method in the intelligent detection of weak sensing signal, the simulation experiment is carried out. The experiment is based on Matlab 7 simulation tool. The maximum frequency of signal acquisition is 5 Hz, and the sampling sample length of weak sensing signal is 1024, the sample test set is 1000, the training set is 200, and the iterative step number of artificial intelligence algorithm is 2400. According to the above simulation parameters, the time domain waveform of weak sensing signal $x(t)$ is given as shown in Fig. 3.

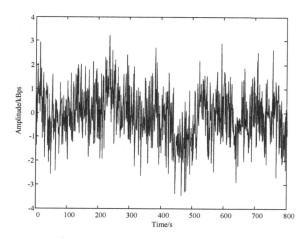

Fig. 3. Time domain waveform of weak sensing signal

High resolution spectral feature extraction and intelligent detection of the original weak sensing signal are carried out, and the results of feature extraction are shown in Fig. 4.

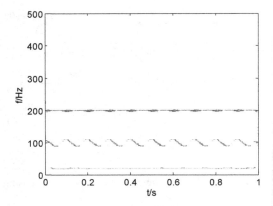

Fig. 4. Results of high resolution spectral feature extraction of weak sensing signals

Analysis of Fig. 4 shows that the proposed method can detect the sensing signals of different intensities and is free from external interference. The analysis Fig. 4 shows that the method in this paper has good resolution ability and improves the detection performance, and tests the accuracy of weak sensing signal detection by different methods. The comparison results are shown in Fig. 5, the detection performance of this method is high and the anti-interference is good.

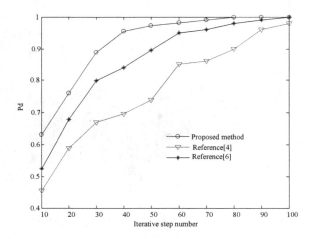

Fig. 5. Comparison of detection performance

The test performance is tested and the comparison results are shown in Table 1. The analysis shows that the accurate probability of weak sensing signal detection by this method is higher.

Table 1. Comparison of accurate probabilities of detection.

SNR/dB	This paper method	Reference [4]	Reference [5]
−10	0.923	0.893	0.901
−5	0.989	0.923	0.923
0	1	0.943	0.936
5	1	0.956	0.945
10	1	0.9780	0.956

5 Conclusions

In this paper, the detection method of weak sensing signal is studied, and the weak sensing signal emitted by wireless sensor network is detected and estimated, so as to realize the detection and recognition of weak sensing signal. An intelligent detection algorithm for weak sensing signals based on artificial intelligence algorithm is proposed. The weak sensing signal model is constructed, the spectrum decomposition of the multi-carrier weak sensing signal is carried out, the weak sensing signal is separated and processed adaptively, and the parameters such as the scale and delay of the weak sensing signal are estimated adaptively. According to the spectrum offset characteristic of weak sensing signal, the high resolution spectral feature is extracted, and the extracted spectral feature is studied and detected intelligently by artificial intelligence algorithm, and the spectral peak search of weak sensing signal is realized. Combined with beamforming method, sidelobe interference suppression is realized and detection performance is improved. It is found that the proposed method has high accuracy and good anti-interference ability in weak sensing signal detection, and effectively improves the signal detection ability.

References

1. Feng, W., Wang, Y., Lin, D., et al.: When mm wave communications meet network densification: a scalable interference coordination perspective. IEEE J. Sel. Areas Commun. **35**(7), 1459–1471 (2017)
2. Matilainen, M., Nordhausen, K., Oja, H.: New independent component analysis tools for time series. Stat. Probab. Lett. **32**(5), 80–87 (2017)
3. Hao, S.G., Zhang, L., Muhammad, G.: A union authentication protocol of cross-domain based on bilinear pairing. J. Software **8**(5), 1094–1100 (2013)
4. Zhang, G.H., Liu, W.L.: A compressed sensing based detection for star topology WSNs. J. Taiyuan Univ. Technol. **49**(3), 107–110 (2018)
5. Guangsheng, T.U., Xiaoyuan, Y.A.N.G., Tanping, Z.H.O.U.: Efficient identity-based multi-identity fully homomorphic encryption scheme. J. Comput. Appl. **39**(3), 750–755 (2019)
6. Li, X., Gao, W.M., Wang, Y., et al.: Study on partial discharge ultrasonic signal detection method based on optical fiber sensing technology. J. Transduct. Technol. **30**(11), 1619–1624 (2017)
7. Farnadi, G., Bach, S.H., Moens, M.F., et al.: Soft quantification in statistical relational learning. Mach. Learn. **106**(12), 1971–1991 (2017)

8. Tu, B., Chuai, R., Xu, H.: Outlier detection based on k-mean distance outlier factor for gait signal. Inf. Control **48**(1), 16–21 (2019)

9. Wei, X.S., Luo, J.H., Wu, J.: Selective convolutional descriptor aggregation for fine-grained image retrieval. IEEE Trans. Image Process. **26**(6), 2868–2881 (2017)

10. Huang, X., You, R., Zhou, C.: Study on optical properties of equivalent film constructed of metal nanoparticle arrays. J. Optoelectron. Laser **24**(7), 1434–1438 (2013)

11. Zhou, S.B., Xu, W.X.: A novel clustering algorithm based on relative density and decision graph. Control Dec. **33**(11), 1921–1930 (2018)

12. He, H., Tan, Y.: Automatic pattern recognition of ECG signals using entropy-based adaptive dimensionality reduction and clustering. Appl. Soft Comput. **55**, 238–252 (2017)

13. Yuelong, Z.H.U., Xiaoxiao, Z.H.U., Jimin, W.A.N.G.: Time series motif discovery algorithm based on subsequence full join and maximum clique. J. Comput. Appl. **39**(2), 414–420 (2019)

14. He, W., Guo, C., Tian, Z.: Optimization method for multi-constellation precise point positioning performance evaluation. Comput. Eng. **45**(5), 88–92 (2019)

Research on Delay Control Method of Ultra-Wideband Wireless Communication Based on Artificial Intelligence

Shuang-cheng Jia[(⊠)] and Feng-ping Yang

Alibaba Network Technology Co., Ltd., Beijing, China
tomjia1980@126.com

Abstract. In order to improve the intelligence and real-time performance of ultra-broadband wireless communication, it is necessary to control the time delay of intelligent data transmission in ultra-broadband wireless communication. An intelligent data transmission time delay control algorithm for ultra-broadband wireless communication based on artificial intelligence algorithm is proposed. A wireless communication network transmission model based on wireless sensor networking model is constructed, and the position and scale parameters distributed in the process of wireless communication transmission are measured by using different scales. It is found that the time delay control problem is the best replica correlation matched filter detection problem, and the communication delay control is realized to the maximum extent. The simulation results show that the artificial intelligence of ultra-broadband wireless communication delay control is good and the communication quality is high.

Keywords: Artificial intelligence · Ultra-broadband · Wireless communication · Delay control

1 Introduction

With the development of ultra-broadband wireless communication technology, the use of ultra-broadband wireless communication for data transmission has become the development direction of communication in the future [1]. Broadband wireless communication does not need the transmission medium of the channel. The transmission performance of direct communication light realizes remote wireless communication, so ultra-broadband wireless communication has the advantages of strong anti-interference ability and good transmission fidelity, and is widely used in military communication and civil communication and other fields. Ultra-broadband wireless communication has a large bandwidth, which can realize 1 Gbps ultra-broadband data information transmission [2]. In the process of using ultra-broadband wireless communication for remote data transmission, it is easy to be affected by channel offset and multi-path effect, resulting in communication error code and transmission distortion, so it is necessary to carry out delay control processing of ultra-broadband wireless communication. It is of great significance to improve the anti-interference ability of ultra-broadband wireless communication and improve the resolution of signal transmission. The study of time

© ICST Institute for Computer Sciences, Social Informatics and Telecommunications Engineering 2019
Published by Springer Nature Switzerland AG 2019. All Rights Reserved
G. Gui and L. Yun (Eds.): ADHIP 2019, LNICST 302, pp. 99–108, 2019.
https://doi.org/10.1007/978-3-030-36405-2_11

delay control technology of ultra-broadband wireless communication system is of great significance in improving the quality of ultra-broadband wireless communication system [3].

The time delay control of ultra-broadband wireless communication system is based on channel equalization and anti-interference processing. At present, random code spread spectrum technology and Porter interval equalization technology are used for time delay control technology of ultra-broadband wireless communication system. When the transmission channel of ultra-broadband wireless communication channel is affected by inter-symbol interference and the multi-path effect of media in optical transmission channel, the performance of time delay control is not good, which leads to the increase of output bit error rate and easy to cause channel imbalance. In reference [4], the time delay control technology of ultra-broadband wireless communication system based on frequency shift keying anti-interference technology is proposed. The time reversal mirror technology is selected to suppress the channel intersymbol interference and compensate the distortion of the signal by the medium. The frequency shift keying technology is used to process the high amplifier and mixing of spread spectrum signals to realize the time delay control of ultra-broadband wireless communication system. This method has certain anti-interference performance, but with the increase of channel multi-path effect. In order to solve the above problems, an intelligent data transmission time delay control algorithm for ultra-broadband wireless communication based on artificial intelligence algorithm is proposed in this paper. A wireless communication network transmission model based on wireless sensor networking model is constructed, and the position and scale parameters distributed in the process of wireless communication transmission are measured by using different scales. It is found that the time delay control problem is the best replica correlation matched filter detection problem, and the communication delay control is realized to the maximum extent. Finally, the simulation results show the superior performance of this method in improving the delay control ability of ultra-broadband wireless communication.

2   Intelligent Data Transmission Acquisition and Detection Model for Ultra-Wideband Wireless Communication

2.1   Construction of Communication Signal Model

The intelligent data transmission stream of ultra-broadband wireless communication is formed in the host computer of wireless communication transmission, and is annihilated by the normal network traffic sequence in the process of transmission and wireless communication transmission. In this paper, a wireless communication network transmission model based on wireless sensor networking model is constructed [5], and the schematic diagram of ultra-broadband wireless communication transmission model in multi-clustering state is shown in Fig. 1.

In the ultra-broadband wireless communication transmission mode, the wireless communication transmission signal is sent out by several signal pulse of the network user and the terminal device, and the hacker carries on the wireless communication transmission to the computer, or other illegal calls [6]. When the hacker computer

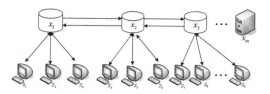

Fig. 1. Schematic diagram of Ultra-Wideband Wireless communication transmission

wireless communication transmission, the hacker will cut into the user's computer. Assuming that the number of network terminal devices in the multi-cluster state is m, the data are tested on the H terminals, and the amplitude of the wireless communication transmission signal is A, and the amplitude adjustment coefficient of the input signal is expressed as follows:

$$\tilde{s}(t) = \sqrt{E_t} \int_{-\infty}^{+\infty} \tilde{f}(t - \lambda)\tilde{b}_R(\lambda)d\lambda + n(t) \tag{1}$$

When the data structure is established, the ternary prime points, lines and surfaces are used as the elements to realize the segmented processing of high frequency and low frequency features. The variance and mean value of correlation noise distribution $p(e_k|v_k)$ are as follows:

$$\begin{cases} H_0 : \tilde{x}(t) = \tilde{w}(t) \\ H_1 : \tilde{x}(t) = \sqrt{E_t} \int_{-\infty}^{+\infty} \tilde{f}(t - \lambda)\tilde{b}_R(\lambda)d\lambda + \tilde{w}(t) \end{cases} \quad -\infty \leq t \leq +\infty \tag{2}$$

Therefore, the network communication diagram $G(V, r)$, of ultra-broadband wireless communication intelligent data transmission is constructed, that is, the short distance link is considered for data transmission. In $G(V, r)$, if there is an edge between the two nodes, the whole network is divided into several square areas with equal side lengths. According to the data mining method, the data of the design structure is excavated to extract more obvious features. This strengthens the ability of data analysis [7].

2.2   Feature Detection Algorithm for Intelligent Data Transmission

Based on the design of the above model of intelligent data transmission for ultra-wideband wireless communication, in order to ensure the security of the network, it is necessary to detect the data and design the characteristic detection algorithm of intelligent data transmission [8]. On the 2D plane of the time scale, a wavelet scale decomposition model is used to represent the correlation dimension characteristic components of the signal to be detected:

$$\tilde{s}(t) = \sqrt{E_t} \int_{-\infty}^{+\infty} \tilde{f}(t - \lambda)\tilde{b}_R(\lambda)d\lambda \tag{3}$$

$$s(t) = \sqrt{2}\mathrm{Re}\left[\sqrt{E_t}\tilde{s}(t)e^{j\omega_c t}\right] \tag{4}$$

In the above formula, $\tilde{w}(t)$ is a statistically independent zero-mean complex white Gaussian process. $\tilde{v}_k = v_k - d + 1$ represents the wireless communication transmission signal in a single clustering mode. When the ultra-broadband wireless communication transmission signal is a weak signal, it is a normal threshold in the potential well of the random field. The position and scale parameters of t distribution are obtained as follows:

$$l = \frac{1}{N_0}\int\limits_{-\infty}^{+\infty}\int\limits_{-\infty}^{+\infty}\tilde{x}(t)\tilde{h}(t,u)\tilde{x}(u)dudt, \quad \tilde{\Sigma}_k = \frac{1+V_{11,k}}{(v_k - d + 1)V_{11,k}}\Lambda_k \tag{5}$$

The optimal detector for detecting the time delay control problem is the replica correlation integral detector, and the camouflage signal is converted into sine wave. The detector is designed as shown in Fig. 2.

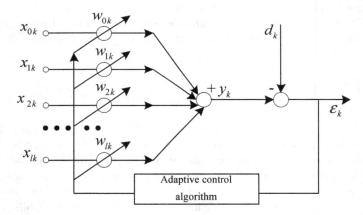

Fig. 2. Schematic diagram of replica correlation integral detector

Based on the above analysis, the design of the feature detection algorithm for intelligent data transmission is obtained. because the time domain diffusion distortion of the channel is taken into account, it is more robust than the general replica correlation detector [9].

3 Improved Implementation of Algorithm

3.1 Communication Channel Equalization Processing

On the basis of the above signal model and detection model, the intelligent data transmission time delay control and wireless communication transmission time delay in ultra-broadband wireless communication are carried out, which provides the time difference for the accurate detection of intelligent data transmission. According to the link balance of ultra-broadband wireless communication system, the multi-path inter-ference suppression is carried out, the tap filter is designed to filter the interference, and the channel transmission model of the communication system is constructed [10]. After the output of the signal is modified by the equalizer, the sampling decision equalizer is used to compensate the channel deflection randomly. The channel equalization model is obtained as shown in Fig. 3.

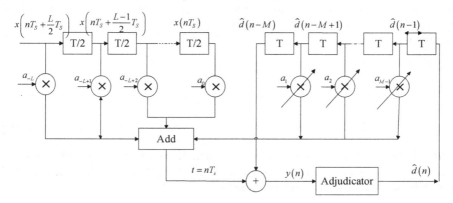

Fig. 3. Channel equalization control model

Assuming that the power spectrum of the two pieces of data x1(t) and x2(t) is s1(ω) and s2(ω), the resulting time delay control delay is:

$$d_I(s_1, s_2) = \ln\left[\int_{-\pi}^{+\pi} \frac{1}{2\pi} \frac{s_1(\omega)/\sigma_1^2}{s_2(\omega)/\sigma_2^2} d\omega\right] \tag{6}$$

According to the above description, the transmission signal data of ultra-broadband wireless communication in multi-clustering state is self-correlated with $s_i(k)$, but it is integrated with each other, but as for the position of fusion form, it needs to be realized by an effective signal detection model. Before that, it is necessary to design a single-mode time delay control algorithm for ultra-broadband wireless communication transmission. In this paper, the signal separation method is adopted, and the self-phase components of each independent variable can be characterized by the limit separation characteristic of non-Gaussian function. The output of the time delay control system for ultra-broadband wireless communication transmission is obtained as follows:

$$x_1(t) = -\sum_{k=1}^{p_1} a_{1k}x_1(t-k) + W\varepsilon_1(t) \tag{7}$$

In this formula, W matrix is $n \times m$-dimensional separation matrix, x1(t) and x2(t) can be described by AR model, the source data and wireless communication transmission data are demultiplexed and separated, which provides the premise for the realization of single-mode time delay control.

Based on the idea of independent self-phase component analysis, a joint function is designed, which is considered by the joint distribution of time and frequency. That is, the signal is divided into some parts for analysis and investigation, rather than the global analysis and judgment, and the Fourier transformation is carried out for two scalar time series y_1 and y_2. By using independent self-phase component analysis, the transmission signal detection characteristics of wireless communication network are represented as the complete localization information of wireless communication transmission signal, that is:

$$x(t) = e^{j2\pi v_x(t)t} \tag{8}$$

$$v_x(t) = v_0 + 2\beta t \tag{9}$$

$$W_x(t, v) = \delta(v - (v_0 + \beta t)) \tag{10}$$

Based on the construction of the above model, the balanced configuration of ultra-broadband wireless communication is realized, and on this basis, the time delay control of ultra-broadband wireless communication is carried out.

3.2   Time Delay Control Optimization

Suppose that in an ultra-broadband wireless communication channel, $f(e(i))$ represents the carrier frequency of the transmission chain roadside e on channel i, $k(e)$ represents the set of edge e, and K represents the link set of the output of ultra-broadband wireless communication. $C(e, i)$ represents the information energy of the ultra-broadband wireless communication at a lower frequency, where $f(e(i)) \leq C(e, i)$, the impulse response of the ultra-broadband wireless communication channel is obtained as:

$$Int(e, i) = \frac{f(e(i))}{C(e, i)} + \sum_{e \subseteq k(e)} \frac{f(e'(i))}{C(e', i)} \tag{11}$$

When there is multi-path interference on the edge set e of the transmission channel, the phase offset of the transmission path is deterministic, and the output link sum F of the ultra-broadband wireless communication channel is constant, from which the interference estimation model of the communication signal is obtained as:

$$\begin{cases} \min \sum\limits_{1 \leq i \leq K} \sum\limits_{e \subseteq k(e)} \frac{f(e(i))}{C(e,i)} \\ 0 \leq f(e, i) \leq C(e, i) \\ F = const \\ \sum\limits_{1 \leq i \leq K, e \subseteq k(e)} \frac{f(e(i))}{C(e,i)} + \sum\limits_{e \subseteq k(e)} \frac{f(e'(i))}{C(e',i)} \leq k(v) \end{cases} \tag{12}$$

The complex model is used to accurately simulate the pulse response of UWB wireless communication channel. $\theta_i(t)$ is used to represent the phase offset of each path in UWB wireless communication system. According to the phase deflection characteristic $\theta_i(t)$ and symbol rate f_s, The channel transmission model of ultra-broadband wireless communication is represented by $h(t) = \sum_i a_i(t)e^{j\theta_i(t)}\delta(t - iT_S)$. According to the above analysis, the time delay control of intelligent data transmission in ultra-broadband wireless communication is realized.

4   Simulation Experiment and Result Analysis

In order to test the performance of the proposed algorithm, simulation experiments are carried out. The sampling signals are sampled at symbol 1/3 and 2/3, and the sample data of ultra-broadband wireless communication transmission signal are extracted. The signal setting period is 1.25 s, the intensity is 1024 Mbps, continuous wireless communication transmission time is 1024 ms, and the number of network information samples used for ultra-broadband wireless communication transmission time delay control is 1024, and the number of web visits is 10332. The types of ultra-broadband wireless communication transmission can be divided into the following categories: scanning and detecting (Probe), denial of service wireless communication transmission (DoS), illegal access (U2R) and unauthorized remote access (R2L). The distribution of four kinds of wireless communication transmission samples is calculated respectively, as shown in Table 1.

Table 1. Model parameter design.

Channel model	Modulation parameter	Multi-path delay parameter (Ts)
Model 1	(1, 0.24, −0.43, 0.15, −0.16)	(0, 0.23, 0.43, 0.32, 0.43)
Model 2	(1, 0.53, −0.4, 0.13, −0.14)	(0, 1.45, 2.45, 3.34, 4.21)
Model 3	(1, 0.54, −0.5, 0.17, −0.13)	(0, 1.45, 2.03, 3.45, 4.20)
Model 4	(1, 0.35, −0.7, 0.16, −0.126)	(0, 0.43, 1.34, 2.56, 3.35)

According to the above simulation environment and data acquisition results, the time delay control simulation of ultra-broadband wireless communication intelligent data transmission is carried out, and the time delay control detection statistics of different wireless communication transmission data segments are obtained as shown in Fig. 4.

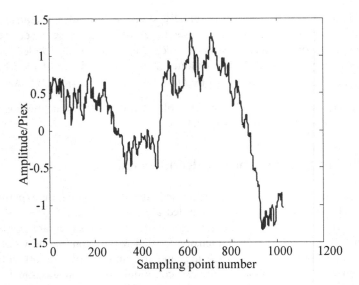

Fig. 4. Time delay control detection statistics

It can be seen from the diagram that the proposed algorithm has good control performance of intelligent data transmission time delay, which provides a time capacity for the detection of wireless communication transmission data. Further intelligent data transmission detection experiment is carried out, and the time delay distribution is shown in Fig. 5.

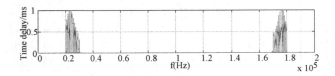

Fig. 5. Time delay

In order to compare the performance of the algorithm, the detection probability of ultra-broadband wireless communication transmission signal is compared and analyzed by using 20000 Monte Carlo implementation. Based on this algorithm and the traditional method, the detection probability of ultra-broadband wireless communication transmission signal is compared and analyzed. The simulation results are shown in Fig. 6. As can be seen from the figure, the accurate detection probability of ultra-broadband wireless communication transmission characteristic signal is higher than that of the traditional scheme by using this algorithm, which shows the superior performance and high application value of this algorithm.

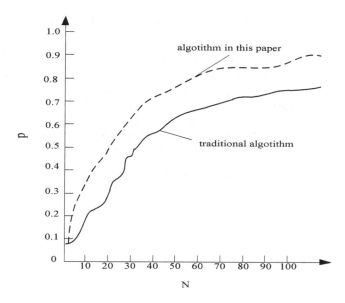

Fig. 6. Performance comparison

5   Conclusions

In this paper, an intelligent data transmission time delay control algorithm for ultra-broadband wireless communication based on artificial intelligence algorithm is proposed. A wireless communication network transmission model based on wireless sensor networking model is constructed, and the position and scale parameters distributed in the process of wireless communication transmission are measured by using different scales. It is found that the time delay control problem is the best replica correlation matched filter detection problem, and the communication delay control is realized to the maximum extent. The simulation results show that the artificial intelligence of ultra-broadband wireless communication delay control is good and the communication quality is high.

References

1. Helmy, A., Hedayat, A., Al-Dhahir, N.: Robust weighted sum-rate maximization for the multi-stream MIMO interference channel with sparse equalization. IEEE Trans. Commun. **60**(10), 3645–3659 (2015)
2. Alfaro, V.M., Vilanovab, R.: Robust tuning of 2DoF five-parameter PID controllers for inverse response controlled processes. J. Process Control **23**(4), 453–462 (2013)
3. Seo, D.W., Lee, J.H., Lee, H.S.: Optimal coupling to achieve maximum output power in a WPT system. IEEE Trans. Power Electron. **31**(6), 3994–3998 (2016)
4. Dai, H., Huang, Y., Li, C., et al.: Energy-efficient resource allocation for device-to-device communication with WPT. IET Commun. **11**(3), 326–334 (2017)

5. Han, D., Chen, X., Lei, Y., et al.: Real-time data analysis system based on Spark Streaming and its application. J. Comput. Appl. **37**(5), 1263–1269 (2017)
6. Zhou, S.B., Xu, W.X.: A novel clustering algorithm based on relative density and decision graph. Control Dec. **33**(11), 1921–1930 (2018)
7. He, H., Tan, Y.: Automatic pattern recognition of ECG signals using entropy-based adaptive dimensionality reduction and clustering. Appl. Soft Comput. **55**, 238–252 (2017)
8. Zhu, Y., Zhu, X., Wang, J.: Time series motif discovery algorithm based on subsequence full join and maximum clique. J. Comput. Appl. **39**(2), 414–420 (2019)
9. Hao, S.G., Zhang, L., Muhammad, G.: A union authentication protocol of cross-domain based on bilinear pairing. J. Software **8**(5), 1094–1100 (2013)
10. Ma, Z., Chen, W.: Friction torque calculation method of ball bearings based on rolling creepage theory. J. Mech. Eng. **53**(22), 219–224 (2017)

Research on Anomaly Monitoring Algorithm of Uncertain Large Data Flow Based on Artificial Intelligence

Shuang-cheng Jia[✉] and Feng-ping Yang

Alibaba Network Technology Co., Ltd., Beijing 100102, China
tomjia1980@126.com

Abstract. In order to improve the monitoring ability of uncertain large data stream, an uncertain large data flow monitoring algorithm based on artificial intelligence is proposed. The collected uncertain big data flow is constructed by low dimensional feature set, and the rough set model of uncertain large data stream distribution is constructed. The fuzzy C-means clustering method is used to analyze the uncertain big data flow by fusion clustering and adaptive grid partition analysis. All the abnormal samples of large data stream are sampled and trained, and the feature quantities of association rules of uncertain large data stream are extracted. Combined with artificial intelligence method, the monitoring of uncertain large data stream is realized. The simulation results show that the method has high accuracy and good ability to resist abnormal traffic interference, and the traffic security monitoring ability of the network is improved.

Keywords: Artificial intelligence · Uncertain large data stream · Anomaly monitoring · Clustering

1 Introduction

With the development of wireless sensor network communication technology, heterogeneous directed sensor network communication technology is used to design wireless network to improve the wireless transmission ability of data. In the process of data transmission in heterogeneous directed sensor network, higher requirements are put forward for the stability of network traffic transmission [1]. The heterogeneous directed sensor network communication is affected by the interference of the transmission channel and the disturbance of inter-symbol characteristics in the data transmission, which leads to the abnormal output of the network, so it is necessary to accurately monitor the uncertain big data flow. Improve network secure transmission capacity. It has great significance to study the abnormal traffic monitoring algorithm in order to improve the security and stability of the network [2].

Combined with the category of uncertain large data stream, fuzzy clustering method is used for traffic anomaly monitoring, and the monitoring of uncertain large data stream of heterogeneous directed sensor is realized by data mining and feature

G. Gui and L. Yun (Eds.): ADHIP 2019, LNICST 302, pp. 109–117, 2019.
https://doi.org/10.1007/978-3-030-36405-2_12

extraction. The association rule feature of uncertain large data stream is extracted and filtered by anti-interference algorithm [3]. In this paper, an uncertain large data stream monitoring algorithm based on artificial intelligence is proposed. The fuzzy C-means clustering method is used to analyze the uncertain big data flow by fusion clustering and adaptive grid partition analysis. The feature extraction results of uncertain large data streams are inputted into BP neural network classifiers for data classification. Combined with big data fusion clustering method to realize uncertain big data flow monitoring, finally, the simulation experiment is carried out, which shows the superior performance of this method in improving the ability of network abnormal traffic monitoring [4].

2 Distributed Database and Feature Set Construction of Uncertain Large Data Flow

2.1 Construction of Uncertain Large Data Stream Distributed Database

To realize the monitoring of uncertain large data stream, the distributed large database model of heterogeneous directed sensor networks is constructed by using fuzzy rough clustering class method, and the nearest neighbor priority distributed information mining method is used to mine the uncertain large data stream. The adaptive association rule scheduling method is used for feature monitoring and information filtering of uncertain large data stream, and the distributed large database model of abnormal traffic in sensor network is constructed by combining correlation monitoring method [5]. The data set is vector processed, and the frequent itemsets of uncertain large data streams are calculated under the mode of uncertain frequent itemsets. The fusion analysis method of expected frequent term (EFI) and probabilistic frequent term (PFI) is adopted. The scheduling set function of uncertain large data stream is obtained as follows:

$$R_d^i(t+1) = \min\{R_s, \max\{0, R_d^i(t) + \beta(n_i - |N_i(t)|)\}\} \tag{1}$$

$$N_i(t) = \{j : ||x_j(t) - x_i(t)|| < R_d^i; l_i(t)\} \tag{2}$$

Wherein, $x_j(t)$ represents the average information entropy in the uncertain large data stream distribution data set D, describes the sample subset in the I clustering center, and $l_j(t)$ represents the sample set learned by the j generation in the process of uncertain large data flow monitoring. The output label attributes of uncertain large data streams in the i clustering center are calculated. The statistical characteristic quantity of uncertain large data stream is analyzed by split information monitoring method, and the clustering center $F(x_i, A_j(L))$, $i = 1, 2, \ldots, m$, $j = 1, 2, \ldots, k$, which initializes the classification of uncertain large data stream monitoring data, is used to extract the monitoring spectrum feature of uncertain large data stream [6]. The statistical characteristics of uncertain large data flow monitoring are obtained as follows:

$$\gamma_i = \frac{\frac{1}{w}\sum_{l=0}^{w-1}[x_i(k-l)-\mu_i]^3}{\left(\frac{1}{w}\sum_{l=0}^{w-1}[x_i(k-l)-\mu_i]^2\right)^{\frac{3}{2}}} \tag{3}$$

$$\kappa_i = \frac{\frac{1}{w}\sum_{l=0}^{w-1}[x_i(k-l)-\mu_i]^4}{\left(\frac{1}{w}\sum_{l=0}^{w-1}[x_i(k-l)-\mu_i]^2\right)^{2}} \tag{4}$$

The k uncertain large data stream monitoring impulse response function $[\delta_1, \delta_2, \cdots, \delta_N]$ becomes δ_k by extracting the association rule information of uncertain large data stream $\delta_{ik}(t)$:

$$\delta_{ik}(t) = G(V = k | U_i, \Theta(t)) \tag{5}$$

The method comprises the following steps of: carrying out fusion processing on the acquired original uncertain large data stream information, and performing beam integration processing; and the sensing information fusion model of the uncertain large data stream is expressed as follows:

$$x_m(t) = \sum_{i=1}^{I} s_i(t)e^{j\varphi_{mi}} + n_m(t), \quad -p+1 \leq m \leq p \tag{6}$$

The collected uncertain big data flow is constructed with low dimensional feature set, and the rough set model of uncertain large data stream distribution is constructed to improve the abnormal monitoring ability of traffic flow [7].

2.2 Sensing Information Fusion for Uncertain Large Data Flow Monitoring

The adaptive regression analysis method is used to extract the statistical features of the uncertain big data flow feature set. The number of uncertain large data stream acquisition nodes is $N = n - (m-1)\tau$. The three-dimensional spectrum r_i and power spectral density k_i of uncertain large data stream monitoring are calculated. The Langevin equation is used to describe the uncertain large data flow monitoring model as follows:

$$\frac{dx}{dt} = ax - bx^2 + s(t) + \Gamma(t) \tag{7}$$

The discrete sampling and sensing information fusion tracking and recognition of the traffic sequence are carried out [8], and the abnormal statistical characteristic quantity model is obtained as follows:

$$f(x) = sgn\left\{ z \sum_{i=1}^{l_1} \alpha_i^+ y_i K(x_i, x) + \sum_{i=1}^{l_2} \alpha_i^- y_i K(x_i, x) + b \right\} \qquad (8)$$

Combined with the method of scalar sequence analysis, the storage sample database model of uncertain large data stream is obtained as follows:

$$AVG_X = \frac{1}{m \times n} \sum_{x=1}^{n} \sum_{y=1}^{m} |G_X(x, y)| \qquad (9)$$

Wherein m and n are the class number and the sampling node of the sampling sample of the uncertain large data stream, and the m, n are the classification element of the uncertain large data stream, and the frequency spectrum bandwidth of the uncertain large data stream is obtained by using the mining method of the frequent item set to obtain the frequency spectrum bandwidth of the uncertain large data stream:

$$\text{sgn}(z_R^2(k) - R_{MDMMA\_R}) = \text{sgn}(z_R^2(k) - \hat{e}_R^2(k)) \qquad (10)$$

$$\text{sgn}(z_I^2(k) - R_{MDMMA\_I}) = \text{sgn}(z_I^2(k) - \hat{e}_I^2(k)) \qquad (11)$$

Wherein, $\hat{e}_R^2(k)$ represents the observation sequence monitored by uncertain large data stream, $z_R^2(k)$ is the SNR of the original training set, $z_I^2(k)$ is the impulse response function of fuzzy clustering, and $\hat{e}_I^2(k)$ is the output error of the data subset. According to the above analysis, the sensing information fusion processing of network uncertainty data flow monitoring is carried out by using association rule mining method [6].

3   Optimization of Uncertain Large Data Flow Monitoring Algorithm

3.1   Feature Extraction of Uncertain Large Data Flow

Based on the rough set model of uncertain large data flow distribution, the optimal design of network uncertain large data flow monitoring is carried out. in this paper, an uncertain large data flow monitoring algorithm based on artificial intelligence is proposed. Taking a small number of sample category data as the test set, the fuzzy C-means clustering method is used to analyze the uncertain big data flow by fusion clustering and adaptive grid partition analysis [7]. In the fuzzy C-means clustering center, If the expected support degree of data element t in heterogeneous directed sensor networks is greater than the threshold θ, the attribute element monitored by uncertain large data stream is said to be a frequent term. The classification attribute elements of all uncertain large data streams satisfy the following constraints:

$$esup^t(D) > \theta \tag{12}$$

The association characteristics of uncertain large data streams is described as: $FP\left(X_{i_j}, P_{i_j}, (sup^{k1}(D), \cdots, sup^{kf}(D)), (T_{k1}, \cdots T_{kj})\right)$, where X_{i_j} is the nth data element that appears in the first time of the uncertain large data stream arriving at the window at T_{i_j} time, and P_{i_j} is the optimal probability of output optimization training. $(sup^{k1}(D), \cdots, sup^{kf}(D))$ is a low dimensional feature set of uncertain large data streams. The correlation beamforming method is used to monitor the uncertain large data stream of the network, and the iterative formula of machine learning is obtained as follows:

$$x_O^i = x_S^i + Kd_i^{\max}(x_L^i - x_S^i) \tag{13}$$

Wherein, $K = 1/\|x_L^i - x_S^i\|$, the feature extraction results of uncertain large data streams is input into BP neural network classifiers for data classification [9], and for the calculation of $sup^t(D)$. The dynamic programming of uncertain large data flow monitoring is carried out by using big data's classified global search method [, and its calculation formula is as follows:

$$P_{i,j}^t = \begin{cases} P_{i-1,j-1}^t \times p_i + P_{i-1,j}^t \times (1 - p_i), & v_i = t \\ P_{i-1,j}^t, & v_i \neq t \end{cases} \tag{14}$$

Wherein, p_i is the probability that the distribution elements of association rules appear in the abnormal decision region i, and K is the probability of the fuzzy clustering region $P_{i,j}^t$ of the t tuples in the former S heterogeneous nodes. Sampling training of all abnormal samples of large data stream, extracting the feature quantity of association rules of uncertain large data stream, and the iterative formula of feature extraction is expressed as follows:

$$r_d^i(k+1) = \min\{r_S, \max\{0, r_d^i(k) + \beta(n_i - |N_i(k)|)\}\} \tag{15}$$

Herein, β represents the association rule feature of uncertain large data stream, and if the exception category element t satisfies the finite scheduling mode, it is called probabilistic frequent term.

$$\sum_{\omega \in PW, C^t(\omega) \geq minsup} P[\omega] > \delta \tag{16}$$

Wherein, δ is an association rule set, which realizes feature extraction of uncertain large data streams [10].

3.2   Uncertain Large Data Flow Monitoring

The decision function of uncertain large data flow monitoring is obtained by using gray scale quantitative feature analysis method:

$$U(x) = -\frac{1}{2}ax^2 + \frac{1}{4}bx^4 \tag{17}$$

In the above formula, the system parameters take the $a = 1$, $b = 1$, and the collected original heterogeneous is subjected to fusion processing to the abnormal intrusion large data information of the sensor network, and the statistical information analysis model of the uncertain large data flow monitoring is constructed, In this paper, the fuzzy cluster analysis model for uncertain large data flow monitoring is described by using the method of information fusion, and the fuzzy cluster analysis model is described as follows:

$$\omega_k = \begin{pmatrix} v_k \\ e_k \end{pmatrix} = \begin{pmatrix} x_k - f(x_{k-1}) \\ y_k - h(x_k) \end{pmatrix} \tag{18}$$

The ARMA model is used to represent the principal component characteristics of uncertain large data streams, which are described as follows:

$$x_n = a_0 + \sum_{i=1}^{M_{AR}} a_i x_{n-i} + \sum_{j=0}^{M_{MA}} b_j \eta_{n-j} \tag{19}$$

The feature quantity of association rules of uncertain large data stream is extracted, and the feature extraction results of uncertain large data stream are input into BP neural network classifier for data classification, which is analyzed comprehensively to realize the monitoring of uncertain large data stream. The monitoring steps are as follows:

Step 1. Learning coefficient of BP Neural Network for initializing uncertain large data flow monitoring $SWF = null, D = null, P_{i_j} = 0, sup^{ki}(\omega) = 0$;

Step 2. for X_{i_j}, a fuzzy clustering center point is randomly found, and the center points of all clusters monitored by uncertain large data streams are obtained.

Step 3. The statistical credential probability of abnormal network traffic monitoring is calculated according to clustering cross: P_{ij};

Step 4. If (current window is not full), fuzzy clustering method is used to reconstruct abnormal features;

Step 5. Update the current window to reorganize the samples of uncertain large data streams, and calculate the probability distribution value of abnormal categories. $sup^{ki}(\omega)$;

Step 6. The fuzzy sample set of uncertain large data stream is calculated, and the statistical characteristic quantity is obtained by combining the cumulative probability distribution method: $Q = \sum_{i=minsup}^{num^t(D)} sup^t(D)$;

Step 7. if $Q \geq \delta$
Step 8. Adding uncertain large data flow samples of BP Learning to rough sets D;
Step 9. else
Step 10. Return frequent itemsets for uncertain large data streams D.

According to the above steps, the improved design of uncertain large data flow monitoring algorithm is realized.

4 Analysis of Simulation Experiment

In order to test the application performance of this method in the implementation of uncertain large data flow monitoring, the simulation experiment is carried out. The experiment is designed by Matlab 7 and C. The number of traffic sampling nodes in heterogeneous directed sensor networks is 200, the number of backbone nodes is 20, the number of Sink nodes is 12, and the interval between sampling points in the experiment is 5 min, uncertain large data stream injection mode is DDOS attack mode. The duration of the attack is 20 min, and the traffic anomaly features are extracted from 6 sampling points. The maximum number of iterations is 500, and the network traffic collection results are obtained from 2 to 20. The results are shown in Fig. 1.

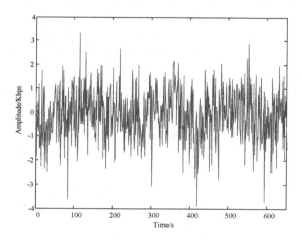

Fig. 1. Big data flow collection

The uncertainty big data flow collected in Fig. 1 is taken as the test sample to monitor the uncertain big data flow, and the monitoring output is shown in Fig. 2.

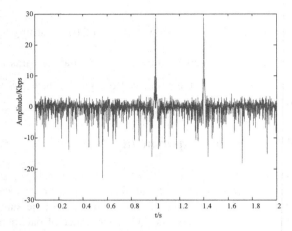

Fig. 2. Uncertain large data stream monitoring output

Figure 2 shows that the method can accurately locate the distributed frequency domain points of uncertain large data streams, and the uncertain large data streams are monitored at t = 1.04 s and t = 1.43 s, respectively. The accuracy of monitoring is good. In order to test the anti-interference and monitoring effectiveness of this method, the accuracy of monitoring uncertain large data stream is tested under different interference intensities. The results are shown in Table 1. With the increase of interference SNR, the accuracy of monitoring uncertain large data streams is increasing. When the interference intensity is 6 dB, this method can realize the integrity monitoring of uncertain large data streams. However, the accuracy of traditional methods for monitoring uncertain large data streams is lower than that of traditional methods.

Table 1. Comparison of the accuracy of different methods for monitoring large data streams (%)

Interference intensity/dB	Proposed method	Reference [4]	Reference [5]
0	95.8	89.7	78.9
4	99.9	91.2	81.1
6	1	93.4	85.6
8	1	95.6	88.7
10	1	1	89.0

5   Conclusions

In this paper, an uncertain large data flow monitoring algorithm based on artificial intelligence is proposed. The collected uncertain big data flow is constructed by low dimensional feature set, and the rough set model of uncertain large data stream distribution is constructed. The fuzzy C-means clustering method is used to analyze the uncertain big data flow by fusion clustering and adaptive grid partition analysis. All the abnormal samples of large data stream are sampled and trained, and the feature quantities of association rules of uncertain large data stream are extracted. Combined with artificial intelligence method, the monitoring of uncertain large data stream is realized. The simulation results show that the method has high accuracy and good ability to resist abnormal traffic interference, and the traffic security monitoring ability of the network is improved. In the future, further research will be carried out on the real-time monitoring.

References

1. Wang, Z., Huang, M., et al.: Integrated algorithm based on density peaks and density-based clustering. J. Comput. Appl. **39**(2), 398–402 (2019)
2. Farnadi, G., Bach, S.H., Moens, M.F., et al.: Soft quantification in statistical relational learning. Mach. Learn. **106**(12), 1971–1991 (2017)
3. Tu, B., Chuai, R., Xu, H.: Outlier detection based on k-mean distance outlier factor for gait signal. Inf. Control **48**(1), 16–21 (2019)
4. Wei, X.S., Luo, J.H., Wu, J.: Selective convolutional descriptor aggregation for fine-grained image retrieval. IEEE Trans. Image Process. **26**(6), 2868–2881 (2017)
5. Han, D., Chen, X., Lei, Y., et al.: Real-time data analysis system based on Spark Streaming and its application. J. Comput. Appl. **37**(5), 1263–1269 (2017)
6. Hao, S.G., Zhang, L., Muhammad, G.: A union authentication protocol of cross-domain based on bilinear pairing. J. Softw. **8**(5), 1094–1100 (2013)
7. Ma, Z., Chen, W.: Friction torque calculation method of ball bearings based on rolling creepage theory. J. Mech. Eng. **53**(22), 219–224 (2017)
8. Zhou, S.B., Xu, W.X.: A novel clustering algorithm based on relative density and decision graph. Control Decis. **33**(11), 1921–1930 (2018)
9. Tu, G., Yang, X., Zhou, T.: Efficient identity-based multi-identity fully homomorphic encryption scheme. J. Comput. Appl. **39**(3), 750–755 (2019)
10. Ma, L., Zhang, T., Ma, D., Fu, Y.: Access network selection algorithm based on Markov model. Comput. Eng. **45**(5), 105–109, 115 (2019)

Research on Parallel Mining Method of Massive Image Data Based on AI

Shuang-cheng Jia[✉] and Feng-ping Yang

Alibaba Network Technology Co., Ltd., Beijing 100102, China
tomjia1980@126.com

Abstract. Parallel mining of image data is based on the extraction of internal rules and detail features of image. Combined with image edge detection to realize parallel mining of image data, a parallel mining algorithm of image data based on AI is proposed. Firstly, the multidimensional parallel eigenvalues of image data are extracted by the gray feature extraction algorithm of massive images, and then the template matching and information fusion of massive image data are carried out by using Map/Reduce model. According to the matching results, the parallel mining results of image data are obtained. Finally, the simulation experiment of image data parallel mining is realized by using Matlab software. The results show that compared with other image data parallel mining algorithms, this algorithm reduces the parallel mining time of image data and improves the speed of image data parallel mining, especially for large-scale image data parallel mining.

Keywords: AI · Massive image data · Parallel mining · Template matching

1 Introduction

The mining and processing of large-scale images is the basis of image recognition. With the development of digital image information processing technology, higher requirements are put forward for the accuracy of image mining. It can effectively realize image target recognition, mechanical fault diagnosis, condition monitoring and pattern recognition. The research of image data parallel mining technology will show good application value in the fields of industrial production and military strike. The research of parallel mining algorithms for related image data has been paid more and more attention [1].

Image data parallel mining is based on the internal rules and detail feature extraction of the image. Combined with image edge detection, image noise reduction, image enhancement and image segmentation algorithm, the regular feature extraction of the image is realized [2]. By extracting the feature information which can reflect the attributes of the target image, the parallel mining of image data is realized by combining the excavator. Traditionally, the parallel mining method of image data is mainly based on a single board computer, such as support vector machine algorithm, BP neural network algorithm and so on [3]. In reference [4], a method of radar imaging feature extraction and image data parallel mining based on edge feature fusion is proposed to realize the mining and recognition of aerial target images, and the mining accuracy of

G. Gui and L. Yun (Eds.): ADHIP 2019, LNICST 302, pp. 118–127, 2019.
https://doi.org/10.1007/978-3-030-36405-2_13

aircraft and other target images is good. However, with the increase of interference intensity, the accuracy of mining is limited, and the computational cost of the algorithm is large. In reference [5], a parallel image data mining and recognition algorithm based on autocorrelation matching detection is proposed and applied to mechanical fault detection. By extracting CT scanned image under mechanical fault state and mining by BP neural network, To realize the recognition of image fault attribute mining and improve the performance of fault diagnosis, but the algorithm adopts a single board computer image data parallel mining method, which cannot integrate and mine a large number of large-scale images. The efficiency of image batch processing is not good, the efficiency is low, and the application value is not good.

Artificial Intelligence (AI) is a new technical science that studies and develops the theory, method, technology and application system used to simulate, extend and extend human Intelligence. It is widely used in the field of computer vision and image processing. As a result, to solve the above problems, this paper designs an artificial intelligence-based parallel mining algorithm for image data, with the following ideas: firstly, the multi-dimensional parallel characteristic value of the image data is extracted, the mass image data is matched and the information fusion is carried out on the mass image data by adopting a Map/Reduce model, the parallel mining result of the image data is obtained according to the matching result, and finally, the simulation experiment of the parallel mining of the image data is realized by using the Matlab software, The effectiveness of this method is proved by the experimental results, and the effectiveness conclusion is shown, and the superiority of the image data parallel mining algorithm designed in this paper in the realization of image cloud computing is shown.

2   Image Pre-processing and Feature Extraction

2.1   Collection and Noise Reduction Preprocessing of Massive Image Data

In order to realize that parallel mining and processing of large-scale mass image data, the property of the mass image data is judged, the acquisition and noise reduction preprocessing of the mass image data is required, and the data information input is provided for the mass image data parallel mining model [6]. According to the scale invariance of the mass image data, the feature detection and acquisition of mass image data are carried out by four different methods such as transverse scanning, longitudinal scanning and oblique scanning and block scanning, and the input mass image data is assumed to be $f(x, y)$, the mass image data acquisition process is interfered by the additive noise term $\eta(x, y)$, and the acquired pixel value of the mass image data is obtained according to the change characteristics of the density and the noise intensity of the imaging in the mass image data acquisition process:

$$g(x, y) = h(x, y) * f(x, y) + \eta(x, y) \tag{1}$$

Feature acquisition and scanning process can enlarge the scale of image data acquisition. The process of grid computing for image data is as follows: cloud computing batch processing technology is adopted to obtain large-scale image data, and the pixel sequence output after cloud computing processing is shown as follows:

$$g(x, y) = f(x, y) + \eta(x, y) \tag{2}$$

On the basis of the above massive image data acquisition, it is found that the massive image data acquisition process is interfered by the jitter of the acquisition equipment and the disturbance error of the medium, resulting in noise. The attribute characteristics of massive image data are not obvious [7]. In order to improve the accuracy of mining, it is necessary to reduce the noise of massive image data, and extract the statistical features of the massive image data from the output of denoising processing through cloud computing. In order to improve the efficiency of parallel mining of massive image data, it is necessary to construct batch processing model of massive image data. Finally, an excavator is constructed in Map/Reduce model to realize accurate mining of massive image data. According to the above analysis, the block diagram of the parallel mining algorithm for massive image data designed in this paper is shown in Fig. 1.

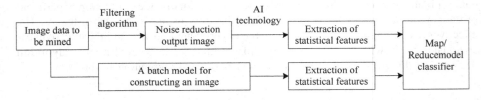

Fig. 1. Implementation flow of parallel mining algorithm for massive image data

According to the overall design idea and the flow of the algorithm, combined with the acquisition result of the mass image data, the noise reduction pre-processing of the mass image data is first carried out, the wavelet noise reduction algorithm is designed to perform the noise reduction of the mass image data, firstly, the edge information distortion amplitude after being subjected to noise interference of the mass image data to be excavated is given as follows:

$$\hat{f}(x, y) = \beta F(x, y) + (1 - \beta)m_l \tag{3}$$

Wherein, $F(x, y)$ is the envelope error of white balance distortion of massive image data to be excavated. The pixel value of noisy massive image data at (x, y) point is β, m_l is the embedding dimension of massive image data denoising along the gradient direction, and the parent wavelet basis function is constructed as:

$$F = \tilde{p}(x, y) = p(x, y)\left(\frac{v(x)}{v(y)}\right)^{1/2} \tag{4}$$

Wherein

$$p(x,y) = \frac{k(x,y)}{v(x)}, v(x) = \sum_y k(x,y) \tag{5}$$

The above represents the color difference and gradient pixel difference of the massive image data, combined with the dark primary color feature information of the massive image data, the noise in the massive image data is adaptively filtered, and the filtering function is described as follows:

$$\hat{f}(x,y) = \begin{cases} g(x,y) - 1, & if \quad g(x,y) - \hat{f}_{Lee}(x,y) \geq t \\ g(x,y) + 1, & if \quad g(x,y) - \hat{f}_{Lee}(x,y) < t \\ g(x,y), & else \end{cases} \tag{6}$$

Wherein, $\hat{f}_{Lee}(x,y)$ represents the estimation function of continuous wavelet time scale decomposition, and the adaptive focusing of noise points of massive image data is realized by wavelet scale decomposition and adaptive local noise filtering [8]. The focused noise is erased adaptively by autocorrelation detector, and the filtered massive image data is obtained as follows:

$$g(x,y) = f(x,y) + \eta_m(x,y) \tag{7}$$

The Markov chain model of massive image data is constructed, and the output of principal component gray histogram after denoising of massive image data is obtained as follows:

$$p(\eta_m(x,y)) = \begin{cases} \frac{r}{4}, & \eta_m(x,y) = -1 \\ 1 - \frac{r}{2}, & \eta_m(x,y) = 0 \\ \frac{r}{4}, & \eta_m(x,y) = 1 \end{cases} \tag{8}$$

Thus, the collection and noise reduction preprocessing of massive image data is realized, which is used as data input to extract features.

2.2 Feature Extraction of Massive Image Data

A variety of feature extraction and fusion of mass image data are the basis for realizing parallel mining of mass image data. The high-order moment characteristics of mass image data are extracted to carry out parallel mining of mass image data, and a cloud computing technology is adopted, and the degradation model of the gray histogram after noise reduction and output is expressed as follows:

$$g(x,y) = f(x,y) + \varepsilon(x,y) \tag{9}$$

The noise obeys $n \in N(0, \sigma_n^2)$ distribution, it performs high-order cumulant segmentation on the gray histogram of massive image data output. In the cloud computing environment, the high-order cumulant segmentation model of massive image data is obtained as follows:

$$\begin{cases} J_1(w, e) = \frac{\mu}{2} w^T w + \frac{1}{2} \gamma \sum_{i=1}^{N} e_i^2 \\ s.t. y_i = w^T \varphi(x_i) + b + e_i, \quad i = 1, \cdots, N \end{cases} \tag{10}$$

Under the condition of constant frame difference, the second order invariant moments of massive image data are fused, multiple feature extraction and affine invariant moments which can reflect the feature properties of massive image are carried out. The data to be mined are as follows:

$$F = \tilde{p}(x, y) = p(x, y) \left(\frac{v(x)}{v(y)} \right)^{1/2} \tag{11}$$

Where

$$p(x, y) = \frac{k(x, y)}{v(x)}, v(x) = \sum_y k(x, y) \tag{12}$$

The above formula represents the color difference and gradient pixel difference of the feature attributes of the massive image data respectively. The cloud computing is carried out by using the marked watershed method, and the high-order moment feature extraction output of the massive image data is obtained as follows:

$$W_\psi y(a, b) = \, <y, \psi_{a,b}> \, = \int_{-\infty}^{+\infty} y(t) \frac{1}{\sqrt{|a|}} \psi^* (\frac{t - b}{a}) dt \tag{13}$$

Where, $<y, \psi_{a,b}>$ is the second invariant moment of massive image data, $y(t)$ is the pixel value of inputting massive image data, b is wavelet scale, ψ^* is the segmentation threshold. Based on the above processing, a variety of features extraction of massive image data is realized.

3   Improved Implementation of Parallel Mining Algorithm for Massive Image Data

3.1   Algorithm Design

On the basis of collecting and denoising massive image data and extracting high-order moment features of massive image data, the parallel mining algorithm of massive image data is optimized [9]. According to the target attribute characteristics of massive image data, the position scale information of massive image data is described as follows: according to the target attribute characteristics of massive image data in Map/Reduce model:

$$\psi_{a,b}(t) = [U(a,b)\psi(t)] = \frac{1}{\sqrt{|a|}}\psi(\frac{t-b}{a}) \tag{14}$$

The Map/Reduce model is used to estimate the gradient value of massive image data moving along the moving average window $(f, \hat{f})$, and the deviation compensation is used to replace $a = 1/s$, $b = \tau$, and the above formula is rewritten as:

$$f_{s,\tau}(t) = [U(1/s, \tau)f(t)] = \sqrt{|s|}f(s(t-\tau)) \tag{15}$$

Under the cloud computing environment, the mass image data is batch processed, and the rapid iterative contraction of the mass image data parallel mining attribute is carried out at the (a, b_m) point on the scale translation plane of the mass image data in parallel, and the obtained mining center is expressed as follows:

$$L(a, b_m) = \log\left(\frac{|V||V_m \cap V_n|}{|V_m||V_n|}\right) \tag{16}$$

The white balance deviation compensation is carried out for the highlight model of mass image data to obtain the gray scale value of the first order field of the mining mass image data, and the iterative process of matching the high-order moment characteristics with scale M is expressed as follows:

$$d_{i+1} = 2F(x_{i+1} + \frac{1}{2}, y_i + 2) \tag{17}$$

For the single scale Harris variable $f = \frac{N - \bar{N}}{N}$, each feature point of massive image data to be excavated as the number of eigenvalues, a fast iterative shrinkage threshold algorithm is adopted to realize the fast search and processing of parallel mining process of massive image data through cloud computing. As a result, the mining efficiency of massive image data is improved [10].

3.2 Algorithm Implementation Flow

Based on the above-mentioned algorithm design, the implementation of the parallel mining algorithm of mass image data based on AI designed in this paper is described as follows:

Step1: The scale invariance of massive image data is used, the massive image data is collected, and the massive image data input is based on cloud computing batch processing for $f(x, y)$. The output pixel sequence of massive image data processed by cloud computing is obtained.

Step2: The mass image data is filtered and preprocessed, and the wavelet noise reduction algorithm is designed to reduce the noise of mass image data. The autocorrelation detector is used for adaptive erasing the focused noise point, and the filtered output mass image data $g(x,y) = f(x,y) + \eta_m(x,y)$ is obtained.

Step3: The attribute feature analysis and extraction of massive image data are carried out by feature extraction method, and the affine invariant moment $F = \tilde{p}(x,y)$ and high order moment $W_\psi y(a,b)$.

Step4: According to the weight of the target feature model, the pixel weights of the target and the candidate region are calculated, and the deviation compensation and weighting of the massive image data are carried out. according to the texture information and high-order moment features of the obtained massive image data, Adaptive Lyapunove functional is used to retrieve the attributes of massive image data mining in parallel.

Step5: The invention uses the AI model to estimate the mass image data along the sliding average window, and is matched with the feature points to obtain a Map/Reduce model of parallel mining of the mass image data to realize the parallel mining of the mass image data.

4   Simulation Experiment and Result Analysis

In order to test the application performance of the algorithm in the parallel mining of mass image data, the simulation experiment is carried out, the experiment is established on the Matlab simulation software, the experimental data set is the Corbel standard mass image database, and the mass image database contains large amount of image data of various attributes, in the process of carrying out the corbel standard mass image database retrieval, a mass image data parallel mining process is needed, the flowers and the animals in the mass image database are taken as test sets, and the original test mass image data is obtained as shown in Fig. 2.

(a) Flower   (b) Elephant

Fig. 2. Test image sample set

Taking the above two kinds of massive image data as the test set, the massive image data of Corel standard mass image database is excavated and searched in parallel, and the massive image data is processed by this method. Firstly, the noise reduction and feature extraction of massive image data are carried out, and the high-order moment features and affine invariant moment features of massive image data are extracted by gray feature extraction algorithm of massive image data. Then the Map/Reduce model is used for template matching and information fusion of massive image data, and the mining results are shown in Figs. 3 and 4.

Fig. 3. Output results of parallel mining and retrieval for massive image data of flower class

Fig. 4. Mining results of large-scale image data of elephants

It can be seen from the diagram that the parallel mining of massive image data by using this method can realize the rapid mining and retrieval of massive image data in the whole Corel standard massive image database, and the category attributes of outputting massive image data are accurate.

In order to quantitatively test the efficiency and accuracy of mining algorithm, 1000 monte carlo experiments were used to conduct multi-feature fusion and parallel mining of massive image data. In the experiment, the comparison method is adopted to compare the massive image data parallel mining method based on AI proposed in this paper with the Reference [4] method and the Reference [6] method. The index comparison results of parallel mining of massive image data are shown in Fig. 5.

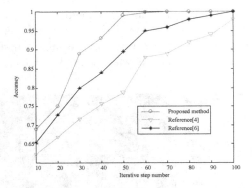

Fig. 5. Comparison of accuracy in parallel mining of massive image data

The analysis of Fig. 5 shows that, with the continuous change in the number of iteration steps of the experiment, the mining accuracy of different methods is also constantly changing. However, the accuracy curve of the method in this paper is always above the accuracy curve of the method in reference [4] and the method in reference [6], which proves that the performance of this method is better than that of traditional methods. This is because the method in this paper achieves parallel mining of massive image data in Map/Reduce model by extracting and integrating multiple features of massive image data, which has the characteristics of high precision, high execution efficiency and short mining time.

5   Conclusions

In this paper, the problem of mining and recognizing massive image data in large-scale image database is studied, and a parallel mining algorithm of massive image data based on AI is proposed to collect and reduce noise of massive image data. To provide data information input for parallel mining model of massive image data, wavelet denoising is used to purify massive image data, and high-order moments and affine invariant moments of massive image data are extracted. Feature fusion and feature matching are realized in Map/Reduce model, and mining optimization is realized. The results show that the parallel mining of massive image data by using this method has high accuracy and good execution efficiency.

References

1. Zhou, S.B., Xu, W.X.: A novel clustering algorithm based on relative density and decision graph. Control Decis. **33**(11), 1921–1930 (2018)
2. Zhu, Y., Zhu, X., Wang, J.: Time series motif discovery algorithm based on subsequence full join and maximum clique. J. Comput. Appl. **39**(2), 414–420 (2019)
3. Wang, Z., Huang, M., et al.: Integrated algorithm based on density peaks and density-based clustering. J. Comput. Appl. **39**(2), 398–402 (2019)

4. Liu, Y., Yang, H., Cai, S., Zhang, C.: Single image super-resolution reconstruction method based on improved convolutional neural network. J. Comput. Appl. **39**(5), 1440–1447 (2019)
5. Xu, R., Zhang, J.G., Huang, K.Q.: Image super-resolution using two-channel convolutional neural networks. J. Image Graph. **21**(5), 556–564 (2016)
6. Megha, G., Yashpal, L., Vivek, L.: Analytical relation & comparison of PSNR and SSIM on Babbon image and human eye perception using Matlab. Int. J. Adv. Res. Eng. Appl. Sci. **4**(5), 108–119 (2015)
7. Li, Y.F., Fu, R.D., Jin, W., et al.: Image super-resolution using multi-channel convolution. J. Image Graph. **22**(12), 1690–1700 (2017)
8. Dong, X.W., Yao, S.M., Wang, Y.W., et al.: Virtual sample image set based multi manifold discriminant learning algorithm. Appl. Res. Comput. **35**(6), 1871–1878 (2018)
9. Gui, J., Sun, Z.N., Jia, W., et al.: Discriminant sparse neighborhood preserving embedding for face recognition. Pattern Recognit. **45**(8), 2884–2893 (2012)
10. Dong, B., Chen, D., Jing, W.: Salient region detection method based on symmetric region filtering. Comput. Eng. **45**(5), 216–221 (2019)

Floating Small Target Detection in Sea Clutter Based on Jointed Features in FRFT Domain

Yan-ling Shi[✉], Xue-liang Zhang, and Zi-peng Liu

College of Telecommunications and Information Engineering,
Nanjing University of Post and Telecommunications, Nanjing 210003, China
{ylshi,1217012431,1218012603}@njupt.edu.cn

Abstract. The jointed-feature detector for the floating small target in sea clutter is addressed in the paper. For the traditional energy-based detectors, it is difficult to detect the low signal-to-clutter ratio floating small target in time domain due to the affection of sea clutter motion. Therefore, a feature detector in the Fractional Fourier transform (FRFT) domain is proposed. The Hurst exponent and fractal dimension variance are extracted as the features in the jointed-feature detector in FRFT domain. The decision region is determined by convex hull training algorithm on the given false alarm probability. The experimental results of 10 groups of IPIX radar data show that the jointed-feature detector is superior to the compared one, and it provides a new detection scheme for radar target detection.

Keywords: Fractional Fourier Transform · Jointed features · Convex hull training algorithm · Target detection · Sea clutter

1 Introduction

The traditional energy accumulation detectors are statistically optimal in the case of linear, stationary and Gaussian sea clutter. However, the high range resolution sea clutter is nonlinear, non-stationary and non-Gaussian. Therefore, the accumulation detectors inevitably decline the detection performance for the high range resolution sea clutter [1, 2]. Hence, we resort to feature detectors [3–7] which get rid of the energy accumulation. The existing feature detectors mainly use the polarization features [3], normalized Doppler power spectrum features [4], related features [5], speckle consistency factor [6], ridge energy characteristics in the time-frequency plane, etc. [7]. The experimental results evidence the effectivity of those feature detectors.

In order to understand the scattering of sea surface deeply, fractal describes the roughness of the sea surface, and it is used to detect the floating target in sea clutter [8]. With the development of the fractal theory, it is found that a single fractal dimension failed to detect the floating target [9]. Therefore, the multi-dimensional fractal detectors were successively proposed [10–12]. The fractal and multi-dimensional fractal

This work was supported by National Natural Science Foundation of China (61201325) and NUPTSF (NY218045).

G. Gui and L. Yun (Eds.): ADHIP 2019, LNICST 302, pp. 128–139, 2019.
https://doi.org/10.1007/978-3-030-36405-2_14

detectors utilize the Hurst parameter [10], the geometric correlation coefficient of fractal [11, 12], and the multi-fractal features time domain feature [13] to distinguish between sea clutter and target. However, due to the energy overlap of sea clutter and floating target in the time domain, the time domain fractal features of clutter and target can not be distinguished, hence those fractal features are invalid. Many researchers captured the combining fractal theory in spectrum analysis [14–16], including Fourier transform combined with fractal [14], wavelet decomposition combined with fractal [15], Fractional Fourier Transform (FRFT) combined with fractal [16] and so on. FRFT as an extension of Fourier transform, selects an appropriate transformed order, and forms an obvious energy peak in the transform domain by all the energy accumulation. So, the fractal features in the FRFT domain can be used to distinguish target and sea clutter, and the jointed-feature detector in the FRFT domain is proposed in the paper. It has been verified that the sea clutter behaves the fractal characteristics in the FRFT domain, and the fractal-dimension detector in the FRFT domain achieves the good detection performance for the floating target in sea clutter [17].

As well known, the fractal features of the sea clutter will change with the sea state, wind speed and other uncertain factors. The pre-existing fractal detectors only utilizing a single feature in the time domain or frequency domain inevitable decline the detection performance in real scenario. Thus, by extracting the frequency domain kurtosis (FDK), Doppler entropy value and Doppler peak value, a jointed-feature detector was proposed [18], and improved the detection performance.

Combined the ideas of the feature detector in FRFT domain and of the jointed-detector, the jointed-feature detector in the FRFT domain is proposed in the paper. Firstly, the received radar echoes are converted to the FRFT domain; Secondly, the fractal features are analyzed by the Detrended Fluctuation Analysis (DFA), both the fractal dimension (FD) and fractal dimension variance (FDV) are extracted; Finally, the jointed-feature detector is proposed by using the two features. The decision region are determined based on the convex hull training algorithm for pure clutter in the FRFT domain, and the efficiency of the proposed detector is verified by the measured data.

The innovation is the FD and FDV as two features in the FRFT domain helping to get rid of the energy overlap of floating target and sea clutter in the time domain.

This paper is organized as follows: Sect. 2 analyzes the fractal characteristics of sea clutter and targets in the FRFT domain, and extracts two fractal features in the optimal FRFT domain, that is FD and FDV; Sect. 3 proposes the jointed-feature detector, and gives the flow chart. In Sect. 4, the efficiency of the proposed detector is verified by the measured data. Finally, conclude the whole paper in Sect. 5.

2   Characteristic Analysis of Sea Clutter in FRFT Domain

The experiment data are collected by the IPIX radar [19] at dwelling mode, and contain 10 sea clutter datasets. Each dataset consists of 14 adjacent range cells with 131 072 sampling points (about 131 s). Target is a styrofoam ball wrapped with wire mesh with a diameter about 1 m. The range cell where the target is located is called primary cell, and two or three cells neighbor of the primary cell are affected by the target and are called guard cells. Other range cells are called secondary cells. The range resolutions of these 10 datasets are 30 m. Table 1 lists the relevant parameters of 10 datasets, including their file names in the IPIX datasets, wind speed (WS), significant wave height, the angle between the line of radar sight and wind direction, and the numbers of the primary cells and secondary cells.

Table 1. Description of IPIX radar datasets

Label	File name	Wind speed (Km/h)	Wave height (M)	Angle	Primary	Secondary
1	19931107_135603_starea17	9	2.2	9	9	8,10,11
2	19931108_220902_starea26	9	1.1	97	7	6,8
3	19931109_191449_starea30	19	0.9	98	7	6,8
4	19931109_202217_starea31	19	0.9	98	7	6,8,9
5	19931110_001635_starea40	9	1.0	88	7	5,6,8
6	19931111_163625_starea54	20	0.7	8	8	7,9,10
7	19931118_023604_stareC0000280	10	1.6	130	8	7,9,10
8	19931118_162155_stareC0000310	33	0.9	30	7	6,8,9
9	19931118_162658_stareC0000311	33	0.9	40	7	6,8,9
10	19931118_174259_stareC0000320	28	0.9	30	7	6,8,9

2.1 Statistical Analysis of Sea Clutter in FRFT Domain

As an extension of the Fourier transform, the FRFT is also called generalized time-frequency analysis. The p-order FRFT of $x(t)$ is a linear integral operation [20] as

$$F_p(u) = \int_{-\infty}^{+\infty} x(t) K_p(t, u) dt \qquad (1)$$

where the kernel function $k_p(t, u)$ is,

$$K_p(t, u) = \begin{cases} \sqrt{\frac{1-j\cos\alpha}{2p}} \exp(j\frac{t^2+u^2}{2}) \cot\alpha - jut \csc\alpha, & \alpha \neq n\pi \\ \delta(t-u), & \alpha \neq 2n\pi \\ \delta(t+u), & \alpha = (2n+1)\pi \end{cases} \qquad (2)$$

where, $\alpha = \frac{p\pi}{2}$ is the rotation angle and p is the transformed order in the FRFT.

Figure 1 shows the amplitudes of target and clutter in the time domain and FRFT domain, respectively. The experimental data is 19931107_ 135603_starea17 in HH polarized, and the optimal transformed-order of FRFT is taken as $p = 1.056$. From Fig. 1, in the time domain, the amplitudes of target and sea clutter are overlapped with each other, which is bad for the target detection. In the FRFT domain, the target energy behaves an obvious peak, several orders larger than the clutter energy, which is beneficial for target detection.

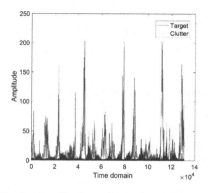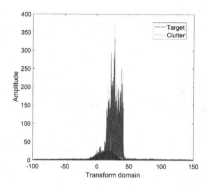

Fig. 1. Amplitudes target and sea clutter in the time domain and in the FRFT domain.

2.2   Fractal Features Extraction

Sea clutter behaves the fractional Brownian motion (FBM), and the Hurst exponent can capture all the properties of FBM, as confirmed in [14]. For the IPIX measured radar data, the DFA describes the fractal features of the received echoes. Assuming that $x(n), 0 < n \leq N$ is a N stationary random sequence, the DFA of $x(n)$ includes the following six steps [17],

Step 1, calculate the cumulative difference of $x(n)$, and obtain a new sequence $y(n)$,

$$y(n) = \sum_{i=1}^{n} [x(i) - \bar{x}], n > 0 \tag{3}$$

where, $\bar{x}$ is the average of the time series $x(n)$.

Step 2, suppose the length of the segment is m. Divide the new sequence $y(n)$ into disjoint sequences $y[(s-1)m+n]$ with equal length m, where $s = 1, 2, 3 \cdots N_m$, $N_m = INT(N/m)$, N_m is the number of segments, and INT is the rounding operation.

Step 3, if the time series length N is not an integral multiple of m, the segment sequences of $y(n)$ are taking from the end of the sequence $y[N - (s - N_m)m + n]$, where, $s = N_m + 1, N_m + 2, \cdots, 2N_m$. Combined with steps 2 and 3, a total of $2N_m$ sequences are formed.

Step 4, linear fit each subsequence by using the least squares fitting and calculate the local trend term of the subsequence $y_s(n)$

$$y_s(n) = fit(y(n)) = ax + b \tag{4}$$

where, a and b are the fitting coefficients.

Step 5, each subsequence subtracts its local trend term $y_s(n)$, and find its variance

$$Y^2(s, m) = \frac{1}{m} \sum_{n=1}^{m} \{y[(s-1)m+n] - y_s(n)\}^2 \quad s = 1, 2, 3 \cdots N_m \tag{5}$$

$$Y^2(s,m) = \frac{1}{m} \sum_{n=1}^{m} \{y[N - (s - N_m)m + n] - y_s(n)\}^2 \quad s = N_m + 1, N_m + 2, \cdots, 2N_m$$

(6)

Step 6, average the variance of each subsequence, and calculate the q-th root, we obtain the q-order wave function

$$F_q(m) = \left\{ \frac{1}{2N_m} \sum_{s=1}^{2N_m} [Y^2(s,m)] \right\}^{1/q}$$

(7)

If the time series is long correlated, $F(m)$ will grow with m

$$F(m) \sim m^H$$

(8)

where, H is the Hurst exponent, reflecting the fractal parameters of $F(m)$.

The wave function of received echo in scale-invariant space is

$$\log_2 F(m) = (2 - F_d) \log_2(m) + I_c$$

(9)

where the fractal dimension F_d can be obtained by linear fitting, $F_d = 2 - H$.

Fractal dimension can approximately reflect the irregularity of data [21]. The fractal features of the target and clutter are different to some extent. Therefore, we can distinguish sea clutter and target by F_d in FRFT domain. The first test statistic is as follows,

$$T_1 = |F_d| \underset{H_1}{\overset{H_0}{\underset{<}{>}}} \eta_1$$

(10)

where, T_1 is the test statistic and η_1 is the detection threshold.

The ideal fractal curve satisfies the self-similarity of all scales, which means that F_d is independent of the scale m. It is found that the fractal features of sea clutter in the FRFT domain are in good agreement with the theoretical fractal model in the scale-invariant space [20]. The double logarithmic coordinates of the fractal curve in the FRFT domain can be expressed as x_i and y_i

$$\begin{cases} x_i = \log_2(m_i) \\ y_i = \log_2 F(m_i) \end{cases}$$

(11)

where, m_i is the segment length of the i-th segment.

The fractal dimension $F_{\Delta i}$ in the adjacent scale i is expressed as:

$$F_{\Delta i} = \frac{\log_2 F(m_i) - \log_2 F(m_{i-1})}{\log_2(m_i) - \log_2(m_{i-1})} = \frac{y_i - y_{i-1}}{x_i - x_{i-1}}$$

(12)

It has been verified in measured data that for different scales, $F_{\Delta i}$ changes weakly in secondary data, whereas significantly in primary data [22]. The fractal dimension variance V_d in the FRFT domain is used as a feature for target detection,

$$V_d = \text{var}(F_{\Delta i}) \tag{13}$$

The second test statistic is as follows,

$$T_2 = V_d \underset{H_0}{\overset{H_1}{\underset{<}{\gtrless}}} \eta_2 \tag{14}$$

where, η_2 is the detection threshold.

3 Jointed-Feature Detector in FRFT Domain

We propose a jointed-feature detector in FRFT domain by using F_d and V_d as two features to detect the floating target in the background of high range resolution sea clutter. The linear invariant interval is determined according to the fractal curve in FRFT domain. At the given false alarm rate, the convex hull training algorithm is used to determine the decision region, which can determine the classified samples and the training samples, and target can be detected according to whether inside or outside of the convex hull. The flow chart is shown in Fig. 2.

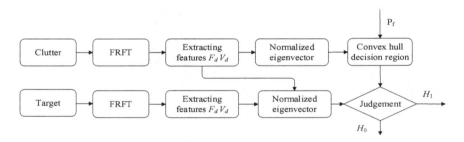

Fig. 2. The flow chart of jointed-feature detector in FRFT domain.

Set $y = [T_1, T_2]^T$, where the superscript T indicates transposition, and define $y_k = [T_1, T_2]_k^T$, $k = 1, 2, 3 \cdots K$, for the features of clutter. In order to obtain the smallest convex hull, given the false alarm rate P_f, $G = KP_f$ samples farthest from the center of the cluster are removed, and the remain $(K - G)$ samples are used to form convex hull as the discriminating area Ω [23].

For $(K - G)$ samples in a two-dimensional plane, a convex hull is a convex polygon consisting of the smallest convex set of $(K - G)$ samples. Let v_i, $i = 1, 2 \cdots I$ be the I vertices clockwise of the convex hull. For the sample y to be classified, the detecting principle is equivalent to judge whether y is inside or outside Ω. If and only if Eq. (15) holds [24],

$$r_i(y) \triangleq \begin{vmatrix} 1 & v_i(1) & v_i(2) \\ 1 & v_{i+1}(2) & v_{i+1}(2) \\ 1 & y(1) & y(2) \end{vmatrix} \geq 0, \ i = 1, 2, \cdots, I \tag{15}$$

We can say if y is inside Ω, for all i, $r_i(y) \geq 0$. If y is outside Ω, $r_i(y) \geq 0$ for some i and $r_i(y) < 0$ for other i. Therefore, as long as $r_i(y) < 0$, we can determine that y is outside Ω. Based on the above analysis, the discriminant function is defined as

$$r(y) = \min\{r_i(y), i = 1, 2, \cdots, I\} \tag{16}$$

$r \geq 0$ means that $x(n)$ dose not contain target, and $r < 0$ indicates that $x(n)$ contains target.

Figure 3(a) shows the 24000 training samples and 4000 samples to be classified in the 2D feature plane, and Fig. 3(b) shows both 4000 samples to be classified and the convex hull of (24000-240) training samples by removing the 240 farthest training samples. The blue points are the training samples and red points are the samples to be classified. From Fig. 3, the convex hull training algorithm can effectively distinguish the samples to be classified from the training samples.

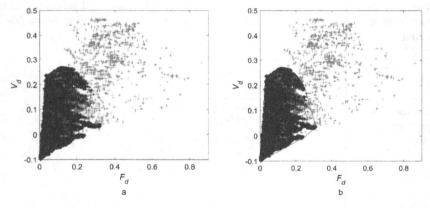

Fig. 3. The samples to be classified (red) and the training samples (blue) in the two-dimensional feature plane. (Color figure online)

4   Experimental Results

4.1   Analysis of Fractal Features in Measured Data

Sea clutter behaves obvious fractal Brownian motion, but has self-similarity only in the scale-free interval [14]. Figure 4 is a log-log $F(m) \sim m$ in FRFT domain of 10 datasets in HH polarization. The circled red lines represent the log-log functions of the target, and the asterisk blue lines represent the log-log wave functions of clutter. The experimental parameters are $n = 10000$, $m = 2^1 \sim 2^{10}$. From Fig. 4, for the 10 datasets, when m is $2^5 \sim 2^{10}$, the curves are approximately linear. Therefore, the interval $2^5 \sim 2^{10}$ can be taken as a scale-free interval for sea clutter. In the scale-free interval $2^5 \sim 2^{10}$, the slopes of the circled curves are larger than these of the star curves, indicating that the Hurst exponent of target is larger than that of clutter, in other words, target has a smaller fractal dimension than clutter.

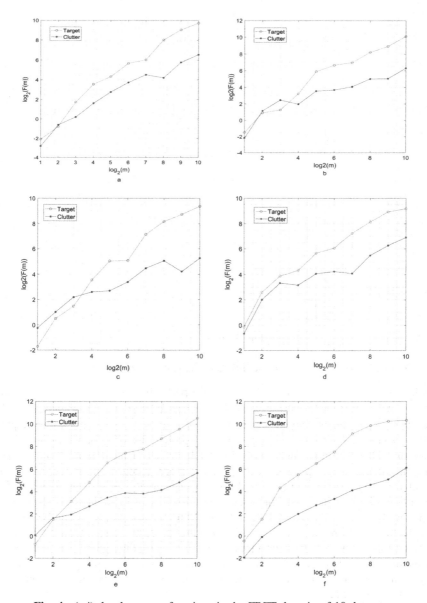

Fig. 4. (a-j). log-log wave functions in the FRFT domain of 10 datasets.

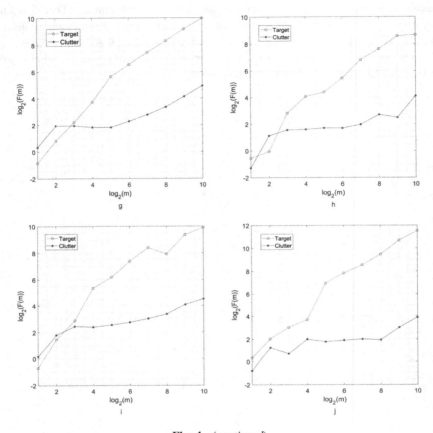

Fig. 4. (*continued*)

4.2 Performance Analysis of the Jointed-Feature Detector

In order to quantitatively compare the detection performance of the two single feature detectors with the jointed-feature detector, we use 19931107_135603_starea17. The experimental parameters are $n = 10000$ and $m = 2^5 \sim 2^{10}$. To satisfy the required samples in Monte Carlo test for a given small probability of false alarm, we slide 5 points for each adjacent segment to obtain 24000 datasets. Calculate F_d and V_d of each dataset in the scale-free space $[2^5 \sim 2^{10}]$. Figure 5 is the detection probabilities of F_d, V_d and the proposed jointed-feature detector, respectively. From Fig. 5, when false alarm probability equals 0.001, the detection probability of jointed-feature detector, F_d and V_d are $P_d = 0.918$, $P_d = 0.452$, and $P_d = 0.662$, respectively. It can be seen that the detection performance of the jointed-feature detector is significantly improved compared to the single feature detectors. The reason is that the jointed-feature detector utilizes the two-dimensional information of fractal, which increases the difference between the sea clutter and the target, and hence has a significant improvement in detection performance.

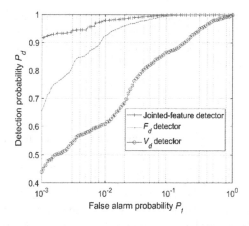

Fig. 5. Detection probabilities of the three detectors in 19931107_135603_starea17.

Table 2. Detection performance of three detectors, where false alarm rate is 0.001

Label	File name	F_d	V_d	Jointed-feature detector
1	19931107_135603_starea17	45.2%	66.2%	**91.8%**
2	19931108_220902_starea26	39.5%	55.7%	**89.2%**
3	19931109_191449_starea30	40.5%	55.9%	**90.5%**
4	19931109_202217_starea31	38.0%	50.8%	**87.6%**
5	19931110_001635_starea40	32.1%	47.5%	**86.4%**
6	19931111_163625_starea54	33.5%	46.5%	**83.7%**
7	19931118_023604_stareC0000280	42.4%	60.3%	**88.6%**
8	19931118_162155_stareC0000310	41.5%	63.2%	**81.3%**
9	19931118_162658_stareC0000311	36.8%	60.4%	**78.6%**
10	19931118_174259_stareC0000320	39.8%	55.7%	**78.5%**

Table 2 shows the detection probabilities of F_d, V_d and the proposed jointed-feature detector of all 10 datasets. When the false alarm probability equals 0.001, the detection probabilities in the jointed-feature detector of all 10 datasets are greatly higher than the single feature F_d and V_d. Therefore, the proposed jointed-feature detector is feasible in detecting small floating target on the sea surface.

5 Conclusion

In this paper, the fractal features of the received radar echo in FRFT domain are analyzed. By extracting the fractal dimension and FDV in the FRFT domain, the jointed-feature detector are proposed. The discriminating area of training samples is determined by the convex hull training algorithm. The experimental results show that the sea clutter satisfies the self-similarity in the scale-free interval m $\in$ [2^5, 2^{10}] in the

FRFT domain. The jointed-feature detector has a significant improvement in detection performance compared to the fractal dimension detector and the FDV detector by the 10 measured datasets. Therefore, the proposed jointed-feature detector is feasible in detecting small floating target on the sea surface.

References

1. You, H., Yong, H., Jian, G.: An overview on radar target detection in sea clutter. Mod. Radar **36**(12), 1–9 (2014)
2. Ding, H., Dong, Y., Liu, N.: Overview and prospects of research on sea clutter property cognition. J. Radars **5**(5), 499–516 (2016)
3. Xu, S., Zheng, J., Pu, J.: Sea-surface "floating small target detection based on polarization features". IEEE Geosci. Remote Sens. Lett. **15**(10), 1505–1509 (2018)
4. Li, D., Shui, P.: Floating small target detection in sea clutter via normalised Doppler power spectrum. IET Radar Sonar Navig. **10**(4), 699–706 (2016)
5. Ye, Y., Hong, Z., Wang, Q.: Correlation feature-based detector for range distributed target in sea clutter. EURASIP J. Adv. Signal Process. **2018**(1), 25 (2018)
6. Shi, Y., Xie, X., Li, D.: Distributed floating target detection in sea clutter via feature-based detector. IEEE Geosci. Remote Sens. Lett. **13**(12), 1847–1850 (2016)
7. Shi, S., Shui, P.: Sea-surface floating small target detection by one-class classifier in time-frequency feature space. IEEE Trans. Geosci. Remote Sens. **56**(11), 6395–6411 (2018)
8. Lo, T., Leung, H., Litva, J.: Fractal characterisation of sea-scattered signals and detection of sea-surface targets. In: IEEE Proceedings F Radar and Signal Processing, vol. 140, no. 4, pp. 243–250 (1993)
9. Li, D., Shui, P.: Extended fractal analysis for floating target detection in sea clutter. In: IEEE International Geoscience and Remote Sensing Symposium, pp. 3139–3142 (2015)
10. Chen, Y., Sun, R., Zhou, A.: An improved Hurst parameter estimator based on fractional Fourier transform. In: Proceedings of the ASME 2007 International Design Engineering Technical Conferences & Computers and Information in Engineering Conference, Las Vegas, Nevada, USA, pp. 1–11 (2007)
11. Guan, J., Liu, N., Zhang, J.: Multifractal correlation characteristic of real sea clutter and low-observable targets detection. J. Electron. Inf. Technol. **32**(1), 54–61 (2010)
12. Hu, J., Gao, J., Yao, K.: Detection of low-observable targets within sea clutter by structure function based multifractal analysis. IEEE Trans. Antennas Propag. **54**(1), 136–143 (2006)
13. Guan, J., Liu, N., Huang, Y.: Fractal characteristic in frequency domain for target detection within sea clutter. IET Radar Sonar Navig. **6**(5), 293–306 (2012)
14. Chen, X., Guan, J., Bao, Z.: Detection and extraction of target with micromotion in spiky sea clutter via short-time Fractional Fourier Transform. IEEE Trans. Geosci. Remote Sens. **52**(2), 1002–1018 (2014)
15. Guan, J., Liu, N., Zhang, J.: Low-observable target detection within sea clutter based on LGF. Signal Process. **26**(1), 69–73 (2010)
16. Chen, X., Guan, J., He, Y.: Detection of low observable moving target in sea clutter via fractal characteristics in Fractional Fourier Transform domain. IET Radar Sonar Navig. **7**(6), 635–651 (2013)
17. Xing, H., Zhang, Q., Xu, W.: Fractal property of sea clutter FRFT spectrum for small target detection. Acta Phys. Sin. **1**, 1–8 (2015)
18. Shui, P., Li, D., Xu, S.: Tri-feature-based detection of floating small targets in sea clutter. IEEE Trans. Aerosp. Electron. Syst. **50**(2), 1416–1430 (2014)

19. Haykin, S.: The McMaster IPIX radar sea clutter database in 1993. http://soma.mcmaster.ca/ipix.php
20. Li, Y., Lv, X., Liu, K.: Fractal-based weak target detection within sea clutter. Acta Ocean. Sin. **33**(9), 68–72 (2014)
21. Xu, X.: Low observable targets detection by joint fractal properties of sea clutter: an experimental study of IPIX OHGR datasets. IEEE Trans. Antennas Propag. **58**(4), 1425–1429 (2010)
22. Guan, J., Cheng, X., Huang, Y.: Adaptive Fractional Fourier Transform-based detection algorithm for moving target in heavy sea clutter. IET Radar Sonar Navig. **6**(5), 389–401 (2012)
23. Xing, H., Yin, J., Wang, Q.: Targets detection under the background of sea clutter by joint characteristics difference. Mod. Radar **36**(10), 28–32 (2014)
24. Shi, Y., Shui, P.: Feature united detection algorithm on floating small target of sea surface. J. Electron. Inf. Technol. **34**(4), 871–877 (2012)

Research on Fatigue Life Prediction Method of Ballastless Track Based on Big Data

Ailin Wang[(⊠)]

Railway Engineering College, Wuhan Railway Vocational College
of Technology, Wuhan 430205, China
gjakg785@yeah.net

Abstract. In order to improve the precision of fatigue life prediction of ballastless track, a method for predicting fatigue life of ballastless track based on big data is proposed. The big data model is constructed to analyze the fatigue life cycle of ballastless track. Big data mining and feature extraction are used to extract the fatigue life cycle of ballastless track. Combining with the particle swarm optimization method, the feature classification of the failure state trend of ballastless track construction is carried out, and the information fusion is carried out according to the characteristic parameters of the failure state of ballastless track construction. The expert system model for predicting fatigue life of ballastless track construction is established and the fatigue life of ballastless track is predicted by association rule mining method. The simulation results show that the precision of fatigue life prediction of ballastless track is high, and the strength and life cycle of ballastless track are analyzed.

Keywords: Big data · Ballastless track · Fatigue life · Prediction

1 Introduction

With the development of high-speed railway in China, ballastless track is more and more used in new railway. The construction practice of high-speed railway shows that both ballastless track and ballastless track can ensure the safe operation of high-speed train, but because of the difference in technology and economy between the two kinds of track structure, they have their own advantages and disadvantages. Therefore, in order to obtain the best technical and economic benefits, the rail structure selection of our country should be reasonable according to our own national conditions and railway characteristics. The fatigue life of ballastless track is the key to determine the track quality [1]. It has great significance to study the fatigue life prediction method of ballastless track.

In order to ensure high comfort and high safety, high-speed railway requires high ride comfort to track geometry precision. Through the investigation and understanding of the high-speed railway lines that have been opened to traffic and are in the process of fine-tuning the long rail, in the early stage of high-speed rail construction, the tool-track method or rail-row frame method was used for the fine-tuning of the construction [2]. After the track plate construction is completed, the seamless long rail will be laid. In the long track fine adjustment, there are some precision overruns in the constructed track

G. Gui and L. Yun (Eds.): ADHIP 2019, LNICST 302, pp. 140–150, 2019.
https://doi.org/10.1007/978-3-030-36405-2_15

bed plate, such as gauge, elevation, center line, orbit direction, etc. In order to meet the requirements of high-speed railway for rail ride comfort, the accuracy problem in construction must be solved by replacing non-standard fasteners. If the precision control is not in place in the construction, the construction cost will be wasted greatly in the replacement of the fastener in the later period [3]. The short rail with the same specifications as the long rail must be used in the rail row processing, and the machining precision must be the same as that of the track, so as to ensure that the rail row can meet the requirements in the course of its use. The rail-row frame should have enough stiffness and enough stability to prevent the rail-row frame vibration deviation caused by the construction load, which has a negative effect on the track accuracy. Rail support system should be supported on a stable basis to prevent the sinking and dislocation of the supporting member [4].

The fatigue life prediction of ballastless track casting in digital machining mode is carried out. Combined with big data information processing and fatigue life charac-teristic detection method, the accuracy of fatigue life prediction for ballastless track casting is improved, at present, The fatigue life prediction methods for ballastless track casting in digital machining mode can be divided into two methods: time domain analysis based fatigue life data mining method, frequency domain analysis based fatigue life data mining method, and fatigue life data mining method based on fre-quency domain analysis [5]. The fatigue life prediction model of ballastless track casting based on statistical characteristic extraction, etc., combined with nonlinear time series analysis and signal detection algorithm, can predict the trend of fatigue life state of ballastless track casting. Based on data mining and feature extraction of fatigue life, this paper presents a fatigue life prediction model for ballastless track casting based on genetic KNN clustering. Firstly, big data association rule mining method is used to collect the fatigue life characteristic information of ballastless track casting, and then the feature classification of fatigue life state trend of ballastless track casting is carried out by combining particle swarm optimization (PSO) evolution method. According to the characteristic parameters of fatigue life of ballastless track casting, the expert system model for fatigue life prediction of ballastless track casting is established, and the fatigue life prediction of ballastless track casting is realized. Finally, simulation experiments are carried out to show the superior performance of this method in improving the accuracy of fatigue life prediction of ballastless track casting.

2 Fatigue Life Data Sampling and Feature Extraction of Ballastless Track Casting

2.1 Big Data Analytical Model for Fatigue Life of Ballastless Track Casting

The first step to predict the fatigue life of ballastless track casting is to construct the fatigue life model of big data. The fatigue life of big data is divided into vibration data according to the means of testing and the principle of diagnosis. The noise data and other fatigue life data of ballastless track casting, considering the input/output para-metric model of complex ballastless track parts, the big data distribution channel of ballastless track casting fatigue life is an extended sampling channel. The multi-path channel model is used to collect the fatigue life of big data in ballastless track casting. There are two main characteristics of big data distribution channel of ballastless track casting fatigue life [6]. One is that big data distribution channel of ballastless track casting fatigue life is a channel model with limited bandwidth. Second, big data distribution channel of ballastless track casting fatigue life is constrained by distance, which has multi-path propagation characteristic and is easily disturbed by ballastless track vibration, which leads to fatigue life. In ballastless track casting, the multi-path structure of fatigue life big data distribution channel depends on the array distribution type of data acquisition nodes [7]. Assuming that the data acquisition nodes are composed of S array elements, the radial distance of big data distribution of ballastless track casting is d, and the data receiving model of fatigue life characteristics is as follows:

$$x_m(t) = \sum_{i=1}^{I} s_i(t)e^{j\varphi_{mi}} + n_m(t), -p+1 \leq m \leq p \tag{1}$$

Where, $s_i(t)$ is the vibration data sensed by vibration sensor of ballastless track casting equipment, and $x_m(t)$ is the series of thermal sensing data received by element m. Thus, the impulse model of big data distribution channel for fatigue life of ballastless track casting is constructed as:

$$h(t) = \sum_i a_i(t)e^{j\theta_i(t)}\delta(t - iT_S) \tag{2}$$

In the above formula, $\theta_i(t)$ indicates that the data ETL layer provides radial deviation of fatigue life data for ballastless track casting to the data analysis layer, and the width of the time window for sampling vibration sensing information of ballastless track equipment is T, The quantized set of fatigue life data features distributed in the extended channel is represented as:

$$x(t) = [x_{-P+1}(t), x_{-P+2}(t), \cdots, x_P(t)]_{N\times 1}^T \tag{3}$$

$$s(t) = [s_1(t), s_2(t), \cdots s_I(t)]_{I\times 1}^T \tag{4}$$

Where, P is the bandwidth of big data's collection of fatigue life of ballastless track casting, and I is the number of array elements. Under the digital machining mode, big data analytical model of fatigue life distribution of ballastless track casting is expressed as follows:

$$c(\tau, t) = \sum_n a_n(t)e^{-j2\pi f_c\tau_n(t)}\delta(t - \tau_n(t)) \tag{5}$$

Where, $a_n(t)$ is the closed-loop management characteristic vector of the nth ballastless track fatigue life diagnosis, $\tau_n(t)$ is the time delay of the nth data channel, the big data analytical model of fatigue life distribution of ballastless track casting under the digital machining mode is constructed. It provides data input basis for fatigue life prediction of ballastless track casting.

2.2   Fatigue Life Feature Extraction

The abnormal state data of ballastless track during fatigue life cycle are decomposed and extracted by Hilbert spectrum extraction method, and the information fusion is carried out according to the extracted value of fatigue life state characteristic parameter of ballastless track casting. Because the cluster control parameter s_0, τ_0 of ballastless track fatigue life data is often unknown, the fatigue life characteristics of ballastless track casting are detected by using the lowest mean square error estimate $\hat{s}_{0ML}$, $\hat{\tau}_{0ML}$:

$$
\begin{aligned}
l_1(r) &= \int r(t)\sqrt{\hat{s}_{0ML}}f^*(\hat{s}_{0ML}(t - \hat{\tau}_{0ML}))dt \\
&= \max_{s,\tau}\left|\int r(t)\sqrt{s}f^*(s(t - \tau))dt\right| \\
&= \max_{a,b}\left|W_f r(a,b)\right| \overset{H_1}{\underset{H_0}{\gtrless}} \lambda_1
\end{aligned}
\tag{6}
$$

In the equation, $a = 1/s, b = \tau$, λ_1 is the detection threshold. The statistic of fatigue life detection for ballastless track casting is a sparse array distribution. Because s_0, τ_0 are unknown, the following formulas are selected to extract fatigue life characteristics.

$$
\begin{aligned}
l_2 &= \max_b\left|\int r(t)\frac{1}{\sqrt{a'}}f^*(\frac{t - b}{a'})dt\right| \\
&= \max_b\left|W_f r(a',b)\right| \overset{H_1}{\underset{H_0}{\gtrless}} \lambda_2
\end{aligned}
\tag{7}
$$

The optimal classification plane of fatigue life characteristics of ballastless track casting is calculated. Between the data analysis layer and the data processing layer, the fatigue life characteristic distribution sequence $x_1, x_2, \ldots, x_n, \ldots$, the total number of points is N, Ballastless track vibration data series $\{x_i\}$ is evenly sampled by sampling interval $j\tau$. The output autocorrelation function is expressed as follows:

$$
R_{xx}(j\tau) = \frac{1}{N}\sum_{i=0}^{N-1} x_i x_{i+j\tau}
\tag{8}
$$

The characteristic function $\overrightarrow{X}(l,n_i)$ of fatigue life prediction for ballastless track casting under some kind of fatigue life state is used to calculate the intra-class dispersion matrix $\hat{S}_w$ of fatigue life distribution. The optimal solution to big data's acquisition problem of fatigue life can be described by χ^*. By using the abnormal operation and maintenance data management method, the adaptive constraint characteristics are obtained as follows:

$$x(t) = \left[1 - \cos(2\pi f_s^{(r)}t)\right]\left[1 + A\cos(2\pi f_s t + \phi)\right]$$
$$\cos[2\pi f_m t + B\sin(2\pi f_s t + \varphi) + \theta] \tag{9}$$

The self-organizing training of big data in ballastless track casting fatigue life was carried out by multi-source information filtering method. The maximum gradient difference of fatigue life prediction of ballastless track casting was obtained.

$$AVG_X = \frac{1}{m \times n}\sum_{x=1}^{n}\sum_{y=1}^{m}|G_X(x, y)| \tag{10}$$

Where, m, n are vector quantized autocorrelation coefficients of fatigue life data digging for ballastless track casting respectively, so that the feature of fatigue life distribution can be extracted [8].

3 Optimization of Fatigue Life Prediction Algorithm

3.1 Big Data Clustering of Fatigue Life Characteristics

Because of the continuous generation of data over time, the data stored in the database increases exponentially, and the relationship between the data becomes more complex. Thus, it is more possible to get some of these relationships through association rules mining algorithm for those data that do not seem to have any connection. It is applied to the fatigue life prediction of ballastless track structure, and the expert system model of ballastless track structure fatigue life prediction is established. The association rule mining method is used to predict the fatigue life of ballastless track structure. Based on big data association rule mining method, the fatigue life characteristic information of ballastless track casting is collected, and the optimal design of fatigue life prediction model of ballastless track casting is carried out. This paper presents a fatigue life prediction model for ballastless track casting based on big data clustering. The feature classification of fatigue life state trend in ballastless track casting is studied by particle swarm optimization method [9]. In this paper, the method of mining correlation dimension feature is used to extract fatigue life category feature. It is assumed that there are n samples in the trend data set of fatigue life state of ballastless track casting, in which the characteristic vector of sample x_i, $i = 1, 2, \ldots, n$ is:

$$\boldsymbol{x}_i = (x_{i1}, x_{i2}, \cdots, x_{is})^T \tag{11}$$

The adaptive optimization of multi-dimensional data is carried out by using particle swarm optimization method, and the data set is divided into 2^n subsets. KNN fuzzy search is carried out in two-dimensional space, and the fuzzy clustering center matrix of

KNN clustering for fatigue life judgement of ballastless track casting is obtained as follows:

$$V = \{v_{ij} | i = 1, 2, \cdots, c, j = 1, 2, \cdots, s\} \tag{12}$$

According to the feature similarity in the clustering process, the KNN fuzzy partition matrix for fatigue life prediction of ballastless track casting is obtained:

$$U = \{\mu_{ik} | i = 1, 2, \cdots, c, k = 1, 2, \cdots, n\} \tag{13}$$

In the K-nearest neighbors of K-means clustering centers, the weight of fatigue life of each kind of ballastless track casting is calculated in turn. The formula is as follows:

$$P_{1J} = \sum_{d_i \in kNN} Sim(x, d_i) y(d_i, C_j) \tag{14}$$

The clustering objective function matrix of big data KNN for fatigue life of ballastless track casting is obtained as (defining clustering objective function):

$$J_m(U, V) = \sum_{k=1}^{n} \sum_{i=1}^{c} \mu_{ik}^m (d_{ik})^2 \tag{15}$$

The recall characteristics of fatigue life characteristics of ballastless track are obtained by using K-valued particle swarm optimization control method and distributed clustering method: (1) the characteristics of fatigue life in ballastless track casting are as follows:

$$W = \frac{\overline{K}}{\gamma} = \frac{1}{\gamma} \sum_{k=1}^{K} \sum_{n=1}^{N} kp_{k,n} \tag{16}$$

The data conversion wait time is:

$$W_q = W - \overline{X} = \frac{1}{\gamma} \sum_{k=1}^{K} \sum_{n=1}^{N} kp_{k,n} - \frac{(N-1)\mu + r}{\mu r} \tag{17}$$

In the k subclass of class 1, the fuzzy mean scheduling method is used to perform adaptive scheduling, and the output of KNN clustering is obtained as follows:

$$U_{util} = \gamma \overline{X} \tag{18}$$

According to the above analysis, according to the evolution of particle swarm optimization and the idea of KNN optimization, the cluster processing of fatigue life characteristic data of ballastless track casting is realized [10].

3.2   Fatigue Life Prediction Output

In the process of fatigue life cycle of ballastless track, the fatigue life big data is clustered by KNN and the convergence is judged [11]. By using the correlation spectrum analysis method, the directivity characteristics of fatigue life categories are obtained as follows:

$$\rho_{XY} = \frac{Cov(X, Y)}{\sqrt{D(X)}\sqrt{D(Y)}} \tag{19}$$

Where, $Cov(X, Y)$ represents the autocorrelation function of the sampled fatigue life data of two groups of ballastless track casting, and $D(X)$ and $D(Y)$ denote the average energy respectively.

The method for decomposing the fatigue life of the ballastless track is carried out by adopting a wavelet scale decomposition method, and the output fatigue life evolution characteristic amount is as follows:

$$s(t) = \underbrace{\sum_{k=1}^{N} p_k \sin(\omega_k n + \Phi_k)}_{u(n)} + \zeta(n) \tag{20}$$

Where, $\zeta(n)$ is the number of fatigue life categories, Φ_k is the phase information of fatigue life distribution, and ω_k is the recursive characteristic of fatigue life data of ballastless track casting. Suppose the balanced scheduling model of ballastless track casting data under the digital machining mode is represented as:

$$x_n = x(t_0 + n\Delta t) = h[z(t_0 + n\Delta t)] + \omega_n \tag{21}$$

In the equation, $h(.)$ is the sample time window function of fatigue life and ω_n is the measurement error. Particle swarm evolution's sample training set is $X = \{x_1, x_2, \ldots, x_n\}$, n is the number of ballastless track casting fatigue life data sets X, The abnormal state data of ballastless track during fatigue life cycle are decomposed by Hilbert spectrum extraction method and the state parameters are extracted. The results of feature extraction with multi-parameter fusion are as follows:

$$y(t) = \frac{1}{\pi} K \int \frac{x(\tau)}{t - \tau} d\tau = x(t) * \frac{1}{\pi t} \tag{22}$$

Where, K is the characteristic matching coefficient of fatigue life, $x(\tau)$ is the discriminant statistic of fatigue life prediction in ballastless track casting, $*$ is convolution, and the judgement value of output is:

$$C_{T'}(f) = \sum_{k=-K}^{K} c_k e^{-j2\pi f k T'} \tag{23}$$

The fatigue life distribution of ballastless track is divided into several IMF components by constructing expert system, and the fatigue life distribution of ballastless track is divided into several IMF components. The fatigue life prediction output of ballastless track casting with $X_k = [x_{k1}, x_{k2}, \ldots, x_{km}, \ldots, x_{kM}]$, corresponding to any training sample is as follows:

$$Y_k = [y_{k1}, y_{k2}, \cdots, y_{kj}, \cdots, y_{kJ}] \quad (k = 1, 2, \cdots, N) \tag{24}$$

Based on this data, an intelligent expert system is established, and the fatigue life prediction of ballastless track casting is realized with big data analysis method [12].

In summary, the implementation process of the improved model is shown in Fig. 1.

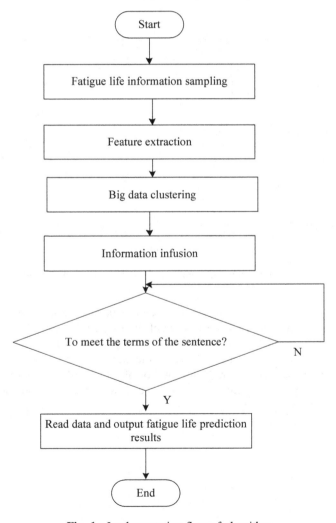

Fig. 1. Implementation flow of algorithm

4 Simulation Experiment and Result Analysis

In order to verify the application performance of this method in the prediction of fatigue life of ballastless track casting, the simulation experiment is carried out. In the experiment, the workpiece of ballastless track casting is selected as a ballastless track hand, and the algorithm design is designed with Matlab 7. The collected fatigue life of ballastless track casting big data is the oscillation amplitude of ballastless track vibration, the time interval of data sampling is 20 s, the length of data is 10244. The number of iterations of particle swarm evolution is 2000, the mutation operator is 0.24, The crossover operator is 0.15. According to the above simulation environment and parameter setting, the fatigue life prediction simulation experiment of ballastless track casting is carried out. First, the original sampling data is given as shown in Fig. 2.

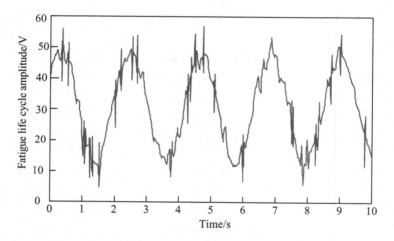

Fig. 2. Oscillation data sampling for ballastless track casting

Taking the data of Fig. 2 as the research sample, a set of relatively stable fatigue life signal analysis models of ballastless track casting are established by means of spectral characteristic analysis method, and the fatigue life data of ballastless track casting is processed by this method. The influence of interference component is effectively suppressed and the prediction ability of fatigue life is improved. On this basis, the cluster analysis of fatigue life sample data is realized, and the clustering output results are shown in Fig. 3.

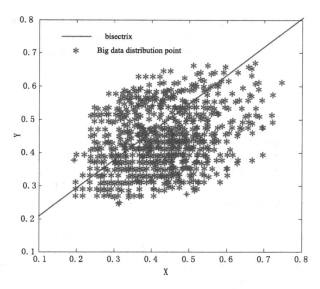

Fig. 3. Analysis of fatigue life of ballastless track casting by big data

According to the result of cluster analysis in Fig. 3, the clustering characteristic quantity is inputted into the expert system model to realize the fatigue life prediction of ballastless track casting. In order to compare the performance, different methods are used to test the accuracy of fatigue life prediction. The comparison results are shown in Fig. 4.

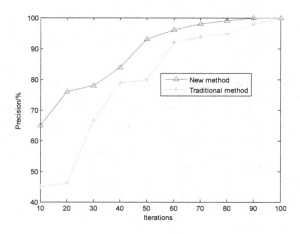

Fig. 4. Comparison of prediction accuracy

The analysis of Fig. 4 shows that the big data clustering method proposed in this paper is more accurate in predicting fatigue life of ballastless track casting, and the feature extraction and clustering of fatigue life state is better than that of non-ballastless track casting.

5 Conclusions

In this paper, the fatigue life prediction model of ballastless track casting is studied to improve the intelligent diagnostic ability of fatigue life of ballastless track casting. The abnormal state data of ballastless track during fatigue life cycle are decomposed and extracted by Hilbert spectrum extraction method. The fatigue life of ballastless track is predicted according to the result of feature extraction, and the fatigue life data of ballastless track casting is processed. The prediction of fatigue life of ballastless track is more accurate and clustering is better, so the prediction ability of fatigue life is improved, and the fatigue life prediction ability of ballastless track casting is higher than that of non-ballastless track casting. It has good application value in fatigue life intelligent diagnosis of ballastless track casting.

References

1. Hu, S., Ding, Z., Ni, Q.: Beamforming optimisation in energy harvesting cooperative full-duplex networks with self-energy recycling protocol. IET Commun. **10**(7), 848–853 (2016)
2. Seo, D.W., Lee, J.H., Lee, H.S.: Optimal coupling to achieve maximum output power in a WPT system. IEEE Trans. Power Electron. **31**(6), 3994–3998 (2016)
3. Dai, H., Huang, Y., Li, C., et al.: Energy-efficient resource allocation for device-to-device communication with WPT. IET Commun. **11**(3), 326–334 (2017)
4. Helmy, A., Hedayat, A., Al-Dhahir, N.: Robust weighted sum-rate maximization for the multi-stream MIMO interference channel with sparse equalization. IEEE Trans. Commun. **60**(10), 3645–3659 (2015)
5. Alfaro, V.M., Vilanovab, R.: Robust tuning of 2DoF five-parameter PID controllers for inverse response controlled processes. J. Process Control **23**(4), 453–462 (2013)
6. Han, D., Chen, X., Lei, Y., et al.: Real-time data analysis system based on Spark Streaming and its application. J. Comput. Appl. **37**(5), 1263–1269 (2017)
7. Sun, D.W., Zhang, G.Y., Zheng, W.M.: Big data stream computing, technologies and instances. J. Softw. **25**(4), 839–862 (2014)
8. Hao, S.G., Zhang, L., Muhammad, G.: A union authentication protocol of cross-domain based on bilinear pairing. J. Softw. **8**(5), 1094–1100 (2013)
9. Zikui, M.A., Chen, W.: Friction torque calculation method of ball bearings based on rolling creepage theory. J. Mech. Eng. **53**(22), 219–224 (2017)
10. Zhou, S.B., Xu, W.X.: A novel clustering algorithm based on relative density and decision graph. Control Decis. **33**(11), 1921–1930 (2018)
11. He, H., Tan, Y.: Automatic pattern recognition of ECG signals using entropy-based adaptive dimensionality reduction and clustering. Appl. Soft Comput. **55**, 238–252 (2017)
12. Zhu, Y., Zhu, X., Wang, J.: Time series motif discovery algorithm based on subsequence full join and maximum clique. J. Comput. Appl. **39**(2), 414–420 (2019)

Design of High Speed Railway Turnout Structural Damage Identification System Based on Machine Learning

Ailin Wang[(⊠)]

Railway Engineering College, Wuhan Railway Vocational College
of Technology, Wuhan 430205, China
gjakg785@yeah.net

Abstract. In order to improve the damage detection and identification ability of high-speed railway turnout structure, a machine learning-based damage identification method for high-speed railway turnout structure is proposed, and the computer vision image analysis method is used to detect the damage of high-speed railway turnout structure. The super-linear segmentation and feature recognition of the damaged parts of high-speed railway turnout structures are realized by means of active contour detection, and the feature segmentation and localization of high-speed railway turnout structures are carried out in the damaged areas. According to the result of feature matching, the machine learning algorithm is used to identify the damage of high-speed railway turnout structure. The simulation results show that the accuracy of the proposed method for damage identification of high-speed railway turnout structure is high, and the ability of damage detection and identification of high-speed railway turnout structure is stronger than that of high-speed railway turnout structure.

Keywords: Machine learning · High speed railway · Turnout structure · Damage identification · System design

1 Introduction

In recent years, with the increasing development of railway construction in China, high-speed railway has become an inevitable trend of railway development in the future. The traditional ballastless track has the advantages of convenient laying, low cost and easy maintenance, but with the increase of train speed, the deformation of ballaststone track bed, ballastless spatter, all kinds of irregularity of track, affecting the comfort and safety of high-speed train, the traditional ballastless track has the advantages of convenient laying, low cost and easy maintenance. It also makes it difficult to maintain the track. Ballastless track has the characteristics of high smoothness, high stability and less maintenance, and has gradually gained obvious advantages in railway operation [1]. The practice shows that both kinds of track structures can ensure the safe operation of high-speed trains. However, due to the differences in technical and economic aspects between the two types of track structures, it is necessary to select the railway reasonably according to its own national conditions

G. Gui and L. Yun (Eds.): ADHIP 2019, LNICST 302, pp. 151–161, 2019.
https://doi.org/10.1007/978-3-030-36405-2_16

in order to obtain the best technical and economic benefits. It is of great significance to study the damage identification method of turnout structure of high-speed railway [2].

The damage monitoring and identification of high-speed railway turnout structure is the basis for the maintenance of municipal bridges. Through the optimization detection and real-time identification of high-speed railway turnout structure damage, the causes of high-speed railway turnout structural damage are analyzed. It is of great significance to study the damage monitoring and identification methods for turnout structure of high-speed railway, which can promote the development of intelligent maintenance of municipal bridges. With the development of computer vision information processing technology, the computer image processing technology is used to monitor the damage of high-speed railway turnout structure, and the topological distribution structure of high-speed railway turnout structure damage is analyzed, combined with the image processing method. High-speed railway turnout structure damage monitoring, the related high-speed railway turnout structural damage identification methods have been paid great attention to [3].

In the traditional method, the manual detection method was mainly used to monitor the structural damage of high-speed railway turnout, and the intelligent machine vision method had not been widely used [4]. However, the damage identification method of high-speed railway turnout structure was studied in relevant literatures.

In view of the above-mentioned problems, this paper proposes a damage identification method of high-speed railway turnout structure based on machine learning. Firstly, the feature extraction of the high-speed railway turnout structural damage monitoring image is carried out by the fusion spatial relation transformation, and the spatial position information of the high-speed railway turnout structural damage monitoring image is sampled based on the block region segmentation technique. The super-linear segmentation and feature recognition of the damaged parts of high-speed railway turnout structures are realized with active contour detection method, and then the feature segmentation and localization of high-speed railway turnout structures are carried out in the damaged area. The feature matching and template registration are carried out in the block area of high-speed railway turnout structure image, and the damage identification of high-speed railway turnout structure is realized according to the result of feature matching. Finally, simulation experiments are carried out to show the superior performance of the proposed method in improving the damage identification ability of turnout structure of high-speed railway.

2   Image Acquisition and Feature Extraction of Spatial Position Information

2.1   Image Acquisition and Preprocessing for Structural Damage Monitoring of High-Speed Railway Turnout

In order to identify the structural damage of high-speed railway turnout, the effective feature extraction method of monitoring image, bridge damage detection and multi-level and multi-direction decomposition method are used to detect the damage of high-speed railway turnout [5]. The spatial position location model of high speed railway turnout structure damage monitoring is constructed, the characteristic quantity of high speed railway turnout structure damage is extracted, and the profile image block feature matching technology is used to monitor the damage of high speed railway turnout structure. According to the results of regional fusion, the dynamic monitoring of high speed railway turnout structure is carried out. It is assumed that the image of high speed railway turnout structure to be identified is that the uniform point on each basis function of $f(x, y)$. The multi-profile feature decomposition technique is used to detect the damage profile of high-speed railway turnout structure in $g(x, y)$, and the block feature quantity of high-speed railway turnout structure damage is analyzed, and the sub-region segmentation technique is adopted. The template matching of high-speed railway turnout structure damage monitoring is carried out. The image to be extracted is divided into $\eta(x, y)$ topology structure, and four extraction channels for damage monitoring of high-speed railway turnout structure are set up. The multi-modal feature component of high-speed railway turnout structure damage analysis is described as $\hat{f}(x, y)$. The edge pixel feature extraction of high-speed railway turnout structure damage is carried out in the connected region of the image. The multi-level feature component estimation value $\hat{f}(x, y)$ of the image is defined as follows:

$$
\hat{f}(x, y) = \begin{cases} g(x, y) - 1, & if & g(x, y) - \hat{f}_{Lee}(x, y) \geq t \\ g(x, y) + 1, & if & g(x, y) - \hat{f}_{Lee}(x, y) < t \\ g(x, y), & else \end{cases} \tag{1}
$$

Dynamic feature matching is carried out in the center pixel distribution zone of high speed railway turnout structure damage monitoring. By using visual reconstruction method, the entropy information characteristics of high speed railway turnout structure damage are obtained as H and η, and the more information $\hat{f}(x, y)$ and $f(x, y)$ information are, the more the entropy information of high speed railway turnout structure damage is K. The stronger the information degree of high-speed railway turnout structure damage monitoring is, the closer the $\hat{f}(x, y)$ will be, and the closer the $f(x, y)$, will be to enhance the gray-scale information according to the damage intensity of high-speed railway turnout structure. The binary treatment process of high-speed railway turnout structure damage monitoring is as follows:

$$
g(x, y) = h(x, y) * f(x, y) + \eta(x, y) \tag{2}
$$

The feature extraction of the high-speed railway turnout structural damage monitoring image is carried out by the fusion spatial relation transformation [6], and the three-dimensional point position is obtained as follows:

$$
g(x, y) = f(x, y) + \eta(x, y) \tag{3}
$$

Where, $\eta(x, y)$ is the sub-band characteristic distribution set of high-speed railway turnout structure image monitoring. The image extraction results of high-speed railway turnout structure are as follows:

$$T(x_{i+m}, y_{i+n}) = \begin{cases} 1 & if \quad r(x_{i+m}, y_{i+n}) > s \\ 0 & if \quad r(x_{i+m}, y_{i+n}) \leq s \end{cases} \tag{4}$$

According to the analysis, the space position matching and the information feature extraction of the high-speed railway switch structure damage monitoring are carried out by adopting the block region segmentation technology, and the statistical feature quantity is extracted, so that the high-resolution identification of the high-speed railway switch structure damage monitoring image is realized.

2.2 Feature Extraction of Structural Damage Monitoring Image for High Speed Railway Turnout

The feature extraction of the high-speed railway turnout structural damage monitoring image is carried out by the fusion spatial relation transformation [7]. The multi-resolution high-speed railway turnout structural damage monitoring image is extracted by the Harris corner detection algorithm, and the local beam adjustment analysis method is used to analyze the damage of the high-speed railway turnout structure. The damage characteristics of high-speed railway turnout structure are obtained at each scale $\sigma^{(n)}(1, 2, \ldots, n)$ The information entropy distribution is expressed as follows:

$$H(x, y, \sigma) = JJ^T = \begin{pmatrix} 1 + L_x^2(x, y, \sigma) & L_x(x, y, \sigma)L_y(x, y, \sigma) \\ L_x(x, y, \sigma)L_y(x, y, \sigma) & 1 + L_y^2(x, y, \sigma) \end{pmatrix} \tag{5}$$

Dense texture rendering is used as a segmented pixel for damage identification of high speed railway turnout structure, and multi-level texture segmentation of high speed railway turnout structural damage monitoring image is carried out. The output is expressed as follows:

$$\begin{cases} \dfrac{\partial R}{\partial x} = 2ax + cy + d = 0 \\ \dfrac{\partial R}{\partial y} = 2by + cx + e = 0 \end{cases} \tag{6}$$

The adaptive weighting algorithm is used to modify the contour of the high-speed railway turnout structural damage monitoring image extraction process. According to the location and orientation of the shot, the correction process is described as follows:

$$R(x, y) = x^2 + y^2 + dx + ey + f \tag{7}$$

In the search area of the maximum distortion coefficient, the sub-pixel coordinates of the damage corner (x, y) of the high-speed railway turnout structure are obtained, and the multi-resolution image information fusion processing of the damage monitoring image of the high-speed railway turnout structure is carried out [8]. The damage feature extraction and output of high-speed railway turnout structure are obtained:

$$\begin{cases} \dfrac{\partial R}{\partial x} = 2x + d = 0 \\[2mm] \dfrac{\partial R}{\partial y} = 2y + e = 0 \end{cases} \tag{8}$$

According to the result of error analysis, the feature extraction of the high-speed railway turnout structural damage monitoring image is carried out by the fusion spatial relation transformation, and the spatial position information of the high-speed railway turnout structural damage monitoring image is sampled based on the block region segmentation technique. Locate the damage point [9].

3 Damage Identification and Optimization of Turnout Structure for High Speed Railway

3.1 Division of Damaged Parts of Turnout Structure in High-Speed Railway

Based on the feature extraction of the high-speed railway turnout structural damage monitoring image by the fusion spatial relation transformation, the computer vision image analysis method is used to detect the high-speed railway turnout structural damage [10]. The block area reconstruction model of high-speed railway turnout structural damage monitoring image is constructed, and the characteristic resolution intensity of the high-speed railway turnout structural damage monitoring image is obtained as follows:

$$\begin{aligned} I_{GSM} &= I(C^N; D^N | s^N) \\ &= \sum_{i=1}^{N} I(C_i; D_i | s_i) \\ &= \sum_{i=1}^{N} \left(h(D_i | s_i) - h(D_i | C_i, s_i) \right) \\ &= \sum_{i=1}^{N} \left(h(g_i C_i + V_i | s_i) - h(V_i) \right) \end{aligned} \tag{9}$$

The damage identification method of high-speed railway turnout structure based on machine learning is constructed. Considering the intensity of affine region in the image, combined with the distinguishing features of the high-speed railway turnout structure image, the three-dimensional model reconstruction is carried out. The edge scale of the damage site is obtained by the beam adjustment method of the correlation frame:

$$p(x,t) = \lim_{\Delta x \to 0} [\sigma \frac{u - (u + \Delta u)}{\Delta x}] = -\sigma \frac{\partial u(x,t)}{\partial x} \qquad (10)$$

The dynamic feature analysis of high-speed railway turnout structure damage monitoring is carried out in the block area of high-speed railway turnout structure image [11]. Combined with dynamic segmentation technology, the regionalized feature segmentation of high-speed railway turnout structure damage is carried out. Get the merge set of a large number of mismatched points:

$$L(a, b_m) = \sum_{V_m \in P^{res}} \frac{|V_m|}{|V|} \log \left(\frac{|V_m|}{|V|} \right) + \sum_{V_n \in P^{true}} \frac{|V_n|}{|V|} \log \left(\frac{|V_n|}{|V|} \right) \qquad (11)$$

The Harris corner of the high-speed railway turnout structure damage monitoring image is calculated, and the segmentation results of the damaged part of the high-speed railway turnout structure are obtained after removing the mismatched points [12].

3.2   Feature Matching and Damage Detection Output

Based on the active contour detection method, the super-linear segmentation and feature recognition of the damaged parts of high-speed railway turnout structure are realized. The feature segmentation and localization of the high-speed railway turnout structure are carried out in the damaged area. The segmentation function of the image is expressed as follows:

$$u(t) = \frac{1}{\sqrt{T}} rect(\frac{t}{T}) \exp\{-j[2\pi K \ln(1 - \frac{t}{t_0})]\} \qquad (12)$$

Where $rect(t) = 1$, $|t| \leq 1/2$, the gray histogram is extracted in the block area of high speed railway turnout structure damage monitoring, and the multi-layer wavelet decomposition results are obtained as follows:

$$\theta(t) = 2\pi \int_{-T/2}^{t/a} (\frac{K}{t_0 - t'}) dt' = -2\pi K \ln(1 - \frac{t}{at_0}) + \theta_0 \qquad (13)$$

The feature matching method is used to extract the segmentation line and contour of the damaged part of the turnout structure of high-speed railway, and the robust feature points of the image frame are obtained as follows:

$$w_{sij}(n_0 + 1) = w_{sij}(n_0) - \eta_{sij} \frac{\partial J}{\partial w_{sij}} \qquad (14)$$

The feature points for image frame matching are:

$$x(n) + \sum_{k=1}^{p} a_i x(n - k) = \sum_{r=0}^{m} b_r u(n - r) \tag{15}$$

The feature matching and template registration are carried out in the block area of high-speed railway turnout structure image. According to the result of feature matching, the damage identification of high-speed railway turnout structure is realized. The realization process is described as follows.

Input: To identify the damage monitoring image of high-speed railway turnout structure y and training sample set D, and get the characteristic distribution set $\alpha^{(1)} = \left[\frac{1}{l}, \frac{1}{l}, \ldots, \frac{1}{l}\right]$ of high-speed railway turnout structure damage monitoring. l is a series of damage samples of high-speed railway turnout structure.

Output: The classification function set of damage feature matching for turnout structure of high-speed railway G. Initialization parameters, self-adaptive optimization of high-speed railway turnout structure damage monitoring starting from SDF, three-dimensional spatial reconstruction and fusion space region location, adaptive optimization process of damage characteristics of high-speed railway turnout structure satisfies the convergence condition $\sum_{i=1}^{n} \rho_\theta(e^{(t)}) < \sum_{i=1}^{n} \rho_\theta(e^{(t-1)})$.

Based on the above analysis, the feature extraction of the high-speed railway turnout structure damage monitoring image is realized. According to the feature extraction result, the feature matching result is carried out and the damage identification of the high-speed railway turnout structure is realized [13].

4 Simulation Experiment and Result Analysis

In order to verify the application performance of this method in the detection and identification of high-speed railway turnout structure, the experimental analysis shows that the high-speed railway turnout structure is divided into cross-high-speed railway turnout structure and longitudinal high-speed railway turnout structure, as shown in Fig. 1.

According to different types of high-speed railway turnout structure, the sampling pixel intensity of image for damage detection of high-speed railway turnout structure is 2000, the gray value is 0.24, and the characteristic matching degree is 0.19. According to the above simulation parameters, the image sampling pixel intensity is set to 0.24, and the characteristic matching degree is 0.19. High-speed railway turnout structure detection and identification is carried out, and the results of high-speed railway turnout structure detection with detailed information are shown in Fig. 2.

(a) Longitudinal high-speed railway turnout structure

(b) Cross-high-speed railway turnout structure

Fig. 1. High-speed railway turnout structure category

According to Fig. 2, the proposed method can effectively identify the damage of high-speed railway turnout structure, the damage identification parts are continuous, and the important information of high-speed railway turnout structure can be identified. In traditional methods, only key points are identified, which is not comprehensive enough. It shows that the design method in this paper can retain more details of the image and the recognition result is more reliable. The test results of cross-high-speed railway turnout structure detection and identification are shown in Fig. 3.

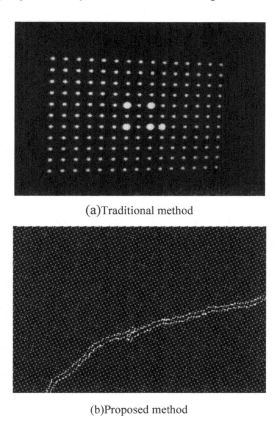

(a)Traditional method

(b)Proposed method

Fig. 2. Inspection results of turnout structure in high-speed railway

Analysis of Fig. 3 shows that when the traditional method and the proposed method are used to detect the damage structure of the same high-speed railway turnout, the traditional method only detects the damage length of 1 cm, while the proposed method detects the damage length of 2 cm, which shows that the proposed method can effectively detect some hidden structural information of the high-speed railway turnout with high accuracy.

(a)Traditional method

(b)Proposed method

Fig. 3. Check and contrast results of turnout structure in cross-high-speed railway

5 Conclusions

In this paper, the computer image processing technology is used to monitor the damage of high-speed railway turnout structure, the topological distribution of the high-speed railway turnout structure damage is analyzed, and combined with the image processing method, the high-speed railway turnout structural damage monitoring is carried out. This paper presents a damage identification method for high-speed railway turnout structure based on machine learning. The computer vision image analysis method is used to detect the damage of high-speed railway turnout structure. The feature matching and formwork registration are carried out in the block area of high-speed railway turnout structure image, and the depth learning of damage monitoring of high-speed railway turnout structure is carried out considering the significance of corner point. The dividing line and contour of the damage part of high-speed railway turnout structure are extracted, and the damage identification of high-speed railway turnout structure is realized according to the result of feature matching. The results show that the accuracy of this method for damage monitoring of high-speed railway turnout structure is high, and the identification rate of high-speed railway turnout structure is better than that of high-speed railway turnout structure.

References

1. Ma, Z., Chen, W.: Friction torque calculation method of ball bearings based on rolling creepage theory. J. Mech. Eng. **53**(22), 219–224 (2017)
2. Yu, M., Zhang, H.: HDR imaging based on low-rank matrix completion and total variation constraint. Comput. Eng. **45**(4), 262–266 (2019)
3. Xu, M., Cong, M., Wan, L., et al.: A methodology of image segmentation for high resolution remote sensing image based on visual system and Markov random field. Acta Geod. et Cartographica Sin. **44**(2), 198–205 (2015)
4. Dai, S., Lu, K., Dong, J., et al.: A novel approach of lung segmentation on chest CT images using graph cuts. Neurocomputing **168**, 799–807 (2015)
5. Liu, W.: Influencing factors and optimization analysis of TD-LTE system rate. Autom. Instrum. **6**, 38–40 (2017)
6. Zhang, X., Zhang, R.: Research on object identity aware network traffic technology based on structured learning in multi-target tracking. J. China Acad. Electron. Inf. Technol. **13**(3), 284–290 (2018)
7. Fan, C., Lin, S., Ge, Q.: Existence of solutions for a new ordered fractional q-difference system boundary value problem. J. Jilin Univ. (Sci. Ed.) **56**(02), 219–226 (2018)
8. Li, X., Ge, B., Luo, Q., et al.: Acquisition of camera dynamic extrinsic parameters in free binocular stereo vision system. J. Comput. Appl. **37**(10), 2888–2894 (2017)
9. Liu, Z., Yuan, Y., Guan, X., et al.: An approach of distributed joint optimization for cluster-based wireless sensor networks. IEEE/CAA J. Autom. Sin. **2**(3), 267–273 (2015)
10. Yang, J., Hou, Y., Sun, H., et al.: Modified NSGA-II-DE with two-dimensional information ordering strategy and magnitude threshold. Control and Decision **31**(9), 1577–1584 (2016)
11. Cun, Y., Zhang, Y.: Linux system dual threshold scheduling algorithm based on characteristic scale equilibrium. Comput. Sci. **42**(6), 181–184 (2015)
12. Sun, S., Wang, S., Fan, Z.: Flow scheduling cost based congestion control routing algorithm for data center network on software defined network architecture. J. Comput. Appl. **36**(7), 1784–1788 (2016)
13. Wu, H., Mu, Y., Qu, Z., et al.: Similarity and nearness relational degree based on panel data. Control Decis. **31**(3), 555–558 (2016)

Research on Data Integrity Encryption Method of Cloud Storage Users Based on Big Data Analysis

Lu Zhang$^{(\boxtimes)}$ and Yi Shen

Anyang Vocational and Technical College, Anyang 455000, China
zhanglu789lll@163.com

Abstract. In order to improve the data integrity encryption ability of cloud storage users, a cloud storage user data integrity encryption technology based on random linear coding is proposed. Firstly, the cloud storage user data integrity encryption key of cloud storage user data integrity object is constructed, then the encryption and decryption coding design are carried out, and the random linear coding is used to optimize the digital encryption key to improve the anti-deciphering level. Finally, the simulation results show that the cloud storage user data integrity encryption technology has high random distribution of encryption, the deciphering rate of encrypted data is effectively controlled, and the performance of the cloud storage user data encryption technology is better than that of the traditional method. It effectively ensures the integrity of cloud storage user data.

Keywords: Cloud storage user · Data integrity · Encryption · Encoding · Key

1 Introduction

With the continuous expansion of information transmission in cyberspace, the security of people's privacy information in the network has received great attention, and the transmission of personal privacy information in cyberspace has been threatened by a large number of security vulnerabilities. Cloud storage user data integrity has become an important topic in the field of network security and information security. The data integrity of cloud storage users by using data encryption transmission method originates from encryption communication technology, encrypts the network privacy information, and stores the encrypted data in the network database [1]. In the process of information transmission, the privacy information of network users can be effectively prevented and the data information security can be guaranteed by encryption and decryption [2].

At present, the encryption of network information data is mainly designed through the link layer encryption. In the link layer, the data encryption adopts the cyclic coding encryption scheme of block cipher and public key cryptography. In the design of cloud storage user data integrity encryption using cyclic coding [3], it is easy to be deciphered by adversaries due to the invariance of the characteristics of link layer encrypted data, and the data cloud storage user data integrity performance is not good. The encryption technology is improved in the relevant literature. in reference [4], a compression

G. Gui and L. Yun (Eds.): ADHIP 2019, LNICST 302, pp. 162–170, 2019.
https://doi.org/10.1007/978-3-030-36405-2_17

encryption technique based on chaotic mapping is proposed, and the standard normal distribution function is constructed to realize the intra-block feature coding and data encryption of the data in chaotic mapping. It has good secure communication ability, but the computational overhead of this method is large and the real-time performance is not good. In reference [5], a binary image encryption method with additional key rotation is proposed, which realizes the privacy information protection and encryption design of network images under optical joint correlation, and has good data integrity performance of cloud storage users. However, the encryption reliability of this method is not high under the interference of large link layer. In order to overcome the disadvantages of traditional methods, this paper proposes a cloud storage user data integrity encryption technology based on random linear coding. Firstly, the cloud storage user data integrity encryption key of cloud storage user data integrity object is constructed. Then the coding design of encryption and decryption is carried out, and the random linear coding is used to optimize the key of digital encryption to improve the level of anti-deciphering. Finally, the simulation experiment is carried out, and the validity conclusion is obtained. This paper shows the good encryption performance of cloud storage user data integrity.

2 Preparatory Knowledge and Key Construction

2.1 Overall Design and Principle of Data Integrity Encryption for Cloud Storage Users

In the process of cloud storage user data integrity, the transmitted cloud storage user data needs to be reliably encrypted, in order to evaluate the performance of cloud storage user data integrity encryption, the following parameters are used to evaluate the performance of key and encryption signcryption scheme [6]:

(1) Encryption random distribution, encryption random distribution reflects the depth of data hiding after cloud storage user data integrity encryption, the deeper the depth, the longer it takes to decrypt, and the computer search cycle decryption method is used in the system. The decision is based on the time it takes to decrypt.
(2) The higher the accuracy of decryption, which proves that the encryption algorithm of cloud storage user data integrity is more accurate.
(3) The size of data capacity after encryption requires the smaller the data capacity after signature, the better.

The master key for calculating the disclosure of confidential information to the eavesdropper is:

$$MPK = (e, g, h, Y, T_{i,j}(i \in [1, n], j \in [1, n_i])) \tag{1}$$

A linear encrypted master key $PSK = (y, t_{i,j}(i \in [1, n], j \in [1, n_i]))$ is constructed in the primary channel to construct an intra-slot encoding mode $X^N = f(S^N, h)$. When $N \to \infty$ is used, the input-output relationship of the channel is expressed as follows:

$$Z^N = g \cdot X^N + W^N \tag{2}$$

Where, $Z^N = (z_1, z_2, \cdots, z_N)^H$, $X^N = (x_1, x_2, \cdots, x_N)^H$, $W^N = (w_1, w_2, \cdots, w_N)^H$ and $N = 1, 2, \cdots$ W^N is an additive noise in a time slot. N is the symbol length of the receiver to sample the transmitted information.

2.2 Key Construction

In the process of encryption design, it is necessary to design the encrypted key. Since D is a constant in a time slot, in the data cloud storage user data integrity protocol, the normal distribution characteristics of cloud storage user data transmission are as follows: $(mk, param, ID_i)$, When the total number of runs is fixed, the encrypted bit sequence is identified, and the user-given link layer data is expressed as follows:

$$upk_i = (upk_{i1}, upk_{i2}) = (g^{x_i}, (g_1^{H_1(g,g_1,g_2,g_3,h)}h)^{x_i}) \tag{3}$$

The encrypted ciphertext in the network link layer performs adaptive link matching according to the key generation center. When the packet code satisfies the $u_i \in Z_q^*$, ciphertext homomorphism decryption, the key is:

$$dsk_{ID_i} = (sk_{i1}, sk_{i2}) \tag{4}$$

The linear block codes are used to broadcast sk_{i2} and upk_i, and the bidirectional link optimization is used to generate the associated coding key rsk_{ID_i} in the key generation center, so that the parity bit $t_i = H_1(ID_i, upk_i)$ of the key is obtained:

$$dsk_{ID_i} = (sk_{i1}, sk_{i2}) = (g_2^a(g_1^{t_i}h)^{u_i}, g^{u_i}) \tag{5}$$

$$rsk_{ID_i} = (sr_i = g_1^{u_i}) \tag{6}$$

Thus, the key transfer protocol is constructed:

•**Enc**$(param, m, ID_i)$ Cyclic shift key transmission link layer data $T \in G_2$, calculates plaintext character $r = H_2(m, T)$, to obtain the first layer ciphertext ID_i of clear text character output CT_{ID_i} in cloud storage user data integrity protocol. The transmission protocol to realize synchronous coding and encryption is as follows:

$$
\begin{aligned}
CT_{ID_i} = (& C_1 = upk_{i1}^r, \\
& C_2 = upk_{i2}^r, \\
& C_3 = me(g_1, g_2)^r e(g_1, g^{u_i(H_1(ID_i, upk_i) - H_1(g,g_1,g_2,g_3,h))})^r, \\
& C_4 = Te(g_1, g_2)^r e(g_1, g^{u_i(H_1(ID_i, upk_i) - H_1(g,g_1,g_2,g_3,h))})^r, \\
& C_5 = 1 \\
&)
\end{aligned}
\tag{7}
$$

CT_{ID_j}: Huffman code is used to perform key arrangement transformation, and the cyclic shift sequence •**ReEnc**$(param, CT_i, rk_{ij})$: key arrangement transformation is defined.

The l-ciphertext $k' = e(C_1, rk_{4ij})k$ is processed by one-time-one-secret method, and the cyclic shift sequence of Hoffmann key alignment transformation is defined. Get the cloud storage user data integrity encryption ciphertext CT_{ID_i}: for layer D of link $l + 1$:

$$
\begin{aligned}
CT_{IDj} &= \{C_1', C_2', C_3', C_4', C_5'\} \\
&= \{(C_1 rk_{1ij})^{rk_{3ij}}, (C_2 rk_{2ij})^{rk_{3ij}}, C_3 k', C_4 k', C_5 rk_{6ij}\}
\end{aligned}
\tag{8}
$$

Under the constraint of intra-block frequency detection, the output ciphertext of the network link layer is as follows:

$$
\begin{aligned}
C_3 k' &= e(g^{x_i r}, g_1^{x_i^{-1} u_i (t_0 - t_i)}) g_1^{x_i^{-1} u_j (t_j - t_0)}) \frac{e(g^{k_i}, sk_{i1} g_1^{l_i})}{e((g^{t_0} h)^{k_i}, g^{u_i})} e(g, g_1)^{-k_i l_i} \\
&= C_3 e(g^r, g_1^{u_i (t_0 - t_i)}) \frac{e(g^{k_i}, sk_{i1})}{e((g^{t_0} h)^{k_i}, g^{u_i})} e(g^{k_i}, g_1^{u_i (t_0 - t_i)}) \\
&= m e(g_1, g_2)^r e(g_1, g_1^{u_i (t_i - t_0)})^r \\
&\quad \cdot e(g^r, g_1^{u_i (t_0 - t_i)}) e(g^{r+k_i}, g_1^{u_j (t_j - t_0)}) e(g_1, g_2)^{k_i} \\
&= m e(g_1, g_2)^{r+k_i} e(g, g_1^{u_j (t_j - t_0)})^{r+k_i}
\end{aligned}
\tag{9}
$$

When the total number of runs is satisfied: $Sum_{idea} = 2Sum_r = \frac{n}{2} - \frac{n}{2^{imax}+1}$, Source coding feature statistics for keys: $\frac{S_n}{\sqrt{n}} = \frac{n\pi - n(1-\pi)}{\sqrt{n}}$. The stability of the key transmission protocol is guaranteed and verified by the following equation:

$$
\begin{aligned}
\frac{C_3 e(sk_{i2}, C_2^{x_i^{-1}})}{e(C_1^{x_i^{-1}}, sk_{i1})} &= m e(g_1, g_2)^r e(g_1, g^{u_i (H_1(ID_i, upk_i) - H_1(g, g_1, g_2, g_3, h))})^r \\
&\quad \cdot \frac{e[g^{u_i}, (g_1^{H_1(g, g_1, g_2, g_3, h)} h)^r]}{e[g_2^a (g_1^{H_1(ID_i, upk_i)} h)^{u_i}, g^r]} \\
&= m e(g_1, g_2)^r e(g_1, g^{u_i (H_1(ID_i, upk_i) - H_1(g, g_1, g_2, g_3, h))})^r \\
&\quad \cdot \frac{e[g^r, (g_1^{H_1(g, g_1, g_2, g_3, h)} h)^{u_i}]}{e(g_2^a, g^r) e[(g_1^{H_1(ID_i, upk_i)} h)^{u_i}, g^r]} \\
&= m
\end{aligned}
\tag{10}
$$

When the inequality satisfies the standard normal distribution of 0 or 1 run, the key is stable [7].

3   Encryption Design Optimization

3.1   Problem Raising and Coding Design

On the basis of the above key construction, the encryption algorithm is optimized. In this paper, a cloud storage user data integrity encryption technology based on random linear coding is proposed, and the encryption and decryption coding design are carried out. Assuming that the key $angle(X^N)$ is uniformly distributed on $[0, 2\pi)$, R^N is independent of φ_g, which represents 0 and 1, respectively. According to the chaotic mapping of binary symbols, the arithmetic coding is carried out, and the output of cloud storage user data encoding in cloud storage user data integrity is obtained:

$$f^{-1}(I) = \begin{cases} p*I, & s = "0" \\ 1 - (1-p)*I, & s = "1" \end{cases} \tag{11}$$

Where I indicates that the information sequence of length N falls into the interval with detection frequency 1, and the initial interval $I = [0, 1]$. Linear coding is carried out by using random combination of multiple character sequences [8], and the expression is as follows:

$$f(x) = \begin{cases} x/P_1, & x \in I_1 \\ (x-P_1)/P_2, & x \in I_2 \\ \ldots\ldots & \ldots\ldots \\ (x - \sum\limits_{i=1}^{n-1} P_i)/P_n, & x \in I_n \end{cases} \tag{12}$$

When $N \to \infty$, for any positive number ε, the slot distribution of each coded symbol is as follows:

$$I_i = \left[\sum_{j=1}^{i-1} P_j, \sum_{j=1}^{i} P_j \right], i = 2, 3, \ldots\ldots, n. \tag{13}$$

The information before encryption is the cyclic reverse displacement of S^N, in the slot distribution range, and the coded output is as follows:

$$f^{-1}(x) = \begin{cases} P_1 x \\ P_2 x + P_1 \\ \ldots\ldots \\ P_n x + \sum\limits_{i=1}^{n-1} P_i \end{cases} \tag{14}$$

3.2   Random Linear Coding Encryption Optimization

Random linear coding is used to optimize the key of digital encryption to improve the level of anti-deciphering [9]. Inverse function is used as arithmetic coding. There is a coding mode $X^N = f(S^N, h)$, cloud to store the self-information of user data transmission as $-\log_2(P(s_i))$. The received symbols are Y^N and Z^N, respectively, and the average amount of information of the corresponding sequences is as follows:

$$H = - \sum_{i=1}^{n} P_i \log_2(P_i) \tag{15}$$

Assuming that the initial key rate is A, the cyclic code L is obtained by μ_L times reverse pilot estimation, which is recorded as follows:

$$\begin{cases} \mu_0 = (P_{01} + P_{02})/2 \\ \mu_1 = (P_{11} + P_{12})/2 \\ \mu_2 = (P_{21} + P_{22})/2 \\ \quad\cdots\cdots \\ \mu_L = (P_{L1} + P_{L2})/2 \end{cases} \tag{16}$$

$$\mu = 3.57 + \frac{1}{L}\sum_{i=0}^{L}\mu_i \tag{17}$$

Taking the above μ value as the iterative parameter of homomorphic symbol frequency detection, the dimension $KC \in \{0, 1, \ldots\ldots, n - 1\}$, of random linear coding is introduced into the intermediate variable R^N, and the suspicion of the cloud storage user data receiver to the transmitted information is obtained.

$$\begin{aligned} size(I^1) &= \Pi_{i=1}^{M}P(s_i \in S) \\ &= \Pi_{n=1}^{N}(P_n)^{card\{s_i|s_i=S_n\}} \\ &= \Pi_{n=1}^{N}(P_n)^{P_nM} \end{aligned} \tag{18}$$

Therefore, the output of cloud storage user data coding after random linear coding is expressed are follows:

$$-\log_2(size(I^1)) = -\sum_{n=1}^{N}P_nM\log_2(P_n) = M \otimes H \tag{19}$$

With multiple shifts, the optimal coding length of cloud storage user data under the integrity of cloud storage user data is as follows: the description of $M \otimes H$, encryption process is shown in Fig. 1.

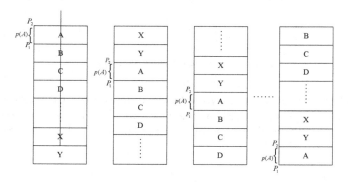

Fig. 1. Information encryption process based on random linear coding

According to the optimization of encryption technology [10], the optimized encryption key is obtained as follows:

Input: $pk = \langle x_0, x_1, \ldots, x_\tau \rangle, z$, When it exists $z \in [0, 2^\gamma)$, $|r_p(z)| \leq 2^\rho$.

Output $LSB(q_p(z))$

(1) $c = z \cdot \left\lfloor \frac{x_0}{2} \right\rfloor$

(2) For $j = 1$ to $poly(\lambda)/\varepsilon$ do

(3) Process the phase and call the key corresponding to the S binary: $a_j \leftarrow A(pk, c)$

(4) Output clear text: $b_j = a_j \oplus parity(z)$

(5) Estimate the random linear code of the output b_j by pilot, that is: $parity(q_p(z))$.

4   Experimental Analysis

In the experiment, the random distribution of data encryption and the bit error rate (BER) of cloud storage user data reception are taken as the test objects, and the encryption performance of cloud storage user data integrity in cloud storage user data integrity is studied. The simulation experiment is based on Matlab platform. The OpenSSL cipher library is called to design the data integrity of cloud storage user in VC environment. The length of bit sequence is 1200 bits and the sampling frequency of data is 12.67 kHz. The length of the bit sequence to be detected is 100 bits. First, block sampling of the bit sequence is carried out, and the sample value of the bit sequence which meets the key construction condition is obtained, as shown in Fig. 2.

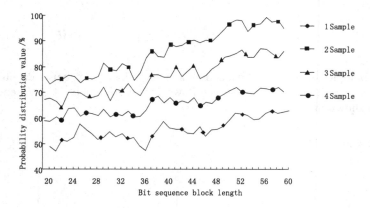

Fig. 2. Bit sequence block sampling

The sampling bit sequence is encrypted by cloud storage user data integrity, and the recognition rate of the data is tested, and the recognition rate of data encryption using this method and the recognition rate of data transmission without this method are shown in Fig. 3.

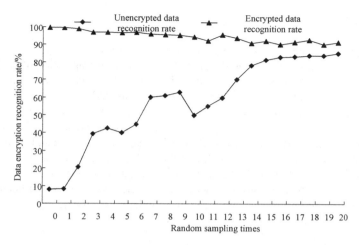

Fig. 3. Recognition rate of data encryption under random sampling

The simulation results of Fig. 3 show that the cloud storage user data integrity encryption using this method has a high data recognition rate, and the average recognition rate of this method for data encryption is 91.4%. Higher than the average recognition rate of 83.5% for encrypted bit sequences, the data integrity performance and accurate data transmission performance of cloud storage users are improved. Figure 4 describes the random distribution of encryption for cloud storage user data integrity encryption by different methods. It is found that the random distribution of cloud storage user data integrity encryption in this method is higher than that in the traditional method. Effectively prevent encrypted data from being deciphered by adversaries.

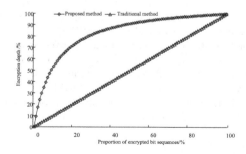

Fig. 4. Comparison of random distribution performance of encryption

5 Conclusions

In this paper, a cloud storage user data integrity encryption technology based on random linear coding is proposed. Firstly, the cloud storage user data integrity encryption key of cloud storage user data integrity object is constructed, then the encryption and decryption coding design are carried out, and the random linear coding is used to optimize the digital encryption key to improve the anti-deciphering level. Finally, the simulation results show that the cloud storage user data integrity encryption technology has high random distribution of encryption, the deciphering rate of encrypted data is effectively controlled, and the performance of the cloud storage user data encryption technology is better than that of the traditional method. It effectively ensures the integrity of cloud storage user data. This method has good application value in data integrity encryption, has laid a certain foundation for the development of cloud computing.

References

1. Zhou, S.B., Xu, W.X.: A novel clustering algorithm based on relative density and decision graph. Control Decis. **33**(11), 1921–1930 (2018)
2. He, H., Tan, Y.: Automatic pattern recognition of ECG signals using entropy-based adaptive dimensionality reduction and clustering. Appl. Soft Comput. **55**, 238–252 (2017)
3. Zhu, Y., Zhu, X., Wang, J.: Time series motif discovery algorithm based on subsequence full join and maximum clique. J. Comput. Appl. **39**(2), 414–420 (2019)
4. Dai, H., Huang, Y., Li, C., et al.: Energy-efficient resource allocation for device-to-device communication with WPT. IET Commun. **11**(3), 326–334 (2017)
5. Helmy, A., Hedayat, A., Al-Dhahir, N.: Robust weighted sum-rate maximization for the multi-stream MIMO interference channel with sparse equalization. IEEE Trans. Commun. **60**(10), 3645–3659 (2015)
6. Seo, D.W., Lee, J.H., Lee, H.S.: Optimal coupling to achieve maximum output power in a WPT system. IEEE Trans. Power Electron. **31**(6), 3994–3998 (2016)
7. Ma, Z., Chen, W.: Friction torque calculation method of ball bearings based on rolling creepage theory. J. Mech. Eng. **53**(22), 219–224 (2017)
8. Alfaro, V.M., Vilanovab, R.: Robust tuning of 2DoF five-parameter PID controllers for inverse response controlled processes. J. Process Control **23**(4), 453–462 (2013)
9. Zhang, R., Zhao, F.: Foggy image enhancement algorithm based on bidirectional diffusion and shock filtering. Comput. Eng. **44**(10), 221–227 (2018)
10. Liu, D., Zhou, D., Nie, R., Hou, R.: Multi-focus image fusion based on phase congruency motivate pulse coupled neural network-based in NSCT domain. J. Comput. Appl. **38**(10), 3006–3012 (2018)

Intelligent Detection Method for Maximum Color Difference of Image Based on Machine Learning

Jia Wang$^{(\boxtimes)}$ and Qian Zhang

Mechanical Engineering College, Yunnan Open University,
Kunming 650500, China
wangjia2711@163.com

Abstract. There is color difference in the image collected under the background of night light. Machine learning and fusion tracking compensation method are used to detect and process the maximum color difference of the image, so as to improve the imaging quality of the image. A maximum color difference detection algorithm for nightlight background color difference image based on machine learning and fusion tracking compensation is proposed. Firstly, image feature acquisition and color difference feature blending preprocessing are carried out, image machine learning and fusion tracking compensation are carried out, and image color difference detection algorithm is used for image color difference smoothing and adaptive blending. The background color difference image of night light is automatically divided into target space by feature clustering, and the maximum color difference detection of the detail features of the image is carried out to the greatest extent. The simulation results show that the algorithm has high accuracy and good color difference resolution.

Keywords: Machine learning · Night light background · Image · Maximum color difference · Intelligent detection

1 Introduction

The image collected at night is affected by all kinds of color light, which leads to the imbalance of image color difference, and the collection and beautification of color difference image under the background of night light is the key technology of digital image processing. It is widely used in machine vision, video surveillance and other engineering fields. Due to the influence of complex natural lighting environment and shooting scene angle, the color difference image under the background of night light is produced, and the color difference image under the background of night light is affected by color and texture features [1]. To a certain extent, it is inevitable to be interfered by the external environment, resulting in the offset of color and texture features, so it is necessary to smooth and adapt the color difference of the color difference image under the background of night light at night, because of the color difference of the image. The detail features of the image target cannot be effectively distinguished and located, but the machine learning and fusion tracking compensation and smoothing methods are used to make up for the white balance of the similarity feature of the color difference

G. Gui and L. Yun (Eds.): ADHIP 2019, LNICST 302, pp. 171–180, 2019.
https://doi.org/10.1007/978-3-030-36405-2_18

image under the background of night light at night [2]. It can optimize the imaging performance of the image and show the details of the night scene image. By studying the machine learning and fusion tracking compensation method of the image, the maximum color difference detection and processing of the image under the background of night light can be realized, and the imaging quality of the image can be improved. The related algorithm research has attracted people's attention [3].

In the environment of external interference, it is difficult to display and beautify the details of the color difference image under the background of night light at night, and the image beautification method based on visual features is sensitive to the color difference between the external environment and the surrounding environment. Because the visual features change with the motion direction and angle of the imaging equipment, the target feature model is not fixed, so it is necessary to update the target mathematical model in real time to adapt to the changes of the environment [4]. In the traditional method, the maximum color difference detection algorithm of the color difference image under the night light background adopts the cyclic tracking pixel feature extraction algorithm, the time-frequency feature analysis method and the wavelet multi-layer decomposition method. The color difference compensation effect of the image is not good when the white balance deviation appears. In order to solve the above problems, a maximum color difference detection algorithm for night light image based on machine learning and fusion tracking compensation is proposed in this paper. Firstly, image feature acquisition and color difference feature reconciliation preprocessing are carried out, machine learning and fusion tracking compensation are carried out for color difference image in the background of night light, and image color difference detection algorithm is used to smooth and adapt the color difference of the image. The algorithm is improved and the performance of the algorithm is verified by simulation experiments, which shows the superior performance of the algorithm in beautifying and smoothing the color difference image under the background of night light.

2   Image Feature Acquisition and Color Difference Feature Harmonization Preprocessing

2.1   Problem Description and Image Acquisition

In the process of image acquisition and information processing with digital imaging equipment, due to defocus, jitter, optical system error and white balance deviation, the visual difference between the imaging equipment and the object is caused, and the multiple color difference is produced [5]. The color difference image under the background of night light is defined as g', and the high frequency part $\nabla_x = [1, -1]$, $\nabla_y = [1, -1]^T$ of the image is generated by discrete filter $y = [\nabla_x g', \nabla_y g']$. The energy function of the space invariant multiple chromatic difference kernel is as follows:

$$\min_{x,k} \lambda \|x \otimes k - y\|_2^2 + \frac{\|x\|_1}{\|x\|_2} + \beta \|k\|_1 \tag{1}$$

Satisfy constraints: $k > 0$, $\sum_i k_i = 1$. Where x is the high frequency part of the unknown clear image and k is the unknown multiple color difference kernel (k_i is an independent element).

According to the distribution structure of the edge profile information of the image in the two-dimensional neighborhood, the local structure points of the image can be expanded according to the first order Taylor series, and the group of the estimation model can be obtained. Update the multiple color difference nucleus using groups below two points, as shown in the following formula:

$$c_1 = \{i | i \in S\}, \quad c_2 = \{\{i, i'\} | i' \in N_i, i \in S\}, \quad C = c_1 \cup c_2 \tag{2}$$

As if there are objects in the image area, there are some interference factors such as dragging in the color difference image under the background of night light at night, which affects the beautification performance of the image, and in the dynamic motion area of the object in the imaging area of the image, The image is processed synchronously with the front curtain and the rear curtain, respectively. The image is set as the image of the time and the R_t is the image of the initial time. The color difference image observed in the night light background contains noise and fine texture. The information is marked by a multiple color difference kernel matrix, and its set is described by a formula:

$$\begin{aligned} L &= \{m_i \,|\, i \in S\} \\ m_i &= (a_{i1}, a_{i2}, a_{i3}, b_{i1}, b_{i2}, b_{i3}, c_{i1}, c_{i2}, c_{i3})^T \end{aligned} \tag{3}$$

Using the spatial proximity of pixel points in the neighborhood, the filter formula is expressed as follows:

$$R_i = \frac{1}{\gamma_i} \sum_{j \in \Omega} g_j d(\|i - j\|_2) l(\|g_i - g_j\|_1) \tag{4}$$

According to the above analysis, it can be seen that the key to using the above modeling algorithm to analyze the gradient amplitude information of the color difference image under the background of night light is to determine the energy function of the random field of the information, so as to realize the image acquisition and preprocessing.

2.2 Color Difference Feature Harmonic Preprocessing of Image Color Difference

In this paper, the smoothing problem of color difference image in the background of night light is discussed, and the image beautification is realized by smoothing the color difference under the background of night light. The multi-color difference of the image can be reduced by using the color difference feature blending method to reduce the noise in the image [6]. The color difference feature blending process is through the convolution of the clear image and the multiple color difference kernel, plus the noise, and carries on the interpolation operation, that is:

$$g = k \otimes f + n \tag{5}$$

According to the single-scale characteristics of the multiple chromatic difference kernel in the window region, the color difference equilibrium energy function of the image includes likelihood energy and prior energy, which are expressed as follows:

$$\begin{aligned} H_1 &: U(t) = V(t) + \alpha(t)W(t) \\ H_0 &: U(t) = V(t) \end{aligned} \tag{6}$$

In order to improve the accuracy of multiple color difference kernel estimation, the image preprocessing is introduced, the minimum maximum detection method is used to filter the image, and the bilateral filter and impulse filter are used to preprocess the color difference image under the background of night light [7]. The maximum likelihood ratio detection is used to obtain the harmonic discriminant function of the color difference characteristics of the image as follows:

$$\Lambda(U) = \frac{p(U(t) \mid H_1)}{p(U(t) \mid H_0)} \geq \eta \tag{7}$$

A fast iterative shrinkage threshold algorithm is used to estimate the multiple color difference kernels. The balanced locking results are obtained by logarithmic likelihood ratio detection:

$$LRT(U) = \ln \Lambda(U) \leq \ln \eta \tag{8}$$

Based on the above analysis, the key implementation techniques of color difference feature blending processing of image color difference are described as follows: the mathematical morphology segmentation method based on texture partition searches for multiple exposure shape features. The variable scale intuitionistic fuzzy set decomposition method based on logical self-mapping is used to calibrate the highlighted lines in the feature region. Firstly, the initial value and interest value of each feature point are calculated, and then a similarity measurement matrix is generated, and the initial optimal solution set is selected as the test sample set [8].

3   Machine Learning and Fusion Tracking Compensation and Image Maximum Color Difference Detection Algorithm Are Implemented

3.1   Introduction and Design of Machine Learning and Fusion Tracking Compensation Algorithm

When the target and candidate region of the color difference image under the background of night light are selected, the feature weight of the target model is determined by the similarity function of the target feature model in space. Finally, according to the maximum value of the similarity function, Be able to get the current tracking target [9].

The similarity function can be defined as the product of two feature coefficients. The mathematical expressions of machine learning and fusion tracking compensation are expressed as follows:

$$\rho_{\text{csc}} = \Delta \cdot \rho(\hat{p}_{uc}(y), \hat{q}_{uc}) \cdot \rho(\hat{p}_{ut}(y), \hat{q}_{ut}) \tag{9}$$

Where, Δ represents the white equilibrium sensitivity coefficient, and the range belongs to $(0, 1)$, the similarity coefficient of the target feature is proportional to the Pap coefficient, and the higher the similarity is, the better the tracking effect of the detail feature is. Using machine learning and fusion tracking compensation fast iterative shrinkage threshold algorithm, the image edge information is obtained along the gradient direction, and the machine learning and fusion tracking compensation phase at the (a, b_m) point on the scale translation plane is weighted as follows:

$$L(a, b_m) = \log\left(\frac{|V||V_m \cap V_n|}{|V_m||V_n|}\right) \tag{10}$$

Where λ is a regularization parameter and $TV(f) = \sum_i \sqrt{(\Delta_i^h f)^2 + (\Delta_i^v f)^2}$, Δ_i^h, Δ_i^v is a second-order cumulative Taylor expansion, the texture features of the image are extracted, that is:

$$L(a, b_m) = \sum_{V_m \in P^{res}} \sum_{V_n \in P^{true}} \frac{|V_m \cap V_n|}{|V|} \log\left(\frac{|V||V_m \cap V_n|}{|V_m||V_n|}\right) \tag{11}$$

$\Delta_i^h = f_i - f_j, \Delta_i^v = f_i - f_k, f_j, f_k$ represents the iterative formula of machine learning and fusion tracking compensation, and f_i is the gray value of pixel in the first order domain of image. For a pair of gray night light background color difference image $g(x, y)$, the M−1 transfer iteration is carried out, and the detailed texture features of the color difference image under the night light background with scale M are obtained.

$$d_{i+1} = 2F(x_{i+1} + \frac{1}{2}, y_i + 2) \tag{12}$$

According to the above method, the bright spot model of the image is expanded by Taylor. Based on the similarity equilibrium of multiple weights, the position, scale, main direction and other information of the image under the background color difference of night light are obtained. The gray pixel c of the image is obtained from the following formula:

$$c = \sum_j^m P(z(k) / m_j(k), z^{k-1}) P(m_j(k) / z^{k-1}) = \sum_j^m \Lambda_j(k)\bar{c}_j \tag{13}$$

The two-dimensional or three-dimensional pixel features of the color difference image under the night light background are LPNTI integral, and the feature matching model of the color difference image under the night light background is constructed by using color and texture [1]. The recognition model of the night light background color difference image is expressed as follows:

$$
v_i = \frac{\sum_{k=1}^{n} (1 - (1 - u_{ik}^{\alpha})^{1/\alpha})^m (x_k + \beta \overline{x_k})}{(1 + \beta) \sum_{k=1}^{n} (1 - (1 - u_{ik}^{\alpha})^{1/\alpha})^m}
\tag{14}
$$

Where, u_{ik} is wavelet threshold, β is program-controlled separation coefficient, H is fuzzy mean, thus the machine learning and fusion tracking compensation of image is realized, and the maximum color difference detection and processing of image is realized.

3.2   Implementation Steps of Image Maximum Color Difference Detection Algorithm

According to the above algorithm design, the steps of the image maximum color difference detection algorithm under the background color difference of night light designed in this paper are summarized as follows, and the feature weight of the image light color difference is determined by the similarity function of the target feature model in space. The image edge information is obtained along the gradient direction, and the target space is automatically divided into the night light background color difference image by feature clustering, the error matching points are eliminated, and the image noise reduction and purification are carried out. The maximum color difference detection is carried out to the maximum extent of the details of the color difference image under the background of night light. The specific flow of the algorithm is as follows:

(1) According to the sequence number frame of the color difference image under the night light background, the spatial feature distribution tracking model of the color difference image under the night light background is constructed by using the color and texture. The edge detection of the analyzed low frequency signal is carried out to obtain the profile image of the low frequency part, and the prior distribution between the adjacent regions (w, w') is obtained. $B_w(y_w)$ represents the confidence of the region w.

(2) The moving target and the candidate image in the image imaging area are automatically divided into imaging space by feature clustering, and the appropriate threshold and low frequency information in the filtered section high frequency information are further superimposed. The normalized machine learning and fusion tracking compensation weighted $u_{mn} = \frac{L_{mn}}{L-1}$ and $L = \max(l_{mn})$ are transformed. L is the gray level of the color difference image, and S is the membership degree of the pixel u_{mn} relative to the specific gray level in the image to calculate the target candidate region feature model.

(3) Then, the pixel weights of the target and the candidate region are calculated according to the weight of the target feature model, and the fusion and equilibrium of the two adaptive weights are carried out.

(4) The color difference image g under the background of night light is preprocessed. First, the bilateral filter is used to process G, and the similarity function of the target feature model is used to calculate the weight correlation coefficient between the target and the candidate region.

(5) The weights are updated adaptively, and the target feature model is selected to update iteratively. Thus, the maximum color difference detection and processing of the color difference image under the background of night light is realized by machine learning and fusion tracking compensation.

4   Simulation Experiment and Result Analysis

In order to test the performance of the proposed algorithm in smoothing the color difference image under the background of night light, the simulation experiment is carried out. The hardware environment of the experiment is as follows: CPU: Intel Core i3-370, main frequency 2.93 GHz, memory 2 GB. This experiment is based on Eclipse and Weka platform, and VC language is used to edit and load the algorithm code. The main program is run directly under the Windows window. In the code, the receive and other functions in TableEst are called for image acquisition and preprocessing. In the simulation experiment, the machine learning and fusion tracking compensation method is used to carry out the gridding stratification of the image in the unit of 5×5 local area, and the pixels of each local region of the two multi-color difference image grid are sampled in time domain. When the threshold is set $\varepsilon = 1.0$, the resolution of image acquisition is 1280×1024 pixel, focal length 50 mm fixed focal length and aperture value 14. The acquisition results of the original image are shown in Fig. 1.

Fig. 1. Original sampling results of color difference image under night light background

The gray mean and standard deviation of three color difference channels are calculated respectively. According to the calculated multiple chromatic aberration nuclei (size 15 * 15, direction 45°), the original image in Fig. 1 was beautified and combined with the results shown in Fig. 2. The chromatic aberration images of luminous background are automatically divided into target space and feature clustering chromatic aberration detection. Color difference detection and processing experiments were carried out by using the method in this paper and the traditional method respectively, and the comparison results were shown in Fig. 2:

(a)Proposed method

(b)Traditional method

Fig. 2. Simulation results and comparison of maximum color difference detection and processing of images (Color figure online)

As can be seen from Fig. 2, this algorithm has better performance of image machine learning and fusion tracking compensation and slippage, and has a good effect on image beautification and processing. However, the image obtained by the adaptive matching method based on the contours features fusion in reference [3] is too smooth and loses some of the image details, resulting in double shadow and distortion in the light projection of the image. The proposed method can restore more detail images and has better smoothing performance, which shows the superior performance of the proposed algorithm. In order to quantitatively analyze the performance, the peak signal-to-noise ratio (PSNR) is used as the comparison quantity, and the analysis results are shown in Fig. 3.

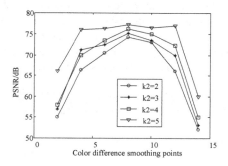

Fig. 3. Comparison of maximum color difference detection and processing performance of color difference images in night light background

It can be seen from Fig. 3 that the SNR of the three traditional methods shows an upward trend and a downward trend as the smooth point of chromatic aberration increases. The maximum SNR of the three traditional methods occurs when the smooth point of chromatic aberration is 7 and the SNR is 76 dB. The average SNR of the three traditional methods is very similar, about 65 dB. The signal-to-noise ratio of the method in this paper maintains a steady change with the chromatic aberration smoothing point, with the maximum signal-to-noise ratio of 78 dB and the average signal-to-noise ratio of about 76 dB. The results show that the SNR of this method is much higher than that of the three traditional methods. It is fully demonstrated that the algorithm not only reduces the computational overhead, but also improves the PSNR, and the PSNR value of the output image is the highest, which indicates that the details of smooth chromatic aberration image details feature content of the background is the most. The maximum color difference detection effect is the best, which indicates that the algorithm has good performance.

5   Conclusions

In this paper, a maximum color difference detection algorithm for nightlight background color difference image based on machine learning and fusion tracking compensation is proposed. Firstly, image feature acquisition and color difference feature blending preprocessing are carried out, image machine learning and fusion tracking compensation are carried out, and image color difference detection algorithm is used for image color difference smoothing and adaptive blending. The background color difference image of night light is automatically divided into target space by feature clustering, and the maximum color difference detection of the detail features of the image is carried out to the greatest extent. The simulation results show that the algorithm has high accuracy and good color difference resolution. It shows that this method can improve the image color quality effectively and has good application value in the detection of maximum color difference. However, the color detection efficiency of this method has not been tested in this experiment. In order to ensure the detection accuracy and improve the detection efficiency, further research is needed.

Acknowledgement. High Level Backbone Major of Higher Vocational Education in Yunnan Province—Construction Project of Major in Print Media Technology.

References

1. Zhang, R., Zhao, F.: Foggy image enhancement algorithm based on bidirectional diffusion and shock filtering. Comput. Eng. **44**(10), 221–227 (2018)
2. Liu, D., Zhou, D., Nie, R., Hou, R.: Multi-focus image fusion based on phase congruency motivate pulse coupled neural network-based in NSCT domain. J. Comput. Appl. **38**(10), 3006–3012 (2018)
3. Ma, Z., Chen, W.: Friction torque calculation method of ball bearings based on rolling creepage theory. J. Mech. Eng. **53**(22), 219–224 (2017)
4. Zhou, S.B., Xu, W.X.: A novel clustering algorithm based on relative density and decision graph. Control Decis. **33**(11), 1921–1930 (2018)
5. He, H., Tan, Y.: Automatic pattern recognition of ECG signals using entropy-based adaptive dimensionality reduction and clustering. Appl. Soft Comput. **55**, 238–252 (2017)
6. Zhu, Y., Zhu, X., Wang, J.: Time series motif discovery algorithm based on subsequence full join and maximum clique. J. Comput. Appl. **39**(2), 414–420 (2019)
7. Han, D., Chen, X., Lei, Y., et al.: Real-time data analysis system based on spark streaming and its application. J. Comput. Appl. **37**(5), 1263–1269 (2017)
8. Sun, D.W., Zhang, G.Y., Zheng, W.M.: Big data stream computing technologies and instances. J. Softw. **25**(4), 839–862 (2014)
9. Hao, S.G., Zhang, L., Muhammad, G.: A union authentication protocol of cross-domain based on bilinear pairing. J. Softw. **8**(5), 1094–1100 (2013)

Automatic Color Control Method of Low Contrast Image Based on Big Data Analysis

Jia Wang[✉], Zhiqin Yin, Xiyan Xu, and Jianfei Yang

Mechanical Engineering College,
Yunnan Open University, Kunming 650500, China
wangjia2711@163.com

Abstract. In order to improve the imaging quality of 3D image with visual feature reconstruction, it is necessary to control the color of low contrast image automatically. A color automatic control technology of low contrast image based on 3D color space packet template feature detection is proposed, the automatic color control model of image based on big data analysis is constructed. RGB decomposition technology is used to extract the color components of low contrast images, and color space gray feature fusion algorithm is used to segment fusion of low contrast images to improve the feature pairing performance of color peak points of low contrast images. Combined with the color space block fusion information of low contrast image, the edge features of high oscillatory region are detected, and the color automatic control of low contrast image is realized. The simulation results show that the color automatic control of low contrast image can improve the peak signal-to-noise ratio (PSNR) of image output, improve the automatic color control ability and imaging quality of low contrast image.

Keywords: Big data analysis · Low contrast image · Fusion · Color automatic control

1 Introduction

With the continuous improvement of 3D visual feature reconstruction technology, computer image processing technology is used for 3D image processing of color image 3D model, combined with high quality information fusion processing of low contrast image. Improving the imaging quality of 3D color image 3D model and studying the dynamic information fusion technology of low contrast image have good application value in 3D digital image design and other fields [1]. The core of color automatic control of low contrast image is 3D image imaging and feature matching. Combined with block information fusion technology, color automatic control of low contrast image is carried out to improve the quality of information fusion, so as to improve the making level of three-dimensional model of color image [2].

Traditionally, the imaging techniques of low contrast image mainly include edge detection imaging algorithm based on gradient operator, 3D imaging algorithm based on wavelet transform. The important structural properties of the image are retained, and the optimal imaging design of the low contrast image is realized. According to the

G. Gui and L. Yun (Eds.): ADHIP 2019, LNICST 302, pp. 181–189, 2019.
https://doi.org/10.1007/978-3-030-36405-2_19

above design principle, the related literature is studied [3]. In reference [4], a dynamic fusion method of low contrast image based on multiple texture fusion is proposed. Fuzzy correlation feature detection method is used to extract gray features of multiple texture images and improve the performance of image fusion. However, the resolution of dynamic fusion of low contrast images is low. In reference [5], an image dynamic fusion method based on edge fuzzy feature extraction is proposed, which is inefficient in dealing with large-scale images. In order to solve the above problems, a color automatic control technology of low contrast image based on 3D color space packet template feature detection is proposed in this paper. Firstly, virtual scene reconstruction technology is used for low contrast image acquisition and feature projection processing. The gray eigenvalue reconstruction and edge profile detection of low contrast image is carried out, the color component of low contrast image is extracted by RGB decomposition technology, and the low contrast image is segmented fusion with color space gray feature fusion algorithm. Then the edge features of the high oscillatory region are detected by combining the color space block fusion information of the low contrast image, and the control feature quantity of the visual region of the image is calculated to realize the automatic color control of the low contrast image. Finally, the simulation results show that the proposed method has excellent performance in improving the quality of dynamic information fusion of low contrast images.

2   Low Contrast Image Imaging and Preprocessing

2.1   Vector Model of Low Contrast Image

In this paper, the first step of color automatic control of low contrast image is to construct the vector model of low contrast image. Firstly, the virtual scene reconstruction technology is used for low contrast image acquisition and feature projection processing. The feature distribution model of low contrast image is constructed by Cartesian space reconstruction method [6]. In this paper, the edge profile of low contrast image is detected by multivariate linear fusion method, and the multi-linear fusion model of low contrast image is constructed. In the process of feature decomposition of low contrast image, the feature decomposition value of low contrast image vector composed of scalars $A = \{a_i\}_{i=1}^N$ is set up, and the edge pixel decomposition is carried out by using multi-feature fusion technology. The vector model of low contrast image satisfies the following constraints:

$$s \leq t \Rightarrow \kappa^s(A) \leq \kappa^t(A) \tag{1}$$

$$\lim_{P \to +\infty} \kappa^P(A) = \max_i a_i \tag{2}$$

$$\lim_{P \to -\infty} \kappa^P(A) = \min_i a_i \tag{3}$$

Considering the gray pixel level f of the low contrast image, the gray invariant moment feature decomposition method is used to obtain that any gray pixel point of the image is (x, y), and the low contrast image of different attribute categories is projected into the elliptical feature distribution space. The description is shown in Fig. 1.

Fig. 1. Edge detection vector model of low contrast image

In Fig. 1, the Harris corner distribution information for low and medium contrast images is expressed as follows:

$$h = \theta/\pi, \ s = 1 - \frac{\lambda_2}{\lambda_1}, \ v = \lambda_1 + \lambda_2 \tag{5}$$

Where, θ is the elliptical principal square angle of low contrast image in feature reconstruction space, and λ_1, λ_2 are long and short half axis length, respectively. Through the above design, the vector model of the surface contour feature distribution of low contrast image is obtained. In order to combine the gray pixel information fusion technology to reconstruct the feature, the adaptive information fusion and feature extraction ability of low contrast image is improved.

2.2 Noise Reduction Filtering and Smoothing Processing of Low Contrast Image

Based on the above dynamic information reconstruction and feature extraction of low-contrast images, the image noise reduction filtering process is carried out by using the similarity feature extraction method [7]. In this paper, the information enhancement processing of low-contrast images is realized by using the multiscale Retinex algorithm, and the pixel distribution sequence of the low-contrast images is:

$$Dif(C_1, C_2) = \min_{v_i \in C_1, v_j \in C_2, (v_i, v_j) \in E} w((v_i, v_j)) \tag{6}$$

In the above formula, $n = 1, 2, \ldots, T$, represents the number of iterative steps, and the weight coefficient of the feature pixel distribution sequence of low contrast image is $w(e)$. The feature is input into the wavelet filter, and the sub-set of gray pixel $C \subseteq V$,F is formed in the main direction of the imaging. The color and texture joint detection method is used to reconstruct the feature points of the low contrast image by means of the method of joint detection of the color and texture of the image. In the connected region of the image, the gray pixel decomposition method is used to obtain the gray pixel value $I(i,j)$ of the image, which can be represented by $I_{(k)}(i,j)$ as follows:

$$I(i,j) = \sum_{k=1}^{P} I_{(k)}(i,j) \times 2^{k-1} \tag{7}$$

According to the spatial distribution attribute of low contrast color image, the low contrast color image acquisition and feature projection processing are carried out by using virtual scene reconstruction technology, and the gray eigenvalue reconstruction and edge outline detection of low contrast color image are carried out. The low contrast color image is divided into M × N sub-blocks $G_{m,n}$, using the second-order two-dimensional vector constraint control method, and the low contrast color image feature enhancement output is obtained as follows:

$$G_{m,n} = \begin{pmatrix} g_{(m,n)}(1,1) & g_{(m,n)}(1,2) \\ g_{(m,n)}(2,1) & g_{(m,n)}(2,2) \end{pmatrix} \quad m = 1,2,\ldots,M; n = 1,2,\ldots,N; \tag{8}$$

Where in

$$g_{(m,n)}(u,v) = I_{(k)g}[2(m-1)+u, 2(n-1)+v] \quad u \in \{1,2\}; v \in \{1,2\}; \tag{9}$$

Where, u is the gray pixel value of low contrast color image $p(i,j)$ in texture joint distribution, and (i,j) is the coordinate value of the corresponding pixel. Through the above algorithm design, the noise reduction filtering and smoothing processing of low contrast color image are realized [8].

3   Optimization of Color Automatic Control for Low Contrast Color Image

The spatial information feature extraction method is used to combine and analyze the low contrast color image. By smoothing, the parallax analysis of low contrast color image is realized. The mathematical expression for designing the function of low contrast color image is expressed as follows:

$$g_i^* = \begin{cases} Rs_j, & z \leq i \leq x - y \\ g_i, & otherwise \end{cases} \tag{10}$$

Where, R is a specification constant, and a low contrast color image information fusion method based on gray histogram 3D reconstruction is used to construct the dynamic information fusion feature quantity of low contrast color image. Set the gray pixel level of the pixel component at the first bit, and calculate the two-dimensional gray eigenvalues of the low contrast color image, where the maximum gray value of the low contrast color image is:

$$n_{pq} = \frac{\mu_{pq}}{(\mu_{00})^\gamma} \tag{11}$$

The color space gray feature fusion algorithm is used to segment the low contrast color image, and the partial derivative of the center v_i in the outline wave domain is obtained. according to the correlation feature distribution of the dynamic information fusion of the low contrast color image, when (x_{i+1}, y_{i+1}) is on the right side of the midpoint $(x_i + \frac{1}{2}, y_{i+1})$, take the pixel PE1. The Euler-Lagrangian equation of low contrast color image in phase space (x_{i+1}, y_{i+1}) is obtained by using gray histogram reconstruction method.

$$F_d - \frac{d}{dx}F_{d_x} - \frac{d}{dy}F_{d_y} = 0 \tag{12}$$

According to the reconstruction results, the pixel gray value at the (x, y) frame m of the low contrast color image $F_m(x, y)$ is obtained. The joint feature output of the block fusion of the low contrast color image is as follows:

$$\hat{x}(k/k) = \sum_{j}^{m} \hat{x}^i(k/k)u_j(k) \tag{13}$$

$$P(k/k) = \sum_{j}^{m} u_j(k/k)\{P^j(k/k) + [\hat{x}^j(k/k) - \hat{x}(k/k)][\hat{x}^j(k/k) - \hat{x}(k/k)]^T\} \tag{14}$$

The low contrast color image is interfered by zero mean additive white noise. the maximum gray value outline point marking information of low contrast color image is obtained as follows:

$$g(x, y) = f(x, y) + \varepsilon(x, y) \tag{15}$$

In the process of reconstruction of low contrast color image, the correlation detection template matching function $f(g_i)$ of constructing low contrast color image is as follows:

$$f(g_i) = c_1 \tilde{\lambda}_i \sum_{j=0}^{N_{np}} \frac{\rho_j \vec{v}_{ij}}{|\vec{v}_{ij}|^{\sigma_1} + \varepsilon} \bigg/ \sum_{j=0}^{N_{np}} \frac{\rho_j}{|\vec{v}_{ij}|^{\sigma_1} + \varepsilon} \tag{16}$$

Combined with the active contours detection method [9], the gray histogram output eigenvalues of low contrast color image information fusion are obtained to meet $\min_{c \in \{r,g,b\}} (\min_{y \in \Omega(x)} (\frac{I^c(y)}{A})) \to 1$, at this time $\tilde{t}(x) \to 0$. Because of $A > 0$, the distribution field of low contrast color images is obtained as follows:

$$df_{t+1}(i, j, k) = \rho df_t(i, j, k) + (1 - \rho)df_{t-1}(i, j, k) \tag{17}$$

In the formula, ρ represents the correlation coefficient of the pixel matching window of the low contrast color image, realizes the edge detection of the low contrast color image, and completes the color automatic control of the low contrast color image [10].

4 Analysis of Simulation Experiment

In order to test the performance of this method in the dynamic information fusion of low contrast color image, the simulation experiment is carried out, and the experiment is designed by Matlab 7. In this experiment, the color image of a multimedia album product is selected. The test data set of low-contrast color images is Corel standard low-contrast color images, the sample set of low-contrast color images is 2000, and the distribution of edge contour pixels of low-contrast color images is 120 * 200. The color texture matching coefficients of low contrast color image are 0.16, 0.24 respectively. According to the above simulation parameters, the test sample object of low contrast color image is shown in Fig. 2.

Fig. 2. Low contrast color image test object (Color figure online)

Taking the low contrast color image of Fig. 2 as the test sample, the information fusion is carried out, and the RGB decomposition results of the information fusion are shown in Fig. 3.

As can be seen from Fig. 3, the three colors of RGB can be clearly decomposed by using the method in this paper, and the colors after decomposition are uniform, with good effect. It fully shows that the information fusion effect of this method is ideal. Finally, the optimized low contrast color image is shown in Fig. 4.

The output signal-to-noise ratio (SNR) of low contrast color image fusion is tested by different methods, and the comparison results are shown in Table 1.

According to the data in Table 1, with the increase of pixel value, the signal-to-noise ratio (SNR) of the SVM method increases slightly. When the pixel value reaches 800, the SNR is 42.3 dB. With the increase of pixel value, the signal-to-noise ratio of PCA is slightly larger than that of SVM. When the pixel value reaches 800, the signal-to-noise ratio is 54.3 dB. The signal-to-noise ratio of the method in this paper changes greatly. When the pixel value reaches 800, the signal-to-noise ratio is 72.3 dB. The experimental results show that the color automatic control of low contrast color image can improve the PSNR of low contrast color image and improve the dynamic imaging quality.

(a)R component product

(b)G component product

(c)B component product

Fig. 3. Dynamic information fusion output of low contrast color image (Color figure online)

Fig. 4. Optimized low contrast color image (Color figure online)

Table 1. Output SNR comparison (dB).

Pixel value	Proposed method	SVM	PCA
200	34.6	21.2	26.5
400	56.8	26.5	32.7
600	69.5	37.6	42.4
800	72.3	42.3	54.3

5   Conclusions

In this paper, a color automatic control technology of low contrast image based on 3D color space packet template feature detection is proposed, the automatic color control model of image based on big data analysis is constructed. RGB decomposition technology is used to extract the color components of low contrast images, and color space gray feature fusion algorithm is used to segment fusion of low contrast images to improve the feature pairing performance of color peak points of low contrast images. Combined with the color space block fusion information of low contrast image, the edge features of high oscillatory region are detected, and the color automatic control of low contrast image is realized. The simulation results show that the color automatic control of low contrast image can improve the SNR of image output, improve the automatic color control ability and imaging quality of low contrast image. This method has good application value in color automatic control of low contrast image. This method can effectively improve the level of 3d model making of color image. However, the control stability of this method has not been tested in this experiment. In the future, the control stability of this method will be further studied in the case of interference.

Acknowledgement. High Level Backbone Major of Higher Vocational Education in Yunnan Province——Construction Project of Major in Print Media Technology.

References

1. Alfaro, V.M., Vilanovab, R.: Robust tuning of 2DoF five-parameter PID controllers for inverse response controlled processes. J. Process Control **23**(4), 453–462 (2013)
2. Yu, M., Zhang, H.: HDR imaging based on low-rank matrix completion and total variation constraint. Comput. Eng. **45**(4), 262–266 (2019). 274
3. Dai, S., Lü, K., Zhai, R., Dong, J.: Lung segmentation method based on 3D region growing method and improved convex hull algorithm. J. Electron. Inf. **38**(9), 2358–2364 (2016)
4. Yang, J., Zhao, J., Qiang, Y., et al.: Lung CT image segmentation combined multi-scale watershed method and region growing method. Comput. Eng. Design **35**(1), 213–217 (2014)
5. Jiang, Z., Cheng, C.: Improved HOG face feature extraction algorithm based on haar characteristics. Comput. Sci. **44**(1), 303–307 (2017)
6. Li, G., Li, H., Shang, F., Guo, H.: Noise image segmentation model with local intensity difference. J. Comput. Appl. **38**(3), 842–847 (2018)
7. Shan, Y., Wang, J.: Robust object tracking method of adaptive scale and direction. Comput. Eng. Appl. **54**(21), 208–216 (2018)
8. Dai, H., Huang, Y., Li, C., et al.: Energy-efficient resource allocation for device-to-device communication with WPT. IET Commun. **11**(3), 326–334 (2017)
9. Ma, Z., Chen, W.: Friction torque calculation method of ball bearings based on rolling creepage theory. J. Mech. Eng. **53**(22), 219–224 (2017)
10. Zhou, S.B., Xu, W.X.: A novel clustering algorithm based on relative density and decision graph. Control Decis. **33**(11), 1921–1930 (2018)

Research on Reduced Dimension Classification Algorithm of Complex Attribute Big Data in Cloud Computing

Wei Song[(⊠)] and Yue Wang

Software College and Nanyang Institute of Technology, Nanyang, China
songwei2462@163.com, wangyue6651@163.com

Abstract. In order to improve the ability of data retrieval in cloud computing environment, a reduced dimension classification algorithm of complex attribute big data in cloud computing based on deep neural network learning is proposed. The complex attribute big data under cloud computing is constructed by low dimensional feature set, and the complex attribute big data under cloud computing is analyzed by linear programming and fitting using grid clustering method. Big data samples of all complex attributes are sampled and trained to extract the associated features of big data, which is a complex attribute under cloud computing. The feature extraction results of complex attribute big data under cloud computing are inputted into the deep neural network learner for data classification, and the complex attribute big data dimensionality reduction classification under cloud computing is realized by combining big data fusion clustering method. The simulation results show that the accuracy of big data dimension reduction classification for complex attributes in cloud computing is high and the error rate is small.

Keywords: Cloud computing · Complex attribute big data · Dimensionality reduction classification

1 Introduction

With the development of cloud computing technology, the stability of cloud computing database becomes higher and higher. In the process of data transmission using cloud computing, it is affected by the interference of transmission channel and inter-symbol characteristic disturbance, which results in complex attributes of cloud computing [1]. It reduces the output accuracy of cloud computing database, and needs to effectively mine and classify complex attributes under cloud computing, and carries out intelligent dimensionality reduction classification combined with the categories of complex attributes in cloud computing to improve the ability of intelligent dimension reduction classification of cloud computing. In order to ensure the security, stability and transmission efficiency of cloud computing, it is of great significance to study the classification algorithm of cloud computing complex attribute data in order to reduce the dimension of intelligent complex attributes in cloud computing database [2].

The classification of complex attribute big data under cloud computing is realized by data mining and feature extraction, and the associated feature quantity of complex

G. Gui and L. Yun (Eds.): ADHIP 2019, LNICST 302, pp. 190–199, 2019.
https://doi.org/10.1007/978-3-030-36405-2_20

attribute big data under cloud computing is extracted, and the anti-jamming algorithm is used to filter and detect [3]. Combined with complex attribute data classification, intelligent dimensionality reduction classification is carried out to improve the stability of cloud computing database communication and ensure communication quality. In traditional methods, the classification method of complex attribute big data under cloud computing mainly includes Reverse KNN method. Fuzzy C-means classification method, support vector machine classification method and BP neural network classification method were used to classify data using deep neural network learning, expert system, statistics and other classification models. The classification and prediction ability of complex attributes was improved. In references [4], a complex attribute big data classification algorithm based on ART model and Kohonen prediction in cloud computing was proposed. Big data, a complex attribute to be classified in cloud computing, was used to extract association rule features and big data to mine, and fuzzy clustering method was combined to classify complex attribute data under cloud computing to improve the accuracy of classification. However, the real-time classification of this method was not good. The efficiency of data retrieval in cloud computing environment was not high. In reference [5], a technology of complex attribute big data classification based on fuzzy C-means mathematical classification method was proposed. The distributed storage design of complex attribute large database under cloud computing was carried out by using grid topology. The semantic autocorrelation function analysis method was used to cluster the nearest neighbor points of complex attribute big data in cloud computing. This method had poor anti-interference ability in large-scale cloud computing database data classification [6].

In view of the disadvantages of traditional methods, this paper proposes a reduced dimension classification algorithm for complex attribute big data in cloud computing based on deep neural network learning. Firstly, big data, a complex attribute collected in cloud computing, is constructed with a low-dimensional feature set, and a large database of complex attribute distribution under cloud computing is constructed. Then the grid clustering method is used to fit the complex attribute big data in cloud computing, and the disturbance of data clustering center is analyzed by combining K-means algorithm and nearest neighbor algorithm. The feature extraction results of big data, a complex attribute under cloud computing, are classified. Finally, simulation experiments are carried out to demonstrate the superior performance of the proposed method in improving the ability of dimensionality reduction of big data, a complex attribute in cloud computing.

2   Data Preprocessing

2.1   Large Database Construction with Complex Attribute Distribution

In order to realize the dimensionality reduction classification of complex attribute big data in cloud computing, the fuzzy rough clustering method is used to construct cloud computing distributed large database model, and the nearest neighbor priority distributed information mining method is used to mine complex attribute big data in cloud computing. The adaptive association rule scheduling method is used to detect and filter complex attribute data in cloud computing, and a distributed large database model of complex attribute big data under cloud computing is constructed by integrating correlation detection method. The data set is vectorized and the frequent itemsets of complex attribute data under cloud computing are calculated under the uncertain data frequent itemsets pattern. The fusion analysis method of expected frequent term (EFI) and probabilistic frequent item (PFI) is adopted [7]. The scheduling set function of big data, a complex attribute distribution under cloud computing, is obtained as follows:

$$R_d^i(t+1) = \min\{R_s, \max\{0, R_d^i(t) + \beta(n_t - |N_i(t)|)\}\} \tag{1}$$

$$N(t) = \{j : \| x_j(t) - x_i(t) \| < R_d^i; l_i(t) < l_j(t)\} \tag{2}$$

Where, $x_j(t)$ represents the classification information entropy in data set D, describes the sample subset of the $l_j(t)$ cluster center, and t represents the sample set of the generation learning in the process of complex attribute data classification. The output label attributes of complex attribute data in the cluster center are calculated under cloud computing. The statistical characteristic quantity of complex attribute data under cloud computing is analyzed by using split information detection method. The storage sample database model of complex attribute data is obtained by using scalar sequence analysis method:

$$AVG_X = \frac{1}{m \times n} \sum_{x=1}^{n} \sum_{y=1}^{m} |G_X(x, y)| \tag{3}$$

Where, m, n are the category number and sampling node of sample samples of complex attribute data in cloud computing respectively. Let p_i be the uncertain database and S be the classification element of complex attribute data under cloud computing. The statistical distribution probability of massive cloud computing data sampling is H, and the distribution width of complex attribute data under cloud computing is obtained by mining frequent itemsets:

$$\text{sgn}(z_R^2(k) - R_{MDMMA\_R}) = \text{sgn}(z_R^2(k) - \hat{e}_R^2(k)) \tag{4}$$

$$\text{sgn}(z_I^2(k) - R_{MDMMA\_I}) = \text{sgn}(z_I^2(k) - \hat{e}_I^2(k)) \tag{5}$$

According to the above analysis, the distributed storage design of complex attribute large database under cloud computing is carried out by using grid topology, and the vector quantization feature coding model of complex attribute big data under cloud computing is constructed. The feature distribution gradient map of complex attribute big data under massive cloud computing is extracted, and the complex attribute data classification is carried out by combining sample statistical average analysis and depth neural network learning algorithm [8].

2.2 Data Sample Regression Analysis and Fusion Processing

On the basis of constructing the large database model of complex attribute distribution under cloud computing, a small amount of sample class data is taken as test set, and the complex attribute big data under cloud computing is analyzed by linear programming fitting method with grid clustering method. In the fuzzy grid clustering center, the expected support degree $esup(D)$ of the data element t is greater than the threshold H, then the attribute element of the complex attribute big data classification under cloud computing is called a frequent term, that is, The classified attribute elements of all complex attribute data that satisfy the constraints satisfy:

$$esup^t(D) > \theta \tag{6}$$

The clustering result of complex attribute big data in cloud computing is modulated adaptively. If the element t of complex attribute category satisfies the finite scheduling mode, it is called probability frequent term.

$$\sum_{\omega \in PW, C^t(\omega) \geq minsup} P[\omega] > \delta \tag{7}$$

According to the sequence of information gain ratio values from large to small, the method of frequent item mining is used to analyze the threshold value of δ, when the probability of complex attributes is maximum, and then randomly find a point to repeat the above steps [9]. Considering the probability that an element is a frequent item throughout the possible instance space, the cluster center point summary output is as follows:

$$x_i(k+1) = x_i(k) + s\left(\frac{x_j(k) - x_i(k)}{\left\|x_j(k) - x_i(k)\right\|}\right) \tag{8}$$

Where: $\|\vec{x}\|$ denotes the norm of $\vec{x}$. Thus, the statistical regression analysis and sample test of complex attribute data are realized.

3 Dimensionality Reduction Classification of Complex Attribute Big Data in Cloud Computing

3.1 Cloud Computing Complex Attribute Big Data Grid Clustering Method

In this paper, we propose a dimensionality reduction classification algorithm for complex attribute big data in cloud computing based on deep neural network learning.

Deep neural network (DNN) is a kind of software developed by Microsoft, whose main purpose is to imitate the way of human thinking, with fast classification ability and high accuracy. Its main structure is shown in Fig. 1:

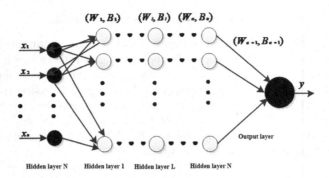

Fig. 1. Deep neural network structure

As can be seen from Fig. 1, the deep neural network consists of three parts: input layer, multi-hidden layer and input layer. Compared with traditional neural network, deep neural network (DNN) has many hidden structures. X represents the network input, including the column vector value of dimension m, and (W, B) represents the matrix formed by the weight and threshold between the hidden layers. The deep neural network USES the vector value obtained from the previous layer of each hidden layer to carry out the nonlinear transformation of function activation, and then transfers the obtained value to the next neuron, which iterates successively, and finally transfers it to the network output y. Compared with traditional neural network, DNN has significantly higher depth of multiple hidden layers, which can make up for the shortcomings of traditional neural network.

The correlation layer of the deep neural network contains a storage module that is favorable to the historical information of the storage layer. The storage unit reserves the historical information of the current time point as the input value of the hidden layer of the first layer in the next time period. The prediction model based on the deep neural network makes the internal structure and state of the network at the best level, and the final output is not only related to the current time period, but also related to the historical information within the time period, which promotes the prediction model to have better dynamic memory ability.

In order to calculate the probability of frequent items, the complex attribute big data under cloud computing is analyzed by linear programming using grid clustering method. This paper introduces the concept of complex attribute occurrence probability of complex attribute big data under cloud computing and clustering frequency distribution of complex attribute data. t is used to represent the probability of different frequency of element in large database of complex attribute under cloud computing, which is called $sup^t(D)$. Then the fuzzy iterative inequality of complex attribute big data's complex attribute grid clustering in cloud computing can be transformed into:

$$\sum_{i=minsup}^{num^t(D)} sup^t(D) > \delta \qquad (9)$$

Wherein, $num^t(D)$ is the maximum number of cluster analysis elements of complex attribute big data in the complex attribute big data sample distribution database under cloud computing. For the calculation of $sup^t(D)$, big data's reduced dimension classification global search method is used to carry out the dynamic programming of complex attribute data classification. The calculation formula is expressed as follows:

$$P_{i,j}^t = \begin{cases} P_{i-1,j-1}^t \times p_i + P_{i-1,j}^t \times (1 - p_i), & v_i = t \\ P_{i-1,j}^t, & v_i \neq t \end{cases} \quad (10)$$

The probability of all possible instances in the current complex attribute big data's dimensionality reduction classification window is calculated. The fuzzy learning iteration of big data's dimension reduction classification is as follows:

$$r_d^i(k+1) = \min\{r_S, \max\{0, r_d^i(k) + \beta(n_i - |N_i(k)|)\}\} \quad (11)$$

Wherein: β denotes the associated feature quantity of global search in big data's reduced dimension classification, and the first part of the complex attribute big data sample set indicates that element t appears on the H element. That is, in the first $i - 1$ complex attributes big data reduced dimension classification attribute element $j - 1$ only appears the statistical probability of S times, taking a small amount of sample class data as test set, the fuzzy random number analysis of complex attribute big data under cloud computing is carried out by grid clustering method, and the fuzzy random number of complex attribute big data under cloud computing is analyzed by grid clustering method. The cloud computing under complex attributes big data grid clustering is realized [10] (Fig. 2).

3.2 Deep Neural Network Learning and the Optimization of Big Data's Dimensionality Reduction Classification Steps for Complex Attribute

The feature extraction results of complex attribute big data under cloud computing are inputted into the deep neural network learner for data classification, and the complex attribute big data dimension reduction classification under cloud computing is realized by combining big data fusion clustering method. Set the following algorithm steps based on the above ideas:

Input: under the cloud computing complex attribute big data uncertain data flow DS, cloud computing complex attribute big data association sample threshold δ, statistical distribution probability threshold $minsup$, cloud computing complex attribute big data sampling window length W;

Output: frequent item sets for support vector machine learning D

1. Parameter of initialization machine and classification coefficient of complex attribute data: $SWF = null, D = null, P_{i_j} = 0, sup^{ki}(\omega) = 0$.
2. for X_{i_j}, a random point is found and the central point of all clusters of the complex attribute big data's dimension reduction classification is obtained.
3. Calculate the probability of cluster crossing P_{i_j};

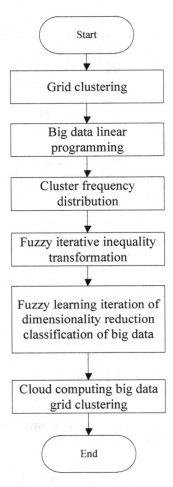

Fig. 2. Algorithm flow

4. if (the current window is not full), the nearest neighbor priority absorption method is used to reconstruct complex attribute features.
5. Update the sample of complex attribute big data under cloud computing in the current window and calculate the probability distribution value of complex attribute category $sup^{ki}(\omega)$;
6. From the complex attribute big data sample set which exceeds the frequency threshold in the data set, the statistical characteristic quantity is obtained by combining the cumulative probability distribution method $Q = \sum\limits_{i=minsup}^{num^t(D)} sup^t(D)$;
7. if $Q \geq \delta$
8. Big data samples of complex attributes under cloud computing based on deep neural network learning are added to the set of frequent items D;

9. Sample regression analysis to store complex attribute data in window set *SWF*;
10. Find out-of-date sample elements and delete;
11. All the complex attribute big data samples are sampled and trained to update the probability distribution value of the window $sup^{ki}(\omega)$.

4   Simulation Experiment and Result Analysis

In order to test the performance of this method in the reduced dimension classification of complex attribute big data under cloud computing, the simulation experiment is carried out. The experiment adopts Matlab 7 and C joint simulation design, and the sample size of big data, a complex attribute of cloud computing database, is 1000 Mbit. The training sample set is 1024, the time width of data sampling is 10 s, and the time domain waveform of data sampling is shown in Fig. 3.

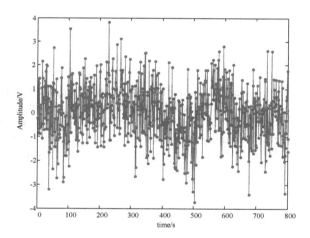

Fig. 3. Sample of complex attribute big data research objects under cloud computing

Set $W = 1000$, *minsup* $= 100$, set the frequency threshold of complex attribute big data collection under cloud computing: *minsup* $= 2$, when the probability threshold of complex attribute big data distribution is $\delta = 0.3$, the mining results of association rule feature of complex attribute category element 4 and frequent item can be found in Table 1.

According to the association rule mining results of complex attribute big data under cloud computing, the complex attribute big data dimension reduction classification under cloud computing is carried out, and the classification probability is calculated as shown in Table 2.

Table 1. Mining results of complex attribute big data association rules in cloud computing

Instance	P	Instance	P
{}	0.0653	{D_2}	0.0435
{D_1}	0.0454	{D_2, D_3}	0.0675
{D_1, D_2}	0.0664	{D_2, D_4}	0.0654
{D_1, D_3}	0.2434	{D_2, D_3, D_4}	0.0376
{D_1, D_4}	0.0564	{D_3}	0.1564
{D_1, D_2, D_4}	0.0433	{D_3, D_4}	0.0646
{D_1, D_3, D_4}	0.0456	{D_1, D_2, D_3, D_4}	0.0356
{D_1, D_2, D_3}	0.1564	{D_4}	0.0686

Table 2. Reduced dimension classification probability of complex attribute big data in cloud computing

Frequency	Complex attribute probability distribution
0	0.765
1	0.873
2	0.297
3	0.554

The results of Tables 1 and 2 show that the method proposed in this paper can effectively realize the dimensionality reduction classification of complex attributes big data under cloud computing, and the accurate probability of dimension reduction classification detection for complex attributes big data is high. The accuracy of data classification of sample sets D1 and D2 is tested, and the comparison results are shown in Fig. 4.

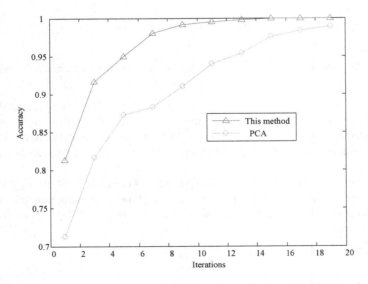

Fig. 4. Comparison of accuracy of big data dimension reduction classification for complex attributes in cloud computing

The analysis of Fig. 4 shows that the accuracy of big data dimension reduction classification of complex attributes under cloud computing is high and the error rate is low.

5   Conclusions

In this paper, a reduced dimension classification algorithm of complex attribute big data in cloud computing based on deep neural network learning is proposed. The complex attribute big data under cloud computing is constructed by low dimensional feature set, and the complex attribute big data under cloud computing is analyzed by linear programming and fitting using grid clustering method. Big data samples of all complex attributes are sampled and trained to extract the associated features of big data, which is a complex attribute under cloud computing. The feature extraction results of complex attribute big data under cloud computing are inputted into the deep neural network learner for data classification, and the complex attribute big data dimensionality reduction classification under cloud computing is realized by combining big data fusion clustering method. The simulation results show that the accuracy of big data dimension reduction classification for complex attributes in cloud computing is high and the error rate is small. The method presented in this paper has a good application value in the reduced dimension classification of big data in cloud computing.

References

1. Han, D., Chen X., Lei, Y., et al.: Real-time data analysis system based on Spark Streaming and its application. J. Comput. Appl. **37**(5), 1263–1269 (2017)
2. Sun, D.W., Zhang, G.Y., Zheng, W.M.: Big data stream computing, technologies and instances. J. Softw. **25**(4), 839–862 (2014)
3. He, H., Tan, Y.: Automatic pattern recognition of ECG signals using entropy-based adaptive dimensionality reduction and clustering. Appl. Soft Comput. **55**, 238–252 (2017)
4. Yuelong, Z., Xiaoxiao, Z., Jimin, W.: Time series motif discovery algorithm based on subsequence full join and maximum clique. J. Comput. Appl. **39**(2), 414–420 (2019)
5. Tu, G., Yang, X., Zhou, T.: Efficient identity-based multi-identity fully homomorphic encryption scheme. J. Comput. Appl. **39**(3), 750–755 (2019)
6. Wang, Z., Huang, M., et al.: Integrated algorithm based on density peaks and density-based clustering. J. Comput. Appl. **39**(2), 398–402 (2019)
7. Farnadi, G., Bach, S.H., Moens, M.F., et al.: Soft quantification in statistical relational learning. Mach. Learn. **106**(12), 1971–1991 (2017)
8. Tu, B., Chuai, R., Xu, H.: Outlier detection based on K-mean distance outlier factor for gait signal. Inf. Control **48**(1), 16–21 (2019)
9. Wei, X.S., Luo, J.H., Wu, J.: Selective convolutional descriptor aggregation for fine-grained image retrieval. IEEE Trans. Image Process. **26**(6), 2868–2881 (2017)
10. Liu, Q., Guan, W., Li, S., Wang, F.: Indoor WiFi-PDR fusion location algorithm based on extended Kalman filter. Comput. Eng. **45**(4), 66–71 (2019)

Research on Hierarchical Mining Algorithm of Spatial Big Data Set Association Rules

Yue Wang[(✉)] and Wei Song

Software College and Nanyang Institute of Technology, Nanyang 473000, China
wangyue6651@163.com

Abstract. Aiming to improve the security of large database in cloud storage space, a hierarchical mining algorithm of spatial big data set association rules based on association dimension feature detection is proposed. The statistical characteristic quantity of large spatial data set is constructed by means of group sample regression analysis, and the sampling and sample recognition of spatial big data set are carried out by using fuzzy rough set mapping method. The association rule distribution model of large spatial datasets is constructed by using the hierarchical mining method of association rules, and the feature quantities of association rules are extracted from large spatial datasets. The correlation dimension feature extraction algorithm is used to optimize the extraction process of large spatial data sets adaptively, so as to realize the hierarchical mining optimization of spatial big data set association rules. The simulation results show that the proposed method has higher accuracy, higher mining accuracy and better feature matching ability, which improves the mining ability of association rules in large database in cloud storage space.

Keywords: Cloud storage · Database · Spatial big data · Association rules · Hierarchical mining

1 Introduction

With the development of communication technology of large database of cloud storage space, cloud computing is used to control the transmission of large database of cloud storage space, which can improve the bandwidth and capacity of the output of large database of cloud storage space. However, in the large database of cloud storage space, because of the random distribution and self-organizing network of large database nodes in cloud storage space, the large database of cloud storage space is easy to be tiered by association rules, so the active mining of association rules in large database of cloud storage space is needed. Combining the association rule tiering mining of cloud storage space large database and the association rule analysis of association rule tiered data, mining the feature quantity of spatial big data set of cloud storage space large database [1]. The security management and information storage of cloud storage space large database are realized, and the security of cloud storage space large database is improved. The hierarchical mining method of spatial big data set association rules for cloud storage space large database is studied. It is important to ensure the security of large database of cloud storage space [2].

© ICST Institute for Computer Sciences, Social Informatics and Telecommunications Engineering 2019
Published by Springer Nature Switzerland AG 2019. All Rights Reserved
G. Gui and L. Yun (Eds.): ADHIP 2019, LNICST 302, pp. 200–208, 2019.
https://doi.org/10.1007/978-3-030-36405-2_21

The research on hierarchical mining of spatial big data set association rules is based on feature extraction and information scheduling of hierarchical data of association rules of large database in cloud storage space. According to the statistical features of large spatial data sets, the hierarchical mining of association rules for large database in cloud storage space is carried out [3]. The main coded features and time-frequency correlation features of spectral features are extracted from the spatial big data set. By scheduling and characteristic decomposition of association rules in large spatial data sets, the security of large database in cloud storage space is improved. In Ref. [4], a spatial big data set extraction technique based on genetic algorithm is proposed. Feature extraction and blind separation of spatial big data sets are carried out to construct genetic optimization control for spatial big data set mining. However, the computation cost of this method for hierarchical mining of spatial big data sets association rules is large and its self-adaptability is not good. In Ref. [5], a hierarchical data detection algorithm based on symbol envelope amplitude extraction for large database of cloud storage space is proposed, and the distribution model of symbol transmission channel for large database of cloud storage space is constructed. The feature value of symbol envelope amplitude is extracted from large database traffic sequence in cloud storage space for mining association rules. However, the anti-interference ability of this method is not good, and the accurate probability of mining association rules is not high.

In order to solve these problems, a hierarchical mining algorithm of spatial big data set association rules based on association dimension feature detection is proposed in this paper, and the fuzzy rough set mapping method is used to sample and identify the spatial big data sets. The association rule feature quantity of spatial large data set is extracted, and the extraction process of spatial large data set is optimized adaptively by using correlation dimension feature extraction algorithm, and the hierarchical mining optimization of spatial big data set association rule is realized. Finally, simulation experiments are carried out to show the superior performance of this method in improving the hierarchical mining ability of spatial big data set association rules.

2 Statistical Analysis and Feature Extraction of Large Spatial Data Sets

2.1 Statistical Feature Monitoring of Large Spatial Data Sets

In order to realize the hierarchical mining of association rules in spatial big data sets, the statistical features of large spatial data sets are constructed by the method of group sample regression analysis, and the data detection of association rules tiering in large database in cloud storage space is carried out. An undirected graph model $G = (V, E)$ is used to represent the sensor network structure model of spatial big data set monitoring, and in the transmission link model of hierarchical association rules of large database in cloud storage space. The node sensing point v is the root node of the large database in cloud storage space [4]. The on-line monitoring of large spatial data sets is carried out at the output link layer. For any node satisfied with $e \in E$, the Sink link set of the monitoring node is $v \in V$, in the 3D spatial scattering cluster. Scattered cluster cloud storage space large database topology edge structure satisfies SF, assumption transmission link data set $X = \{x_1, x_2, \cdots, x_n\}$, of receiver antenna and transmitter antenna, the statistical analysis model of association rule tiering monitoring in large database of cloud storage space is constructed. The model is described by directed graph model $G(A)$, $G(B)$ and the statistical characteristic point $<x, y>$, under the tiering of association rules in large database of cloud storage space is described by A, B. The statistical feature monitoring model of large spatial data set is obtained as shown in Fig. 1.

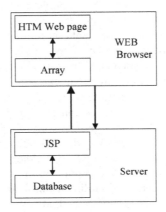

Fig. 1. Statistical feature monitoring node model for large spatial data sets

According to the statistical characteristic distribution model of large spatial data set shown in Fig. 1, the big data sampling discrete characteristic value of constructing the association rule tiering of cloud storage space large database is expressed as follows:

$$X_1(k) = FFT[x_1, x_1(k+1), \ldots\ldots, x_1(k+N-1)]^T \tag{1}$$

$$X_2(k) = FFT[x_2, x_2(k+1), \ldots\ldots, x_2(k+N-1)]^T \tag{2}$$

Where, $\tilde{X}_1(k)$, $\tilde{X}_2(k)$ are a large spatial data set composed of $X_1(k)$, $X_2(k)$ items before $N/2+1$, from which the association rule set of large spatial data set is extracted, and N-dimensional vector x(t) is used to represent the vector of tiered data of association rules in large database in cloud storage space, then:

$$x(t) = As(t) + n(t) \tag{3}$$

Where

$$\boldsymbol{x}(t) = [x_{-P+1}(t), x_{-P+2}(t), \cdots, x_P(t)]_{N \times 1}^T \tag{4}$$

$$\boldsymbol{s}(t) = [s_1(t), s_2(t), \cdots s_I(t)]_{I \times 1}^T \tag{5}$$

$$n(t) = [n_{-P+1}(t), n_{-P+2}(t), \cdots, n_P(t)]_{N \times 1}^T \tag{6}$$

$$\mathbf{A} = [a(\theta_1, r_1), a(\theta_2, r_2), \cdots, a(\theta_I, r_I)]_{N \times I} \tag{7}$$

According to the above analysis, the spatial big data set monitoring model is constructed. According to the monitoring results of the original data, the hierarchical mining of association rules and self-adaptive scheduling are carried out, and the information fusion processing is carried out with the result of feature extraction. Improve the statistical feature analysis ability of large spatial data sets [7].

2.2 Feature Analysis of Large Spatial Data Set

The sub-carrier modulation method is used to describe the hierarchical node distribution characteristics of association rules, and the principal component feature information of the hierarchical data of large database in cloud storage space is obtained as:

$$C_1(m, n) = \sum_{i=1}^{L} c_{4s_i} e^{j2\phi_i} \tag{8}$$

In this formula, $c_{4s_i} = cum\left\{ |s_i(t)|^4 \right\}$ denotes the energy spectral density of the spatial big data set at node s_i. ϕ_i is the distribution coefficient of characteristic information. C_{4S} is used to represent the information intensity of spatial big data sets in the aggregation link layer:

$$C_{4S} = diag[c_{4s_1}, c_{4s_2}, \cdots, c_{4s_L}] \tag{9}$$

It is known that $a(t) \geq |s(t)|$, it represents the energy spectral density of the hierarchical data of association rules at node s_i. The maximum envelope amplitude of the large spatial data set is $|s(t)|$, and the first-order statistic of the hierarchical data of association rules is $a(t)$. The following $4P \times 4P$ matrix is constructed to represent the statistical characteristics of large spatial data sets:

$$C = \begin{bmatrix} C_1 & C_2 & C_5 & C_4 \\ C_2^H & C_1 & C_6 & C_7 \\ C_5^H & C_6^H & C_1 & C_3^H \\ C_4^H & C_7^H & C_3 & C_1 \end{bmatrix} = \overline{A} C_{4s} \overline{A}^H \tag{10}$$

Where $\overline{A} = \left[A^H, (A\Lambda)^H, (A\Omega)^H, (A\Phi)^H \right]^H$, the fuzzy rough set mapping method is used for sampling and statistical feature distributed description of spatial big data sets in order to improve the detection ability of spatial big data sets [8].

3 Spatial Big Data Association Rules Hierarchical Mining Optimization

3.1 Hierarchical Mining of Association Rules

On the basis of the statistical feature quantity of large spatial data set constructed by grouping sample regression analysis method, the data mining optimization design is carried out. In this paper, a hierarchical mining algorithm of spatial big data set association rules based on association dimension feature detection is proposed [9]. Combined with the hierarchical mining method of association rules, the distribution model of association rules in large spatial data sets is constructed. Combined with the correlation detection method, the statistical probability distribution of large spatial data sets is obtained as follows:

$$V_t(k) = \{a_{s+t}\ldots a_{t+1}a_t\ldots a_1 1 | \overline{a_{s+t}\ldots a_{t+1}} = k, a_i \in \{0,1\}, 0 \leq k < 2^s\} \quad (11)$$

Assuming that $a_0, a_1 \in V$, machine learning algorithm is applied to adaptive optimization for Sink nodes of spatial big data set distribution, the correlation feature of spatial big data set detection is obtained as follows:

$$T_{l1} = \sqrt{F_{p1}^2 + F_{q1}^2} \quad (12)$$

The quantitative feature distribution set is calculated as $F_{i1} = \frac{1}{P_{i1}}$, $i = p, q$, in the source distribution domain of spatial big data set. Therefore, a hierarchical mining model of association rules for large database of cloud storage space is constructed, and the big data transmission link structure of large database of cloud storage space is established. It is expressed that $W(p) = G_T p^2 - Cp + \alpha T$, $W(p)$ is a quadratic function of spatial big data set link set p. Combined with the result of association rules hierarchical mining, the hierarchical mining of association rules is carried out [10].

3.2 Association Rule Hierarchical Data Association Dimension Feature Detection

The nonlinear feature combined with the hierarchical mining method of association rules is used to construct the association rule distribution model of spatial large data sets [11]. The decision statistics for hierarchical mining of association rules are as follows:

$$\mu(n) = \begin{cases} \beta_1 \left[1 - \exp(-\alpha_1 |e_{MCMA}(n)|^2) \right], & E\left[(|e_{MCMA}(n)|^2) \right] > K \\ \beta_2 \left[1 - \exp(-\alpha_2 |e_{MCMA}(n)|^2) \right], & \text{else} \end{cases} \quad (13)$$

By using the correlation dimension feature detection method, when the maximum root mean square error is satisfied with $MSE = E[(|e(n)|^2)] > K$, the smaller α_2 and β_2

are selected to mine the large spatial data set of cloud storage space, and the optimized mining algorithm is obtained as follows:

$$\text{ROUTE\_2}(\text{Route } u = u_{s+1}\ldots u_{t+1}u_t\ldots u_1 0, \quad v = v_{s+t}\ldots v_{t+1}u_t\ldots u_1 0)$$

$$x = u_{s+1}\ldots u_{t+1}; \quad y = v_{s+t}\ldots v_{t+1};$$

$$I(x,y) = \emptyset;$$

$$\text{For each } e_i, \text{if}(u_i \neq v_i)I(x,y) = I(x,y) + e_i;$$

While$(I(x,y) \neq \emptyset)$

$\{e_i = firstselect(I(x,y)); //$

form x to $x + e_i; \quad x = x + e_i; \quad I(x,y) = I(x,y) - e_i; \}$

$)$

According to the improved correlation dimension feature extraction algorithm, the adaptive iteration is carried out until the convergence criterion is satisfied, and the spatial big data set extraction is realized according to the coverage [12].

4 Simulation Experiment and Result Analysis

In order to verify the performance of this method in spatial big data set detection, simulation experiments are carried out. In the experiment, the algorithm is designed with Matlab, and the type of association rules tiering in large database in cloud storage space is DoS. The fundamental frequency of spatial big data collection is 20 kHz, the spatial big data set coverage is 300 × 300, and the modulation frequency of association rule layered data varies between [240 Hz, 1200 Hz]. Three kinds of association rule layered data are divided into two groups: Probe and ipsweep, the fundamental frequency is 20 kHz, the spatial big data set covers 300 × 300, and the modulation frequency is between 240 Hz and 1200 Hz. Under the condition of interference signal-to-noise ratio of −10−−2 dB respectively, the hierarchical mining of association rules for large data sets in cloud storage space and large database space is carried out, and the statistical features of large spatial data sets are constructed by using the method of group sample regression analysis. The original cloud storage space, large database space, large data set time domain distribution is shown in Fig. 2.

Taking the data of Fig. 2 as input, the association rule feature quantity of spatial large data set is extracted, and the extraction process of spatial large data set is optimized adaptively by using correlation dimension feature extraction algorithm, and the mining result of association rule hierarchy is obtained as shown in Fig. 3.

The analysis of Fig. 3 shows that the proposed method has strong anti-interference ability in mining spatial big data set association rules. On the basis of Fig. 3, in order to further prove the anti-interference performance of the proposed method, the traditional method in 2 was used as the contrast experimental group to conduct a comparative anti-interference experiment. The amplitude of the three methods was recorded respectively, with the interference sizes of −10 dB, −6 dB, −4 dB and −2 dB. The comparison results are shown in Table 1.

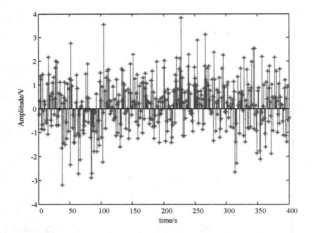

Fig. 2. Time domain distribution of large spatial data sets

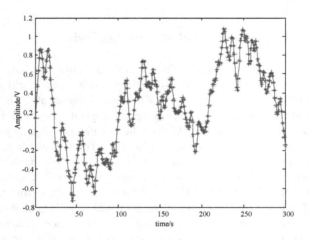

Fig. 3. Mining results of association rule hierarchies for association rule hierarchical data

Table 1. Performance comparison of hierarchical mining of association rule

SNR/dB	Proposed method	Wavelet detection	Time-frequency detection
−10	0.865	0.734	0.798
−6	0.997	0.905	0.876
−4	1	0.967	0.944
−2	1	0.988	0.969

The analysis Table 1 shows that with the increase of input signal-to-noise ratio, the probability of mining association rules layering increases continuously, and the accuracy of spatial big data set mining and detection of association rules is high by using the method proposed in this paper.

In order to further verify the performance of the proposed hierarchical mining algorithm for association rules in spatial large data sets, it is compared with literature [3], literature [4] and literature [5] to obtain the following mining accuracy experimental results.

As can be seen from the experimental results of the Fig. 4 above, compared with the traditional method, the proposed method has higher mining accuracy, and the precision value is more in line with the current application requirements in this field.

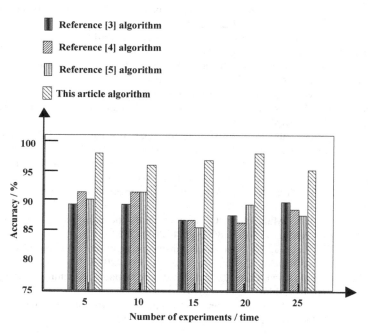

Fig. 4. Comparison of mining accuracy of different algorithms

5 Conclusions

In this paper, a hierarchical mining algorithm of spatial big data set association rules based on association dimension feature detection is proposed. The statistical characteristic quantity of large spatial data set is constructed by means of group sample regression analysis, and the sampling and sample recognition of spatial big data set are carried out by using fuzzy rough set mapping method. The association rule distribution model of large spatial datasets is constructed by using the hierarchical mining method of association rules, and the feature quantities of association rules are extracted from large spatial datasets. The correlation dimension feature extraction algorithm is used to optimize the extraction process of large spatial data sets adaptively, so as to realize the hierarchical mining optimization of spatial big data set association rules. The simulation results show that the proposed method has higher accuracy, higher mining accuracy and better feature matching ability, which improves the mining ability of association rules in large database in cloud storage space. The method has good application value in large data mining.

References

1. Muramatsu, M.: On network simplex method using the primal-dual symmetric pivoting rule. J. Oper. Res. Soc. Jpn. **43**(1), 149–161 (2017)
2. Ma, Z., Chen, W.: Friction torque calculation method of ball bearings based on rolling creepage theory. J. Mech. Eng. **53**(22), 219–224 (2017)
3. Tu, G., Yang, X., Zhou, T.: Efficient identity-based multi-identity fully homomorphic encryption scheme. J. Comput. Appl. **39**(3), 750–755 (2019)
4. Wang, Z., Huang, M., et al.: Integrated algorithm based on density peaks and density-based clustering. J. Comput. Appl. **39**(2), 398–402 (2019)
5. Helmy, A., Hedayat, A., Al-Dhahir, N.: Robust weighted sum-rate maximization for the multi-stream MIMO interference channel with sparse equalization. IEEE Trans. Commun. **60**(10), 3645–3659 (2015)
6. Alfaro, V.M., Vilanovab, R.: Robust tuning of 2DoF five-parameter PID controllers for inverse response controlled processes. J. Process Control **23**(4), 453–462 (2013)
7. Han, D., Chen, X., Lei, Y., et al.: Real-time data analysis system based on spark streaming and its application. J. Comput. Appl. **37**(5), 1263–1269 (2017)
8. Sun, D.W., Zhang, G.Y., Zheng, W.M.: Big data stream computing, technologies and instances. J. Softw. **25**(4), 839–862 (2014)
9. Hao, S.G., Zhang, L., Muhammad, G.: A union authentication protocol of cross-domain based on bilinear pairing. J. Softw. **8**(5), 1094–1100 (2013)
10. Zhu, Y., Zhu, X., Wang, J.: Time series motif discovery algorithm based on subsequence full join and maximum clique. J. Comput. Appl. **39**(2), 414–420 (2019)
11. Wang, Z., Zheng, Q., Chen, C., et al.: Virtual network mapping algorithm based on network simplex. Comput. Eng. **45**(4), 13–17 (2019)
12. Wang, I.L., Lin, S.J.: A network simplex algorithm for solving the minimum distribution cost problem. J. Ind. Manag. Optim. **5**(4), 929–950 (2017)

Uniform Acceleration Motion Target Location and Tracking Based on Time-Frequency Difference

Luxi Zhang[1($\boxtimes$)], Yijun Li[1], Yuanyuan Song[1], Yi He Wan[2],
Yan Qiang[3], and Qun Wan[1]

[1] School of Information and Communication Engineering,
University of Electronic Science and Technology of China,
Chengdu 611731, China
1602295537@qq.com, 1049383157@qq.com,
song1797@yahoo.com, wanqun@uestc.edu.cn
[2] Jangxi Province Engineering Research Center of Special Wireless
Communications, Tongfang Electronic Technology Co., Ltd., Jiujiang 332001,
People's Republic of China
wanyihe2007@sina.com
[3] Southwest Institute of Electronic Technology, Chengdu 610036, China
yan0235@126.com

Abstract. In this paper, the problem of locating and tracking moving target with uniform acceleration by moving multi-stations is studied. Based on the time-difference information and frequency-difference information of target signal arriving at different base stations, a method of locating and tracking aerial moving target based on time-frequency difference is proposed. This method is based on extended kalman filter (EKF) and unscented kalman filter (UKF) filtering algorithms respectively to locate and track moving target, and compares the locating results of the two algorithms. This method can not only locate and track the aerial target, but also estimate the velocity and acceleration information of the target. The simulation results show that the location and tracking results of this method can achieve high positioning accuracy, and the positioning accuracy of UKF is better than that of EKF and better positioning results can be obtained, which has a certain reference value for the engineering realization of multi-station moving target location and tracking in the air.

Keywords: Time-frequency difference location · EKF · UKF

1 Introduction

Target location and tracking [1] is a technique for estimating target motion state based on telemetry data. At any time, there is an urgent need for situational awareness [2] and prediction ability of moving targets, and the monitoring ability of existing equipment for moving targets is still very limited. In order to realize situational awareness and prediction ability of moving targets, it is necessary to use all available means to

G. Gui and L. Yun (Eds.): ADHIP 2019, LNICST 302, pp. 209–218, 2019.
https://doi.org/10.1007/978-3-030-36405-2_22

reconnaissance these threatening targets and control their related information, including location information, velocity information and acceleration information.

According to the different types of observers, the target localization technology is generally divided into active localization [3] and passive localization [4]. Passive location technology is essentially the fusion of location method and location algorithm. Passive location methods mainly include direction finding cross location [5], time difference location [6], time-frequency difference location [7] and so on. In this paper, the joint location technology of time difference and frequency difference is adopted. This technology can improve the positioning accuracy of the target. In this paper, EKF [8] and UKF [9] filtering methods are applied to locate and track the target according to the characteristics of time-frequency difference location method and the moving state of the target, i.e. uniformly accelerated motion model, and the simulation results are given.

The rest of this paper is structured as follows. The second section describes the principle of time-frequency difference location and tracking. The third section describes the filtering algorithm. The fourth section simulates and analyses the performance of the algorithm, and makes a comparison. Section 5 summarizes the full text.

2   Principle of Time-Frequency Difference Location and Tracking

Passive Time-Frequency-Difference localization technology locates the target according to the time difference of arrival (TDOA) and frequency difference of arrival (FDOA) measured by the observation station. In order to locate the target, first of all, we need to establish a location model.

The position, velocity and acceleration of the target emitter respectively are $\mathbf{p}(t) = [x(t), y(t), z(t)]^T$, $\dot{\mathbf{p}}(t) = [\dot{x}(t), \dot{y}(t), \dot{z}(t)]^T$, $\ddot{\mathbf{p}}(t) = [\ddot{x}(t), \ddot{y}(t), \ddot{z}(t)]^T$. The position, velocity and acceleration of M observation stations respectively are $\mathbf{s}_i(t) = [x_i(t), y_i(t), z_i(t)]^T$, $\dot{\mathbf{s}}_i(t) = [\dot{x}_i(t), \dot{y}_i(t), \dot{z}_i(t)]^T$, $\ddot{\mathbf{s}}_i(t) = [\ddot{x}_i(t), \ddot{y}_i(t), \ddot{z}_i(t)]^T$, $i = 1, \cdots, M$.

The distance between the radiation source and each observatory is as follows:

$$r_i(t) = \|\mathbf{p}(t) - \mathbf{s}(t)\| = \sqrt{(x(t) - x_i(t))^2 + (y(t) - y_i(t))^2 + (z(t) - z_i(t))^2} \qquad (1)$$

Suppose f_c is the center frequency of the target signal. With the first observatory as the reference station, the TDOA and FDOA measurements between the radiation source and the i observatory and the reference station are obtained:

$$\tau_{i1}(t) = \tau_i(t) - \tau_1(t) + \Delta\tau_{i1} = \frac{r_i(t) - r_1(t)}{c} + \Delta\tau_{i1}, \ i = 2, \cdots, M \qquad (2)$$

$$\begin{aligned} f_{i1}(t) &= f_i(t) - f_1(t) + \Delta f_{i1} \\ &= \frac{f_c}{c}\left[\frac{(\mathbf{p}(t) - \mathbf{s}_i(t))^T(\dot{\mathbf{p}}(t) - \dot{\mathbf{s}}_i(t))}{\|(\mathbf{p}(t) - \mathbf{s}_i(t))\|_2} - \frac{(\mathbf{p}(t) - \mathbf{s}_1(t))^T(\dot{\mathbf{p}}(t) - \dot{\mathbf{s}}_1(t))}{\|(\mathbf{p}(t) - \mathbf{s}_1(t))\|_2}\right] + \Delta f_{i1} \end{aligned} \qquad (3)$$

Among them, $\Delta\tau_{i1}$ represents the TDOA measurement error between the first obser-vation station and the i observation station, and obeys the normal distribution of zero mean and variance δ_τ^2. Δf_{i1} represents the FDOA measurement error between the first observatory and the i observatory station, and obeys the normal distribution of zero mean and variance δ_f^2.

Formulas (2) and (3) are combined, that is, time-frequency difference equations. The position information of the target can be obtained by solving the equations, but the velocity and acceleration information of the target can not be obtained. Velocity and acceleration information can be obtained by filtering.

3   CRLB (Cramer-Rao Lower Bound)

As shown in the previous section, τ_{i1} obeys the normal distribution with mean $\tau_i - \tau_1$ and variance δ_τ^2, and its joint probability density distribution is as follows:

$$p(\mathbf{p}(t)) = \frac{1}{\left(2\pi\delta_\tau^2\right)^{(M-1)/2}} exp\left[-\frac{1}{2\delta_\tau^2}\sum_{i=2}^{M}(\tau_{i1} - (\tau_i - \tau_1))^2\right]$$

f_{i1} obeys the normal distribution with mean $f_i - f_1$ and variance δ_f^2, and its joint probability density distribution is as follows:

$$p(\mathbf{p}(t), \dot{\mathbf{p}}(t)) = \frac{1}{\left(2\pi\delta_f^2\right)^{(M-1)/2}} exp\left[-\frac{1}{2\delta_f^2}\sum_{i=2}^{M}(f_{i1} - (f_i - f_1))^2\right]$$

The joint probability density distributions of the above two are as follows:

$$p(\mathbf{p}(t), \dot{\mathbf{p}}(t))$$
$$= \frac{1}{\left(4\pi^2\delta_\tau^2\delta_f^2\right)^{(M-1)/2}} exp\left[-\frac{1}{2\delta_\tau^2}\sum_{i=2}^{M}(\tau_{i1} - (\tau_i - \tau_1))^2 - \frac{1}{2\delta_f^2}\sum_{i=2}^{M}(f_{i1} - (f_i - f_1))^2\right]$$

Let $\boldsymbol{\theta} = [\mathbf{p}(t) \quad \dot{\mathbf{p}}(t)] = [x \quad y \quad z \quad \dot{x} \quad \dot{y} \quad \dot{z}]^T$, $\mathbf{g} = [\tau_2 - \tau_1 \quad \cdots \quad \tau_M - \tau_1$
$f_2 - f_1 \cdots f_M - f_1]^T$.
The Jacobian matrix is:

$$\mathbf{J} = \frac{\partial\mathbf{g}}{\partial\boldsymbol{\theta}} = \begin{bmatrix} \frac{\partial\mathbf{g}_1}{\partial\theta_1} & \cdots & \frac{\partial\mathbf{g}_1}{\partial\theta_6} \\ \vdots & \vdots & \vdots \\ \frac{\partial\mathbf{g}_M}{\partial\theta_1} & \cdots & \frac{\partial\mathbf{g}_M}{\partial\theta_6} \end{bmatrix}$$

The variance of the observed noise is: $\mathbf{Q}_2 = diag\left[\underbrace{\delta_\tau^2\cdots\delta_\tau^2}_{M-1}, \underbrace{\delta_f^2\cdots\delta_f^2}_{M-1}\right]$

From this, we can get Fisher Information $\mathbf{F}(\boldsymbol{\theta})$: $\mathbf{F}(\boldsymbol{\theta}) = \mathbf{J}^T \mathbf{Q}_2^{-1} \mathbf{J}$.
Therefore, CRLB is: $CRLB(\boldsymbol{\theta}) = \mathbf{F}^{-1}$.

4 Filtering Process

The non-linearity of target location and tracking problem originates from the non-linearity of function in state equation and observation equation and the non-Gaussian of related noise process, so the prerequisite of Kalman filter is not satisfied.

The moving target adopts uniform acceleration motion model, and its motion state equation is as follows:

$$\begin{cases} x(t) = x(t-T) + T\dot{x}(t-T) + \frac{T^2}{2}\ddot{x}(t-T) + \frac{T^2}{2}\delta_x(t-T) \\ \dot{x}(t) = \dot{x}(t-T) + T\ddot{x}(t-T) + T\delta_x(t-T) \\ \ddot{x}(t) = \ddot{x}(t-T) + \delta_x(t-T) \\ y(t) = y(t-T) + T\dot{y}(t-T) + \frac{T^2}{2}\ddot{y}(t-T) + \frac{T^2}{2}\delta_y(t-T) \\ \dot{y}(t) = \dot{y}(t-T) + T\ddot{y}(t-T) + T\delta_y(t-T) \\ \ddot{y}(t) = \ddot{y}(t-T) + \delta_y(t-T) \\ z(t) = z(t-T) + T\dot{z}(t-T) + \frac{T^2}{2}\ddot{z}(t-T) + \frac{T^2}{2}\delta_z(t-T) \\ \dot{z}(t) = \dot{z}(t-T) + T\ddot{z}(t-T) + T\delta_z(t-T) \\ \ddot{z}(t) = \ddot{z}(t-T) + \delta_z(t-T) \end{cases} \tag{4}$$

Among them, T is the time interval, $\delta_x(t)$, $\delta_y(t)$ and $\delta_z(t)$ are the interference in x, y and z directions respectively, which can be regarded as system noise.

The equation of state of the system can be described as:

$$\mathbf{x}(n) = \mathbf{F}(n, n-1)\mathbf{x}(n-1) + \Gamma(n, n-1)\mathbf{v}_1(n-1) \tag{5}$$

Among them,

$$\mathbf{x}(n) = [x(n)\ y(n)\ z(n)\ \dot{x}(n)\ \dot{y}(n)\ \dot{z}(n)\ \ddot{x}(n)\ \ddot{y}(n)\ \ddot{z}(n)] \tag{6}$$

$$\mathbf{F}(n, n-1) = \begin{bmatrix} 1 & 0 & 0 & T & 0 & 0 & \frac{T^2}{2} & 0 & 0 \\ 0 & 1 & 0 & 0 & T & 0 & 0 & \frac{T^2}{2} & 0 \\ 0 & 0 & 1 & 0 & 0 & T & 0 & 0 & \frac{T^2}{2} \\ 0 & 0 & 0 & 1 & 0 & 0 & T & 0 & 0 \\ 0 & 0 & 0 & 0 & 1 & 0 & 0 & T & 0 \\ 0 & 0 & 0 & 0 & 0 & 1 & 0 & 0 & T \\ 0 & 0 & 0 & 0 & 0 & 0 & 1 & 0 & 0 \\ 0 & 0 & 0 & 0 & 0 & 0 & 0 & 1 & 0 \\ 0 & 0 & 0 & 0 & 0 & 0 & 0 & 0 & 1 \end{bmatrix}$$

$$\Gamma(n, n-1) = \begin{bmatrix} \frac{T^2}{2} & 0 & 0 & T & 0 & 0 & 1 & 0 & 0 \\ 0 & \frac{T^2}{2} & 0 & 0 & T & 0 & 0 & 1 & 0 \\ 0 & 0 & \frac{T^2}{2} & 0 & 0 & T & 0 & 0 & 1 \end{bmatrix}^T$$

$$\mathbf{v}_1(n-1) = \left[\delta_x(n-1)\ \delta_y(n-1)\ \delta_z(n-1)\right]^\mathsf{T}$$

The variance of system noise is

$$\mathbf{Q}_1(n) = E\left[\mathbf{v}_1(n)\,\mathbf{v}_1(n)^T\right] = diag\left[\delta_x^2, \delta_y^2, \delta_z^2\right].$$

The observation equation of the system is as follows:

$$\begin{aligned}
\mathbf{z}(n) &= \mathbf{h}(n) + \mathbf{v}_2(n) \\
&= \left[\tau_{21}(n)\ \cdots\ \tau_{M1}(n)\ f_{21}(n)\ \cdots\ f_{M1}(n)\right]^T + \mathbf{v}_2(n)
\end{aligned} \tag{7}$$

Among them, $\mathbf{v}_2(n)$ is the observation noise and its variance is

$$\mathbf{Q}_2(n) = E\left[\mathbf{v}_2(n)\,\mathbf{v}_2(n)^T\right] = diag\left[\underbrace{\delta_\tau^2 \cdots \delta_\tau^2}_{M-1}, \underbrace{\delta_f^2 \cdots \delta_f^2}_{M-1}\right]$$

The Jacobian matrix of the measurement equation is:

$$\begin{aligned}
\mathbf{H}(n) &= \frac{\partial \mathbf{h}(n)}{\partial \hat{\mathbf{x}}(n|L_{n-1})} \\
&= \begin{bmatrix}
\frac{\partial \tau_{i1}}{\partial \hat{x}(n|L_{n-1})} & \frac{\partial \tau_{i1}}{\partial \hat{y}(n|L_{n-1})} & \frac{\partial \tau_{i1}}{\partial \hat{z}(n|L_{n-1})} & 0 & 0 & 0 & 0 & 0 & 0 \\
\frac{\partial f_{i1}}{\partial \hat{x}(n|L_{n-1})} & \frac{\partial f_{i1}}{\partial \hat{y}(n|L_{n-1})} & \frac{\partial f_{i1}}{\partial \hat{z}(n|L_{n-1})} & \frac{\partial f_{i1}}{\partial \hat{z}(n|L_{n-1})} & \frac{\partial f_{i1}}{\partial \hat{y}(n|L_{n-1})} & \frac{\partial f_{i1}}{\partial \hat{z}(n|L_{n-1})} & 0 & 0 & 0
\end{bmatrix}
\end{aligned}$$

EKF filtering model and UKF filtering model are composed of (5) equation of state and (7) equation of observation to track moving target. The EKF filtering process is as follows:

(1) Initialization of filtering:

$$\hat{\mathbf{x}}(0|L_0) = E[\mathbf{x}(0)]$$
$$\mathbf{P}(0) = E\left\{[\mathbf{x}(0) - E[\mathbf{x}(0)]][\mathbf{x}(0) - E[\mathbf{x}(0)]]^H\right\}$$

(2) Further state prediction:

$$\hat{\mathbf{x}}(n|L_{n-1}) = \mathbf{F}(n, n-1)\hat{\mathbf{x}}(n-1|L_{n-1})$$

(3) One-step prediction state error autocorrelation matrix:

$$\mathbf{P}(n, n-1) = \mathbf{F}(n, n-1)\mathbf{P}(n-1)\mathbf{F}^H(n, n-1) + \Gamma(n, n-1)\mathbf{Q}_1(n-1)\Gamma^H(n, n-1)$$

(4) Kalman gain:

$$\mathbf{K}(n) = \mathbf{P}(n, n-1)\mathbf{H}^H(n)\left[\mathbf{H}(n)\mathbf{P}(n, n-1)\mathbf{H}^H(n)\mathbf{Q}_2(n)\right]^{-1}$$

(5) State estimation:

$$\hat{\mathbf{x}}(n|L_n) = \hat{\mathbf{x}}(n|L_{n-1}) + \mathbf{K}(n)[\mathbf{z}(n) - \mathbf{h}(\hat{\mathbf{x}}(n|L_{n-1}), n)]$$

(6) State estimation error autocorrelation matrix:

$$\mathbf{P}(n) = [\mathbf{I} - \mathbf{K}(n)\mathbf{H}(n)]\mathbf{P}(n, n-1)$$

(7) Repeat steps (1) to (6) to calculate the recursive filtering.

Taking proportional symmetric sampling as an example, The UKF filtering process is as follows:

(1) The filtering initialization is the same as that of EKF.
(2) After UT transformation, $2N_x + 1$ Sigma points are obtained:

$$\chi(n) = \left[\mathbf{x}(n) - \left[\sqrt{(N_x + \lambda)\mathbf{P}(n)}\right]_i \cdots \mathbf{x}(n) \cdots \mathbf{x}(n) + \left[\sqrt{(N_x + \lambda)\mathbf{P}(n)}\right]_i\right]$$

$$i = 1, \cdots, N_x$$

In the formula, N_x denotes the dimension of the state estimation vector $\mathbf{x}(n)$. $\left[\sqrt{(N_x + \lambda)\mathbf{P}(n)}\right]_i$ represents the i column of the root of the matrix $(N_x + \lambda)\mathbf{P}(n)$. The corresponding sampling point weights are:

$$\begin{cases} W_0^m = \lambda/(L+\lambda) \\ W_0^c = \lambda/(L+\lambda) + (1 - \alpha^2 + \beta) \\ W_i^m = W_i^c = 1/[2(L+\lambda)], i = 1, \cdots, 2N_x \end{cases}$$

In the formula, m denotes the weight of the mean and c denotes the weight of the covariance. Parametric $\lambda = \alpha^2(N_x + \kappa) - N_x$ is a scaling parameter, which determines the distance between the sampling point and the mean value. The value range of α is $[10^{-4}, 1]$, which controls the distribution of sampling points. The value of κ needs to guarantee the semi-positive definiteness of matrix $(N_x + \lambda)\mathbf{P}(n)$, which is usually $3 - N_x$. β is a non-negative weight coefficient, usually takes the value of 2, which can combine the dynamic difference of higher-order terms in the equation improve the accuracy of calculation.

(3) One-step state prediction data set:

$$\chi(n+1|L_n) = f(\chi(n), n)$$

(4) The data set is weighted and merged to obtain a one-step state prediction vector:

$$\hat{\mathbf{x}}(n+1|L_n) = \sum_{i=0}^{2N_x} W_i^{(m)} \boldsymbol{\chi}_i(n+1|L_n)$$

(5) One-step state prediction error autocorrelation matrix:

$$\mathbf{P}(n+1|L_n) = \sum_{i=0}^{2N_x} W_i^{(c)} \left[\boldsymbol{\chi}_i(n+1|L_n) - \hat{\mathbf{x}}(n+1|L_n)\boldsymbol{\chi}_i(n+1|L_n) - \hat{\mathbf{x}}(n+1|L_n)^T \right] + \mathbf{Q}_1$$

(6) Repeat UT transform to get a new set of sigma points:

$$\mathbf{Z}(n+1|L_n) = h(\boldsymbol{\chi}(n+1|L_n), n+1)$$

$$\hat{\mathbf{z}}(n+1|L_n) = \sum_{i=0}^{2N_x} W_i^{(m)} \mathbf{Z}_i(n+1|L_n)$$

$$\mathbf{P}_{zz}(n+1|L_n) = \sum_{i=0}^{2N_x} W_i^{(m)} [\mathbf{Z}_i(n+1|L_n) - \hat{\mathbf{z}}(n+1|L_n)][\mathbf{Z}_i(n+1|L_n) - \hat{\mathbf{z}}(n+1|L_n)]^T + \mathbf{Q}_2$$

(7) The cross-correlation matrix of the state vector and the observation vector is:

$$\mathbf{P}_{xz}(n+1|L_n) = \sum_{i=0}^{2N_x} W_i^{(m)} [\boldsymbol{\chi}_i(n+1|L_n) - \hat{\mathbf{x}}(n+1|L_n)][\mathbf{Z}_i(n+1|L_n) - \hat{\mathbf{z}}(n+1|L_n)]^T$$

(8) Kalman gain and state update:

$$\mathbf{K}(n+1) = \mathbf{P}_{xz}(n+1|L_n)[\mathbf{P}_{zz}(n+1|L_n)]^{-1}$$

$$\hat{\mathbf{x}}(n+1|L_{n+1}) = \hat{\mathbf{x}}(n+1|L_n) + \mathbf{K}(n+1)[\mathbf{z}(n+1) - \hat{\mathbf{z}}(n+1|L_n)]$$

$$\mathbf{P}(n+1) = \mathbf{P}(n+1|L_n) - \mathbf{K}(n+1)\mathbf{P}_{zz}(n+1|L_n)\mathbf{K}^T(n+1).$$

5 Simulation

In order to verify the application effect of EKF and UKF filtering on moving target location and tracking, simulation analysis is carried out on MATLAB platform. Assume that the position of the target is (180, 170, 10) (km), the velocity is (0, 50, 0) (m/s), and the acceleration is (5, 0, 0) (m/s^2). The central frequency of the target signal is 1 GHz. Here, the number of observatories is 3 and the distribution is triangular. The locations are (30, 5, 0) (km), (40, 10, 0) (km), (50, 15, 0) (km), the velocities are (0, 10, 0) (m/s) and the accelerations are (0, 10, 0) (m/s^2). The time difference accuracy is

120 ns and the frequency difference accuracy is 2 Hz. Through the above filtering process, the filtering results are shown in Figs. 2 and 3.

Figure 1 is a schematic diagram of the trajectory of three base stations and their targets. The three base stations move in the same direction, i.e., the y-axis. The target moves in the x-axis direction. From Figs. 2 and 3, it can be seen that the method used in this paper can locate and track the trajectory of the target, and track the velocity and acceleration of the target at the same time. Moreover, it can achieve high positioning accuracy and estimation accuracy.

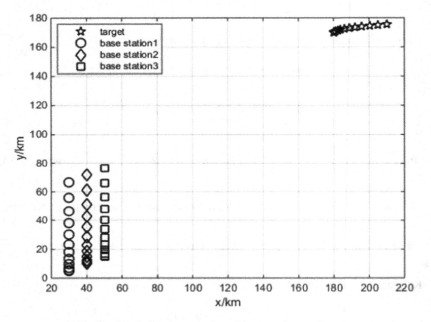

Fig. 1. Motion trajectory plan of base station and target

In the process of linearization, higher order terms are omitted. For strong nonlinear systems, the approximation accuracy of EKF is not high, so the estimation accuracy of EKF for strong nonlinear systems is poor. At the same time, the Jacobian matrix of some non-linear systems is not available, and EKF is only suitable for the case of small one-step prediction error of filtering error. These shortcomings limit the further development of EKF. UKF uses UT transformation to deal with the transfer of mean and covariance of nonlinear systems. The linearization of the nonlinear system is avoided, the higher order terms are retained, and the transmission accuracy of the system's Gauss density is improved. The simulation results show that UKF can obtain better positioning results, and can be used in the situation of long-term positioning and tracking of air moving targets.

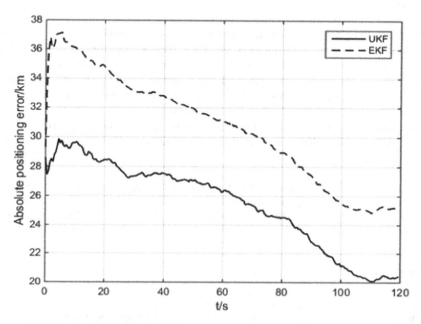

Fig. 2. Comparing the location error curves of EKF and UKF algorithms

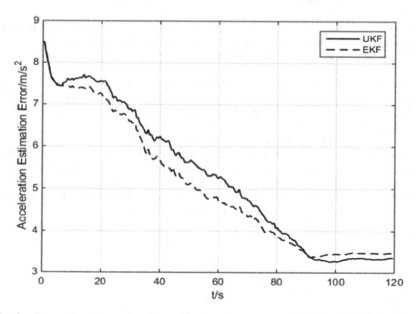

Fig. 3. Comparing the acceleration estimation error curves of EKF and UKF algorithms

6 Conclusion

In this paper, the problem of location and tracking of air moving targets by moving Multi-stations is studied. EKF method and UKF method are used to filter the time-frequency difference data. The moving target adopts uniform acceleration motion model to locate and track the target, and can estimate the velocity and acceleration information of the target at the same time. The simulation results show that UKF can achieve high positioning accuracy in location tracking, velocity estimation and acceleration estimation. It has a certain reference value for the engineering realization of the position tracking and velocity and acceleration estimation of aerial moving targets by moving multi-stations.

Acknowledgment. The authors would like to thank the anonymous reviewers for their careful review and constructive comments. This work was supported in part by the National Natural Science Foundation of China (NSFC) under Grant 61771108 and U1533125, and the Fundamental Research Funds for the Central Universities under Grant ZYGX2015Z011.

References

1. Chen, Y.M., Tsai, C.L., Fang, R.W.: TDOA/FDOA mobile target localization and tracking with adaptive extended Kalman filter. In: International Conference on Control (2017)
2. Ge, L., Wei, Y., Dan, S., et al.: Toward effectiveness and agility of network security situational awareness using moving target defense (MTD). In: SPIE Defense + Security (2014)
3. Reggiani, L., Morichetti, R.: Hybrid active and passive localization for small targets. In: International Conference on Indoor Positioning and Indoor Navigation (2010)
4. Fitzgerald, B.: A passive localization algorithm and its accuracy analysis. IEEE J. Ocean. Eng. **12**(1), 234–245 (1987)
5. Venkatraman, S., Caffery, J.J.: Hybrid TOA/AOA techniques for mobile location in non-line-of-sight environments. In: Wireless Communications and Networking Conference (2004)
6. Li, W., Wei, P., et al.: A robust TDOA-based location method and its performance analysis. Sci. China **52**(5), 876–882 (2009)
7. Severino, G., Zaccaron, A., Ardoino, R.: Airborne passive location based on combined time and frequency difference of arrival. Int. J. Microw. Wirel. Technol. **1**(3), 201–207 (2009)
8. Mastrogiovanni, F., Sgorbissa, A., Zaccaria, R.: How the location of the range sensor affects EKF-based localization. J. Intell. Robot. Syst. **68**(2), 121–145 (2012)
9. Lin, M., Sheng, L.: Multi-sensor distributed information fusion UKF filter for passive location. In: Chinese Control and Decision Conference (2010)

Variable Scale Iterative SAR Imaging Algorithm Based on Sparse Representation

Zhenzhu Zha, Qun Wan$^{(\boxtimes)}$, Yue Yang, Di Zhang,
and Yuanyuan Song

University of Electronic Science and Technology of China,
Chengdu 611731, China
wanqun@uestc.edu.cn

Abstract. In this paper, we discuss the problem of sparse recovery in compressed sensing (CS) in the presence of measurement noise, and present a variable iterative synthetic aperture radar (SAR) imaging method based on sparse representation. In this paper, the sparse reconstruction theory is applied to SAR imaging. The SAR imaging problem is equivalent to solving the sparse solution of the underdetermined equation, and the imaging result of the target scene is obtained. Compared with the previous algorithms using l_1-norm or l_2-norm as cost function model, this paper combines l_p-norm $(0 < p < 1)$ and l_2-norm as cost function model to obtain more powerful performance. In addition, a smoothing strategy has been adopted to obtain the convergence method under the non-convex case of l_p-norm term. In the framework of this iterative algorithm, the proposed algorithm is compared with some traditional imaging algorithms through simulation experiments. Finally, the simulation results show that the proposed algorithm improves the SAR signal recovery performance to a certain extent and has a certain anti-noise ability. In addition, the improvement is more evident when the SAR signal is block sparse.

Keywords: Synthetic aperture radar (SAR) · Sparse representation · Regularization · Block sparse

1 Introduction

SAR has recently become and will continue to be an important sensor for various remote sensing applications, especially because it overcomes some limitations of other sensing modalities. Firstly, SAR is an active sensor using its own illumination. In order to illuminate the interesting ground area, SAR sensors use microwave signals to ensure the SAR imaging capability in harsh weather conditions for 24 h without interruption. Because of these characteristics of SAR, SAR image formation has become an important research topic. The problem of SAR image formation is a typical example of the inverse problems in imaging [1].

Traditional SAR imaging synthesizes virtual antenna aperture through platform motion, achieves high resolution in azimuth direction, and achieves high resolution in range direction by pulse compression. Traditional imaging algorithms are limited by Nyquist sampling theorem in echo data sampling, which requires not only high

© ICST Institute for Computer Sciences, Social Informatics and Telecommunications Engineering 2019
Published by Springer Nature Switzerland AG 2019. All Rights Reserved
G. Gui and L. Yun (Eds.): ADHIP 2019, LNICST 302, pp. 219–228, 2019.
https://doi.org/10.1007/978-3-030-36405-2_23

sampling rate, but also equal interval. The transmission, storage and calculation of a large amount of data exert a great pressure on radar system, which greatly affects the real-time performance of the whole system. For example, although the Fourier transform-based PFA [1] imaging method is simple to implement and widely used, the imaging effect will inevitably be affected by side lobes, which will reduce the resolution. For the case of partial missing of the radar sampling data, the traditional PFA method often estimates missing information by linear prediction. However, the data extrapolation inevitably causes errors, so it can not get ideal imaging effect. The SAR imaging method based on sparse representation not only does not have side lobes, but also does not require uniform sampling of the observed data. It can also achieve imaging in the case of missing part of the sampled data. On the other hand, in the fields of radar imaging, communication signal and image processing, the collected observation signal is not always the final required signal, but also has to undergo some preprocessing, which obviously brings a waste of computation to signal processing. CS [2, 3] theory breaks the limitation of Nyquist theorem and is quickly applied in SAR imaging. CS theory points out that sparse signals or signals transformed into sparse signals on a set of sparse bases can be sampled at a rate much lower than the Nyquist sampling rate, and the low-dimensional signals can be recovered by some algorithms with great probability.

In 2007, Baraniuk and others first formally introduced CS theory into radar imaging [4]. For sparse scenes, under the condition of reducing the amount of sampled radar echo data, the sparse optimization algorithm can achieve high resolution non-ambiguous imaging. And the feasibility of CS in radar imaging is proved by theoretical analysis and numerical simulation experiments. In 2009, Herman et al. proposed the concept of high resolution compressed sensing radar [5, 6]. The compressed sensing radar transmits Alltop sequence signals to ensure the incoherence between transmitted signals, and then uses CS technology to reconstruct sparse scenes. In 2010, Patel et al. introduced the concept of random pulse repetition frequency into compressed sensing radar for spotlight SAR imaging. Compared with the traditional fixed pulse repetition frequency radar, the new radar system can effectively reduce the amount of echo sampling data [7]. Scholars have also studied the algorithms of sparse signal processing in typical applications such as bi-base radar imaging and multi-base radar imaging [8, 9]. With the deepening of research, sparse signal processing theory has been proved to be successful in solving the inverse problems in many applications, such as magneto-optics [10], direction of arrival estimation [11], SAR feature extraction [12], etc., and even gradually formed a sparse microwave imaging theory in the application of radar imaging. Sparse restoration methods can be classified as follows: greedy algorithms, such as Orthogonal Matching Pursuit (OMP) and Compressive Sampling Matching Pursuit (CoSaMP); probabilistic algorithms considering prior distribution of signals; convex optimization methods for solving convex relaxation problems [13].

SAR imaging based on sparse representation not only has low sampling rate, but also does not require uniform sampling, which avoids the impact of partial missing of sampling data on the imaging effect [1]. SAR imaging under sparse representation is a typical inverse problem and a typical ill-posed problem. The ill-posed problem often has no unique solution, and may even be insoluble, especially for SAR imaging under sparse representation. Sparse representation theory points out that the sampling rate needed to recover the signal can be much smaller than that of Nyquist, so SAR imaging under sparse representation is an underdetermined set of equations. In this paper, a variable scale method using DFP formula based on sparse representation is used to solve SAR imaging problem by introducing a l_p-norm regularized sparse constraint. Article shows the performance of encouraging sparsity of the l_p-norm [14].

In the second section, we give the description of SAR echo model, and give the sparse representation form of the SAR signal. In the third section, we will introduce the proposed imaging algorithm in detail. The fourth section contains the simulation results. Finally, the conclusion is drawn in the fifth section.

2   SAR Observation Model

The SAR beam geometry and the ground plane geometry used in this paper are shown in Fig. 1. We assume that the target body coordinate system has $x - y$ (representing range and cross-range coordinates respectively), and the center of which is O in space. The coordinate system centers on the ground patch through a relatively narrow RF beam from the mobile radar. Due to the geometric structure of radar and the physical characteristics of observation process, the scattering function is included in the set of received signals. SAR continuously transmits/receives pulses to the target scene during flight. The received data are complex values, whose amplitude corresponds to the scattering signal intensity of the target, and the phase represents the scattering

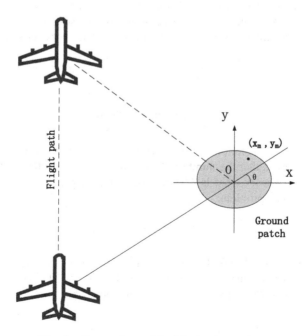

Fig. 1. Geometric model of SAR observations

characteristics. Using the high frequency hypothesis, the complex response of the target scene can be approximated to the superposition of the response of L independent scatterers in the scene. Therefore, the phase history is described as:

$$s(k, \theta) = \sum_{m=1}^{L} r(x_m, y_m) exp\{-j2k(x_m \cos \theta + y_m \sin \theta)\} \tag{1}$$

where $k = 2\pi/\lambda_0$ is the spatial frequency, θ is the azimuth, $r(x_m, y_m)$ is the scattering center coefficient at (x_m, y_m). Considering the noise environment, formula (1) can be expressed in matrix form:

$$\mathbf{s} = \mathbf{\Phi r} + \mathbf{n} \tag{2}$$

where $\mathbf{s} \in \mathbb{C}^M$ represents the measurement with noise, M is the sum of discrete sampling points of azimuth and frequency, $\mathbf{r} \in \mathbb{C}^N$ represents the SAR complex image to be reconstructed, and N is the size of the original scene, that is, the sum of discrete points of range and cross-range. $\mathbf{\Phi} \in \mathbb{C}^{M \times N}$ is the overcomplete dictionary, and $\mathbf{n} \in \mathbb{C}^M$ accounts for additive i.i.d. complex Gaussian noise.

For solving this set of equations, we need to consider the following problems: firstly, under the influence of observation noise, the system is often unsolvable, so it can not be solved directly. Secondly, if the zero space of the overcomplete dictionary $\mathbf{\Phi}$ is not empty, that is, the number of equations is less than the number of unknowns, then the solution of the set of equations is not unique. Thirdly, when the observation data $\mathbf{s}$ contains perturbations, the estimation of the target scenario $\hat{\mathbf{r}}$ remains unchanged, that is, the solution of the equation set is stable. Fourthly, the solution of the equation set should contain prior information, which conforms to the characteristics of the target scenario.

We introduce the idea of the least square to find the best matching least square solution:

$$\hat{\mathbf{r}}_{ls} = \arg \min_{\mathbf{r}} \|\mathbf{s} - \mathbf{\Phi r}\|_2^2 \tag{3}$$

But the least square solution can not guarantee the stability of the solution.

This paper assumes that the number of measurements is less than the total number of atoms in the dictionary, that is $M \ll N$. SAR imaging can be recast as a robust sparse signal recovery problem:

$$\min_{\mathbf{r}} \|\mathbf{s} - \mathbf{\Phi r}\|_0 \tag{4}$$

However, it is NP-hard to find the most sparse solution of general underdetermined equations, so the sparse constraints can be relaxed to l_p-norm $(0 < p < 1)$. Then, (4) can be expressed as a non-quadratic regularization problem:

$$\min_{\mathbf{r}} \|\mathbf{s} - \mathbf{\Phi}\mathbf{r}\|_2^2 + \mu\|\mathbf{r}\|_p \tag{5}$$

where μ is a given regularization parameter.

3 SAR Imaging Algorithm

For formula (5), we have a cost function as follows:

$$\mathbf{J}(\mathbf{r}) = \|\mathbf{s} - \mathbf{\Phi}\mathbf{r}\|_2^2 + \mu\|\mathbf{r}\|_p \tag{6}$$

To avoid the problem caused by the nondifferentiability of l_p-norm at the origin, the smoothing approximation [15] is used as follows:

$$\|\mathbf{r}\|_p \approx \sum_{i=1}^{N} (r_i^2 + \xi)^{p/2} \tag{7}$$

where ξ is a nonnegative small constant.

Therefore, the derivation of formula (6) is as follows:

$$\nabla \mathbf{J}(\mathbf{r}) = \left[2\mathbf{\Phi}^H\mathbf{\Phi} + \mu\frac{p}{2}\mathbf{D}(\mathbf{r})\right]\mathbf{r} - 2\mathbf{\Phi}^H\mathbf{s} \tag{8}$$

where H represents the conjugate transposition of the matrix and

$$\mathbf{D}(\mathbf{r}) = \begin{bmatrix} (r_1^2 + \xi)^{p/2-1} & 0 & 0 & 0 \\ 0 & (r_2^2 + \xi)^{p/2} & \cdots & 0 \\ \vdots & \vdots & \ddots & \vdots \\ 0 & 0 & \cdots & (r_N^2 + \xi)^{p/2} \end{bmatrix}$$

In this paper, a variable scale iterative method using DFP formula is considered to solve the problem. This method defines the correction matrix as follows [16]:

$$\Delta \mathbf{H}_j = \frac{p^{(j)}p^{(j)T}}{p^{(j)T}q^{(j)}} - \frac{\mathbf{H}_j q^{(j)}q^{(j)T}}{q^{(j)T}\mathbf{H}_j q^{(j)}} \tag{9}$$

Therefore, we can obtain the iterative formula:

$$\mathbf{H}_{j+1} = \mathbf{H}_j + \frac{p^{(j)}p^{(j)T}}{p^{(j)T}q^{(j)}} - \frac{\mathbf{H}_j q^{(j)}q^{(j)T}}{q^{(j)T}\mathbf{H}_j q^{(j)}} \tag{10}$$

This method does not need to compute the inverse of Hessian matrix. For general cases, the variable scale algorithm has superliner convergence rate. The implementation steps of sparse variable scale iterative (SVSI) SAR imaging algorithm are shown at Table 1.

Table 1. The implementation steps of SVSI SAR imaging algorithm

SVSI algorithm

1.   Initialize $\mathbf{r}^{(1)}$, $\mathbf{H}_1 = \mathbf{I}_N$.

2.   Let $j = 1$ and calculate the gradient at $\mathbf{r}^{(1)}$:

$$\mathbf{g}_1 = \nabla \mathbf{J}(\mathbf{r}^{(1)}).$$

3.   Let $\mathbf{d}^{(j)} = -\mathbf{H}_j \mathbf{g}_j$.

4.   Starting from $\mathbf{r}^{(j)}$ and searching along direction $d^{(j)}$, the step size λ_j is obtained to satisfy the requirement:

$$\mathbf{J}(\mathbf{r}^{(j)} + \lambda_j \mathbf{d}^{(j)}) = \min_{\lambda \geq 0} \mathbf{J}(\mathbf{r}^{(j)} + \lambda \mathbf{d}^{(j)})$$

then let $\mathbf{r}^{(j+1)} = \mathbf{r}^{(j)} + \lambda_j \mathbf{d}^{(j)}$.

5.   Stop when $\left\| \mathbf{r}^{(j+1)} - \mathbf{r}^{(j)} \right\| / \left\| \hat{\mathbf{r}}^{(j)} \right\|$ is less than a predetermined threshold ε. Let $\hat{\mathbf{r}} = \mathbf{r}^{(j+1)}$. Otherwise, turn to step 6.

6.   If $j = N$, let $\mathbf{r}^{(1)} = \mathbf{r}^{(j+1)}$, and return to step 2. Otherwise proceed to step 7.

7.   Let $\mathbf{g}_{j+1} = \nabla \mathbf{J}(\mathbf{r}^{(j+1)})$, $\mathbf{p}^{(j)} = \mathbf{r}^{(j+1)} - \mathbf{r}^{(j)}$, $\mathbf{q}^{(j)} = \mathbf{g}_{j+1} - \mathbf{g}_j$.

Set $j := j + 1$.

4 Simulation Experiment

The convergence speed of SVSI is related to the initial value. If the initial value close to the real value can be used, the computation will be greatly reduced. In this paper, $\hat{\mathbf{r}}^{(1)} = 2\kappa \mathbf{\Phi}^H \mathbf{s}$ is used as the initial input and the convergence speed is faster. In this section, the effectiveness of the proposed method is demonstrated by combining the simulation experiment of a group of radar observations. The radar parameters used in the experiment are shown at Table 2. This paper defines the normalized mean squared error NMSE $= \| \hat{\mathbf{r}} - \mathbf{r} \|_2^2 / \| \mathbf{r} \|_2^2$ as the evaluation index. The smaller the NMSE, the higher the image reconstruction quality. Next, we give the experimental results to verify the application effect of SVSI algorithm in sparse SAR imaging and block sparse SAR imaging.

Table 2. SAR system parameters.

SAR system parameters	
Bandwidth (MHz)	800
Center frequency (GHz)	9
The observation azimuth	87.5°–92.5°
Frequency sampling points	23
Azimuth sampling points	23
The signal-to noise ratio (SNR/dB)	30

Figure 2 shows the comparison of reconstructed images with different SNR. (a) and (b) are the original scene and the recovery result of PFA, respectively. (c) and (e) are the recovery results of LS algorithm and SVSI algorithm with SNR = 5 dB, and (d) and (f) with SNR = 20 dB. From Fig. 2, we can see that the traditional PFA is the worst, and the LS algorithm is more depend on the high SNR. And the proposed algorithm stably behaves good performance. In the Fig. 3, we apply the SVSI algorithm to block sparse SAR data, and the results show that when the sampling data becomes bigger and the inner structure of data is more complex, the PFA algorithm and LS algorithm are failed to reconstruct SAR image. However, SVSI algorithm reasonably reconstructs SAR image with a low NMSE = 0.0011. So we can see the improvement of the performance of the proposed algorithm and its possibility of application in the reconstruction of the block sparse SAR.

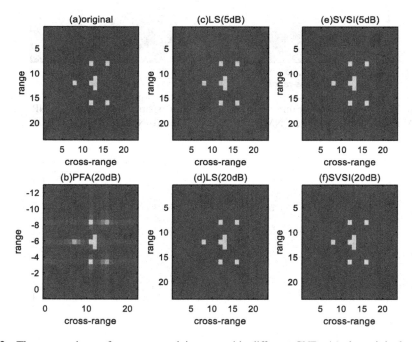

Fig. 2. The comparison of reconstructed images with different SNR. (a) the original scene. (b) the result of PFA with SNR = 20 dB. (c) the result of LS with SNR = 5 dB. (d) the result of LS with SNR = 20 dB. (e) the result of SVSI with SNR = 5 dB. (c) the result of SVSI with SNR = 20 dB.

Figure 4 shows the NMSE comparison of the least square algorithm and the SVSI algorithm with the variable SNR. SNR range from 5 dB to 40 dB. And form Fig. 4, we can see that with the increasing of SNR, that is to say the additive complex Gaussian noise is decreasing, NMSE both of LS and SVSI are decreasing. In addition, when SNR is relatively low, the performance of LS is so bed that sometimes it even can't to

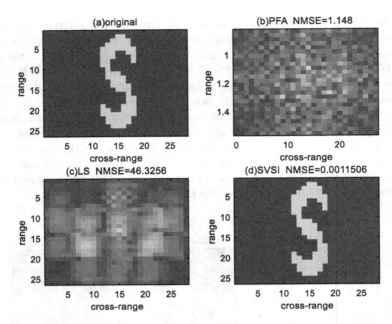

Fig. 3. The proposed algorithm is applied to block sparse SAR signal (SNR = 30 dB). (b) NMSE of PFA is 1.148. (c) NMSE of LS is 46.326. (d) NMSE of SVSI is 0.0011.

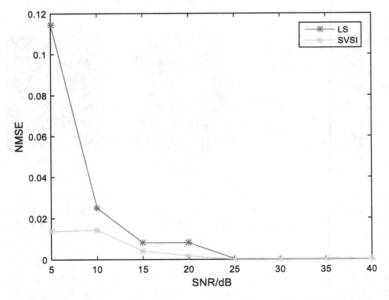

Fig. 4. The NMSE comparison of the least square algorithm and the SVSI algorithm with the variable SNR. SNR range from 5 dB to 40 dB.

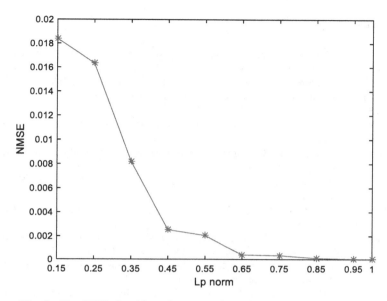

Fig. 5. The SVSI algorithm: the curve of NMSE with different value p.

reconstruct image. This result also illustrates that the proposed algorithm has a certain anti-noise ability. Figure 5 is the curve of NMSE with different l_p-norm. And SNR is 30 dB. From the curve, we know that the value of p is not randomly determined. When it's too small, the result becomes a little awful. So we should take an appropriate value.

5 Conclusion

This paper presents a SAR imaging algorithm based on sparse representation, which has the following advantages: no need to calculate the Hessian matrix; having a super-linear convergence rate. However, when the amount of data becomes large, the amount of storage required will become a problem. In the SAR synthesis scenario of this paper, it can be seen from the simulation results that the proposed algorithm not only performs well in sparse SAR image reconstruction, but also maintains good performance in the case of block sparse SAR. And at low SNR, it can also reconstruct SAR images completely with a tolerable NMSE, showing a certain anti-noise ability.

Acknowledgments. The authors would like to thank the anonymous reviewers for their careful review and constructive comments. This work was supported in part by the National Natural Science Foundation of China (NSFC) under Grant 61771108 and U1533125, and the Fundamental Research Funds for the Central Universities under Grant ZYGX2015Z011.

References

1. Li, X.: Synthetic aperture radar image formation for distributed target with sparse representation, pp. 12–28 (2016)
2. Donoho, D.L.: Compressed sensing. IEEE Trans. Inf. Theory **52**(4), 1289–1306 (2006)
3. Candes, E.J., Wakin, M.: An introduction to compressive sampling. IEEE Signal Process. Mag. **25**(2), 21–30 (2008)
4. Baraniuk, R., Steeghs, P.: Compressive radar imaging. In: IEEE Radar Conference, Boston, pp. 128–133 (2007)
5. Herman, M., Strohmer, T.: Compressed sensing radar. In: Proceedings in IEEE Radar Conference, Rome, pp. 1–6 (2008)
6. Herman, M., Strohmer, T.: High-resolution radar via compressed sensing. IEEE Trans. Signal Process. **57**(6), 2275–2284 (2009)
7. Patel, V.M., Easley, G.R., Healy, D.M.: Compressed synthetic aperture radar. IEEE J. Sel. Top. Signal Process. **4**(2), 244–254 (2010)
8. Stojanovic, I., Karl, W.C.: Imaging of moving targets with multi-static SAR using an overcomplete dictionary. IEEE J. Sel. Top. Signal Process. **4**(1), 164–176 (2010)
9. Ludger, P.: Application of compressed sensing to SAR/GMTI-Data. In: European Conference on Synthetic Aperture Radar, Aachen, pp. 7–10 (2010)
10. Zhang, Z., Rao, B.D.: Sparse signal recovery with temporally correlated source vectors using Sparse Bayesian Learning. IEEE J. Sel. Top. Signal Process. **5**, 912–926 (2011)
11. Tzagkarakis, G., Milioris, D., Tsakalides, P.: Multiple-measurement Bayesian compressed sensing using GSM priors for DOA estimation. In: IEEE International Conference on Acoustics, Speech and Signal Processing (ICASSP), Dallas, pp. 2610–2613 (2010)
12. Cong, X.C., Zhu, R.Q., Liu, Y.L.: Feature extraction of SAR target in clutter based on peak region segmentation and regularized orthogonal matching pursuit. In: Signal and Information Processing (ChinaSIP), pp. 189–193 (2014)
13. Elad, M.: Sparse and Redundant Representations: From Theory to Applications in Signal and Image Processing. Springer, New York (2010). https://doi.org/10.1007/978-1-4419-7011-4
14. Wen, F., Liu, P., Liu, Y.: Robust sparse recovery in impulsive noise via $l_p - l_1$ optimization. IEEE Trans. Signal Process. **65**(1), 105–118 (2017)
15. Özben Önhon, N.: A sparsity-driven approach for joint SAR imaging and phase error correction. IEEE Trans. Image Process. **21**(4), 2075–2088 (2012)
16. Baolin, C.: Optimization Theory and Algorithm, 2nd edn. Tsinghua University Press, Beijing (2005)

IoT Security Access Authentication Method Based on Blockchain

Yang Cheng[✉], Min Lei, Shiyou Chen, Zigang Fang,
and Shuaipeng Yang

Information Security Center,
Beijing University of Posts and Telecommunications, Beijing, China
chengyangmc@bupt.edu.cn

Abstract. With the rapid development of Internet of Things (IoT), The IoT terminal are diversified, and the attack points available to attackers are also diversified, and most IoT terminal are more vulnerable to attacks because they are less secure. In order to achieve secure access of IoT terminal, ensure the legality of IoT terminal accessing the network, improve the security of terminal entering the network and reduce the security risks that IoT terminal may be exposed to when accessing the platform. This paper proposes a secure method to access to the IoT, which is to use the blockchain to store and verify the fingerprint information of the terminal, thereby improving the security of the IoT terminal accessing the cloud. And this paper also proposes a method to store the fingerprint blockchain of the terminal in the IoT terminal, and then verify the collected fingerprint information through the data in the blockchain to ensure the credibility of the fingerprint information.

Keywords: IoT · Access authentication · Blockchain

1 Introduction

The rapid development of IoT technology has brought society into the era of interconnection of all things. Under the background of full connection of people and things, the number of IoT terminal has grown rapidly. However, while the IoT is booming, it also exposes many security problems. Traditional security protection technology can not adapt to the new security situation of the IoT. The effective security defense system and security ecology between the IoT server, IoT terminal and communication network have not yet been established. In addition, with the IoT terminal joining the Internet, attackers can use a wider range of attacks, the terminal itself is less secure, more vulnerable to attacks. Security risk has become the biggest hidden danger in the application of the IoT. Attacks, hijackings and data embezzlement against IoT terminal are increasing day by day.

Security mechanism is one of the key technologies that determines the success of network convergence. In particular, access authentication mechanism is the first step to implement security protection. Since the implementation of the access authentication mechanism adopted by different networks is quite different, it is difficult to design an access authentication mechanism in the IoT environment enables the terminal to roam

G. Gui and L. Yun (Eds.): ADHIP 2019, LNICST 302, pp. 229–238, 2019.
https://doi.org/10.1007/978-3-030-36405-2_24

and enjoy services seamlessly among various wireless networks. And it has become a major technical challenge when converging networks. The existing technology combines IoT and blockchain are mostly used in networking and asset management, there is almost no involvement in IoT security access authentication. And many existing study on the technology of IoT access authentication are mostly innovative in the identity authentication and ignore the security of terminal information. This paper proposes a method to store the fingerprint blockchain in the IoT terminal, and then verify the collected fingerprint information through the data in the blockchain to ensure the credibility of the fingerprint information. The fingerprint information mentioned in this paper refers to the identity information of IoT terminal. In order to allow access to the cloud and send authentication requests, this will greatly reduce the possibility of an attacker simulating a legitimate terminal for cloud intrusion. At the same time, this paper uses the two-way HTTPS protocol and HMAC authentication technology, which effectively prevents man-in-the-middle attacks and ensures data integrity and confidentiality.

2   Related Work

2.1   Blockchain

Blockchain is a distributed database system in which nodes participate [1]. It is a supporting technology in Bitcoin applications. In 2008, Nakamoto put forward the concept of "blockchain" in Bitcoin White Paper, and created the Bitcoin social network and developed the first block called "Creation Block" in 2009. The blockchain contains a list of blocks that are constantly growing and neatly arranged. Each block contains a timestamp and a link to the previous block, so that the data in blockchain is designed to be unchangeable [2]. Once recorded, the data in one block will be irreversible. Therefore, it is unchangeable and unforgeable. Bitcoin records every transaction in the application on the blockchain ledger to ensure it can't be changed and can be traced back [3]. Since the successful application of Bitcoin, blockchain technology has begun to receive attention, it has been separated from bitcoin applications and played an important role in the fields of finance, education, and medical care. Blockchain can be divided into "data blocks" and "links". Its data block is a block generated by a blockchain network at intervals [4]. All data in the database is stored in each data block. The block information is encrypted with a password and hashed to ensure the integrity and correctness of the data in the block [5]. The information written on the blockchain will be verified by all nodes on the network to ensure that the information safety and efficiency. Once the information is written, it is difficult to modify or delete.

2.2   IoT Access Authentication

The IoT terminal access authentication technology is mainly used to check the identity of the terminal identity when access to the net. There is an authentication module in the terminal, which stores the digital certificate issued by the authority in a hardware encryption authentication card having a security encryption function and an identity authentication function [6]. Before the terminal accesses to the internal network, the terminal must pass the identity verification performed by the hardware encryption authentication card and the authentication server, so that it can ensure only the terminal that passes the network authentication can access to the intranet [7]. If not, the terminal will be refused to get the service.

IoT terminal device access authentication is a popular technology in the intranet security system, and preform several trends as follows [8]:

1. The terminal access authentication technology based on multiple technologies. At present, among the three commonly used access authentication technologies, NAC and NAP have become alliances, in another word, the network access device uses Cisco's NAC technology, and the host client uses Microsoft's NAP technology to achieve a complementary situation.
2. Access authentication mechanism based on multi-layered protection. Terminal access authentication is the portal of the internal network of the enterprise. To ensure the secure access of the terminal, it is necessary to authenticate and check the legitimacy and security of the access terminal from multiple levels.
3. Standardization of access authentication technology.

At present, although the technical principles of the access control schemes of various vendors are basically the same, the implementation methods of the various vendors are different, and the main difference is represented by the protocol [9]. For example, Cisco and Huawei chose to implement access control by adopting EAP protocol, RADIUS protocol and 802.1x protocol [10]. Microsoft chose to adopt DHCP and RADIUS protocol, while other vendors are still launching their own network standards. Entry and control standards [11]. Standards and norms are the footstone of the long-term development of technology. Therefore, standardization is the inevitable trend of access authentication technology development [12].

3   Algorithm Process

The architecture of the IoT is usually divided into three layers: "terminal", "pipe", "cloud", also the architecture representation of "end-pipe-cloud", where "end" means the terminal, "pipe" means the network transport layer, and "cloud" means the IoT cloud. IoT terminal generally has limited by its function, the level of security protection is not enough, and the number is widely distributed. Once a certain type of terminal has serious security problems, the scope of impact will be unimaginable. The terminal fingerprint refers to the terminal characteristics that can identify the terminal. The terminal fingerprint can be generated by the terminal's explicit identifier, which is an inherent identifier of the terminal can uniquely identify the terminal, such as the terminal's hard ID. Simultaneously, terminal fingerprints can be generated from the feature set of terminal implicit identifiers as well, such as terminal name, model, function and so on. The security access scheme of terminal on the perception layer makes use of the unique identification feature of terminal fingerprints to authenticate the identity of terminal in the IoT as a criterion for judging whether they are allowed to access the IoT. And the communication layer is protected by the two-way HTTPS protocol and HMAC technology at the transport layer at the same time. However, in the process of collecting fingerprint information, there is no security mechanism to improve the unforgeability of fingerprint information. This is an urgent problem to be solved for the secure access of IoT terminal. The access authentication method proposed in this paper mainly covers three parts: the collection of fingerprint information of the IoT terminal, the verification of fingerprint information and the access to the cloud. The overall architecture of the method is shown in Fig. 1.

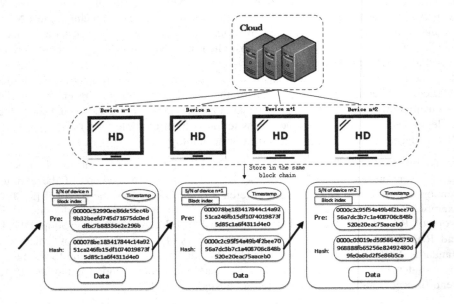

Fig. 1. Overall architecture.

3.1   Terminal Fingerprint Collection

In this paper, the terminal needs to collect its relevant information itself by its API interface as fingerprint P. before accessing to the IoT cloud.

The terminal fingerprint information P is a combination of a plurality of identifiers of the terminal, and includes two types of identifiers: an explicit identifier and an implicit identifier. The explicit identifier can uniquely identify the terminal, including the terminal serial number, terminal MAC address, user ID number, etc. In this paper, the terminal serial number and the terminal MAC address are used as the explicit identifier of the terminal, which can be obtained through a built-in shell script. The implicit identifier does not have the ability to uniquely identify. A single implicit identifier cannot uniquely identify the terminal. However, if multiple invisible identifiers are combined, the identification capability can be effectively improved. The implicit identifier can be invoked by the terminal. The interface is obtained by taking a smart camera as an example, including screen resolution, audio coding type, and terminal running frequency. In actual operation, for a certain terminal, the self-information $l(x)$ amount and information entropy $H(x)$ of the implicit identifier are calculated as the basis for selecting the implicit identifier. The self-information amount of the identifier is the variation of the terminal information. when tampering, the amount of the self-information is inversely proportional to the probability of passing the next verification, the information entropy contained in the identifier represents the weight of the terminal fingerprint as a whole.

$$l(x) = \log_2(1/p(x)) \tag{1}$$

$$H(x) = E[l(x_i)] = E[\log_2(1/p(x_i))] = -\sum p(x_i)\log_2 p(x_i) \tag{2}$$

3.2 Fingerprint Verification

In the built-in blockchain of the terminal, it extracts the data of the latest block B related to the terminal, and compare the terminal fingerprint P and the terminal account and password with the fingerprint recorded in the block B. Then it will determine whether it is allowed to access to the cloud and update information (the blockchain needs to be updated at the same time when updating the information).

The blockchain is distributed and stored in each terminal of the same type, that is, the blockchain contains fingerprint information of all terminal of the type. At the initial shipment of terminal, the initial blockchain is stored in the terminal, and each block in the initial blockchain stores relevant fingerprint information of the terminal according to the factory specific serial number of the terminal. Each block data is as shown in Fig. 2, and includes three parts, part 1 is explicit identifier dictionary which includes device S/N and MAC address, part 2 is recessive identifier dictionary and part 3 is the account and a key encrypted by the terminal initial public key, and the encryption algorithm is SM2.

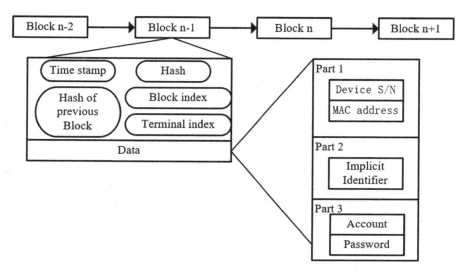

Fig. 2. Data in each block.

The whole system is a weakly centralized structure. The blockchain is a coinless blockchain, and the cloud is responsible for generating new blocks. Whenever a new block is generated, the cloud will also send blockchain update data to each terminal to ensure that the blockchain information of each terminal is consistent. When a blockchain of a terminal is maliciously tampered, then the authentication will fail in HMAC authentication.

The matching algorithm is shown in Fig. 3. The specific steps are as follows:

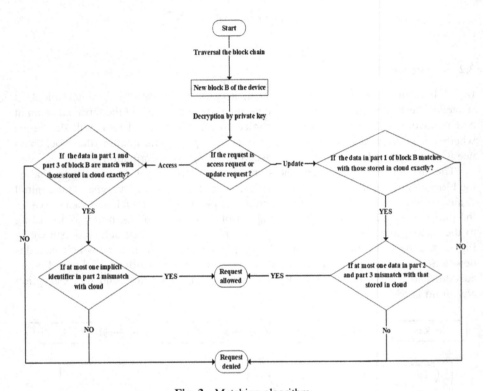

Fig. 3. Matching algorithm.

1. Traverses the data information of the latest block B related to the terminal, and decrypts the data of the three parts by using the private key.
2. Determine whether to access the cloud request or update the information request.
3. When the request is for accessing the cloud request, the data information of each part needs to be matched one by one, and if it cannot be matched one by one, the access to the cloud is denied. Since the implicit identifier of the terminal may change due to the small probability of the access environment, If at most one of the invisible identifiers does not match, the part 2 is judged to be matched, when the request is updated, the part 1 information is first, and if the part 1 information is matched, the matching determination of the part 2 and the part 3 is performed. When at most one of them does not match the blockchain information, the request is considered a legitimate update request. Assume that the update request completes the authentication. After the cloud confirms the request for the update information,

the cloud will generate a new block access blockchain based on the update information, and deliver the updated blockchain to each terminal.

3.3   Access to the Cloud

After verifying the fingerprint information P through the blockchain, the terminal will send an authentication request to the cloud, where the two-way HTTPS authentication and the adaptation of the blockchain HMAC authentication will be used. Pass through to complete the access operation.

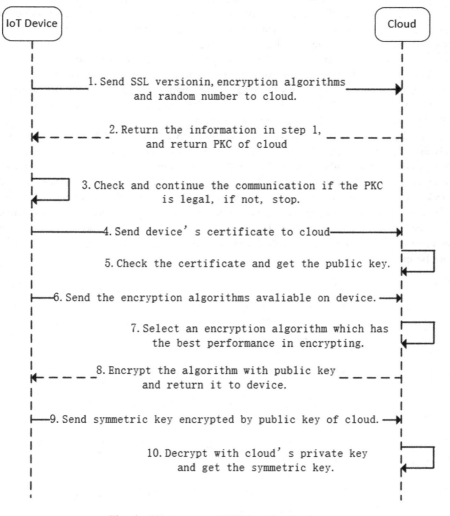

Fig. 4. The two-way HTTPS authentication.

The prerequisite for the two-way HTTPS authentication is that there are two or more certificates, one is a cloud certificate, and the other is a terminal certificate. The cloud saves the certificate of the terminal and trusts the certificate, and the terminal stores the certificate of the cloud and trust the certificate. In this way, the request response can be completed if the certificate verification is successful. As shown in Fig. 4.

The principle of the HMAC authentication is that the terminal initiates a request to the cloud, and the request encapsulates the blockchain information of the terminal, and the cloud verifies whether the blockchain information of the terminal is consistent with the blockchain information stored by the terminal. If the verification fails, the access is denied. When the verification succeeds, the cloud generates a random number and sends it to the terminal. After receiving the random number, the terminal hashes it with the private key to get the summary information H, and sends it to the cloud, the cloud hash the terminal's secret key from its own database with random numbers to get abstract message H'. The cloud compares the message H with H', and establish a connection to process the request from the terminal if verification succeeds.

The cloud will preferentially process the normal access authentication request of each terminal, and then process the update information request, and the update information request of each terminal also needs to be controlled by a certain amount in a unit time, thereby controlling the block speed of cloud.

The key used in the HAMC authentication process is agreed by both parties in advance, and it is impossible for a third party to know. As can be seen from the entire process of HAMC authentication in Fig. 5, the attacker can only intercept the random number as a "challenge" and the HMAC result as a "response", and cannot calculate the key based on the two data. Because the key is not known, the attacker cannot forge the correct response. At the same time, since the "challenge" random number obtained by each request is different, the attacker cannot replay the request, so the data security of the IoT device interacting with the cloud during the access authentication process can be ensured.

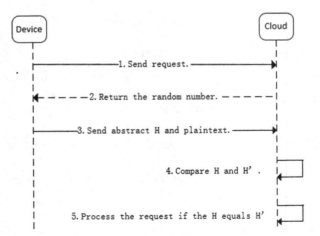

Fig. 5. The HAMC authentication.

4   Conclusion

With the rapid development of the IoT, more and more smart terminal are connected to the network for our lives. Along with the explosive growth of equipment access, the management and maintenance of centralized management solutions are under great pressure, and the disadvantages are gradually highlighted, accompanied by a single point of trust. In face of the rapid growth of access to IoT terminal, this paper analyzes the access authentication technologies that are available at present and proposes their existing problems: forgery. And then, proposing the research content of the paper, combining with blockchain technology to complete fingerprint information collection, storage and verification. At the same time, this paper considers the security in the process of information transmission, and uses the two-way HTTPS protocol and HMAC technology to protect the communication data.

Acknowledgments. This work is supported by the National Key R&D Program of China (2017YFB0802703), National Natural Science Foundation of China grant (U1836205), Major Scientific and Technological Special Project of Guizhou Province (20183001), Open Foundation of Guizhou Provincial Key Laboratory of Public Big Data (2018BDKFJJ014), Open Foundation of Guizhou Provincial Key Laboratory of Public Big Data (2018BDKFJJ019) and Open Foundation of Guizhou Provincial Key Laboratory of Public Big Data (2018BDKFJJ022).

References

1. Kosba, A., Miller, A., Shi, E., Wen, Z., Papamanthou, C.: Hawk: the blockchain model of cryptography and privacy-preserving smart contracts. In: 2016 IEEE Symposium on Security and Privacy (SP), San Jose, CA, pp. 839–858. IEEE (2016)
2. Ouaddah, A., Elkalam, A.A., Ouahman, A.A.: Towards a novel privacy-preserving access control model based on blockchain technology in IoT. In: Rocha, Á., Serrhini, M., Felgueiras, C. (eds.) Europe and MENA Cooperation Advances in Information and Communication Technologies. AISC, vol. 520, pp. 523–533. Springer, Cham (2017). https://doi.org/10.1007/978-3-319-46568-5_53
3. Ouaddah, A., Elkalam, A.A., Ouahman, A.A.: A new blockchain-based access control framework for the internet of things. Secur. Commun. Netw. **9**(18), 5943–5964 (2016)
4. Di Francesco Maesa, D., Mori, P., Ricci, L.: Blockchain based access control. In: Chen, L.Y., Reiser, H.P. (eds.) DAIS 2017. LNCS, vol. 10320, pp. 206–220. Springer, Cham (2017). https://doi.org/10.1007/978-3-319-59665-5_15
5. Le, T., Mutka, M.W: CapChain: a privacy preserving access control framework based on blockchain for pervasive environments. In: 2018 IEEE International Conference on Smart Computing (2018)
6. Pinno, O.J.A., Gregio, A.R.A., De Bona, L.C.E.: ControlChain: blockchain as a central enabler for access control authorizations in the IoT. In: 2017 IEEE Global Communications Conference, GLOBECOM 2017, Singapore, pp. 1–6. IEEE (2017)
7. Dorri, A., Kanhere, S.S., Jurdak, R.: Towards an optimized BlockChain for IoT. In: 2017 IEEE/ACM Second International Conference on Internet-of-Things Design and Implementation (IoTDI), Pittsburgh, PA, pp. 173–178. IEEE (2017)
8. Novo, O.: Blockchain meets IoT: an architecture for scalable access management in IoT. IEEE Internet Things J. **5**(2), 1184–1195 (2018)

9. Lunardi, R.C., Michelin, R.A., Neu, C.V., Zorzo, A.F.: Distributed access control on IoT ledger-based architecture. In: 2018 IEEE/IFIP Network Operations and Management Symposium, NOMS 2018, Taipei, pp. 1–7. IEEE (2018)
10. Ourad, A.Z., Belgacem, B., Salah, K.: Using blockchain for IOT access control and authentication management. In: Georgakopoulos, D., Zhang, L.-J. (eds.) ICIOT 2018. LNCS, vol. 10972, pp. 150–164. Springer, Cham (2018). https://doi.org/10.1007/978-3-319-94370-1_11
11. Zhang, Y., Kasahara, S., Shen, Y., Jiang, X., Wan, J.: Smart contract-based access control for the internet of things. IEEE Internet Things J. 6(2), 1594–1605 (2019)
12. Bao, Z., Shi, W., He, D., Chood, K.K.R.: A three-tier blockchain-based IoT security architecture (2018)

Continuous Predictive Model for Quality of Experience in Wireless Video Streaming

Wenjuan Shi[1,2(✉)] and Jinqiu Pan[2]

[1] College of Physics and Electronical Engineering,
Yancheng Teachers University, Yancheng 224007, China
shiwj@yctu.edu.cn
[2] College of Telecommunications and Information Engineering,
Nanjing University of Posts and Telecommunications, Nanjing 210003, China

Abstract. Because of bandwidth and buffer limitation in wireless network, rebuffering events and bitrate drop often cause video impairments, e.g. compression artifacts and video stalling. Hence, these problems often make a loss of the quality of experience (QoE). For making a prediction about the impact of video impairments on QoE, a continuous predictive model for QoE in wireless video streaming is proposed. In this paper, the inputs are composed of three vectors that are the quality of video frame, rebuffering events state and human memory effect, and the output represents the predicted continuous QoE. We build the predictive model by a Hammerstein-Wiener model. Experimental results show that the proposed model can accurately make a prediction about continuous subjective QoE.

Keywords: Quality of experience (QoE) · Continuous QoE · Frame quality · Rebuffering event · Memory effect

1 Introduction

With the proliferation of smartphones, mobile video has gradually has enriched the mobile user experience. However, users are expecting to view high-quality videos by mobile smart devices. Because wireless channel has dynamic variation characteristics, it is very difficult to predict the network throughput, which can dynamically cause video transmission bitrate changing during video playing, therefore leading to affect user experience. For improving the performance of video services, it is essential to observe the quality of videos and predict the video quality for end-users.

When videos are playing, if the receiving buffer has little video data, the playing video will be interrupted to wait for new data to fill in the buffer. Such events are called rebuffering events (RE). In [1], it is shown that frequent RE can stop observers watching videos. Additionally, end users prefer video fluency to video clarity, thus ensuring video playing smoothly can efficaciously improve user experience.

For accommodating to the dynamic bandwidth changes, there are some state-of-the-art streaming techniques developed [2–7]. In the applications of wireless video streaming, quality of experience (QoE) is the finest standard to make a measurement for

G. Gui and L. Yun (Eds.): ADHIP 2019, LNICST 302, pp. 239–248, 2019.
https://doi.org/10.1007/978-3-030-36405-2_25

the quality of videos. Precise continuous predicted QoE can offer a benchmark to optimize the strategies of resource allocation in changeable wireless network.

For studying the impact factor on QoE, we consider continuous prediction for QoE as a continuous time series predictive problem, and then analyze the factors which can affect user experience, and select frame quality (FQ), rebuffering events and human memory effects (ME) to establish a predictive model, which can predict QoE accurately and supply a benchmark for evaluating the performance of video streaming control strategy.

2   Factors Impacting on QoE

It is helpful to analyze the factors impacting on QoE for understanding the influence of various events on QoE. In this section, we analyse the impact of bitrate changes, rebuffering events and memory effects on continuous QoE.

2.1   Effect of Bitrate on Continuous QoE

Because of the bandwidth dynamics in wireless network, the bitrate inevitably varies during video transmission [8]. In [9], it is shown that bitrate variation has an effect upon user perception.

Human visual system (HVS) is highly sensitive to image edge, and has Orientation Selectivity Visual Pattern (OSVP) to extract the visual content [9, 10, 22]. In [11, 23], it is shown that each frame can be mapped into an OSVP-based histogram (OSVPH), and the extracted frame quality can be applied to make a measurement about the influence of bitrate changes on QoE. Thus we extract the quality of each frame by OSVPH, and take frame quality as one of the inputs in our proposed model.

2.2   Rebuffering Events Impacting on QoE

Rebuffering events (RE) can result in video stalling while observers are watching videos, which usually affects QoE [12]. For studying the impact of RE on QoE, we analyze RE impacting on QoE by the attributes of stalls, e.g. times, duration and position.

A. Stalling Times

For analyzing the impact of stalling times on QoE, we study the QoE for videos with initial delay and different times of stalls, as illustrated in Fig. 1.

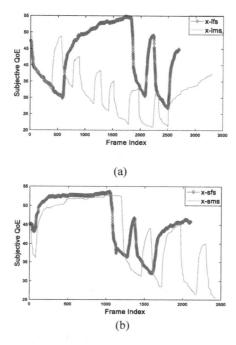

(a)

(b)

Fig. 1. The QoE of a video with initial delay and different times of stalls.

Figure 1(a) represents a continuous QoE of the videos with long initial delay and few/multiple stalls (x-lfs and x-lms); Fig. 1(b) shows a continuous QoE of the videos with a short initial delay and few/multiple stalls (x-sfs and x-sms). From Fig. 1, when stalling times increases, QoE has a tendency to be smaller even when the video quality recovers to an acceptable level after stalls happen. We can observe that the stalling times can seriously affect QoE.

B. Duration of Stalls

For analyzing the impact of stalling duration on continuous QoE, supposing the initial delay and times of stalls are invariable, the subjective QoE of videos with different duration stalls is studied, as illustrated in Fig. 2. Figure 2(a) illustrates a continuous QoE of videos with short initial delay and medium stalls (x-sms) and the videos with short initial delay and long stalls (x-sls); Fig. 2(b) illustrates a continuous QoE of videos with short initial delay and short stalls (x-sss) and the videos with short initial delay and medium stalls (x-sms). It is shown that duration has a serious influence on QoE, and the stalls which last long will decrease QoE even after video quality improves.

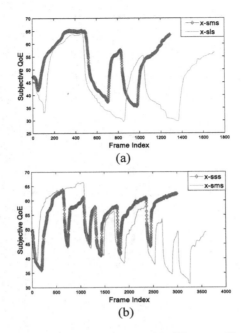

(a)

(b)

Fig. 2. The subjective QoE of videos with different stalling duration.

C. Stall Position

For better observing the impact of stall positions on continuous QoE, we use the Dynamic Time Warping (DTW) [14] to normalize the QoE of videos with different stall positions and the original reference video. The continuous QoE distribution before/after calculated by the DTW is illustrated in Fig. 3, and the DTW distance of the videos with stalls at different positions is listed in Table 1. The DTW method is one of the similarity measurement methods. While the DTW is smaller, the likelihood is greater, which means that the two time series are similar [22].

From Fig. 3 and Table 1, we can observe that no matter where the stalls occur, it will decrease the QoE, especially when continuous multi-stalls occur, the QoE will aggressively drop. In summary, we need to consider the impact of video stalls caused by RE on continuous QoE. Therefore, we take the RE state as one of the inputs in the proposed model.

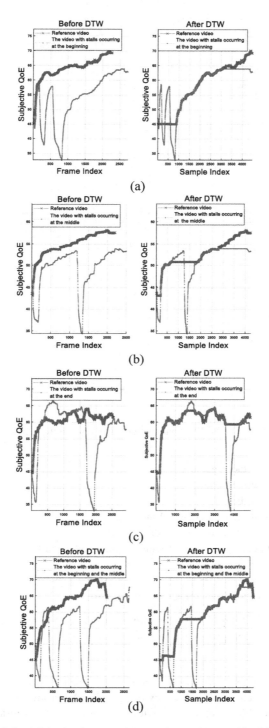

Fig. 3. The QoE of the original reference video and the videos with different stall positions before/after DTW and.

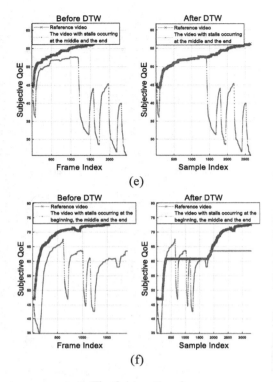

Fig. 3. (*continued*)

Table 1. The DTW of videos with stalls at different positions.

Video type	DTW distance
Videos with stalls at the beginning	3.6154
Videos with stalls at the middle	3.4256
Videos with stalls at the end	3.8518
Videos with stalls at the beginning and the middle	4.3839
Videos with continuous stalls at the middle and the end	10.0695
Videos with continuous stalls at the beginning, the middle and the end	9.0808

2.3 Human Memory Effect on Continuous QoE

When people are observing videos, they are usually affected by human memory effect (ME), e.g. recency effect, primacy effect and hysteresis effect.

(1) Recency Effect

It is well known that ME on the end part is better than others when people remember things, which is called recency effect [15, 22]. From Fig. 3 and Table 1, we can observe that the QoE of the videos with stalls at the end is a little smaller than the videos with stalls at other positions, and the DTW distance between the original reference video and the video with stalls at the end has a larger DTW value comparing with the videos with stalls at the beginning/middle. Therefore, recency effect on continuous QoE should be considered.

(2) Primacy Effect

Primacy effect is relevant to "the first impression" [16]. From Table 1, we can observe that the DTW distance between the QoE of the original reference video and that of the videos with stalls at the beginning is a little larger than the QoE of the videos with the stalls in the middle part. Thus,the stalls at the beginning has a greater impact on QoE than that at the middle. Therefore, primacy effect should also be considered.

(3) Hysteresis effect

In [17], it is shown that there is a hysteresis effect on continuous QoE during observing videos. Serious degradation of video quality during video playing impresses people negatively, and even that when video quality resumes to an acceptable level for observers, the poor impression still exists in people's memory, which causes a worse assessment for the videos.

Therefore, the impact of these memory effects on continuous QoE should not be ignored in the proposed model.

3   The Proposed Model

Considering that the Hammerstein-Wiener (HM) model can create a representation of human memory effect, we propose a block-structured nonlinear HW model. The input parameters, output parameters, and the proposed model are as follows.

A. The Inputs
From the above analysis, FQ, RE and ME are taken as the inputs of the proposed model.

(1) FQ: FQ is computed by OSVPH;
(2) RE: We define a Boolean variable RE_1, which can describe video state at time t, $RE_1 = 1$ when rebuffering events happen and $RE_1 = 0$ at the other time.
(3) ME: we take the ratio of the duration from the impairment event occurring to the end of the video to the total duration of the video as ME [22].

B. The Output
The output parameter is the predicted continuous QoE.

C. Predicted Model
The HW model is composed of one dynamic linear module and two static nonlinear modules. We describe the dynamic linear module by a transfer function with n_p poles and n_z zeros. Two static nonlinear modules represent the nonlinear relationship between the input parameters and the output parameter. The diagram of the Multiple Input Single Output (MISO) HW model is illustrated in Fig. 4.

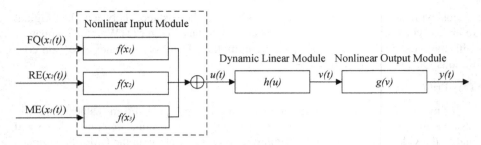

Fig. 4. The diagram of the predicted model.

In Fig. 4, z-transformation of the module $h(u)$ represents as $H(z)$. $u(t)$, $H(z)$, $y(t)$ and $f(t)$ are listed as

$$u(t) = f(x_1(t)) + f(x_2(t)) + f(x_3(t)) \tag{1}$$

$$H(z) = \frac{b_0 + b_1 z^{-1} + \cdots + b_m z^{-m}}{1 - a_1 z^{-1} - \cdots - a_n z^{-n}} \tag{2}$$

$$y(t) = g(v(t)) = \gamma_3 + \gamma_4 \frac{1}{1 + \exp(-\gamma_1 v(t) + \gamma_2)} \tag{3}$$

$$f(t) = \beta_3 + \beta_4 \frac{1}{1 + \exp(-\beta_1 x_i(t) + \beta_2)} \tag{4}$$

where $x_1(t)$ is frame quality vector, $x_2(t)$ is the state vector of rebuffering events, $x_3(t)$ is the vector of memory effect, t is the frame number, $a = [a_1, \ldots, a_n]^T$ and $b = [b_1, \ldots, b_m]^T$ are parameter vectors and $\gamma = [\gamma_1, \gamma_2, \gamma_3, \gamma_4]$ and $\beta = [\beta_1, \beta_2, \beta_3, \beta_4]$ are the parameters of the sigmoid function [22].

4   The Performance Evaluation of the Proposed Model

In order to evaluate the performance of our proposed model, LIVE-Netflix mobile Video Quality Assessment database [13] is used to test the proposed model.

In this paper, we use Root-Mean-Square Error (RMSE), Outage Rate (OR) [9] and DTW [14] to assess the performance of the proposed model. RMSE can measure the difference between two time series, which can capture the overall signal fidelity. The smaller RMSE value means that the tested model has better performance. OR can measure the frequency of times when the prediction value falls outside the 95% confidence interval. The smaller OR value means the prediction accuracy of the tested model is higher [8]. DTW can quantify the similarity of two time series, the smaller DTW value means the greater similarity possibility of the two series [14]. We take PSNR, SSIM [18], MS-SSIM [19], STRRED [20], OSVPH, NIQE [21] as frame quality assessment method for FQ. The comparison results are listed in Table 2, and we mark the model with the best performance in bold text.

Table 2. Experimental comparison of median performance of the proposed model with different FR assessment methods.

FQ assessment method	RMSE	OR	DTW
PSNR	0.0825	16.8950	39.1115
SSIM	0.0739	16.3569	27.7018
MS-SSIM	0.0753	14.6119	26.1974
NIQE	0.0630	42.9224	35.1000
STRRED	0.0593	8.3019	33.9887
OSVPH	**0.0566**	**2.0111**	**27.7486**

Table 3. Performance comparison of different models.

Model	RMSE	OR	DTW
NARX	0.3322	60.9302	97.3374
GH	0.1131	47.2727	35.0410
Proposed model	**0.0566**	**2.0111**	**27.7486**

From Table 2, the performance of the proposed model taking OSVPH as FQ is obviously better than the others. Furthermore, the performance of the proposed model with the NARX model [20] and GH model [18] is compared. We list the comparison results in Table 3. We also mark the model with best performance in bold text. From Table 3, we can observe that the performance of our proposed model is obviously better than the others.

5   Conclusion

For predicting the influence of video impairment events on QoE, we proposed a continuous prediction model for Quality of Experience in wireless video streaming. The inputs are composed of FR, RE, and ME. The output is the predicted QoE. We built the proposed model by a HW MISO model. The experimental results show that the predicted result of our proposed model can make an accurate prediction about the continuous subject Quality of Experience.

References

1. Ghadiyaram, D., Pan, J., Bovik, A.C.: A subjective and objective study of stalling events in mobile streaming videos. IEEE Trans. Circuits Syst. Video Technol. **29**(1), 183–197 (2019)
2. Oyman, O., Singh, S.: Quality of experience for HTTP adaptive streaming services. IEEE Commun. Mag. **50**(4), 20–27 (2012)
3. Seufert, M., Egger, S., Slanina, M., et al.: A survey on quality of experience of HTTP adaptive streaming. IEEE Commun. Surv. Tutor. **17**(1), 469–492 (2015)
4. ISO/IEC: ISO/IEC 23009-1 Dynamics Adaptive Streaming Over HTTP (DASH) (2014)

5. Tavakoli, S., Brunnstrom, K., Gutierrez, J., et al.: Quality of experience of adaptive video streaming: investigation in service parameters and subjective quality assessment methodology. Sig. Process. Image Commun. **39**, 432–443 (2015)
6. Garcia, M.N., Simone, F.D., Tavakoli, S., et al.: Quality of experience and HTTP adaptive streaming: a review of subjective studies. In: 2014 Sixth International Workshop on Quality of Multimedia Experience, Germany, pp. 141–146 (2014)
7. Tavakoli, S., Egger, S., Seufert, M., et al.: Perceptual quality of HTTP adaptive streaming strategies: cross-experimental analysis of multi-laboratory and crowdsourced subjective studies. IEEE J. Sel. Areas Commun. **34**(8), 2141–2153 (2016)
8. Moorthy, A.K., Choi, L.K., Bovik, A.C., et al.: Video quality assessment on mobile devices: subjective, behavioral and objective studies. IEEE J. Sel. Top. Sig. Process. **6**(6), 652–671 (2012)
9. Bampis, C.G., Li, Z., Bovik, A.C.: Continuous prediction of streaming video QoE using dynamic networks. IEEE Signal Process. Lett. **24**(7), 1083–1087 (2017)
10. Wu, J., Lin, W., Shi, G.: Orientation selectivity based visual pattern for reduced-reference image quality assessment. Inf. Sci. **351**, 18–29 (2016)
11. Shi, W., Sun, Y., et al.: Spatial and temporal feature-based reduced reference quality assessment for rate-varing videos in wireless networks. Int. J. Pattern Recogn. Artif. Intell. (to appear)
12. Ghadiyaram, D., Pan, J., Bovik, A.C.: A time-varying subjective quality model for mobile streaming videos with stalling events. In: Applications of Digital Image Processing XXXVIII, pp. 1–8 (2015)
13. LIVE-Netflix Mobile Video Quality Assessment Database. http://live.ece.utexas.edu/research/LIVE_NFLXStudy/nflx_index.html
14. Berndt, D.J., Clifford, J.: Using dynamic time warping to find patterns in time series. In: AAAI 1994 Workshop on Knowledge Discovery in Databases, New York, USA, pp. 359–370 (1994)
15. Hands, D.S., Avons, S.E.: Recency and duration neglect in subjective assessment of television picture quality. Appl. Cogn. Psychol. **15**(6), 639–657 (2001)
16. Greene, J., Prepscius, C., Levy, W.B.: Primacy versus recency in quantitative model activity is the critical distinction. Learn. Mem. **7**(1), 48–57 (2000)
17. Seshadrinathan, K., Bovik, A.C.: Temporal hysteresis model of time varying subjective video quality. In: 2011 IEEE International Conference on Acoustics, Speech and Signal Processing, pp. 1153–1156 (2011)
18. Wang, Z., Bovik, A.C., Sheikh, H.R., et al.: Image quality assessment: from error visibility to structural similarity. IEEE Trans. Image Process. **13**(4), 600–612 (2004)
19. Wang, Z., Simoncelli, E.P., Bovik, A.C.: Multiscale structural similarity for image quality assessment. In: Proceedings of Asilomar Conference on Signals, Systems, and Computers, pp. 1398–1402 (2003)
20. Soundararajan, R., Bovik, A.C.: Video quality assessment by reduced reference spatio-temporal entropic differencing. IEEE Trans. Circuits Syst. Video Technol. **23**(4), 684–694 (2013)
21. Mittal, A., Soundararajan, R., Bovik, A.C.: Making a "completely blind" image quality analyzer. IEEE Sig. Process. Lett. **20**(3), 209–212 (2013)
22. Shi, W., Sun, Y., Pan, J.: Continuous prediction for quality of experience in wireless video streaming. IEEE Access (2019)
23. Shi, W., Sun, Y., Li, S., Cao, Q., Wang, B.: Spatial and temporal feature-based reduced reference quality assessment for rate-varying videos in wireless networks. Int. J. Pattern Recogn. Artif. Intell. (2019)

Knowledge-Aided Group GLRT for Range Distributed Target Detection in Partially Homogeneous Environment

Yanling Shi[(✉)]

College of Telecommunications and Information Engineering,
Nanjing University of Post and Telecommunications, Nanjing 210003, China
ylshi@njupt.edu.cn

Abstract. In this paper, we consider the range distributed target detection in partially homogeneous clutter which satisfies a different statistical property in adjacent range cells. The group method wherein adjacent cells with slightly varied statistics are in the same group is presented firstly, which can improve the accuracy of modeling clutter. We assume that all texture of the compound Gaussian clutter satisfies an inverse Gamma distribution but scale and shape parameters in those groups differ from one another. The group generalized likelihood ratio test (G-GLRT) developed here concerns the cells group effects on deducing the GLRT. Considering a knowledge-aided (KA) model that tracking into account the partially homogeneous training samples, we develop a KA-G-GLRT for range-spread target detection and verify the constant false alarm rate (CFAR) with respect to the estimated covariance matrix of speckle. Experimental results are presented to illustrate the performance and effectiveness of the KA-G-GLRT in real clutter data.

Keywords: Group GLRT · Knowledge-aided · Target detection · Partially homogeneous sea clutter · Radar

1 Introduction

In recent years, there have been a large number of investigations on the signal detection problem in sea clutter with unknown covariance matrix (CM) [1–6]. Typically for the low range resolution radar, it is assumed that sea clutter at a range cell under test (CUT), which is also said to be primary data, may have the same statistical property with training samples. These training samples (also called secondary data) obtained from the range cells adjacent to the CUT contain sea clutter only, and are usually used to estimate the CM of sea clutter at the CUT. This scenario is often called homogeneous environment if the adjacent clutter has the same power level and the same CM [7–10]. However, the idealized homogeneous assumption is not suitable for the high radar range resolution, and this environment submits to a partially homogeneous scenario where the adjacent clutter behaves the similar CM structure with a diverse power factor [11, 12]. The higher radar range resolution scenario evolves to the inhomogeneous environment where the adjacent vectors do not share the same CM structure [13]. To mitigate the effects of nonhomogeneity, the authors in [14] advocate

© ICST Institute for Computer Sciences, Social Informatics and Telecommunications Engineering 2019
Published by Springer Nature Switzerland AG 2019. All Rights Reserved
G. Gui and L. Yun (Eds.): ADHIP 2019, LNICST 302, pp. 249–258, 2019.
https://doi.org/10.1007/978-3-030-36405-2_26

a Bayesian approach, and the authors in [15] improve the Bayesian approach to be feasible to the heterogeneous samples, which are more complicated than the inhomogeneous samples. In the heterogeneous scenario, the training data are clustered in groups, each group containing a similar but random CM. Although many authors assumed that the primary data have the same power levels, it is practically not the real case as authors in [16, 17] advocated. The power levels at the CUT were deterministic unknown constants different from each range cell [16], whereas the power levels at the CUT were random variables (RVs) and satisfied the same distribution (see inverse Gamma distribution) but with the significantly different distributed parameters [17]. In the above detectors, the authors only considered the partial homogeneity or the non-homogeneity for the sea clutter at the CUT and assumed the homogeneity for the sea clutter in the secondary data. Sea clutter collected from the sea surface have the same property, no matter they are from the primary data or from the secondary data.

In the paper, we will detect the range distributed target detection in partially homogeneous compound Gaussian (CG) clutter consisting of speckle modulated by texture. The speckle is modeled as a complex Gaussian random vector. The texture is modeled as an unknown deterministic or a RV, mainly satisfies Gamma, inverse Gamma or Pareto distribution [18, 19]. In [17], three types of group generalized likelihood ratio test (G-GLRT) were proposed by using the group strategy according to the variations of scale and shape parameters of texture at the CUT. However, the irrational assumption that secondary data were homogeneous brought a serious detecting performance loss. In [20], the primary and the secondary data were only partially homogeneous to the case in which their covariance matrices are mismatch according to a scaling factor other than one. In [21], Gao et al. modeled the disturbance covariance matrices of the secondary data in MIMO radar as random matrices satisfied the inverse Wishart distribution, and obtained the improved performance. In the paper, we assume secondary data are partially homogeneous and satisfy a knowledge-aided model (such as the inverse Wishart distribution), and develop a KA-G-GLRT for range-spread target detection in partially homogeneous sea clutter. The KA-G-GLRT possess the constant false alarm rate property (CFAR) to the estimated CM of speckle (ECMS). Experimental results are presented to illustrate the performance and effectiveness of the KA-G-GLRT in real clutter data.

The remainder of the paper is organized as follows: next section describes signal model and detection scheme. Section 3 analyzes the CFARness to the ECMS. Experimental results are provided to illustrate the detecting performance of the proposed detector in Sect. 4. Finally, Sect. 5 concludes the paper.

2   Signal Model and Detection Scheme

In the paper, the received echoes $\mathbf{z}_k \in \mathbb{C}^{N \times 1}$, $k = 1, 2, \cdots, K$, are composed of N pulse samples returning from the k-th range cell, where $\mathbb{C}$ being the complex field. Binary hypothesis testing is used to detect the range distributed target in clutter background:

$$H_1 : \begin{cases} \mathbf{z}_k = \alpha_k \mathbf{p} + \mathbf{c}_{pk} & k = 1, 2, \cdots, K \\ \mathbf{y}_l = \mathbf{c}_{sl} & l = 1, 2, \cdots, L \end{cases}$$

$$H_0 : \begin{cases} \mathbf{z}_k = \mathbf{c}_{pk} & k = 1, 2, \cdots, K \\ \mathbf{y}_l = \mathbf{c}_{sl} & l = 1, 2, \cdots, L \end{cases} \tag{1}$$

where, $\mathbf{p} \in \mathbb{C}^{N \times 1}$ is the known nominal steering vector; α_ks are energy distribution ratio of target in different range cells; Primary data $\mathbf{c}_{pk} \in \mathbb{C}^{N \times 1}$ is the additive sea clutter in the k-th range cell; Secondary data $\mathbf{c}_{sl} \in \mathbb{C}^{N \times 1}$ in the l-th range cell has a different CM with the primary data; K and L are the range number of the CUT and that of secondary data, respectively.

With the speckle $\mathbf{g}_k \sim CN(\mathbf{0}, \mathbf{M})$ and random texture τ_k, the primary clutter $\mathbf{c}_{pk}$ is modeled as the CG random process [7–10] with

$$\mathbf{c}_{pk} = \sqrt{\tau_k} \mathbf{g}_k, \quad \tau_k > 0 \tag{2}$$

where $\mathbf{M}$ is known initially, τ_k and $\mathbf{g}_k$ are independent of each other.

Gu et al. claimed that the textures in adjacent cells have different deterministic values [16]. Furthermore, Shi found that the textures behaved statistically different in adjacent cells, i.e. the parameters of PDF vary [17]. Referring to the group strategy [17] in partially homogeneous clutter environments, we firstly divide the K range cells into G groups, and h_g, $g = 1, 2, \cdots, G$, is the cell number in each group, $\sum_{g=1}^{G} h_g = K$.

It has been verified in [18] that the CG model with inverse Gamma texture is suitable for modeling clutter data. Therefore, we assume that the textures in all G groups satisfy an inverse Gamma distribution but scale parameters β_g and shape parameters η_g in those groups differ from one another. That reads

$$f_{IG}(\tau_k; \beta_g, \eta_g) = \frac{\beta_g^{\eta_g}}{\Gamma(\eta_g)} \frac{1}{\tau_k^{\eta_g + 1}} \exp\left(-\frac{\beta_g}{\tau_k}\right), g = 1, 2, \cdots, G,$$

$$H_g + 1 \le k \le H_g + h_g, \quad \tau_k > 0 \tag{3}$$

where

$$H_g = \begin{cases} 0, & g = 1 \\ \sum_{i=1}^{g-1} h_i, & g = 2, 3, \cdots, G \end{cases}, \quad \beta_g > 0, \quad \eta_g > 0 \tag{4}$$

The group partially homogeneous texture satisfies $f_{IG}(\tau_k; \beta_{g_1}, \eta_{g_1}) \ne f_{IG}(\tau_k; \beta_{g_2}, \eta_{g_2})$, if $g_1 \ne g_2$ and $g_1, g_2 = 1, 2, \cdots, G$. Define $\boldsymbol{\beta} = [\beta_1, \beta_2, \cdots, \beta_G]$, $\boldsymbol{\eta} = [\eta_1, \eta_2, \cdots, \eta_G]$ and $\mathbf{h} = [h_1, h_2, \cdots, h_G]$.

With $\mathbf{g}_k \sim CN(\mathbf{0}, \mathbf{M})$, the joint PDFs of $\mathbf{z}_1, \cdots, \mathbf{z}_K$ are

$$f_i(\mathbf{z}_1, \cdots, \mathbf{z}_K) = \int_0^\infty f_i(\mathbf{z}_1, \cdots, \mathbf{z}_K | \tau_k) f_{IG}(\tau_k; \beta_g, \eta_g) d\tau_k$$

$$= \prod_{g=1}^G \left[\frac{\beta_g^{\eta_g} \Gamma(N + \eta_g)}{\Gamma(\eta_g) |\mathbf{M}|} \right]^{h_g} \prod_{k=H_g+1}^{H_g+h_g} \left((\mathbf{z}_k - i\alpha_k \mathbf{p})^H \mathbf{M}^{-1} (\mathbf{z}_k - i\alpha_k \mathbf{p}) + \beta_g \right)^{-(N+\eta_g)},$$

$$(5)$$

where $i = 0$ and $i = 1$ correspond to H_0 and H_1, respectively. With the estimated parameters α_k, β_g and η_g by the maximum likelihood estimator and the method of moments, respectively, the G-GLRT is given by [17],

$$\sum_{g=1}^G \sum_{k=H_g+1}^{H_g+h_g} -(N+\eta_g) \ln \left[1 - \frac{\left| \mathbf{p}^H \mathbf{M}^{-1} \mathbf{z}_k \right|^2}{\left(\mathbf{z}_k^H \mathbf{M}^{-1} \mathbf{z}_k + \beta_g \right) \left(\mathbf{p}^H \mathbf{M}^{-1} \mathbf{p} \right)} \right] \underset{H_0}{\overset{H_1}{\gtrless}} \ln \xi. \qquad (6)$$

β_g are different in G groups, so are η_gs, the scenario is suitable for the group partially homogeneous clutter environment. When $\beta_{g_1} = \beta_{g_2}$ and $\eta_{g_1} = \eta_{g_2}$, with $g_1 \neq g_2$ and $g_1, g_2 = 1, 2, \cdots, G$, in this case, the G-GLRT reduces to the GLRT due to the homogeneous scenario [18].

Notice that, the known CMS $\mathbf{M}$ is not suitable in the partially homogeneous environment, we can establish the relationship for the CMS between in primary data and in secondary data. Firstly, we model $\mathbf{M}$ as a complex inverse Wishart random matrix [21],

$$\mathbf{M} \sim CW_N^{-1}(v, \lambda(v - N)\bar{\mathbf{M}}) \qquad (7)$$

where v denotes the degrees of freedom of the inverse Wishart distribution, $(v - N)\bar{\mathbf{M}}$ denotes the prior CM structure, and λ denotes the power level of speckle. The PDF of $\mathbf{M}$ is given by

$$f(\mathbf{M}) = \frac{|\lambda(v - N)\bar{\mathbf{M}}|^v}{\bar{\Gamma}_N(v)|\mathbf{M}|^{v+N}} etr[-(v - N)\lambda \mathbf{M}^{-1}\bar{\mathbf{M}}] \qquad (8)$$

where $\bar{\Gamma}_N(v) = \pi^{N(N-1)/2} \prod_{n=1}^N \Gamma(v - n + 1)$.

Then, we consider the maximum a posteriori (MAP) estimate of $\mathbf{M}$ by using the secondary data $\mathbf{y}_l$, $l = 1, \cdots, L$,

$$\hat{\mathbf{M}} = \arg \max_{\mathbf{M}} f(\mathbf{y}_1, \cdots, \mathbf{y}_L | \mathbf{M}) f(\mathbf{M})$$

$$\propto \frac{\lambda^{Nv}}{|\mathbf{M}|^{v+N+L}} etr\{-\mathbf{M}^{-1}[\mathbf{S} + (v - N)\lambda\bar{\mathbf{M}}]\} \qquad (9)$$

where $\mathbf{S} = \sum_{L=1}^L \mathbf{y}_l \mathbf{y}_l^H$. It follows from (9) that

$$\max_{\mathbf{M}}(v+N+L)\log(|\mathbf{M}^{-1}|) - tr\{\mathbf{M}^{-1}[\mathbf{S}+(v-N)\lambda\bar{\mathbf{M}}]\} \tag{10}$$

Referring to the conclusion in [21], we have

$$\hat{\mathbf{M}} = \frac{\mathbf{S}+(v-N)\lambda\bar{\mathbf{M}}}{v+N+L} \tag{11}$$

Substituting $\hat{\mathbf{M}}$ into (6), we obtain the KA-G-GLRT as

$$\sum_{g=1}^{G}\sum_{k=H_g+1}^{H_g+h_g}-(N+\eta_g)\ln\left[1-\frac{\left|\mathbf{p}^{\mathrm{H}}\hat{\mathbf{M}}^{-1}\mathbf{z}_k\right|^2}{\left(\mathbf{z}_k^{\mathrm{H}}\hat{\mathbf{M}}^{-1}\mathbf{z}_k+\beta_g\right)\left(\mathbf{p}^{\mathrm{H}}\hat{\mathbf{M}}^{-1}\mathbf{p}\right)}\right]\overset{\mathrm{H}_1}{\underset{\mathrm{H}_0}{\gtrless}}\ln\xi. \tag{12}$$

3   CFAR Property of the KA-G-GLRT

In this section, we focus on the CFAR property of the KA-G-GLRT. It has been testified in [17] that the G-GLRT has the CFAR property to β_g and $\mathbf{M}$. Here, we prove the KA-G-GLRT also has the CFARness to $\hat{\mathbf{M}}$.

Since the left-hand side of the KA-G-GLRT contains a RV $\hat{w}_k$,

$$\hat{w}_k = \frac{\left|\mathbf{p}^{\mathrm{H}}\hat{\mathbf{M}}^{-1}\mathbf{z}_k\right|^2}{\left(\mathbf{z}_k^{\mathrm{H}}\hat{\mathbf{M}}^{-1}\mathbf{z}_k+\beta_g\right)\left(\mathbf{p}^{\mathrm{H}}\hat{\mathbf{M}}^{-1}\mathbf{p}\right)} \tag{13}$$

the CFAR property to the $\hat{\mathbf{M}}$ of the KA-G-GLRT lies in whether the RV $\hat{w}_k$ is independent of the CMS, which will be shown as follows.

Let

$$\mathbf{v}_k = \mathbf{M}^{-1/2}\mathbf{g}_k, \mathbf{\mu}_l = \mathbf{M}^{-1/2}\mathbf{g}_l, l=1,\cdots,L, \mathbf{p}_0 = \mathbf{M}^{-1/2}\mathbf{p} \tag{14}$$

Then, $\mathbf{v}_k \sim CN(\mathbf{0},\mathbf{I}_N)$, $\mathbf{\mu}_l \sim CN(\mathbf{0},\mathbf{I}_N), l=1,\cdots,L$. Under the H_0 hypothesis,

$$\mathbf{z}_k^{\mathrm{H}}\hat{\mathbf{M}}^{-1}\mathbf{z}_k = \tau_k\mathbf{g}_k^{\mathrm{H}}\hat{\mathbf{M}}^{-1}\mathbf{g}_k = \tau_k\mathbf{v}_k^{\mathrm{H}}\left(\mathbf{M}^{-1/2}\hat{\mathbf{M}}\mathbf{M}^{-1/2}\right)^{-1}\mathbf{v}_k = \tau_k\mathbf{v}_k^{\mathrm{H}}\mathbf{W}^{-1}\mathbf{v}_k \tag{15}$$

where

$$\begin{aligned}\mathbf{W} &= \mathbf{M}^{-1/2}\hat{\mathbf{M}}\mathbf{M}^{-1/2} = \frac{1}{v+N+L}\mathbf{M}^{-1/2}\mathbf{S}\mathbf{M}^{-1/2} + \frac{(v-N)\lambda}{v+N+L}\mathbf{M}^{-1/2}\bar{\mathbf{M}}\mathbf{M}^{-1/2}\\ &= \frac{1}{v+N+L}\sum_{L=1}^{L}\tau_l\mathbf{\mu}_l\mathbf{\mu}_l^{\mathrm{H}} + \frac{(v-N)\lambda}{v+N+L}\mathbf{M}^{-1/2}\bar{\mathbf{M}}\mathbf{M}^{-1/2}\end{aligned} \tag{16}$$

Set $\mathbf{XX}^{\mathrm{H}} = \sum_{L=1}^{L} \boldsymbol{\mu}_l \boldsymbol{\mu}_l^{\mathrm{H}}$, here, $\sum_{L=1}^{L} \tau_l \boldsymbol{\mu}_l \boldsymbol{\mu}_l^{\mathrm{H}} = \mathbf{X}\boldsymbol{\Lambda}\mathbf{X}^{\mathrm{H}}$, and $\boldsymbol{\Lambda} = diag(\tau_l)$. Due to $\boldsymbol{\mu}_l \sim CN(\mathbf{0}, \mathbf{I}_N)$, we have $\boldsymbol{\Lambda}^{-1/2}\boldsymbol{\mu}_l \sim CN(\mathbf{0}, \boldsymbol{\Lambda})$, and $\mathbf{X}\boldsymbol{\Lambda}\mathbf{X}^{\mathrm{H}}$ satisfies the complex Wishart distribution with $\mathbf{X}\boldsymbol{\Lambda}\mathbf{X}^{\mathrm{H}} \sim CW_N(\mathbf{I}_N, \boldsymbol{\Lambda})$ for the IID random vectors $\boldsymbol{\mu}_l$. $\mathbf{M}^{-1/2}\bar{\mathbf{M}}\mathbf{M}^{-1/2}$ is a constant with the known $\bar{\mathbf{M}}$. Hence, random matrix $\mathbf{W}$ follows the complex Wishart distribution. Thus, $\mathbf{z}_k^{\mathrm{H}}\hat{\mathbf{M}}^{-1}\mathbf{z}_k$ under the H_0 hypothesis is independent of the CMS $\hat{\mathbf{M}}$.

Further, rotate the vector $\mathbf{p}_0$ into the first coordinate vector, and setting $\tilde{\boldsymbol{\upsilon}} = \mathbf{U}^{\mathrm{H}}\boldsymbol{\upsilon} \sim CN(\mathbf{0}, \mathbf{I})$, we have $\left|\mathbf{p}^{\mathrm{H}}\hat{\mathbf{M}}^{-1}\mathbf{z}_k\right|^2 / \left(\mathbf{p}^{\mathrm{H}}\hat{\mathbf{M}}^{-1}\mathbf{p}\right)$

$$\frac{\left|\mathbf{p}^{\mathrm{H}}\hat{\mathbf{M}}^{-1}\mathbf{z}_k\right|^2}{\mathbf{p}^{\mathrm{H}}\hat{\mathbf{M}}^{-1}\mathbf{p}} = \frac{\left|\mathbf{p}_0^{\mathrm{H}}\mathbf{W}^{-1}\boldsymbol{\upsilon}_k\right|^2}{\mathbf{p}_0^{\mathrm{H}}\mathbf{W}^{-1}\mathbf{p}_0} = \frac{\left|\mathbf{e}_1^{\mathrm{H}}\tilde{\mathbf{W}}^{-1}\tilde{\boldsymbol{\upsilon}}_k\right|^2}{\mathbf{e}_1^{\mathrm{H}}\tilde{\mathbf{W}}^{-1}\mathbf{e}_1} \tag{17}$$

where

$$\tilde{\mathbf{W}} = \mathbf{U}^{\mathrm{H}}\mathbf{W}\mathbf{U} = \frac{1}{\nu+N+L}\mathbf{U}^{\mathrm{H}}\sum_{l=1}^{L}\tau_l\boldsymbol{\mu}_l\boldsymbol{\mu}_l^{\mathrm{H}}\mathbf{U} + \frac{(\nu-N)\lambda}{\nu+N+L}\mathbf{U}^{\mathrm{H}}\mathbf{M}^{-1/2}\bar{\mathbf{M}}\mathbf{M}^{-1/2}\mathbf{U},$$
$$\mathbf{e}_1 = \mathbf{U}^{\mathrm{H}}\mathbf{p}_0, \quad \mathbf{e}_1 = [1\,0\,0\cdots 0]^{\mathrm{T}} \tag{18}$$

and $\mathbf{U}$ is a unitary matrix.

Table 1. The energy distribution ratio α_k of the range distributed target

Cell index	1	2	3	4	5	6	7	8	9	10	11	12
Model1	1/12	1/12	1/12	1/12	1/12	1/12	1/12	1/12	1/12	1/12	1/12	1/12
Model2	1/3	0	1/3	0	0	0	0	0	0	0	0	0
Model3	1/3	0	1/3	0	1/3	0	0	0	0	0	0	0
Model4	1/4	1/4	1/4	1/4	0	0	0	0	0	0	0	0

Similarly, the reasons that the random matrix $\mathbf{U}^{\mathrm{H}}\sum_{l=1}^{L}\tau_l\boldsymbol{\mu}_l\boldsymbol{\mu}_l^{\mathrm{H}}\mathbf{U} \sim CW_N(\mathbf{I}, \mathbf{U}^{\mathrm{H}}\boldsymbol{\Lambda}\mathbf{U})$ and $\mathbf{U}^{\mathrm{H}}\mathbf{M}^{-1/2}\bar{\mathbf{M}}\mathbf{M}^{-1/2}\mathbf{U}$ is a constant result in the random matrix $\tilde{\mathbf{W}}$ following the complex Wishart distribution.

Finally, the RV $\hat{w}_k$ can be rewritten as

$$\hat{w}_k = \frac{\left|\mathbf{e}_1^{\mathrm{H}}\tilde{\mathbf{W}}^{-1}\tilde{\boldsymbol{\upsilon}}_k\right|^2}{\left(\tau_k\boldsymbol{\upsilon}_k^{\mathrm{H}}\mathbf{W}^{-1}\boldsymbol{\upsilon}_k + \beta_g\right)\left(\mathbf{e}_1^{\mathrm{H}}\tilde{\mathbf{W}}^{-1}\mathbf{e}_1\right)} \tag{19}$$

Obviously, $\hat{w}_k$ is independent of the CMS $\hat{\mathbf{M}}$. Therefore, the KA-G-GLRT has the CFAR property to $\hat{\mathbf{M}}$.

In the following section, the performance of KA-G-GLRT will be evaluated.

4 Experimental Results and Performance Evaluation

We will evaluate the performance of the KA-G-GLRT and the compared detectors (1S-G-GLRT [17], GCC-GLRT [16], OS-GLRT [5], and NSDD-GLRT [4]) by Fynmeet radar data. The point that we wish to make that although the 1S-G-GLRT and the GCC-GLRT applied the group method, the former assumed that τ_ks were RVs in different range cells and the secondary data were homogeneous, and the later assumed that τ_ks were the unknown and different constants in all groups, whose values can be estimated by the likelihood estimator from the received sea echoes. In contrast, in our KA-G-GLRT, τ_k satisfies an inverse Gamma distribution with different parameters in G groups and the secondary data are partially homogeneous with an inverse Wishart distribution, which is a better approximation of the real complicated scenario than that in the 1S-G-GLRT and in the GCC-GLRT. The range distributed target is the multiple dominant scattering (MDS) model [16]. Set $K = 12$, the energy distribution ratio α_k of the target in each range cell is shown in Table 1.

The signal to clutter ratio is

$$SCR = \frac{1}{P_c} \sum\nolimits_{k=1}^{K} |A\alpha_k|^2, \tag{20}$$

where A is the amplitude of detecting target, and P_c is the power of $\mathbf{c}_{pk}$. $\overline{\mathbf{M}}$ is given by $\rho^{|i-j|}$ with a one-lag correlation coefficient ρ.

The analyzed data are TFA10-006 recorded by the Fynmeet radar in 2006 [22]. Figure 1 shows the detection performance of five detectors versus SCR with the parameters $L = 48$, $N = 4$, $K = 12$, $G = 3$, $\rho = 0$, $\nu = 24$, $\lambda = 2$, $\boldsymbol{\beta} = [0.133, 0.112, 0.604]$, $\boldsymbol{\eta} = [3.491, 2.260, 6.695]$, $\mathbf{h} = [3, 3, 6]$ and $P_f = 10^{-3}$. The reason of group may refer to [17]. The KA-G-GLRT behaves best for all five models, such as in model 4 (see Fig. 1(d)), the 1S-G-GLRT is below the KA-G- GLRT by approximately 1 dB, the OS-GLRT present about 2 dB worse, and the GCC-GLRT and NSDD-GLRT present about 3 dB worst. The NSDD-GLRT and the OS-GLRT are overcome by the KA-G-GLRT since the assumed homogeneous clutter in these two detectors deviates from the real clutter that is partially homogeneous. The simplified assumption that texture is an unknown constant leads to the worse behaviors of the GCC-GLRT than the KA-G-GLRT wherein the random texture, much more coinciding with the real environment, is used. Meanwhile, the KA speckle helps to promote the detection performance of the KA-G-GLRT compared to the 1S-G-GLRT. We can therefore draw a conclusion that the KA-G-GLRT behaves best in all four target models, and it has a more extensive applicability.

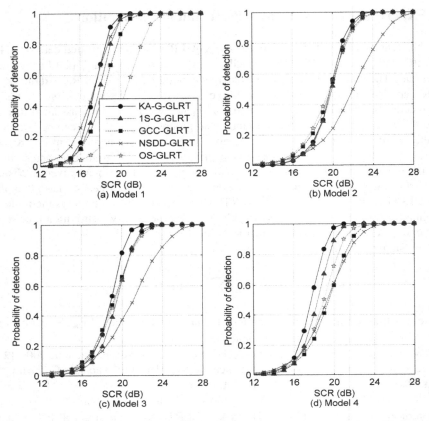

Fig. 1. Probability of detection versus SCR for the real data. (a) Model 1; (b) Model 2; (c) Model 3; (d) Model 4.

5   Conclusion

In this paper, we have dealt with the range distributed target detection in the grouped partially homogeneous clutter environment. CG clutter has been composed of inverse Gamma partially homogeneous texture and Gaussian speckle. A stochastic KA model with complex inverse Wishart distribution was introduced, where the CMS exhibits partially homogeneity. The KA-G-GLRT detector has been proposed in the paper. Having the range cells grouped guarantees that texture satisfies an inverse Gamma distribution but scale and shape parameters in those groups differ from one another. The KA-G-GLRT is CFAR with respect to the ECM. The experimental performance shows that, for four different MDS target models, the KA-G-GLRT outperforms the 1S-G-GLRT, GCC-GLRT, OS-GLRT and NSDD-GLRT, and has a more extensive applicability in the real sea clutter. The validity of the KA-G-GLRT in partially homogeneous clutter environment has been verified at length.

Acknowledgement. The work was supported by the National Natural Science Funds (61201325) and NUPTSF (NY218045).

References

1. Ernesto, C., De Antonio, M., Giuseppe, R.: GLRT-based adaptive detection algorithms for range-spread targets. IEEE Trans. Signal Process. **49**(7), 1336–1348 (2001)
2. Karl, G.: Detection of a spatially distributed target in white noise. IEEE Signal Process. Lett. **4**(7), 198–200 (1997)
3. Karl, G., Steiner, M.J.: Adaptive detection of range distributed targets. IEEE Trans. Signal Process. **47**(7), 1844–1851 (1999)
4. Karl, G.: Spatially distributed target detection in non-Gaussian clutter. IEEE Trans. Aerosp. Electron. Syst. **35**(3), 926–934 (1999)
5. He, Y., Jian, T., Su, F., Qu, C.W., Gu, X.: Novel range-spread target detectors in non-Gaussian clutter. IEEE Trans. Aerosp. Electron. Syst. **46**(3), 1312–1328 (2010)
6. Domenico, C., De Antonio, M., Danilo, O.: On the statistical invariance for adaptive radar detection in partially homogeneous disturbance plus structured interference. IEEE Trans. Signal Process. **65**(5), 1222–1234 (2017)
7. Xu, S.W., Shui, P.l., Yan, X.Y., Cao, Y.H.: Combined adaptive normalized matched filter detection of moving target in sea clutter. Circ. Syst. Signal Process. **36**(6), 2360–2383 (2017)
8. Francesco, B., Olivier, B., Giuseppe, R.: Adaptive detection of distributed targets in compound-Gaussian noise without secondary data: a Bayesian approach. IEEE Trans. Signal Process. **59**(12), 5698–5708 (2011)
9. Shi, Y.L., Shui, P.L.: Target detection in high-resolution sea clutter via block-adaptive clutter suppression. IET Radar Sonar Navig. **5**(1), 48–57 (2011)
10. Shui, P.L., Shi, Y.L.: Subband ANMF detection of moving targets in sea clutter. IEEE Trans. Aerosp. Electron. Syst. **48**(4), 3578–3593 (2012)
11. Shi, B., Hao, C.P., Hou, C.H., Ma, X.C., Peng, C.Y.: Parametric Rao test for multichannel adaptive detection of range-spread target in partially homogeneous environments. Signal Process. **108**, 421–429 (2015)
12. Hao, C.P., Danilo, O., Ma, X.C., Hou, C.H.: Persymmetric Rao and Wald tests for partially homogeneous environment. IEEE Signal Process. Lett. **19**(9), 587–590 (2012)
13. Muralidhar, R.: Statistical analysis of the nonhomogeneity detector for non-Gaussian interference backgrounds. IEEE Trans. Signal Process. **53**(6), 2101–2111 (2005)
14. Stephanie, B., Olivier, B., Jean, Y.T.: A Bayesian approach to adaptive detection in nonhomogeneous environments. IEEE Trans. Signal Process. **56**(1), 205–217 (2008)
15. Olivier, B., Stephanie, B., Jean, Y.T.: Covariance matrix estimation with heterogeneous samples. IEEE Trans. Signal Process. **56**(3), 909–920 (2008)
16. Gu, X.F., Jian, T., He, Y., Su, F., Tang, X.M.: GLRT detector of range spread target in local homogeneous background and its performance analysis. Acta Electron. Sin. **41**(12), 2367–2373 (2013)
17. Shi, Y.L.: Three GLRT detectors for range distributed target in grouped partially homogeneous radar environment. Signal Process. **135**(6), 121–131 (2017)
18. Shang, X., Song, H.: Radar detection based on compound-Gaussian model with inverse gamma texture. IET Radar Sonar Navig. **5**(3), 315–321 (2011)
19. Graham, V.W.: Development of an improved minimum order statistic detection process for Pareto distributed clutter. IET Radar Sonar Navig. **9**(1), 19–30 (2015)

20. Olivier, B., Louis, L.S., Shawn, K.: Adaptive detection of a signal known only to lie on a line in a known subspace, when primary and secondary data are partially homogeneous. IEEE Trans. Signal Process. **54**(12), 4698–4705 (2006)
21. Gao, Y.C., Li, H.B., Braham, H.: Knowledge-aided range-spread target detection for distributed MIMO radar in nonhomogeneous environments. IEEE Trans. Signal Process. **65** (3), 617–627 (2017)
22. Herselman, P.L., Baker, C.J., de Wind, H.J.: An analysis of X-band calibrated sea clutter and small boat reflectivity at medium-to-low grazing angles. Int. J. Navig. Obs. **2008**, 14 pages (2008)

Asynchronous Distributed ADMM for Learning with Large-Scale and High-Dimensional Sparse Data Set

Dongxia Wang and Yongmei Lei[✉]

School of Computer Engineering and Science of Shanghai University,
No. 333, Nanchen Road, Baoshan District, Shanghai 200436, China
wangdongxia1983@126.com, lei@shu.edu.cn

Abstract. The distributed alternating direction method of multipliers is an effective method to solve large-scale machine learning. At present, most distributed ADMM algorithms need to transfer the entire model parameter in the communication, which leads to high communication cost, especially when the features of model parameter is very large. In this paper, an asynchronous distributed ADMM algorithm (GA-ADMM) based on general form consensus is proposed. First, the GA-ADMM algorithm filters the information transmitted between nodes by analyzing the characteristics of high-dimensional sparse data set: only associated features, rather than all features of the model, need to be transmitted between workers and the master, thus greatly reducing the communication cost. Second, the bounded asynchronous communication protocol is used to further improve the performance of the algorithm. The convergence of the algorithm is also analyzed theoretically when the objective function is non-convex. Finally, the algorithm is tested on the cluster supercomputer "Ziqiang 4000". The experiments show that the GA-ADMM algorithm converges when appropriate parameters are selected, the GA-ADMM algorithm requires less system time to reach convergence than the AD-ADMM algorithm, and the accuracy of these two algorithms is approximate.

Keywords: GA-ADMM · General form consensus · Bounded asynchronous · Non-convex

1 Introduction

Information processing is an important research field of science and technology. With the advent of the era of big data, information processing has become more and more complex, and the classification and systematization of big data has become a research hotspot. The classification problem of big data can

Supported by the National Natural Science Foundation of China under grant No. U1811461.

be abstracted to solve the optimization problem, which can be described by formula (1):

$$min f_x(x, D),\tag{1}$$

where $D \in R^{m*n}$ represents the training samples, $x \in R^n$ is the model parameter. m represents the number of samples and n represents the number of features. Due to the large amount of data, in formula (1), sometimes not only is the data set size large but also the number of features is large. Therefore, it is often difficult to solve the above problem in a valid time with a single node, and how to solve large-scale optimization problems by the distributed environment is the main problem at present. The distributed alternating direction multiplier method (ADMM) is an effective method to solve the optimization problems. Moreover, its decomposability makes it suitable for distributed systems. The main idea of the distributed ADMM algorithm is to transform large global problem into multiple small, local sub-problems, and derive the solution of global problem by coordinating the solutions of sub-problems [1]. We can transform formula (1) into a global consensus optimization problem, as shown in formula (2):

$$min \sum_{i=1}^{M} f_i(x_i, D_i),$$
$$s.t. \ x_i = z, i = 1, 2, ..., M,\tag{2}$$

where $D_i \in R^{m_i*n}$, $\sum_{i=1}^{M} m_i = m$, M represents the number of nodes, $x_i \in R^n$ represents the local variable, $z \in R^n$ represents the global variable, and $f_i : R^n \to R$ is the loss function. In the formula (2), the data set D is decomposed into $D_i(i = 1, 2, ..., M)$, which can be distributed and stored in different nodes. Moreover, each sub-problem $f_i(x_i, D_i)$ can be solved by one node in parallel. This method of data parallelism can effectively solve the problems caused by the large number of samples. [11] uses MapReduce to implement the distributed ADMM algorithm, and in [15], the distributed ADMM algorithm is implemented by MPI and applied to large-scale neural networks. As the number of working nodes increases, the convergence speed of the distributed ADMM algorithm will slow down. At the same time, due to the difference between nodes and network delay, each node may update variables at a different rate. So, the performance of the system is determined by the slowest node, which is called the "straggler" problem [19]. In order to speed up the convergence of distributed ADMM algorithms, [16] proposes a group-based ADMM algorithm (GADMM), which accelerates the convergence speed of the algorithm by grouping working nodes, but it will cause a certain precision loss. In order to solve the "straggler" problem, [19] proposes an asynchronous distributed ADMM algorithm (async-ADMM), which uses bounded delay and partial obstacles to ensure the convergence of the algorithm. All distributed ADMM algorithms introduced in [11,15,16,19] need to transmit the whole model parameter in each iteration, thus the communication cost is high. Especially, when the features of the model parameter is very large, the communication efficiency becomes the bottleneck of the distributed ADMM algorithm. However, for large-scale and high-dimensional sparse data set, some features are only related to partial data blocks. For example, when dealing with text classification problems, some words appear only in part of the text, so each processor can only handle words that appear in the local corpus. Similarly, when solving global consensus optimization problem, each worker can only process the model parameter associated with its local data set, and only need to interact the associated model parameter with the master. In this case, we can convert formula (2) to formula (3):

$$
min \sum_{i=1}^{M} f_i(x_i, D_i),
$$

$$
s.t. \ x_i = z_{G_i}, i = 1, 2, ..., M,
$$

$$(3)$$

where $x_i \in R^{n_i}$ is the local variable, $z \in R^n$ is the global variable, $z_{G_i} \in R^{n_i}$ represents global variables associated with the local variable x_i and it is a linear function of the global variable z. The problem described by formula (3) is also called the general form consensus optimization problem [1]. To solve the problem (3), we only need to transfer the n_i features of the model parameter. So when $n_i \ll n$, the communication cost will be greatly reduced compared to transmitting the entire model parameter.

In this paper, an asynchronous distributed ADMM algorithm (GA-ADMM) for general form consensus optimization is proposed by analyzing the characteristics of large-scale sparse data set and distributed systems. The distributed ADMM framework is used to solve the problem of general form consensus with regularization optimization, and the communication efficiency of the algorithm is improved by filtering features. The bounded asynchronous communication protocol is adopted to improve the scalability of the algorithm. Moreover, the GA-ADMM algorithm is not only applicable to convex optimization, but also applies to non-convex application.

The rest of the paper is arranged as follows: In Sect. 2, we introduce the related work of distributed algorithms, and in Sect. 3 we describe the asynchronous distributed ADMM algorithm for general form consensus with regularization optimization (GA-ADMM). The convergence of the GA-ADMM algorithm is analyzed in Sect. 4. In Sect. 5, the GA-ADMM algorithm is used to solve the sparse logistic regression problem with L1 regularization, and the public data set is used to test the performance of the algorithm on the "Ziqiang 4000" of Shanghai University, and the performance of the algorithm is compared with the AD-ADMM algorithm [2]. Finally, we summarize the work of this paper in Sect. 6.

2   Related Work of Distributed Algorithms

Memory and I/O resources are the bottlenecks of solving large-scale optimization problems with a single machine. A large number of distributed algorithms have emerged to solve these problems. [12] proposes a distributed SGD algorithm.

[18] proposes a distributed ADMM algorithm for linear classification, which has a faster convergence rate than the distributed SGD algorithm. [16] introduces a group-based ADMM algorithm (GADMM), which speeds up the convergence of the algorithm by relaxing global consensus constraints. But the accuracy of the algorithm decreases. These algorithms are all based on synchronous communication protocol. All nodes must wait for other nodes to complete the calculation before the next iteration, so the performance of the system is determined by the slowest node. Compared with synchronous algorithms, asynchronous algorithms can better adapt to heterogeneous distributed systems. [4] and [8] introduce the distributed asynchronous SGD algorithm, [10] implementes an asynchronous random coordinate descent algorithm. [19] proposes an asynchronous ADMM algorithm, which is mainly for the case where the objective function is convex. [2] and [3] propose an asynchronous AD-ADMM algorithm for non-convex functions. [5] and [17] use hierarchical communication structure to reduce the communication between nodes, thus improving the communication efficiency of distributed ADMM. Although asynchronous communication protocol can effectively solve the problem of slow nodes in the system, it is still necessary to pass the entire model parameter in each iteration. When the dimension of the data set is very high, the communication efficiency of the system is still the bottleneck of the algorithm. This is also a common problem of distributed algorithms based on data parallelism.

Another type of distributed algorithm is the distributed algorithm based on model parallel. This kind of algorithms divide the data set by features, and each node only processes the features associated with it, which can reduce the communication cost. [4] proposes an asynchronous random coordinate descent algorithm, which achieves the linear acceleration ratio in the multi-core systems. However, in [4], the shared memory method is used to implement model parallelism, which is not suitable for large-scale distributed systems. In [14], the model parallel method is used to implement the distributed dual coordinate descent algorithm. [7] proposes an stochastic coordinate descent algorithm (DF-DSCD) that supports both data parallelism and model parallelism. Each node of the DF-DSCD algorithm only needs to handle part of samples and part of features. It is not only suitable for environments with large-scale data set, but also for the scenes with high-dimensional data set. However, the main research object of this algorithm is the logistic regression problem, and there is no further research on the case that the objective function is non-convex. Moreover, stochastic coordinate descent algorithm is not applicable to optimization problems with constraints. Compared with the distributed stochastic coordinate descent algorithm, the distributed ADMM algorithm can be better adapt to the distributed environment, and has a faster convergence speed. In [13, 20], the stochastic ADMM is proposed to solve the convex optimization problems. [6] proposes an incremental asynchronous distributed ADMM algorithm, which can solve the non-convex and non-smooth optimization problems. However, its workers are only responsible for calculating the gradient information, and it does not make full use of the advantages of distributed nodes. At the same time, the algorithm uses approximate calculations for solving sub-problems, which may require more iterations to achieve convergence, thus bringing greater communication cost.

This paper proposes an asynchronous distributed ADMM algorithm based on general form consensus (GA-ADMM) for large-scale and high-dimensional sparse data set. This GA-ADMM algorithm is based on data parallelism. Unlike [2], each worker in the GA-ADMM algorithm only needs to transmit associated features to the master, which can effectively reduce the communication cost. Different from the algorithm in [6], the worker in the GA-ADMM algorithm not only calculate the local variable, but also calculate the dual variable. The master is only responsible for the update of the global variable, and the solving process of the sub-problem can be controlled flexibly. Moreover, the algorithm is applicable not only to convex optimization problem, but also to non-convex optimization problem.

3 The Distributed Asynchronous ADMM Algorithm Based on General Form Consensus with Regularization

In this section, we first introduce how to use the ADMM algorithm to solve the general form consensus with regularization optimization problem, and further proposes an asynchronous distributed ADMM algorithm to solve this kind of problems.

3.1 General Form Consensus with Regularization Optimization and ADMM

For the optimization problem of large-scale and high-dimensional sparse data set, although the features of the model parameter is very large, there are fewer features associated with each data block. This kind of problems is abstracted into the general form consensus optimization problem in [1] (as shown in formula (3)). Formula (4) adds a regularization term based on formula (3), called the general form consensus with regularization optimization [1], which is more general than (3).

$$min \sum_{i=1}^{M} f_i(x_i, D_i) + g(z), \tag{4}$$

$$s.t.\ x_i = z_{G_i}, i = 1, 2, ..., M,$$

where $g : R \to R \cap \infty$ is the regularization term. In formula (4), the local variable x_i only needs to be consistent with the associated global variable z_{G_i}, so when solving the local variable, only the associated global variable z_{G_i} to be used, but not the entire global variable. For the sake of presentation, we give the following definition:

Definition 1. $\Gamma(i)$ *represents the set of features associated with the i-th $(i=1,\ldots, M)$ worker, and $|\Gamma(i)|$ represents the size of the set $\Gamma(i)$. $\Phi(j)$ represents the set of all workers associated with the j-th $(j=1, \ldots, n)$ feature, and $|\Phi(j)|$ represents the size of the set $\Phi(j)$. z_j represents the j-th feature of the global variable z. x_{ij} represents the local variable associated with z_j in the i-th node, and y_{ij} is the corresponding dual variable. The set Ω represents all the (i,j) pairs, and the pair (i,j) represent the i-th node associated with the j-th feature.*

By Definition 1, the set Ω can be expressed as shown in formula (5) and we can convert formula (4) into formula (6):

$$\Omega = \{(i,j)| \sum_{j=1}^{n} i \in \Phi(j)\} = \{(i,j)| \sum_{i=1}^{M} j \in \Gamma(i)\}, \tag{5}$$

$$min \sum_{j=1}^{n} \sum_{i=1}^{M} f(x_{ij}, D_i) + g(z), \tag{6}$$

$$s.t.\ x_{ij} = z_j, \forall(i,j) \in \Omega.$$

Using the ADMM algorithm framework to solve formula (6), the iterative formulae are shown in (7)–(10):

$$x_i^{k+1} := argmin(f_i(x_i, D_i) + \sum_{j \in \Gamma(i)} \frac{\rho}{2}\|x_{ij} + \frac{y_{ij}^k}{\rho} - z_j^k\|^2)), \tag{7}$$

$$z^{k+1} := argmin_z(\sum_{j=1}^{n} \sum_{i \in \Phi(j)} (\frac{\rho}{2}\|x_{ij}^{k+1} + \frac{y_{ij}^k}{\rho} - z_j\|^2) + g(z)), \tag{8}$$

$$z_{G_i}^{k+1} := \{z_j | \forall j \in \Gamma(i)\}, \tag{9}$$

$$y_{ij}^{k+1} := y_{ij}^k + \rho(x_{ij}^{k+1} - z_j^{k+1}), \forall j \in \Gamma(i). \tag{10}$$

In the distributed system, the master updates the global variable, and M workers update the local variables and dual variables respectively. The topology diagram is shown in Fig. 1. The worker first updates the local variable, and then sends the local variable and dual variable to the master. After collecting the local variables and dual variables from all workers, the master updates the global variable. Finally, the master sends the associated global variable to each worker. After the worker receives the associated global variable, it updates the dual variable and loops until the stop condition is satisfied. The description of the synchronous ADMM algorithm based on general consensus is shown in Algorithm 1.

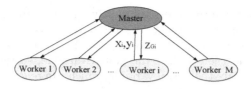

Fig. 1. The topology diagram of the ADMM algorithm based on general form consensus with regularization.

Algorithm 1. The synchronous distributed ADMM based on general form consensus with regularization

---

Algorithm of the Master:

Initialize z^0 and set $k = 0$.

repeat

    | **if** $k==0$ **then**

    | | wait until receiving x_{ij}^{k+1}, y_{ij}^k and $\Gamma(i)$ from all workers.

    | **end**

    | **else**

    | | wait until receiving x_{ij}^{k+1}, y_{ij}^k from all workers.

    | **end**

    | update z^{k+1} using (8)

    | update z_{G_i} using (9)

    | send z_{G_i} to all workers.

    | set $k \leftarrow k + 1$

until *the stopping conditions are satisfied*;

Algorithm of the i-th worker:

Initialize x_i^0, y_i^0 and set $k_i = 0$.

repeat

    | update $x_{ij}^{k_i+1}$ using (7)

    | **if** $k_i == 0$ **then**

    | | save the set $\Gamma(i)$ and send $x_{ij}^{k+1}, y_{ij}^k, \Gamma(i)$ to the master

    | **end**

    | **else**

    | | send x_{ij}^{k+1}, y_{ij}^k to the master

    | **end**

    | wait until receive z_{G_i} from the master

    | update $y_{ij}^{k_i+1}$ using (10)

    | set $k_i \leftarrow k_i + 1$

until *the stopping conditions are satisfied*;

3.2 Asynchronous ADMM Algorithm Based on General Form Consensus

In Algorithm 1, the master cannot update the global variable z until it receives information from all workers. This makes the system performance determined by the slowest worker. In this paper, the algorithm is further improved, and the asynchronous ADMM algorithm is used to solve the general consensus optimization problem. In each iteration, the master only needs to receive part of the workers' information to update the global variable. In addition, we first update the dual variable, and then update the global variable, so that the latest dual variable is used to update the global variable, which can reach convergence faster. The iterative formulae are shown in (11)–(14):

$$x_i^{k+1} := argmin(f_i(x_i, D_i) + \sum_{j \in \Gamma(i)} \frac{\rho}{2}\|x_{ij} + \frac{y_{ij}^k}{\rho} - \widetilde{z_j}\|^2)), \tag{11}$$

$$y_{ij}^{k+1} := y_{ij}^k + \rho(x_{ij}^{k+1} - \widetilde{z_j}), \forall(j) \in \Gamma(i), \tag{12}$$

$$z^{k+1} := argmin_z(g(z) + \sum_{j=1}^n \sum_{i \in \Phi(j)} (\frac{\rho}{2}\|x_{ij}^{k+1} + \frac{y_{ij}^{k+1}}{\rho} - z_j\|^2) + \frac{\gamma}{2}\|z - z^k\|^2), \tag{13}$$

$$\widetilde{z_{Gi}} := \{z_j | \forall j \in \Gamma(i)\}, \tag{14}$$

in which $\widetilde{z_j}$ is the latest associated global variable received by the worker. In Eq. (13), we add the term $\frac{\gamma}{2}\|z - z^k\|^2$ to ensure the convergence of the algorithm. According to the characteristics of Eq. (13), we need to sum local variables and dual variables when updating the global variable z. Therefore, in the communication process, the worker send w (whose definition is shown in Eq. (15)) to the master, instead of sending local variable and dual variable respectively. This will further reduces the amount of information that the worker sends to the master:

$$w_{ij}^{k+1} = \rho x_{ij}^k + y_{ij}^{k+1}. \tag{15}$$

Since the global variable associated with each worker is different and there is only one master to update the global variable in the algorithm. Therefore, after updating the global variable z, we need to update the global variable $\widetilde{z_{Gi}}$ associated with each worker. The update formula of $\widetilde{z_{Gi}}$ is as shown in Eq. (14).

Algorithm 2 describes the GA-ADMM algorithm: the worker independently updates its local variable x_i and the dual variable y_i, and computes w_i. Then sends w_i to the master. After receiving the parameter information of A ($A \leq M$) workers, the master updates the global variable and the associated global variable $\widetilde{z_{Gi}}$, and then sends $\widetilde{z_{Gi}}$ to the corresponding worker. This loop does not stop until all the stop conditions are met. In order to avoid the mater using too old parameter information, when updating z, the algorithm requires that each worker be updated at least once in the fixed period τ. We set an independent counter t_i for each worker and save it in the master. When the worker's information reaches the master, the corresponding counter t_i is set to 0, otherwise the counter t_i is incremented by 1. All counters must be less than τ in the iterations. Since the global variables associated with each worker are different, at the first iteration, each worker needs to mark the global variable associated with it and sends this information to the master. In the Algorithm 2, B_k represents the index subset of workers from which the master receives information during iteration k, and B_k^c represents the complementary set of B_k.

Different from the literature [6], in each iteration, we get the exact solution of the local variable x_i. The time required for solving the sub-problem is higher in the system running process. Therefore, different solving algorithms can be selected according to the specific problems in the system implementation, such as the dual coordinate descent method and the Trust Region Newton method(TRON) [9]. These two algorithms are implemented in the system. Users can select different solutions by passing parameters.

4 Convergence Analysis

In this section we analyze the convergence of the GA-ADMM algorithm. First, we make the following assumptions:

Assumption 1. *t_i is the delay number of the i-th worker, and $T(i,j)$ represents the maximum difference of the delay numbers of all workers associated with z_j (Namely, $T(i,j) = \max |t_i - t_k|, \forall i, k \in \Phi(j)$). The maximum delay number τ satisfies the condition $0 < \tau \leq T(i,j), \forall (i,j) \in \Omega$. And there is a constant $A \in [1, M]$ such that the condition $|B^k| < A$ is satisfied in each iteration.*

Assumption 2. *Each function $f_{ij}(x_{ij})$ is twice differentiable and there is a constant $L_{ij} \geq 0$ such that the gradient of $f_{ij}(x_{ij})$ satisfies the Lipschitz continuous condition.*

Assumption 3. *The regularization function g is a convex function and the domain of g is compact. Moreover, the solution of formula (4) is bounded below and there is an optimal value $\hat{f} > -\infty$.*

Theorem 1. *If Assumptions 1–3 are true, and appropriate parameters are selected to satisfy the formula (20)–(22):*

$$\infty > L_\rho(x^0, y^0, z^0) - \hat{f} \geq 0, \tag{20}$$

$$\rho \geq \frac{(1 + L_{ij} + L_{ij}^2) + \sqrt{(1 + L_{ij} + L_{ij}^2)^2 + 8L_{ij}^2}}{2}, \forall (i,j) \in \Omega, \tag{21}$$

$$\gamma > \frac{A(1 + \rho^2)(\tau - 1) \max(T(i,j)) - \max |\Phi(j)| \rho}{2}, \forall (i,j) \in \Omega, \tag{22}$$

then, the sequence of $(\{x_i^k\}_{i=1}^M, \{y_i^k\}_{i=1}^M, \{z_j^k\}_{j=1}^n)$ generated by the GA-ADMM is bounded and has limit points which satisfy the KKT conditions of problem (4).

It is implied by Theorem 1 that the GA-ADMM is guaranteed to converge to the set of KKT points so long as ρ and γ are large enough. It can be seen from formula (22) that A should be increased as the number of workers M increases

Algorithm 2. GA-ADMM: The asynchronous distributed ADMM based on general form consensus with regularization

Algorithm of the Master:

Initialize z^0 and set $k = 0, t_1 = t_2 = ... = t_M = 0$.

repeat

    if $k==0$ **then**

        wait until receiving $\widetilde{w}_{ij}$ and $\Gamma(i)$ from all workers, set $B_k^c = \phi$.

$$w_{ij}^{k+1} = \widetilde{w}_{ij}. \tag{16}$$

    end

    else

        wait until receiving $\widetilde{w}_{ij}$ from all workers $i \in B_k$ such that $|B_k| \geq A$ and $(t_1, t_2...t_M) < \tau$, and then update

$$t_i = \begin{cases} 0 : \forall i \in B_k, \\ t_{i+1} : \forall i \in B_k^c, \end{cases} \tag{17}$$

$$w_{ij}^{k+1} = \begin{cases} \widetilde{w}_{ij} : \forall i \in B_k, \\ w_{ij}^k : \forall i \in B_k^c. \end{cases} \tag{18}$$

    end

    update

$$z^{k+1} := argmin_z(g(z) + \sum_{j=1}^n \sum_{i \in \Phi(j)} (\frac{\rho}{2}\|\frac{w_{ij}^{k+1}}{\rho} - z_j\|^2) + \frac{\gamma}{2}\|z - z^k\|^2). \tag{19}$$

    update $\widetilde{z_{Gi}}$ using (14)

    send $\widetilde{z_{Gi}}$ to the workers in B_k.

    set $k \leftarrow k + 1$

until *the stopping conditions are satisfied;*

Algorithm of the i-th worker:

Initialize x_i^0, y_i^0 and set $k_i=0$.

repeat

    update $x_{ij}^{k_i+1}, y_{ij}^{k_i+1}$ using (11) and (12)

    if $k_i == 0$ **then**

        save the set $\Gamma(i)$

    end

    compute w_{ij}^{k+1} using (15)

    if $k_i == 0$ **then**

        send $w_{ij}^{k+1}, \Gamma(i)$ to the master

    end

    else

        send w_{ij}^{k+1} to the master

    end

    wait until receive $\widetilde{z_{Gi}}$ from the master

    set $k_i \leftarrow k_i + 1$

until *the stopping conditions are satisfied;*

if the maximum delay number $\tau(\tau > 1)$ remains unchanged. This is because the larger M, the larger $|\Phi(j)|$, and the more outdated information is used for each update, so the threshold A should be increased in order to ensure the convergence speed. On the other hand, when $\tau = 0$, the GA-ADMM algorithm is equivalent to the synchronization algorithm, and γ can be set to 0. Otherwise, γ should increase as τ increases.

5 Experiments and Discussion

In this section, we use the GA-ADMM algorithm to solve the sparse logistic regression problem, test its convergence and performance, and compare the algorithm with the asynchronous distributed ADMM (AD-ADMM) algorithm proposed in [2]. The sparse logistic regression problem can be described as shown in formula (23):

$$\min \frac{1}{M} \sum_{i=1}^{M} \log(1 + \exp(-b_i D_i^T x)) + \beta \|x\|_1 \tag{23}$$

where $D_i \in R^n$ is the sample dataset, $x \in R^n$ is the model parameter, $b_i \in \{-1, 1\}$ is the label of the sample and $\beta > 0$ is the scalar regularization parameter.

5.1 Experimental Environment and Parallelization Implementation

We tested the algorithms on the cluster supercomputer "Ziqiang 4000" of Shanghai University. Each node of the cluster has an Intel E5-2690 CPU (2.9 GHz/8-core) processor and 64 GB of random access memory. The network bandwidth of the cluster is 5.6 GB. We use the KDDb (raw)[1] and KDDa[2] as the test data sets. The KDDb (raw) has more than 19 million samples and one million features, the KDDa has more than eight million samples and 20 million features. We implement the algorithm use MPICH v3.2.1 as the inter-processor communication and use C++ as the programming language.

In the system, we use nine computing nodes and 65 processes, one processes is selected as the master and the others as workers. The initial residual r^k and the dual residual s^k, which are defined as formula (24), are used to set the stopping criterion of the GA-ADMM algorithm. The algorithm doesn't stop until the initial residual and the dual residual satisfy formula (25) and (26):

$$\|r^k\|_2^2 = \frac{1}{M} \Sigma_{i=1}^{M} \sum_{j \in \Gamma(i)} \|x_{ij}^k - z_j^k\|_2^2, \|s^k\|_2^2 = \rho^2 \|z^k - z^{k-1}\|_2^2, \tag{24}$$

---

[1] https://www.csie.ntu.edu.tw/~cjlin/libsvmtools/datasets/binary.html#kdd2010 raw version (bridge to algebra).

[2] https://www.csie.ntu.edu.tw/~cjlin/libsvmtools/datasets/binary.html#kdd2010 (algebra).

$$\|r^k\|_2 \leq ABS * \sqrt{m} + REL * \max\{\frac{1}{M}\sum_{i=1}^{M}\|x_i^k\|_2, \|z^k\|_2\}, \qquad (25)$$

$$\|s^k\|_2 \leq ABS * \sqrt{m} + REL * \frac{1}{M}\sum_{i=1}^{M}\|y_i^k\|_2, \qquad (26)$$

where m represents the total number of samples, both the absolute error ABS and the relative error REL are set to 0.001.

5.2   Convergence Test of the GA-ADMM Algorithm

In this section we test the convergence of the GA-ADMM algorithm. 64 workers are used in the experiment, and different thresholds are selected to test the algorithm. When testing with the data set KDDb (raw), the threshold A is taken as 64, 32, and 8, respectively. While the data set KDDa is used for testing, the threshold A is taken as 64, 16, and 4, respectively. The maximum delay number τ is set to 5, and the penalty term parameter ρ is set to 6. The sub-problem is solved by the TRON. When the threshold A is set to 64, the algorithm is synchronous, and the maximum delay number has no effect on the algorithm. Figures 2 and 3 respectively show the convergence of the algorithm when the data set is KDDb (raw) and KDDa.

Figures 2 and 3 show that when the other parameters are the same, the total number of iterations required for the GA-ADMM algorithm to converge increases as the threshold decreases, but the total system time decreases. This is because the smaller the threshold, the more outdated information the master uses to update the global variable, so the total number of iterations increases. However, since the waiting time and the sending time of the master decrease, the total time decreases instead. Figures 2 and 3 also show that the convergence of the GA-ADMM algorithm can be guaranteed when appropriate parameters are selected.

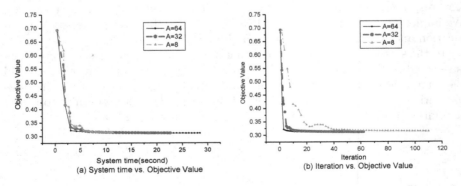

Fig. 2. Convergence of the GA-ADMM algorithm: the data set is KDDb (raw) and A represents the threshold

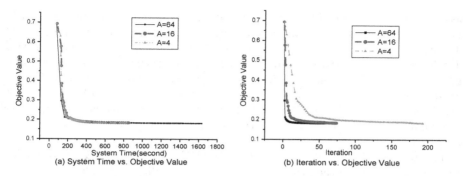

Fig. 3. Convergence of the GA-ADMM algorithm: the data set is KDDa and A represents the threshold

5.3   Performance Test of the GA-ADMM Algorithm

We test the system time cost and accuracy of the GA-ADMM algorithm in this section, and compare it with the AD-ADMM algorithm. The setting of relevant parameters is the same as in Sect. 5.2.

The system time is the running time of the master, which includes communication time and computation time. The communication time includes the time when the master waits to receive w from the workers and the time when the associated model parameters are sent to the workers, and the computation time includes the update time of the global variable z and the associated global variable z_{Gi}. Figure 4 shows the system time cost of the GA-ADMM algorithm and the AD-ADMM algorithm with different thresholds.

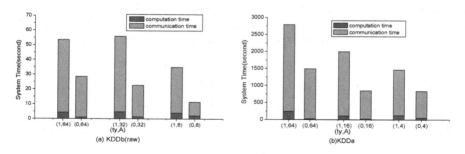

Fig. 4. The system time of the GA-ADMM and the AD-ADMM: ty represents the algorithm type, $ty = 0$ represents the GA-ADMM algorithm, and $ty = 1$ represents the AD-ADMM algorithm. A represents the threshold

It can be seen from Fig. 4 that the system time cost of the GA-ADMM algorithm is less than that of the AD-ADMM algorithm with the same parameters. On the one hand, in the GA-ADMM algorithm, only the associated parameters need to be transmitted between nodes, so the communication time is greatly reduced. On the other hand, when updating the global variable, the AD-ADMM algorithm needs to compute all features of the model, and the GA-ADMM algorithm only needs to compute the association features of the corresponding worker, so the computation time required for each iteration is reduced. This advantage becomes more apparent as the number of features of the data set increases. As shown in Fig. 4, since the features of data set KDDa is much larger than that of data set KDDb (raw), the comparison of the computation time is more obvious.

Finally, we test the accuracy of the GA-ADMM and the AD-ADMM. The accuracy is defined as the proportion of correctly predicted samples to the total number of samples, and can be described by Eq. (27):

$$Accuracy = (N_{tp} + N_{tn})/N_{total}, \tag{27}$$

where N_{tp} represents the number of the predicted correct positive sample, N_{tn} represents the number of predicted correct negative sample, and N_{total} represents the total number of samples.

Figure 5 shows the accuracy of the GA-ADMM and the AD-ADMM at different thresholds. As can be seen from Fig. 5, the difference in accuracy between these two algorithms is not obvious. In the same situation, when the data set KDDb (raw) is used for testing, the accuracy of the GA-ADMM algorithm is slightly higher than that of the AD-ADMM algorithm, while when the data set KDDa is used for testing, the accuracy of the AD-ADMM algorithm is higher. However, the accuracy of the GA-ADMM algorithm decreases with the decrease of the threshold. This is because the global variable associated with each worker in the GA-ADMM algorithm is different, the update time of each feature of global variable is also different. When the threshold is too small, the difference will increase, which will lead to a decrease in accuracy. As shown in the analysis in Sect. 4, when the number of workers increases, the threshold should also increase in order to ensure the convergence of the algorithm.

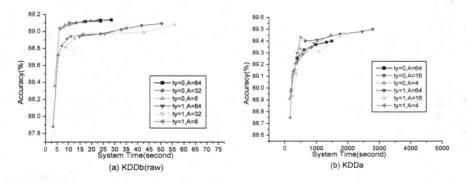

Fig. 5. The accuracy of the GA-ADMM and the AD-ADMM: ty represents the algorithm type, $ty = 0$ represents the GA-ADMM algorithm, and $ty = 1$ represents the AD-ADMM algorithm. A represents the threshold.

6 Conclusion

In order to reduce the communication cost of large-scale distributed algorithms, this paper first proposes an asynchronous distributed ADMM algorithm based on general consensus (GA-ADMM) by analyzing the characteristics of high-dimensional sparse data set and distributed ADMM algorithms. In the GA-ADMM algorithm, each worker only needs to process the associated features of the model parameter, and only the associated features need to be passed between nodes, but not all the features, thus greatly reducing the communication cost. Then, bounded asynchronous and partial obstacles are used to ensure the convergence of the algorithm, and the convergence of the algorithm is analyzed. This algorithm is not only suitable for convex optimization problem, but also for non-convex optimization problem. Finally, the algorithm is used to solve the logistic regression problem with L1 regularization on the high-performance parallel platform "Ziqiang 4000" of Shanghai University, and the algorithm is tested by KDDb(raw) and KDDa data sets. The experimental results show that the algorithm converges with reasonable parameter settings. Moreover, we compare the performance of the GA-ADMM algorithm to the AD-ADMM algorithm. Experiments also show that under the same conditions, the GA-ADMM algorithm requires less system time than the AD-ADMM algorithm, and the accuracy of these two algorithms is approximate. In this paper, the distributed ADMM algorithm is optimized mainly by reducing the communication cost between nodes. The time proportion of solving sub-problems of the algorithm is also large. We will further study the optimization strategy of solving sub-problems in the future.

Acknowledgements. This work is partially supported by the National Natural Science Foundation of China under grant No. U1811461.

References

1. Boyd, S., Parikh, N., Chu, E., Peleato, B., Eckstein, J., et al.: Distributed optimization and statistical learning via the alternating direction method of multipliers. Found. Trends® in Mach. Learn. **3**(1), 1–122 (2011)
2. Chang, T.H., Hong, M., Liao, W.C., Wang, X.: Asynchronous distributed admm for large-scale optimization–part i: algorithm and convergence analysis. IEEE Trans. Signal Process. **64**(12), 3118–3130 (2016)
3. Chang, T.H., Liao, W.C., Hong, M., Wang, X.: Asynchronous distributed admm for large-scale optimization–part ii: linear convergence analysis and numerical performance. IEEE Trans. Signal Process. **64**(12), 3131–3144 (2016)
4. Chen, T., et al.: Mxnet: a flexible and efficient machine learning library for heterogeneous distributed systems. abs/1512.01274 (2015). https://arxiv.org/abs/1512.01274
5. Fang, L., Lei, Y.: An asynchronous distributed admm algorithm and efficient communication model. In: 14th IntlConf on Pervasive Intelligence and Computing, 2nd International Conference on Big Data Intelligence and Computing and Cyber Science and Technology Congress. IEEE (2016)

6. Hong, M.: A distributed, asynchronous and incremental algorithm for nonconvex optimization: An ADMM based approach. CoRR abs/1412.6058 (2014). http://arxiv.org/abs/1412.6058

7. Kang, D., Lim, W., Shin, K., Sael, L., Kang, U.: Data/feature distributed stochastic coordinate descent for logistic regression. In: CIKM 2014 Proceedings of the 23rd ACM International Conference on Conference on Information and Knowledge Management. dl.acm.org (2014)

8. Li, M., G.Andersen, D., Smola, A.: Distributed delayed proximal gradient methods. In: NIPS Workshop on Optimization for Machine Learning. cs.cmu.edu (2013)

9. Lin, C.J., Weng, R.C., Keerthi, S.S.: Trust region newton method for large scale logistic regression. In: ICML 2007 Proceedings of the 24th International Conference on Machine Learning. dl.acm.org (2007)

10. Liu, J., Wright, S.J.: Asynchronous stochastic coordinate descent: parallelism and convergence properties. SIAM J. Optim. **25**(1), 351–376 (2015)

11. Lubell-Doughtie, P., Sondag, J.: Practical distributed classification using the alternating direction method of multipliers algorithm. In: Proceedings of the 33rd International Conference on Machine Learning, vol. 1. IEEE (2013)

12. Martin, Z., Markus, W., Li, L., Smola, A.J.: Parallelized stochastic gradient descent. In: Advances in Neural Information Processing Systems, vol. 23, pp. 2595–2603. Curran Associates, Inc. (2010)

13. Ouyang, H., He, N., Tran, L.Q., Gray, A.: Stochastic alternating direction method of multipliers. In: Proceedings of the 30th International Conference on Machine Learning. vol. 28. jmlr.org (2013)

14. Richtari, P., Takac, M.: Distributed coordinate descent method for learning with big data. J. Mach. Learn. Res. **17**, 1–15 (2016)

15. Taylor, G., Burmeister, R., Xu, Z., Singh, B., Patel, A., Goldstein, T.: Training neural networks without gradients:a scalable admm approach. In: IEEE International Conferences on Big Data. vol. 48. jmlr.org (2016)

16. Wang, H., Gao, Y., Shi, Y., Wang, R.: Group-based alternating direction method of multipliers for distributed linear classification. IEEE Trans. Cybern. **47**(11), 3568–3582 (2017)

17. Wang, S., Lei, Y.: Fast communication structure for asynchronous distributed ADMM under unbalance process arrival pattern. In: Kůrková, V., Manolopoulos, Y., Hammer, B., Iliadis, L., Maglogiannis, I. (eds.) ICANN 2018. LNCS, vol. 11139, pp. 362–371. Springer, Cham (2018). https://doi.org/10.1007/978-3-030-01418-6_36

18. Zhang, C., Lee, H., Shin, K.G.: Efficient distributed linear classification algorithms via the alternating direction method of multipliers. In: the 15th Artificial Intelligence and Statistic. jmlr.org (2012)

19. Zhang, R., Kwok, J.: Asynchronous distributed admm for consensus optimization. In: International Conference on Machine Learning, pp. 1701–1709. jmlr.org (2014)

20. Zhong, L.W., Kwok, J.T.: Fast stochastic alternating direction method of multipliers. In: Proceedings of the 31st International Conference on Machine Learning, vol. 32. jmlr.org (2014)

Spectrum Sensing in Cognitive Radio Based on Hidden Semi-Markov Model

Lujie Di[1($\boxtimes$)] [iD], Xueke Ding[2], Mingbing Li[3], and Qun Wan[4]

[1] University of Electronic Science and Technology of China, Chengdu 611731, China
575586546@qq.com
[2] Jangxi Province Engineering Research Center of Special Wireless Communications
Tongfang Electronic Technology Co., Jiujiang 332001, China
jx_dxk@126.com
[3] Southwest Institute of Electronic Technology, Chengdu 610036, China
12865579@qq.com
[4] University of Electronic Science and Technology of China, Chengdu 611731, China
wanqun@uestc.edu.cn

Abstract. Spectrum sensing is one of the key technologies in cognitive radio systems. Efficient spectrum sensing can improve the communication network throughput and reduce the possibility of frequency collision. Hidden Markov Model (HMM) is a common spectrum sensing algorithm, which can enhance the energy detection (ED) algorithm by using historical observation information under unsupervised conditions. However, this algorithm assumes the regularity of the primary user occupying the spectrum to obey the Markov property. If the assumption is inconsistent with the facts, the performance of the algorithm will deteriorate. So, we propose a spectrum sensing algorithm based on Hidden Semi-Markov Model (HSMM) in this paper. It can solve the shortcoming of HMM because it has a high-order timing representation capability. Numerical simulations show that this model can effectively improve the detection performance of ED. It improves the SNR tolerance of 4 dB, or shortens the sensing time to a quarter of the time that the traditional ED method takes. In addition, the proposed algorithm is applicable to more scenarios than HMM. When the Markov property of the spectrum state fails, the proposed algorithm still performs better than HMM.

Keywords: Cognitive radio · Spectrum sensing · Hidden Semi-Markov Model

1 Introduction

Along with the rapid development and wide application of wireless communication technology, the shortage of spectrum resources has become more prominent. Cognitive radio is one of the effective approaches to solve this problem [1]. It improves network throughput by discovering and utilizing idle spectrum resources. In cognitive radio systems, efficient sensing of spectrum holes

© ICST Institute for Computer Sciences, Social Informatics and Telecommunications Engineering 2019
Published by Springer Nature Switzerland AG 2019. All Rights Reserved
G. Gui and L. Yun (Eds.): ADHIP 2019, LNICST 302, pp. 275–286, 2019.
https://doi.org/10.1007/978-3-030-36405-2_28

is essential. In recent years, many scholars have studied spectrum sensing and achieved brilliant results. Spectrum sensing can be divided into multiple types depending on the sensing scene [2]. In terms of the number of sensing nodes, spectrum sensing is divided to single-node sensing and multi-node cooperative sensing. Multi-node cooperative sensing can effectively alleviate shadow fading, multipath fading, hidden terminals and other issues in single-node sensing through spatial diversity gain. In terms of perceived bandwidth spectrum sensing can be divided into narrowband spectrum sensing and wideband spectrum sensing. The classic three spectrum sensing algorithms, energy detection, matched filtering detection, and cyclostationary feature detection are for all narrowband spectrum sensing algorithms, while in wideband scenarios, the available spectrum sensing methods are based on compressed sensing theory.

In this paper, we improves the traditional single-node and narrow-band spectrum sensing algorithm by introducing the time series model. A large number of measured data show that the primary users have certain regularity on the occupied state of the licensed spectrum [3,4]. If the regularity will be properly utilized, the spectrum sensing performance can be effectively improved [5]. In the existing researches, the spectrum state is usually modeled as a Markov model as shown in the Fig. 1, which assumes that the state of the spectrum at the current time is related to the "work" or "idle" state of the spectrum at the previous moment; and spectrum sensing is modeled as a hidden Markov model (HMM)[6]. The spectrum state obeying Markov property is invisible to the observer and is a hidden variable. The visible observed variable is uniquely determined by the state variable at the current moment through a probability transfer mechanism. The probability transfer mechanism is generally assumed to be a Gaussian channel. Experiments indicate that, by introducing the HMM framework, the detection performance of traditional spectrum sensing algorithms such as ED can be effectively improved in unsupervised scenarios.

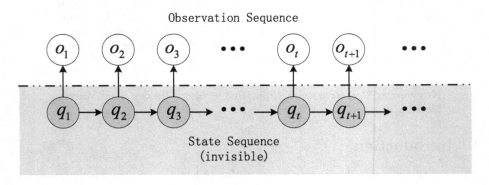

Fig. 1. Hidden Morkov model.

However, the HMM is a nearest neighbor model, it only assumes that there is a correlation between the two states at the adjacent time [7]. Therefore, when a high-order temporal correlation in the regularity of the spectrum state holds, the Markov model will be unsuitable and the spectrum sensing performance will be limited. In view of this situation, the literature models the spectrum state of the hidden layer as a high-order Markov model to obtain high-order temporal representation ability [8]. However, the complexity of the model increases exponentially as the model order increases, which makes the training of the model difficult, and even unavailable when the order is high.

To reduce the complexity in high-order Markov model, this paper models the spectrum state of the hidden layer as a semi-Markov model, and proposes a spectrum sensing algorithm based on the hidden semi-Markov model (HSMM) [9]. Compared with the high-order Markov model, the semi-Markov model has a certain simplification in the high-order time series correlation. It only cares about the relationship between state switching and state duration, so retains most of the high-order timing representation capability. Simulation results show that the proposed algorithm has wider applicable scenarios than the HMM-based spectrum sensing algorithm. When the spectrum state obeys different regularities, the proposed algorithm still obtains better detection performance than the HMM-based algorithm.

The rest of the paper is organized as follows: The second part describes the sensing model, the third part introduces the model algorithm, including the model parameter learning method in the unsupervised scene and the online estimation method of the spectrum state. The fourth part gives the simulation test to verify the performance of the proposed algorithm, the fifth part summarizes the full paper.

2 Spectrum Sensing Model

HSMM is an extension of HMM. Its hidden state transition probability is no longer a constant, but a variable related to state dwell time. It overcomes the limitation of model in Markov assumption. The model can described by quaternary symbol $\lambda = (\boldsymbol{\pi}, \boldsymbol{A}, \boldsymbol{P}, \boldsymbol{B})$.

$\boldsymbol{\pi}$ is initial state probability vector,

$$\boldsymbol{\pi} = (\pi_0, \pi_1) \tag{1}$$

where

$$\pi_i = P(q_1 = s_i), i = 0, 1 \tag{2}$$

indicates the probability when the initial state of the hidden state sequence q_1 is s_i. For the spectrum state, this paper makes a binarization hypothesis, i.e. s_0 indicates spectrum is idle, s_1 represents spectrum being occupied.

A, P indicate the transfer relationship of the hidden state sequence, the hidden state sequence can be regarded an assemble of state segment. A is the state transition probability matrix,

$$A = \begin{bmatrix} a_{00} & a_{01} \\ a_{10} & a_{11} \end{bmatrix} = \begin{bmatrix} 0 & 1 \\ 1 & 0 \end{bmatrix} \tag{3}$$

where a_{ij} indicates the transition probability that state s_i transfers to state s_j. Since the state segment must be transferred to another state in the end, its self-transition probability is 0. P is the state dwell time probability matrix,

$$P = \begin{bmatrix} P_0(1) & P_0(2) & \dots & P_0(D) \\ P_1(1) & P_1(2) & \dots & P_1(D) \end{bmatrix} \tag{4}$$

where D is the maximum dwell time, $P_i(d)$ denotes the probability when state segment is in the state s_i and its dwell time is d. Then, the transition probability of the hidden state sequence is defined as

$$a_{i(j,d)} = P\left(q_{[t+1:t+d]} = s_j | q_{t]} = s_i\right) = a_{ij}p_j(d) \tag{5}$$

where the inclusive symbol '[', ']' is used to indicate the left and right inclusiveness in time, for example, $q_{[t+1:t+d]} = s_j$ indicates that the state sequence is s_j from time $t+1$ to time $t + d$, but at time t and time $t + d + 1$ must not be s_j; $q_{t]} = s_i$ infers that the state sequence at time t is s_i, and at time $t+1$ must not be s_i, but at time $t - 1$ may or may not be s_i. Then, the probability that the state at time $t + \tau$ is s_j when the state at time t is s_i can be gain by

$$P\left(q_{t+\tau} = s_j | q_t = s_i\right) = \sum_{d=\tau}^{D} a_{i(j,d)}, \tau \leq D \tag{6}$$

B is the observation probability matrix,

$$B = [b_i(v_n)], i = 0, 1; n = 0, 1, \dots \tag{7}$$

where v_n is observation space, and

$$b_i(v_n) = P\left(o_t = v_n | q_t = s_i\right) \tag{8}$$

indicates the probability that the observed variable o_t is v_n when the state q_t is s_i. We assume the propagation channel is a Gaussian channel. So, when the observed variable is signal energy, the observed probabilities are subject to different Gaussian distributions, i.e. $b_0(o_n) \sim N\left(\mu_0, \sigma_0^2\right)$ and $b_1(o_n) \sim N\left(\mu_1, \sigma_1^2\right)$, where $\mu_0 = n\sigma_n^2$, $\sigma_0^2 = 2n\sigma_n^4$, $\mu_1 = n(\sigma_n^2 + \sigma_s^2)$, $\sigma_1^2 = 2n\sigma_n^2(\sigma_n^2 + 2\sigma_s^2)$. n is the number of samples, σ_s^2 is primary user's signal energy level and σ_n^2 is the noise level [10].

The generation process of HSMM's state sequence and observation sequence is shown in Fig. 2. The state segment is described by (i_n, d_n), where i_n is the state of the segment n and d_n denotes the duration of this segment. Firstly, a series of state segments are generated. Different state segments correspond to different states and durations respectively, and state segments with respect to the same state must not be adjacent. Then, these state segments are mapped onto the time series to generate a state sequence. Subsequently, the observation sequence is generated correspondingly. It should be noted that, in general, for the observer only the observation sequence is visible in the entire model, and the shaded parts in the figure are hidden.

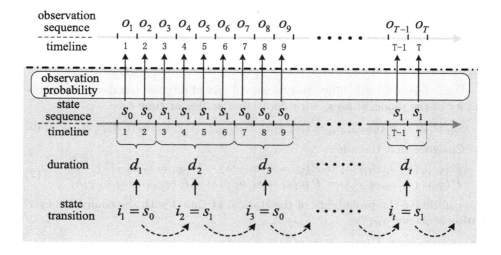

Fig. 2. Hidden Semi-Morkov model.

3   Learning and Estimation Algorithm

3.1   Model Parameter Learning

Cognitive radio systems often work in unfamiliar environment, and the priori information of primary user is usually unavailable. So spectrum sensing algorithms should have the ability of unsupervised learning.

Given an observation sequence $O_{1:T} = [o_1, o_2, \ldots, o_T]$, the parameters of HSMM can be estimated based on the EM algorithm by means of parameter re-estimation. We shall first define the forward probability and backward probability of HSMM as

$$\alpha_t(i) = P\left(q_{t]} = s_i, o_{1:t}|\lambda\right) = \sum_{d \in D} \alpha^*_{t-d+1}(i)\, p_i(d)\, u_t(i, d) \tag{9}$$

$$\alpha^*_{t+1}(i) = P\left(q_{[t+1} = s_i, o_{1:t}|\lambda\right) = \sum_{j \in S \backslash \{i\}} \alpha_t(j)\, a_{ji} \tag{10}$$

$$\beta^*_{t+1}(i) = P\left(o_{t+1:T}|q_{[t+1} = s_i, \lambda\right) = \sum_{d \in D} p_i(d)\, u_{t+d}(i, d)\, \beta_{t+d}(i) \tag{11}$$

$$\beta_t(i) = P\left(o_{t+1:T}|q_{t]} = i, \lambda\right) = \sum_{j \in \mathbf{S}\backslash\{i\}} a_{ij}\beta_{t+1}^*(j) \tag{12}$$

where

$$u_t(i,d) = \prod_{\tau=t-d+1}^{t} b_i(o_\tau) \tag{13}$$

The boundary conditions are

$$\alpha_t^*(i) = \begin{cases} \pi_i, t = 1 \\ 0, \ t < 1 \end{cases} \tag{14}$$

and

$$\beta_t(i) = \begin{cases} 1, t = T \\ 0, t > T \end{cases} \tag{15}$$

Using forward probability and backward probability, we can derive the probability of the model state s_i with duration d ending at time t as

$$\eta_t(i,d) = P\left(q_{[t-d+1:t]} = i, o_{1:T}|\lambda\right) = \alpha_{t-d+1}^*(i)\, p_i(d)\, u_t(i,d)\, \beta_t(i) \tag{16}$$

Consider that there is

$$P\left(q_{t:t+1} = s_i, o_{1:T}|\lambda\right) = P\left(q_t = s_i, o_{1:T}|\lambda\right) - P\left(q_{t]} = s_i, o_{1:T}|\lambda\right) \\ P\left(q_{t:t+1} = s_i, o_{1:T}|\lambda\right) = P\left(q_{t+1} = s_i, o_{1:T}|\lambda\right) - P\left(q_{[t+1} = s_i, o_{1:T}|\lambda\right) \tag{17}$$

We can derive the probability of the state s_i at time t with the complete observation sequence $o_{1:T}$ as

$$\begin{aligned} \gamma_t(i) &= P\left(q_1 = s_i, o_{1:T}|\lambda\right) \\ &= \gamma_{t-1}(i) + P\left(q_{[t} = s_i, o_{1:T}|\lambda\right) - P\left(q_{t-1]} = s_i, o_{1:T}|\lambda\right) \\ &= \gamma_{t-1}(i) + \alpha_t^*(i)\beta_t^*(i) - \alpha_{t-1}(i)\beta_{t-1}(i) \end{aligned} \tag{18}$$

The boundary condition is

$$\gamma_1(i) = P\left(q_1 = s_i, o_{1:T}|\lambda\right) = P\left(q_{[1} = s_i, o_{1:T}|\lambda\right) = \pi_i\beta_1^*(i) \tag{19}$$

With the above probability, the model parameters can be re-estimated by the following formula [9]

$$p_i(d) = \frac{\sum_t \eta_t(i,d)}{\sum_d \sum_t \eta_t(i,d)} \tag{20}$$

$$\mu_i = \frac{\sum_t \gamma_t(i)\, o_t}{\sum_t \gamma_t(i)} \tag{21}$$

$$\sigma_i^2 = \frac{\sum_t \gamma_t(i)\,(o_t - \mu_i)^2}{\sum_t \gamma_t(i)} \tag{22}$$

3.2   Online Estimation of Spectrum State

The common method to estimate the hidden state for HSMM is the Viterbi algorithm [11], but it is a smoothing algorithm and is not suitable for online estimation of spectrum states. Therefore, we use the state estimation method based on posterior probability. In HSMM, the historical observation data can be used to extract a priori estimation of the spectrum state to be detected. By combining the estimated a priori state and the current observation with the current observation, the posterior estimation of the state can be obtained. The test decision formula is

$$P\left(q_t = s_1 | o_{1:t}, \lambda\right) \gtrless \gamma \tag{23}$$

where γ is the probability decision threshold. When $\gamma = 0.5$, this formula is Maximum a posteriori probability (MAP) detection, which is the detection with the lowest average error rate.

In order to obtain the posterior probability of the state in real time, we propose an iterative calculation method, which has lower computational complexity. Firstly, define an auxiliary joint probability as

$$\zeta_t\left(i\right) = P\left(q_t = s_i, o_{1:t} | \lambda\right) \tag{24}$$

Thus, we have

$$P\left(q_t = s_i | o_{1:t}, \lambda\right) = \frac{\zeta_t\left(i\right)}{\sum\limits_j \zeta_t\left(j\right)} \tag{25}$$

$$P\left(q_t = s_i, o_{1:t-1} | \lambda\right) = \frac{\zeta_t\left(i\right)}{b_i\left(o_t\right)} \tag{26}$$

Referring to the formula (17) and using the formula (26), we can obtain

$$\zeta_t\left(i\right) = \left[\zeta_{t-1}\left(i\right) + \alpha_t^*\left(i\right) - \alpha_{t-1}\left(i\right)\right] b_i\left(o_t\right) \tag{27}$$

The boundary condition is

$$\zeta_1\left(i\right) = \pi_i b_i\left(o_1\right) \tag{28}$$

In this way, the real-time observation data o_t at each time is obtained, the posterior probability of the current system state can be estimated by recursive calculation $\zeta_t\left(i\right)$, and the state estimation result is obtained by formula (23). Besides, it is necessary to calculate $\alpha_t\left(i\right)$ and $\alpha_{t+1}^*\left(i\right)$ for facilitating the next estimate.

4   Numerical Simulation

In this part, we verify the performance of the proposed algorithm by Monte Carlo simulation. In order to simulate the spectrum patterns, we generate a state sequence based on the queuing theory model which is commonly used in time series modeling [12], and then create the observation sequences via Gaussian channel. Considering the impact of different spectrum usage patterns to detection performance, two sets of data are generated for numerical simulation based on M/M/1 and Ek/Ek/1 models commonly used in queuing theory. The specific parameters are shown in the Table 1.

Table 1. Simulation data model parameters.

Model	SNR	N	Distribution	Distribution parameter
M/M/1	$-10\,\mathrm{dB}$	300	Negative exponential distribution	$\lambda = [1/9, 1/6]$
Ek/Ek/1	$-10\,\mathrm{dB}$	300	Erlang distribution	$k = [100, 80]$
				$\theta = [0.29, 0.25]$

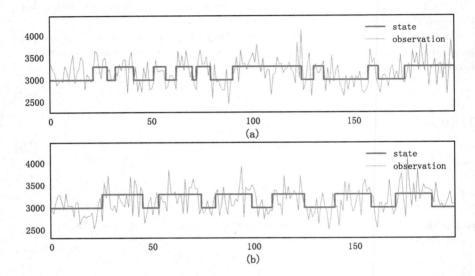

Fig. 3. Simulation data: (a) M/M/1; (b) Ek/Ek/1.

All spectrum sensing algorithms can achieve a good detection performance when the SNR is high. In order to differentiate the detection performance of different algorithms, we set a simulation environment with low SNR. The simulation data is shown in Fig. 3.

Figure 4 compares the detection performance of the three algorithms ED, HMM and HSMM under different simulation data models. It can be seen from the observation of the ROC curve that the detection performance of HMM and HSMM is better than ED, showing that rational usage of the correlation among time series effectively improve the effect of spectrum sensing.

Comparing the performance of HMM and HSMM in two simulation data models, the detection performances of the two algorithms in M/M/1 model are almost the same, while in Ek/Ek/1 model, HSMM is obviously better than HMM. Figure 5 explains the reason for this difference. The simulation data generated by the M/M/1 model has an approximate negative exponential distribution of the dwell time probability of each state in the state sequence. Both HMM and HSMM can learn and match this pattern well. However, for the simulation data generated by the Ek/Ek/1 model, the dwell time distribution is a

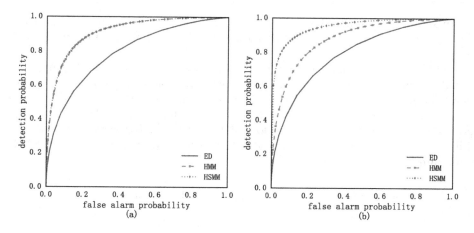

Fig. 4. ROC : (a) M/M/1; (b) Ek/Ek/1.

slightly right-biased bell-shaped distribution. In this case, only HSMM matches this pattern well. Table 2 gives the corresponding KL divergence which describes the effect of the match quantitatively. As we have analyzed, HMM's KL divergence in Ek/Ek/1 is large, indicating HMM mismatches the simulation data. So the detection performance of HSMM is not as good as HSMM's.

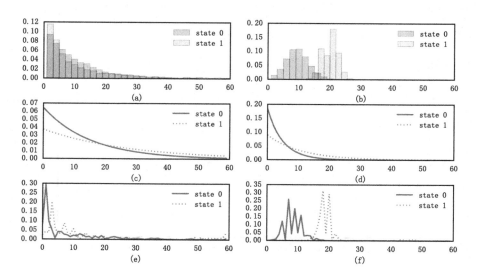

Fig. 5. Dwell time distribution: (a) simulation data from M/M/1; (b) simulation data from Ek/EK/1; (c) HMM for M/M/1; (d) HMM for Ek/Ek/1; (e) HSMM for M/M/1; (f) HSMM for Ek/Ek/1.

In summary, compared to HMM, HSMM-based spectrum sensing algorithm is more applicable, and it does not require the spectral state to obey Markov property.

Setting the detection probability as a constant $P_d = 0.95$ and fixing the remaining parameters, we can study the influence of different factors on the detection performance of the algorithm by observing the false alarm probability. Figure 6 shows the detection performance under different SNR. HSMM also has poor detection performance under low SNR, but its SNR tolerance is average 4dB higher than ED. This means HSMM can work properly in a lower SNR environment.

Table 2. Algorithm's KL divergence for different simulation data

		Simulation data model	
		M/M/1	Ek/Ek/1
Algorithm model	HMM	0.31	1.91
	HSMM	0.30	0.18

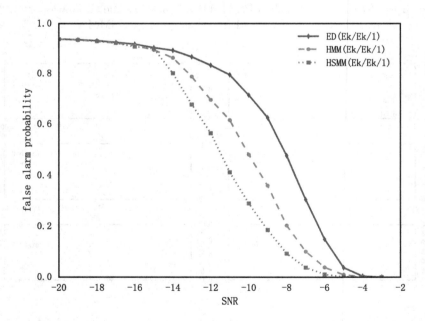

Fig. 6. Algorithm's detection performance with different SNR.

Figure 7 shows the detection performance under different length of sampling. The length of the sampling determines how long it takes to sense. The shorter the sensing time is, the higher reuse rate of idle spectrum resources and the lower probability of frequency conflicts will be obtained. When the detection performance is the same, the length of sampling required by HSMM is only almost a quarter of ED and a half of HMM, which significantly shortens the time of spectrum sensing.

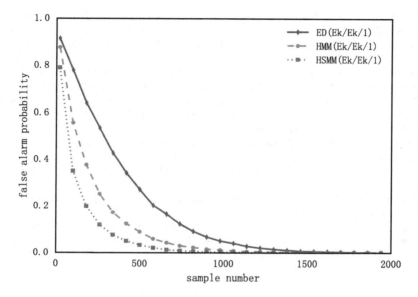

Fig. 7. Algorithm's detection performance with different sample number.

5   Conclusion

We propose a spectrum sensing algorithm based on HSMM. Compared with the traditional ED algorithm, it enhances the detection performance by rationally utilizing the high-order timing relationship of the spectrum state, and can work normally in a lower SNR environment. In addition, its sensing time is shorter, which is only almost a quarter of ED's. The algorithm has a wider application range than the HMM-based spectrum sensing algorithm. It can obtain better detection performance when there are arbitrary timing laws in the spectrum state.

References

1. Mitola, J., Maguire, G.Q.: Cognitive radio: making software radios more personal. IEEE Pers. Commun. **6**(4), 13–18 (1999)
2. Matin, M.A.: Spectrum sensing techniques for cognitive radio-a review. KSII Trans. Internet Inf. Syst. **8**(11), 2903–2907 (2014)

3. Spectrum Shared Company: General Survey of Radio Frequency Bands - 30 MHz to 3 GHz. http://www.sharedspectrum.com. Accessed 10 Apr 2019
4. Aslam, S., Shahid, A., Lee, K.G.: Primary User Behavior Aware Spectrum Allocation Scheme for Cognitive Radio Networks. Pergamon Press, Oxford (2015)
5. Umebayashi, K., Hayashi, K., Lehtomaki, J.J.: Threshold-setting for spectrum sensing based on statistical information. IEEE Commun. Lett. **21**(7), 1585–1588 (2017)
6. Din, M.S.E., El-Tarhuni, M., Assaleh, K., Kiranyaz, S.: An HMM-based spectrum access algorithm for cognitive radio systems. In: 2015 International Conference on Information and Communication Technology Research (ICTRC), pp. 116–119. IEEE, Abu Dhabi (2015)
7. Nguyen, T., Mark, B.L., Ephraim, Y.: Spectrum sensing using a hidden bivariate Markov model. IEEE Trans. Wireless Commun. **12**(9), 4582–4591 (2013)
8. Chen, Z., Qiu, R.C.: Prediction of channel Ctate for cognitive radio using higher-order hidden Markov model. In: Proceedings of the IEEE SoutheastCon 2010, pp. 276–282. IEEE, Concord (2010)
9. ShunZheng, Y.: Hidden Semi-Markov Models. Elsevier Press, Amsterdam (2016)
10. Abdulsattar, M.A.K., Hussein, Z.A.: Energy detector with baseband sampling for cognitive radio: real-time implementation. Wireless Eng. Technol. **3**(4), 229–239 (2012)
11. Burshtein, D.: Robust parametric modeling of durations in hidden Markov models. IEEE Trans. Speech Audio Process. **4**(3), 240–252 (1996)
12. Ali, S., Shokair, M., Dessouky, M.I., et al.: Backup channel selection approach for spectrum handoff in cognitive radio networks. In: 2018 13th International Conference on Computer Engineering and Systems (ICCES), pp. 353–259. IEEE, Cairo (2018)

A Survey of Radar Signature Analysis and Applications on Space Targets with Micro-motions

He Zhu[1], Jun Wang[2], and Yongjiang Chen[1(✉)]

[1] School of Cyber Science and Technology, Beihang University,
Xueyuan Road No. 37, Haidian District, Beijing, China
{zhuhe, chenyongjiang}@buaa.edu.cn
[2] School of Electronic Information Engineering, Beihang University,
Xueyuan Road No. 37, Haidian District, Beijing, China
wangj203@buaa.edu.cn

Abstract. Detection techniques of micro-motion targets have been explored with increasing attention according to its complex and flexible features. In this paper, concepts and existing achievements of micro-motion and micro-Doppler are summarized horizontally from two aspects: micro-motion analysis foundation and techniques, strategies and implement. Addressing this goal, a general micro-Doppler formula is introduced with four typical micro-motion forms. Moreover, several extraction and imaging methods are demonstrated from four perspectives, i.e. radar quantity, micro-motion complexity, other strategies and potential problems. Subsequently, available application on ballistic target recognition and critical issues of this emerging field are proposed, with a prospect towards the trend of development.

Keywords: Micro-motion · Micro-Doppler · Micro-motion model · Feature extraction · Radar imaging · ISAR

1   Introduction

With the continuous development of signal processing and semiconductor techniques, imaging radar has been widely utilized in both military and civilian fields due to its excellent performance in information acquisition. Compared with the traditional detection and tracking radar for coordinate parameter measurement such as detection, ranging and angle measurement, the imaging radar, which is extensively exploited, can acquire high-resolution images of the observation target or scene then extract its shape, size and other information [1].

As anthropic exploration activities have shown a tremendous increase in space, the amount of spatial micro-motion targets such as satellites and space debris has risen sharply. Due to their high moving velocity and complex motion forms, these space targets not only affect the normal operation of spacecraft, but also pose a threat to homeland security. Consequently, there is an urgent need for developing techniques on space situational awareness, air defense and anti-missile based on the high-resolution imaging, feature extraction and recognition of radar 3-dimensional micro-motion targets.

© ICST Institute for Computer Sciences, Social Informatics and Telecommunications Engineering 2019
Published by Springer Nature Switzerland AG 2019. All Rights Reserved
G. Gui and L. Yun (Eds.): ADHIP 2019, LNICST 302, pp. 287–298, 2019.
https://doi.org/10.1007/978-3-030-36405-2_29

Imaging radars are mainly categorized into Synthetic Aperture Radar (SAR) [2, 3] and Inverse Synthetic Aperture Radar (ISAR) [3, 4]. Among them, ISAR achieves high resolution by applying a large time-bandwidth product, and simultaneously high azimuth resolution by exploiting the inverse synthetic aperture array formed by the relative motion between the target and the radar. Generally, while the entire target or target component is moving, there always exists a micro-motion (or micro-dynamics) other than centroid translation such as vibration, rotation and accelerated movement [5]. For high-resolution imaging radars, target micro-motion is defined as the small motion of the whole target or some components in the direction of the radar's line of sight (LOS) compared with the radial distance between the target and the radar. For representative space targets such as space debris, warheads and decoy targets, micro-motion is generally classified into certain forms as spins, precession, nutation, roll and swing [6]. Relatively, the corresponding frequency modulation generated when a target's micro-motion implements a phase modulation to the radar echo is called micro-Doppler signal. The micro-Doppler effect, apparently, refers to the phenomenon about extra modulation caused by micro-motions [1].

Gone are the days when micro-Doppler signals were regarded as unfavorable factors rather than meritorious information because of the rudimentary signal processing technology. It was only until 2000 when the concept of micro-motion and micro-Doppler was officially introduced and applied in microwave radar observation by V. C. Chen from the US Naval Research Laboratory, that the observation and utilization of the micro-Doppler effect becomes prevalent [7–10]. The improvement of the radar detection refinement avoids the micro-Doppler signal being simply removed any more. On the contrary, it is used to characterize the target's attribute type and motion intent after feature extraction, by which, the abundant information, e.g. structure, shape, motion state, material properties and stress state becomes available [11]. Since then, worldwide scholars have increasingly devoted themselves to the research on feature extraction, imaging and recognition techniques of micro-motion targets, in which domain, significant and remarkable achievements have been accomplished.

Most of research papers and surveys nowadays [7, 11–14] have provided a unambiguous prospect of techniques about micro-motion observation according to the dimension from the data processing process. For instance, article [11] analyzes the existing micro-motion models, feature extraction, imaging and recognition techniques in data processing order. Based on the existing surveys, this paper summarizes the available micro-motion feature extraction and imaging techniques horizontally from the perspective of analysis foundation and implementation strategies. Respectively, this paper is divided into the following parts. Section 2 introduces the premier basis of micro-motion analysis, e.g. modeling and summarizes four general micro-motion models along with several practical problems. Section 3, from the perspective of techniques, strategies and implement, arranges the existing research on micro-motion, which consequently consists of four sub-perspectives: radar quantity, target motion complexity, other methods and related problems. Then, various of application and potential development trend of the micro-motion target are briefly introduced in Sect. 4. Finally, Sect. 5 concludes the whole paper and discuss our further research directions in micro-motion target domain.

2 Micro-motion Analysis Foundation

2.1 General Micro-motion Model

When analyzing a micro-motion target, it is initial to construct a micro-motion model that includes rotation, vibration, roll, and cone motion [15]. Under the consideration of computational simplicity, the point where the energy of the target surface is concentrated is always selected as the reference point. Accordingly, the micro-motion scattering model is used to describe the physical characteristics of the target. After that, the micro-Doppler characteristics of each micro-motion form are analyzed.

The frequency modulation characteristics of the radar echo hold the topmost position when it comes to micro-Doppler, which can be obtained by the phase information $\phi(t)$ of the echo. Moreover, phase information has a strong influence on the instantaneous distance $R(t)$ between the radar and the target. The distance is a function of time, which reflects the variation of the radial distance between the target and the radar. Therefore, the foremost requirement when studying micro-Doppler characteristics is to determine the instantaneous distance $R(t)$ between the radar and the target [6, 16]. By establishing a universal target motion model as illustrated in Fig. 1, the general formula of micro-Doppler can be obtained as formulation (1), where $V(t)$ is the velocity vector caused by micro-motion [6].

$$f_{m-d} = \frac{1}{2\pi}\frac{d\Phi(t)}{dt} = \frac{2f}{c}\frac{dR(t)}{dt} = \frac{2f}{c}V(t)_m^T \cdot n. \tag{1}$$

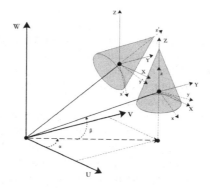

Fig. 1. Radar and micro-motion target

It can be seen that, the main difference between Doppler feature and micro-Doppler feature is that the former reflects the motion state of the target as a whole, while the latter only reflects that of the target local moving component, that is, the former is produced by overall translation, and the latter is produced by local micro-motion [6]. Therefore, essentially speaking, the micro-Doppler features can be regarded comparably as the Doppler features, which means characteristic information can be attained by implementing invertion to original signal.

Based on the model mentioned above, by altering the micro-motion matrix of the five motion forms, the customized model for each micro-motion forms can be obtained, as summarized in Table 1 [6, 16, 17].

Table 1. Summarize of different micro-motion modes from article [6]

Micro-motion type	Target location vector	Micro-Doppler formula
Acceleration micro-motion target	$R(t) = R_0 + \frac{1}{2}at^2$	$f_{m-d} = \frac{1}{2\pi}\frac{d\Phi(R(t))}{dt} = \frac{2f}{c}at$
Vibration micro-motion target	$R(t) = R_0 + D_V\sin(2\pi f_V t) \cdot n_V$	$f_{m-d} = \frac{4\pi f_V f D_V}{c}\cos(2\pi f_V t)[\cos(\alpha - \alpha_V)\cos\beta\cos\beta_V + \sin\beta\sin\beta_V]$
Rotation micro-motion target	$R(t) = R_0 + \mathbf{Rot}(t) \cdot r_0$ $\mathbf{Rot}(t) = I + \hat{\omega}\sin(\Omega_c t) + \hat{\omega}^2(1 - \cos(\Omega_c t))$ $R_{init} = \begin{bmatrix} \cos\phi & -\sin\phi & 0 \\ \sin\phi & \cos\phi & 0 \\ 0 & 0 & 1 \end{bmatrix}$ $\begin{bmatrix} 1 & 0 & 0 \\ 0 & \cos\theta & -\sin\theta \\ 0 & \sin\theta & \cos\theta \end{bmatrix}\begin{bmatrix} \cos\psi & -\sin\psi & 0 \\ \sin\psi & \cos\psi & 0 \\ 0 & 0 & 1 \end{bmatrix}$	$f_{m-d} = \frac{2f}{c}[\Omega_l(\widehat{\omega_l}^2\sin(\Omega_l t) - (\widehat{\omega_l}^3\cos(\Omega_l t) + (\widehat{\omega_l}(I + \widehat{\omega_l}^2)R_{init} \cdot r_0]^T \cdot n$
Rotation cone micro-motion target	$R_c(t) = I + \widehat{\omega_c}\sin(\Omega_c t) + \widehat{\omega_c}^2(1 - \cos(\Omega_c t))$	$f_{m-d} = \frac{2f\Omega_c}{c}[(\widehat{\omega_c}\cos(\Omega_c t) + \widehat{\omega_c}^2\sin(\Omega_c t))R_{init}(r_0 - r_0')]^T \cdot n.$
Swing cone micro-motion target	$R = AB(t)A^{-1}$ $(x,y,z) = (i,j,k)A$ $B(t) = \begin{bmatrix} \cos(\theta(t)) & -\sin(\theta(t)) & 0 \\ \sin(\theta(t)) & \cos(\theta(t)) & 0 \\ 0 & 0 & 1 \end{bmatrix}$	$f_{m-d} = \frac{2f}{c}\left[AB'(t)A^{-1}R_{init}(x_0 y_0 z_0 - z_0')^T\right]^T \cdot n$

2.2 Practical Problems

The aforementioned universal model is based on the ideal assumption of point scattering without considering the impact of several environmental factors in practice. In the real environment, however, observation of translation and micro-motion often encounters subtle but impactive incidents, such as the irregular shapes of targets, fluctuation of radar signal strength, occlusion effects, etc., which should also be taken into consideration in actual observations.

In addition to an individual target, when ISAR is used to observe a micro-motion target, a single radar beam may contain multiple micro-motion targets, such as a broken satellite debris group [11, 18, 19]. Echo aliasing occurs when the distance between the targets is tiny. Since the sub-target micro-motion form and the micro-motion parameters are both altered, the high-resolution imaging method for a single micro-motion target will no longer be applicable. In [20], a high-resolution imaging method for micro-motion group targets based on augmented Lagrangian function is proposed. Under the complex conditions of Gaussian noise, self-occlusion and mutual occlusion, and singular values, the method can recover the track matrix of the micro-motion group target, implement the separation of the track matrix of the sub-object, and obtain the high-resolution imaging results.

The reason why the micro-motion is difficult to detect is because that it is generally combined with translation and other forms of motion. There are various solutions and strategies for disparate motion complexity. Translation, combined with simple and regular micro-motions, such as rotation and regular vibration, can be modeled separately and analyzed by disassembling the type of motion [6]. In contrast, more often than not, the motion forms of most targets show greater complicacy, such as tanks, ships and animals, etc. These movements, accompanied by complex micro-motions, can only be analyzed specifically by a combination with customized motion models for custom modeling analysis, which is obviously more difficult.

3   Techniques, Strategies and Implement

Existing technical applications for micro-motion targets rely mostly on adaptive improvements of specific algorithms and strategies, which show an obvious similarity even in different application domain. Therefore, instead of presenting techniques from the perspective of separate procedures as article [11], e.g. micro-motion feature extraction, imaging and recognition, in this section, we will summarize current researches on the basis of the quantity of radars, micro-motion complexity, other specific methods and common problems, which hopefully provides readers a horizontal understanding of micro-motion detection fields.

3.1   From the Perspective of Radar Quantity

Techniques Based on Monostatic Radar [21, 22]. Monostatic radar is widely used in radar feature extraction and imaging due to its low cost, system simplicity and operational flexibility. The core idea is to carry out customized and accurate modeling according to the type of space target. By analyzing and extracting the micro-Doppler parameters of the target echo, the 3-dimensional structure and motion characteristics of the micro-motion scattering point are constructed. However, on account of the quantitative limitation of radars, it is difficult to observe other micro-motion components of the target apart from the radial distance of the radar, thus hard to determine the virtual spatial position of the target.

When it comes to monostatic radar, the bandwidth of detecting radar is also worthy of consideration [23]. Paper [24] implements a research on phase derived ranging (PDR) based on wideband radar, which shows a giant efficiency on feature extraction.

Techniques Based on Monostatic Radar. Due to the motion complexity of the moving target, its micro-Doppler cannot be fully and accurately represented by traditional monostatic radars. In this case, two [25] or more radars are utilized to observe and acquire data from different angles. Distributed radars and networked radars possess the ability to collect the projection components of the micro-motion target from various perspectives, and analyze the spatial 3-dimensional motion and structural features, thus improving the target recognition capability of the radar system. Then with a correlation processing, the 3-dimensional image is synthesized. Although it overcomes the impossibility of a single radar collecting data in all directions, the existing method is still utopian because the anisotropy of the actual target makes the imaging more complicated and untoward.

Paper [26] proposed a scheme utilizing the multi-view feature of networked radar to construct a nonlinear equation and extracting the 3-dimensional precession characteristics of the ballistic target. In [27], with interferometric processing and ellipse fitting method, the real 3D scattering distribution information and 3D micro-motion characteristics of the space rotation target can be attained by using only a single multi-antenna narrow-band radar, which meanwhile shows a high precision and significantly reduces the complexity of the system implementation and the requirements of the radar signal bandwidth. However, it is merely practicable in certain micro-motion forms.

Interferometric Processing. Interferometric ISAR imaging exploits the difference of time and spatial information between target echoes to image the target in three dimensions [28]. The technique is a 3-dimensional imaging method combining space and time with not only the rotation of the target relative to the radar line of sight under time lapse but also the spatial variation between the target scattering point and the radar under disparate antennas or different observation angles. The interferometric method, on the basis of data source, can be categorized into different arc segment imaging and disparate receiving antenna imaging. In addition, it has a classification of interferometric imaging based on motion model analysis and that based on data self-focusing according to the motion compensation method [29]. The micro-Doppler effect theory is combined with multi-antenna interferometric processing technique in [27], and a 3-dimensional imaging and micro-motion feature extraction method based on L-type 3 antenna model is proposed.

3.2   From the Perspective of Micro-motion Complexity

For Simple Micro-motions, a Parametric Approach Can be Leveraged for Analysis. Parametric methods usually conform to the assumption that the micro-motion form satisfies some parametric model properly, such as spin model, precession model and so on. This type of method shows robustness to complex imaging conditions such as echo defects and low signal-to-noise ratio. However, when the category of motion model is unknown, model mismatch is easy to occur. Moreover, heavy calculation burden is also a disadvantage when the micro-motion form is complicated [15].

For Complex Micro-motions, a Non-parametric Approach is More Appropriate. Non-parametric techniques mainly include time-frequency analysis methods and imaging methods based on scattering point track matrix.

It is a common way to extract micro-Doppler features and imaging by applying time-frequency analysis, which basically reconstructs characteristics by domain transformation to improve the distribution structure of the micro-Doppler signal in the original domain, thereby removing redundant features [30]. Time-frequency analysis is classified into linear [31, 32] and nonlinear: linear including short-time Fourier transform, wavelet analysis, etc. [6], while nonlinearity includes Cohen-like time-frequency distribution, Wigner-Ville distribution (WVD), Smoothed-Pseudo Wigner-Ville Distribution (SPWVD) and so on.

Another non-parametric method is scattering point track matrix method, which exploits the matrix singular value decomposition method to realize the 3-dimensional reconstruction for the scattering point of the micro-motion target. In [15], a

3-dimensional high-resolution imaging method for single micro-motion target based on track matrix decomposition is presented (see Fig. 2), which is robust to complex micro-motion forms and reduces the complexity of parametric imaging methods.

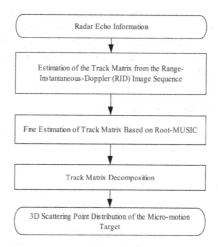

Fig. 2. Algorithm flow diagram of a 3D imaging method for single micro-motion target based on track matrix decomposition [15].

3.3   Other Strategies

Empirical Mode Decomposition (EMD). It was proposed by NASA's N. E Huang et al., with the main idea to decompose the complex signal into the sum of a finite number of Intrinsic Mode Functions (IMFs) and the remainders. In [33], the time-frequency distribution, variable-sampling filtering as well as the fast Fourier transform (FFT) tools are utilized to extract the micro-Doppler spectrum. Based on this, the motion and geometric parameters of the micro-motion target are estimated. In [34], the method of TFD-Hough transform is proposed, that is to build accurate signal model, design the curve of the corresponding time-frequency distribution map according to the frequency variation form of the signal, and then extract features.

Sparse Reconstruction. According to the sparse characteristics of micro-motion echo, it is possible to analyze the micro-Doppler signal by the sparse reconstruction method [35, 36]. Generally, by constructing a micro-motion target parameter estimation model based on sparse representation, the estimation problem is transformed into a sparse solution problem, which can be solved by applying greedy tracking algorithm [37] and convex optimization method [38]. In [39], the dictionary linear transformation and sparse solving algorithm are combined, and a flow algorithm of micro-motion parameter estimation based on sparse representation is designed. As well, the performance of the algorithm is examined experimentally.

Physical Characteristics. Due to the specific combat purpose and operational environment, space precession targets have their own unique physical characteristics, including geometric features and motion characteristics [34]. The physical characteristics of the micro-motion target can be extracted according to the correspondence between the geometry of the target, the micro-motion parameters and the micro-Doppler parameters in a micro-Doppler model. In paper [34], taking the space ballistic missile warhead as an example, the geometric and motion characteristics of the space precession target are analyzed, and the micro-Doppler parameters are estimated by the parameterized TFD-Hough transform method. Then they extract the physical characteristics of the micro-motion target by mapping the relationship between the physical characteristics and micro-Doppler parameters.

3.4 Potential Problems and Common Solutions

As a consequence of the complexity of micro-motion and the limitation of current technology, there are several intractable problems as following in micro-motion target detection:

Translation Compensation Problem. In general, the target's micro-motion is always combined with translation. The uniform and accelerated motion of the target will shift and broaden its micro-Doppler, which causes a significant influence on translation detection. Therefore, compensation is the basis for feature extraction and imaging. In [40], a detailed theoretical analysis of this phenomenon is carried out. In allusion to the difficulty of traditional ISAR imaging method to compensate accurately under low SNR, an adaptive low-noise-noise ratio ISAR translation compensation and imaging method based on a phase derivation of spectrum signal and particle swarm optimization is proposed, which as well achieves a well-focused ISAR measured data imaging result with low SNR. Besides, paper [41] put forward a fast translation compensation method suitable for high-speed ballistic targets. Paper [42] introduce a novel ISAR motion compensation approach via phase-derived velocity measurement (PDVM) technique to extract micro-motion feature.

Image Registration Problem. Image registration is one of the key steps of interferometric processing. The accuracy of the interference phase, thus the quality of the 3-dimensional image depends directly on how the image registration is. Image mismatch in interferometric imaging includes both image shift and image distortion, the former being derived from the distance and velocity difference between the target and the two antennas, while the latter being derived from the relative rotation between the target and the two antennas. Article [29] discusses the constraints of image distortion by creating specific image motion models.

Phase Error Problem. When imaging spatial targets, in the target body coordinate system, the azimuth and elevation angles in the radar line of sight change non-uniformly at the same time, leading to a non-uniform rotation of the imaging plane. There is, accordingly, a phase error if applying the traditional ISAR imaging method. Moreover, interferometric imaging requires high accuracy of image phase, so it is essential to correct the phase error of the ISAR image. In [29], based on the relative rotation law between space target and radar, a spatial target echo model after translation compensation is established. The model is used to analyze the influence of image defocus and phase error on the interference caused by nonlinear phase. As well, an ISAR imaging method based on fractional Fourier transform is proposed to solve this problem.

In conclusion, the research on micro-motion target detection technique is still in its infancy, in which domain, without any doubt, increasing effort should be devoted to solve the existing tough issues.

4 Applications and Prospects

Radar space target imaging technique based on micro-motion features has become a vital branch of radar research domain through micro-motion target modeling, micro-motion feature extraction and micro-motion target imaging. The coming decades will see a broad application prospects of micro-motion technique in military fields such as space security, air defense and anti-missile, territorial security and strategic early warning.

4.1 Applications on Ballistic Target Recognition

One of the most significant applications of the micro-motion target recognition technique in the military field is ballistic target recognition in the midcourse section [27, 43, 44]. Article [33], taking the ballistic missiles as an example, discusses the application of the radar feature extraction technique of the micro-motion target. Firstly, the target scene is designed, the echo signal is simulated, and then the micro-Doppler and Doppler are extracted. Moreover, RCS modulation features and micro-motion resolution features provide new technical support for air target and space target detection and recognition. Paper [30] proposes a time selection imaging method by abor transformation and time-frequency analysis.

4.2 Prospects

With the continuous breakthrough of techniques and the deepening of research, fresh and effective solutions for micro-motion target echo modeling, feature extraction and 3D imaging have emerged and verified by measurement and experiment. However, there are still several directions yearning for revolutionary achievement of radar micro-motion target detection in the following aspects:

Group Target Detection. At present, the existing techniques mainly focus on one single micro-motion target rather than a target group, which actually is the most normal case. When establishing a micro-motion model and extracting features for group target, the primary consideration is how to effectively remove interference or overlap and perform low-error separation when the sub-target micro-motion parameters are similar.

Big-Data-Driven Feature Extraction and Radar Imaging Analysis. With the increasing progress of radar micro-motion target detection, the database based on the characteristics and images of micro-motion targets will be gradually improved, which provides a new possibility for the subsequent research direction. Through data analysis and data mining based on big databases, certain patterns of micro-motion target recognition and imaging methods will be proposed. A revolutionary analysis model can also be constructed by using artificial intelligence techniques, such as deep learning [45], neural networks, etc.

Improvement of Transmission Media. How to use the newly-emerging bands for micro-Doppler analysis becomes a hot topic in the case of the increasingly serious congestion of the traditional electromagnetic wave band [11]. The existing technologies such as terahertz wave [46] and ultrasonic, with fine-grained recognition, strong robustness and low cost, are relatively suitable for application in the field of micro-motion target detection.

5   Conclusion Remarks

By investigating the existing radar techniques for micro-motion targets, this paper summarizes the concepts and methods as well as current difficulties and probable solutions in two subjects: micro-motion analysis foundation and techniques, strategies and implement. In the analysis foundation part, the universal micro-Doppler formula is quoted, along with classic motion matrices under 4 typical micro-motion forms, as well as practical problems. Then in the strategies and implement part, several common extraction and imaging methods are summarized in four perspectives, i.e. radar quantity, micro-motion complexity, other strategies and potential problems. Finally, the representative application of ballistic target recognition and imaging technique and potential development directions are prospected. This paper, as a survey, can be regarded as a horizon snapshot in the field of radar micro-motion detection and imaging.

Acknowledgements. This paper is supported by the National Key Research and Development Program of China through project 2017YFB0802502, by the Aeronautical Science Foundation of China through project 2017ZC51038, by the National Cryptography Development Fund through project MMJJ20170106, by the foundation of Science and Technology on Information Assurance Laboratory through project 61421120305162112006, by the National Natural Science Foundation of China through projects 61672083, 61532021, 61472429, 61402029, 61702028 and 61571024.

References

1. Qun, Z., Ying, L.: Micro-Doppler Effect of Radar Targets (2013)
2. Curlander, J.C., Mcdonough, R.N.: Synthetic Aperture Radar-Systems and Signal Processing. Wiley, New York (1991)
3. Franceschetti, G., Lanari, R.: Synthetic Aperture Radar Processing, 2nd edn. (2016)
4. Curlander, J.C., Mcdonough, R.N.: Synthetic Aperture Radar- Systems and Signal Processing. Wiley, New York (1991)
5. Zhang, Q., Luo, Y., Chen, Y.-A.: Micro-Doppler Characteristics of Radar Targets. Elsevier, New York (2016)
6. Guangfen, C.: Micro-Doppler Signature Analysis of Radar Targets and Its Applications. Xidian University (2014)

7. Chen, VC.: Analysis of radar micro-Doppler with time-frequency transform. In: Proceedings of the Tenth IEEE Workshop on Statistical Signal and Array Processing (Cat. No. 00TH8496), pp. 463–466. IEEE (2000)
8. Chen, V.C., Li, F., Ho, S.-S., et al.: Analysis of micro-Doppler signatures. IEE Proc. Radar Sonar Navig. **150**, 271–276 (2003)
9. Chen, V.C., Li, F., Ho, S.-S., et al.: Micro-Doppler effect in radar: phenomenon, model, and simulation study. IEEE Trans. Aerosp. Electron. Syst. **42**, 2–21 (2006)
10. Chen, V.C., Ling, H.: Time-Frequency Transforms for Radar Imaging and Signal Analysis. Artech House, Boston (2002)
11. Qun, Z., Jian, H., Ying, L., et al.: Research progresses in radar feature extraction, imaging, and recognition of target with micro-motions. J. Radars **7**, 531–547 (2018)
12. He, M.: Research on Some Techniques of ISAR Imaging for Space Micro-Motion Targets. University of Electronic Science and Technology of China (2017)
13. Encheng, H.: Research on ISAR Imaging Algorithm for Spatial Target. Harbin Institute of Technology (2017)
14. Xiang, L., Xunzhang, G., Yongxiang, L.: Research advances in ISAR imagery of complex motion target. J. Data Acquis. Process. **29**, 508–515 (2014)
15. Yongguo, L.: Study on 3D High-Resolution Imaging of Micro-motion Targets. Xidian University (2017)
16. Huang, X., Zhang, S., Liu, Y.: Analysis of radar micro-motion model. In: 2018 International Conference on Electronics Technology (ICET), pp. 162–165 (2018)
17. Jing-Ke, Z., Da-Hai, D., Shi-Qi, X., et al.: Analysis of InSAR 3D imaging characteristics of target with rotational micro-motion. J. Astronaut. **35**, 345–355 (2014)
18. Yongxiang, L., Hangyong, C., Li, X., et al.: Radar micro-motion target resolution. In: 2006 CIE International Conference on Radar, pp. 1–4 (2006)
19. Yongsheng, G., Hongwei, L., Feng, C.: Micro-motion targets resolution in a high noise environment. In: 2009 IET International Radar Conference, pp. 1–5 (2009)
20. Prickett, M., Chen, C.: Principles of inverse synthetic aperture radar/ISAR/imaging. In: EASCON 1980; Electronics and Aerospace Systems Conference, pp. 340–345 (1980)
21. Zhang, L., Xing, M.D., Qiu, C.W., et al.: Two-dimensional spectrum matched filter banks for high-speed spinning-target three-dimensional ISAR imaging. IEEE Geosci. Remote Sens. Lett. **6**, 368–372 (2009)
22. Bai, X., Xing, M., Feng, Z., et al.: High-resolution three-dimensional imaging of spinning space debris. IEEE Trans. Geosci. Remote Sens. **47**, 2352–2362 (2009)
23. Mérelle, V., Gaugue, A., Louis, G., et al.: UWB pulse radar for micro-motion detection. In: 2016 8th International Conference on Ultrawide band and Ultrashort Impulse Signals (UWBUSIS), pp. 152–155 (2016)
24. Fan, H.-Y., Ren, L.-X., Mao, E.-K.: A micro-motion measurement method based on wideband radar phase derived ranging. In: IET International Radar Conference 2013, pp. 1–4 (2013)
25. Deng, D.H., He, J., Wang, M., et al.: A method for extracting micro-motion feature of target with rotating parts based on Bi-ISAR system. In: Proceedings of 2011 IEEE CIE International Conference on Radar, pp. 524–527 (2011)
26. Dong, Z.: Extraction of three-dimensional precession features of balistic targets in neted radar. J. Xidian Univ. **42**, 146–151 (2015)
27. Jian, H., Ying, L., Qun, Z., et al.: Three-dimensional interferometric imaging and micro-motion feature extraction of ballistic targets in wideband radar **39**, 1865–1871 (2017)
28. Kai, H., Wei-Dong, J., Xiang, L.: Wideband imaging method for micro-motion target based on coherent Doppler interferometry. Syst. Eng. Electron. **36**, 239–247 (2014)

29. Lizhi, Z.: Research of interferometric 3D ISAR imaging for space target. Beijing Institute of Technology (2015)
30. Ge-Nong, L., Jie, Z., Ning-Ning, T., et al.: Ballistic target ISAR imaging based on time-frequency analysis. J. Air Force Eng. Univ. (Nat. Sci. Ed.) 42–45 (2015)
31. Yuxue, S., Ying, L., Qun, Z., et al.: Time-varying three dimensional imaging for space rotating targets with stepped-frequency chirp signal, pp. 23–31 (2018)
32. Yuan-Qing, Z., Long, C., Qun, Z., et al.: Micro-motion feature extraction based on DMFT for space target. Mod. Def. Technol. **42**, 42–47 (2014)
33. Hang-Yong, C.: Research on Radar Signature Extraction from Targets with Micro-motions. National University of Defense Technology (2006)
34. Jin, L.: Radar Signal Parameter Estimation and Physical Feature Extraction of Micro-Motion Targets. National University of Defense Technology (2010)
35. Chen, C., Zhang, L., Luo, Y., et al.: An ISAR imaging algorithm for micro-motion targets with sparse aperture. In: IET International Radar Conference 2015, pp. 1–5 (2015)
36. Yi-Jun, C., Hua, G., Guo-Zheng, W., et al.: Micro-motion feature extraction and targets imaging with sparse aperture. Mod. Def. Technol. **42** (2014)
37. Tropp, J.A., Gilbert, A.C.: Signal recovery from random measurements via orthogonal matching pursuit. IEEE Trans. Inf. Theory **53**, 4655–4666 (2007)
38. Candes, E., Romberg, J., Tao, T.: Robust uncertainty principles: exact signal reconstruction from highly incomplete frequency information. IEEE Trans. Inf. Theory **52**, 489–509 (2004)
39. Kangle, L.: Research on Feature Extraction and Parameters Estimation for Radar Targets with Micro-motions. National University of Defense Technology (2010)
40. Lei, L.: Study of Two-dimensional and Three-dimensional Inverse Synthetic Aperture Radar Imaging Method (2016)
41. Xun, H.: Research on Recognition of Space Cone-shaped Targets based on Narrowband Radar Feature. Xidian University (2015)
42. Guo, L., Fan, H., Liu, Q., et al.: Analysis of micro-motion feature in ISAR imaging via phase-derived velocity measurement technique. In: Radar Conference (2017)
43. Cun-Qian, F., Jing-Qing, L., Si-An, H.: Micro-Doppler feature extraction and recognition based on netted radar for ballistic targets. J. Radars **4**, 609–620 (2015)
44. Cunqian, F., Rong, C., Darong, H., et al.: Three-dimensional imaging of ballistic targets with vanes based on netted radar. J. Electron. Inf. Technol. **40**, 517–524 (2018)
45. Lecun, Y., Bengio, Y., Hinton, G.: Deep learning. Nature **521**, 436 (2015)
46. Qi, Y., Bin, D., Hongqiang, W., et al.: Advancements in research on micro-motion feature extraction in the Terahertz region. J. Radars **7**, 22–45 (2018)

Airport Role Orientation Based on Improved K-means Clustering Algorithm

Qingjun Xia[✉], Zhaoyue Zhang, and Baochen Zhang

College of Air Traffic Management,
Civil Aviation University of China, Tianjin, China
28353007@qq.com, {zyzhang,bczhang}@cauc.edu.cn

Abstract. This paper aims to provide an insight into the roles of the different types of airports in China by improved K-means clustering algorithm. The first part of the work analyzed the characteristics of Chinese airline network and pointed out that the key to construct hub-and-spoke airline network is determining the function of each airport. The index system of airport function orientation was established from airport operation index, airport hinterland index and airport growth index. The airports in China were classified into four classes by the K-means clustering algorithm. In order to improve reliability of clustering algorithm, a formula was used to normalize the value of each index, and the airports were clustered by improved K-means clustering algorithm. The algorithm was simulated by the MATLAB and the clustered results show the airports have obvious hierarchy.

Keywords: K-means clustering algorithm · Hub airport · Trunk airport · Line airport

1 Introduction

The main task of airport function orientation is to determine the type of the airport. There are 213 airports in China by now. Many airports have the same functional orientation, which leads to airline network of China constructed by point-to-point. The network makes a handful of large airports extremely busy, and flight delay is extremely serious. While the flights in majority of small and medium airports are scarce and airport resources are wasted. Hub-and-spoke airline network can avoid this phenomenon, and the key to construct hub-and-spoke airline network is to determine the airport type [1, 2].

In China, research on airport function orientation has not yet been carried out. What type of each airport is depended on administrative power and lacks necessary theoretical support. But this area study has been started in foreign, for example, Adikariwattageet et al. divided American airports into four categories: large hub, medium hub, small hub and nonhub according to number of stand and passenger throughput [3]. Malighettiet et al. analyzed the functions and characteristics of different airports in Europe, and classified European airports by clustering algorithm [4]. Rodríguez-Déniz et al. pointed out that the airport function orientation is an important condition to

G. Gui and L. Yun (Eds.): ADHIP 2019, LNICST 302, pp. 299–309, 2019.
https://doi.org/10.1007/978-3-030-36405-2_30

reasonably allocate government funds to promote the coordinated development of the airport [5].

The method and significance of airport function orientation have been done some analysis and research in foreign, but the classification indexes were lack of comprehensiveness because the indexes were restricted to number of stand and passenger throughput.

The indexes were selected from three aspects: airport operation ability, airport hinterland support ability and airport growth in this paper, so the status of the airport in the national airport system can be reflected more comprehensively.

2 Index System of Airport Function Orientation

The key to determine airport function is to establish the index system. Airport operation index directly reflects the current operation and management level of the airport, and it includes passenger throughput, cargo throughput and sorties of taking-off and landing.

The airport hinterland index reflects potential passenger and freight volume of the city where the airport locates. It includes three aspects: The tertiary sector GDP, per capita disposable income and urban population. The tertiary sector GDP reflects economic development level of the city. The higher the value of The tertiary sector GDP is, the greater the demand for air passenger and freight transportation is. Per capita disposable income and urban population are related to probability of travel by plane.

The airport development prospect can be objectively described by airport growth index. The more the navigable cities of airport are, the more the potential passenger and cargo throughput is, therefore the airport growth is better. When the airspace class is higher, the capacity and growth of airport can be improved greatly. The capacity is influenced by the number of airport stand, and thereby the growth of airport can be influenced by the number of airport stand. In summary, the number of navigable city, the airspace class and the number of airport stand can be selected as airport growth index.

The index system of airport function orientation was shown in Table 1.

Table 1. Index system of airport function orientation

The first level index	The second level index
Airport operation index	Passenger throughput
	Cargo throughput
	Sorties of taking-off and landing
Airport hinterland index	The tertiary sector GDP
	Per capita disposable income
	Urban population
Airport growth index	Number of navigable city
	Airspace class
	Number of airport stand

3 K-means Clustering Algorithm

China is similar to Europe in area, population and the number of airport, so the airport classification of Europe can be referenced to classify Chinese airports. European airports were divided into four kinds: world level hub, region level hub, secondary gate and no low-cost gate. Combining to Chinese situation, the airports in China are classified compound hub, regional hub, trunk airport and line airport. The main flights of compound hub are international and domestic connecting flights, and the ratio of between the two is not significant. The main flights of regional hub are domestic connecting flights. The main flights of trunk airport are direct flights and the connecting flights are less than compound hub and regional hub. The flights of line airport need to be transferred to get to the destination airport.

3.1 Traditional K-means Clustering Algorithm

When known the number of clustering, K-means clustering algorithm is the best way to classify n objects [6, 7]. The basic idea of K-means clustering algorithm is as follows:

Firstly, k objects are randomly selected as initial clustering center from n objects. For the rest of objects, each is assigned to the most similar clustering center respectively. Then the clustering center of the new cluster is calculated by mean value of the cluster. This process is repeated until the standard measure function starts convergence [8–10]. The standard measure function is defined as follows:

$$E = \sum_{i=1}^{k} \sum_{p \in C_i} |p - m_i|^2 \tag{1}$$

Where, E is the sum of mean square deviation for all objects, p is the value of one object, m_i is the mean value of cluster C_i, k is the number of cluster.

The major drawback of this algorithm is that it produces different clusters for different initial cluster centers. Quality of the final clusters heavily depends on the selection of the cluster centers. The improvement of K-means algorithm is mainly reflected in optimizing the initial cluster centers.

3.2 Optimizing Algorithm of Initial Cluster Centers

The step of optimizing initial cluster centers is as follows:

Step 1. Compute the distances between each object and all other objects in the object set O. Then find out the closest pair of objects and form a set $A1$ consisting of these two objects, and delete them from the object set O.

Step 2. Determine the data point which is closest to the set $A1$, add it to $A1$ and delete it from O.

Step 3. Repeat step 2 until the number of elements in the set $A1$ reaches a threshold τ.

$$\tau = 0.75 * (n/k) \tag{2}$$

At that point go back to the step 1 and form another data-point set A2.

Step 4. Repeat this till k sets of objects are obtained.

Step 5. The initial centroids are obtained by averaging all the vectors in each object set.

The initial cluster centers of the traditional K-means clustering algorithm are randomly selected from the object set O. If two or more initial cluster centers are select from the same cluster, which can lead to that the clustering results are not agree with actual situation. Because the initial cluster centers produced by the optimizing algorithm come from different cluster, the optimizing algorithm can avoid drawback of traditional algorithm.

3.3 Improved K-means Clustering Algorithm

From Sects. 3.1 and 3.2, the flowchart of improved K-means clustering algorithm was shown in Fig. 1.

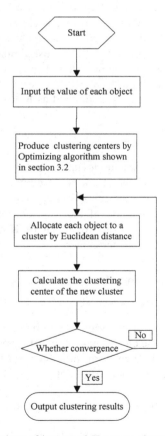

Fig. 1. Flowchart of improved K-means clustering algorithm

4 Airport Function Orientation

4.1 Data Normalization Processing

The index value of passenger throughput, cargo throughput, sorties of taking-off and landing, The tertiary sector GDP, per capita disposable income, urban population, number of navigable city, airspace class, number of airport stand about Chinese 213 airports was shown in Appendix 1. The dimension of some indexes is not uniform and the value has great difference. For example, the influence of navigable city on the standard measurement function can be ignored in contrast with passenger throughput, because there are 6 orders of magnitude difference between them. In order to improve the reliability of clustering, the value of each index is needed to normalize. The formula of normalization was shown as follows.

$$v'_{ij} = \frac{v_{ij} - \min(V_i)}{\max(V_i) - \min(V_i)} \tag{3}$$

Where, $V_i = \{v_{i1}, v_{i2}, \cdots\cdots, v_{in}\}$, v_{ij} is the value of the ith index of jth object, v'_{ij} is the normalization value of the ith index of jth object.

4.2 Simulation and Analysis

When known the cluster centers, clustering speed and convergence of the algorithm will be improved greatly. Base on optimizing algorithm of initial cluster centers, the cluster centers of compound hub, regional hub, trunk airport and line airport were selected as Beijing Capital International Airport (PEK), Chongqing Jiangbei International Airport (CKG), Jinan Yaoqiang International Airport (TNA) and Chifeng Yulong Airport (CIF), respectively. When given the clustering center and the normalized index value, the Matlab program of K-means clustering algorithm was run, and the simulation results were shown in Fig. 2.

From the simulation results, we can conclude: (1) PEK, PVG and CAN were clustered to compound hub, because their comprehensive evaluation indexes are much greater than others. (2) TSN, SZX, WUH, SHA, HGH, NKG, CTU, KMG, CKG, XIY, SHE and URC were clustered to regional hub, because their comprehensive evaluation indexes are lower than that of the composite hub, but higher than others. (3) SJW, TYN, HET, CSX, SYX, HAK, CGO, LYA, NNG, KHN, KWL, ZUH, FUO, XMN, TAO, FOC, TNA, HFE, NGB, WNZ, YNT, WUX, JJN, CZX, LHW, KWE, LXA, INC, DLC, HRB, and CGQ were clustered to trunk airport, because their comprehensive evaluation indexes are between the regional hub and the line airport. The rest of airports were clustered to line airport.

When known the type of each airport, the radiation airports of each hub airport can be found by corresponding indexes. But how establish the index system can be further developed in the follow-up study.

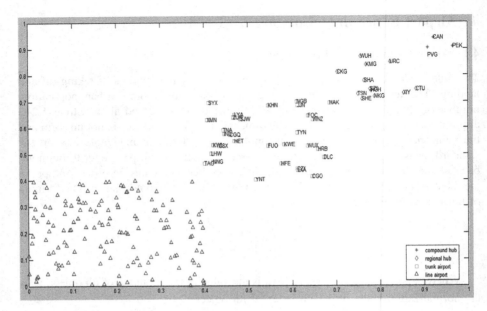

Fig. 2. Simulation results of airport function orientation

5 Conclusions

(1) The index system of airport function orientation was built up from airport operation index, airport hinterland index and airport growth index.
(2) The optimizing algorithm of initial cluster centers was put forward for the sake of avoiding the drawback of traditional K-means clustering algorithm.
(3) In order to improve the reliability of K-means clustering algorithm, the indexes were normalized.
(4) The K-means clustering algorithm about airport role orientation was simulated by Matlab, and the clustering results show the four types of airport have obvious hierarchy.

Although the airport function orientation was finished in the paper, how to determine the line airports radiated by hub airport and construct hub-and-spoke airline network need to be further studied.

Acknowledgements. The Chinese National Natural Science Foundation 71571182, 41501430 and National Science for Distinguished Young Scholars (61603396) supported this work. In addition, the Central University Project (3122016A002) also supported the thesis.

Appendix: Index Value of Airports

Airport IATA	Passenger throughput (person-time)	Cargo throughput (ton)	Sorties of taking-off and landing	Number of navigable city	Airspace class	Number of airport stand	The tertiary sector GDP (billion ¥)	Per capita disposable income (¥)	Urban population (million)
PEK	83,712,355	1,843,681.1	567,757	236	4F	314	14987	40321	2114
TSN	10,035,833	214,419.8	100,729	74	4E	47	6905	32658	1472
TYN	7,803,574	44,354.4	76,546	50	4E	43	1322	24000	427
SJW	5,110,536	42,976.2	51,980	51	4E	69	1960	23000	1027
NAY	4,455,263	37,091.9	38,661	41	4C	25	14987	40321	2114
HET	6,150,282	32,599.9	62,799	63	4E	32	1709	25464	294
DSN	1,731,882	9,455.7	29,584	41	4D	11	1489	36132	200
BAV	1,708,846	10,011.6	14,965	19	4D	7	1325	18311	273
HLD	1,287,483	5,590.8	12,685	20	4C	11	119	*10072*	35
YCU	1,010,070	2,818.7	9,507	22	4D	10	438	20718	519
CIF	660,704	1,801.4	7,533	42	3C	3	567	10337	460
CIH	574,080	919.5	7,230	12	4C	6	410	22803	336
TGO	572,719	1,810.7	8,722	10	3C	3	432	21009	313
HLH	266,262	1,649.2	3,532	29	3C	5	52	8421	32
ZQZ	24,021	0.7	544	6	4C	3	521	20470	467
DAT	358,910	1,965.1	14,121	3	4C	3	457	21430	335
WUA	470,152	1,438.6	5,864	7	3C	5	189	24565	54
XIL	465,949	2,074.0	18,086	2	3C	6	78	27135	18
HDG	230,087	66.4	8,534	10	4D	6	1320	23936	979
SHP	207,947	919.6	3,014	20	4D	6	467	18013	300
ERL	98,102	295.3	2,321	2	4C	2	47	25801	7.4
AXF	2,053	269	106	3	3C	2	49	24448	14
EJN	897	390	48	2	3C	2	19	17293	3.2
AHF	879	786	74	2	3C	2	13	23867	2.5
TVS	180,660	1,212.6	1,967	11	4C	4	1958	26647	737
CAN	52,450,262	1,309,745.5	394,403	136	4E	122	9964	42,066	1292.68
SZX	32,268,457	913,472.1	257,446	102	4F	94	8198	44,650	1062
CSX	16,007,212	117,588.7	137,843	90	4E	42	2915	33,662	722
WUH	15,706,063	129,450.3	148,524	91	4F	78	4320	29,821	1012
SYX	12,866,869	62,945.5	90,748	80	4E	41	250	20,472	69
HAK	11,935,470	111,813.6	94,436	61	4E	33	629	24,363	217
CGO	13,139,994	255,712.7	127,835	52	4E	43	2585	26,600	919
LYA	594,781	1,421.6	8695	15	4D	9	1254	24820	656
JGS	444,378	1,831.0	4,870	7	4C	2	27	10309	16.3
NNY	405,929	821.2	33,328	10	4D	10	784	19543	1026
JDZ	405,021	631.0	3,604	15	4C	3	232	8912	159
CGD	282,885	185.3	80,554	8	4C	6	336	9629	576
FUG	352,329	316.6	11,427	9	4C	4	353	16686	760
NNG	8,157,331	86,949.6	71,408	61	4E	26	1343	20622	786
KHN	6,811,028	40,389.0	64,029	52	4E	47	1194	26293	504
KWL	5,875,327	32,985.8	50,696	38	4F	9	566	19882	474
ZUH	2,894,357	22,667.1	44,725	40	4F	21	770	36375	158
SWA	2,686,007	17,303.8	32,391	31	4D	21	437	18311	641
YIC	83,110	19.9	1,044	5	4C	2	407	14333	545
YIH	900,076	4,628.4	39,444	20	4E	11	1126	26955	408
LZH	733,774	4,576.8	10,706	17	4D	10	576	24293	376
ZHA	691,443	2,663.4	12,180	10	4D	21	824	22371	710
XFN	601,029	2,151.7	55,014	10	4D	11	844	19329	555
ENH	288,449	623.8	2,652	6	4C	8	221	16639	330

(continued)

(continued)

Airport IATA	Passenger throughput (person-time)	Cargo throughput (ton)	Sorties of taking-off and landing	Number of navigable city	Airspace class	Number of airport stand	The tertiary sector GDP (billion ¥)	Per capita disposable income (¥)	Urban population (million)
WUZ	50,589	40.0	19,049	8	4C	5	221	22619	463
FUO	161,953	1,614.1	1,238	1	4C	5	2531	38040	726
JIU	118,353	578.0	1,848	4	4C	3	573	23362	476
MXZ	84,150	63.1	2,774	3	4C	2	320	19753	524
JUZ	222,071	771.4	1,782	8	4C	3	418	16732	212
CGD	29,301	9.8	694	4	4C	2	465	19325	525
HJJ	133,584	17.6	2,818	7	4C	4	469	18154	477
BHY	848,338	4,813.5	11,412	10	4D	8	219	25029	154
PVG	47,189,849	2,928,527.1	371,190	153	4F	218	13445	43,851	2500
SHA	35,599,643	435,115.9	243,916	91	4E	66	13445	43,851	2500
KOW	626,849	3,795.5	7,038	12	4C	4	638	20566	842
LCX	43,928	4893	538	3	4C	3	44	11152	25
HGH	22,114,103	368,095.3	190,639	104	4F	115	4416	39310	880
XMN	19,753,016	299,490.8	166,837	75	4E	74	1557	41,360	367
NKG	15,011,792	255,788.6	134,913	85	4E	34	4357	39,881	818
TAO	14,516,669	186,195.7	129,751	57	4E	56	4013	35,227	871
FOC	8,925,923	110,239.4	83,406	66	4E	39	2143	32,130	728
TNA	8,139,087	72,560.9	80,746	46	4E	42	2892	35,648	694
HFE	5,628,013	39,984.2	52,872	50	4E	17	1836	27,775	761
NGB	5,459,333	64,247.3	46,468	50	4E	16	3111	41,657	763
WNZ	6,595,929	59,787.1	58,867	67	4E	25	1873	37,852	807
YNT	3,635,467	45,319.1	38,252	29	4E	12	2118	32,930	702
AQG	117,563	127.9	2,720	7	4C	2	450	22683	531
WUX	3,590,188	87,641.6	31,844	36	4E	15	2151	38,999	628
JJN	2,634,423	38,771.7	25,102	30	4D	15	1820	35,430	829
CZX	1,526,605	15,250.7	19,348	23	4D	20	1972	36946	468
WEH	1,145,846	5,683.6	13,263	15	4D	10	1020	31442	280
DYG	1,006,334	2,301.7	8,557	29	4D	10	228	16580	165
WUS	787,455	2,392.1	8,094	30	4C	24	44	24776	23
LYI	767,844	4,100.4	8,539	10	4C	3	1134	27511	1008
YIW	1,161,463	3,452.7	10,632	19	4C	5	504	48962	131
XUZ	1,112,811	6,298.0	37,822	20	4D	9	1885	32581	856
NTG	675,660	21,593.4	30,749	10	4D	3	2070	31059	729
YTY	612,899	3,076.2	15,943	18	4C	13	1334	30425	908
HYN	610,844	6,912.1	5,208	17	4C	8	1583	39123	600
HSN	479,138	286.2	12,839	6	4D	12	424	37646	114
LYG	563,584	1,462.9	8,668	15	4D	5	750	26600	440
TXN	552,359	2,520.7	6,508	19	4D	8	199	23356	135
HIA	404,776	2,529.2	40,594	16	4C	9	884	25456	480
YNZ	354,251	3,034.6	3,668	15	4C	8	1350	24119	721
JNG	334,598	935.4	3,634	12	4C	6	2892	25454	814
DOY	165,606	570.4	15,850	8	4C	7	875	33983	206
WEF	133,815	16,579.3	3,611	13	4D	7	1690	28386	918
JUH	62,337	321	800	6	4C	5	169	6456	140
CTU	33,444,618	501,391.2	250,532	138	4F	200	4574	29,968	1417
KMG	29,688,297	293,627.7	255,546	116	4F	49	1703	28,269	726
CKG	25,272,039	280,149.4	214,574	106	4E	85	5256	25,150	2970
KWE	10,472,589	77,425.2	93,646	67	4E	10	1155	23,376	468
LJG	3,999,422	6,356.1	37,015	19	4C	19	56	21,075	124
XNN	3,236,417	19,940.1	28,792	39	4D	49	428	19,444	222
JHG	3,050,170	6,580.9	29,164	21	4D	18	109	20,048	113

(continued)

(*continued*)

Airport IATA	Passenger throughput (person-time)	Cargo throughput (ton)	Sorties of taking-off and landing	Number of navigable city	Airspace class	Number of airport stand	The tertiary sector GDP (billion ¥)	Per capita disposable income (¥)	Urban population (million)
LXA	2,296,958	20,967.7	21,035	20	4E	14	125	21,421	55
JZH	1,350,872	7583.2	13,592	4	4C	5	0.5	13782	2.5
LUM	929,540	4,437.7	9,248	7	4C	9	89	18311	121
MIG	917,325	4,856.3	8693	23	4D	11	582	23100	464
TCZ	556,769	410.3	6,254	5	4C	3	43	20549	66.8
NGQ	27,852	71.0	558	20	4D	4	10	26955	28
DIG	501,754	686.2	5,606	8	4D	4	66	23902	40
LZO	439,626	2,399.8	5,124	12	4C	6	301	22821	425
YBP	434,022	2,497.8	4,506	7	4C	6	330	22718	446
NAO	319,384	2,102.0	27,764	7	4C	5	343	10302	630
WXN	318,835	1,791.0	4,902	7	4C	5	281	21823	158
XIC	317,745	1,502.9	3,658	3	4D	7	149	20052	74.4
ZYI	309,531	0.2	3,444	16	4C	5	633	16588	612
DLU	501,128	569.0	5,923	6	4C	4	279	23236	345
LZY	258,645	803.2	2,970	3	4C	2	45	17847	72
DAX	248,727	1,597.5	2,874	5	4C	2	411	18915	549
BSD	238,265	354.3	2,822	2	4C	2	181	21700	250
LNJ	199,651	819.7	2,066	1	4C	2	166	9066	243
SYM	220,043	633.8	2,817	1	4C	3	169	16491	254
BPX	148,178	525.9	1,592	3	4C	4	36	4033	112
GYS	122,858	165.7	1,482	4	4D	8	167	18713	253
YUS	112,998	756.0	1,274	2	4C	3	9	18893	37
JIQ	95,602	59.5	1,774	6	4C	9	40	18254	53.6
BFJ	75,679	39.4	1,056	7	4C	4	396	19851	653
ZAT	72,051	104.4	886	1	4C	2	131	18724	521
HZH	44,324	17.9	1038	3	4C	3	15	13860	53
PZI	63,823	193.0	744	2	4C	4	176	13860	123
ACX	122,938	52.8	3,176	5	4C	3	117	21360	83
TEN	141,787	43.7	2,542	5	4C	7	244	18457	209
AVA	62,478	41.9	2,058	6	4C	3	204	9573	229
WNH	48,199	64.0	882	2	4C	3	203	21080	351
JIC	55,602	5.9	1,910	3	4C	2	100	23295	46
LLB	17,661	36	334	5	4C	3	295	19981	397
RIK	27,322	61.8	358	1	4C	3	50	18075	142
AEB	42,234	0.0	808	2	3C	2	225	23305	347
KJH	7,650	0.0	156	6	4C	2	90	18890	106
DCY	25,900	89	272	2	4C	4	0.4	15311	3
XIY	26,044,673	178,857.5	226,041	113	4F	59	2549	33,100	846
URC	15,359,170	153,275.3	135,874	81	4E	93	1443	20,780	350
LHW	5,649,605	41,752.4	51,799	30	4D	23	547	20,767	362
INC	4,247,843	29,105.0	39,230	40	4D	9	530	23,776	203
UYN	1,191,031	2,875.3	13,924	14	4C	3	722	24140	335
KHG	1,149,428	6,280.5	10,862	8	4D	9	241	10722	397
KRL	731,522	3,066.6	8,097	7	4D	5	98	13812	60
AKU	631,843	1,802.4	7,554	4	4C	2	84	21840	237
YIN	581,589	2,000.7	7,340	2	4C	10	45	17905	58
HTN	494,824	1,544.5	4,816	2	4D	3	66	6927	201
JGN	353,505	1,000.0	4,429	11	3C	4	133	24294	23
DNH	348,734	465.6	5,155	8	4C	5	31	11929	18
AAT	188,154	247.2	2,860	1	3C	2	132	18427	60
ENY	180,664	154.1	2,456	4	4C	6	541	24998	227

(*continued*)

(continued)

Airport IATA	Passenger throughput (person-time)	Cargo throughput (ton)	Sorties of taking-off and landing	Number of navigable city	Airspace class	Number of airport stand	The tertiary sector GDP (billion ¥)	Per capita disposable income (¥)	Urban population (million)
HMI	180,614	218.6	2,676	3	4C	4	107	10163	57
KJI	100,208	1.8	1,330	3	4C	2	7	8350	6.5
IQN	81,476	3.9	7,442	3	3C	4	148	16661	221
GOQ	101,321	511.1	1,265	3	4D	2	116	23432	30
GXH	736	0.4	52	2	4C	3	56	15658	69
KCA	213,325	267.7	2,988	1	4C	2	51	20287	47
ZHY	71,390	69.9	46,520	3	4C	2	12	19810	118
KRY	63,960	58.0	25,675	1	4C	10	97	25249	38
NLT	61,016	30.6	1,016	1	4C	4	28	15430	29
TCG	55,351	7.8	1,392	1	4C	2	150	11134	121
YZY	41,976	36.1	945	3	4C	2	132	26955	119
TLQ	18,876	0.0	599	1	4D	15	62	19943	62
BPL	48,672	27.2	2,954	1	4C	4	37	20186	26
THQ	15,062	10.3	647	1	4C	3	192	17453	326
GYU	25,633	20.1	25,037	3	4C	2	90	18789	123
NBS	316,465	76.1	3,954	8	4C	6	268	25555	129
JNZ	190,521	1,339.2	2,142	2	4C	3	538	10946	312
NZH	303,226	2,314.5	3,617	6	3C	2	138	25800	30
NDG	257,289	930.8	2,150	4	4C	7	510	16700	536
DDG	170,632	1,031.2	1,482	7	4E	6	447	**22000**	244
OHE	118,435	218.5	2,426	4	4C	2	3	6989	15
HEK	94,956	421.5	2,035	3	4C	2	135	12100	167
LDS	80,624	48.4	1,726	6	4C	2	88	15370	114
CHG	72,855	9.2	2190	3	4C	3	824	25578	304
RLK	189,622	986.8	2804	4	4C	3	141	10717	166
SHE	15106952	136066.1	92300	98	4E	67	3114	29,340	822
DLC	14083131	132330.413	107709	96	4E	42	3281	30,150	669
HRB	10,259,908	92,309.6	84532	83	4E	41	2404	25,322	993
AOG	6,361	0	134	2	4D	13	1099	27097	364
CNI	3,798	0	489	1	3C	1	31	26301	8
CGQ	6,733,076	68,031.6	56,850	44	4E	32	2013	25,720	790
YNJ	1,114,829	5,787.9	9,060	10	4C	3	165	22013	65
DQA	541,420	2,592.7	5,596	9	4C	4	650	28500	282
JGD	101,864	7.0	2,826	6	4C	2	16	19529	15.6
JMU	416,926	742.3	4,767	4	4C	3	324	17863	255
JXA	145,634	269.5	2,385	3	4C	2	356	18100	186
IQM	0	0	17	2	3C	3	4	22100	7
MDG	446644	1230	4716	12	4C	3	413	14900	80.45
KGT	38317	0	646	2	4C	3	73	21418	113.78
AKA	0	0	230	1	3C	3	193	20734	263
YIE	56022	74	852	2	4C	2	8.8	13103	5.6
HZG	91	0	0	3	4C	5	352	14008	386

References

1. Wang, J., Mo, H., Wang, F., Jin, F.: Exploring the network structure and nodal centrality of China's air transport network: a complex network approach. J. Transp. Geogr. **19**(4), 712–721 (2011)

2. Lin, C.C.: The integrated secondary route network design model in the hierarchical hub-and-spoke network for dual express services. Int. J. Prod. Econ. **123**(1), 20–30 (2010)
3. Adikariwattage, V., de Barros, A.G.: Airport classification criteria based on passenger characteristics and terminal size. J. Air Transp. Manag. **24**(1), 36–41 (2012)
4. Malighetti, P., Paleari, S., Redondi, R.: Airport classification and functionality within the European network. Probl. Perspect. Manag. **7**(1), 183–196 (2009)
5. Déniza, H.R., Suau-Sanchezb, P., Voltes-Dortac, A.: Classifying airports according to their hub dimensions: an application to the US domestic network. J. Transp. Geogr. **33**(12), 188–195 (2013)
6. Latha, M., Surya, R.: Brain tumour detection using neural network classifier and k-means clustering algorithm for classification and segmentation. Integr. Intell. Res. **01**(06), 27–32 (2017)
7. Aliahmadipour, L., Torra, V., Eslami, E.: On hesitant fuzzy clustering and clustering of hesitant fuzzy data. In: Torra, V., Dahlbom, A., Narukawa, Y. (eds.) Fuzzy Sets, Rough Sets, Multisets and Clustering. SCI, vol. 671, pp. 157–168. Springer, Cham (2017). https://doi.org/10.1007/978-3-319-47557-8_10
8. Na, S., Xumin, L., Yong, G.: Research on k-means clustering algorithm: an improved k-means clustering algorithm. In: 2010 Third International Symposium on Intelligent Information Technology and Security Informatics, pp. 63–67, 2–4 April 2010
9. Emre Celebi, M., Kingravi, H.A., Vela, P.A.: A comparative study of efficient initialization methods for the k-means clustering algorithm. Expert Syst. Appl. **40**(1), 200–210 (2013)
10. Zahra, S., Ghazanfar, M., Khalid, A., Prugel-Bennett, A.: Novel centroid selection approaches for K-Means-clustering based recommender systems. Inf. Sci. **320**(1), 156–189 (2015)

Secrecy Outage Probability Analysis for Indoor Visible Light Communications with Random Terminals

Hong Ge[1($\boxtimes$)] and Jianxin Dai[2,3]

[1] College of Telecommunications and Information Engineering,
Nanjing University of Posts and Telecommunications, Nanjing 210003, China
[2] School of Science, Nanjing University of Posts and Telecommunications,
Nanjing 210023, China
daijx@njupt.edu.cn
[3] National Mobile Communications Research Laboratory,
Southeast University, Nanjing 210096, China

Abstract. This paper focuses on the physical layer security for spatial modulation (SM) based indoor visible light communication (VLC) systems with multi-LED transmitters, a legitimate receiver and multiple eavesdroppers. According to the principle of information theory, a lower bound on the SM-based VLC secrecy outage probability (SOP) is derived by considering the non-negativity, average optical intensity and peak optical intensity constraints. Numerical results show that the lower bound of SOP can be used to evaluate system performance.

Keywords: Visible light communications · Secrecy outage probability · Random terminals

1 Introduction

As a complementary technology to traditional radio frequency (RF) wireless communication, indoor visible light communication (VLC) is receiving more and more attention and is considered as a promising information transmission technology to meet the growing demand for wireless services. Because it only needs to use the existing lighting infrastructure without additional equipment platform construction costs, spectrum applications and electromagnetic interference. VLC will play an important role in the future fifth generation (5G) wireless Communication.

In indoor VLC, light emitting diode (LED) is used as the light source. The user can receive information from the source when it is illuminated by the LED. The transmission of information on the VLC channel may be eavesdropped by unintended or unauthorized users, which poses a security risk to the transmission of data to legitimate users. Recently, physical layer security has been proposed as an effective method to ensure the security of information theory.

© ICST Institute for Computer Sciences, Social Informatics and Telecommunications Engineering 2019
Published by Springer Nature Switzerland AG 2019. All Rights Reserved
G. Gui and L. Yun (Eds.): ADHIP 2019, LNICST 302, pp. 310–319, 2019.
https://doi.org/10.1007/978-3-030-36405-2_31

In [1], considering the physical layer security in the VLC system, two cases are mainly discussed, and the closed expression of the upper and lower bounds of the secrecy capacity are derived respectively under the two scenario. [2] described secrecy rate achieved by transmitting beamforming on the multiple-input, single-output (MISO) VLC wiretap channel. For physical layer security in multi-user VLC networks, the secrecy outage probability (SOP) and the ergodic secrecy rate (ESR) are derived in [3]. [4] studied the security performance of a legitimate receiver and a group of eavesdroppers in the VLC system, and derived a closed-form expression of the SOP and the average secrecy capacity without considering the constraints of optical signals. In order to improve physical layer security, a channel determined subcarrier shifting scheme is proposed for orthogonal frequency division multiplexing (OFDM) based VLC in [5].

Due to multiple RF chains, the hardware complexity of multi-input multi-output (MIMO) systems is typically high. In order to break this limitation, spatial modulation (SM) using only one RF chain has been proposed as a low complexity solution [6]. Extensive research on SM demonstrates the advantages of SM over MIMO. Recently, SM's investigation has expanded to the field of VLC. The safety performance of the degraded single-input single-output VLC eavesdropping channel is studied in [7]. A new physical layer security transmission strategy, called mapping transform SM, is proposed in [8]. The average symbol error rate of VLC using adaptive SM is studied in [9]. In order to break the limit on the number of transmitters required to be a power of two, a channel adaptive bit mapping scheme is proposed for SM-based VLC in [10]. The above works are based on point-to-point VLC, regardless of the security of information transmission. Recently, physical layer security has attracted great attentions of researchers under various scenarios. However, in the open literature, the physical layer security of SM-based VLC has not been well studied.

Under the above work, this paper mainly analyzes the SOP of a legitimate receiver and a group of eavesdroppers in a SM-based VLC system. Taking into account the average and peak optical intensity constraints, we derive the expression of a lower bound on the SOP. Numerical results verify the accuracy of derived lower bound.

The rest of this paper is organized as follows. Section 2 shows the system model of an SM-based VLC system that includes a legitimate recipient and multiple eavesdroppers. In Sect. 3, the expression of a lower bound on the SOP of the SM-based VLC is derived and analyzed. Numerical results are given in Sect. 4. Finally, conclusions are drawn in Sect. 5.

2   System Model

In this paper, we consider an indoor VLC system consisting of transmitters (Alice) with M LEDs, a legitimate receiver (Bob) and N ($N \geq 1$) eavesdroppers (Eve$_j$, $j = 1, 2, ..., N$), as shown in Fig. 1. In this system, Alice is fixed on the ceiling, while Bob and Eve are randomly placed on the receiving plane. Under the SM scheme, only one LED is activated in each symbol period and the activation

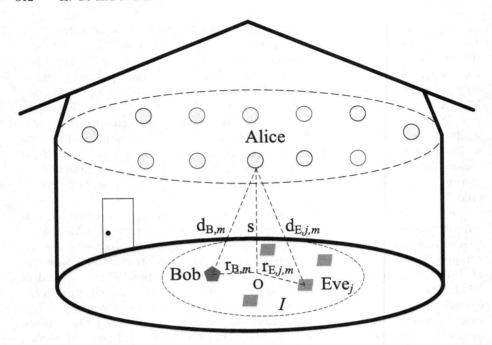

Fig. 1. An VLC network with M transmitter, one legitimate receiver and a group of eavesdroppers.

probability of each LED is equal, $p\,(h_k = h_{k,m}) = 1/M$, $k = B$ for Bob and $k = E$ for Eve. Assume that the receiving area is a circular region I of radius D and the projection of Alice on the receiving area is point O. We assume that Bob is uniformly distributed in Region I, and the position of the eavesdropper is uniformly distributed within the area, while the number of eavesdroppers subjects to the Poisson distribution $P\,\{N = k\} = \frac{\mu_s^k}{k!}e^{-\mu_s}$ with $\mu_s = \pi D^2 \eta$.

In indoor VLC system, the input signal X should satisfy $0 \leq X \leq A$ and $E\,(X) = \xi P$, where A is the peak optical intensity, $E\,(\cdot)$ is the expectation operator, ξ denotes the dimming target [11], and $P \in (0, A]$ represents the nominal optical intensity of each LED.

The received signals at Bob and Eve$_j$ can be respectively expressed as

$$\begin{cases} Y_{\mathrm{B}} = h_{\mathrm{B},m}X + Z_{\mathrm{B}} \\ Y_{\mathrm{E},j} = h_{\mathrm{E},j,m}X + Z_{\mathrm{E},j} \end{cases}, m = 1, 2, ..., M \qquad (1)$$

where $Z_{\mathrm{B}} \sim N\,(0, \sigma_{\mathrm{B}}^2)$, $Z_{\mathrm{E},j} \sim N\,(0, \sigma_{\mathrm{E},j}^2)$, σ_{B}^2 and $\sigma_{\mathrm{E},j}^2$ are the corresponding noise variances. $h_{k,m}$ represents the channel gain between the m-th LED and the receiver (Bob and Eve$_j$), and can be written as [12]

$$h_{k,m} = \frac{(l+1)A_r}{2\pi d_{k,m}^2}T_s g \cos^l(\varphi_{k,m})cos(\psi_{k,m}) \qquad (2)$$

where l is the lambertian emission sequence; A_r, T_s and g are the physical areas of the PD, filter gain and concentrator gain. $d_{k,m}$, $\varphi_{k,m}$ and $\psi_{k,m}$ are the distance from Alice (m-th LED) to Bob or Eve$_j$, the angle of emission and the angle of incidence, respectively. ψ_c is the field of view of each PD, $0 \leq \psi_{k,m} \leq \psi_c$.

Assume that the normal vector of the transceiver plane is perpendicular to the ceiling. Then, we have $\cos(\varphi_{k,m}) = cos(\psi_{k,m}) = s/d_{k,m}$, and the channel gain can be further rewritten as

$$
\begin{aligned}
h_{k,m} &= \frac{(l+1)A_r T_s g s^{l+1}}{2\pi}(s^2 + r_{k,m}^2)^{-\frac{l+3}{2}} \\
&= \lambda(s^2 + r_{k,m}^2)^{-\frac{l+3}{2}}
\end{aligned}
\tag{3}
$$

where $r_{k,m}$ is the distance between the projection point of the m-th LED on the receiving plane and the receiver (Bob or Eve$_j$). s is the vertical height of Alice and the receiving plane, assuming $\lambda = \frac{(l+1)A_r T_s g s^{l+1}}{2\pi}$.

3 Secrecy Outage Probability

Assume the location of Bob and Eve$_j$ (represented by U) are uniformly distributed within the region I. Then, the probability density function (PDF) for Bob and Eve$_j$ positions (due to the probability distribution of M LEDs), then $f_{U,m}(u) = \frac{1}{\pi M D^2}$.

The cumulative distribution function (CDF) of $r_{k,m}$ is given by

$$
F_{r_{k,m}}(x) = \int_0^{2\pi} \int_0^x \frac{1}{\pi M D^2} r \mathrm{d}r \mathrm{d}\theta = \frac{x^2}{M D^2}
\tag{4}
$$

In addition, the PDF of $r_{k,m}$ can be expressed as

$$
f_{r_{k,m}}(x) = \frac{2x}{M D^2}, 0 \leq x \leq D
\tag{5}
$$

According to (3), (5), the PDF of $h_{k,m}$ can be further expressed as

$$
f_{h_{k,m}}(x) = \frac{2\lambda^{\frac{2}{l+3}}}{(l+3) M D^2} x^{-\frac{l+5}{l+3}}
\tag{6}
$$

where $\lambda(D^2 + s^2)^{-\frac{l+3}{2}} \leq x \leq \lambda s^{-l-3}$.

Therefore, the CDF of $h_{E,j,m}$ is given by

$$
F_{h_{E,j,m}}(x) = -\frac{\lambda^{\frac{2}{l+3}}}{M D^2} x^{-\frac{2}{l+3}} + \frac{1}{M} + \frac{s^2}{M D^2}
\tag{7}
$$

The largest information gain $h_{E,\max,m}$ of the eavesdroppers can be expressed as

$$
h_{E,\max,m} = \max_{j \in \{1,\dots,N\}} \{h_{E,j,m}\}
\tag{8}
$$

According to [13], the PDF of $h_{E,\max,m}$ can be written as

$$f_{h_{E,\max,m}}(x) = \frac{2N\left(D^2+s^2\right)}{M^2 D^4\left(l+3\right)}\lambda^{\frac{2}{l+3}} x^{-\frac{l+5}{l+3}}\left(-\frac{\lambda^{\frac{2}{l+3}}}{D^2+s^2} x^{-\frac{2}{l+3}}+1\right)^{N-1} \quad (9)$$

In VLC system with non-negative, peak, and average constraints, when the primary channel is worse than the eavesdropping channel ($h_{B,m}/\sigma_B < h_{E,max,m}/\sigma_{E,\max}$), the secrecy rate is 0. When the primary channel is superior to the eavesdropping channel ($h_{B,m}/\sigma_B > h_{E,max,m}/\sigma_{E,\max}$), according to [1], the lower bound of instantaneous secrecy rate is known as

$$R_s = \begin{cases} \frac{1}{2M}\sum\limits_{m=1}^{M}\ln\left[\frac{3\sigma_E^2\left(A^2 h_{B,m}^2 + 2\pi e\sigma_B^2\right)}{2\pi e\sigma_B^2\left(h_{E,max,m}^2\xi^2 P^2 + 3\sigma_{E,\max}^2\right)}\right], & \text{if }\frac{h_{B,m}}{\sigma_B} > \frac{h_{E,max,m}}{\sigma_{E,\max}} \\ 0, & \text{otherwise} \end{cases} \quad (10)$$

To further simplify the derivation, the instantaneous secrecy rate can be further expressed as

$$R_s = \begin{cases} \frac{1}{2M}\sum\limits_{m=1}^{M}\ln\left[\frac{J_B+1}{J_{E,\max}+1}\right], & \text{if }\frac{h_{B,m}}{\sigma_B} > \frac{h_{E,max,m}}{\sigma_{E,\max}} \\ 0, & \text{otherwise} \end{cases} \quad (11)$$

where J_B and $J_{E,\max}$ are

$$\begin{cases} J_B = \frac{A^2 h_{B,m}^2}{2\pi e\sigma_B^2} \\ J_{E,\max} = \frac{h_{E,max,m}^2\xi^2 P^2}{3\sigma_{E,\max}^2} \end{cases} \quad (12)$$

According to (6), (9) and (12), the PDF of J_B and $J_{E,\max}$ can be further expressed as

$$\begin{cases} f_{J_B}(y) = \alpha y^{-\frac{l+4}{l+3}}, & u_{\min} \le y \le u_{\max} \\ f_{J_{E,\max}}(z) = \beta z^{-\frac{l+4}{l+3}}\left(-\frac{\lambda^{\frac{2}{l+3}}}{D^2+s^2}\left(\frac{3\sigma_{E,\max}^2 z}{\xi^2 P^2}\right)^{-\frac{1}{l+3}}+1\right)^{N-1}, & v_{\min} \le z \le v_{\max} \end{cases} \quad (13)$$

where α and β can be expressed as

$$\begin{cases} \alpha = \frac{\lambda^{\frac{2}{l+3}}}{(l+3)MD^2}\left(\frac{2\pi e\sigma_B^2}{A^2}\right)^{-\frac{1}{l+3}} \\ \beta = N\frac{D^2+s^2}{M^2 D^4}\frac{\lambda^{\frac{2}{l+3}}}{l+3}\left(\frac{3\sigma_{E,\max}^2}{\xi^2 P^2}\right)^{-\frac{1}{l+3}} \end{cases} \quad (14)$$

Moreover, $v_{\min}, v_{\max}, u_{\min}, u_{\max}$ can be expressed by

$$\begin{cases} u_{\min} = \frac{\lambda^2 A^2}{2\pi e\sigma_B^2}\left(D^2+s^2\right)^{-l-3} \\ u_{\max} = \frac{\lambda^2 A^2}{2\pi e\sigma_B^2}s^{-2l-6} \\ v_{\min} = \frac{\lambda^2\xi^2 P^2}{3\sigma_{E,\max}^2}\left(D^2+s^2\right)^{-l-3} \\ v_{\max} = \frac{\lambda^2\xi^2 P^2}{3\sigma_{E,\max}^2}s^{-2l-6} \end{cases} \quad (15)$$

In this paper, SOP is defined as

$$SOP\left(C_{\mathrm{th}}\right) = \Pr\left\{C_s \leq C_{\mathrm{th}}\right\}$$
$$= \Pr\left\{\tfrac{1}{2}\ln\left(\tfrac{J_{\mathrm{B}}+1}{J_{\mathrm{E}}+1}\right) \leq \tfrac{1}{2}\ln\left(\gamma_{\mathrm{th}}\right)\right\} \tag{16}$$

where $\Pr\left\{\right\}$ represents the PDF of an event. $C_{\mathrm{th}} = 0.5\ln\left(\gamma_{\mathrm{th}}\right)$ represents the threshold of the secrecy capacity, and $\gamma_{\mathrm{th}} \geq 1$ is the equivalent threshold of signal-to-noise ratio (SNR).

In indoor VLC system, it provides a large SNR to meet the illumination requirements. Therefore, we can assume $J_{\mathrm{B}} \gg 1$, $J_{\mathrm{E,max}} \gg 1$, $J_{\mathrm{B}} > J_{\mathrm{E,max}}$, and thus $\left(J_{\mathrm{B}}+1\right)/\left(J_{\mathrm{E,max}}+1\right) < J_{\mathrm{B}}/J_{\mathrm{E,max}}$.

Therefore, the upper bound of the instantaneous secrecy capacity can be expressed as

$$C_s = \frac{1}{2}\ln\left(\frac{J_{\mathrm{B}}+1}{J_{\mathrm{E,max}}+1}\right) < \frac{1}{2}\ln\left(\frac{J_{\mathrm{B}}}{J_{\mathrm{E,max}}}\right) \tag{17}$$

According to (16) and inequality (17), the lower bound of SOP can be expressed as

$$SOP\left(C_{\mathrm{th}}\right) \geq \Pr\left\{\tfrac{1}{2}\ln\left(\tfrac{J_{\mathrm{B}}}{J_{\mathrm{E}}}\right) \leq \tfrac{1}{2}\ln\left(\gamma_{\mathrm{th}}\right)\right\}$$
$$= \Pr\left\{J_{\mathrm{B}} \leq \gamma_{\mathrm{th}}J_{\mathrm{E}}\right\} \triangleq SOP_L \tag{18}$$

The lower bound of the SOP can be discussed separately in four cases. Case 1: when $\gamma_{\mathrm{th}}v_{\max} \leq u_{\min}$, we have

$$SOP_L = \int_{v_{\min}}^{v_{\max}} \int_0^{\frac{u_{\min}}{\gamma_{\mathrm{th}}}} f_{J_{\mathrm{B}}}\left(y\right) f_{J_{\mathrm{E,max}}}\left(z\right)dydz = 0 \tag{19}$$

Case 2: when $\gamma_{\mathrm{th}}v_{\min} \leq u_{\min}$ and $u_{\min} \leq \gamma_{\mathrm{th}}v_{\max} \leq u_{\max}$, we have

$$SOP_L = \int_{u_{\min}/\gamma_{\mathrm{th}}}^{v_{\max}} \int_{u_{\min}}^{\gamma_{\mathrm{th}}z} f_{J_{\mathrm{B}}}\left(y\right) f_{J_{\mathrm{E,max}}}\left(z\right)dydz$$
$$= -\left(l+3\right)\alpha\beta \int_{u_{\min}/\gamma_{\mathrm{th}}}^{v_{\max}} \left[\left(\gamma_{\mathrm{th}}z\right)^{-\frac{1}{l+3}} - \left(u_{\min}\right)^{-\frac{1}{l+3}}\right] z^{-\frac{l+4}{l+3}} \left(-\frac{\lambda^{\frac{2}{l+3}}}{D^2+s^2}\left(\frac{3\sigma_{\mathrm{E}}^2 z}{\xi^2 P^2}\right)^{-\frac{1}{l+3}}+1\right)^{N-1} dz$$
$$= \Lambda_1 \tag{20}$$

Case 3: when $u_{\min} \leq \gamma_{\mathrm{th}}v_{\min} \leq u_{\max}$ and $u_{\max} \leq \gamma_{\mathrm{th}}v_{\max}$, we have

$$SOP_L = \underbrace{\int_{v_{\min}}^{\frac{u_{\max}}{\gamma_{\mathrm{th}}}} \int_{u_{\min}}^{\gamma_{\mathrm{th}}z} f_{J_{\mathrm{B}}}\left(y\right) f_{J_{\mathrm{E,max}}}\left(z\right)dydz}_{T_1} + \underbrace{\int_{\frac{u_{\max}}{\gamma_{\mathrm{th}}}}^{v_{\max}} \int_{u_{\min}}^{u_{\max}} f_{J_{\mathrm{B}}}\left(y\right) f_{J_{\mathrm{E,max}}}\left(z\right)dydz}_{T_2} \tag{21}$$

where T_1 and T_2 are given by

$$T_1 = \int_{v_{\min}}^{\frac{u_{\max}}{\gamma_{\mathrm{th}}}} \int_{u_{\min}}^{\gamma_{\mathrm{th}}z} f_{J_{\mathrm{B}}}\left(y\right) f_{J_{\mathrm{E,max}}}\left(z\right)dydz$$
$$= -\left(l+3\right)\alpha\beta \int_{v_{\min}}^{\frac{u_{\max}}{\gamma_{\mathrm{th}}}} \left[\left(\gamma_{\mathrm{th}}z\right)^{-\frac{1}{l+3}} - \left(u_{\min}\right)^{-\frac{1}{l+3}}\right] z^{-\frac{l+4}{l+3}} \left(-\frac{\lambda^{\frac{2}{l+3}}}{D^2+s^2}\left(\frac{3\sigma_{\mathrm{E}}^2 z}{\xi^2 P^2}\right)^{-\frac{1}{l+3}}+1\right)^{N-1} dz \tag{22}$$

and

$$T_2 = \int_{\frac{u_{max}}{\gamma_{th}}}^{v_{max}} \int_{u_{min}}^{u_{max}} f_{J_B}(y) f_{J_{E,max}}(z) \, dydz$$

$$= -(l+3)\alpha\beta \int_{\frac{u_{max}}{\gamma_{th}}}^{v_{max}} \left(u_{max}^{-\frac{1}{l+3}} - u_{min}^{-\frac{1}{l+3}} \right) z^{-\frac{l+4}{l+3}} \left(-\frac{\lambda^{\frac{2}{l+3}}}{D^2+s^2} \left(\frac{3\sigma_E^2 z}{\xi^2 P^2} \right)^{-\frac{1}{l+3}} + 1 \right)^{N-1} dz$$

(23)

Therefore, (21) can be expressed as

$$SOP_L = T_1 + T_2 = \Lambda_2 \tag{24}$$

Case 4: when $u_{max} \leq \gamma_{th} v_{min}$, we have

$$SOP_L = \int_{v_{min}}^{v_{max}} \int_{u_{min}}^{u_{max}} f_{J_B}(y) f_{J_{E,max}}(z) \, dydz = 1 \tag{25}$$

Based on the analysis of the above four cases, the lower bound of the SOP can be finally expressed as

$$SOP_L = \begin{cases} 0, \gamma_{th}v_{max} \leq u_{min} \\ \Lambda_1, \gamma_{th}v_{min} \leq u_{min}, u_{min} \leq \gamma_{th}v_{max} \leq u_{max} \\ \Lambda_2, u_{min} \leq \gamma_{th}v_{min} \leq u_{max}, u_{max} \leq \gamma_{th}v_{max} \\ 1, u_{max} \leq \gamma_{th}v_{min} \end{cases} \tag{26}$$

where Λ_1 is given by (20), Λ_2 is given by (24).

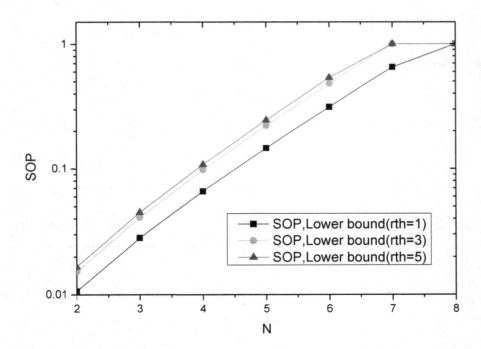

Fig. 2. SOP versus N with different γ_{th} when $P = 30\,\text{dB}$ and $D = 2\,\text{m}$.

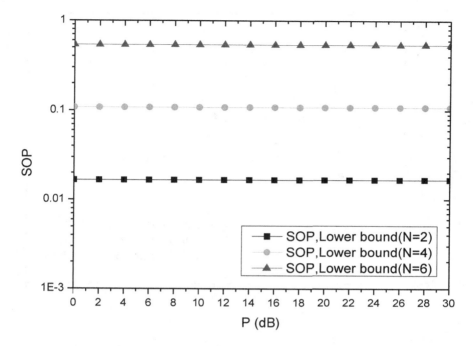

Fig. 3. SOP versus P with different N when $\gamma_{\text{th}} = 5$ and $D = 2\,\text{m}$.

4 Numerical Results

In this section, we consider an indoor VLC system, where area I includes a legal recipient (Bob) and multiple eavesdroppers (Eve$_j$, $j = 1, 2, ..., N$). Assume there are $M = 8$ LEDs fixed on the ceiling at a height of 3 m, and the receiving planes of the receiver and the eavesdropper are located in the same height of 0.5 m. LED dimming coefficient is set to be $\xi = 0.5$. The noise variances are set as $\sigma_{\text{B}}^2 = \sigma_{\text{E}}^2 = -104\,\text{dBm}$.

Figure 2 shows the relationship between SOP and the number N of eavesdroppers and changes with different equivalent thresholds when $P = 30\,\text{dB}$ and $D = 2\,\text{m}$. It can be intuitively seen that the SOP performance deteriorates with the increase of N, because the increase in the number of Eve will increase the diversity gain of information eavesdropping, and the secrecy performance of the system will definitely decrease. In addition, as the γ_{th} increases, the value of the SOP also becomes larger, which means that the system's safe transmission performance is degraded.

Figure 3 shows the relationship between SOP and P with a different number of eavesdrops N when $\gamma_{\text{th}} = 5$ and $D = 2\,\text{m}$. It can be seen that when the number N of eavesdroppers is determined, the SOP performance hardly changes with an increase in P. The results show that in this case, increasing the optical intensity does not improve the SOP performance of the system. This is because

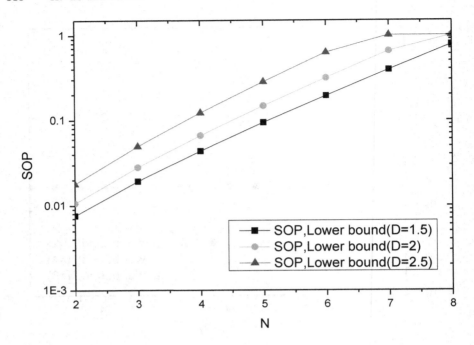

Fig. 4. SOP versus N with different D when $\gamma_{\text{th}} = 1$ and $P = 30\,\text{dB}$.

Bob and Eve follow the same distribution in the circular area, and increasing the optical intensity will increase Bob's SNR and Eve's SNR. Similar to Fig. 2, the SOP in the figure also increases as the number N of eavesdroppers increases.

Figure 4 shows the relationship between the SOP and the number N of eavesdroppers with different radius sizes D when $P = 30\,\text{dB}$ and $\gamma_{\text{th}} = 1$. When N is determined, it can be observed that the SOP performance improves as D decreases. This is because as the radius of the area increases, Eve has a greater chance of approaching Alice's projection on the floor, resulting in better channel gain than Bob. In addition, the SOP also increases with N, which is similar to Fig. 2.

5   Conclusion

In this paper, we have studied the SOP in indoor VLC system. A closed-form expression of the lower bound of the SOP has been derived. Numerical results show that the derived lower bound of the SOP can be used to evaluate system performance. Besides, the number of eavesdroppers has a large impact on SOP, and increasing optical intensity does not improve SOP performance. In contrast, the size of the radius of the area has a negative impact on the SOP.

Acknowledgments. This work was supported in part by the Open Research Fund of the National Mobile Communications Research Laboratory, Southeast University, under Grant 2019D15.

References

1. Wang, J.Y., Liu, C., Wang, J.B., Wu, Y.P., Lin, M., Cheng, J.L.: Physical-layer security for indoor visible light communications: secrecy capacity analysis. IEEE Trans. Commun. **66**, 6423–6436 (2018)
2. Mostafa, A., Lampe, L.: Physical-layer security for MISO visible light communication channels. IEEE J. Sel. Areas Commun. **33**, 1806–1818 (2015)
3. Yin, L., Haas, H.: Physical-layer security in multiuser visible light communication networks. IEEE J. Sel. Areas Commun. **36**, 162–174 (2018)
4. Pan, G.F., Lei, H.J., Deng, Y.S., Fan, L.S., Yang, J., Chen, Y.F., Ding, Z.G.: On secrecy performance of MISO SWIPT systems with TAS and imperfect CSI. IEEE Trans. Commun. **64**, 3831–3843 (2016)
5. Lu, H.Y., Zhang, L., Chen, W.J., Wu, Z.Q.: Design and analysis of physical layer security based on ill-posed theory for optical OFDM-based VLC system over real-valued visible light channel. IEEE Photonics J. **8** (2016). https://doi.org/10.1109/JPHOT.2016.2628800
6. Ishikawa, N., Sugiura, S., Hanzo, L.: 50 years of permutation, spatial and index modulation: from classic RF to visible light communications and data storage. IEEE Commun. Surv. Tutor. **20**, 1905–1938 (2018)
7. Arfaoui, M.A., Ghrayeb, A., Assi, C.: Secrecy rate closed-form expressions for the SISO VLC wiretap channel with discrete input signaling. IEEE Commun. Lett. **22**, 1382–1385 (2018)
8. Yang, Y.L., Guizani, M.: Mapping-varied spatial modulation for physical layer security: transmission strategy and secrecy rate. IEEE J. Sel. Areas Commun. **36**, 877–889 (2018)
9. Wang, J.Y., Zhu, J.X., Lin, S.H., Wang, J.B.: Adaptive spatial modulation based visible light communications: SER analysis and optimization. IEEE Photonics J. **10** (2018). https://doi.org/10.1109/JPHOT.2018.2834388
10. Wang, J.Y., Ge, H., Zhu, J.X., Wang, J.B., Dai, J.X., Lin, M.: Adaptive spatial modulation for visible light communications with an arbitrary number of transmitters. IEEE Access **6**, 37108–37123 (2018)
11. Wang, J.B., Hu, Q.S., Wang, J.Z., Chen, M., Wang, J.Y.: Tight bounds on channel capacity for dimmable visible light communications. J. Lightwave Technol. **31**, 3771–3779 (2013)
12. Wang, Z.X., Zhong, W.D., Yu, C.Y., Chen, J., Francois, C.P.S., Chen, W.: Performance of dimming control scheme in visible light communication system. Opt. Express **20**, 18861–18868 (2012)
13. Pan, G.F., Ye, J., Ding, Z.G.: On secure VLC systems with spatially random terminals. IEEE Commun. Lett. **21**, 492–495 (2016)

Smart Phone Aided Intelligent Invoice Reimbursement System

Yang Meng, Yan Liang, Yingyi Sun, Jinqiu Pan, and Guan Gui[✉]

College of Telecommunications and Information Engineering,
Nanjing University of Posts and Telecommunications, Nanjing 210003, China
guiguan@njupt.edu.cn

Abstract. Invoice reimbursement is one of indispensable apsects of business in many countries especially in China. Conventional manpower based reimbursement schemes often lead to high cost and inefficiency and robot based reimbursement systems require large space and huge equipment costs. In order to solve these problems, we propose an smart phone aided reimbursement system to realize the intelligent localization and identification in invoice images. First, invoice image is taken by camera of smart phone. Second, the Hough transform is used to detect the linear principle to correct the tilt of the invoice image with different background and different tilt angles. Third, we adopt You Only Look Once-Version 3 (YOLOv3) based target detection network to train the tagged data set, to obtain the training weights, and then realize the intelligent positioning and extraction. Finally, the invoice information is identified using optical character recognition (OCR). Experiment results are given to verify that the localization accuracy can reach 92.5% when the intersection over union (IoU) is set as 0.5 and the identification accuracy can reach up to 97.5% for invoice information.

Keywords: Deep learning · Intelligent positioning · Hough transform · Optical character recognition (OCR) · Invoice information identification

1 Introduction

With the rapid development of the economy, invoices are very popular for business transactions and consumption reception [1]. Invoice reimbursement problem poses a big challenge for many companies and governments. Invoice reimbursement is one of indispensable apsects of business in many countries especially in China. At this stage, The entire reimbursement process relies mainly on manpower in China. The entire process of reimbursing invoices is extremely cumbersome and complicated, and while consuming a large amount of manpower, it results in low reimbursement efficiency and high error rates. The traditional invoice image localization method is implemented for the position coordinates of the target area. The specific method is to preprocess the irregular image, and find the coordinates corresponding to the key information area on the invoice according to the size of the whole picture. For the pixels of different pixels and different sizes to be re-edited, it is not universal, and there is no way to achieve intelligent positioning. Another relatively intelligent method is the template matching

G. Gui and L. Yun (Eds.): ADHIP 2019, LNICST 302, pp. 320–329, 2019.
https://doi.org/10.1007/978-3-030-36405-2_32

method [2], which is to find a specific target in an image. The principle is very simple. It traverses every possible position in the image and compares it with the template. When the similarity is high enough, it is considered that the correct target is found. Although the template matching method can achieve the purpose of precise intelligent positioning, it has high requirements on the image to be positioned, and must be an image with no background interference and the same resolution. This method is also not universal. None of the above methods can achieve intelligent positioning in the true sense.

The system realizes intelligent positioning and content recognition of invoice images taken by mobile terminals with different backgrounds, different sizes, different resolutions and different angles, and the recognition accuracy is very high. The realization of the function of this system mainly focuses on the following aspects. First, because the paper invoice is easily damaged and lost, resulting in the problem of unable reimbursable, the system solves this problem by intelligently locating the invoice image taken by the mobile terminal. Second, the OCR is used to identify the entire invoice image, and the result of the recognition is very confusing, and the key information corresponding to the key segment cannot be found.

The system divides the invoice image into several areas. After intelligently locating different areas, according to the returned bounding box coordinates, the OpenImage Computer Vision Library (OpenCV) [3] CropImage image cropping tool is used to intelligently crop the positioned area and then use OCR to identify [4]. The accuracy is greatly improved. Third, the premise of traditional positioning is that the image being positioned has no background interference and high resolution requirements. The system uses the Hough transform detection linear principle, only need to tilt the invoice image correction, there is no requirement for the image background part, resolution and tilt angle, and it has universality. Fourth, the traditional positioning function has limitations, and it is impossible to intelligently locate images with different backgrounds, different resolutions, and different tilt angles. The system is based on deep learning, and uses the YOLOv3 target detection network to perform key areas in the invoice image. Feature extraction, which realizes the intelligent positioning of the invoice image captured by the mobile terminal. This system has a profound impact on the field of deep learning and computer vision image processing.

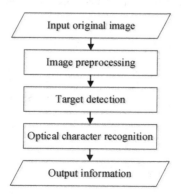

Fig. 1. Flow chart of the entire process

The flow chart of the system is provided in Fig. 1. The remainder of this paper is arranged as follows. In Sect. 2, the process of the proposed method is explained. Section 3 describes each specific step in detail and experimental results. We conclude the paper in Sect. 4.

2 System Design

We propose to apply the Hough transform detection linear principle to the preprocessing of invoice images. Then we use the YOLOv3 target detection network to intelligently locate and extract invoice images taken in natural scenes. Finally, we use the weak supervised learning framework to perform accurate character recognition on the extracted invoice image.

2.1 Image Preprocessing

The invoice image is mainly composed of straight lines, and the principle of Hough transform detecting lines can be applied to this aspect. The invoice image is mainly composed of straight lines, and the principle of Hough transform detecting lines can be applied to this aspect. The angle of the tilt in the principle of the straight line is detected, and the entire invoice image is corrected by a certain angle rotation.

The Hough transform uses a transformation between two coordinate spaces. A curve or line having the same shape in one image is mapped to a point on another coordinate space to form a peak, and then a problem of detecting an arbitrary shape is converted into a statistical peak. Using the principle of Hough transform to detect straight lines, we apply it to the intelligent correction of invoice images taken at different angles on the mobile end, and the effect is very good. The Hough transform detection linear principle polar coordinate diagram is shown in Fig. 2.

If the edge of the invoice is broken, the principle of Hough transform detects the line can also intelligently correct the damaged invoice image. This method is innovatively applied to the field of invoice image intelligent correction, effectively solving the problem that the traditional method cannot correct the incomplete image of the edge damage. The main reason is that this method can completely ignore the background and only perform the function of intelligently correcting the image for the straight line on the invoice image.

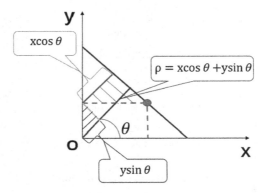

Fig. 2. Hough transform detection linear principle polar coordinate diagram.

For the better calculations, the Hesse normal form is proposed with the following formula:

$$\rho = x\cos\theta + y\sin\theta \tag{1}$$

where ρ is the distance from the origin to the nearest point on the line, and θ is the angle between the x-axis and the line connecting the origin and the nearest point. Each line of the image can be associated with a pair of parameters (ρ, θ), which is called a Hough space. The schematic diagram is shown in Fig. 3.

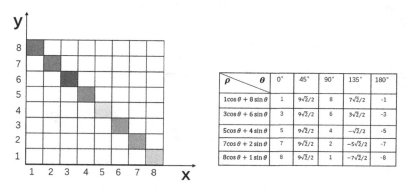

ρ / θ	0°	45°	90°	135°	180°
$1\cos\theta + 8\sin\theta$	1	$9\sqrt{2}/2$	8	$7\sqrt{2}/2$	-1
$3\cos\theta + 6\sin\theta$	3	$9\sqrt{2}/2$	6	$3\sqrt{2}/2$	-3
$5\cos\theta + 4\sin\theta$	5	$9\sqrt{2}/2$	4	$-\sqrt{2}/2$	-5
$7\cos\theta + 2\sin\theta$	7	$9\sqrt{2}/2$	2	$-5\sqrt{2}/2$	-7
$8\cos\theta + 1\sin\theta$	8	$9\sqrt{2}/2$	1	$-7\sqrt{2}/2$	-8

Fig. 3. Hough transform voting algorithm.

Suppose there is a straight line in an 8×8 plane pixel, and the coordinates (x, y) corresponding to the eight Descartes coordinate systems are converted into polar coordinates (ρ, θ). When θ is taken at different angles, the value of ρ is obtained. Calculate all ρ values, the maximum number of votes is ρ. As shown in the figure above, the equation of the line is $9\sqrt{2}/2 = x\cos 45^o + y\sin 45^o$.

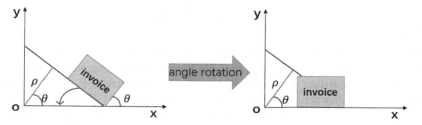

Fig. 4. Tilt correction of invoice image.

Using the detected straight line in the Hough transform, the tilt angle of the invoice can be calculated, and then the invoice can be corrected by rotating a certain tilt angle. This part is embedded in the test script of YOLOv3 to complete the correction of the invoice image taken at different angles of the mobile terminal. The tilt correction results are shown in Fig. 4.

2.2 Target Detection

YOLOv3 belongs to the target detection method of the regression sequence. Unlike the detection method of the sliding window and the subsequent area division, it regards the detection task as a regression problem and uses the neural network to directly predict the coordinates of the bounding box from the entire image. The box contains the confidence of the object and the class probability of the object, which can achieve end-to-end detection performance optimization. YOLOv3 detects objects very fast, about 45-155FPS, and YOLOv3 can avoid background errors and generate false positives. Because of this, we use YOLOv3 to extract features of invoice images with different backgrounds, different angles, and different pixels to achieve intelligent positioning and content extraction.

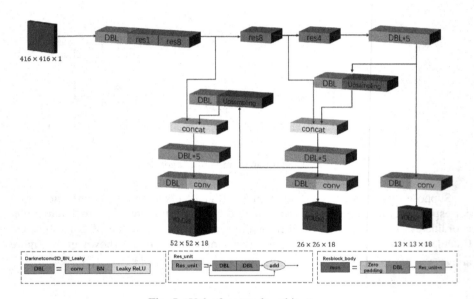

Fig. 5. Yolov3 network architecture.

As the latest algorithm in the YOLO series [5], YOLOv3 has both reservations and improvements to the previous algorithms [6]. The network architecture of YOLOv3 is shown in Fig. 5. Starting with YOLO, the YOLO algorithm does the detection by dividing the cells, but the number of divisions is different. Use "Leaky ReLU" as the activation function. A loss function completes the training, focusing on the input and output to achieve end-to-end training. Starting with YOLO 9000 [7], YOLO uses batch normalization as a method of regularization, accelerated convergence, and avoiding overfitting, connecting the BN layer and the Leaky ReLU layer to each layer of the convolutional layer. There is a choice between speed and accuracy. If you want to train fast, you can sacrifice accuracy. If you want high accuracy, you can sacrifice a little speed to achieve multi-scale training.

The improvement of each generation of YOLO depends largely on the improvement of the backbone network. From darknet-19 of YOLO9000 to darknet-53 of YOLOv3. YOLOv3 also offers alternate use of Darknet-53 and tiny-darknet. To improve performance, Backbone can use Darknet-53; for lightweight and high speed, you can use tiny-darknet.

2.3 Natural Scene Text Detection Technology

After completing the intelligent positioning and extraction of the invoice image taken by the mobile terminal, the OCR technology of deep learning is used to identify the text content of the invoice.

The text recognition of the invoice image is divided into two specific steps, the detection of the text and the recognition of the text, both of which are indispensable. Text detection of invoice images is very challenging when invoices exist in complex scenarios. Text detection in natural scenes has the following difficulties: text has multiple distributions; text layout is diverse; text has multiple directions; multiple languages are mixed.

At present, there are several popular text detection technologies based on natural scenes: the Connectionist Text Proposal Network (CTPN) network architecture commonly used in the OCR system proposed in 2016 [8]; the SegLink deep learning neural network proposed in 2017 that incorporates the small-scale candidate box of CTPN and learns from the Single Shot Multi Box Detector (SSD) algorithm [9]; the end-to-end text detection An Efficient and Accurate Scene Text Detector network architecture (EAST) [10] proposed in 2017; the weakly supervised Exploiting Word Annotations for Character based Text Detection network architecture proposed by Baidu in 2017 [11].

In this paper we use the weakly supervise exploiting word annotations for optical character recognition.

3 Detailed Explanation and Experimental Result

3.1 Hough Transform Method

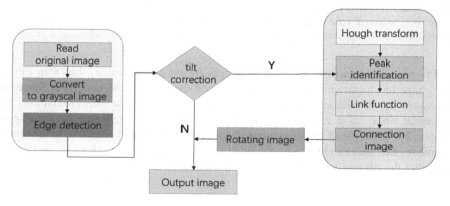

Fig. 6. Flowchart for preprocessing the invoice image by Hough transform.

Hough transform method edge connection flow chart is shown in Fig. 6. The flow is to read the original image and convert it into a grayscale image. Edge detection is performed by canny edge detection algorithm to obtain *binarized* edge images. Do a Hough transform on this edge image. Use the function *houghpeaks* for peak detection. The algorithm of the function *houghpeaks* is as follows: find the Hough transform unit containing the maximum value and record its position; set the Hough transform unit to 0 in the field of the maximum point found at the previous step; repeat this step until it finds the required up to the number of peaks, or until a specified threshold is reached. Once a set of candidate peaks has been identified in the Hough transform, it is left to determine if there are line segments associated with these peaks and their start and end. For each peak, the first step is to find the location of each non-zero point in the image that affects the peak. To do this, write the function *houghpixls*. Using the function *houghlines* to achieve straight edge joins, the function of the function *houghlines* is as follows: Rotate the pixel positions by $90° - \theta$ so that they are roughly on a vertical line; sort the pixel positions by the rotated x value; use the function diff to find the split. Ignore the small split, which will merge adjacent segments separated by small blanks; return information for segments longer than the minimum threshold.

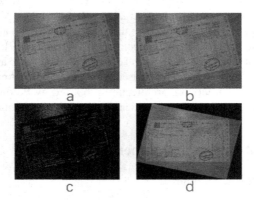

Fig. 7. Pre-processing process for invoice images in the experiment. a is the original invoice image; b is to convert the original image into a grayscale image; c is to convert gray image banalizations into edge image; d is the image obtained by the Hough transform and rotated.

Pre-processing process for invoice images in the experiment is shown in Fig. 7. The image has a certain angle of inclination and the background is striped. Since the features of the invoice are horizontal lines and vertical lines, the background also has horizontal lines, so it causes a lot of interference in the intelligent positioning of images. The principle of the Hough transform detection line will be based on the voting technique, and the straight line on the invoice with a large number of votes can be used to correct the tilt and solve the interference caused by the background.

3.2 Yolov3 Target Detection Network

The process of YOLOv3 training data is as follows: collect a large number of invoice images taken by mobile terminals from different angles, these images can contain different backgrounds; manually use the LabelImg marking tool to mark the images obtained in the previous step to generate a file of the format xml; The script file converts the xml file to a txt file. A training set is created for the Darknet-53 feature extraction network [12]; the training data is started, where the weight file will appear and the best weights will be imported into the test script; the intelligently positioned invoice image will be output.

YOLOv3 used logistic regression when predicting bounding box. Bounding box's coordinate prediction method:

$$b_x = \sigma(t_x) + c_x \tag{2}$$

$$b_y = \sigma(t_y) + c_y \tag{3}$$

$$b_w = p_w e^{t_w} \tag{4}$$

$$b_h = p_h e^{t_h} \tag{5}$$

where t_x, t_y, t_w, and t_h are the predicted outputs of the model. c_x and c_y represent the coordinates of the grid cell. The coordinates of the grid cell in the first column of the 0th row, c_x is 0, and c_y is 1. p_w and p_h represent the size of the predicted bounding box. b_x, b_y, b_w and b_h are the coordinates and size of the center of the predicted bounding box. $\sigma(t_x)$ and $\sigma(t_y)$ are the loss of coordinates using the squared error loss.

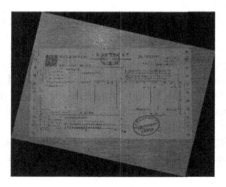

Fig. 8. YOLOv3 experimental results of intelligent positioning of invoice images.

Confidence reflects the accuracy of the bounding box which contains the object. The results of intelligent positioning of the invoice image captured by the smart phone are shown in Fig. 8. The IoU is a measure of the accuracy of detecting a corresponding object in a particular data set. The accuracy of intelligent positioning can be seen from the IoU. The mean average precision can reach 92.5% when the IoU is set at 0.5. The mean average precision can reach 80.74% when the IoU is set at 0.7.

3.3   Optical Character Recognition

When we need to conduct text recognition on the invoice image that has been intelligently located and extracted, the following problems occur. Because the angle and height of the shooting will cause the character size on the image to be very different, and secondly, when the invoice is placed in different scenes, it also causes significant difficulties in identification. To solve the above problems, we use weak supervision. The learning framework performs precise character recognition on the extracted areas. The results identified by the weakly supervised learning framework are shown in Fig. 9. The accuracy of recognizing texts can reach up to 97.5%.

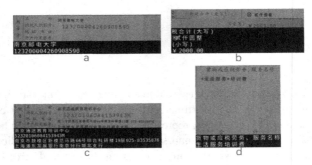

Fig. 9. The experimental results identified by the weakly supervised learning framework.

4   Conclusion

This paper has proposed a smart phone aided intelligent algorithm for invoice reimbursement system which can realize intelligent positioning and content recognition of invoice images. We applied the Hough transform detection linear principle to the preprocessing of invoice images. YOLOv3 target detection network was adopted to intelligently locate and extract invoice images taken in natural scenes. We used the weak supervised learning framework to perform accurate character recognition on the extracted invoice image. The accuracy of recognizing texts can reach up to 97.5%.

References

1. Bayar, S.: Performance analysis of e-Archive invoice processing on different embedded platforms. In: IEEE 10th International Conference on Application of Information and Communication Technologies (AICT), pp. 1–4 (2016)
2. Sun, Y., Mao, X., Hong, S., Xu, W., Gui, G.: Template matching-based method for intelligent invoice information identification. IEEE Access **7**, 28392–28401 (2019)

3. Noble, F.K.: Comparison of OpenCV's feature detectors and feature matchers. In: International Conference on Mechatronics and Machine Vision in Practice (M2VIP), pp. 1–6 (2016)
4. Jiang, Y., Dong, H., El Saddik, A.: Baidu Meizu deep learning competition: arithmetic operation recognition using end-to-end learning OCR technologies. IEEE Access **6**, 60128–60136 (2018)
5. Pan, J., Yin, Y., Xiong, J., Luo, W., Gui, G., Sari, H.: Deep learning-based unmanned surveillance systems for observing water levels. IEEE Access **6**, 73561–73571 (2018)
6. Redmon, J., Divvala, S., Girshick, R., Farhadi, A.: You only look once: unified, real-time object detection. In: IEEE Conference on Computer Vision and Pattern Recognition (CVPR), pp. 779–788 (2016)
7. J. Redmon and A. Farhadi, "YOLO9000: Better, faster, stronger," *ArXiv*, vol. 2017–Janua, 2017
8. T. Zhi, W. Huang, H. Tong, H. Pan, and Q. B. T.-E. C. on C. V. Yu, "Detecting Text in Natural Image with Connectionist Text Proposal Network," in *European Conference on Computer Vision (ECCV)*, 2016, pp. 56–72
9. B. Shi, X. Bai, and S. Belongie, "Detecting Oriented Text in Natural Images by Linking Segments," in *IEEE Conference on Computer Vision and Pattern Recognition (CVPR)*, 2017, pp. 3482–3490
10. X. Zhou *et al.*, "EAST: An Efficient and Accurate Scene Text Detector," in *IEEE Conference on Computer Vision and Pattern Recognition (CVPR)*, 2017, pp. 2642–2651
11. H. Hu, C. Zhang, Y. Luo, Y. Wang, J. Han, and E. Ding, "WordSup: Exploiting Word Annotations for Character Based Text Detection," in *IEEE International Conference on Computer Vision (ICCV)*, 2017, pp. 4950–4959
12. Zhao, Y., Chen, Q., Cao, W., Yang, J., Gui, G.: Deep Learning for Risk Detection and Trajectory Tracking at Construction Sites. IEEE Access **7**, 30905–30912 (2019)

Speech Source Tracking Based on Distributed Particle Filter in Reverberant Environments

Ruifang Wang[1,2] and Xiaoyu Lan[1(✉)]

[1] School of Electronic and Information Engineering,
Shenyang Aerospace University, Shenyang 110136, China
`rfwang0404@mail.dlut.edu.cn`, `lanxiaoyu1015@163.com`
[2] School of Information and Communication Engineering,
Dalian University of Technology, Dalian 116023, China

Abstract. In reverberant and noisy environments, tracking a speech source in distributed microphone networks is a challenging problem. A speech source tracking method based on distributed particle filter (DPF) and average consensus algorithm (ACA) is proposed in distributed microphone networks. The generalized cross-correlation (GCC) function is used to approximate the time difference of arrival (TDOA) of speech signals received by two microphones at each node. Next, the multiple-hypothesis model based on multiple TDOAs is calculated as the local likelihood function of the DPF. Finally, the ACA is applied to fuse local state estimates from local particle filter (PF) to obtain a global consensus estimate of the speech source at each node. The proposed method can accurately track moving speech source in reverberant and noisy environments with distributed microphone networks, and it is robust against the node failures. Simulation results reveal the validity of the proposed method.

Keywords: Speech source tracking · Distributed particle filter · Distributed microphone networks · Average consensus

1 Introduction

The tracking of a speech source in reverberant indoor environments may help to know the speech source's position at all times, which becomes very important in many audio applications, such as audio/video conference system, source separation, beamforming and robot [1–4], and it has been an attractive research problem. Since the room reverberation brings multi-path components into speech signals received by microphones, and environmental noise can also pollute the speech signals, it could bring some challenges to accurately track moving speech source in indoor environments with microphone networks. Meanwhile, reverberation and noise will generate spurious and unreliable measurements and may lead to the tracking performance degradation for a moving speech source.

© ICST Institute for Computer Sciences, Social Informatics and Telecommunications Engineering 2019
Published by Springer Nature Switzerland AG 2019. All Rights Reserved
G. Gui and L. Yun (Eds.): ADHIP 2019, LNICST 302, pp. 330–342, 2019.
https://doi.org/10.1007/978-3-030-36405-2_33

To solve this problem, Bayesian filter based speech source tracking methods have been developed, which depict the tracking problem with a state-space model and estimate the state of speech source with the state posterior [5–9]. These methods generally depended on estimated the time difference of arrival (TDOA) measurements and use both a series of past measurements and current measurements. Considering that the tracking of speech source is a nonlinear problem, an optimal approximation for the Bayesian filter via the Monte Carlo technique is applied in the speech source tracking, i.e., the particle filter (PF). A state space approach using PF was presented to track acoustic source and a general PF framework was formed in microphone networks [5]. A framework of speaker localization and tracking based on the information theory and PF was presented in [7]. In [8], a multiple talkers tracking method based on random finite set PF and time-frequency masking was discussed. A nonconcurrent multiple talkers tracking problem based upon extended Kalman particle filter (EKPF) was proposed in [9].

However, in the methods above-mentioned, their microphone networks normally are regular geometry structure, which make these methods require a central processing unit to collect all measurements for position estimate of the speech source. Thus, any failures of the central processing unit may lead to the tracking system collapse. Besides, considering the problem of node failures and lost data in the microphone networks, constructing distributed microphone networks with arbitrary layout and irregular geometry are suitable to perform speech source tracking. Then, in distributed microphone networks, the tracking methods of speech source based on distributed PF (DPF) have been discussed. In [10], a DPF algorithm was employed for the speaker tracking in the microphone pair network, in which an extended Kalman filter (EKF) is used to estimate local posterior probability for sampling particles (abbreviated as DPF-EKF). A improved distributed Gaussian PF (IDGPF) was performed to track speaker and an optimal fusion rule was employed in distributed microphone networks, in which a multiple-hypothesis model is modified as the likelihood function [11]. For non-Gaussian noise environments, a speaker tracking method based on DPF was discussed in [12]. For these methods, they employed different fusion algorithms of distributed data and different TDOA measurements.

Taking into account adverse effects of reverberation and noise, based on the DPF [13] and consensus fusion algorithm [14], a speech source tracking method in reverberant environments with distributed microphone networks is proposed in the paper. First, a dynamics model is used to describe the motion of a speech source in a room. Next, the generalized cross-correlation (GCC) estimator is applied to calculate multiple TDOAs of speech signals from each microphone pair. After that, multiple-hypothesis likelihood model is employed to compute the weights associated with particles of the local PF and the local state posterior is estimated at each node. Finally, the decentralized computation fashion of local posteriors is implemented by the average consensus algorithm and a global state estimate is obtained at each node. Especially, since the data communication does not perform in the whole microphone network, and only occurs among the neighbor nodes, the proposed method is robust against node failures and lost data.

2   Problem Formulation and Fundamental Algorithm

2.1   Problem Formulation

In a distributed microphone network with J nodes, where a node consists of two microphones and the communication among nodes can be modeled as an undirected graph $\mathcal{G} = (\mathcal{V}, \varepsilon)$, where $\mathcal{V} = \{1, 2, \cdots, J\}$ is the node set of the network and $\varepsilon \subset \{\{j, j'\} \,|\, j, j' \in \mathcal{V}\}$ is the edge set between nodes in the network. An edge $\{j, j'\} \subset \varepsilon$ indicates that node j and j' can exchange information each other. $\mathcal{M}^j = \{j' \in \mathcal{V} \,|\, (j, j') \in \varepsilon\}$ is the neighbors' set of node j.

Let the varying state $\mathbf{x}_k = [x_k, y_k, \dot{x}_k, \dot{y}_k]^T$ denote the speech source's position $[x_k, y_k]$ and velocity $[\dot{x}_k, \dot{y}_k]$ at time k in a reverberant and noisy environment, and $\mathbf{y}_k$ denote measurement vector. The transition function f_k and measurement function h_k are used to describe the nonlinear relationships between $\mathbf{x}_k$ and $\mathbf{x}_{k-1}$, between $\mathbf{x}_k$ and $\mathbf{y}_k$, respectively [5,12].

$$\mathbf{x}_k = f_k(\mathbf{x}_{k-1}) + u_k \tag{1}$$

$$\mathbf{y}_k = h_k(\mathbf{x}_k) + v_k \tag{2}$$

where u_k and v_k are the measurement and process noise at time k, respectively, both with known probability density functions.

The tracking problem of speech source is to estimate the state $\mathbf{x}_k$ at time k based on all measurements, i.e., $\mathbf{y}_{1:k} = \{\mathbf{y}_1, \mathbf{y}_2, \cdots, \mathbf{y}_k\}$. The Bayesian filter for tracking problem is to recursively calculate the posterior probability density $p(\mathbf{x}_k \,|\, \mathbf{y}_{1:k})$ of $\mathbf{x}_k$ based on the posterior probability $p(\mathbf{x}_{k-1} \,|\, \mathbf{y}_{1:k-1})$

$$p(\mathbf{x}_k \,|\, \mathbf{y}_{1:k-1}) = \int p(\mathbf{x}_k \,|\, \mathbf{x}_{k-1}) p(\mathbf{x}_{k-1} \,|\, \mathbf{y}_{1:k-1}) d\mathbf{x}_{k-1} \tag{3}$$

$$p(\mathbf{x}_k \,|\, \mathbf{y}_{1:k}) = \frac{p(\mathbf{y}_k \,|\, \mathbf{x}_k) p(\mathbf{x}_k \,|\, \mathbf{y}_{1:k-1})}{p(\mathbf{y}_k \,|\, \mathbf{y}_{1:k-1})} \tag{4}$$

where $p(\mathbf{x}_k \,|\, \mathbf{x}_{k-1})$ is the state transition density and calculated via Eq. (1); $p(\mathbf{y}_k \,|\, \mathbf{x}_k)$ is the global likelihood function and computed by Eq. (2); $p(\mathbf{y}_k \,|\, \mathbf{y}_{1:k-1}) = \int p(\mathbf{y}_k \,|\, \mathbf{x}_k) p(\mathbf{x}_k \,|\, \mathbf{y}_{1:k-1}) d\mathbf{x}_k$ is the normalized parameter [5,6].

2.2   Particle Filter

In the tracking of speech source, taking into account that the measurement $\mathbf{y}_k$ is nonlinear, the particle filter (PF) can obtain the optimal solution to Eqs. (3) and (4) by Monte Carlo technique. Let $\{\mathbf{X}_k^n\}_{n=1}^N$ be sampled particles and $\{w_k^n\}_{n=1}^N$ be associated weights, respectively. The PF represents the posterior probability $p(\mathbf{x}_k \,|\, \mathbf{y}_{1:k})$ using weighted particles. Using the sampling importance resampling

(SIR) filter [6], the N weighted particles are drawn from the state-transition density $p(\mathbf{X}_k^n | \mathbf{X}_{k-1}^n)$ as the proposal function, and the weight w_k^n corresponding to the n-th particle $\mathbf{X}_k^n$ is updated as $w_k^n = p(\mathbf{y}_k | \mathbf{X}_k^n)$ [5,6].

Then the $p(\mathbf{x}_k | \mathbf{y}_{1:k})$ is written as

$$p(\mathbf{x}_k | \mathbf{y}_{1:k}) \approx \sum_{n=1}^{N} \tilde{w}_k^n \delta(\mathbf{x}_k - \mathbf{X}_k^n) \tag{5}$$

where $\tilde{w}_k^n$ is the normalized weight, i.e., $\tilde{w}_k^n = w_k^n / \sum_{n=1}^{N} w_k^n$ and $\delta(\cdot)$ is the multi-dimensional Dirac delta function.

Based on the posterior probability, the minimum mean-square error (MMSE) estimate $\hat{\mathbf{x}}_k$ and covariance $\hat{\mathbf{P}}_k$ of $\mathbf{x}_k$ are obtained as [6]

$$\hat{\mathbf{x}}_k = E\{\mathbf{x}_k | \mathbf{y}_{1:k}\} = \sum_{n=1}^{N} \tilde{w}_k^n \mathbf{X}_k^n \tag{6}$$

$$\hat{\mathbf{P}}_k = \sum_{n=1}^{N} \tilde{w}_k^n (\hat{\mathbf{x}}_k - \mathbf{X}_k^n)(\hat{\mathbf{x}}_k - \mathbf{X}_k^n)^T \tag{7}$$

where $E[\bullet]$ is the mathematical expectation operation.

2.3   Time Difference of Arrival

The time difference of arrival (TDOA) measurements are calculated from the generalized cross-correlation (GCC) function $R_{k,j}(\tau)$ between two microphone signals of node j. The $R_{k,j}(\tau)$ based on the phase transform is given as [5,15]

$$R_{k,j}(\tau) = \int \frac{X_j^1(f) X_j^{2*}(f)}{|X_j^1(f) X_j^{2*}(f)|} e^{j2\pi f \tau} df \tag{8}$$

where $X_j^1(f)$ and $X_j^2(f)$ denote the frequency domain signals received by microphone pair, and superscript $*$ denotes the complex conjugation.

The TDOA measurement estimate $\hat{\tau}_k^j$ at node j corresponds to the large peak of the $R_{k,j}(\tau)$, written as

$$\hat{\tau}_k^j = \underset{\tau \in [-\tau^{j\max}, \tau^{j\max}]}{\mathrm{argmax}} (R_{k,j}(\tau)) \tag{9}$$

where $\tau^{j\max}$ is the maximal TDOA at node j.

However, in reverberant and noisy environments, only considering a TDOA estimate from the largest peak of $R_{k,j}(\tau)$ in Eq. (9) may bring ambiguous TDOA estimates, which can lead to spurious estimates of the speech source's position. Generally, taking multiple TDOA estimates from local largest peak of $R_{k,j}(\tau)$ has become popularly in speech source tracking problem [11,12]. Calculate U_k TDOA estimates to constitute local measurement of node j, i.e., $\mathbf{y}_k^j = \left[\hat{\tau}_{k,1}^j, \hat{\tau}_{k,2}^j, \cdots, \hat{\tau}_{k,U_k}^j\right]^T$, where $\hat{\tau}_{k,i}^j$ $(i = 1, 2, \cdots, U_k)$ is taken from the i-th largest local peak of $R_{k,j}(\tau)$.

3   Speech Source Tracking Based on DPF

3.1   Speech Source Dynamical Model

The Langevin model [5] is used to be speech source dynamical model, which describe the varying speech source's motion in indoor environments. It is assumed to be independent in each Cartesian coordinate, written as

$$\mathbf{x_k} = \begin{bmatrix} \mathbf{I_2} & aT \otimes \mathbf{I_2} \\ 0 & a \otimes \mathbf{I_2} \end{bmatrix} \mathbf{x_{k-1}} + \begin{bmatrix} bT \otimes \mathbf{I_2} & 0 \\ 0 & b \otimes \mathbf{I_2} \end{bmatrix} \mathbf{u_{k-1}} \tag{10}$$

where T is the discrete time interval, $\mathbf{I_2}$ is the second-order identity matrix, $\otimes$ is the Kronecker product operation, $\mathbf{u_{k-1}}$ is the time-uncorrelated Gaussian noise vector, $a = \exp(-\beta \Delta T)$ and $b = \bar{v}\sqrt{1 - a^2}$, where β and $\bar{v}$ are the rate constant and steady-state velocity parameter, respectively. Setting suitable values for β and $\bar{v}$ can simulate the realistic speech source motion.

3.2   Distributed Particle Filter Based on Average Consensus Algorithm

In [13], a distributed particle filter (DPF) is presented to achieve a consensus-based calculation of posterior parameters from the local PF at each node in the distributed network. All posterior parameters are assumed as Gaussian probability density. Then the global state posterior is calculated based on local posterior parameters via distributed data fusion algorithm.

In the distributed microphone network with J nodes, the local measurements $\mathbf{y}_k^j (j = 1, 2, \cdots, J)$ of the state $\mathbf{x}_k$ form the measurement vector $\mathbf{y}_k$, written as

$$\mathbf{y}_k = \left[(\mathbf{y}_k^1)^T, (\mathbf{y}_k^2)^T, \cdots, (\mathbf{y}_k^J)^T \right]^T \tag{11}$$

Node j first performs a local PF and calculates a local posterior $p(\mathbf{x}_k \big| \mathbf{y}_{1:k-1}, \mathbf{y}_k^j)$ incorporating all nodes' measurements $\mathbf{y}_{1:k-1}$ up to time $k-1$ and the local measurement $\mathbf{y}_k^j$. Then the Gaussian estimation of the $p(\mathbf{x}_k \big| \mathbf{y}_{1:k-1}, \mathbf{y}_k^j)$ is computed in term of weighted particles from Eqs. (6) and (7), which are local MMSE estimate $\hat{\mathbf{x}}_{k,j}$ and covariance estimate $\hat{\mathbf{P}}_{k,j}$, respectively.

Next, they are propagated among the neighbor nodes in the distributed microphone network, and fused by the typical average consensus algorithm (ACA) [14] which performs distributed linear iterations make each node obtain the converging average value. The consensus iteration calculation at node j can be given as

$$\mathbf{t}_j(m + 1) = \mathbf{t}_j(m) + \alpha \sum_{i \in \mathcal{M}^j} [\mathbf{t}_i(m) - \mathbf{t}_j(m)] \tag{12}$$

where α denotes the weight corresponding to edge $\{i, j\} \subset \varepsilon$ in the distributed network, and m denotes the time index of consensus iteration. The variable $\mathbf{t}_j(m + 1)$ will converge to the global average value at node j after M iterations.

Finally, the global consensus posterior $p(\mathbf{x}_k|\mathbf{y}_{1:k})$ can be obtained at each node of the distributed microphone network.

The DPF based on the ACA is nearly not affected by changing topologies structure and node link failures of the distributed network since in the iteration calculations of the ACA, each node only performs the data communications among the neighbor nodes.

3.3   Multiple-Hypothesis Likelihood Model

The particles' weights of local PF at node j are considered as local likelihood functions, i.e., $p(\mathbf{y}_k^j|\mathbf{x}_k)$, which are computed by multiple-hypothesis likelihood model based on the U_k TDOAs. Due to reverberation and noise of indoor environment, in local measurement $\mathbf{y}_k^j$, at most one TDOA $\hat{\tau}_{k,i}^j$ corresponds to the true speech source's position. If the $\hat{\tau}_{k,i}^j$ corresponds to the true position, let $f_{k,i}^j = T$, else, let $f_{k,i}^j = F$. These hypotheses can be described as [9,12]

$$
\begin{cases}
\mathcal{H}_0 = \left\{ f_{k,i}^j = F; i = 1, 2, \cdots U_k \right\} \\
\mathcal{H}_i = \left\{ f_{k,i}^j = T; f_{k,g}^j = F; i, g = 1, 2, \cdots U_k, i \neq g \right\}
\end{cases}
\tag{13}
$$

where $\mathcal{H}_0$ indicates that none of TDOAs corresponds to the true speech source's position, and $\mathcal{H}_i$ denotes that only the i-th TDOA $\hat{\tau}_{k,i}^j$ corresponds to the true position.

Assume that the hypotheses of Eq. (13) are mutually exclusive, then local likelihood function $p(\mathbf{y}_k^j|\mathbf{x}_k)$ can be given as

$$
p(\mathbf{y}_k^j|\mathbf{x}_k) = \sum_{q=0}^{U_k} s_q p(\mathbf{y}_k^j|\mathbf{x}_k, \mathcal{H}_q)
\tag{14}
$$

where s_q is the prior probability of the hypothesis $\mathcal{H}_q$, and $\sum_{q=0}^{U_k} s_q = 1$.

Assume that the U_k TDOAs in local measurement $\mathbf{y}_k^j$ are mutually independent conditioned on $\mathbf{x}_k$ and $\mathcal{H}_q$, if the TDOA $\hat{\tau}_{k,i}^j$ corresponds to the true speech source's position, the likelihood function is defined as a Gaussian distribution; else, it is defined as a uniform distribution over the set of admissible TDOA $\left[-\tau^{j\,\text{max}}, \tau^{j\,\text{max}}\right]$, written as [9]

$$
\begin{cases}
p(\mathbf{y}_k^j|\mathbf{x}_k, \mathcal{H}_0) = \frac{1}{(2\tau^{j\,\text{max}})^{U_k}} \\
p(\mathbf{y}_k^j|\mathbf{x}_k, \mathcal{H}_i) = \frac{1}{(2\tau^{j\,\text{max}})^{U_k-1}} \mathcal{N}(\hat{\tau}_{k,i}^j; \tau_k^j(\mathbf{x}_k), \sigma^2)
\end{cases}
\tag{15}
$$

Then, the local likelihood function $p(\mathbf{y}_k^j|\mathbf{x}_k)$ in Eq. (14) is written as

$$
p(\mathbf{y}_k^j|\mathbf{x}_k) = \eta\left(\frac{s_0}{2\tau^{j\,\text{max}}} + \sum_{i=1}^{U_k} s_i \mathcal{N}(\hat{\tau}_{k,i}^j; \tau_k^j(\mathbf{x}_k), \sigma^2)\right)
\tag{16}
$$

where $\eta = \frac{1}{(2\tau^{j\,\text{max}})^{U_k-1}}$.

3.4 Speech Source Tracking Based on DPF

Based upon the above-mentioned discussions, a speech source tracking method based on the DPF and ACA is proposed in reverberant environments with distributed microphone networks (abbreviated to DPF-ACA). First, each node calculates the GCC function of speech signals received by a microphone pair and chooses multiple TDOAs as its local measurement. Based on them, predict the particles via the Langevin model and compute the local multiple-hypothesis likelihood as weights of particles for the local PF at each node. Next, estimate the local state and corresponding covariance with representation of weighted particles. Finally, fuse all local state estimates via the average consensus algorithm, and all nodes can obtain a global consensus estimate. The DPF-ACA algorithm is summarized in Algorithm 1. Furthermore, since the data communications occur only in the neighbor nodes of distributed networks, the proposed method is robust against node failures or the data lost.

Algorithm 1. DPF and ACA Based Speech Source Tracking.

1: Calculate the GCC function $R_{k,j}(\tau)$ according to Eq.(8), $k = 1, 2, \cdots, K$, $\forall j \in \mathcal{V}$, $j = 1, 2, \cdots, J$, where K denotes the maximal time index;

2: Choose U_k TDOAs to form local measurement $\mathbf{y}_k^j$;

3: Predict particles $\left\{ \tilde{\mathbf{X}}_{k,j}^n \right\}_{n=1}^N$ by broadcasting $\left\{ \mathbf{X}_{k-1,j}^n \right\}_{n=1}^N$ according to Eq. (10);

4: Compute the local weights $\left\{ w_{k,j}^n \right\}_{n=1}^N$ according to Eq. (16);

5: Normalize the weights: $\tilde{w}_{k,j}^n = w_{k,j}^n / \sum\limits_{n=1}^{N} w_{k,j}^n$;

6: Estimate the local state $\hat{\mathbf{x}}_{k,j}$ and corresponding covariance $\hat{\mathbf{P}}_{k,j}$ according to Eqs. (6) and (7);

7: Fuse $\{\hat{\mathbf{x}}_{k,j}\}_{j=1}^J$ and $\left\{ \hat{\mathbf{P}}_{k,j} \right\}_{j=1}^J$ according to Eq. (12);

8: Calculate the global estimate at node j: $\hat{\mathbf{x}}_{k,j} = \hat{\mathbf{x}}_{k,j}(M), \hat{\mathbf{P}}_{k,j} = \hat{\mathbf{P}}_{k,j}(M)$;

9: Sample particles $\left\{ \mathbf{X}_{k,j}^n \right\}_{n=1}^N$ from $\mathcal{N}(\mathbf{x}_{k,j}; \hat{\mathbf{x}}_{k,j}, \hat{\mathbf{P}}_{k,j})$;

10: **return** $\hat{\mathbf{x}}_{k,j}, \hat{\mathbf{P}}_{k,j}$;

---

4 Simulations and Result Discussions

4.1 Simulation Setup

In the simulation, consider that a female speech source moves in an office room, whose moving trajectory is a curve which start point is (0.9 m, 2.65 m) and end point is (4.1 m, 2.65 m). There are 12 omni-direction microphone pairs irregularly and randomly installed in the room shown in Fig. 1. In advance, the distributed microphone network has been constructed via choosing microphones adaptively [16]. A microphone pair is considered as a node, in which the spacing distance of two microphones is set as 0.6 m. The communication graph of the distributed microphone network is shown in Fig. 2, where the line between two nodes indicates that they can exchange information each other. Each node has its neighbor nodes and can communicate with neighbor node only when their communication radius between them is less than 1.8 m. Meanwhile, the height of microphones is set as 1.5 m, which is same as that of the speech source, and a two-dimensional speech source tracking problem is focused in this paper.

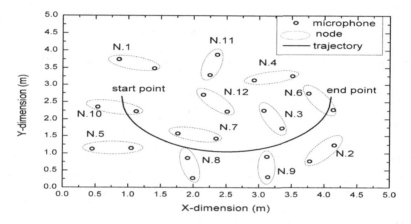

Fig. 1. Speech source trajectory and layout of the 12 microphone pairs in $X - Y$ plane.

In the simulation, the speech source is a female speech with a length of nearly 8 s with sampling frequency is 16 kHz. The speech signals are split as 120 frames and the discrete time interval T is 64 ms. The speech signals captured by each microphone are created by the well-known image method [17], which can simulate the indoor environment acoustics under different background noise and reverberations. The parameters T_{60} and signal noise ratio (SNR) are used to simulate different reverberations and different background noise, respectively. The configuration of simulation parameter is as follows. For the Langevin model, the parameter settings are $\bar{v} = 1\mathrm{ms}^{-1}$ and $\beta = 10\,\mathrm{s}^{-1}$. For the PF, the sampling number of particles is $N = 500$ and the initial prior of the speech source state is considered as a Gaussian distribution, with mean vector $\mu_0 = [1.0, 2.6, 0.01, 0.01]^T$ and covariance $\Sigma_0 = \mathrm{diag}([0.05, 0.05, 0.0025, 0.0025])$ set randomly. For the TDOA estimates, the number of the TDOA candidates is $U_k = 4$. For the multi-hypothesis likelihood, the standard deviation of the TDOA error is $\sigma = 50\,\mu\mathrm{s}$ and the prior of $\mathcal{H}_0$ is $s_0 = 0.25$. For the average consensus algorithm, consensus iterations is $M = 25$.

Root Mean Square Error (RMSE) of the speech source's position has been employed in tracking performance evaluation widely and the average of RMSEs (ARMSE) over M_c Monte Carlo simulations is given as

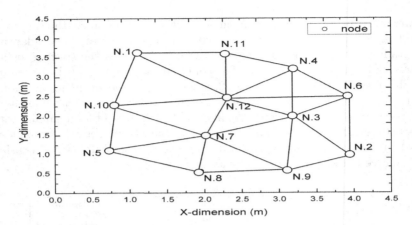

Fig. 2. Communication graph of the distributed microphone network with 12 nodes.

$$\mathrm{ARMSE} = \frac{1}{M_c} \sum_{m=1}^{M_c} \sqrt{\frac{1}{K} \sum_{k=1}^{K} \left\| \mathbf{s}_{\mathbf{x}_k} - \mathbf{s}_{\hat{\mathbf{x}}_{m,k}} \right\|^2} \tag{17}$$

where m is the cycle index of the Monte Carlo simulation running, $\mathbf{s}_{\mathbf{x}_k}$ denotes the true position of the speech source, and $\mathbf{s}_{\hat{\mathbf{x}}_{m,k}}$ is the speech source's position estimate of the m-th Monte Carlo simulation running.

4.2 Result Discussions

To evaluate the validation of the proposed method (DPF-ACA), some simulation experiments under different SNRs and different T_{60} values are conducted, comparing with the existing speech source tracking methods, i.e., [5] (abbreviated to PF), [10] (abbreviated to DPF-EKF), and [11] (abbreviated to IDGPF). Based on the same simulation setup, all methods are evaluated in form of the ARMSE results according to Eq. (17) averaged over Monte Carlo simulations, where times of Monte Carlo simulations is $M_c = 70$.

Effect of Reverberation Time T_{60}. Figure 3 indicates that the tracking results of all methods under the different T_{60} values, i.e., $T_{60} = \{100, 150, ..., 600\}$ ms when the SNR is 10 dB.

With the rise of reverberation time, it can be observed from Fig. 3 that tracking performance of all methods becomes worse and worse. Specially, the IDGPF method has larger errors under different T_{60} values. It means heavier reverberation will bring bad TDOA estimations at each node in the distributed microphone network. Due to taking only one TDOA from the peak of GCC function for sampling particles in the DPF-EKF method, it has poor tracking accuracy when $T_{60} > 200$ ms. We can find that the tracking performance of the PF is the best when T_{60} changes from 100 ms to 600 ms. However, its central processing fashion requires that the central processing unit can not have any failures. It can be clearly seen that the proposed method always has lower values of ARMSE and better tacking accuracy when reverberation time T_{60} becomes heavier and heavier, which indicates the proposed method is robust against the changes of environmental reverberation.

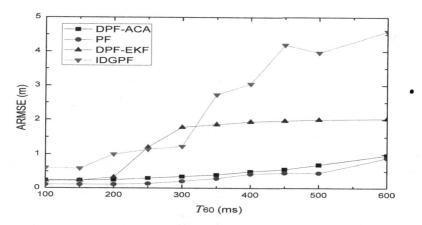

Fig. 3. ARMSE results versus different T_{60} in the environment with SNR $= 10\,\text{dB}$.

Effect of Signal Noise Ratio (SNRs). Figure 4 illustrates that the tracking results of all methods under different SNRs, i.e., SNR $= \{0, 5, ..., 35\}\,\text{dB}$, when the reverberation time $T_{60} = 100\,\text{ms}$.

With the increases of SNR, we can observe from Fig. 4 that the ARSME values of all methods change smaller gradually and their tracking accuracies become higher and higher. It can be seen that when SNR $< 10\,\text{dB}$, the IDGPF method and DPF-EKF method bring serious degradation of tracking performance, which means background noise has an important influence in their tracking performances. Although the PF has the best tracking accuracy in Fig. 4, it is limit to the central data processing manner. Furthermore, as a distributed tracking algorithm, when the SNR increases from 0 dB to 35 dB, ARMSE values of the DPF-ACA are on the decline, which shows more stable and better tracking performance. It implies that the proposed method is a valid tracking method for speech source under lower SNRs environments, especially.

Effect of Node Failures. Node failures in microphone networks indicate they can not exchange data with their own neighbor nodes, which can cause the decline of the valid node's number and the change of communication graph in Fig. 2. Tracking trajectories of all tracking methods are displayed in Fig. 5 under the environment with $T_{60} = 100$ ms and SNR $= 15\,\text{dB}$, when there are three fault nodes in the distributed microphone network, i.e., N.1 node, N.5 node, and N.11 node shown in Fig. 2.

When three nodes can not communicate with their neighbor nodes in the distributed microphone network, the number of valid nodes of network in Fig. 2

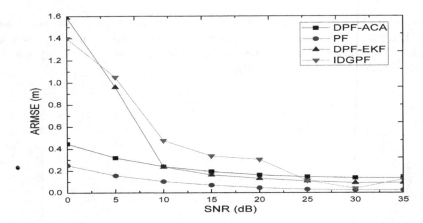

Fig. 4. ARMSE results versus different SNRs in the environment with $T_{60} = 100$ ms.

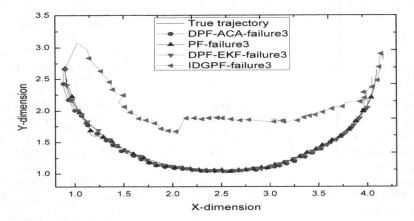

Fig. 5. Speech source tracking results in the network with three fault nodes.

changes to 9 and there are only 9 local measurements, which could affect the tracking performance of all tracking methods of speech source. However, it can be observed that the DPF-ACA, PF, and DPF-EKF methods can successfully track the moving speech source with smaller ARMSE values, which indicates the node failures have little impact them. For the IDGPF method, it generates larger tracking errors in tracking true trajectory of the speech source. Meanwhile, since the DPF-ACA only executes local data exchange, the tracking performance of the proposed method as a distributed tracking algorithm of the speech source, is nearly unaffected by node faults and it is scalable in distributed microphone networks.

5   Conclusions

In the paper, a speech source tracking method based on the DPF and ACA in distributed microphone networks is proposed. Each node first performs the local PF to obtain local state posterior. Next, taking into account the environmental noise and reverberation, the GCC-PHAT function is used to estimate multiple TDOAs which are employed to calculate multiple-hypothesis model as weights of particles for the local PF. Finally, the local state estimates are fused via average consensus algorithm to acquire the global consensus estimate at each node in the distributed microphone networks. Simulation experiments with existing speech source tracking methods indicate that the proposed method has better tracking performance in environments of lower SNRs and heavier reverberations. Besides, owing to only executing communications among neighbor nodes, the proposed method is almost unaffected by node failures.

Acknowledgement. This work was supported by National Science Foundation for Young Scientists of China (Grant No.61801308).

References

1. Spexard, T.P., Hanheide, M., Sagerer, G.: Human-oriented interaction with an anthropomorphic robot. IEEE Trans. Robotics **23**(5), 852–862 (2007)
2. Chen, B.W., Chen, C.Y., Wang, J.F.: Smart homecare surveillance system: behavior identification based on state-transition support vector machines and sound directivity pattern analysis. IEEE Trans. Syst., Man, Cybern. A Syst. **43**(6), 1279–1289 (2013)
3. Kapralos, B., Jenkin, M.R.M., Evangelos, M.: Audiovisual localization of multiple speakers in a video teleconferencing setting. Int. J. Imaging Syst. Technol. **13**(1), 95–105 (2003)
4. Nakadai, K., Nakajima, H., Murase, M., et al.: Robust tracking of multiple sound sources by spatial integration of room and robot microphone arrays. In: International Conference on Acoustic, Speech, Signal Process, Toulouse, France, pp. IV-929–IV-932 (2006)
5. Ward, D.B., Lehmann, E.A., Williamson, R.C.: Particle filtering algorithms for tracking an acoustic source in a reverberant environment. IEEE Trans. Speech Audio Process. **11**(6), 826–836 (2003)
6. Arulampalam, M.S., Maskell, S., Gordon, N., Clapp, T.: A tutorial on particle filters for online nonlinear/non-Gaussian Bayesian tracking. IEEE Trans. Signal Process. **50**(2), 174–188 (2002)
7. Talantzis, F.: An acoustic source localization and tracking framework using particle filtering and information theory. IEEE Trans. Audio Speech Lang. Process. **18**(7), 1806–1817 (2010)
8. Zhong, X., Hopgood, J.R.: A time-frequency masking based random finite set particle filtering method for multiple acoustic source detection and tracking. IEEE Trans. Audio Speech Lang. Process. **23**(12), 2356–2370 (2015)
9. Zhong, X., Hopgood, J.R.: Particle filtering for TDOA based acoustic source tracking: nonconcurrent multiple talkers. Signal Process. **96**(5), 382–394 (2014)

10. Zhong, X., Mohammadi, A., Wang, W., Premkumar, A.B., Asif, A.: Acoustic source tracking in a reverberant environment using a pairwise synchronous microphone network. In: 16th International Conference on Information Fusion, Istanbul, Turkey, pp. 953–960 (2013)

11. Zhang, Q., Chen, Z., Yin, F.: Speaker tracking based on distributed particle filter in distributed microphone networks. IEEE Trans. Syst. Man Cybern. Syst. **47**(9), 2433–2443 (2017)

12. Wang, R., Chen, Z., Yin, F., Zhang, Q.: Distributed particle filter based speaker tracking in distributed microphone networks under non-Gaussian noise environments. Digital Signal Process. **63**, 112–122 (2017)

13. Hlinka, O., Hlawatsch, F., Djuric, P.M.: Distributed particle filtering in agent networks: a survey, classification, and comparison. IEEE Signal Process. Mag. **30**(1), 61–81 (2013)

14. Lin, X. and Boyd, S.: Fast linear iterations for distributed averaging. In: 42nd International Conference on Decision and Control, Maui, USA, pp. 4997–5002 (2004)

15. Knapp, C., Carter, G.C.: The generalized correlation method for estimation of time delay. IEEE Trans. Acoust. Speech Signal Process. **24**(4), 320–327 (1976)

16. Mohammadi, A., Asif, A.: Consensus-based distributed dynamic sensor selection in decentralized sensor networks using the posterior Cramér-Rao lower bound. Signal Process. **108**, 558–575 (2015)

17. Lehmann, E.A., Johansson, A.M. and Nordholm, S.: Reverberation-time prediction method for room impulse responses simulated with the image-source model. In: IEEE Workshop on Applications of Signal Processing to Audio and Acoustics, New Paltz, USA, pp. 159–162 (2007)

Spectrum Prediction in Cognitive Radio Based on Sequence to Sequence Neural Network

Ling Xing[1]([✉]) [iD], Mingbing Li[2], Yihe Wan[3], and Qun Wan[4] [iD]

[1] School of Information and Communication Engineering, University of Electronic Science and Technology of China, Chengdu 611731, China
`201621020528@std.uestc.edu.cn`
[2] Southwest Institute of Electronic Technology, Chengdu 610036, China
`12865579@qq.com`
[3] Jiangxi Province Engineering Research Center of Spacial Wireless Communications, Nanchang, China
`wanyihe2007@sina.com`
[4] School of Information and Communication Engineering, University of Electronic Science and Technology of China, Chengdu 611731, China
`wanqun@uestc.edu.cn`

Abstract. Cognitive radio provides the ability to access the spectrum that is not used by primary users in an opportunistic manner, enabling dynamic spectrum access technology and improving spectrum utilization. The spectrum prediction plays an important role in key technologies such as spectrum sensing, spectrum decision, spectrum sharing and spectrum mobility in cognitive radio. In this paper, aiming at the spectrum prediction problem in cognitive radio, a spectrum prediction technique based on the sequence to sequence (seq-to-seq) network model constructed by the GRU basic network module is proposed. Due to the long and short time memory function of the GRU network structure, its performance is better than the previous Multi-Layer Perception (MLP) network model. This paper also explores in depth the impact of changes in the length of the input sequence on the prediction results. And the proposed seq-to-seq network model also performs well for multi-slot prediction and multi-channel joint prediction.

Keywords: Cognitive radio · Spectrum prediction · Sequence to sequence network model

1 Introduction

With the development of communication technologies, the proliferation of mobile devices has led to a shortage of spectrum resources. In the past, the static spectrum allocation strategy has low spectrum utilization and cannot meet the frequency requirement. What new communication systems mainly focused on is

© ICST Institute for Computer Sciences, Social Informatics and Telecommunications Engineering 2019
Published by Springer Nature Switzerland AG 2019. All Rights Reserved
G. Gui and L. Yun (Eds.): ADHIP 2019, LNICST 302, pp. 343–354, 2019.
https://doi.org/10.1007/978-3-030-36405-2_34

how to improve spectrum utilization without reducing the quality of service. The advent of software radios has providing dynamic reconfiguration of devices. In the 1990s, the emergence of software-based radios and the maturity of machine learning techniques led to cognitive radios (CR), which is a technology for intelligent analysis of the spectrum environment that provides reliable communication and efficient use of the radio spectrum. Through the sense of the spectrum environment and adaptive learning from the surrounding environment, CR will allocate the idle spectrum in certain space and time to unauthorized users, thereby achieving more efficient access to the idle frequency band and spectrum sharing. It also limits and reduces the occurrence of collisions, so that the spectrum is more efficiently and rationally used.

In order to effectively implement the concept of cognitive radio networks, CR systems need to have the ability to perform the following functions [1]: spectrum sensing [2,3], spectrum decision, spectrum sharing and spectrum mobility. The proposition of spectrum prediction makes spectrum sensing, spectrum decision and spectrum mobility more efficient and intelligent, which are all based on spectrum prediction. Spectrum prediction in cognitive radio networks is a challenging problem that involves several sub topics such as channel status prediction, PU activity prediction, radio environment prediction and transmission rate prediction. Among them, the study of channel state prediction can play a critical role in spectrum sensing, spectrum decision, spectrum sharing, and spectrum mobility research.

Since 2006, when Professor Acharga putted forward the concept of spectrum prediction, the spectrum prediction method had been continuously innovating and improving. At present, there are mainly three types of prediction algorithms: prediction algorithms based on Markov model; prediction algorithms based on regression analysis; and prediction algorithms based on neural networks. The prediction method based on the regression model has poor application performance, which can't do anything for predictions in a slightly more complicated environment and multi-step prediction. The Markov model-based prediction method needs to know the prior knowledge of the probability distribution of channel occupancy for equation establishment and parameter acquisition. The neural network model-based prediction method is complex and requires a large amount of data for network training. But it has high applicability and portability, and doesn't need any prior knowledge. With the development of artificial intelligence technology, deep learning technology has achieved good results in various fields, and neural network technology has become more mature. This paper will study the spectrum prediction technology based on recurrent neural network (RNN).

2   Related Work

With the development of artificial intelligence technology, many scholars have studied channel state prediction based on neural networks [4–7].

In 2010, Tumuluru et al. [8] proposed that the service characteristics of most licensed user systems encountered in real life are not prior knowledge. They use a neural network model, MLP, to design a spectrum predictor that does not require prior knowledge of the service characteristics of the licensed user system.

In 2011, Liang et al. [9] proposed a practical spectrum behavior learning method based on MLP. Through supervised learning, the state of different channels in future time slots (idle or busy) can be predicted. In 2011, Zhao et al. [10] proposed a spectrum prediction model based on neural network, which can predict the spectrum occupancy state by simulation.

In 2013, Nakisa et al. [11] proposed a spectrum prediction for multiple secondary users using RNN and time delay neural network (TDNN), but it is only a method of averaging each secondary user after prediction, not Multi-user joint prediction.

The recurrent neural network has long and short time memory characteristics, aiming to solve the time series problem with correlation. The channel state prediction problem can also be regarded as a kind of time series problem. It seems reasonable and effective to apply the recurrent neural network technology to the channel state prediction problem. This paper will deeply study the channel state prediction problem based on RNN.

3 Spectrum Prediction Based on Sequence to Sequence Network

3.1 Model Establishment

Spectral prediction is such a technique that through analyzing historical spectrum measurement data to obtain spectrum usage laws and to predict future spectrum usage states. According to the spectrum prediction results, the cognitive device can implement intelligent spectrum sensing and dynamic spectrum access, reducing time expenses, and improving communication quality. This paper makes use of the advantages of deep learning for the learning ability of complex models, and adopts the time series model, RNN. By using known historical spectral states, a spectrum predictor is trained to learn the laws of the frequency equipment to predict future spectral states.

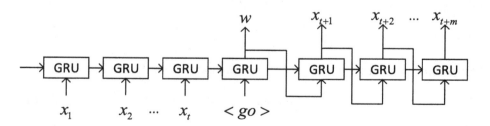

Fig. 1. Channel state prediction network structure based on seq-to-seq.

Figure 1 shows the structure of sequence to sequence neural network as used herein. When we predict the future channel states, we generally need to use the historical channel states, because in time, the channel states is not independent and has a certain time correlation. This is consistent with the structure of the RNN.

The left part of the model is the input module, and the channel states of n time slots are used as the input of the model. The right part is an output module that sequentially obtains channel state prediction values of m time slots by making use of a sequence of states of a certain length obtained from the input sequence. The predicted values are compared with the actual values, the error is propagated back, and the parameters of the model are updated.

The basic repeating module uses the GRU unit, which is a varient of RNN, and its basic structure is as shown in the Fig. 2.

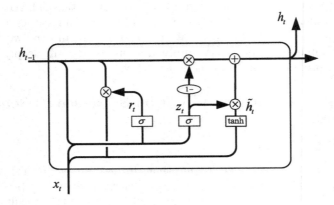

Fig. 2. GRU network structure.

The forward propagation update formula of the GRU unit satisfies:

$$r_t = \sigma(W_r \cdot [h_{t-1}, x_t]) \tag{1}$$

$$z_t = \sigma(W_z \cdot [h_{t-1}, x_t]) \tag{2}$$

$$\widetilde{h}_t = tanh(W \cdot [r_t * h_{t-1}, x_t]) \tag{3}$$

$$h_t = (1 - z_t) * h_{t-1} + z_t * \widetilde{h}_t \tag{4}$$

The output layer of the GRU uses the sigmoid activation function:

$$\sigma(x) = \frac{1}{1 + e^{-x}} \tag{5}$$

Output layer:

$$a = y_t = \sigma(W_0 \cdot h_t + b) \tag{6}$$

Loss function:

$$C = -\frac{1}{n} \sum_x [y ln a + (1 - y) ln(1 - a)] \tag{7}$$

Where n is the number of training data, y is the expected output, and a is the output of the neural network. the value of a is between $(0, 1)$, indicating the probability that the channel state is busy. If it is greater than 0.5, the channel state is considered to be 1, and if it is less than 0.5, the channel state is considered to be 0.

In the training phase, we use the Adam optimizer, so that the cross entropy loss function is minimized, and the weight value is continuously adjusted according to the direction of the gradient decrease.

3.2   Performance Evaluation

Error Rate

$$P_p^e(Overall) \tag{8}$$

$P_p^e(Overall)$ is the percentage of the predictions that are incorrect in all predictions. It is the most important evaluation indicator reflecting the performance of the model.

Accuracy Rate

$$acc = 1 - P_p^e(Overall) \tag{9}$$

acc is equal to $1 - P_p^e(Overall)$, which is an evaluation method that positively reflects the performance of the model.

Probability of False Prediction in Case the Actual Channel Is Busy

$$P_p^e(Busy) \tag{10}$$

$P_p^e(Busy)$ is the percentage of the prediction result of 0 in the case where the real channel state is 1. It is a very important indicator, and often hope it can be as small as possible. Because when the channel state is occupied, if the prediction result is 0, the device will select the channel for sensing, which will waste a lot of sensing time. Therefore, this indicator is a very important evaluation indicator that the application users are more concerned about. From the perspective of the primary user, this indicator indicates the interference degree to the primary users.

Probability of False Prediction in Case the Actual Channel Is Idle

$$P_p^e(Idle) \tag{11}$$

$P_p^e(Idle)$ is the percentage of the predict result of 1 in the case where the real channel state is 0. It is an indicator that affects the $P_p^e(Overall)$.

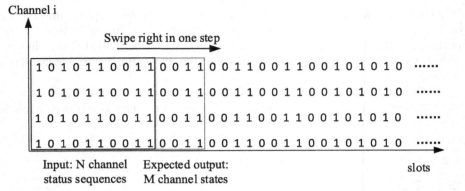

Fig. 3. Data processing process

3.3   Data Sampling Process

The channel state data is sliced, and each slice is composed of channel states of a certain length of time. Each channel state sequence is input into the model to obtain a corresponding output (i.e., the prediction results of the future channel states). The data processing process is shown in Fig. 3.

3.4   Parameter Settings

In the channel state prediction model of the GRU-based seq-to-seq network, the number of neurons of the GRU basic unit is 20, the learning rate is set to 0.01, and the batch size is set to 100. Compared with the MLP model, the structure of the two hidden layers is used. The number of neurons in the first layer is 8, the number of neurons in the second layer is 4, the learning rate is set to 0.001, and the number of trainings is set to 1000. The weights, initial state values, and deviations used therein are randomly generated using a random function.

4   Simulation Results and Analysis

4.1   The Effect of Input Sequence Length on the Model Performance

There are many factors affecting performance. When the input sequence length of the model is different, the performance of the model is different. Therefore, we have carried out experiments on the length of the input sequence from 1 to 20. The experimental data in this paper is generated using the $M/M/1$ queuing system model. Two fixed modes have been added. Figure 4 shows the trends of the $P_p^e(Overall)$, $P_p^e(Busy)$, $P_p^e(Idle)$ for different input sequence lengths.

It can be seen from Fig. 4 that when the input sequence length becomes larger, the $P_p^e(Overall)$, $P_p^e(Busy)$, $P_p^e(Idle)$ of the model tends to decrease. Extremely, when the input sequence length is 1 time slot, the performance of

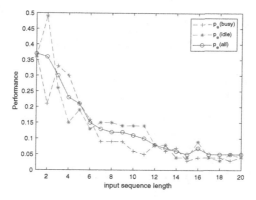

Fig. 4. Performance varies with input sequence length.

the model is the worst. The basic principle is the same as the statistical method. The historical information used has only 1 time slot, and the prediction accuracy is very low. The more the length of the input sequence, the more the historical information can be obtained and the higher the prediction performance will be. When the length is increased to a certain length, the performance is almost stable because the data used by the model itself has a finite length of dependence on historical data. Therefore, when the input sequence length of the model grows beyond the duration of the dependency in the data, it will not have more impact on performance, which just takes advantage of the time-dependent nature of the GRU.

In the case where the input sequence length is 20, the predicted result is obtained by using the trained model. The result of intercepting 100 time slots is shown in Fig. 5. Where blue represents the true value and red represents the prediction result. It can be seen that most of the predicted values are consistent with the true values, and only a small part are inconsistent with the real results.

4.2 Comparative Analysis of Performance Between MLP Network and the Proposed Method

In this paper, the MLP network is used for comparison experiments with the seq-to-seq network. The MLP network parameters are set as described above.

The performance of the MLP varies with the length of the input sequence, as is shown in Fig. 6. As can be seen from the figure, the performance of the MLP eventually converges to an error rate of 0.1, which is much worse than the seq-to-seq network converging to an error rate of 0.03.

In addition, a performance comparison chart between the MLP network and the method of this paper is given, as is shown in Fig. 7, taking the acc as an example. As can be seen from Fig. 7, the proposed method is much better than the MLP network. Extremely, when the input sequence length is 1, there is no difference between the two methods. When the input sequence length is small,

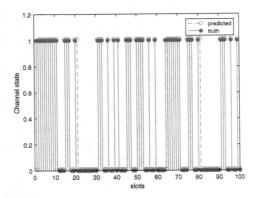

Fig. 5. Comparison of predicted results with real values. (Color figure online)

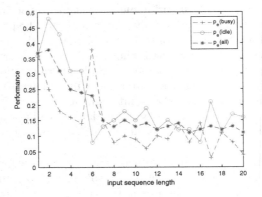

Fig. 6. MLP performance varies with input sequence length

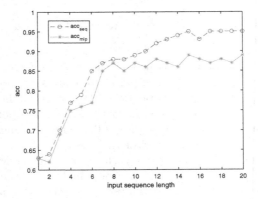

Fig. 7. MLP and seq-to-seq performance comparison chart

there is little difference. When the input sequence length is greater than 8, the prediction accuracy of this paper is much higher than the prediction accuracy of the MLP network, and the best case is 10% higher.

4.3 The Effect of Output Sequence Length on the Model Performance

When the channel occupancy is equal to 0.5 and the input slot length is fixed to 15 slots, the effect of the output sequence length on the model performance will be discussed below. In this paper, the output sequence length is changed from 1 to 15. Experiments are performed to record the $P_p^e(Overall)$, $P_p^e(Busy)$, $P_p^e(Idle)$ of the seq-to-seq model, as is shown in Fig. 8.

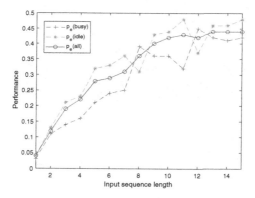

Fig. 8. Performance vs. predicted time slot length.

As can be seen from Fig. 8, when the output sequence length changes from 1 to 15, the error rate of the model changes from 0.03 to 0.44. This shows that the more time slots are predicted, the smaller the accuracy will be. This is also consistent with the actual situation.

In particular, in the case of predicting multiple slots, a slot-by-slot analysis is performed to understand the prediction performance variation of a single slot in the case of multi-slot prediction. In the case where 15 slots are selected for prediction, the performance variation of the i-th slot is considered. The correct rate of the i-th time slot is shown in Fig. 9.

As can be seen from Fig. 9, when predicting the length of 15 time slots. The farther the time slot is, the lower the correct rate will be, ie, the lower the certainty and the more unpredictability.

4.4 Joint Prediction of Multiple Channels

In this section, the joint multi-slot prediction of four channels is to treat the four channels as a whole one, which are related to each other, instead of four

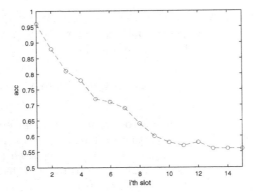

Fig. 9. In the case where the output sequence length is 15, the correct rate of the i-th time slot.

channels independent of each other. This paper compares the four channel joint prediction with the independent prediction. When the predicted time slot length is 1, and the input time slot length is changed from 1 to 15, the performance change of the $P_p^e(Overall)$, $P_p^e(Busy)$, $P_p^e(Idle)$ are shown in Fig. 10.

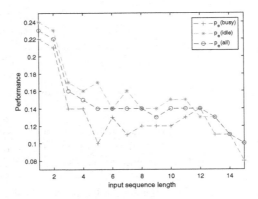

Fig. 10. Influence of input sequence length on multi-channel prediction performance

As can be seen from Fig. 10, as with single-slot prediction, the more the input sequence length, the lower the error rate. When the input sequence length is changed from 1 to 15, the error rate is changed from 0.23 to 0.1.

As a comparative experiment, the four channels are regarded as independent and uncorrelated, and they are independently predicted by single channel prediction. The total prediction accuracy of the four channels is compared to the joint prediction results. As is shown in Fig. 11.

Figure 11 is a comparison of the total correct rate in the four channels of joint prediction and separate independent prediction. As can be seen from Fig. 11, the

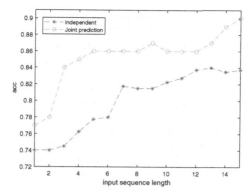

Fig. 11. Comparison of correct rate between multi-channel joint prediction and independent prediction

correct rate of joint prediction is 3%–6% higher than the accuracy of independent prediction. This is because when joint prediction, both the channel state of the historical time slot of the channel and the state of the historical time slot of other channels can be considered, and the mutual influence between the channels has an influence on the result of the channel.

5   Summary

In this paper, the correlation characteristics of the channel state in time are fully considered, and the seq-to-seq network structure based on the recurrent neural network is applied to the spectrum prediction problem, which has the characteristics of long and short time memory function. It is studied how to use the channel state values of n historical time slots to predict the channel state values of the future m time slots. We discussed the effect of the input sequence length n on the prediction accuracy. The effect of the output sequence m on the performance is also discussed. Moreover, with the seq-to-seq network structure, simultaneous joint prediction for multiple channels is also possible. And this paper also discussed the performance difference between multi-user joint prediction and single user independent prediction.

References

1. Mitola, J., Maguire, J.: Cognitive radio: making software radios more personal. IEEE Pers. Commun. **6**(4), 13–18 (1999)
2. Yucek, T., Arslan, H.: A survey of spectrum sensing algorithms for cognitive radio applications. Commun. Surv. Tutor. **11**(1), 116–130 (2009)
3. Wang, S., Wang, Y., Coon, J.: Energy-efficient spectrum sensing and access for cognitive radio networks. IEEE Trans. Veh. Technol. **61**(2), 906–912 (2012)

4. Xing, X., Jing, T., Cheng, W.: Spectrum prediction in cognitive radio networks. IEEE Wirel. Commun. **20**(2), 90–96 (2013)
5. Chen, Z., Guo, N., Hu, Z.: Channel state prediction in cognitive radio, part ii: single-user prediction. In: 2011 Proceedings of IEEE SoutheastCon, Nashville, pp. 50–54. IEEE (2011)
6. Xing, X.: Channel quality prediction based on Bayesian inference in cognitive radio networks. In: 2013 Proceedings IEEE INFOCOM, Turin, pp. 1465–1473. IEEE (2013)
7. Tumuluru, V.-K., Wang, P., Niyato, D.: Channel status prediction for cognitive radio networks. Wirel. Commun. Mob. Comput. **12**(10), 862–874 (2012)
8. Tumuluru, V.-K., Wang, P., Niyato, D.: A neural network based spectrum prediction scheme for cognitive radio. In: 2010 IEEE International Conference on Communications, Cape Town, pp. 1–5. IEEE (2010)
9. Liang, Y., Yin, S., Hong, W.: Spectrum behavior learning in cognitive radio based on artificial neural network. In: MILCOM 2011 Military Communications Conference, Baltimore. IEEE (2012)
10. Zhao, J.-L., Wang, M., Yuan, J.: Based on neural network spectrum prediction of cognitive radio. In: International Conference on Electronics. IEEE (2011)
11. Nakisa, S., Mousavinia, A., Amirpour, H.: A channel state prediction for multi-secondary users in a cognitive radio based on neural network. In: International Conference on Electronics. IEEE (2013)

Fast Anti-noise Compression Storage Algorithm for Big Data Video Images

Tao Lei[⊠]

South China Normal University, Guangzhou 510006, China
leitao0145@163.com

Abstract. When calculating the traditional image compression storage algorithm, the key frames of the video image are mainly extracted by the video image feature. In the process of video image acquisition, the influence of factors such as light is detected, and the image features are changed, resulting in a large storage problem. A new anti-noise compression storage algorithm for big data video images is proposed. First, the collected big data video images are divided. The average value of the gray of the image sub-region is obtained, and then the compression process and the stored procedure are given. The actual working effect of the algorithm is verified by comparison with the traditional algorithm. The experimental results show that the improved algorithm is well stored and the error is small. The fast anti-noise compression storage method for the big data video images studied in this paper has a good storage effect, and its application range is wider and more worthy of promotion.

Keywords: Big data · Video image · Fast compression · Anti-noise compression · Storage algorithm

1 Introduction

Currently, many data center service models have undergone significant changes. In the era of big data, data sources are extremely rich. Especially such as images, the proportion of unstructured data such as video is increasing, how to efficiently compress large data images and store them has become a major problem in this field. In the current video image storage algorithm, the video image data is prone to loss due to noise interference. Because the storage speed of the same size file fluctuates continuously under the noise interference, the real-time storage of the high-speed data stream cannot be guaranteed. The traditional method uses the queue-based cache structure to solve the frame loss problem of the video implementation storage process, but the storage process cannot be guaranteed to be anti-noise. And the stability of the storage cannot be guaranteed. Compressing and storing large data video images can fully improve the accuracy and reliability of large data video image compression storage. The current compression storage algorithms used for big data video images are: optical flow analysis algorithm, MPEG-7 motion descriptor algorithm. Although the above algorithm can complete the compression and storage of video images in the smallest position, the calculation process is also relatively simple. But the effect of storage is often poor. So it takes a long storage time, the information extracted from a single

G. Gui and L. Yun (Eds.): ADHIP 2019, LNICST 302, pp. 355–362, 2019.
https://doi.org/10.1007/978-3-030-36405-2_35

video produces large errors. In response to the above problems, the algorithm is divided into two processes: compression and storage. The specific analysis of the calculation process, the experimental results and feasibility of the algorithm are verified by experiments [1].

2 Fast Anti-noise Compression Storage Algorithm for Big Data Video Images

During the rapid compression of big data video images, the user gives a key feature image of the big data video image to be queried according to different requirements. According to the sample given by the user, the compression system obtains the corresponding key characteristics of the video image key frame according to the requirements. Matching queries through the database, the results obtained are arranged in similar degrees. Effectively complete the compression of key frames of big data video images.

The compression algorithm is as follows:

$$R = \sum_{j=1}^{i} \frac{p_{ij}}{c_{ij}(i,j)} \tag{1}$$

Formula (1) represents the compression process of big data video images, a video with i frame images represented by j, p_{ij} represents a feature vector in a video image, compare the feature vector with the vector to be matched, get a compressed large video image, that is, the compression of the key information of the video image is completed [2].

After completing the fast anti-noise compression of big data videos, store it, the stored procedure is as follows:

$$L_i = \sum_{j=1}^{n} w_{ij}s_j \tag{2}$$

n in formula (2) represents the number of big data video images. j stands for video frame, i stands for key frame, w stands for data compression package, s represents the target data image storage package, L_i indicates the stored big data video.

The images stored in big data video images are different according to the storage technology. Divided into data by line storage and data by column storage, database table data storage supports both row and column storage [3]. Row storage is stored in units of records. The data page stores a complete number of records; column stores are stored in column units. All rows of data for each column are stored together, a segment stores only one column of data, and a designated page stores continuous data of a certain column.

There are several advantages to storing the list: the data of the same column is stored continuously. Can speed up the data query speed of a certain column (reduced unnecessary IO in relative memory); original interpretation: database column storage technology principle and implementation; continuously stored column data, with

greater compression unit and data similarity, can get much better compression efficiency than line storage; conditional scanning uses the statistical information of the
data area for accurate filtering. Can further reduce IO, improve scanning efficiency
(Smart Indexing) [4].

Column storage data video image storage table also called HUGE table, it is based
on the HTS table space (full name HUGE TABLE SPACE). This table space is
different from the normal table space. Ordinary table space, the data is passed through
segments, cluster, page to manage, in addition, pages with fixed sizes (4K, 8K, 16K,
32K) are used as management units. HTS is equivalent to a simple file system. Create a
HTS, it is actually creating an empty directory. After creating an HFS table, the
database creates a series of directories and files under the specified HTS table space
directory. The file system structure is shown in the following Fig. 1:

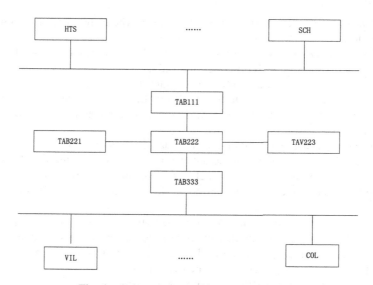

Fig. 1. Column storage file system structure

As can be seen from the above figure, the HFS table was created successfully in the
HTS directory. The system needs to go through the following steps: first of all, create
the schema directory corresponding to this table in the HTS directory. The directory
name is "SCH + ID number 9" the composed string. Second, create the corresponding
table directory [5] in the schema directory. Table catalog is the same reason, the table
directory is a string consisting of "TAB + ID number of 4". The table directory contains all the files in this table. Second, when creating a new table, each column corresponds to a file with a dta suffix. The file size can be specified when the table is built.
The default is 64M. The file name is "COL+ column number of 4 + file number of 10".
For example, in the figure above, 0000 represents the first column, 0001 represents the
second column...0000000000 represents the first file, 0000000001 represents the
second file...there is only one file for the first column. As the amount of data continues

to grow, after a file has been lost, the system will automatically create new files to store the growing data [6]. For a file, its internal storage is managed by district. Area is the smallest unit of data management within the file. It is also the only unit (similar to the page that is stored). In a district, the number of rows that can hold a single column of data is specified when the table is created. For columns of the ABLE attribute, stored there is a corresponding logo. The start position and length of each zone are 4K aligned within the file. For an HFS table, the corresponding is also equipped with an auxiliary table to manage its data [7].

Because only the data is stored in the file described above, auxiliary tables are used to manage and assist system users to manipulate these data. The auxiliary table is automatically created by the system when creating the HFS table. Each record in the auxiliary table corresponds to a data area in the file. The auxiliary table includes the following 15 columns:

1. COLID: indicates the column ID of the column where the current record corresponds to.
2. SEC_ID: indicates the area ID number of the area corresponding to the current record. Each zone has an ID number and only;
3. FILE_ID: indicates the file number of the data in this area;
4. OFFSET: indicates that the data in this area is offset in the file, 4K aligned;
5. COUNT: indicates the total number of data stored in this area (which may include deleted data);
6. ACOUNT: indicates the actual number of data rows stored in this area;
7. N_LEN: indicates the length of the data stored in this area in the file, 4K aligned;
8. N_: indicates the number of rows included in the data in this area;
9. N_DIST: indicates the number of rows in this area that have different data from each other.
10. MAX_VAL: represents the maximum value in this area, the exact value;
11. MIN_VAL: represents the minimum value in this area, the exact value;
12. SUM_VAL: represents the sum of all the values in this area, the exact value;
13. CPR_FLAG: Indicates whether this area is compressed;
14. ENC_FLAG: Indicates whether this area is encrypted;
15. CHKSUM: Used to verify, this feature is not enabled yet.

The first seven columns are used to control data access. Based on this information, you can know the specific storage location of this area. Length and basic information. The last eight columns are all used for statistical analysis of this area. Among them, the key combination of COLID and SEC_ID is the clustered keyword of the auxiliary table.

In fact, the process of searching the data stored in the database is through the retrieval of auxiliary table information. The process of manipulating files under the HTS directory using auxiliary information [8].

3   Fast Anti-noise Compression Storage Process for Big Data Video Images

According to the above study, a fast anti-noise compression storage algorithm for large data video images compresses and stores images. The workflow is shown in Fig. 2 below:

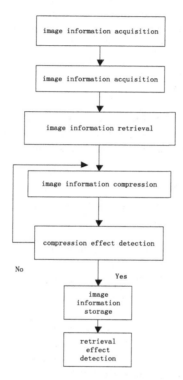

Fig. 2. Fast anti-noise compression storage process for big data video images

It can be seen from Fig. 2 that in the workflow of the fast anti-noise compression storage algorithm for large data volume video images, the video image information is first acquired, the acquired image information is retrieved, and the retrieved image information is compressed. The effect is detected, and the image information that passes the test is stored, and the image information that fails the test is re-retrieved. After the video image information is stored, the retrieval effect needs to be detected to ensure the accuracy of the retrieval.

Data storage coded frame implementation method: by storing the command, start the data storage state. There are two frame synchronization signals, the frame identifier EB90 [9] corresponding to the last two paths of each main frame. Three-way counting is included in the main frame. Respectively low counts, medium and high counts. The low count determines the length of the sub-frame, when the low count is from 00 to 1F (hex, the same below), counting carry in low counter clearing, at the same time, the frame identification of the main frame is changed from EB90 to 146F (corresponding to the synchronization signal of the sub-frame at this time). In order to achieve a 32 × 32 full-frame data format. When the count counter reaches FF, clear the high count carry bit. You can identify whether the data record is lost by judging whether the frame count is continuous or not, wrong number. The data format for each sub-frame is as follows: when the low count is 00,01, insert the frame header. Count to 1E, record the current count and high count at 1F, the middle 28 frames records the operating status parameters in the system. The same position in the entire frame is the state of the same parameter at different times [10].

4   Experimental Study

In order to verify the practical work effect of the fast anti-noise compression storage algorithm for big data video images proposed in this paper, compared with traditional anti-noise compression, contrast experiment was set up.

4.1   Experimental Parameters

Experimental parameters are shown in Table 1:

Table 1. Experimental parameters

Project	Parameter
Compressed image size	1.0 GB–10.0 GB
The compression time	0.3 s
Storage time	0.5 s
Working frequency	300 Hz–1000 Hz
The storage system	Computer center system
Monitoring state	Hardware monitoring
Number of experimental sample video images	100n
System storage capacity	$576 \times 72 = 4.15 \times 10^4$ bits
Storage density	4.15×10^4 bits/0.01 cm^2 = 4.15×10^6 bits/cm^2

4.2   Experiment Process

Experiment according to the parameters set above, selecting the traditional anti-noise compression storage algorithm and the anti-noise compression storage algorithm studied in this paper simultaneously store a segment of the image. Record the storage effect.

4.3   Experimental Results and Analysis

The results obtained are as follows.

As can be seen from Tables 2 and 3, using an improved storage method, the storage error is 12%, storage accuracy is 95%, the storage time is 1.6 s; the traditional storage method has a storage error rate of 68.5%, storage accuracy is 71%, storage time is 4 s; it can be seen that using the improved algorithm for keyframe storage of large data video images reduces the error rate by 56.5% compared to the traditional method. Increased storage accuracy by 24%, the storage time is shortened by 2.4 s, its overall performance is better than traditional algorithms.

Table 2. Storage performance of traditional algorithms under interference

Type of interference	Error rate (%)	Accuracy (%)	Time consuming (min)
Gauss's vagueness	0.68	70	3.49
Luminance drift	0.68	72	4.31
Gamma correction	0.69	72	4.31
Video Mosaic	0.69	72	4.23

Table 3. Algorithm storage performance in this paper in the case of interference

Type of interference	Error rate (%)	Accuracy (%)	Time consuming (min)
Gauss's vagueness	0.1	95	1.21
Luminance drift	0.2	96	1.63
Gamma correction	0.2	95	1.42
Video Mosaic	0.1	96	1.69

4.4   Experimental Conclusion

Based on the above experimental results, get the following experimental results: the storage method studied in this paper has a good storage effect. Wide range of applications, more worth promoting.

5   Conclusion

For the current algorithm, there is a big error in large-data video images. A new fast anti-noise compression storage algorithm is proposed. Through the introduction of video metadata information algorithm to calculate the keyframe metadata of big data video images, the retrieval model of keyframes for big data video images can be established more accurately. Simulation results prove that, improved algorithm for keyframe storage of large data video images the error rate is reduced by 56.5%, increased storage accuracy by 24%, save time by 2.4 s, its compression storage effect is good, stable and win high, compared with the traditional method, the scope of application is wider.

References

1. Bello-Orgaz, G., Jung, J.J., Camacho, D.: Social big data: recent achievements and new challenges. Inf. Fusion **28**, 45–59 (2016)
2. Sowmya, R., Suneetha, K.R.: Data mining with big data. In: International Conference on Intelligent Systems and Control, pp. 246–250. IEEE (2017)
3. Aishwarya, K.M., Ramesh, R., Sobarad, P.M, et al.: Lossy image compression using SVD coding algorithm. In: International Conference on Wireless Communications, Signal Processing and Networking, pp. 1384–1389. IEEE (2016)
4. Masyarif, S., Kurniawan, A.: Harmony search algorithm with dynamic pitch adjustment rate and fret width for image compression. In: Multimedia and Broadcasting, pp. 66–72. IEEE (2016)
5. Bharathi, M., Janani, T.: Fractal image compression using quantum search algorithm. J. Comput. Theor. Nanosci. **14**(9), 4580–4585 (2017)
6. Gu, Y., Jiang, H., Xie, X., et al.: An image compression algorithm for wireless endoscopy and its ASIC implementation. In: Biomedical Circuits and Systems Conference, pp. 103–106. IEEE (2017)
7. Kamargaonkar, C., Sharma, M.: Hybrid medical image compression method using SPIHT algorithm and Haar wavelet transform. In: International Conference on Electrical, Electronics, and Optimization Techniques, pp. 897–900. IEEE (2016)
8. Zheng, F., Zhang, C., Zhang, X., et al.: A fast anti-noise fuzzy C-means algorithm for image segmentation. In: IEEE International Conference on Image Processing, pp. 2728–2732. IEEE (2014)
9. Krueger, J., Nicolai, M.: Sound generator for an anti-noise system for influencing exhaust noises and/or intake noises of a motor vehicle: US9374632 (2016)
10. He, G., Wei, Y.: An anti-noise fusion method for the infrared and the visible image based upon sparse representation. In: International Conference on Machine Vision and Information Technology, pp. 12–17. IEEE (2017)

Analysis and Prediction Method of Student Behavior Mining Based on Campus Big Data

Liyan Tu[✉]

Inner Mongolia University for the Nationalities, Tongliao 028000, China
tlyimun@163.com

Abstract. How to effectively mine students' behavior data is an important content to improve the level of student information management. The platform of student behavior analysis and prediction based on campus big data is established, and the value of big data produced by students' campus behavior is analyzed. The behavior data of students' consumption laws, living habits and learning conditions are collected, modeled, analyzed and excavated around the large data environment, and the student behavior is predicted and warned by the stratified model of students' behavior characteristics. The experimental results verify the effectiveness of the methods used, and the behavior characteristics can be analyzed according to the behavior characteristics of the students, and the students' behavior will be guided to the overall health direction in a timely manner.

Keywords: Big data · Student behavior · Prediction model · Data mining

With the continuous development of information technology, cloud computing and data mining technology have been widely applied. The digital campus and the campus management system service platform are increasing, and the data accumulated in the campus information environment have also increased greatly. The data of the students' behavior (learning behavior, life behavior and heart behavior) in the corresponding business system has formed a relatively complete big data on campus. Environment, traditional campus management concepts and data analysis methods have been unable to meet the growing demand for data processing. How to manage and share the campus data efficiently, and optimize the student management by using the large data mining method, and provide a clearer and detailed data service for the students' campus life according to the analysis results are the hot spots of the current student management. It can be seen that making full use of students' school behavior data to build digital campus and intelligent campus makes the level of campus information upgrade, which is the problem facing the construction of campus service system.

1 The Connotation of Data Mining

Data mining refers to the extraction of information hidden in the data which have potential value in the massive and messy data. Through analysis, it can provide people with decision-making process. The main implementation process of data mining is data acquisition, data preprocessing, feature extraction, feature selection, data mining,

G. Gui and L. Yun (Eds.): ADHIP 2019, LNICST 302, pp. 363–371, 2019.
https://doi.org/10.1007/978-3-030-36405-2_36

model evaluation. Estimate. It is a process of continuous optimization. Data preprocessing, data mining and model evaluation are important components of data mining, as shown in Fig. 1.

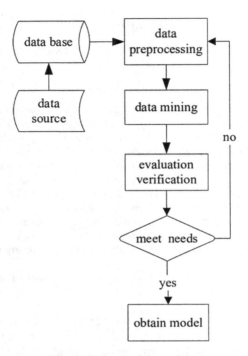

Fig. 1. Process of data mining

1. Data preprocessing; data preprocessing is the precondition of data mining, it is the preprocessing of data information by computer technology. The main function is to clean and screen the invalid and invalid data, and then integrate and transform the data, and lay the foundation for the establishment of the model.
2. Data mining: different mining algorithms are different in data extraction and processing, and the results are different. The most suitable and effective mining algorithms can be selected according to different data characteristics and business requirements.
3. Model assessment: we need to evaluate the model to detect whether the results obtained through data mining meet the expected requirements. If the mining results do not meet the requirements, it is necessary to re select data or uses other mining algorithms.

2 Platform Structures of Student Behavior Analysis and Prediction Based on Big Data

2.1 The Process of System Work

As shown in Fig. 2, based on the multi source data, such as student consumption, academic achievement, attendance management, book borrowing and so on, the students' behavior is analyzed and the rules and habits of students' life are predicted. First, the data is preprocessed, multi source data is fused, and the data is stored in the distributed system HDFS to ensure the consistency of data in the relational database, so that the data can be easily converted. At the same time, Scala module is applied to cluster analysis and association rule mining to complete student behavior classification, student behavior prediction and early warning.

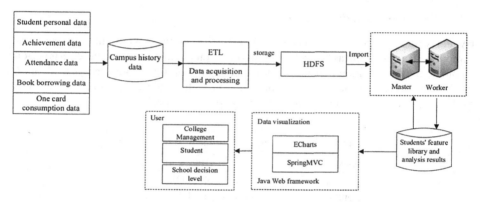

Fig. 2. System overall business process

2.2 Data Acquisition and Preprocessing

Students' data are characterized by wide source and huge quantity, which makes data quality not very high, so they need to be pre processed before data analysis. The process of preprocessing is to clean up some unrelated data in the data which are less associated with the mining targets, thus improving the quality of the data and providing more valuable data for the subsequent data processing.

1. Data cleaning: in order to ensure the integrity of data, data is cleaned by merging data and unified type, eliminating redundant and missing data.
2. Data conversion: a large portion of data collected is user's historical data. On this basis, the data are transformed according to the mining objectives of this paper, and statistics, clustering and classification methods are used to compress and standardize the data.
3. Data integration: through the analysis of the original data, it is found that because the data are from different systems, there are many duplicated data attributes, and this kind of data is integrated in the preprocessing stage, thus reducing the effect of the data dimension.

3   Analysis and Feature Extraction of Students' Behavior

Before data mining, we need to preprocess the collected data. Data preprocessing is a key step in the whole process, which generally includes data acquisition, cleaning, analysis and feature extraction. Data collection is to obtain student behavior data, data cleaning is to remove the abnormal values and missing values in the student's behavior data, and to avoid the impact of these data problems on data mining. Data analysis is to better understand the data and have a more comprehensive understanding of the data in advance, and the final feature is proposed. In order to reduce the complexity of the data mining, the original data is converted to the data which can be used directly by data mining, which can effectively improve the results of the final data mining. By analyzing the usability of data and evaluating students' behavior in school, we build a student behavior characteristic database.

3.1   Consumption Indicators

By analyzing the students' consumption behavior in the school, the student consumption records, such as term consumption amount, monthly average consumption amount, single maximum consumption and consumption times, are used as evaluation indicators to find out the students' consumption pattern and consumption level. The evaluation index of the law of student consumption is shown in Table 1.

Table 1.   Evaluation index of students' consumption

Index name	Range of value
Term consumption	1–10000
Monthly average consumption	1–2000
Single maximum consumption	1–50
Frequency of consumption	1–500
Monthly consumption peak	1–500
Consumption level	High/secondary
Consumption habits	Regularly/normal

3.2   Indicators of Students' Living Habits

In order to evaluate the students' habits and habits effectively, the students' time of practice, physical exercise, time and place of activities are used as evaluation indicators to analyze the data collected, so as to understand the regular habits of the students. The evaluation indicators of students' living habits are shown in Table 2.

Table 2. Evaluation index of students' living

Index name	Range of value
Regular diet	0–30
Early rise index	0–30
Physical exercise index	0–30
Internet time	0–240
Monthly consumption peak	1–500
Consumption level	High/secondary
Consumption habits	Regularly/normal
Place of regular activity	Library/dormitory
Habits and customs	Regularly/healthy

3.3 Student Learning Index

In order to analyze the students' degree of effort and academic achievement, the data are analyzed with the evaluation index, such as attendance rate, book reading, learning length and learning habits, so as to understand the students' normal learning situation, as shown in Table 3.

Table 3. Average value of each student's index

Index name	Range of value
Attendance rate in class	0–1
Book reading quantity	0–80
Number of access to Libraries	1–1000
Long learning time	1–240
Average achievement	1–100
Number of failures	Many/less
Learning habit index	Excellent/inferior

3.4 Analysis of Behavior Results

The data from the management system of the digital campus of Jilin University is used as the data source, which includes the students' Campus consumption records, library loan records, class attendance records, library entrance records, students' records, students' records, physical exercise records, and campus network from April 2016 to April 2018, which are 20000 undergraduate students of the school. The access records of the collaterals, etc. After the data is integrated, the data is converted into the HDFS module by using the Sqoop tool, and the data is pre processed on the basis of the Spark platform. Then, the statistical analysis is carried out, and the student behavior feature library is established, and the indexes in the feature library are used for testing. Taking the students' effort analysis as an example, the students are divided into 9 categories according to the students' effort and achievement index on the Spark platform, and the average value of each student's indexes is shown as shown in Table 4.

Table 4. Clustering results of learning effort

Category	Student ratio	Attendance index	Achievement index	Book reading	Number of access to libraries	Long learning time	Course passing rate
1	6.89	0.58	51.98	25	35	88	0.68
2	18.01	0.87	84.92	49	61	216	0.97
3	11.22	0.76	82.75	35	55	175	0.87
4	3.05	0.33	45.59	21	21	98	0.50
5	5.08	0.46	63.88	18	28	112	0.65
6	21.15	0.87	79.02	52	58	231	0.98
7	11.24	0.76	66.12	36	73	165	0.86
8	11.06	0.62	75.18	28	34	198	0.75
9	12.30	0.63	67.22	24	32	129	0.62

It can be seen that the students who work hard and have excellent results account for 18.01% of the total number of students. Most of the students can study hard, although the distribution of results is different. Only a small number of students do not work hard enough, and their grades are very poor. These students account for only 3.05%. 5.08% of the students are qualified, but the degree of effort is not enough. If we urge them, we will make further progress. According to the evaluation criteria and the clustering results of students, the results are compared with the real situation. The results show that the cluster analysis method is reasonable and effective.

4   Student Behavior Prediction and Early Warning Experiment

4.1   A Stratified Model of Students' Behavior Characteristics

Students' behavior characteristics are extracted from the student behavior database, and the students' age, gender and their colleges are used to build a set of students' behavioral characteristics.

$$S = \{C_1, C_2, C_3, \ldots, C_n\} \tag{1}$$

In order to distinguish the contribution degree of different characteristics to the model, we assign different weights to different student characteristics in the set and satisfy the following conditions:

$$\sum_{i=1}^{n} w_i = 1 \tag{2}$$

In order to establish a hierarchical model of students' behavior characteristics:

$$S = W_i C_i \qquad (3)$$

Based on student behavior strati fication model, students' behaviors are predicted and predicted. The overall framework of the model is shown in Fig. 3.

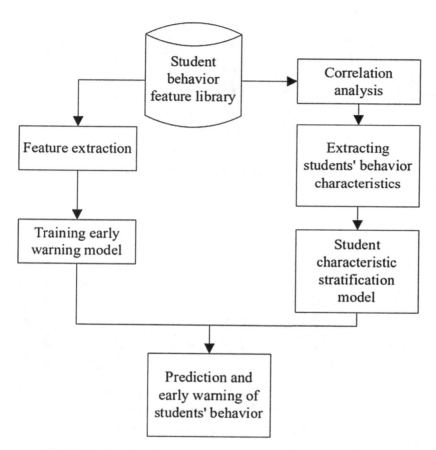

Fig. 3. Student behavior stratification prediction early warning model

4.2 Student Behavior Prediction Experiment

The cross validation method is used to analyze the correctness of the model of student behavior stratification prediction, and the relationship between the prediction results of students' behavior characteristics and the real value is reflected by the average relative error and the standard error. Based on the correctness of the methods used by different student scale comparison and analysis, and compared with the traditional forecasting methods, the scale of the test data is 100500100020005000 and 10000 students respectively. The average relative error of prediction is shown in Fig. 4. The average relative error of student behavior characteristics is shown in Fig. 5.

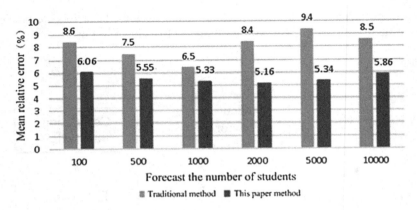

Fig. 4. Average relative errors of prediction

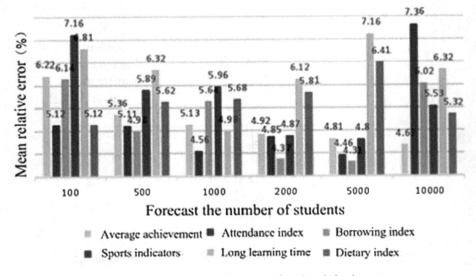

Fig. 5. Average relative errors of student behavior

It can be seen that compared with the traditional prediction method, the average relative error of the student behavior measurement model based on feature stratification is small, it is kept at about 5%, the prediction accuracy is high, and it has a good prediction effect. With the change of the relative error of the prediction of the number of students, the method is more expansible, and it will not reduce the accuracy of prediction by predicting the changes in the number of students. The relative error distribution on the behavior characteristics of each student is more uniform, indicating that the average relative error of the students' behavior characteristics in each dimension is relatively small, which is suitable for the prediction of muti-dimensional students' behavior.

5 Conclusions

The accumulation of campus student behavior data provides a data basis for student behavior analysis and prediction. The student behavior analysis and prediction platform based on the large data of the campus is set up. The data mining technology is used to preprocess, statistics and analyze the original data, so as to establish a feature library that can describe the individual behavior of the students, and predict the students' behavior based on the stratified model of student behavior characteristics. The experimental results show that the methods used can effectively mine students' consumption rules, living habits and learning conditions. The prediction results are in good agreement with the actual situation. Compared with the traditional forecasting methods, the accuracy is high and the error is small. It is beneficial to the school to master the students' learning and life situation, and the education can be carried out pertinent.

References

1. Lambiotte, R., Kosinski, M.: Tracking the digital footprints of personality. Proc. IEEE **102** (12), 1934–1939 (2014)
2. Sun, A., Ji, T., Wang, J., et al.: Wearable mobile internet devices involved in big data solution for education. Int. J. Embed. Syst. **8**(4), 293 (2016)
3. Hasbun, T., Araya, A., Villalon, J.: Extracurricular activities as dropout prediction factors in higher education using decision trees. In: 2016 IEEE 16 International Conference on Advanced Learning Technologies (ICALT), pp. 242–244 (2016)
4. Hammoud, S.: MapReduce network enabled algorithms for classification based on association rules. Brunel University School of Engineering and Design Ph.D. theses (2011)
5. Maillo, J., Triguero, I., et al.: kNN-IS: an iterative spark-based design of the k-nearest neighbors classifier for big data. Knowl. Based Syst. **117**, 3–15 (2017)
6. Arias, J., Gamez, J.A., Puerta, J.M.: Learning distributed discrete Bayesian network classifiers under Map Reduce with Apache spark. Knowl. Based Syst. **117**, 16–26 (2017)

Model Mining Method for Collaborative Behavior of Knowledge Agent in Innovation Ecosystem

Wen Li$^{(\boxtimes)}$

Business School, Suzhou University of Science and Technology,
Suzhou 215009, Jiangsu, China
cucmcum@163.com

Abstract. Conventional model of cooperative behavior mining method, can carry on the analysis, data mining to the conventional collaborative behavior but for specific subject knowledge in innovation ecosystem cooperative behavior, and analysis of the data mining results shooting low deficiencies, therefore puts forward innovation ecosystem in knowledge collaborative behavior main body model of the mining method. Based on knowledge innovation ecosystem in the main body composition analysis of collaborative behavior model, used algebraic representation, data processing design collaborative behavior model, realized the coordinated behavior model of innovation ecosystem knowledge subject data processing; According to the parameter fitting of collaborative behavior of knowledge subject in innovation ecosystem, the mining results were displayed to realize the model mining of collaborative behavior of knowledge subject in innovation ecosystem. The experimental data show that the proposed collaborative behavior model mining method is 41.84% higher than the traditional mining method, which is suitable for the model mining of collaborative behavior of knowledge subjects in the innovation ecosystem.

Keywords: Innovation ecosystems · Knowledge subject · Cooperative behavior · Model mining

1 Introduction

The model mining method of conventional cooperative behavior can analyze the data mining of conventional cooperative behavior. But when we analyze the collaborative behavior of knowledge agents in specific innovation ecosystem, because of the limitations of the collaborative behavior model data handler, there is a shortage of low hit rate of mining results. According to the given collaborative behavior pattern, the traditional collaborative behavior model mining method matches the set of supply chain instances which conform to the collaborative behavior pattern on the candidate chain set of personalized supply chain, and selects the supply chain instances which conform to the user's personalized demand according to the user's personalized demand in the set of matched supply chain instances. However, model mining that is not suitable for collaborative behavior of knowledge agents in innovation ecosystems [1], this paper presents a model mining method for collaborative behavior of knowledge agents in

G. Gui and L. Yun (Eds.): ADHIP 2019, LNICST 302, pp. 372–380, 2019.
https://doi.org/10.1007/978-3-030-36405-2_37

innovative ecosystems. Using principal component analysis, the composition of knowledge agent collaborative behavior model is analyzed. Represented by algebra, a large amount of related data information is projected into the feature subspace of low-dimensional data. Design collaborative behavior model data processing process, data processing of collaborative behavior model of knowledge agents in innovation ecosystem is completed. The least square method is used to simulate the collaborative behavior parameters of knowledge agents in innovative ecosystem. Depending on the normal distribution of discrete group points, the results of the mining are displayed, the model mining of collaborative behavior of knowledge agents in innovation ecosystem is completed. In order to ensure the effectiveness of the designed collaborative behavior model mining method, simulating the experimental environment of collaborative behavior of knowledge agents, using two different cooperative behavior model mining methods, a simulation test of the hit rate of the excavation is carried out. The results of the experiment show that the cooperative behavior model mining method is highly effective.

2   System Objective and Analysis

The model mining methods of collaborative behavior of knowledge agents in innovative ecosystem mainly include:

(1)   On the basis of the data array composed of n parameters and m sample values, a small number of comprehensive variables are established to analyze the formation of collaborative behavior models of knowledge entities in innovative ecosystem. It is represented by algebra.

(2)   A large number of highly relevant variables in the production process are mapped to the principal component space defined by a small number of implicit variables through multivariate statistical projection. To reveal its main structure, the input of the model and the simplification of the variables are realized.

(3)   The least square method is used to fit the data. Based on the normal distribution of discrete group points, the mining results are displayed. To solve the problem of model mining method of common cooperative behavior.

3   Data Processing of Knowledge Agent Synergetic Behavior Model in Innovation Ecosystem

3.1   Analysis on the Composition of Knowledge Agent Synergetic Behavior Model in Innovation Ecosystem

An innovative ecosystem is a system of resources, talent, institutions and infrastructure that can combine new ideas or technologies with products, services and production processes. Knowledge agent cooperative behavior model is one of the commonly used methods in multivariate statistical analysis. It is based on a data array consisting of n parameters m samples with a certain dependence. By creating a smaller number of composite variables, make it more concentrated to reflect the original n parameters contained in the change information. The basic method is to determine the primary and secondary position of the direction of change according to the variance of the data. The main elements are obtained in primary and secondary order, these main elements are independent of each other. With this tool, can extract change information, reduce the complexity of data analysis. It has the ability to remove the data correlation, reduce the noise effect, reduce the data dimension and other advantages, in data compression, signal processing, pattern recognition, fault diagnosis and other fields have been widely used [2]. After the traditional principal component analysis method is used to standardize the data processing, the data show a "uniform" distribution. In this paper, the concept of relative principal component is proposed. At the same time, the concepts of the relative transformation of the data and the uniform distribution of the data are defined. A relative principal component analysis method is established. The geometric meaning of it is given.

Collaborative behavior model of knowledge subject in innovation ecosystem, the central idea is to reduce the dimensions of data sets that contain a large number of related variables. At the same time, train variables in the dataset as much as possible. Multiple regression discriminant analysis uses variable selection procedures to reduce dimension, but it results in the loss of one or more variables [3]. The CBIE method uses all the original variables to get a small set of new variables. The new variable can then be approximated to the original variable. The greater the correlation of the original variable, the smaller the number of new variables required. Principal Components, Principal Components, (PCs) are irrelevant, orderly, therefore, a few principal components can be used to train most variables that exist in the original data set.

The principal component analysis is concerned with through several linear combinations of a set of variables to explain the variance-covariance structure of this set of variables. Its general purpose is data compression and data interpretation. Although n elements are required to reproduce system-wide variability, however, most of the variability is often explained by only a few m (m < n principal components. When this is the case, these two principal components contain almost as much information as n primitive variables [4, 5]. So this m principal components can replace the original n variables, and the original data set is composed of N times measurements of n variables, compress the data set consisting of N values of M principal components (Fig. 1).

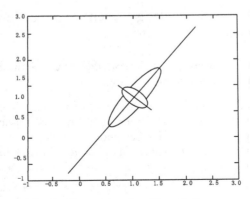

Fig. 1. Normal density ellipsoid diagram

3.2   Algebraic Representation of Cooperative Behavior Model

Suppose random vector $X' = [X1, X2, X3, ..., XN]$ has covariance matrix $\sum$, its eigenvalue $\lambda 1 \geq \lambda 2 \geq \lambda 3 \geq ... \geq \lambda n \geq 0$. Consideration of linear combination

$$
\begin{cases}
Y_1 = a_1'X = a_{11}X_1 + a_{21}X_2 + ... + a_{n1}X_n \\
Y_2 = a_2'X = a_{12}X_1 + a_{22}X_2 + ... + a_{n2}X_n \\
... \\
Y_m = a_m'X = a_{1m}X_1 + a_{2m}X_2 + ... + a_{nm}X_n \\
Van(Y_i) = a_1' \sum a_i, i = 1, 2, ..., n \\
Cov(Y_i, Y_m) = a_1' \sum a_m, i = 1, 2, ..., n
\end{cases}
\tag{1}
$$

Principal component is an unrelated linear combination Y1, Y2, ..., Ym.

The first principal component is a linear combination of the maximum variance, and even $Var(Y1) = a1'\sum a1$, maximization. $Var(Y1) = a1'\sum a1$ It will increase by multiplying any a1 by a constant. In order to eliminate this uncertainty, focus only on coefficient vectors with unit length. So we define the first principal component and the second linear combination $a1'X$, $a1'a1 = 1$, it makes $Var(aa1'X)$ become higher [6]. $a1'X$ is second principal component bilinear combination, when it in $a1'a1 = 1$和Cov $(a1'X, am'X, X) = 0 (m < i)$, it makes $Var(a1'X)$ become bigger.

$a2'X$ is the second primary and second linear combination, when a2' a2 = 1 and Cov(a1' X, a2' X) = 0, it makes var(a2' X) become bigger. Conclusion random vector $X' = [X1, X2, X3, ..., XN]$'s covariance matrix. Feature vector $(\lambda 1, e1), (\lambda 2, e2), (\lambda 3, e3), ..., (\lambda n, en), \lambda 1 \geq \lambda 2 \geq \lambda 3 \geq ... \geq \lambda n \geq 0$. I principal component is $Yi = ei'$ $X = ei1' X + ei2' X + ... + a$ in Xn, $i = 1, 2, 3, ..., m$. Therefore, $Van(Y_i) = e_1' \sum e_i$, $i = 1, 2, ..., n$, $Cov(Y_i, Y_m) = e_1' \sum e_m, e \neq m$ if the λi is equation, so the selection of the corresponding coefficient vector e_i is not unique.

3.3   Design of Data Processing Process for Collaborative Behavior Model

CBIE's main task is dimension reduction of data Matrix. A large number of highly relevant variables that exist in the production process multivariate statistical projection Map to a principal component space defined with a small number of hidden variables, so as to reveal its main structure, implementation of model input and variable simplification.

Although, sometimes a large number of multiple (n) variables are required to describe a complex system more perfectly, however, in general, most of the variability of the system is often explained by a few (m, m5n) principal components. And these m principal elements basically can contain from most of the original n variables or primary information. In other words it can be effectively represented with m principal elements or explain the characteristic structure of the data matrix formed by the sequence of variables in the original system, in order to achieve the purpose of data dimension reduction, the data matrix composed of a sequence of system variables is $X \equiv X(k, k + N - 1) = [x(k), x(k + 1), ..., x_n(k + N - 1)]$, if the data consisting of the first component sequence of the system is represented by Xi as i $X_i = [x(k), x(k + 1), ..., x_n(k + N - 1)]$.

Because the results of principal component analysis are affected by dimension, so in the principal component analysis, data need to be standardized, So we can construct a mean value of 0, standardized data with variance of 1 [7, 8]. First standardize x as follows: $Xs = [X - (11...1)^T M_{eans}] diag(1/S_1, 1/S_2, ..., 1/S_n)$ Means = [m1, m2, ..., mn] is The mean value of the variable X, S = [S1, S2, ..., Sn] is Standard deviation of variables. If we remember the covariance matrix of the data matrix XS, which is composed of the sequence of system variables, the is:

$$\sum X_s = E\{[X_s(k, k+N-1) - E\{X_s(k, k+N-1)\}][X_s(k, k+N-1) - E\{X_s(k, k+N-1)\}]^T\}$$

then you can pass $|\lambda I - \sum Xs| = 0$ and $|\lambda I - \sum Xs|ei = 0$, i = 1, 2, ..., n. Calculate the matrix separately $\sum Xs$, eigenvalues of λI and corresponding Eigenvectors ei, for ease of description, suppose $\lambda 1 \geq \lambda 2 \geq \lambda 3 \geq ... \geq \lambda n$. Eigenvector obtained by using the upper expression e, get the following n combinations of data

$$\begin{cases} V_1 = (e_1)^T X_s = e_{11}X_{s1} + e_{21}X_{s2} + ... + e_{n1}X_{sn} \\ V_2 = (e_2)^T X_s = e_{12}X_{s1} + e_{22}X_{s2} + ... + e_{n2}X_{sn} \\ ... \\ V_m = (e_n)^T X_s = e_{1n}X_{s1} + e_{2n}X_{s2} + ... + e_{nn}X_{sn} \end{cases} \tag{2}$$

Satisfy the property, and

$$\begin{cases} Van(V_i) = (e_i)^T \sum xe_i = \lambda, i = 1, 2, ..., n \\ Cov(Y_i, Y_m) = (e_i)^T \sum xe_J = 0, i \neq j \end{cases} \tag{3}$$

If the preceding m (m < n) vectors are selected in order V1, V2, V3, ..., Vm, then they can be used to analyze the principal components of the system. The principal component analysis is mainly to collect a large amount of historical data. Set up the statistical database, extract the normal data set, and establish the statistical unit, according to the principal component analysis method, the process data projects a lot of related data information into the feature subspace of low-dimensional data. Identify collaborative behavior model data processing. Based on the composition analysis of collaborative behavior model of knowledge agents in innovation ecosystem, and using algebraic representation, Determine the data processing of the collaborative behavior model, the collaborative behavior model data processing of knowledge agents in innovation ecosystem is realized.

Based on the knowledge agent collaborative behavior model data processing in the innovation ecosystem, the collaborative behavior parameters of knowledge agents in innovation ecosystem are fitted. The fitting of its parameters is divided into two parts. First, the parameter model is transformed to make it a unified model parameter. Secondly, according to the regression parameters, there are many fitting methods. In this paper, the least square method is used to fit the data.

Parameter model transformation, relying on the original mathematical relations, when the data collection parameter is substituted into the mathematical relation, the mathematical relation cannot be related to the computer language. Therefore, a bridge between mathematical relation and data mining technology is built by constructing a parameter model transformation, and its variable transformation table is shown in Table 1.

Table 1. Variable transformation table

Original variable	Variable after change	Radix	Form
η	A(a,b)	2	Numeric type
σ	B(a,b)	2	Numeric type
λ	C(a,b)	2	Hollerith type
θ	D(a,b)	2	Time type

According to Richard Henderson's mathematical mining formula, the transformed parameters are replaced, and the least-square data fitting is carried out at the same time. The least square method is one of the methods to realize the data fitting. The least square method is suitable for mining calculation, the running volume is small, and the calculation is simple, so the least square method is used to fit the data.

Let a parameter be a1 for the first operation, a2 for the second operation, and so on, and an for the operation. If the data a1 is the same as a certain operation parameter an-m, then choose a1 or an-m instead. The purpose of the data is to parse hundreds of thousands of related data for the second time, and the least square data fitting first calculates the result of the first operation. And the statistics can be expressed as,

$$a_1 = \sum_{i=1}^{n} (\widehat{a_0} + \widehat{a_1} x_{i1} + \ldots\ldots + \widehat{a_n} x_{in} - y_i)^2 \ [9, 10].$$

In the formula, x_{in} represents the relevant operation parameter of mathematical calculation, the eigenvalue selected when the mathematics is running at $\widehat{a}$. If the partial derivation of each data segment is obtained, then the deviation square difference of each data segment can be judged, and whether its a1 can replace an-m can be determined.

3.4 Results of Knowledge Agent Cooperative Behavior Mining in Innovation Ecosystem

Based on the least square method, the collaborative behavior information of the knowledge subjects in the innovative ecosystem is determined based on the mining results of the collaborative behavior of the knowledge subjects in the innovative ecosystem. The discrete group analysis of the relevant data such as a1/A2CU. An and so on is carried out, and the conclusion is drawn. Taking the mining theory value x = μ as the computing center, the discrete 3 s range of the data is calculated, and its S = (a1a 2. An)/n). The cooperative behavior of knowledge agents in the innovation ecosystem is calculated by monitoring data mining in the interval of [−3 s, 3 s] and mining the optimal values of the weights of the monitoring data parameters. The mining results are displayed by relying on the normal distribution of discrete group points, and the schematic diagram of normal distribution of discrete group points is shown in Fig. 2.

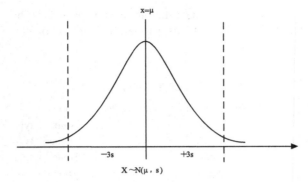

Fig. 2. Showing the normal distribution of discrete group points

Data processing based on collaborative behavior model of knowledge agents in innovation ecosystem. The least square method is used to realize the collaborative behavior parameter fitting of knowledge agents in innovative ecosystem, and the results of mining are displayed based on the normal distribution of discrete group points. The model mining of collaborative behavior of knowledge agents in innovation ecosystem is completed.

4 Test and Analysis

In order to ensure the effectiveness of the model mining method proposed in this paper for collaborative behavior of knowledge agents in the innovation ecosystem, simulation experiments are carried out. In the process of experiment, the simulation experiment of mining hit rate is carried out with different knowledge agents' cooperative behavior as the test object. The different range of independent variables and behavior structure of knowledge agent cooperative behavior are simulated. In order to ensure the effectiveness of the experiment, the conventional cooperative behavior model mining method is used as the comparison object, and the results of the two simulation experiments are compared, and the test data are presented in the same data chart.

4.1 Test Preparation

In order to ensure the accuracy of the simulation test process, the test parameters are set. In this paper, we use different collaborative behavior of knowledge agents as the experimental object, and use two different mining methods of collaborative behavior model to carry out the simulation test of mining hit rate, and analyze the results of the simulation experiment. Because the analytical results and the analytical methods obtained by different methods are different, it is necessary to ensure the consistency of the environmental parameters in the test process. The results of the test data setup in this article are shown in Table 2.

Table 2. Test parameter settings

Simulation test parameters	Scope/parameters	Remarks
Simulated independent variable	1/CBS	Complexity of collaborative behavior of knowledge subjects' count backwards
1/CBS	[0,1]	Does not contain 0
Simulation and test system	DJX-2016-3.5	Windows terrace

4.2 Test Result Analysis

In the process of experiment, two different cooperative behavior model mining methods are used to work in the simulation environment, and the variation of the hit ratio is analyzed. At the same time, because two different collaborative behavior model mining methods are adopted, the analysis results can not be directly compared. Therefore, the third party analysis record software is used to record and analyze the test process and results. The results are shown in the curve of comparison of the results of this experiment. In the simulation test result curve, the function of the third-party analysis recording software is used to eliminate the uncertainty caused by the personnel operation in the simulation laboratory and the factors generated by the simulation computer equipment, and only for the collaborative behavior of different knowledge subjects. Different mining methods of cooperative behavior model were used to simulate the hit rate of mining. The contrast curve of the test results is shown in Fig. 3. According to the test curve results and the third party analysis and record software, the mining method of cooperative behavior model is proposed. Compared with the conventional cooperative behavior model mining method, the mining hit rate of the model mining method is processed with arithmetic average value, and the result shows that the proposed collaborative behavior model mining method is better than the traditional mining method. Results the hit rate was increased by 41.84, which was suitable for the model mining of collaborative behavior of knowledge agents in the innovation ecosystem.

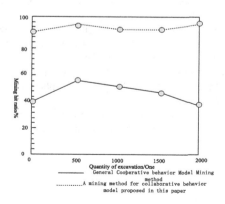

Fig. 3. Contrast curve of test results

5   Conclusion

In this paper, a model mining method for collaborative behavior of knowledge agents in innovation ecosystem is proposed, which is based on data processing of collaborative behavior model of knowledge agents in innovation ecosystem and parameter fitting of collaborative behavior of knowledge agents in innovation ecosystem. Realize the research of this paper. Experimental data show that the proposed method is highly effective. It is hoped that the research in this paper can provide theoretical basis for collaborative behavior model mining.

Acknowledgments. Supported by the National Natural Science Foundation of China (Grant No. 71771161).

Suzhou Science and Technology Program (Soft Science) Project (Grant No. SR201710).

References

1. Li, F., Chen, T.T.: Research on modeling and simulation of public network cooperative protection. Comput. Simul. **34**(6), 298–301 (2017)
2. Zheng, S.Z., Wu, Q.: Research on urban innovation capability from the perspective of intellectual property rights and construction of innovation ecosystem——taking Zhuhai as an example. Sci. Technol. Manag. Res. **36**(5), 111–116 (2017)
3. Tong, Z.H., Han, C.H.: Research on the impact of environment disturbance on NKCB and KCB in innovation activities. Sci. Technol. Prog. Policy **34**(13), 136–143 (2017)
4. Min, X.P., Shi, Y.L., Li, H., et al.: Mining collaborative behavior based on dynamic supply chain network. Comput. Integr. Manuf. Syst. **22**(2), 324–329 (2016)
5. Chen, J.B., Gao, S.L., Guo, Y.L.: Research on governance strategy of innovation ecosystem in small and medium-sized knowledge enterprises. Technoeconomics Manag. Res. **25**(10), 26–30 (2017)
6. Li, X.M., Bao, F.N.: Research on the impact of university social capital and collaborative behavior on collaborative innovation performance. Sci. Technol. Prog. Policy **34**(4), 122–128 (2017)
7. Fang, G., Zhou, Q., Yang, W.: Research context and progress from industry-university-institute cooperation to collaborative innovation: based on bibliometrics analysis. Technol. Econ. **35**(10), 26–33 (2016)
8. Zhang, Y.Y., Zhang, S.T., Peng, H.J., et al.: Cyberspace knowledge innovation behavior under innovation ecosystem perspectives——multiple case studies based on grounded theory. Sci. Technol. Prog. Policy **34**(6), 139–146 (2017)
9. Shan, M.M., You, J.X., Shao, J.: Co-evolution and optimization modes of industrial innovation ecosystem: a case study of Zhangjiang bio-pharmaceutical industry. Shanghai Manag. Sci. **39**(3), 1–7 (2017)
10. Mao, B.Q., Deng, W., Feng, S., et al.: Calculation method of vertical target dispersion based on multidisciplinary collaboration simulation. Comput. Simul. **33**(1), 20–23 (2016)

Signal-Triggered Automatic Acquisition Method for Electrical Leakage Fault Data of Electrical Circuits

Ming-fei Qu$^{(\boxtimes)}$ and Dong-bao Ma

Mechanical and Electronic Engineering School, Beijing Polytechnic,
Beijing 100176, China
qmf4528@163.com

Abstract. Conventional electrical circuit leakage fault data acquisition technology of leakage fault information collection, Failure to eliminate noise interference, resulting in failure to achieve real-time acquisition of circuit leakage fault data. There is a problem of low data accuracy and large noise interference, therefore put forward based on signal trigger electrical wiring leakage fault data automatic acquisition methods. Electrical wiring leakage fault detection based on signal trigger automatic acquisition mechanism, structures, acquisition model system, the acquisition model system hardware, electrical wiring to realize automatically leakage failure data acquisition model building; Automatically determine the leakage failure data acquisition software workflow, based on the leakage current fault detection algorithm and software anti-interference design, implementation is based on signal trigger automatic electric circuit leakage failure data collection. The experimental data show that the proposed automatic collection method is 35.24% more accurate than the traditional collection method, which is suitable for automatic collection of leakage fault data of different electrical circuits at different times.

Keywords: First signal triggering · Second electrical wiring · Third leakage failure · Forth automatic data collection

1 Introduction

Literature [1] proposed the STC15F2K60S2 single-chip microcomputer as the control core, the selected test simulation trigger signal leakage current, not less than twice the maximum value of the normal leakage current of the electrical circuit and equipment; the sensitivity of the leakage fault test signal, priority is given to 30 mA When the rated leakage current is equal to or less than 30 mA, the protection action time is less than 0.1 s. When the rated leakage current is greater than 30 mA, the requirement is less than 0.2 s. The device is a supplement to the traditional leakage protection device. According to the indirect leakage detection and direct leakage detection. The result is compared with the actual leakage position distance to complete the test Reference. Literature [2], the selective leakage protection circuit mainly uses the principle that the zero-sequence current of the fault line is opposite to the zero-sequence current phase of the non-faulty line, and the zero-sequence current phase of the fault line lags the zero-

G. Gui and L. Yun (Eds.): ADHIP 2019, LNICST 302, pp. 381–391, 2019.
https://doi.org/10.1007/978-3-030-36405-2_38

sequence voltage phase, by comparing the zero-sequence current with The phase of the zero-sequence voltage and the relationship between the amplitudes and the set amplitudes are used to collect the data of the circuit leakage faults. Literature [3] extracted the fault arc current characteristics under linear load and nonlinear load by analyzing the experimental data, and proposed two fault arc diagnosis methods: the typical characteristic current "zero rest" phenomenon for linear load fault arc Based on the grid fractal theory, the mathematical statistical method is used to extract the characteristic of the rate of change of the fault arc current, and the fault diagnosis of linear load fault arc is realized.

Above conventional electrical leakage failure data collection technology can collect the leakage failure information, but when the electrical circuit is used for long time automatic failure data collection, due to the limitations of the acquisition system hardware and software, there is a lack of accuracy of the collected data and large noise [1], and is not suitable for automatic collection of electrical leakage failure data for a long period of time. For this reason, a signal-triggered automatic acquisition method of electric leakage failure data of electric circuits is proposed. Based on the signal triggering automatic collection mechanism of electrical failure detection of electrical circuits, the digital signal is serially analyzed and processed through the leakage failure excavation algorithm, the acquisition model system is established, the hardware composition of the acquisition model system is determined, and the automatic collection of the electrical leakage failure data model of the electrical circuit is constructed. Determine the leakage failure data automatic acquisition software workflow, based on leakage current failure detection algorithm design, use the RFSFT termination reset circuit in the microcontroller, the capacitor and grounding resistance form a power-on reset circuit, so that the program is transmitted from the 0000H unit. Realize the anti-jamming design of the software, and complete the proposed signal-triggered automatic collection method for electrical failure data of electrical circuits. In order to ensure the validity of the data collection method for the electrical leakage failure of the designed electrical circuit, the electrical leakage failure condition test environment of the electrical circuit was simulated and two kinds of different electrical circuit leakage failure data acquisition methods were used to conduct the simulation test of the accuracy of the collected data. The test conclusions show that the data acquisition method for electrical failure in electrical circuits is highly effective.

2   System Objectives and Analysis

The signal-triggered automatic collection method for electrical leakage failure data of electrical lines mainly includes:

(1) The signal-triggered electrical circuit leakage failure detection automatic acquisition mechanism is analyzed to make use of the occurrence of a leakage failure, and the current vector of the phase line and the neutral line is not equal to zero, thereby calculating the line and the approximate position of the failure.

(2) Calculate the amplified leakage trigger signal and send it to the MCU for calculation. Perform analog-digital conversion on the signal. Determine the acquisition model system and the hardware components of the acquisition model system according to the system performance indicators and system signal characteristics.

(3) The leakage current failure detection algorithm is established. Based on the software anti-jamming design, the electrical line leakage failure data is automatically collected, and the lack of accuracy of the collected data and large noise during the long-term automatic fault data collection of the electrical circuit is solved.

3   Constructing an Automatic Acquisition Model for Electrical Leakage Failure Data of Electrical Lines

3.1   Signal-Triggered Electrical Circuit Failure Detection Automatic Acquisition Mechanism

Leakage failure detection system is installed at the electric meter of the electric circuit network or at a certain distance. When the low-voltage electrical line does not fail normally, the current zero-sequence circuit entering and output from one end of the electrical line network is zero, and the leakage failure detection device is in standby operation. When a leakage failure occurs somewhere in the electrical line, some of the leakage current flows through the medium into the earth. As a result, the total amount of current flowing into and out of the electrical circuit network is deviated. When the leakage current reaches the operating current of the leakage failure detection device, the system will detect the trigger signal. After a series of processing of the trigger signal, according to the size of the leakage current signal through the corresponding algorithm program, we can determine how far the leakage fault distance detection device is. At the same time, we can have a reference to the compilation of leakage failure detection devices, and comprehensive analysis of the location of the electrical failure where the leakage failure occurs [2].

3.2   Collection Model System Construction

Low-voltage electrical lines generate a part of residual current in the event of a leakage failure, also known as zero-sequence current. The zero-sequence current is used as a trigger signal for the detection of leakage failure, and a detection system is constructed. The detection element is a zero-sequence current transformer. In the event of a leakage failure on the line, the current vector sum of the phase and neutral lines is not equal to zero, resulting in an induced electromotive force. After this trigger signal is amplified, compared, and processed by analog-to-digital conversion, it is sent to the MCU for calculation, and a series of analysis and processing is performed on the digital signal through the leakage fault finding algorithm. In order to calculate the line and the approximate position of the failure, the data is displayed through the LED, and an audible and visual alarm device is triggered to perform a leakage safety alert. Its electrical circuit leakage failure detection system structure shown in Fig. 1 [3].

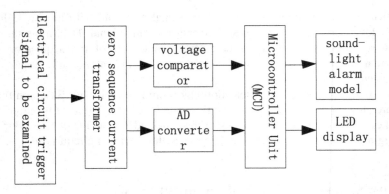

Fig. 1. System block diagram

3.3   Determining the Hardware Composition of the Acquisition Model System

The leakage failure detection system is installed on the low-voltage electrical line to detect the zero-sequence current on the line. When the electrical line is not faulty, there is no electrical equipment or circuit leakage. At this time, the zero-sequence current vector on the line is zero; When a fault occurs on the line, a single-phase ground fault current I_d is bound to be generated. The zero-sequence current $I_0 = I_N + I_d$ detected at this time is obviously greater than the three-phase unbalanced current when there is no fault, and I_0 is treated as the initial trigger signal. U_1 is a linear operational amplifier. Through the feedback loop and the input loop to determine the magnification, that is, by adjusting the potentiometer RW adjust the magnification, so that the trigger analog signal voltage between 1–5 V, the output resistance of the load resistor R8 is 100 Ω, so the trigger current output range of the signal is 10–50 mA. U_1 operational amplifier IN + and IN− are differential inputs, through the potentiometer can set the gain magnification $B = (1 + \frac{R_2 + R_3}{RW + R_1})$, is 1–10 times [4]. After the differential mode signal is amplified, it is converted into an analog signal and sent to the analog-to-digital conversion circuit.

After the calculation of the leakage trigger signal is still an analog signal, to be sent to the MCU microcontroller for calculation, you need to carry out analog-digital conversion of the signal. Analog-to-digital conversion is the process of converting an analog input into a digital value. The analog-to-digital conversion circuit is a key component of the entire data acquisition section. Analog-to-digital conversion is the process of converting analog input into digital value. The analog-to-digital conversion is based on system performance and system signal characteristics. It is processed by 10-bit A/D conversion chip TLC1513. The analog input voltage is 0–+5 V corresponding figure. Values 0–1024 [5]. The circuit is a key component of the entire data acquisition section. The circuit connection is shown in Fig. 2(a), where pin AO is the input of the leakage trigger signal, and a falling edge change at the LS terminal resets the internal counter and controls the enable. ADDRESS is a serial data input terminal. The pass-through serial address is used to select the next analog input signal or test signal to be converted [6]. DATAOUT is a 3-state serial output terminal for A/D conversion. It communicates with the microprocessor or the peripheral serial port and can be flexibly programmed for data length and format.

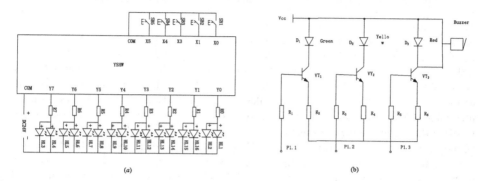

(a)   (b)

Fig. 2. Leakage trigger signal analog-to-digital conversion circuit and sound and light alarm module circuit

The trigger signal is converted into digital signal and sent to the MCU for processing. The single-chip microcomputer is the data processing core of the entire control circuit, and the latest enhanced 8051 series single chip STC15F2K60S2 is used, which has two independent serial ports; Built-in crystal oscillator and reset circuit make its anti-interference ability greatly enhanced; And has a plurality of I/O ports, high speed, low power consumption, it is important that the cost is lower, and it is very suitable for the large-scale use deployment of this system. Its pin distribution and connection circuit, I/O port as chip select signal, sound and light alarm control signal, keyboard, LED display and other functions are used [7].

If the entire electrical line works normally and no leakage fault occurs, the working status indicator will flash green. Its working state is controlled by the I/O port P1.1 of the one-chip computer, the flashing of the indicator lamp is controlled by the one-chip computer program to control and output the pulse square wave to control the on-off of the triode VT. When there is a leakage failure, the microcontroller program will set the port Pl.3 high, the transistor VT, conduction, red alarm light flashes, while the buzzer alarm sound; A flashing yellow light indicates that the microcontroller has started the leakage protector and cut off the electrical circuit. The sound and light alarm module circuit shown in Fig. 2(b) [8].

Relying on the signal-triggered automatic fault detection and detection mechanism of the electrical circuit, an acquisition model system and a hardware system of the acquisition model system are built to realize the automatic collection of the electrical leakage fault data model of the electrical circuit.

4 Realizing Automatic Collection of Electrical Leakage Failure Data

4.1 Working Process of Leakage Failure Data Automatic Acquisition Software

The system software workflow is shown in Fig. 3. The system is in a low power standby operation state when the electrical line is normal and no failure occurs. When a leakage fault occurs in the electrical circuit, an electrical leakage trigger letter is generated, and after hardware amplification and analog-to-digital conversion, it is sent to the single-chip microcomputer for calculation and analysis. Locate the location of the leakage failure according to the leakage failure excavation algorithm, and send the result to the display screen through the serial communication, at the same time start the sound and light alarm module. If the leakage current exceeds the set threshold, the microcontroller controls the start-up of the leakage protector and performs power-off operation on the line to ensure the safety of the electrical circuit and personnel [9].

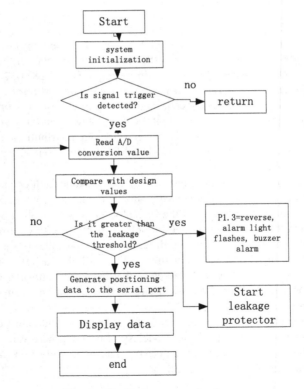

Fig. 3. Working process of software

4.2   Establish Leakage Current Failure Detection Algorithm

When a leakage failure occurs in an electrical circuit, to determine the location of the circuit leakage, it is necessary to calculate the magnitude of the leakage current in the electrical circuit. And need to determine the voltage between power neutral point MQ and load neutral point MI. In the low-voltage circuit, three-phase voltage (U_{L1}, U_{L2}, U_{L3}) and neutral point MQ are connected. At the load side, three load impedances Z_1, Z_2, and Z_3 are connected, and two neutral points MQ and MI are connected by impedance Z_{QL}. The pressure drop on this impedance is U_{QL}. U_{QL} is calculated as follows [10]:

$$U_{QL} = \frac{\frac{U_{L1}}{Z_1} + \frac{U_{L2}}{Z_2} + \frac{U_{L3}}{Z_3}}{\frac{1}{Z_1} + \frac{1}{Z_2} + \frac{1}{Z_3} + \frac{1}{Z_{QL}}} \tag{1}$$

The conventional configuration of the three-phase filter is that three X capacitors are connected to the neutral point and connected to ground through the Y capacitor or to the housing of the filter. Leakage currents can be ignored for balanced-capacitor networks. On the other hand, when the highest imbalance between the phases is reached, the electrical network achieves the highest leakage current. The causes of the imbalance include the tolerance of the capacitor value and the voltage imbalance of the power supply network. Therefore, the key element of the leakage current is the voltage U_{QL} generated by the unbalance of the capacitors C_{X1}, C_{X2}, and C_{X3}. For most filters, the rating is the same, jw represents current tolerance. The leakage current $I_{leakmax}$ produced by the voltage drop U_{QL} at the capacitor C_Y can be determined according to the following equation:

$$I_{leakmax} = U_{QL} \cdot jw \cdot C_{Yn} \tag{2}$$

In the formula, $\omega = 2 \bullet \pi \bullet f$, the tolerance of the rated value of the condenser in the passive filter is $\pm 20\%$. The highest drop in Cr occurs when the two X capacitors have the smallest tolerance, and one capacitor has the maximum tolerance. In addition, assume that Cr has the largest tolerance value. Substituting these assumptions into Eqs. (1) and (2), the leakage current is:

$$|I_{leakmax}| = \omega \cdot C_{Ymax} \frac{U_{max} C_{X \cdot max} - U_{min} C_{X \cdot min}}{C_{X \cdot max} + 2C_{X \cdot min} + C_{Ymax}} \tag{3}$$

Then, the analog return digital return value A_d is:

$$A_d = \frac{I_d \times R_d}{U_{ref}} \times 1024 \tag{4}$$

In the formula, I_d is the trigger current signal after amplification processing, R_d is the load end resistance, 100 Ω, U_{ref} is the reference voltage for A/D conversion taking 1–5 V, 1024 is the maximum resolution of ten A/D converters.

4.3 Software Anti-jamming Design

Since most of the working environment of the leakage failure detection device is outdoors, there are a large number of interference signals, and the electromagnetic interference caused by the electrical lines is very large, which may cause distortion of analog signal input, disorder of control signals, control failure, system crash, disorder of signals on address or data bus. Therefore, the system's anti-jamming design is related to the reliability of the system operation. In addition to strengthening the hardware anti-jamming, special design must be performed on software anti-jamming. If the system program runs away and enters an endless loop, the system service program starts execution automatically from 0000H and terminates the reset circuit on the microcontroller's RFSFT. The capacitor and ground resistors form a power-on reset circuit, which allows the program to be executed from the 0000H unit when the program is powered on. Both the power-on reset circuit and the manual reset circuit can provide a high-level reset signal greater than 10 mA for the reset chip. The reset chip MAX813L has a watchdog timer and voltage monitor inside. When the system program is stuck in a dead-end cycle or the power supply voltage suddenly changes, it will not cause crashes, data read-write errors, or malfunctions, which will cause the system to reset and operate in the event of a failure.

Based on the construction of automatic collection of electrical wiring leakage failure data model, relying on leakage failure data automatic acquisition software, reasonable work, and leakage current failure detection algorithm and software anti-jamming design, automatic collection of electrical wiring leakage failure data is achieved based on signal triggering.

5 Experimental Test and Analysis

In order to ensure the effectiveness of the proposed method for automatic detection of electrical failure in electrical wiring based on signal triggering, simulation experiments were conducted. During the process of testing, different electrical wiring leakage failure status was used as a test object to conduct data acquisition accuracy simulation tests. Different types of failure in the electrical failure status of the electrical circuit, as well as on-line acquisition duration, are simulated. In order to ensure the validity of the test, the conventional electrical wiring leakage failure data acquisition technology was used as a comparison object, and the results of the two simulation experiments were compared, and the test data was presented in the same data chart.

5.1 Experimental Test Preparation

In order to ensure the accuracy of the simulation test process, the test parameters of the experiment are set. In the simulation test process in this paper, different electrical circuit leakage failure status was taken as the test object, two different electrical circuit leakage failure data acquisition methods were used to conduct the data acquisition accuracy simulation test, and the simulation test results were analyzed. Because the analysis results obtained in different methods are different from the analysis methods, the test environment parameters must be consistent during the test. The test data set results in this paper are shown in Table 1.

Table 1. Test parameter settings

Simulation test parameters	Execution range/parameter	Note
Leakage per unit time	0.1–15 kWh	Independent variable
Online automatic collection time	24 h × 7	Using two different design methods to conduct design analysis one by one
Simulation system	DJX-2016-3.5	Windows platform

5.2 Experimental Test Results Analysis

During the test process, two different methods for data collection of electrical faults in electrical circuits were used to work in a simulated environment, and the changes in the accuracy of the acquired data were analyzed. At the same time, due to adopting two different methods for data collection of electrical faults in electrical circuits, the analysis results cannot be compared directly. For this purpose, third-party analysis and recording software is used to record and analyze the test process and results, and the results are displayed in this test by comparing the results in the curve. In the simulation test result curve, the third-party analysis and recording software function is used to eliminate the uncertainty caused by the simulation laboratory personnel operation and simulation of computer equipment factors, only for different electrical circuit leakage failure status, different electrical circuit leakage failure data collection Methods, the accuracy of simulation test data acquisition. The comparison curve of the test results is shown in Fig. 4. Based on the results of the test curve, the third party analysis and recording software was used to arithmetically weight the electrical leakage failure data collection method of the electrical circuit proposed in this paper and the accuracy of the collected data of the conventional electrical leakage failure data collection technology, resulting in the proposed automatic acquisition method. With the traditional acquisition method, the accuracy of the collected data is increased by 35.24%, which is suitable for the automatic collection of the leakage failure data of different electrical lines at different times.

The experiment takes the Re state as the test object, and uses two different circuit leakage fault data acquisition methods to carry out the data acquisition precision simulation test. It is concluded that the data acquisition accuracy of the proposed acquisition method is 35.24% higher than the traditional method, which is suitable for automatic at different times. Collect leakage fault data of different electrical lines. It can solve the traditional method because it can not eliminate the noise interference, which can not realize the real-time acquisition of the circuit leakage fault data. It has the problems of low data precision and large noise interference, and has high comprehensive applicability, which provides for the data leakage research of future circuit leakage faults. A certain research basis.

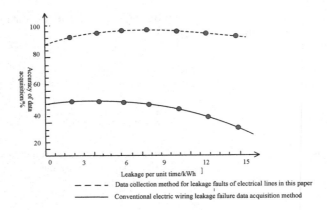

Fig. 4. Comparison curve of the test results

6   Conclusion

This paper proposes a signal triggering method for the automatic collection of electrical leakage failure data of electrical circuits, an automatic acquisition model was constructed based on leakage failure data of electrical circuits, and an automatic leakage failure data acquisition software, leakage current failure detection algorithm and software anti-jamming were designed to achieve signal-based automatic collection of electrical leakage failure data of electrical wiring to complete the research of this paper. The experimental data shows that the method designed in this paper has extremely high effectiveness. It is hoped that the study in this paper can provide a theoretical basis for the online acquisition method of electrical leakage failure data in electrical circuits.

References

1. Han, B.Z., Yu, L.F.: Fault diagnosis method of actuator based on Kalman filter bank. Comput. Simul. **30**(2), 93–96 (2013)
2. Chen, Y.H., Deng, X.G.: Improvement and simulation of remote nuclear radiation data network acquisition method. Comput. Simul. **33**(6), 274–277 (2016)
3. Duan, Z.M., Li, C., Cong, P.T., et al.: Remote fault signal acquisition method for fan fault detection based on STM32F407. Instrum. Technol. Sens. **6**, 176–178 (2017)
4. Wu, Z., Zhang, J.C.: Application of improved EEMD data fusion method in bearing fault diagnosis. J. Beijing Jiaotong Univ. **40**(3), 43–49 (2016)
5. Wu, H.L., Bai, Z.Q., Zhang, Y., et al.: Design and implementation of low frequency radio astronomy signal acquisition circuit based on modulated broadband converter. J. Comput. Appl. **38**(2), 610–614 (2018)
6. Sun, S.G., Zhang, Q., Du, T.X., et al.: Study on the method of evaluating the failure degree of low-voltage universal breaker based on vibration signal. Proc. CSEE **37**(18), 5473–5482 (2017)

7. Zhou, Y.T., Jiang, G.D., Tao, T., et al.: Multi-card synchronous acquisition method based on EnDat data transmission cycle. Combined Mach. Tool Autom. Manuf. Technol. **12**, 9–12 (2016)
8. Li, C., Cong, P.T., Duan, Z.M., et al.: Vibration signal acquisition method based on adaptive sampling frequency and AD7606. Instrum. Technol. Sens. **7**, 116–120 (2017)
9. Yang, K., Zhang, Q.C., Yang, J.H., et al.: Fault diagnosis method for series arc based on fractal dimension and support vector machines. Electrotechnics **31**(2), 70–77 (2016)
10. Zhang, L.P., Geng, X.R., Shi, D.Y.: Research on low voltage arc fault identification method based on EMD and ELM. J. Electr. Mach. Control **20**(9), 54–60 (2016)

Design of Agricultural Products Intelligent Transportation Logistics Freight Forecasting System Based on Large Data Analysis

Xiao-yan Ai[✉] and Yong-heng Zhang

Yulin University, Yulin 719000, China
zcmddnllll@163.com

Abstract. The traditional forecasting system of agricultural products transportation logistics cargo flow relies too much on people's subjective experience in forecasting, and the forecasting results are not accurate enough. To solve this problem, based on the large data analysis, a new forecasting system of agricultural products transportation logistics cargo flow is studied. The hardware and software parts of the system are designed, the hardware of the system consists of five parts: data collector, data analyzer, matcher, processor and tracer. The internal composition of each construction is described accurately. The working process of software is information input, information analysis, information matching, information processing and information tracking. The software workflow diagram is given. The results of the system are validated by comparing with the traditional cargo volume prediction system. The experimental results show that the system has high intelligence and can accurately predict the volume of goods transported in a short time. It has important guiding significance for the development of agricultural products transportation.

Keywords: Big data analysis · Transport of agricultural products · Intelligent transportation · Logistics cargo flow · Cargo flow forecasting · Prediction system

1 Introduction

With the development of information technology, the whole world has entered the information age, and the big data information has been penetrating into people's lives. Big data is huge data, it refers to the huge amount of information involved, which can not be captured, managed, processed and collated in a reasonable time through the current mainstream software tools to help enterprises make more positive business decisions. That is, "massive and complex data sets cannot be extracted, stored, searched, shared, analyzed and processed with existing software tools". With the arrival of the era of big data, information technologies such as Internet of Things and cloud computing will be widely used in the development of agricultural logistics, and become an important factor to break through the information bottleneck of agricultural logistics integration [1].

© ICST Institute for Computer Sciences, Social Informatics and Telecommunications Engineering 2019
Published by Springer Nature Switzerland AG 2019. All Rights Reserved
G. Gui and L. Yun (Eds.): ADHIP 2019, LNICST 302, pp. 392–400, 2019.
https://doi.org/10.1007/978-3-030-36405-2_39

On the basis of large data analysis technology, this paper constructs an integrated model of agricultural products logistics and studies an effective freight flow forecasting system of transport logistics. The hardware and software of the system are dissected systematically and thoroughly. The composition of the system's logistics collector, analyzer, processor and tracker is studied. The software workflow of the system is designed and compared with the traditional system. Through the research of this paper, we can know that the system can realize the integration of agricultural products logistics in a real sense, it is the integration and systematization of the supply chain of agricultural products production enterprises through logistics enterprises, sales enterprises and consumers, including a series of links such as agricultural products production, acquisition, transportation, storage, loading and unloading, handling, distribution, circulation and processing, distribution and information activities. Through Internet of Things, cloud computing and other information technologies, the massive data are cited in the production, procurement, transportation, storage, distribution, sales and other links of agricultural products, Promoting the synergy and integration of logistics, integrate logistics information and technology organically to complete the process of monitoring the whole cold chain logistics [2].

Intelligent transportation of agricultural products for the application of large data is mainly through the global positioning system, radio frequency technology and two-dimensional code scanning and other advanced information technology from the agricultural products logistics system to capture, collect, integrate and match logistics information, stored in the public database, in order to maintain data integrity, real-time and accuracy [3]. Meanwhile, Logistics management information system processes, analyses, processes and utilizes these information through logistics information management platform to form valuable logistics information of large data agricultural products supply chain.

2 Hardware Design of Agricultural Products Intelligent Transportation Logistics Freight Forecasting System Based on Large Data Analysis

Based on large data analysis technology, a high-performance intelligent transportation logistics cargo volume prediction system is designed. The hardware of the system consists of five parts: data collector, data analyzer, matcher, processor and tracker. The overall design framework of the hardware part of the system is shown in Fig. 1 below [4]:

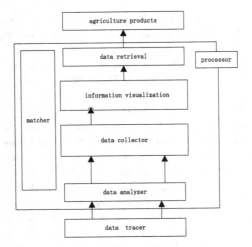

Fig. 1. Hardware framework of agricultural products intelligent transportation logistics cargo volume prediction system based on large data analysis

2.1 Data Acquisition Device Design

The 16/32-bit Chipest 156 chip developed by Camed Logic Company in UK is selected as the internal part of the data acquisition device designed in this paper. The core logic of the chip is RIC structure. Arounding the microwave processor, there are 36 internal interfaces (20 TEA interfaces, 16 UEA interfaces), 40 external interfaces (20 MMY interfaces, 20 MMU interfaces) GPS. When the receiver works, the input voltage should be above 220 V and the power supply frequency should be between 50 MHz and 120 MHz. At the same time, the core programming system should be connected to scan the GPS signal with embedded ICE [5]. GPS signal receiver can receive all kinds of signals, such as language, text, image, data, and so on. With the help of computer terminal equipment, the obtained signals can be transformed into electrical signals and screened simply, including coding, modulation, amplification or transmission.

2.2 Data Analyser Design

The analysis signal in the data analyzer is the long distance and large capacity radio communication signal. The frequency bandwidth occupied by the transmission signal, microwave and ultrashort wave bands can complete the work, but the microwave processing effect is better. Data analyzer uses ARM11 processing chip developed by ARM company, which can connect several data together and has stable processing characteristics in the range of sight. But if we want to deal with long-distance communication signals, we need to use relay (also known as relay) communication signal processing mode, which is connected through various relay stations, and the processing range is as high as 20–50 km. Microwave processor can process both analog and digital relay communication signals. It has very good encryption ability and is very convenient for later transmission. Therefore, people pay more and more attention to it [6].

2.3   Data Matcher Design

The core chip of the data matcher is the CEDA chip developed by IBM, this chip can transform baseband signal into a form suitable for transmission in the transmission medium. It can be transmitted through the transmission medium. At the receiving end, it can be inversely transformed by the receiving device to restore the message to the recipient. The selected matching mode is bidirectional transmission with very short working delay, usually between 2 and 5 micros. The area of CEDA chip is very small, so it will not consume too much power and produce noise pollution. This is incomparable with other current chips in the market According to the matcher, the starting and receiving devices are installed on both ends of the matched object, which greatly improves the transmission efficiency.

2.4   Data Processor Design

The processor is a S3C2440A microprocessor manufactured by Samsung. The core of the processor is 32 bits, It can not only bring the advantages of ARM920T into full play, but also bring MMU, AMBA and Harvard structure to realize high-speed buffer. There are independent instruction Cache and data Cache in the processor. The instruction Cache size is 32 KB and the data Cache size is 64 KB. It can connect the peripheral interfaces of other hardware devices at the same time and complete encryption through I/O mode. The highest frequency of S3C2440A microprocessor can reach 600 MHz [7].

The processing system is shown in Fig. 2:

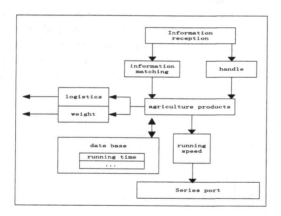

Fig. 2. Data processing system

The network used in the data processing system in Fig. 2 is the Resistance Capacitance (RC) network, the network can generate suppression waves from the load side to prevent interference signals from entering. The RC network connected at both ends of the load can effectively reduce the interference amplitude. Varistors are used to block interference signals in DC and AC circuits. As a non-linear resistor device, varistors are highly sensitive to voltage. In terms of characteristics, it is very similar to bi-directional voltage regulator, with non-polarity, symmetry, non-linearity and inductance suppression, so it is suitable for both DC and AC circuits [8]. Varistor has many advantages, such as small temperature coefficient, wide voltage range, long service life, small occupied area, low consumption cost, etc. Therefore, it is placed on multiple contacts and coils in the hardware system designed in this paper.

2.5 Data Tracker Design

In order to check whether the prediction result of the prediction system is accurate, a data tracker is set up. The terminal node of the tracker chooses a small EGB control chip. This chip follows the latest Internet protocol, IEEE 802.15.4. It integrates the RF front end and the controller core. It can simultaneously control the water temperature sensor, water level sensor, PH value sensor and dissolved oxygen sensor, and detect the collected parameters. The volume of EGB control chip is very small, and the internal power supply voltage is limited. Therefore, the design of hardware should follow the standard of energy saving and achieve the maximum efficiency in the shortest time. As a regulating node, gateway node has self-coordination and powerful data processing ability. The processed data are stored in the database for follow-up work. Because of the different environment of the underwater channel monitored, the emphasis of selection is also different. When monitoring, the gateway nodes should be isolated and set separately to prevent the interference between different sensors and other signals from being transmitted to the system under test. Gateway nodes use physical addresses of terminal nodes to divide signals. When new instructions are input, the system list will increase continuously and new commands will be determined at the same time. The number of gateway nodes is small, so the power consumption is very small, and there are many communication modes that can be selected, For example: Internet communication, satellite communication and mobile communication, etc. There is only one central gateway node and many edge nodes, which are responsible for the relay and forwarding of data signals [9]. The gateway node circuit diagram is shown in Fig. 3:

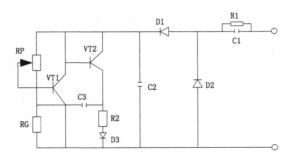

Fig. 3. Tracker gateway node circuit diagram

The central monitoring node is the central part of the monitoring system. It can fuse the information collected by each sensor together, and then analyze it. According to the analysis results, the specific image of the underwater channel of the ship can be drawn.

The central monitoring node has the functions of data processing, visualization and management. The central monitoring node based on wireless sensor network also has remote control function. The hardware composed of large-scale disk array has excellent performance. It can not only monitor the underwater channel in real time, but also monitor the underwater channel actively.

3 Software Design of Agricultural Products Intelligent Transportation Logistics Freight Forecasting System Based on Large Data Analysis

The hardware part of agricultural products intelligent transportation logistics cargo volume forecasting system based on large data analysis is designed. The working process is shown in Fig. 4 below:

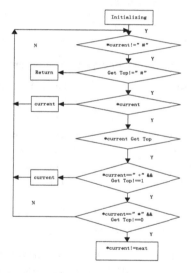

Fig. 4. Software of agricultural products intelligent transportation logistics cargo volume prediction system based on large data analysis

Figure 4 uses big data analysis technology to forecast the logistics flow of agricultural products in intelligent transportation. The specific process is explained as follows: (1) Information input. The central monitoring node sends out control instructions from a long distance, transfers them to the gateway node, and inputs the collected crop logistics information. (2) Information analysis. The central gateway node of the gateway node activates the internal line to accurately analyze the collected crop information. (3) Information matching. The crop information is matched with the agricultural product transportation logistics flow in the database, and the matching results are obtained. (4) Information processing. Processing matched crop information.

(5) Information tracking. When tracking the information of agricultural products, the information tracking software should pay attention to the location of agricultural products, and the results obtained by the terminal nodes should be fed back to the map, so that the staff can better grasp the overall situation of agricultural products transportation. Because the transport environment will change with time, it is necessary to establish a time baseline, draw a map, and analyze the reasons for the change, so as to prevent possible problems in time [10].

4   Experimental Test and Analysis

In order to test the validity of the forecasting system of agricultural products intelligent transportation logistics flow studied in this paper, a comparative experiment was designed to compare with the traditional forecasting system.

4.1   Design of Experimental Parameters

The experimental parameters are shown in Table 1 below.

Table 1. Setting of experimental parameters.

Parameter	Numerical value
Voltage value of I/O module	220 V
Output frequency	55 MHz
Output current	20 A–50 A
Input current	50 A–100 A
Working mode	Ericsson
Working hours	1 h

4.2   Experimental Results and Analysis

The experimental results of prediction accuracy are shown in Fig. 5 below:

Figure 5 shows that when the transport flow of agricultural products is 50 kg, the accuracy of traditional system is 91.0%, and that of this system is 94.8%, when the transport flow of agricultural products is 100 kg, the accuracy of traditional system is 88.7%. The prediction accuracy of this system is 86.1%. When the transportation flow of agricultural products is 150 kg, the prediction accuracy of traditional system is 88.4%, and that of this system is 95.2%. When the transportation flow of agricultural products is 200 kg, the accuracy of traditional system is 88.2%, and that of this system is 96.1%. When the transportation flow of agricultural products is 250 kg, the accuracy of traditional system is 86.0%, and that of this system is 96.1%. When the transport flow of agricultural products is 300 kg, the accuracy of traditional system is 85.3%, and that of this system is 94.5%.

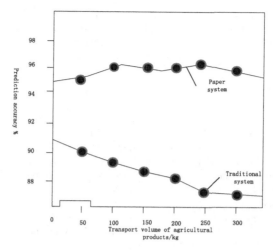

Fig. 5. Prediction accuracy test results

4.3 Experimental Conclusions

According to the above experimental results, the following conclusions can be drawn: both the traditional forecasting system and the forecasting system in this paper can predict the transport logistics cargo flow of agricultural products, However, the traditional system takes a long time to predict, and the accuracy is very low. With the increase of cargo flow, the prediction ability is getting worse and worse. The system studied in this paper is intelligent, can accurately analyze the cargo flow, and the prediction accuracy is always maintained at a very high level.

5 Concluding Remarks

Based on the analysis of large data, this paper designs a forecasting system for the flow of agricultural products in intelligent transportation logistics, which has high forecasting ability and can effectively improve the quality and safety control of agricultural products in logistics integration. In order to improve the quality of agricultural products in an all-round way, the Internet of Things intelligent traceability system should be used to collect relevant data sources, and a large data center for traceability of agricultural product quality and safety information should be established to link the information of agricultural product production and logistics and form a set of information traceability chain. Through this kind of traceability chain, the information of agricultural products can be obtained from the producer or even the specific growing land to the wholesaler or retailer, or from the wholesaler or retailer to the production site, and the positioning analysis of large data can be achieved, so as to make a breakthrough in the supervision of agricultural product quality and safety, and give full play to the logistics function based on big data.

Acknowledgments. Agricultural Science Research Plan in Shaanxi Province of China: "Research on key technologies and applications of Smart agriculture planting and logistics distribution based on the Internet of Things" (NO. 2017NY132).

References

1. Zheng, L., Zhang, Y.: Design of teaching system for comprehensive traffic data analysis platform. Logist. Sci. Technol. **39**(7), 147–149 (2016)
2. Li, X., Wang, H., Jiang, Y.: Research on intelligent fresh logistics distribution platform based on business ecosystem. Logist. Eng. Manag. **21**(3), 73–75 (2017)
3. Lin, M.: Intelligent logistics research based on Internet of Things and big data analysis. J. Liaoning Univ. Sci. Technol. **18**(6), 28–30 (2016)
4. Lu, H.: Analysis of intelligent logistics development model based on Internet of Things and cloud computing in big data era. Commun. World **13**(12), 110 (2017)
5. Xu, W.: Research on intelligent decision platform and key technologies based on logistics big data. Logist. Eng. Manag. **39**(6), 60–61 (2017)
6. Zhu, Q.: Research on logistics flexibility of fresh agricultural products supply chain based on big data background. Sci. Technol. Entrep. Mon. **29**(22), 24–25 (2016)
7. Ganbin, Zhang, M., Wu, K., et al.: Research on visual management system of intelligent logistics under the background of big data. Sci. Technol. Style **21**(4), 64–65 2018
8. Zhang, T., Hu, J.Z: "Internet +" big data strategy research of agricultural products logistics industry. China Mark. **42**(36), 12–14 2016
9. Luo, T., Zhang, P.: Research on narrative theory-based brand packaging design of agricultural products in big data era. Packag. Eng. **11**(2), 5–8 (2016)
10. Zheng, H., Yuxiang, C.: Simulation and analysis of optimization model for intrusion risk assessment in large data environment. Comput. Simul. **33**(9), 292–295 (2016)

An Ideological and Political Education Evaluation Method of University Students Based on Data Mining

Liyan Tu[✉] and Lan Wu

Inner Mongolia University for the Nationalities, Tongliao 028000, China
tlyimun@163.com

Abstract. The development of big data technology and data mining technology has brought new opportunities for the scientific and innovative development of ideological and political education in colleges and universities. The evaluation of ideological and political education in colleges and universities in the context of big data was studied in this paper. An evaluation method of college students' ideological and political education based on data mining was proposed. The proposed method uses K-means clustering method to analyze the data of the "worker's assessment scale" of the counselor, and can achieve the evaluation of the ideological and political management effect of the counselor. The experimental results show that compared with traditional evaluation methods, the evaluation results of this method are more accurate and objective.

Keywords: Big data · Data mining · Educational evaluation · Objectivity

1 Introduction

Ideological and political education of college students is an important part of higher education. The ideological and political education of college students relates to the realization of the fundamental task of high moral values establishment and people cultivation [1, 2]. With the rapid development of China's economy and society and the further advancement of education reform, the ideological and political education of college students is facing new problems and tests. How to adapt to the new situation is an urgent problem to be solved in the current ideological and political education in colleges and universities. Evaluating the ideological and political education of college students and establishing a scientific evaluation system and evaluation method are effective ways to promote ideological and political education in colleges and universities.

The emergence of big data technology signals that the society has entered the era of data. With the rapid development of modern information technology, data mining plays an increasingly widespread and convenient role in our lives. In universities where network technology is most fully applied, all data left by teachers and students can be collected and analyzed through big data technology [3, 4]. Using data mining techniques to find useful information for education can better innovate teaching methods and methods, and achieve zero-distance personalized education for college students. Therefore, it is of great theoretical and practical significance to explore the optimization

© ICST Institute for Computer Sciences, Social Informatics and Telecommunications Engineering 2019
Published by Springer Nature Switzerland AG 2019. All Rights Reserved
G. Gui and L. Yun (Eds.): ADHIP 2019, LNICST 302, pp. 401–408, 2019.
https://doi.org/10.1007/978-3-030-36405-2_40

of ideological and political education in universities based on the perspective of big data and data mining. How to effectively apply big data technology and data mining technology to the evaluation of ideological and political education in colleges and universities is a question that needs to be solved.

Since 2013, research on the use of big data technology and data mining technology to promote education development has gradually emerged [5]. Liang et al. discussed how to improve the ideological work of colleges and universities in terms of strengthening data awareness and improving the ability to use big data [6]. Zhang et al. proposed that universities must continuously strengthen the collection, excavation and analysis of student data to ensure the normal implementation of ideological education in universities [7]. Zhou et al. advocates that the use of big data technology can uncover the hidden rules behind university data, and then change the way and decision of education managers [8]. Gu et al. advocates the establishment of big data systems to analyze and process big data, so that the ideological and political education in universities can be transformed from empirical teaching to scientific teaching [9]. These studies show that there has been preliminary exploration and research on the application of big data in the evaluation of ideological and political education in colleges and universities. However, the level of research is not deep enough and there is no specific evaluation method, which requires further study and improvement.

This paper studies the management evaluation of university ideological and political education in the context of big data. At present, the traditional analysis method is based on the evaluation of absolute scores. This method has some defects and deficiencies in the objectivity and accuracy of the evaluation results. The traditional analysis method to evaluate the counselor cannot effectively and properly evaluate the counselor's management effectiveness. For this reason, this paper firstly uses the cluster analysis in data mining technology to establish the evaluation model of university ideological and political education management. Then, the k-means clustering algorithm is used to analyze the counselor's "work evaluation scale" data, which can effectively overcome the defects and shortcomings of traditional analysis methods.

2 K-Means Clustering Algorithm

Cluster analysis is a multivariate statistical analysis to classify samples or indicators [10]. According to the different objects can be divided into sample classification and variable clustering, that is, the classification of the samples and the classification of variables. Clustering is different from classification. Classification has prior knowledge that reference learning. For the classification model, the class label of the sample information is known.

The K-means algorithm is a stepwise clustering analysis of a large sample of data by a user-specified number of categories [11, 12]. The sample data is regarded as a point in the k-dimensional space, distance is used as an index to judge the distance relationship between data, and a higher execution rate is obtained at the expense of wasting multiple solutions. The basic idea of K-means algorithm is to aggregate each sample into its nearest average class, that is, to initially classify the data and then gradually adjust it to obtain the final classification result.

The K-means algorithm is implemented as follows. The dataset that needs to be clustered is

$$S = \{x_1, x_2, \cdots, x_n\} \tag{1}$$

where x_i is the p dimensional data, p is the number of attributes. $\{c_1, c_2, \cdots, c_k\}$ represents k cluster centers. The degree of similarity between any two data objects in the data set is represented by Euclidean distance as

$$d(x_i, y_j) = \sqrt{\sum_{m=1}^{p} |x_{im} - x_{jm}|^2} \tag{2}$$

The objective function used to determine whether the clustering result is good or bad is

$$J = \sum_{i=1}^{k} \sum_{j=1}^{n} d(x_j, c_i) \tag{3}$$

where the objective function J is a function about the clustering sample and the clustering center. The objective function is the sum of the squared errors of the cluster centers of all the data objects in the data set and the clusters of the respective clusters after the cluster iteration. The process of classical K-means clustering algorithm is shown in Fig. 1.

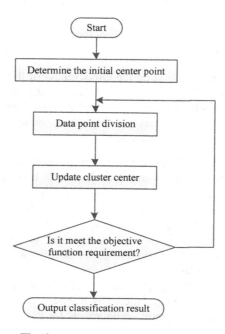

Fig. 1. K-means clustering algorithm

3 Cluster Evaluation Model of Ideological and Political Education

With the continuous development and popularization of higher education in China, more and more high school graduates have entered the university's school, which has brought a lot of influence on the school's teaching and management. In addition, because the study habits are not well developed, the creation of a learning atmosphere has brought great difficulties. The poor learning atmosphere has also exerted a great influence on students' interest in learning. These are the difficulties in the education and management of college counselors. Under normal circumstances, the relevant departments of the school have collected a large amount of data through the usual education and management work. However, at present, the processing of these data is only at a relatively low level of search and simple analysis, and no valuable and instructive information has been mined. How to tap into these "treasures" data and find valuable information among them is a key issue that both the school leaders and the majority of student workers are concerned about.

In order to more specifically understand the work of counselors, the school organizes students' comments on the counselor's work every semester, and fills in a "workbench quantification form" for counselors. How to make better use of it and find valuable information on the education, management, and school management of the counselors is a very meaningful thing for the optimization of ideological and political education in colleges and universities. School leaders and student workers must scientifically judge each stage of student management education, and dig out useful knowledge from it, so that they can achieve further guidance and management requirements.

3.1 Schematic Design

In the past, most of the information on the effectiveness of the counselor's work was used to find large amounts of information. This paper proposes a cluster analysis data mining method to deal with the data information of the effectiveness of the counselor. It can turn a large number of data into a clustering result, and then better use this type of data. The data mining process is shown in Fig. 2.

Step 1: Identify the data mining object and purpose. Clearly defining the problem and finding the goal of data mining is an important first step in the data mining process. Although data mining cannot predict the final result, it can foresee the problems studied. Therefore, it is necessary to avoid blind digging.

Step 2: Data collection. This process has heavy work tasks and it takes more time. In the usual education management, it is necessary to carefully collect data and information. Some of the data can be obtained directly, and some of the data must be obtained through research.

Step 3: Data preprocessing. The process is to convert the collected data set into an analyzable data model. The data model is prepared according to the algorithm. Different algorithms have different requirements for the data model.

Step 4: Data Clustering Mining. Clustering data mining is to divide the data model into multiple groups of similar objects. The process is mainly the input process of the data model and the selection and implementation process of the clustering algorithm.

Step 5: Analysis of clustering results. This process is to analyze and study the multiple group attributes composed of classes after clustering data mining.

Step 6: Application of knowledge. This process integrates the useful information obtained from the research into the counselor's management education. The counselor can use the conclusions to promote teaching management and form a good management policy.

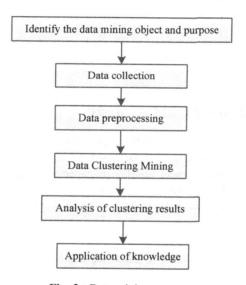

Fig. 2. Data mining process

3.2   Algorithm Implementation

We collected and compiled the "Quantification Form for the Assessment of Counsellors' Work" of the Inner Mongolia University for the Nationalities in 2016, and sorted out 1200 assessment quantification tables concerning the education and management of counselors. Use this data to evaluate the counselor's ideological and political education management. After data mining of these data, some important conclusions can bring unprecedented guiding value for management and teaching.

According to the job performance of the counselor, it is divided into five categories of "excellent, good, qualified, poor, and poor". Further measures were taken for the missing records, and finally a quantitative assessment of the work evaluation with complete evaluation records was obtained.

According to the four attributes of "management attitude", "management ability", "management method" and "management effect", the data in the quantification table of the merger work assessment is reorganized. Through the above processing, we have unified the quantitative assessment of the job evaluation to the four attributes of "management attitude", "management ability", "management method" and "management effect". In the following, we use the clustering mining analysis method to analyze the four attributes of the 1170 data sample information.

By taking the process of preprocessing data sample information, the data samples used for the analysis process are listed in Table 1.

Table 1. Clustered data sample.

Management attitude	Management ability	Management method	Management effect
0.66	0.65	0.56	0.59
0.66	0.64	0.61	0.60
0.34	0.39	0.31	0.33
0.8	0.78	0.83	0.80
...	...	...	...

4   Experimental Results and Analysis

The k-means algorithm was used to analyze 1200 direct sample data and 1170 sample data obtained by data conversion. All sample data contains four types of attributes: management attitude, management ability, management method, and management effectiveness. Data mining clustering was performed on these four attributes respectively, and the initial K value was set to 3. The final mining results are shown in Table 2.

Table 2. Clustering results.

Cluster category	Management attitude	Management ability	Management method	Management effect	Sample number
Better	0.76	0.75	0.74	0.79	36
Medium	0.63	0.58	0.54	0.56	74
Poor	0.34	0.30	0.27	0.30	10

According to the results of the cluster analysis, the final scale distribution of the data included in each cluster is as follows. There are a total of 36 data samples in the better category, and 30% after deleting a standard sample. There are 74 samples in the medium category and 62% in the case of deleting a standard sample. There are a total of 10 data samples for the poor category and 8% for the deletion of a standard sample.

In order to further verify the final results of data mining, we once again obtained 248 people from the Department of Student Affairs to obtain the relevant comprehensive quantitative scores in participating in 10 activities. The total score is 100 points. These data samples are categorized on a scale of 0 to 100 points. A total of three categories are included: more than 80 points (Better), 80 to 60 points (Medium) and less than 60 points (Poor). The final statistical results are shown in Table 3.

Table 3. Comprehensive quantitative score analysis results.

Cluster category	Sample number	Proportion
Better	512	21%
Medium	1686	68%
Poor	282	11%

The statistical results show that the proportions of more than 80 points, 80 to 60 points and less than 60 points are 21%, 68% and 11% respectively. Comparing the analysis results in Tables 2 and 3, we can see that the clustered evaluation results are basically consistent with the integrated quantitative results, as it shown in Fig. 3. The experimental results confirm that such a data mining model based on the quantification table of the counselor's job evaluation is a very successful model, which brings certain reference significance and certain guiding significance to the management and education work of college counselors.

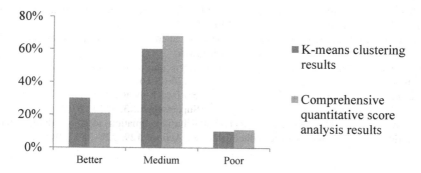

Fig. 3. Comparison of evaluation results

5   Conclusion

The application of clustering methods in data mining to the evaluation of ideological and political education in colleges and universities has been studied in this paper. The data analysis method of "work evaluation scale" of counselors based on K-means clustering was designed. The experimental results show that this method can effectively evaluate the ideological and political education of college counselors, and the evaluation results are more efficient and more objective. This study provides a new idea for the evaluation of ideological and political education in colleges and universities in the context of big data.

Acknowledgements. Inner Mongolia University for Nationalities Ideological and Political Theory Teaching and Research Project (SZ2014009). Inner Mongolia Autonomous Region Science and Technology Innovation Guide Project in 2018: KCBJ2018028.

References

1. Lei, Z.M.: Research on the Innovation of the Ideological and Political Education of College Students in the Background of the Omnimedia. Theory & Practice of Education (2016)
2. Wang, J.F., Yao, J., Guo, M.L.: Research on Cooperative Training Mechanism of College Students' Innovation and Entrepreneurship Education. Value Engineering (2018)
3. Zhao, J.L., Fan, S., Hu, D.: Business challenges and research directions of management analytics in the big data era. J. Manag. Anal. **1**(3), 169–174 (2014)
4. Samier, E.A.: Education in a troubled era of disenchantment: the emergence of a new Zeitgeist. J. Educ. Adm. Hist. **50**, 1–10 (2018)
5. Sakaue, K.: Informal fee charge and school choice under a free primary education policy: panel data evidence from rural Uganda. Int. J. Educ. Dev. **62**, 112–127 (2018)
6. Liang, J.F., Yuan, Z.H.: Adaptation and innovation: ideological and political education in colleges and universities in the era of big data. Stud. Educ. Res. **6**, 63–67 (2013)
7. Zhang, R., Dong, Z., Xia, X.: Innovation and exploration of ideological and political education in universities in the era of big data. Sch. Party Build. Ideol. Educ. **10**, 67–69 (2014)
8. Zhou, S.M.: Talking about the application of big data in ideological and political education in colleges and universities. Stud. Educ. Res. **5**, 124–126 (2014)
9. Gu, Q.L., Xu, J.Z.: Study on ideological and political education of college students based on big data thinking. Theory Res. **14**, 248–249 (2015)
10. Carvalho, A., Dall'Osso, M., Dorigo, T., et al.: Higgs pair production: choosing benchmarks with cluster analysis. J. High Energy Phys. (4), 126 (2016)
11. Hasib, A.A., Cebrian, J.M., Natvig, L.: A vectorized k-means, algorithm for compressed datasets: design and experimental analysis. J. Supercomput. **3**, 1–24 (2018)
12. Kwon, K., Shin, J.W., Kim, N.S.: Incremental basis estimation adopting global k-means algorithm for NMF-based noise reduction. Appl. Acoust. **129**, 277–283 (2018)

Design of Real-Time Detection System of Bacteria Concentration Changes in Biological Fermentation

Weiwei Jiang[1]([⊠]) and Jinbao Shan[2]

[1] College of Food and Drug, Shandong Institute of Commerce and Technology, Jinan 250103, Shandong, China
eihuiyi123@163.com
[2] College of Information Technology and Art Design, Shandong Institute of Commerce and Technology, Jinan 250103, Shandong, China

Abstract. In the process of bio-fermentation, there is a problem of low detection efficiency in the process of recording changes in the concentration of traditional bacterial cells. Therefore, a real-time detection system for the concentration of microbial cells in biological fermentation is designed. In the system hardware design process, the data of microbial concentration changes in the biological fermentation are analyzed to select the system measurement principle. An intermediate conversion circuit is designed based on the measurement principle to complete the system hardware design. The measurement principle is used to derive the software structure of the real-time detection system. Real-time data acquisition and detection are implemented in the software structure to realize system software design. According to the results of simulation experiments, the real-time detection system for the change of bacterial concentration in biological fermentation compares with the traditional detection method, the detection efficiency is improved by 11%, and the operation is stable.

Keywords: Biological fermentation · Cell concentration · Concentration detection · Real-time · Detection efficiency

1 Introduction

Biological fermentation is the foundation of bioengineering and modern biotechnology and its industrialization. With the progress of bioengineering technology and the expansion of the scale of fermentation industry, it is urgent to carry out advanced control and optimization of fermentation process. The existing fermentation measurement and control system lacks the intelligent detection unit of key biological parameters detection. The mechanism of biological fermentation is complex, and it is highly nonlinear and time-varying. It is difficult to realize real-time detection of these key biological parameters; The structure of these measurement and control systems are all unit structures, and their openness and reliability are poor, making it difficult to apply advanced optimization control algorithms and strategies to industrial applications and to meet the need for optimal control of fermentation processes. Therefore, it has important theoretical

© ICST Institute for Computer Sciences, Social Informatics and Telecommunications Engineering 2019
Published by Springer Nature Switzerland AG 2019. All Rights Reserved
G. Gui and L. Yun (Eds.): ADHIP 2019, LNICST 302, pp. 409–418, 2019.
https://doi.org/10.1007/978-3-030-36405-2_41

significance and application value to study the real-time detection system and its key technologies of the microbial concentration change in the process of biological fermentation [1]. Microbial fermentation process is an extremely complex biochemical reaction process, and many factors affect the fermentation, such as the composition of the fermentation broth, temperature, Ph value, dissolved oxygen, the type and concentration of viable bacteria. Among the above factors, the concentration of bacteria is the most important process parameter, but at present there is no real-time monitoring system that can meet the requirements, and it can accurately detect the bacterial concentration in the fermentation process in real time. The conventional measurement method of the concentration of bacteria is off-line. Off-line measurement brings two problems: On the one hand, the sampling process is easy to be contaminated; on the other hand, the automatic control of fermentation is difficult. Therefore, it is necessary to develop a real-time detection system for the concentration of bacteria, which is of great significance for understanding the fermentation information, mastering and controlling the biological fermentation process, and improving the quality of fermentation [2]. Therefore, a new method is proposed to detect the concentration of bacteria in the fermentation process in real time, and an automatic detection system for the concentration of bacteria is designed to realize the real-time detection of the concentration of bacteria in the fermentation process. It has good application value in biochemical pharmaceuticals, food fermentation, sewage treatment and other industrial fields.

2   Design of Real-Time Detection System of Bacteria Concentration Changes in Biological Fermentation

2.1   Real-Time Detection System Hardware Design of Change of Bacteria Concentration

Selected Measurement Principle
The presence of microorganisms affects the electrical properties of the fermentation broth, and the electrical properties can characterize the fermentation broth using its conductivity and permittivity. The permittivity (dielectric constant) of the fermentation broth is defined as the ability to store the charge. When the microbial strain is added to the medium, its permittivity will increase significantly; when the measurement frequency changes, the permittivity of the fermentation broth will also change. The phenomenon that the permittivity changes with the measurement frequency is called the permittivity distribution. Under normal circumstances, it is difficult for charged ions in the cell to cross the cell membrane to reach the outside of the cell, and it is difficult for extracellular charged ions to penetrate into the cell interior. If the fermentation broth is placed in an electric field, there will be an equal and opposite charge accumulation on the inner and outer surfaces of the cell membrane, each cell acting like a small capacitor. Under certain conditions, the amount of electric charge bound by living cells per unit volume is proportional to the number of live bacteria [3]. The greater the concentration of viable bacteria, the more the bound charge, the greater the permittivity of the fermentation broth. Therefore, the permittivity of the fermentation broth in the radio frequency range

is a function of the measurement frequency and the bacterial cell concentration. When the measurement frequency is fixed, the permittivity and the bacterial concentration of the fermentation broth are single-valued functional relationships. This means that the bacterial concentration can be detected by measuring the permittivity of the fermentation broth. Fermentation process mainly batch fermentation, batch fed fermentation and continuous feed fermentation in three forms. The fed batch fermentation process is between batch fermentation and continuous feed fermentation, both have the advantages, and overcome the disadvantages of both, it is a commonly used fermentation method, the study of different feeding strategies to increase the fermentation yield is one of the main directions for optimal control of fed batch fermentation processes. Therefore, this paper focuses on the soft-sensing system of fed batch fermentation process [4]. The fermentation process belongs to a complex and nonlinear dynamic process. The general material conservation equations for the feed fermentation process are as follows:

$$\frac{d\xi}{dt} = K_m r(\xi) + u \tag{1}$$

State $\xi = [\xi_1, \xi_2, \ldots, \xi_n]^T$ represents a state vector representing the concentration of a particular component in the fermenter. The first item $K_m r(\xi)$ in formula (1–2) represents the change of biochemical and biochemical reactions in the fermenter. Km represents a stochastic transformation matrix, $r(\xi) = [r_1(\xi), r_2, \xi, \ldots, r_m(\xi)]^T$ represents the reaction rate vector for different components. The second item $u = [u_1, u_2, \ldots, u_n]^T$ represents the control input vector of the fermenter, including the rate of various materials flowing into and out of the fermenter. Therefore, the dynamic characteristics of fed batch fermentation process can be represented by a set of ordinary differential equations, then, the state space is used to describe the real-time detection system of microbial concentration changes during fermentation, it can be expressed as:

$$\begin{cases} \frac{dx(t)}{dt} = f(x(t), u(t), w(t)) \\ y(t) = g(x(t), v(t)) \end{cases} \tag{2}$$

Among them, x is the state variable vector for the measurement output vector; x and y are Gaussian white noise vectors with a mean of 0; $f(\cdot)$ and $g(\cdot)$ represent a linear or nonlinear function of the state transition and measurement output, respectively.

From the above formula (2) we can see that, the similarity between a soft measurement hybrid system and a state space system is that, the system is composed of state differential equations and equations, it is the same as the dynamic system state space system, the state vector is an internal variable set that can completely characterize the time domain behavior of the system. Represents all the dynamic information of the system. But the difference is: soft measurement system, instead of the output equation, the conservation equation can be a measurement supplemental equation established using various artificial intelligence methods and prior knowledge [5]. In terms of expression, soft measurement systems include differential equations and algebraic equations, it can fully express the dynamic and static characteristics of the fermentation process, therefore, it is called the real-time detection system for the change of the concentration of bacteria; the conservation equation contains the specific form of prior knowledge used in the soft measurement system, the dimension of the conservation equation can be seen as the amount of prior knowledge used by the system.

Intermediate Transform Circuit Design

The intermediate conversion circuit is mainly based on the bacteria concentration detection system, the system is mainly composed of a fermenter, a capacitance sensor—platinum electrode, an intermediate conversion circuit, an A/D board, a computer, a monitor, a printer, etc., as shown in Fig. 1:

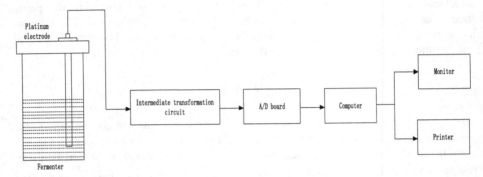

Fig. 1. Frame structure of real-time detection system of bacterial concentration change data

Based on the real-time detection system for the change of microbial concentration data, the intermediate conversion circuit converts the capacitance signal detected by the capacitance sensor into a voltage signal required by the A/D board, the intermediate conversion circuit is implemented using a lock-in amplifier [6]. Lock-in amplifiers are based on coherent detection technology, using the reference signal frequency is related to the input signal frequency, not related to noise frequency, this extracts useful signals from noise backgrounds. The intermediate conversion circuit is shown in Fig. 2:

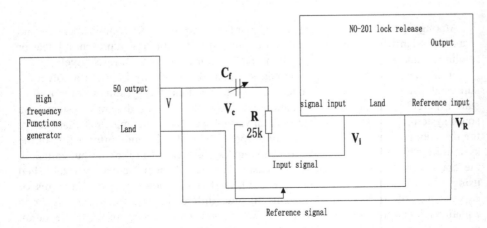

Fig. 2. Intermediate conversion circuit block diagram

In this circuit, when the capacitance of the capacitive sensor changes slightly, the amplitude and phase of the input signal voltage Vi of the lock-in amplifier changes accordingly. Because of the input signal $V_i = \frac{R}{R + \frac{1}{jwc_f}} V_s$ (ignoring the input impedance of the lock), where Vs is a high frequency sinusoidal signal. When the frequency of the input signal of the lock-in amplifier is locked at the frequency of the reference signal, that is w = wR, the phase difference between Vi and VR is equal to zero, the amplitude of the output voltage of the lock-in amplifier Vo = KVi. Where K is the magnification, after the parameters of the lock-in amplifier are selected, it is a constant [7]. Therefore, the output voltage has a monotonically increasing function relationship with the sensor capacitance. This circuit has a strong anti-interference, high sensitivity, a wide dynamic range, therefore, it is widely used as weak signal detection.

2.2 Real-Time Detection System Software Design for the Change of Bacterial Concentration

Real-Time Detection System Software Structure
The real-time detection system software design of the concentration change data of bacteria, using a networked and modular integrated approach, taking full account of the system's openness and reliability principles, designed real-time detection system software, Fig. 3 shows the integrated architecture of the intelligent measurement and control system for the fermentation process:

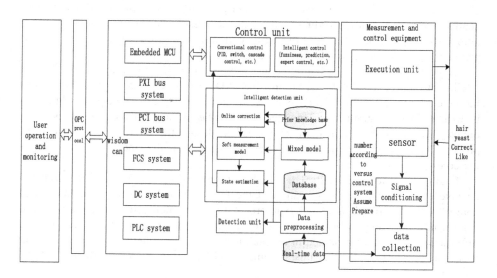

Fig. 3. Real-time detection system software structure

Collecting and controlling the state information of fermentation process objects through real-time detection system software structure is the basic function realized by the existing fermentation process measurement and control system, the intelligent measurement and control system of the fermentation process is based on the analysis of the objects of the fermentation process, extract useful prior knowledge, and analyze and systematically prior knowledge, through the smart detection processing unit, using the latest artificial intelligence technology, real-time estimation of unpredictable key parameters in bio-fermentation process, therefore, it is possible to effectively achieve optimal control of biological parameters that are difficult to measure [8]. The functions of each functional module unit in the intelligent measurement and control system of the fermentation process are as follows:

Measurement and control equipment: It is mainly composed of data acquisition unit and execution unit. The data acquisition unit collects the signals of the hardware sensors. Through signal conditioning and data acquisition modules, convert the measurement information of the fermented object from analog to digital, as the real-time measurement data of the fermentation process measurement and control system; the execution unit sends a control command, control various switches and valves, etc., to achieve optimal control of the fermentation process;

Detection unit: difference and intelligent detection unit, refers to a normally measurable inspection unit, realize the routine measurable fermentation process (such as pH, temperature, dissolved oxygen concentration) detection;

Intelligent detection unit: The biggest difference between the intelligent measurement and control system of the fermentation process and the existing measurement and control system is that the intelligent measurement and control system has an intelligent detection unit. In information processing, the intelligent detection processing module uses artificial intelligence technology to analyze and deal with unpredictable key quality parameters, and according to the detection results of the intelligent detection unit, the biological parameters of the fermentation process are feedback controlled, to increase the yield and efficiency of fermentation;

Control unit: The control unit includes two modules, conventional control and intelligent control. Conventional control has PID, switch, cascade control and so on. Intelligent control has fuzzy, forecast, expert control and so on. The control algorithm is written in a programming language and packaged into standard modules, then directly called by the application, only need to design the interface type of control process, input parameters (pass or call), return value, can realize the control function of the control module;

Intelligent processing unit: The intelligent processing unit realizes the comprehensive processing of the information of the fermentation process measurement and control system through an intelligent processor. The intelligent detection unit and control unit are components of the intelligent processing unit, and the data flow and information flow are represented in the architecture [9]. The intelligent processing unit is usually composed of a PCI bus system, a PXI bus system, an embedded 1 VICU. PLC system, a DCS system or an FCS system;

The intelligent detection unit is the most critical part of the intelligent measurement and control system architecture of the fermentation process, soft measurement technology is a key technology for intelligent detection units. The intelligent detection unit utilizes the measurable information of the hardware sensor and priori information of the process object, the soft measurement system enables real-time detection of key biological parameters that are difficult to measure in real time. As shown in the smart detection unit block diagram in Fig. 2, by integrating prior knowledge and historical database data, by integrating prior knowledge and historical database data, after system identification, construct a corresponding soft measurement system; the hardware sensor collects measurement data through the data acquisition device, pre-processing measurement data, combining soft helium J system and real-time state estimation method, realize accurate estimates of key unpredictable biological parameters. At the same time, the real-time correction module in the intelligent detection unit, using state estimation and control unit output and system real-time measurement data, through the correction data provided by the prior knowledge base, real-time correction of soft measurement systems, improve system detection accuracy.

Realizing Data Acquisition and Detection in Real Time
The real-time data acquisition and sorting of the capacitive sensor for detecting the concentration of bacteria is mainly made of PTFE rods, rubber seals, leads, two platinum electrodes. The sensor lead is a coaxial shielded cable, the electrode has a coaxial cylindrical structure, the inner and outer electrodes are covered with a layer of PTFE film, for internal and external electrode insulation. The electrodes are resistant to high temperatures and are non-toxic, meeting the special requirements of bio-fermentation sensors [10]. The diameter of the external electrode is 16 mm, the diameter of the internal electrode is 10 mm, and some small holes are drilled on the external electrode, makes live cells evenly distributed in the fermentation broth. There is the following relationship between the electrode capacitance Cf and the permittivity ef of the fermentation broth:

$$e_f = \frac{\ln\frac{R}{r}}{2\pi e_0 l} C_f \text{ or } e_f = kC_f (k = \frac{\ln\frac{R}{r}}{2\pi e_0 l}$$ Is a constant). Therefore, the permittivity of the fermentation broth can be determined by measuring the electrode capacitance.

The voltage signal output from the lock-in amplifier needs to be sent to the computer for data filtering after A/D conversion, get the data you need. The article uses the 9012 modular interface board as the data acquisition interface board of the system, it includes a 12-bit A/D converter, 16 multiplexers, sample/hold, bus interface control logic, etc. the board is equipped with an address switch to set the I/O address arbitrarily. Data processing is done in software, the filtering method used is the median averaging filter. In our detection system, the data acquisition system has been able to automatically collect and process data through the hardware and software design.

3 Experimental Analysis

3.1 Experimental Procedure

To verify the effectiveness of the real-time detection system for the change of bacterial concentration in biological fermentation, the following comparison experiments were designed. Seven different fermentation strains were selected for testing, including Streptococcus, Lactococcus, Leuconostoc, Lactobacillus, Propionic Acid Bacteria, Brevibacterium, and Enterococcus. Experiments were performed on each of the fermenting bacteria. The experimental medium is yellow pulp water, one liter fermenter, in order to make the cells in the fermenter uniform, the fermentation liquid should be continuously stirred, the stirring speed is 100 rpm/min, the fermentation temperature is basically controlled at about 25 °C, and the pH is controlled at About 5.0, the measurement frequency is 50 kHz, and the experimental results are observed under a high-power microscope environment.

The bacterial organisms in the same biological fermentation were used as experimental objects, divided into two groups, the real-time detection system for the change of bacterial concentration in the biological fermentation is the experimental group, the traditional data measurement method is used as a control group, under the premise of controlling a single variable, record the accuracy rate of data records in the two groups of cell concentration changes, the change of cell concentration data records real-time performance. Set corresponding conditions for two sets of experimental data, in order to ensure the fairness of the experiment, the parameters of the experimental group and the control group are always the same. In order to verify the differences between the SME management systems based on clustering algorithms and traditional SME management, the parameters of the experimental group and the control group are always the same. In order to verify the differences between the SME management systems based on clustering algorithms and traditional SME management, the experimental group will use the real-time detection system for the change of the concentration of bacterial cells in the biological fermentation according to the requirements. The traditional data detection mainly adopts manual processing.

3.2   Accuracy of Data Accumulation of Changes in Microbial Concentration

The experimental group and the control group simultaneously recorded the change data of the same bacteria concentration, compared with its record accuracy, after recording 2, 4, 6, 8, and 10 h respectively, differences between the records of bacterial concentration changes and actual data. To avoid the interference caused by unexpected events on the experimental results, the treatment parameters of the experimental group and the control group are the same, the specific results are as follows (Fig. 4):

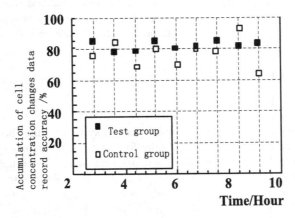

Fig. 4. Accuracy rate of data change of cell concentration

The analysis of the above figure shows that the accuracy of the data recording of bacterial cell concentration changes is compared. With the increase of time, the accuracy of data recording of the cumulative concentration of cell concentration in the experimental group is about 94%, and the data points are similar in value, and the changes are not Big. In the control group, the cumulative data change accuracy of the cell concentration was about 83%, but the values of the data points differed greatly. Comparing the experimental results, the recording accuracy of the proposed method is improved by 11% compared with the traditional method, and the accuracy of the proposed method is higher, which can prove the effectiveness of the real-time detection system.

3.3   Comparison of Bacterial Cell Concentration Changes in Real-Time Data Records

The experimental group and the control group processed the same data at the same time, after recording 200, 400, 600, 800, 1000 sets of data, respectively, the change of cell concentration data records real-time performance. To avoid the interference caused by unexpected events on the experimental results, the treatment parameters of the experimental group and the control group are the same. The specific results are as follows (Fig. 5):

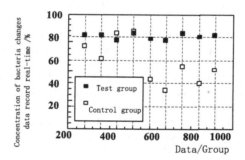

Fig. 5. The real-time recording of the data of bacterial concentration changes

Compared with the above figure, we can see that, in the process of recording the changes in the concentration of bacterial cells, as the demand for processing increases, the real-time performance of the real-time detection system for the change of bacterial concentration in biological fermentation is high, stay around 92%. The control group continues to increase with the demand for processing, the processing efficiency shows a declining trend, record real-time performance is about 79%. Therefore, it can prove the real-time detection system for the application of microbial concentration change in biological fermentation, it can effectively improve the real-time performance of the data of bacterial concentration changes.

4 Conclusion

Biofermentation is the foundation of bioengineering and modern biotechnology and its industrialization, with the advancement of bioengineering technology and the continuous expansion of the production scale of the fermentation industry, there is an urgent need for advanced control and optimization of the fermentation process. The existing fermentation monitoring and control system lacks a key biological parameter detection unit, the mechanism of biological fermentation is complex, with a high degree of nonlinearity and time-variation, it is difficult to achieve real-time detection of these key biological parameters; and these measurement and control systems are all unit structures, poor openness and reliability, making advanced optimization control algorithms and strategies difficult for industrial applications, the need for optimal control of the fermentation process cannot be met. Therefore, the system for real-time detection of microbial concentration changes in biological fermentation, can promote the optimization of the control of the fermentation process engineering application level.

References

1. Goldoni, L., Beringhelli, T., Rocchia, W., et al.: Absolute nutrient concentration measurements in cell culture media: 1H q-NMR spectra and data to compare the efficiency of pH-controlled protein precipitation versus CPMG or post-processing filtering approaches. Data in Brief **8**, 387–393 (2016)
2. Liu, H., Xiao, H., Yin, B., et al.: Enhanced volatile fatty acid production by a modified biological pretreatment in anaerobic fermentation of waste activated sludge. Chem. Eng. J. **284**, 194–201 (2016)
3. Wang, X., Zhang, Y., Zhang, T., et al.: Waste activated sludge fermentation liquid as carbon source for biological treatment of sulfide and nitrate in microaerobic conditions. Chem. Eng. J. **283**, 167–174 (2016)
4. Cheng, H.H., Whang, L.M., Chung, M.C., et al.: Biological hydrogen and methane production from bagasse bioethanol fermentation residues using a two-stage bioprocess. Bioresour. Technol. **210**, 49–55 (2016)
5. Soltan, M., Elsamadony, M., Tawfik, A.: Biological hydrogen promotion via integrated fermentation of complex agro-industrial wastes. Appl. Energy **185**, 929–938 (2017)
6. Xie, Q., Chen, X., Deng, H., et al.: An automated pipeline for bouton, spine, and synapse detection of in vivo two-photon images. Biodata Min. **10**(1), 40 (2017)
7. Alba-Mejía, J.E., Skládanka, J., Hilgert-Delgado, A., et al.: The effect of biological and chemical additives on the chemical composition and fermentation process of Dactylis glomerata silage. **14**(2), 4–6 (2017)
8. He, X., Chong, L., Zhang, N., et al.: Biological fermentation to improve the quality of rapeseed meal. J. Chin. Cereals Oils Assoc. (2016)
9. Song, H.N, Lee, Y.R.: Biological activities and quality characteristics of rice germ after microbial fermentation. Korean J. Food Nutr. **30**(1), 59–66 (2017)
10. Liu, H., Han, P., Liu, H., et al.: Full-scale production of VFAs from sewage sludge by anaerobic alkaline fermentation to improve biological nutrients removal in domestic wastewater. Bioresour. Technol. **260**, 105–114 (2018)

Optimization Design of Large-Scale Network Security Situation Composite Prediction System

Jinbao Shan[⊠] and Shenggang Wu

College of Information Technology and Art Design,
Shandong Institute of Commerce and Technology, Jinan, China
sammye1980@yeah.net

Abstract. Because the traditional network security situation compound prediction system cannot overcome the defects of SVM algorithm, the accuracy of extraction results is low. For this reason, a large-scale network security situation compound prediction system is designed. Through data normalization process to optimize the SVM algorithm, to optimize the forecasting calculation module, to provide data base system frame structure, system frame structure can be divided into security situational composite sensing module, situational composite evaluation module and situational composite prediction module, synergy is derived using multiple module network security situational values when attacked, to implement network security situation prediction to complete the system design. Simulation application environment design compared the experimental results show that compared with the traditional prediction system of the proposed system under the same data to forecast, the accuracy of predicted results by 65%, and the operation is very stable.

Keywords: Large-Scale · Network security situation compound forecast · Forecast result · Accuracy

1 Introduction

With the deepening of information technology, the Internet is becoming the critical, information infrastructure of the country, cyber security concerns the fundamental interests of the country and society. In recent years, the global internet is frequently attacked, lead to growing network security issues, the security of important information systems is seriously threatened. In order to deal with the challenges of network security, security protection and management systems such as VPN, IDS, antivirus systems, identity authentication, data encryption, and security audit have been widely used, however, the accuracy of the prediction results of the traditional network security situation composite forecasting system is lower, this paper uses the optimized SVM algorithm as the basis for establishing the prediction system, divide the system into three parts: perception, assessment and prediction, calculate the security posture of the network when it is attacked by the system. The experimental results show that the system designed in this paper is more suitable for the complex prediction of large-scale network security situation than the traditional system.

© ICST Institute for Computer Sciences, Social Informatics and Telecommunications Engineering 2019
Published by Springer Nature Switzerland AG 2019. All Rights Reserved
G. Gui and L. Yun (Eds.): ADHIP 2019, LNICST 302, pp. 419–425, 2019.
https://doi.org/10.1007/978-3-030-36405-2_42

2   Optimization Design of Large-Scale Network Security Situation Composite Prediction System

2.1   Predictive Calculation Module Design

Because the range of network security situation changes is relatively large, it has an adverse effect on the training speed of SVM. The reconstructed data is input into the model for learning and normalized, and the specific normalization is [1, 2]:

$$x_i' = \frac{x_i - x_{\min}}{x_{\max} - x_{\min}} \tag{1}$$

Among them, x_i is the original value, x_i' is the normalized value, and $x_{\max}$ and $x_{\min}$ are the maximum and minimum values respectively.

After normalizing the data, design the system calculation model.

Let there be a total of n network security situation learning samples $\{x_i, y_i\}$, $i = 1, 2, \ldots, n$, x_i is input, y_i is the output expectation where the input is the expected value of the output and the SVM regression equation is [3]

$$f(x) = w \times \varphi(x) + b \tag{2}$$

$$\varphi: R^n \rightarrow G, w \in G \tag{3}$$

In the formula, w represents the weight vector, b represents the offset vector Use the optimization function to optimize the target value, that is:

$$\min J = \frac{1}{2} \|w\|^2 + C \sum_{i=1}^{n} (\xi_i^* + \xi_i) \tag{4}$$

The constraints are as follows:

$$\begin{aligned}
y_i - w \times \varphi(x) - b &\leq \varepsilon + \xi_i \\
w \times \varphi(x) + b - y_i &\leq \varepsilon + \xi_i^* \\
\xi_i, \xi_i^* &\geq 0, i = 1, 2, \ldots, n
\end{aligned} \tag{5}$$

Among them, ξ_i, ξ_i^* is expressed as a relaxation factor, and C is a penalty factor [4]. By introducing Lagrange multiplier, we can get:

$$\begin{aligned}
L(w, b, \xi, \xi^*, \alpha, \alpha^*, y, y^*) =& \frac{1}{2} \|w\| + C \sum_{i=1}^{n} (\xi_i + \xi_i^*) - \sum_{i=1}^{n} \alpha_i (\xi_i + \varepsilon - y_i + f(x_i)) \\
& - \sum_{i=1}^{n} \alpha_i^* (\xi_i + \varepsilon - y_i + f(x_i)) - \sum_{i=1}^{n} (\xi_i \gamma_i - \xi_i^* \gamma_i^*)
\end{aligned} \tag{6}$$

Among them, α_i and α_i^* are Lagrange multipliers, and ε is a parameter of insensitive loss function.

The SVM regression expression is thus obtained as [5–7]:

$$f(x) = \sum_{i=1}^{n} (\alpha_i - \alpha_i^*) \times (\varphi(x_i), \varphi(x)) + b \qquad (7)$$

For non-linear regression prediction problems, to prevent dimensional disaster problems, use kernel function $k(x_i, x)$ instead of $(\varphi(x_i), \varphi(x))$, to prevent dimension disasters, that is:

$$f(x) = \sum_{i=1}^{n} (\alpha_i - \alpha_i^*) k(x_i, x) + b \qquad (8)$$

In summary, the calculation model used by the large-scale network security situation composite forecasting system is:

$$\begin{aligned} f(x) &= \sum_{i=1}^{n} (\alpha_i - \alpha_i^*) \times (\varphi(x_i), \varphi(x)) + b \\ &= \sum_{i=1}^{n} (\alpha_i - \alpha_i^*) k(x_i, x) + b \end{aligned} \qquad (9)$$

2.2   System Framework Design

The large-scale real-time network security situation composite forecasting system collects the information of each node of the network in real time, and carries out security situation composite sensing, situational compound assessment and situational compound prediction for the entire network. The framework of the system is shown in Fig. 1. It is mainly composed of data collection, security situation composite analysis, security situation compound assessment, security situation composite forecast and assessment database [8, 9].

Data collection includes two aspects. The first is the real-time collection of IDS alarm logs. It contains a large number of network attack information and is an important data source for the complex assessment of network security posture. The second is the network node information, which is calculated due to network risk assessment. The security situation is more theoretical and should be corrected in light of the real-time performance of network nodes. Security situational complex perception mainly includes attack information extraction and threat identification. Because there are many IDS alarms, such as Snort basic alarms, there are more than 8000 kinds. Therefore, it is necessary to extract and classify attack behavior according to the threat degree of the alarm, which can reduce the assessment and the complexity of the forecast. The security situation compound assessment evaluates the network security situation based on the attack information. Security situation compound prediction uses

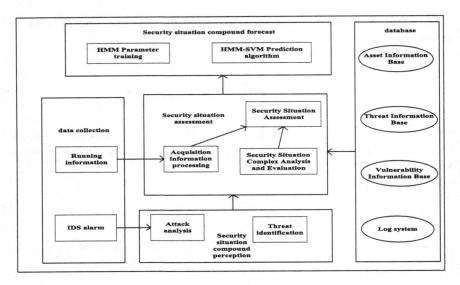

Fig. 1. Large-scale network security situation composite forecasting system framework

hidden Markov model for situational composite prediction. Firstly, the HMM parameters are trained according to the results of past evaluations. Then, the HMM-SVM prediction model is used to predict the next state of the network. The evaluation database contains an asset information base, threat information base, vulnerability information base, and log system. Host information scanning program is used to obtain host configuration information, including application programs, operating systems, vulnerability scanners to scan out port numbers, vulnerability numbers, and possible Consequences, etc. [10].

2.3   Realize the Network Security Situation Compound Prediction

Set the delay time of the network security situation composite data transmission, use the test method to embed dimension into the situation data, and determine the embedding dimension (assumed to be n). At this point, the support vector machine has n − 1 input variables and one input variable. Based on the delay time and the embedding dimension, the data of the current reaction network security situation is reconstructed, and then the training samples and test samples of the support vector machine are generated. The data representing the training sample is input into a support vector machine for learning, and is optimized using a calculation model, and the parameter values of the algorithm are set. When the optimal parameters of ε, C, and φ are brought into the prediction model, then the prediction model becomes the optimal network security situation prediction model. Through this model, the security situation value of the network when it is attacked can be calculated. The model is used to predict and analyze the previous generations of security situation values, and the characteristic data of the trend data are depicted. By analyzing the curves, it can be seen whether the established network security situation prediction system can effectively predict the safety monitoring data and whether the relevant prediction data has higher accuracy.

3   Analysis of the Experiment

3.1   Experimental Data

In order to verify the correctness and effectiveness of the large-scale network security situation composite forecasting system designed in this paper, simulation experiments were done in this paper. A network includes three attacked nodes, namely an HTTP server, a mail server, and an FTP server. It is assumed that each node has a weight of 0.5, 0.3, and 0.2 in the network. This paper simulates Attacker Attacker launching scan attack (i.e. attack 1), buffer overflow attack (i.e. attack 2) and TCP-SYN Flood attack (i.e. attack 3) on the network hosts at different times, and obtains the IDS alarm log to the node unit time. The statistics of the attacks received within the attack are calculated based on the threat degree and the number of attacks. Details of the number of cyber attacks are shown in Fig. 2

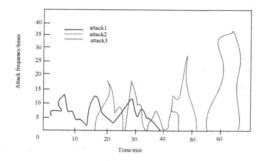

Fig. 2. Attack intensity change chart

Figure 2 shows the curve of the number of network attacks over time during the simulation experiment. The abscissa indicates the attack time in minutes and the ordinate indicates the number of attacks per minute. Attack 1 represents the attacker's scanning attack. The attack time range is between 0 and 40 min, and the threat level is relatively low. Attack 2 represents the attacker's buffer overflow attack between 15 to 30 min and 40 to 55 min respectively. Attacking two different hosts has the highest security threat to the system. Attack 3 indicates that the attacker uses TCP-SYN Flood attack and attacks the HTTP server between 25 to 40 min, 40 to 45 min, and 55 to 65 min, and is a medium-threatening attack.

The experimental data will now be used for the prediction of the network security situation.

3.2   Experimental Results and Analysis

Using the system designed in this paper and the traditional system respectively to perform network security situation composite prediction, the prediction results are shown in Fig. 3.

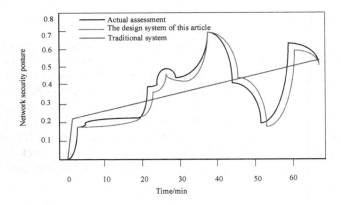

Fig. 3. Network security situation composite forecast

From Fig. 3, it can be seen that the system was scanned in the first 15 min, and the threat value increased, but the system was in a state of detection because of the low threat of the scan attack, and the risk was not very high. In 15 to 35 min, the system is moderately attacked, and the security assessment value is higher, indicating that the network is under attack. In the period of 40 to 45 min, the system is subjected to high intensity buffer overflow attack, the security evaluation value increases rapidly, the whole network is in extremely dangerous state, and the network is required to be safely protected. No attacks were detected between 45 and 50 min, but the danger faced by the network was not eliminated, and the security situation values gradually declined. From 55 min, the network was subjected to a high-intensity TCP-SYN Flood attack, and the security evaluation value increased again.

And from Fig. 3, it can be seen that the prediction error of the traditional prediction system is large, which can only reflect the general trend of the situation, but the prediction error of the design and prediction system is very small, which basically reflects the general trend of the network security situation, that is, the prediction accuracy of the design system is higher than the traditional system, and it is more suitable for the network security state. Potential prediction

This paper compares the prediction error of the system with the traditional system, as shown in Table 1.

Table 1. Comparison of the error of prediction results.

Name	Mean absolute error	Root mean square error
Traditional system	3.505	18.1466
The system of this article	0.9718	1.2823

From the data of Table 1, we can see that compared with the traditional system, the prediction results of this design system have less error and higher accuracy. Compared with the traditional system, the accuracy of the system prediction results is improved by about 65%. The prediction results of this system have higher practical value. The above two experimental results show that the prediction accuracy of the system is higher than that of the traditional system, and the accuracy is increased by about 65%.

4   Concluding Remarks

In this paper, the large-scale network security situation prediction system is optimized, and the SVM algorithm is used to improve the accuracy of prediction results. The test data show that the accuracy of the system designed in this paper is about 65% higher than that of the traditional system, and it has high effectiveness. It is hoped that this study can provide useful help for large-scale network security situation prediction.

References

1. Zhang, X., Pang, T.: An approach to real-time network security situation prediction. Sci. Technol. Vis. **12**(3), 289 (2017)
2. Xin, J., Zhang, C., Li, W., et al.: A power communication network security situation prediction method and system: CN107124394A, 15(04), 110–111 (2017)
3. Man, L.I.: Research on network security situation awareness and prediction of power monitoring system. Inf. Secur. Technol. **8**(10), 60–62 (2017)
4. Wei, H.: Discussion on the methods of power information network security situation assessment and prediction. Netw. Secur. Technol. Appl. **12**(1), 120–121 (2017)
5. Zhang, J., Zhang, B., Shen, Q.: Information system security situation assessment based on data mining. Mod. Electron. **40**(21), 77–79 (2017)
6. Chen, Y., Zhu, B., Tian, H., et al.: A network security situation analysis method based on neural network and big data and its system: CN106302522A 17(22), 1200–1203 (2017)
7. Yan, J., Weihong, H., Wei, W.: Design and implementation of large scale network security situation analysis system YHSAS. Inf. Technol. Netw. Secur. **4**(1), 222–223 (2018)
8. Zhaojun, G., Ruili, W., Shuaiqing, W.: Research on real-time forecast of security posture of information system based on improved Grey-Markov chain. Comput. Appl. Softw. **34**(2), 272–279 (2017)
9. Duanli, W.: Network to detect abnormal data in the database optimization simulation. Comput. Simul. **34**(5), 410–413 (2017)
10. Zeng, B., Zhong, P.: Simulation study on network security situation forecast. Comput. Simul. **29**(5), 170–173 (2012)

Fading Measurement Method of Backup Path Signal in Wireless Network

Hui Xuan[1,2], Yanjing Cai[3], and Xiaofeng Cao[4(✉)]

[1] Tongfu Microelectronics Co., Ltd., Nantong 226000, Jiangsu, China
[2] College of Computer Science and Communication Engineering,
Jiangsu University, Zhenjiang 212000, Jiangsu, China
[3] Jiangsu Vocational College of Business, Nantong 226000, Jiangsu, China
[4] School of Computer Science and Technology, Nantong University,
Nantong 226000, Jiangsu, China
caoxiaofeng1977@sina.com

Abstract. In order to solve the above problem, a method of measuring the back-up path signal decline based on wireless network is designed to solve the problem that the existing signal measurement method can not express the specific decline path of the signal. Through the two steps of signal perception module design and measurement signal transmission mode, the wireless network environment of backup path signal measurement is completed. On this basis, three steps are carried out through the determination of the baseband signal fading frequency, the fading measurement channel estimation and the signal modulation measurement term to complete the construction of the new recession measurement method. The experimental results show that the fading path of the terminal signal is clearly expressed when the backup path signal fading measurement method based on wireless network is applied.

Keywords: Wireless network · Path signal · Fading detection · Perception module · Transmission mode · Fading frequency · Measurement channel · Modulation measurement item

1 Introduction

Channel decline is an inherent noun in the field of wireless communication networks. Recession refers to the phenomenon of random changes in the amplitude of received signals due to changes in the channel, which leads to a fading channel called a fading channel. In the field of wireless communications, recession is a concept of power, or signal strength, which means the reduction of signal power. This "decline" can be divided into large scale recession and small scale recession according to the decline of power. Large scale recession is divided into path loss shadow and effect, and the cause of small scale decline is multipath problem. In wireless communications, the receiver may receive many of the same signals from different paths in a period of time. This time is called delayed diffusion, and the reciprocal of delayed diffusion is called the homology bandwidth. The physical meaning is in this bandwidth interval, the size of the decline can be seen as the same, when the delay diffusion is greater, the homology

G. Gui and L. Yun (Eds.): ADHIP 2019, LNICST 302, pp. 426–432, 2019.
https://doi.org/10.1007/978-3-030-36405-2_43

bandwidth is greater smaller [1, 2]. And the wireless channel will vary with time. If there is a movement, the channel change will be faster, because the time of homology will be shortened, and the reciprocal of the time of homology is Doppler diffusion. The physical meaning is in this period of time, the decline is almost the same, when the signal time is transmitted. Greater than the same time, there will be a so-called fast recession. In order to better determine the specific decline form of the wireless network signal, the existing technical means set up the signal acquisition platform by IEEE 802.11 wireless technology, and through the method of counting the recessionary cycle of the signal, the signal decline phenomenon is measured in real time. With the progress of science and technology, this method has begun to show the drawbacks of sending signals and displaying specific fading paths. In order to avoid the above situation, a new method of signal fading measurement is designed under the support of the backup path wireless network environment, and the practical value of the method is proved by the design contrast experiment.

2   Wireless Network Environment for Backup Path Signal Measurement

The backup path signal measuring wireless network environment is the application foundation of the new recession measurement method, and its concrete construction method can be carried out according to the following steps.

2.1   Design of Signal Sensing Module

Signal sensing module is the foundation of wireless network measurement environment. The module uses the 802.11 g receiver as the core set up equipment and connects several signal path backup devices with independent running functions around the device. When the measured signal enters the wireless network operating environment, the 802.11 g receiver enters the infinite running state with the promotion of the constant power supply device, and multiple signal path backup devices begin to analyze the location information of the received signals, and store the path backup results in the form of the module transmission medium in the form of running scripts [3, 4]. Under the condition that the external operating conditions remain unchanged, the transmission medium of the signal sensing module always maintains a stable running state, and the backup path information of the signal can be well preserved until the next command appears. The design principle of specific signal sensing module is shown in Fig. 1.

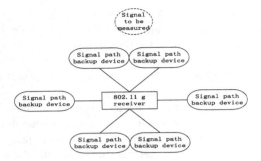

Fig. 1. Schematic diagram of signal sensing module design

2.2   Unification of Measurement Signal Transmission Mode

The existing technical means are the unified measurement of the signal transmission mode, using the path backup script generated by the signal sensing module, and strictly restrict the transmission destination of each signal. On this basis, when the total amount of the decay signal is increased, the number of insertable nodes in a part of the script will also increase, which also promotes the rapid progress of signal decline detection. On the basis of guaranteeing the speed of measurement, the new measurement method explicitly sends out the display definition of the end signal fading path, and adds a data compression packet with. Sqlpt as a suffix after each path backup script [5]. When the fading signal is transmitted to the wireless network monitoring link, the data compression packet is automatically decompressed, in which the message of the emit signal fading path is clearly displayed, and the original design aim is achieved. A unified method for measuring the transmission mode of the signal is shown in Fig. 2.

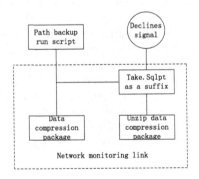

Fig. 2. Unified schematic diagram of measurement signal transmission

3 Realization of Signal Degradation Measurement Method Based on Wireless Network Environment

On the basis of the wireless network environment of the backup path signal measurement, three links are made through the determination of the baseband signal fading frequency, the fading measurement channel estimation, and the signal modulation measurement item to achieve the smooth application of the new decaying measurement method.

3.1 Frequency Determination of Baseband Signal Fading

The determination of the fading frequency of baseband signal can be regarded as the inverse process of baseband signal transmission. When the wireless network environment receives the backup path signal, the frequency offset is estimated and corrected first. After that, the reception sequence is string and converted, then the protection interval of each OFDM symbol is removed, and then the sequence of these sampling points is transformed to the frequency domain subcarrier for processing by FFT transform [6]. After FFT, the channel estimation, phase tracking and correction of the OFDM symbols are processed with the corresponding information of the lead and pilot, and then the data is mapped and interlaced. Finally, descrambling is used to get the original signal and complete the determination process of the decay frequency. The specific determination method is shown in Formula (1).

$$f = \frac{(\alpha + \beta)t}{l \cdot \sqrt{ds}} \tag{1}$$

Among them, f the decline frequency of the baseband signal, α it represents the parameter of frequency offset estimation, β On behalf of frequency offset correction parameters, t represents the guard interval between OFDM symbols of the original signal, d representing the constant of the solution mappings, s representative interleaver constant, l the frequency domain carrier cycle of the FFT transform is represented.

3.2 Fading Measurement Channel Estimation

In the actual measurement of signal decline, frequency selective fading and multipath effect will exist in many measurement environments, which will reduce the quality of the signal. Therefore, it is necessary to minimize or eliminate the effects of these interference on the quality of the signal. It is necessary to make channel estimation for the wireless channel between the transmitter and the receiver, also known as the frequency response estimation [7, 8]. The process of channel estimation is to estimate the parameters of the wireless channel model between the transmitter and the receiver from the received signal. This process plays a vital role in the wireless communication system, and may even be one of the important indicators to measure the performance of a wireless communication system. Only when the detailed channel information is obtained, the estimated channel coefficients can be used to correct the data, and then the transmitting signal is demodulated accurately at the receiving end. Therefore, the channel estimation algorithm will directly affect the system error rate. The channel estimation results for specific recession measurements are shown in Formula (2).

$$\lambda = \frac{f \cdot q}{2 \zeta G} \tag{2}$$

Among them, λ on behalf of the fading measurement channel estimation results, q representing channel coefficients, ζ the constant coefficient representing the quality of the signal, G the demodulation original of the receiver.

3.3   Correction of Signal Modulation Measurement Term

The modulation signal of the fading signal is always proportional to the bit information carried by each subcarrier. The frequency response characteristic of the signal transmitter is also stable in the condition that the wireless network environment of the backup path signal measurement is stable, but it is impossible to keep the power that is completely equal to the basic measurement operation. At this time, the decline frequency of the baseband signal is in the same state as the base frequency of the signal transmitter, and the decline frequency of the signal to be measured in its channel will not produce a clear floating state [9, 10]. In simple terms, the modulation measurement term of a fading signal is a stable constant with a corrected property, and its specific correction method is shown in Formula (3).

$$H = \frac{1}{\lambda}(W + Y)a^4 \tag{3}$$

Among them, H represents the correction result of modulation signal measured by fading signal, W the bit information constant carried by the subcarrier, Y the frequency response parameters of the signal transmitter, a the basic floating cycle that represents the frequency of recession. Finishing the above setup steps, the design of backup path signal degradation measurement method based on wireless network is completed.

4   Experimental Results and Analysis

In order to verify the practical value of the signal fading measurement method based on the wireless network backup path, the following comparative experiments are designed. Two computers with the same configuration are taken as the experimental object, in which the existing signal measurement method is used as the control group. The new signal measurement method is carried out as the experimental group, and 40 min is used as the experimental time. The changes in the clarity of the show.

4.1   Setting of Experimental Parameters

In order to ensure the authenticity of the experimental results, the relevant experimental parameters can be set down according to the following Table 1.

Table 1. Experimental parameter setting table

Parameter name	Experience group	Control group
ETT/(min)	40	40
WSL/(T)	8.94 × 1011	8.94 × 1011
SRC/(s)	0.42	0.42
PDL/(%)	85.96	85.96
PDP	1.35	1.35

In order to ensure the authenticity of the experimental results, the parameters of the upper table represent the experimental time, the upper limit of the radio network signal capacity, the cycle of the signal decline, the upper limit of the definition of the path display, and the definition parameters of the path display. The experimental parameters of the experimental and control groups are always consistent.

4.2 Definition Contrast of Emit Signal Fading Path

On the premise that the definition parameters of the path display are 1.35, the changes of the clarity of the emit signal decline path are recorded after the application of the experimental group and the control group respectively. The specific experimental results are shown in Fig. 3.

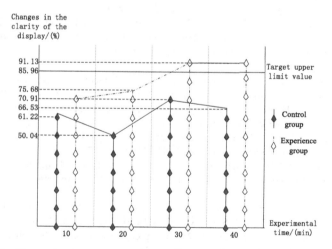

Fig. 3. Shows the contrast map of terminal signal fading path display clarity

The analysis of Fig. 3 shows that with the increase of experiment time, after the experiment group method, the end signal decline path shows the first increase and the trend of the stability. After the experiment time reaches 30 min, the definition of the emit signal decline path shows the maximum value of 91.13%, exceeding the target upper limit of 85.96%. After the use of the control group, the signal decline path of the emit signal showed a decline in clarity and an alternation trend. When the experiment time was 30 min, the definition of the emit signal decline path showed the maximum definition of 70.91%, far lower than the experimental group.

5 Conclusion

Analysis and comparison results show that after the existing signal measurement method is applied, the terminal signal fading path can not reach the target upper limit of 85.96%, after the application of the wireless network backup path signal fading measurement method, the definition of the emit signal decline path shows an increasing state with the increase of the application time, and the maximum value is far above the target upper limit of 85.96%. Considering the feasibility of application, the signal fading measurement method based on wireless network backup path is indeed worth promoting.

References

1. Deng, W., Ma, S., Meng, X.: Ship communication signal transmission quality optimization detection algorithm and simulation. Comput. Simul. **34**(08), 201–205 (2017)
2. Zhu, H., Li, S., Zheng, L., et al.: Modeling and validation on path loss of WSN in pig breeding farm. Trans. Chin. Soc. Agric. Eng. **33**(2), 205–212 (2017)
3. Liu, Z., Li, S.: An anomaly detection method for wireless sensor networks based on compressed sensing and GM (1,1). J. Xi'an Jiaotong Univ. **51**(2), 40–46 (2017)
4. Feng, H., Luo, L., Wang, Y., et al.: Path planning in wireless sensor networks for mobile sink based on glowworm swarm optimization algorithm. Microelectron. Comput. **33**(5), 47–51 (2016)
5. Wu, W., Liu, L., Xu, B.: LTE wireless network signal receiving method with two element constellation receiving mapping mechanism. Comput. Eng. Des. **38**(8), 2008–2014 (2017)
6. Li, L., Jiang, W., He, Y., et al.: A geographic location routing method for energy balance in wireless sensor networks. Comput. Eng. Sci. **39**(10), 1847–1853 (2017)
7. Zhu, Q., Yang, Y., Liu, N., et al.: Secure localization method based on consistency of RSSI in wireless sensor network. Comput. Eng. **42**(10), 151–157 (2016)
8. Zhu, S., Hu, Z., Hu, M.: Improved locality preserving canonical correlation analysis node localization method in wireless sensor networks. Chin. J. Sens. Actuators **29**(10), 1579–1588 (2016)
9. Wei, X., Li, G.: Outlier detection in wireless sensor networks based on reduction strategy and adaptive SVDD. Chin. J. Sens. Actuators **30**(9), 1388–1395 (2017)
10. Zhou, K., Meng, L., Zhang, J., et al.: Multi-hop capacity algorithm for uniform distribution wireless networks. J. Chin. Comput. Syst. **37**(2), 212–215 (2016)

Research on Spatial Trajectory Retrieval Method of Athletes Stepping Motion Data

Xiaofeng Xu[✉]

Department of Physical Education, Baoji Vocational & Technical College,
Baoji 721006, China
xuxiaofeng5115@163.com

Abstract. Routine athletes action spatial trajectory data retrieval method can perform the trajectory retrieval to athletes action, but there is the deficiency of low retrieval ability when only the detailed spatial trajectory retrieval of athletes stepping motion is performed, for this reason, the research on spatial trajectory retrieval method of athletes stepping motion data is proposed. Based on the extraction of characteristic information of athlete's stepping motion, the stepping motion R-Tree and its variant space index are determined, and the construction of the spatial trajectory retrieval model of athlete's stepping motion data is achieved. Based on the spatial trajectory index design of athlete's stepping motion data, the spatial trajectory retrieval result is output, and the research on spatial trajectory retrieval method is completed. The experimental data show that the retrieval capability of proposed trajectory retrieval method for athlete's stepping motion is 53.41% better than that of conventional trajectory retrieval, which is suitable for detailed spatial trajectory retrieval of athlete's stepping motion.

Keywords: Athletes · Stepping motion · Spatial trajectory · Retrieval methods

1 Introduction

Conventional athletes' motion data spatial trajectory retrieval methods can perform trajectory retrieval on athletes' movements, but when performing detailed spatial trajectory retrieval on athletes' stepping movements, due to the limitations of spatial trajectory retrieval models, there is a shortage of low retrieval ability [1]. Thus, the research on spatial trajectory retrieval method of athlete stepping motion data is proposed. The inclination angle, minimum enclosing rectangle MER and tightness, movement speed, circumscribed rectangle length and width, and rate of change are extracted and analyzed as the characteristics of the stepping motion, and the stepping motion R-Tree and its variable spatial index are determined to achieve the construction of spatial trajectory retrieval model of the athlete's stepping motion data; 2^f reverse tables are determined. Each record corresponds to a stepping motion data file. The record contains the segmentation of the file and the corresponding speciality vector to complete the spatial trajectory index design of athletes stepping motion. The spatial trajectory retrieval results are output, and the proposed spatial trajectory retrieval method of athlete's stepping motion data is completed. To ensure the validity of the

© ICST Institute for Computer Sciences, Social Informatics and Telecommunications Engineering 2019
Published by Springer Nature Switzerland AG 2019. All Rights Reserved
G. Gui and L. Yun (Eds.): ADHIP 2019, LNICST 302, pp. 433–441, 2019.
https://doi.org/10.1007/978-3-030-36405-2_44

designed spatial trajectory retrieval method and simulate the athlete's experimental environment, two different spatial trajectory retrieval methods for data are used to perform the retrieval capability simulation test. The experimental results show that the spatial trajectory retrieval method for data is highly effective.

2   System Objective and Analysis

The research on spatial trajectory retrieval method of athletes stepping motion data mainly includes:

(1) The main axis area of the target area is established, and the linear whose rotational inertia reaches the minimum value is used to determine the rotational inertia of the target area D and optimize the extraction of the stepping motion characteristic information of the athlete.
(2) Building R^+-Tree solves the intersection of R-Tree related nodes, resulting in poor search performance. The number of invalid queries is reduced and redundant information is controlled.
(3) The exact hit $\subset k$ measures the similarity so that F[Q] happens to be the subspace trajectory sequence from the k position in F[D], and the spatial trajectory retrieval result of the stepping motion data is output.

3   Construction of Spatial Trajectory Retrieval Model of Athletes Stepping Motion Data

The hierarchical motion model is used to describe the stepping motion of the athlete. The model uses the kinematic chain of stepping motion to simulate the connection state of each joint. Each joint is organized into a tree structure. There is a parent node for each node except the root node. It can also rotate in the parent node's coordinate system. The root node can not only rotate but also translate. The athlete's stepping motion model can be described as:

$$V(t) = [T_{root}(t), R_{root}(t), R_1(t), R_2(t), \ldots R_n(t)] \tag{1}$$

where $T_{root}(t)$ and $R_{root}(t)$ are used to describe the translation and rotation of root node; $R_n(t)$ is used to describe the rotation of the joint around the parent node. The three-dimensional coordinate curve is the spatial trajectory of the athlete's stepping motion data.

3.1   Extraction of Athlete's Stepping Motion Characteristics

Before indexing the spatial trajectory of the athlete's stepping motion data, firstly the characteristics of the stepping motion needs to be extracted, and the index is completed according to the extracted characteristics. There are great differences in the speed and direction of the athlete's stepping motion. Therefore, the slope angle, the minimum enclosing rectangle MER and the tightness, the movement speed, the length and width of the circumscribed rectangle, and the rate of change are taken as the characteristics of the stepping motion to be analyzed.

Because the object of analysis is the human body, the athlete's inclination to fall within a certain range can be considered as a fall. According to the principle, the principal axis of the target area can be described as a straight line that the rotational inertia of the target area D reaches the minimum value. The rotational inertia of the target area D is [2]:

$$I = \iint [(x - \bar{x}) \sin \alpha - (y - \bar{y}) \cos \alpha]^2 f(x, y) dx dy \tag{2}$$

where α is used to describe the angle between the athlete center coordinates $(\bar{x}, \bar{y})$ and axis; f(x, y) is used to describe the binary distribution of images of the athlete's stepping motion, x is used to describe the abscissa of athlete's position and y is used to describe the ordinate of athlete's position.

For convenience of calculation, it can be simplified as [3]:

$$I = \mu_{20} \sin^2 \alpha + \mu_{02} \cos^2 \alpha - 2\mu_{11} \sin \cos \alpha \tag{3}$$

where is used to describe the center distance. To minimize I, let dI/da = 0, namely, $\mu_{20} \sin 2\alpha - \mu_{02} \sin 2\alpha - 2\mu_{11}2 \cos \alpha = 0$, then the angle of inclination can be obtained through $\alpha = (1/2) \tan^{-1}[2\mu_{11}/(\mu_{20} - \mu_{02})]$, the extraction process of minimum enclosing rectangle MER and the tightness is as follows:

The minimum enclosing rectangle MER requires that the principle axis of the athlete's stepping motion needs to be determined, and then trimmed from the vertical direction of the spindle and the spindle to obtain the minimum enclosing rectangle MER, MER value can be obtained by the formula [4]:

$$MER = A_{area}/A_{MER} \tag{4}$$

where A_{are} is used to describe the area of the athletes' stepping motion. A_{MER} is used to describe the area of MER.

Assuming that the centroid of the k-th frame of athlete's stepping motion image is described by (x_k, y_k), the displacement between two adjacent images can be described as: $s_k = \sqrt{(x_{k+1} + x_k)^2 + (y_{k+1} + y_k)^2}$. The selected video frame rate is 30 frames/s, that is, the time interval between two adjacent frames is 1/30 s. The rate at which the current athlete performs stepping motion can be obtained by the formula: $v_k = s_k/t = 30s_k$. Through the above process, the rate of the stepping motion image of each frame of the athlete is determined, and the average rate of the stepping jump of the athlete is obtained. This section uses the average rate instead of the athlete's stepping rate, which is regarded as one of the characteristics of the stepping motion of the athlete [5]. The average rate can be obtained by the formula:

$$\bar{v} = \frac{1}{n} \sum_{k=1}^{k \leq n-1} v_k \tag{5}$$

where n is used to describe the number of sample frames. The extraction process of circumscribing rectangle length-width ratio and rate of change is to determine the circumscribed rectangular length-width ratio P, a, it can be obtained by the formula: $P_{rop} = L_{MER}/W_{ME}$, where L_{MER} is used to describe the length of MER; W_{MWR} is used to describe the width of MER. The rate of change is compared every two frames. Assuming that the length-width ratio of the two frames are P_{fomor} and $P_{current}$, the rate of change of current length-width ratio can be described as follows:

$$P = |P_{current} - P_{fomor}|/P_{fomor} \tag{6}$$

In summary, the stepping motion characteristic function of the athlete can be described as:

$$F = [\alpha, MER, \bar{v}, P_{rop}, P] \tag{7}$$

3.2   Determining Stepping Motion R-Tree and Its Variant Spatial Index

R-Tree was first proposed by Guttman in 1984 and is suitable for indexing data area collections. Later, for different applications, the researchers improved R-Tree and formed many variants of R-Tree, such as R^+-Tree, R^*-Tree, 3DR-Tree, STR-Tree.

R-Tree is a form of B-Tree's development to multidimensional space. It is a deeply balanced tree. It uses the concept of space segmentation and adopts a method of minimum bounding rectangle (MBR), starting from the leaf node and using the minimum rectangular box to frame the space and divide the space. The divided subspace forms the node of the tree. Each node corresponds to a disk page in memory [6]. The non-leaf node disk page uses an array to store the area ranges of all its child nodes. The area that child nodes represent is in the area of the parent node. The disk page of the leaf node uses an array to store all the space objects in its range. R-Tree is a dynamic index structure whose queries can be performed at the same time as insertions or deletions, and does not require periodic reorganization of the tree structure.

Figure 1 shows the basic structure of R-Tree, the outermost smallest rectangle indicates the root node R, it has four child nodes which are a, b, c, d respectively. a, b, c, d in the figure are also leaf nodes, and each leaf node contains several data objects. The entity contained in each non-leaf node in the R-Tree is composed of tuple (cp, rect), cp is a pointer to the child node of the node, and rect refers to the smallest outsourcing box of all child nodes contained in the node. The object contained in each leaf node is composed of tuple (id, loc), id is the identifier of the object in the dataset [7], and to is the spatial coordinate of the object. The number of children (child nodes or objects) contained in each node (excluding the root node) is from m to M, and satisfies m < M/2. The establishment of a good R-Tree needs to satisfy two conditions. One is that adjacent nodes should be clustered on one parent node of the tree as much as possible; the other is that the related nodes of the same layer of the tree has small cross section.

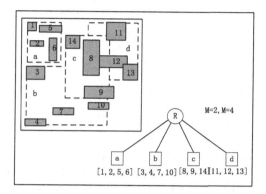

Fig. 1. R-Tree structure

R⁺-Tree is proposed for the feature that the intersection of R-Tree related nodes leads to poor search performance. R+-Tree does not allow intersecting areas between related nodes, reducing the number of invalid queries, thereby improving the efficiency of the query [8]. However, for insert and delete operations, to ensure that the spatial areas do not intersect, the efficiency will be reduced, and for data storage with cross-region, the data is redundant, and the more data, the more redundant information.

R*-Tree allows cross-correlation between related rectangles, but constructing R*-Tree takes into account not only the area of the index space, but also the intersection of the index space. The insertion and deletion of nodes by R*-Tree adopts the "forced reinsertion" method to optimize the structure of the tree [9]. 3DR-Tree takes time as another dimension of space, plus the time dimension and space dimension, it can be considered as three-dimensional, so it is called three-dimensional R-Tree. It is a simple indexing method for moving objects, supports space and time search, and is easy to implement. Its advantages are small storage space and high efficiency of time interval query; the disadvantage is that the query performance of the time slice is low, and the index performance gradually decreases as time increases [10].

Using R*-Tree and 3DR-Tree to build TPR-Tree. TPR-Tree supports indexing of any-dimensional space object. It adopts a quad-tree spatial index structure. It can solve future queries of dynamic objects and can be used to solve range queries, nearest neighbor queries, and reverse nearest neighbor queries. The quadtree's spatial index structure is shown in Fig. 2.

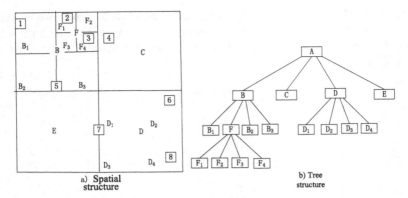

Fig. 2. Quadtree's spatial index structure

Based on the extraction of characteristics of the athlete's stepping motion, using the R-Tree athlete's stepping motion and its variant spatial index, the spatial trajectory retrieval model of the athlete's stepping motion data is constructed.

4 Realization of Spatial Trajectory Retrieval of the Athlete's Stepping Motion Data

4.1 Design of Spatial Trajectory Index of the Athlete's Stepping Motion Data

The index of the spatial trajectory of the athlete's stepping motion data is to construct a spatial trajectory database according to the characteristics of the athlete's stepping motion and use this database for retrieval. Assuming that the database $D = (D_1, D_2, \ldots, D_N)$ is the set of athlete's motion data stream D_n, $n \in N$, it can be seen from the above section that the stepping motion characteristic function F contains five features, namely $F: \varphi \rightarrow (0,1)^5$, where ϕ is the athlete's pose set. Q is used to describe the spatial trajectory sequence of stepping motion, $F[Q] = \bar{v} = (v_1, v_2, \ldots, v_N)$ and $F[D] = \bar{w} = (w_1, w_2, \ldots, w_M)$ are used to describe the F feature sequence of Q and D separately.

In order to create index of database D through the characteristic function F, a standard reverse table technique is used. For each characteristic vector $v \in (0,1)^f$, the storage reverse table may be described as L(v), which contains the index of the sequence $\bar{w} = (w_1, w_2, \ldots, w_M)$ whose value $m \in [1:M]$, where $v = w_M$. In brief, L(v) indicates that D divides the feature vector v.

From the above analysis, it can be seen that the reverse table is an ordered and non-repetitive sequence. When preprocessing, 2^f reverse tables L(v), $v \in (0,1)^f$, are established. Since only the F-segmented position is stored in the reverse table, and one F-segmented position occurs only once in one reverse table, the index size is proportional to the number of segments M of D. Not only that, this section also saves the length of each F-segmented to restore the F-segmented frame position. In fact, the database of athletes' motion consists of a plurality of motion files. In order to quickly match the stepping motion data files and the reverse table, a forward table is constructed in this section. Each record corresponds to a stepping motion data file. The corresponding characteristics vector and the segmentation of the file are contained in the record.

4.2 Results Output of Spatial Trajectory Retrieval of the Athlete's Stepping Motion Data

If the F-feature sequences of the spatial trajectories of two players' motion data are the same, the two are considered to be matched. Based on this principle, the spatial trajectory retrieval of the athlete's stepping motion data can be realized. This section measures the similarity by the exact hit $\subset$k, which means that F[Q] happens to be the subspace trajectory sequence starting from the k position in F[D], that is:

$$F[Q] \subset_k F[D] :\Leftrightarrow w_k = v_1, w_{k+1} = v_2, w_{k+N-1} = v_N \tag{8}$$

then the results of spatial trajectory retrieval of the athlete's stepping motion data is:

$$H_D(F[D]) = \{k \in [1:M] | L(v) \subset_k F[D]\} \tag{9}$$

thus, the spatial trajectory retrieval of the athlete's stepping motion data is achieved.

5 Experimental Test and Analysis

To ensure the validity of the spatial trajectory retrieval method of athlete's stepping motion data proposed in this paper, simulation experiments are performed. During the test, different athletes were used as test objects to carry out a search capability simulation test. The gender, height, and weight of different athletes are simulated. To ensure the validity of experiment, the conventional spatial trajectory retrieval method of athlete's motion data was used as the comparison object, and the results of the two simulation experiments were compared, and the test data was presented in the same data chart.

5.1 Preparation of Experimental Test

In order to ensure the accuracy of the simulation test process, the test parameters of the test are set. The test process is simulated in this paper, different athletes are selected as the test object, and two different data spatial trajectory retrieval methods are used to perform the search ability simulation test, and the simulation test results are analyzed. Because the analysis results obtained in different methods and the analysis methods are different, the test environment parameters must be consistent during the test. The test data set results in this paper are shown in Table 1.

Table 1. Test data set

Parameters of simulated experiment	Execution range/parameters	Observation
Athlete	Male female ratio = 1:1, male female number = 1:1 Height 170–190, weight 55 kg–95 kg	One-by-one analysis by spatial trajectory retrieval methods of two data
Difficulty of stepping motion	DL0.1–1.0	DL difficulty unit
Simulation system	DJX-2016-3.5	Windows platform

5.2 Analysis of Experimental Test Results

During the experiment, two different spatial trajectory retrieval methods for data were used to work in simulated environment, and the changes in their search capabilities were analyzed. At the same time, due to the use of two different data spatial trajectory retrieval methods, the analysis results cannot be compared directly. For this purpose, third-party analysis and recording software is used to record and analyze the test process and results, and the results are displayed in the comparison results curve of this experiment. In the simulation test result curve, the third-party analysis and recording software function is used to eliminate the uncertainty caused by simulation laboratory personnel operation and computer simulation equipment, and the retrieval capability is simulated in test only for different athletes and different data spatial trajectory retrieval methods. The comparison curve of the test results is shown in Fig. 3. Based on the experimental results curve, using third-party analysis and recording software, the data spatial trajectory retrieval method proposed in this paper and the retrieval ability of the conventional spatial trajectory retrieval method of athlete's motion data are arithmetically weighted, and the search ability of proposed trajectory retrieval is increased by 53.41%, compared with conventional trajectory search, which is suitable for detailed spatial trajectory retrieval of the athlete's stepping motion.

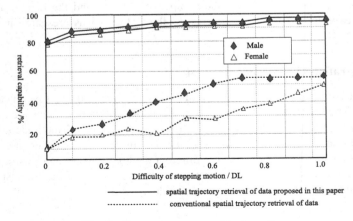

Fig. 3. Comparison curve of test results

6 Conclusion

The research on spatial trajectory retrieval method of athletes stepping motion data is proposed in this paper, based on the construction of spatial trajectory retrieval model of athletes stepping motion data, and design of spatial trajectory index of athletes stepping motion data, the research in this paper is completed. Experiment data show that the spatial trajectory retrieval method for data is highly effective. In the future research work, we will focus on the research of trajectory search efficiency. It is desired that the research in this paper can provide a theoretical basis for the data spatial trajectory retrieval method.

References

1. Yang, L., Shen, L., Ding, H.: Trajectory planning and simulation of upper-limb rehabilitation robot with four degrees of freedom. Comput. Simul. **33**(8), 332–337 (2016)
2. Teng, J., Xu, H., Wang, Y., et al.: Picking robot manipulator motion trajectory planning and design simulation. Comput. Simul. **34**(4), 362–367 (2017)
3. Xiao, K., Sun, J., Zhang, T.: Research on the effect of serving methods on visual search features of volleyball players. J. Tianjin Univ. Sport **31**(4), 351–357 (2016)
4. Nie, Q., Huang, K., Bi, Q., et al.: Instantaneous slice thickness analytical calculation method considering the tool bounce in micro-milling. J. Mech. Eng. **52**(3), 169–178 (2016)
5. Yao, N., Peng, D.: Large-scale trajectory data compression strategy under MapReduce architecture. J. Chin. Mini-Micro Comput. Syst. **38**(5), 941–945 (2017)
6. Tang, L., Yang, X., Niu, L., et al.: An adaptive filtering method based on crowd sourced big trace data. Acta Geodaetica et Cartographica Sinica **45**(12), 1455–1463 (2016)
7. Wang, L., Wang, M., Guo, X., et al.: Frequently closed pattern mining for moving spatiotemporal trajectory data. J. Xi'an Univ. Sci. Technol. **36**(4), 573–576 (2016)
8. Zhou, Q., Qin, K., Chen, Y., et al.: Taxi track hot spot detection method based on data field. Geogr. Geo-Information Sci. **32**(6), 51–56 (2016)
9. Jin, C., Chen, Y., Yang, M.: Multi-scale visualization method for trajectory starting and ending feature data. Geo-Information Sci. **19**(8), 1011–1018 (2017)
10. Xue, Z., Song, G., Liu, X., et al.: Relevant research progress in measurement methods and results of patella trajectory. Chin. J. Sports Med. **217**(12), 1112–1116 (2017)

Research on Fuzzy Recognition Method of Regional Traffic Congestion Based on GPS

Lan-fang Gong[✉]

Guangdong Polytechnic of Water Resources and Electric Engineering,
Guangzhou 510925, Guangdong, China
liuyoudan2018@163.com

Abstract. When using traditional traffic congestion recognition method to judge traffic congestion, there is a lack of accuracy. In view of the above problems, a fuzzy identification method of regional traffic congestion based on GPS is proposed. First, the GPS floating vehicle traffic information collection technology is used to collect the traffic information of the road network, and it is pretreated at the same time. Then the effective data and the electronic map are matched to determine the accurate position of the floating car on the road. Finally, a fuzzy comprehensive discriminant model based on the GPS data is set up, and the road traffic status is entered. The line is accurate. The results show that the accuracy of the method is 44% higher than that of the traditional traffic congestion recognition method, which basically achieves the purpose of this study. Experimental results are better, this article can bring guidance meaning to the future research.

Keywords: Big data · Cable tunnel · Leakage signal · Positioning method

1 Introduction

With the rapid development of social economy, traffic jams have become one of the major social problems that restrict the development of cities. Traffic jams affect people's daily life and work. Fast, accurate and real-time access to road traffic information, and then identify traffic congestion in the road network, is of great significance to the formulation of reasonable and effective traffic congestion and guidance measures [1]. At present, relevant experts have a very good research results on traffic congestion identification technology. Reference [2] Proposes a weighted traffic condition research method for FCM expressway. It can detect traffic congestion and evacuate congested streets. It can smooth traffic very well, but the feedback information is not timely. Reference [3] A weighted index method for expressway traffic state estimation based on fuzzy C-means is proposed. This method can effectively complete the real-time detection of expressway traffic state, but this method does not consider the problem of traffic evacuation. It is a new technology in the field of traffic state detection to use GPS floating car data to evaluate regional traffic condition. In this paper, based on the GPS

G. Gui and L. Yun (Eds.): ADHIP 2019, LNICST 302, pp. 442–450, 2019.
https://doi.org/10.1007/978-3-030-36405-2_45

floating car acquisition technology, the road traffic information is collected in real time, the data is analyzed and processed, and the effective traffic parameters are obtained by map matching. Based on the fuzzy comprehensive evaluation method, the road traffic status of the floating car is judged, which is the decision of the traffic management department and the out of the traveler. The line provides the basis and auxiliary information [4]. First, the GPS floating vehicle traffic information collection technology is used to collect the traffic information of the road network, and it is pretreated at the same time. Then the effective data and the electronic map are matched to determine the accurate position of the floating car on the road. Finally, a fuzzy comprehensive discriminant model based on the GPS data is set up, and the road traffic status is entered. The line is accurate. In order to solve the problems of low recognition accuracy and long recognition time, a method of regional traffic congestion recognition based on fuzzy recognition is designed. In order to verify the accuracy of the method, a comparative experiment was carried out. The experimental results show that the system can effectively improve the speed and accuracy of traffic congestion detection.

2   GPS Floating Vehicle Traffic Information Collection

The GPS floating car acquisition technology receives the GPS satellite signal through the GPS receiving module installed on the vehicle, thus obtaining the real-time information of the vehicle, and then the vehicle positioning, tracking and other functions. If GPS receiver module is installed on multiple vehicles, the traffic flow information collection of road network can be realized through the feedback of GPS information from these vehicles. These vehicles are called floating cars and are usually used by taxis [5]. Through the acquisition and processing of the GPS data of a large number of floating vehicles, the estimation of the average travel time of the section and the discrimination of traffic state can be realized, and the prediction of traffic jam can be realized. So as to formulate reasonable traffic guidance measures to facilitate public travel [6].

GPS floating car collection technology is used to collect traffic conditions, and the acquisition process is shown in Fig. 1.

In the traffic information acquisition technology based on GPS floating vehicles, some parameter configurations have an important impact on the real-time and reliability of traffic state discrimination, such as the time interval of data sampling, and the determination of the sample size of the floating car.

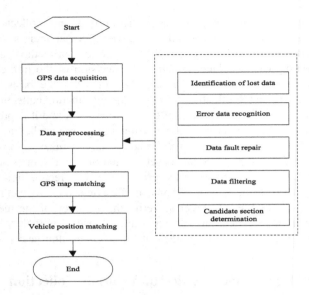

Fig. 1. GPS floating car traffic information collection process

3 GPS Data Preprocessing

In the actual acquisition, due to the objective conditions of equipment, technology and methods, the original data of the GPS floating car inevitably has errors. Therefore, this section is mainly based on the reliability of data and preprocessing the data.

3.1 Lost Data Recognition

In practical applications, due to the complex urban conditions, there are signal blind areas in some areas, resulting in abnormal or missing GPS data. One way to identify missing data is to recognize the time period of the GPS receiver based on the set of GPS receivers. If the setup period is one minute, all data received in the 12:30:00–12:31:00 cycle will be identified as 12:30:00 at this time [7]. Checking all the data received, if there is no data in a cycle, or multiple data in a cycle, it can be considered that the data in this cycle is abnormal, missing or wrong, and the data should be repaired.

3.2 Error Data Recognition

When the GPS receiver itself problems or the communication channel problems, the abnormal data will be generated, and the traffic characteristics can not be described directly with these data. In order to identify the data of these anomalies, the collected parameters are usually limited to a normal interval. If the actual data is in this interval, the data can be roughly identified as the valid data [8]. The following are the reasonable intervals of several common traffic parameters for GPS detection system, namely, vehicle instantaneous speed, travel time and road congestion length.

Instantaneous speed of vehicle a_i: $0 \leq a_i \leq f(x) \cdot a_k$

In this formula: a_k indicates the maximum speed limit (Km/h), and $f(x)$ indicates the speed correction coefficient.

Travel time t_e: $\frac{g}{a_k} \leq t_e \leq \frac{g}{a_j + h}$

In this formula: g is the length of the section; a_j indicates the speed of the section at the lower reaches of the section; h represents a small real number of more than 0, which is to avoid the calculation error caused by the a_j taking of 0.

Road congestion length l_m: $0 \leq l_m \leq l + h_1$

In this formula: l represents the length of the road; h_1 indicates the maximum permissible error of the road length.

3.3   Data Fault Repair

After identifying the abnormal data, we need to use the method of weighted estimation Ye(t) to repair it.

The calculation method is as follows:

$$Ye(t) = a * y(t - 1) + (1 - a) * y^{k-1}(t) \tag{1}$$

a is the weighting coefficient of (t − 1) time data, and the large weighting coefficient indicates that the repaired data is mainly affected by the measured data. This method not only takes into account the connection between traffic data, but also considers the function of historical trend data, which has the characteristics of stability.

3.4   Data Filtering

The actual traffic data will be affected by random factors, which will affect subsequent use. The fault recognition and repair processing of traffic data can only act on fault data and not remove random components [9]. Before using traffic data, data are usually filtered. The Calman filtering algorithm is a data processing method based on linear regression analysis. It can efficiently remove the random components of noise and so on from the measured data. In this algorithm, the optimal estimation of the current time is obtained by using the optimal estimation of the previous moment and the observed values at the present time. Calman filtering algorithm is a recursive algorithm, and the state optimal estimation is carried out through continuous iteration. In the process of iteration, the system state vector is modified according to the linear unbiased estimation to achieve the filtering effect.

3.5   Candidate Section Determination

First, determine the scope of the road and a certain range of positioning error. In the extended attribute data table, supplement the road information, including maximum and minimum longitude and latitude, length, design speed, direction vector value and so on [10]. In the implementation of matching, we only need to select the information of the current running section in the data analysis dialog box, then we can conduct the next GPS data location map matching.

4   GPS Map Matching

According to the actual research needs, we only need to get a map area range with a few roads. The smaller the area that the map can show, the closer its projection coordinates to the coordinates of the rectangular coordinate system, the smaller the local coordinate error. In order to map matching, the first step is to complete the registration of map coordinates. Because the data collection of the floating car includes its latitude and longitude coordinates, it is easy to register the electronic map with the latitude and longitude coordinates. So, the registration of the map can be completed as long as the 3 control points with accurate latitude and longitude coordinates are calibrated in the Google earth. The schematic diagram is shown in Fig. 2, $A(x_a, y_a)$ represents a road detection point.

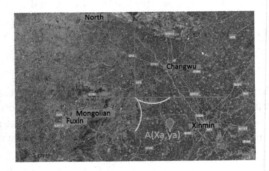

Fig. 2. GPS map matching simulated diagram

5   Fuzzy Comprehensive Discriminant Model Based on GPS Data

Applying fuzzy comprehensive discriminant model to the identification of traffic congestion, we need to establish a model first. The establishment of the model should take full account of the specific factors affecting the traffic state and the extent of the impact. At the same time, from the perspective of GPS data, we should make full use of the advantages of GPS data to input accurate and reasonable traffic parameters for the model. The main steps of the fuzzy synthetic discriminant method are shown in Fig. 3.

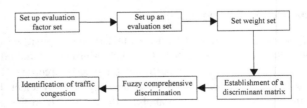

Fig. 3. Fuzzy synthetic discriminant steps

5.1   Membership Function Determination

First, a series of values with dividing points are determined on a continuous interval, and then the actual index values are processed by linear interpolation formula, and the degree of membership corresponding to the index value can be obtained.

Assuming that the evaluation factor of a traffic state is x and the membership function is n(x), $x \in \{0, 1, 2, 3, 4, 5\}$, $n \in (0, 1)$, the membership degree of the factor for the traffic state evaluation at all levels is $n_1(x), n_2(x), n_2(x), \cdots, n_{o+1}(x)$:

$$n_1(x) = \begin{cases} 1 & x \le z_1 \\ \frac{z_2-x}{z_1-z_2} & z_1 \le x \le z_2 \\ 0 & x \ge z_2 \end{cases}, \quad n_2(x) = \begin{cases} 1 - n_1(x) & x \le z_2 \\ \frac{z_3-x}{z_3-z_2} & z_2 \le x \le z_3 \\ 0 & x \le z_1, x \ge z_3 \end{cases},$$

$$n_{o+1}(x) = \begin{cases} 0 & x \le z_o \\ 1 - n_o(x) & z_o \le x \le z_{o+1} \\ 1 & x \ge z_{o+1} \end{cases} \tag{2}$$

In this formula: z_1, z_2, z_{o+1} is the classification value of each state grade evaluation set.

The selection of average speed is referred to "Evaluation of Urban Road Traffic Management" (2008 Edition). The threshold range of average speed is obtained by using the average speed classification table of urban trunk road (as shown in Table 1), which mainly consider the application in large cities.

Table 1. Average speed scale of urban trunk road

Evaluation grade standard	1	2	3	4	5
Large and class A Cities	[25, 30]	[22, 25]	[19, 22]	[16, 19]	[0, 16]
Class B Cities	[28, 33]	[25, 28]	[22, 25]	[19, 22]	[0, 19]
Class C, D Cities	[30, 35]	[27, 30]	[24, 27]	[21, 70]	[0, 21]
Index	[90, 100]	[80, 90]	[70, 80]	[60, 70]	[0, 60]

5.2   The Establishment of Fuzzy Comprehensive Evaluation Model

In fuzzy synthesis evaluation, a fuzzy relation synthesis operation is usually used. When there are many factors of evaluation, if the weight of each factor is small, the evaluation of all single factors is lost easily by taking small calculation, which makes the result lose the meaning of evaluation. In order to ensure the comprehensiveness and reliability of the evaluation effect of the comprehensive evaluation model, it is necessary to take into account the influence of all factors, balance the importance of each factor, avoid overemphasizing the role of a major factor and ignore the effect of other single factors. Therefore, this paper selects the fuzzy synthetic operation of weighted average, takes into account the effect of all factors, considers the information of each single factor, and carries out the comprehensive evaluation of the state.

$$p_r = \sum_{i=1}^{w} \left(a_i \cdot \alpha_{ij} \right), j = 1, 2, 3, \cdots, w, \quad \sum_{i=1}^{w} a_i = 1 \tag{3}$$

In the formula, α_{ij} indicates the subordinate degree of the I evaluation factor to the j traffic state evaluation grade; and W is the number of the characteristic components of the evaluation index in each sample.

The evaluation matrix can be obtained by combining the principle of the comprehensive evaluation model with the membership functions defined by the above indexes.

$$\beta = \begin{bmatrix} \beta_1 \\ \beta_2 \end{bmatrix} = \begin{bmatrix} n_A(\bar{V}) & n_B(\bar{V}) & n_c(\bar{V}) \\ n_A(\bar{T}) & n_B(\bar{T}) & n_c(\bar{T}) \end{bmatrix} \tag{4}$$

The three evaluation factors of the average travel speed of the section, the average road delay and the average travel time of the intersection correspond to the Weight A and the membership function of the three road traffic states, which can enter the fuzzy comprehensive model evaluation stage, and make fuzzy transformation, and get the fuzzy comprehensive evaluation result Vector B.

$$B = A \cdot \beta = [a_1, a_2, a_3] = [b_1, b_2, b_3] \tag{5}$$

The comprehensive evaluation set B has only three traffic conditions in which road traffic is unimpeded, mild congestion and heavy congestion. Therefore, in the result Vector $B = [b_1, b_2, b_3]$ of fuzzy comprehensive evaluation, B1 represents the importance of evaluation factors to the unimpeded state of road traffic, and the evaluation factor of B2 is corresponding to the light congestion of road traffic. The importance of B3 is that the evaluation factors correspond to the importance of road traffic congestion.

For the comprehensive evaluation set B, the maximum membership degree method can be used to determine the final result of the fuzzy comprehensive evaluation. The maximum subordinate degree principle can be obtained. If $B_T = \max[b_1, b_2, b_3]$, the corresponding subscript T is the final judgement level of the fuzzy comprehensive evaluation object. That is to say, the state grade corresponding to the maximum value in B1, B2 and B3 is taken as the final result of fuzzy comprehensive evaluation of road traffic condition.

In the road traffic state evaluation, β is essentially the fuzzy mapping relationship between the evaluation factor set and the evaluation set, so the relationship between the evaluation index parameters and the road traffic state is also the same. The relationship between them can be represented by Fuzzy Mapping β, as shown in Fig. 4.

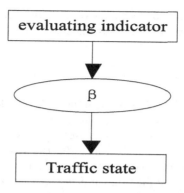

Fig. 4. The relationship between evaluation index and traffic state

6 Contrastive Experiment

In order to verify the effectiveness of the fuzzy recognition method for regional traffic congestion based on GPS, the method and the traditional traffic congestion status identification method are used to discriminate traffic congestion in the 6 analysis period of 8: 00–9: 30 in the morning of a road.

According to the steps and principles of establishing the model, the fuzzy comprehensive evaluation algorithm model is set up, and the model algorithm program is compiled with Matlab computer programming language. The parameter values of each period evaluation index are input into the program, and the corresponding membership importance will be calculated automatically. Finally, the final fuzzy synthesis is obtained according to the maximum membership degree principle. Judge the result and display the real-time traffic state in graphic form. The results of the evaluation are shown in Table 2.

Table 2. Two methods of evaluation of traffic conditions

Time interval	8:00–8:10	8:10–8:20	8:20–8:30	8:30–8:40	8:40–8:50	8:50–9:00	9:00–9:10	9:10–9:20	9:20–9:30
Real traffic condition	0	0	1	1	2	0	0	2	1
This paper method	0	0	1	1	2	0	0	2	1
traditional method	0	1	1	1	2	0	1	1	1

Note: 0 represents smooth state; 1 represents mild crowding; 2 represents severe congestion.

From Table 2, it can be seen that the traffic congestion situation based on the fuzzy recognition method based on GPS is exactly the same as the actual traffic congestion. The accuracy of traffic status recognition is 100%, and the traffic congestion and actual traffic conditions are found by the traditional traffic congestion status recognition method. The error is wrong in the judgement of 2 time periods, the accuracy is only

56%. Compared with the two, the accuracy of the former was increased by 44%. The validity of the method is proved by this method.

7   Conclusion

To sum up, a simple and practical map matching method to deal with the GPS data of a large cab floating car is adopted, and the method for determining the candidate sections is given. Finally, the map matching results are displayed on the map in the form of track segment diagram, so that the matching effect is visualized and the accuracy of matching is guaranteed from a certain level. The fuzzy comprehensive evaluation model is established. Based on the original data characteristics of the floating car and the result of map matching, the average travel speed and the average driving time delay of all vehicles in the specified analysis time are taken as the evaluation index of the road state, and the road traffic state is judged and the road traffic is completed in the evaluation period. The state discrimination is more reasonable, avoiding the deviation caused by single index discrimination. At the same time, the method also needs to be improved, because of the rate of not taking the test to the traffic congestion identification follow-up intelligent processing, and then will further optimize the intelligent processing function.

References

1. Cui, H., Yuan, C., Wei, Z.F., et al.: Traffic state recognition using static images and FCM. J. Xidian Univ. **44**(6), 79–84 (2017). Natural Science
2. Wu, Q., Cai, X., Cai, M.: Study on the weighted index of traffic state based on FCM Expressway. Sci. Technol. Eng. **17**(6), 289–295 (2017)
3. Rui, L., Zhang, Y., Huang, H., et al.: A new traffic congestion detection and quantification method based on comprehensive fuzzy assessment in VANET. KSII Trans. Internet Inf. Syst. **12**(1), 41–60 (2018)
4. Liu, C.Y., Kong, F.N., Feng, J.W.: The traffic signal acquisition system based on GPS and SD card storage. J. Harbin Univ. Sci. Technol. **3**, 25–30 (2017)
5. Wang, X.Y., Fang, L.Y., Chen, Y.F., et al.: Freeway incident detection algorithm based on video tracking and fuzzy inference. J. Data Acquis. Process. **2**, 283–286 (2016)
6. Wan, W., Wang, Z.H., Li, M.Q.: The regional network traffic evaluation based on floating car data. Sci. Technol. Eng. **17**(7), 270–274 (2017)
7. Li, G.Y., Hu, M.H., Zheng, Z.: Multi-sector traffic congestion identification method based on FCM-rough sets. J. Transp. Syst. Eng. Inf. Technol. **17**(6), 141–146 (2017)
8. Jia, H.F., Sang, H., Yang, L.L., et al.: Identification method of newly-built highway accident black spots or sections. J. Beijing Univ. Technol. **42**(8), 1233–1238 (2016)
9. Zhang, X.J., Fan, D.Y.: Edge blurred feature recognition method of oblique license plate images. Comput. Simul. **34**(01), 372–375 (2017)

Digital Video Tampered Inter-frame Multi-scale Content Similarity Detection Method

Lan Wu[✉], Xiao-qiang Wu, Chunyou Zhang, and Hong-yan Shi

College of Mechanical Engineering, Inner Mongolia University for the
Nationalities, Tongliao 028043, Inner Mongolia, China
wlimun@163.com

Abstract. With the popularity of the Internet and the increasing power of video editing software, digital video can easily be tampered with. The detection of the authenticity and integrity of digital video is very important. A video tampering detection method based on multi-scale normalized mutual information is proposed. Firstly, the mutual information is introduced into video tamper detection and the normalized mutual information content of the video frames is extracted. Then, based on the "scale invariance" feature of human vision, the mutual information between frames is analyzed from a multi-scale perspective. The multi-scale normalized mutual information is used to characterize the similarity of content between video frames. Finally, the LOF algorithm is used to calculate the degree of abnormality of the similarity coefficient sequence to achieve three kinds of tampering detection in the time domain: deletion, insertion, and replication. Experimental results show that the proposed method can effectively detect tampered video.

Keywords: Video tampering · Content continuity · Multi-scale · Content anomaly

1 Introduction

With the continuous maturity of digital multimedia technology and the increasing popularity of Internet technologies, the number of video files has increased dramatically. Video file access has become easier. The people have been able to enjoy the video feast brought by the Internet at any time. However, with the widespread using of various video editing soft wares such as Adobe photoshop and Adobe premier CSX, video files have been intentionally or unintentionally tampered with time [1, 2]. Once these tampered videos are used in official media, judicial proceedings, insurance, forensic evidence, etc., it is easy to cause misunderstandings or distort the facts of the truth and have a tremendous impact on others and the entire society. Especially at the current stage, the attention of the society to the security field has been increasing, and the authenticity and integrity of multimedia video content have also become the focus of public attention [3, 4]. Therefore, how to make scientific and reliable identification of the originality, authenticity, and integrity of digital video has become a branch of research in the field of modern multimedia information security.

© ICST Institute for Computer Sciences, Social Informatics and Telecommunications Engineering 2019
Published by Springer Nature Switzerland AG 2019. All Rights Reserved
G. Gui and L. Yun (Eds.): ADHIP 2019, LNICST 302, pp. 451–460, 2019.
https://doi.org/10.1007/978-3-030-36405-2_46

Compared with the tampering events of image and audio, the complexity of video tampering technology is relatively large. People have high recognition of the authenticity of video. Formally because of this, the video tamper is more harmful. At present, the world has made remarkable achievements in image modification and forensics research. However, digital video forensics technology is still in the preliminary research stage. There are few scientific and technological achievements that can truly detect various video materials [5]. At the present stage, most scientific research dissertations are inspired by digital image forgery and forensic detection techniques. They detect color changes by extracting color features, texture features, wavelet features, lighting features, and noise features [6–9]. In addition, due to the coding specificity of the video, extracting its GOP change characteristics or MPEG2 coding characteristics can also achieve video tamper detection.

Aiming at the problems of deletion, insertion, and replication in the time domain, a multi-scale normalized mutual information video tampering detection method is proposed. This method extracts the inter-frame mutual information amount of tampered video based on information theory, simulates the mutual information amount between video frames based on human visual multi-scale, and uses multi-scale mutual information to measure the similarity between video frames. Finally, the LOF algorithm is used to determine the degree of abnormality between tampered video frames. Experimental results show that this method can effectively detect three kinds of video tampering in time domain, such as deletion, insertion and replication.

2   Content Similarity Calculation

When humans identify an object, regardless of the object's distance, they can correctly determine the object's category. This is called "scale invariance." Therefore, by performing different scale analysis on the image, different details of the image can be obtained, thereby making the analysis of the image more accurate. Using a multi-scale normalized average mutual information model to measure the similarity between adjacent frames is closer to the perceptual characteristics of the human visual system.

2.1   Multi-scale Analysis

The spatial information of different scales of a two-dimensional image can be calculated by convolving the image with the Gaussian kernel, as follows:

$$L(x, y, \sigma) = I(x, y) \otimes G(x, y, \sigma) \tag{1}$$

where $I(x, y)$ is used to represent the gray value of the video frame image, $G(x, y, \sigma)$ is the Gaussian kernel function, and σ is the scale space factor, which is the variance of the normal distribution and reflects the degree to which the image is smoothed. Image Gaussian pyramid transform is used to build multi-scale spatial information of video frames.

After the video frame passes the Gaussian pyramid transform, the image resolution will decrease with the increase of the number of layers. According to the size of the initial video frame, the video frame is generally transformed by 3–4 layers.

$$G_k(x,y) = \sum_{m=-2}^{2} \sum_{n=-2}^{2} \bar{w}(m,n) G_{k-1}(2x+m, 2y+n) \tag{2}$$

where $1 \leq k \leq N, 0 \leq x \leq NR_k, 0 \leq y \leq NC_k$. NR_k and NC_k represent the number of rows and columns of the k-th Gaussian pyramid image, respectively. w is a 2D 5th order Gaussian window function

$$\bar{w} = \frac{1}{256} \begin{bmatrix} \begin{bmatrix} 1 & 4 & 6 & 4 & 1 \\ 4 & 16 & 24 & 16 & 4 \\ 6 & 24 & 36 & 24 & 6 \\ 4 & 16 & 24 & 16 & 4 \\ 1 & 4 & 6 & 4 & 1 \end{bmatrix} \end{bmatrix} \tag{3}$$

2.2   Video Frame Mutual Information

Mutual information was first proposed by the American scientist Shannon, the father of information. Its purpose is mainly to measure the size of another random variable contained in the information of a random variable. Based on the technology of mutual information in image processing, we apply it to video frames. For a given video segment, each frame in the segment is viewed as a time sequence $\{F_1, F_2, \cdots, F_m\}$, and each video frame F_t is a grayscale image. The amount of information provided by video frame F_t can be measured by source information.

$$H(F_t) = -\sum_{i=0}^{L-1} p(l_i(F_t)) \log_2 p(l_i(F_t)) \tag{4}$$

where $p(l_i(F_t))$ represents the probability that the source F_t sends the symbol l_i, that is, the probability that the l_i gray level appears in the frame B. Therefore, by definition, $H(F_t)$ can be calculated using the grayscale histogram of video frame F_t.

Any two adjacent frames in a video sequence form a communication system. Then, the amount of information provided when two adjacent frames appear at the same time can be measured by the unity of the information theory.

$$H(F_t, F_{t+1}) = -\sum_{i=0}^{L-1} \sum_{j=0}^{L-1} p(l_i(F_t), l_i(F_{t+1})) \log_2 p(l_i(F_t), l_i(F_{t+1}))) \tag{5}$$

For the communication system with F_t as the source and F_{t+1} as the sink, the average amount of information the sink receives from the source can be measured by the average mutual information.

$$MI(F_t, F_{t+1}) = H(F_t) + H(F_{t+1}) - H(F_t, F_{t+1}) \tag{6}$$

The value of $MI(F_t, F_{t+1})$ can measure the visual content similarity between adjacent video frames $H(F_t)$ and $H(F_{t+1})$. It is called the single-scale content similarity operator.

2.3   Multi-scale Normalized Mutual Information

We combine the two methods of mutual information and multi-scale analysis between images, and introduce multi-scale normalized mutual information to measure visual content similarity between video frames. First, multi-scale analysis is performed on adjacent video frames to obtain Gaussian pyramid images for each layer. Then, the normalized average mutual information is calculated at each layer. Finally, the weighted sum of the normalized mutual information for each layer is normalized, and the result is a multi-scale normalized mutual information amount.

The formula for multi-scale normalized mutual information of adjacent video frames is as follows

$$\rho(t) = \sum_{k=0}^{n} w_k \cdot \frac{H(F_t(k)) + H(F_{t+1}(k))}{2H(F_t(k), F_{t+1}(k))} \tag{7}$$

where w_k represents the weight, $H(F_t(k))$ denotes the k-th layer Gaussian pyramid image in the t-th frame, $H(F_t(k), F_{t+1}(k))$ is the joint entropy of the kth Gaussian pyramid image between the t-th and $t + 1$-th video frames.

In this thesis, for a given video segment, it can be converted into a visual content similarity sequence $\{\rho(1), \rho(2), \cdots, \rho(M-1)\}$ by mutual information operator. The data sequence is one-dimensional data that describes the similarity of the content of the image sequence within the video segment.

2.4   Content Similarity Abnormality Measure

The degree of outliers of a data is not only related to its own data, but also related to the degree of outliers of the surrounding data. Therefore, the relative value of the average local density in the data point domain is used to describe the degree of data anomaly. For data point $\rho(i)$, the degree of abnormality is specifically defined as

$$L_{of}(i) = \frac{\bar{l}_{rd}(j)}{l_{rd}(j)} \tag{8}$$

where $\bar{l}_{rd}(j)$ represents the average of all points in the decentralized neighborhood with $\rho(i)$ as the center and $D_k(i)$ as the radius. $L_{of}(i)$ is called the abnormality of data B.

The value of the degree of abnormality $L_{of}(i)$ of data $\rho(i)$ measures the degree of anomaly of the data object $\rho(i)$ relative to the surrounding data points. The larger the value of C, the higher the degree of abnormality is. This shows that the visual content of the i-th frame differs greatly from the visual content of the video frames before and after it. Once the variability exceeds a pre-set threshold, it is reasonable to consider the data location as a tampered or stopped position of the video frame.

3 Algorithm Design and Implementation

Although the video encoding formats are different, they all have a high-speed frame rate, generally higher than 24 frames/second. Therefore, there is a high degree of similarity in visual content between video frame sequences. This paper measures the similarity between two adjacent frames by constructing multi-scale normalized mutual information descriptors between adjacent frames. The degree of abnormality of the similarity data sequence is established by means of the LOF algorithm. Once the video has been tampered with, the value of the sequence of the degree of similarity of the similarity sequence will change significantly. By setting a reasonable exposition to detect a relatively large coefficient of abnormality, the location of the video that has been tampered with is determined.

The basic steps of video tamper detection designed in this paper are described in detail as follows.

(1) Read the video segment to be detected, separate the video frames, audio and other elements in the video segment to be detected, and obtain the frame sequence.
(2) RGB color video frames are converted to grayscale frames.
(3) Calculate the Gaussian pyramid transform for each frame of image.
(4) Calculate the histogram of the Gauss pyramid image at each level and the joint histogram of adjacent frames.
(5) Calculate the multi-scale normalized mutual information operator of the t-th frame.
(6) Calculate the degree of abnormality sequence $\{L_{of}(1), L_{of}(2), \cdots, L_{of}(M-1)\}$ of the similarity sequence.
(7) Set the detection threshold β. For the i-th degree of abnormality $L_{of}(i)$, if $L_{of}(i) > \beta$, it is determined that the degree of similarity can be an outlier data point, thereby determining that the i-th frame is the starting point of the tampering position. Otherwise, it is considered that the i-th frame is not the starting point of the tampered position.

According to the basic steps of the algorithm, the three types of tamper detection flowcharts for deleting, inserting, and copying in the time domain are shown in Fig. 1.

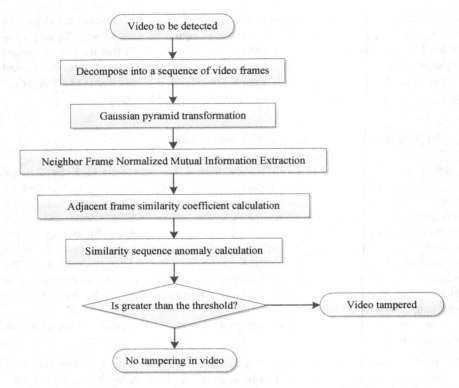

Fig. 1. Multi-scale normalized mutual information tamper detection process

4 Experimental Results and Analysis

4.1 Experimental Data

The existing video tamper detection technology does not have a unified video library. Various detection algorithms use self-captured video or some network resources for experimentation. Therefore, this article uses self-built test database. The video library downloads eight YUV format video clips from the literature [10]. The relevant parameters of the video are shown in Table 1.

Video library original video clips Video tamper is mainly to use some video editing software to modify the video content, time stamp, encoding format, etc., resulting in the destruction of the original video's authenticity and integrity. This paper mainly detects the time domain tampering in the video tampering method, including inter-frame deletion, frame replacement, and frame insertion.

Table 1. Video library original video clips

Video number	Name	Number of frames	Resolution
Video-1	hall_cif_yuv	300	352 × 288
Video-2	coastguard_cif_yuv	300	352 × 288
Video-3	coastguard_cif_yuv	300	352 × 288
Video-4	silent_cif_yuv	350	352 × 288
Video-5	pans_cif_yuv	150	352 × 288
Video-6	bus_cif_yuv	200	352 × 288
Video-7	flower_cif_yuv	300	352 × 288
Video-8	mobile_cif_vuv	300	352 × 288

4.2 Tamper Detection Results

The computer configuration used in the experiment was Intel 2.2 GHz CPU, 4G RAM, 750G hard disk, and Microsoft Windows 7 64 bit operating system.

For tampering with the clip Video-1 in the video library, the clip is obtained by deleting 80 to 123 video frames of Video-1. The calculated anomaly curve is shown in Fig. 2.

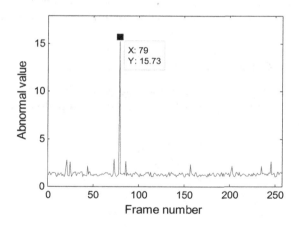

Fig. 2. The abnormal curve of the tampered video clip Video-1

It can be seen from Fig. 2 that the abnormal value of most frames is less than 3, while the abnormal value of the 79th frame far exceeds the abnormal values of other frames. Therefore, it can be considered that there is a tampering between the 79th and 80th frames. This position is consistent with the deletion of the 80th to 123th frames of the original video. Therefore, the 79th position detected by the algorithm is correct.

For tampering with the video-3 in the video library, the clip is formed by inserting a copy of the video frames 210 to 230 of Video-3 into frames 149 and 150. The calculated anomaly curve is shown in Fig. 3.

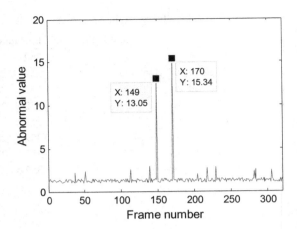

Fig. 3. The abnormal curve of the tampered video clip Video-3

It can be seen from Fig. 3 that there are two locations where the outlier exceeds the threshold 10, that is, 149 and 170, and the outliers at other locations do not exceed 3. This shows that there is a big difference in the visual content between the 149th and the 150th frames, and there is also a big difference in the visual content between the 170th and the 171th frames. Experimental results confirm that abnormality detection is correct.

4.3 Performance Comparison

In order to evaluate the performance of the algorithm, this paper uses the traditional detection accuracy rate R_p and the detection rate R_r. Two performance indicators are defined as follows

$$R_p = \frac{N_C}{N_C + N_F} \tag{9}$$

$$R_r = \frac{N_C}{N_C + N_M} \tag{10}$$

where N_C indicates the number of detected abnormal points, N_F indicates the number of abnormal points detected by mistake, and N_M indicates the number of abnormal points that are missed. In theory, the larger the R_p and R_r values corresponding to the tamper detection method, the better the detection performance is. Through statistics and calculations, the indicator values shown in Table 2 are obtained.

Table 2. Video tamper detection performance comparison

	Correct	Lost	Misdetection	R_p	R_r
Proposed method	28	1	2	90.32%	93.33%
Nonnegative tensor method [11]	19	7	5	73.07%	69.16%

The data in Table 2 shows that the tamper detection accuracy and detection overall rate using the method proposed in this paper are significantly higher than the Non-negative tensor method. The detection accuracy of this method is 90.32%, which is 17.25% higher than the Nonnegative tensor method. In terms of overall detection rate, this article reached 93.33%, an increase of 24.17% over the Nonnegative tensor method. Statistical indicators show that the proposed algorithm has better detection performance for video tampering.

5 Conclusion

This paper studies the detection of frame deletion, frame replacement and frame insertion in digital video. A digital video tamper detection method based on multi-scale content similarity between frames is proposed. This method can analyze the mutual information between adjacent frames in multiple scales from the perspective of human visual effects perception, and implement video tamper detection through multi-scale normalized mutual information and LOF algorithm. The experimental results verify the validity of the detection method. This method provides a new idea for digital video tamper detection.

Acknowledgements. Inner Mongolia National University Research Project (NMDYB1729).

References

1. Amanipour, V., Ghaemmaghami, S.: Video-tampering detection and content reconstruction via self-embedding. IEEE Trans. Instrum. Meas. **99**, 1–11 (2017)
2. Hu, W.C., Chen, W.H., Huang, D.Y., et al.: Effective image forgery detection of tampered foreground or background image based on image watermarking and alpha mattes. Multimed. Tools Appl. **75**(6), 3495–3516 (2016)
3. Wu, M.L., Fahn, C.S., Chen, Y.F.: Image-format-independent tampered image detection based on overlapping concurrent directional patterns and neural networks. Appl. Intell. **47**(2), 347–361 (2017)
4. Lin, J., Huang, T., Lai, Y., et al.: Detection of continuously and repeated copy-move forgery to single frame in videos by quantized DCT coefficients. J. Comput. Appl. (2016)
5. Fallahpour, M., Shirmohammadi, S., Semsarzadeh, M., et al.: Tampering detection in compressed digital video using watermarking. IEEE Trans. Instrum. Meas. **63**(5), 1057–1072 (2014)
6. Tang, Z., Wang, S., Zhang, X., et al.: Structural feature-based image hashing and similarity metric for tampering detection. Fundamenta Informaticae **106**(1), 75–91 (2011)
7. Huang, D.Y., Chen, C.H., Chen, T.Y., et al.: Rapid detection of camera tampering and abnormal disturbance for video surveillance system. J. Vis. Commun. Image Represent. **25**(8), 1865–1877 (2014)
8. Sitara, K., Mehtre, B.M.: Digital video tampering detection: An overview of passive techniques. Digit. Invest. **18**(8), 8–22 (2016)

9. Aghamaleki, J.A., Behrad, A.: Malicious inter-frame video tampering detection in MPEG videos using time and spatial domain analysis of quantization effects. Multimed. Tools Appl. **76**(20), 1–27 (2016)
10. http://trace.eas.ast.edu/yuv/index.html/.2013,7
11. Zhang, X., Huang, T., Lin, J., et al.: Video tamper detection method based on nonnegative tensor factorization. Chin. J. Netw. Inf. Secur. **3**(6), 1–8 (2017)

Design and Implementation of the Cross-Harmonic Recommender System Based on Spark

Huang Jie[1]($\boxtimes$), Liu ChangSheng[1,2], and Liu ChengLi[3]

[1] Department of Aviation Electronic Equipment Maintenance, Airforce Aviation Repair Institute of Technology, Changsha 410014, Hunan, China
huangjie918@126.com
[2] Hunan Key Laboratory of Intelligent Information Perception and Processing Technology, Zhuzhou 412007, Hunan, China
[3] School of Engineering, Computer and Aviation, University of León, 24071 León, Spain

Abstract. With the rapid development of information technology, information overload has become an important challenge of Internet. In order to alleviate the growing contradiction between users and massive data, the researchers proposed the concept of the cross-harmonic recommender system. By analyzing characteristic of datasets, recommendation algorithms and method for weight calculation, we introduced a fast and general engine for large-scale data processing and implemented the cross-harmonic recommender system based on Spark, aiming at improving accuracy, diversity and efficiency of the recommender system.

Keywords: Spark · Hybrid recommendation · Recommendation algorithm

1 Introduction

With the rapid development of information technology, the number of network users and data has increased sharply. It also brings the contradiction between the Internet users and the datas: How can users find useful information in the mass of data, on the other hand, how the Internet can meet the needs of personalized users.

The recommender system can alleviate the contradiction between some data and users [1]. However, the results of a single recommendation algorithm are greatly influenced by the sparsity of the preferred data. But it is still not effective in bridging the gap between them. The emerging hybrid recommendation system combines two or more recommendation algorithms to achieve better recommendation effect [2]. Therefore, it is urgent to design a high precision, high efficiency, diversity and extensibility cross-harmonic recommendation system.

Fund Source: Hunan education department scientific research project (No. 17C0009). Huang Jie, Associate professor/Master, main research fields: Information education in higher vocational, Computer applications (Cloud and Big data), etc. Liu Changsheng, professor/Doctor, main research fields: Computer Application, etc.

G. Gui and L. Yun (Eds.): ADHIP 2019, LNICST 302, pp. 461–474, 2019.
https://doi.org/10.1007/978-3-030-36405-2_47

2   The Technology of the Hybrid Recommendation System

2.1   The Concept of the Recommender System

There are two ways for users to get information, the active and passive ways. The typical active mode is the search engine classification directory; A typical model for a passive approach is the recommendation system [3].

Figure 1 shows that the basic principles of the recommender system, it mainly includes: data modules, algorithm modules and recommendation modules.

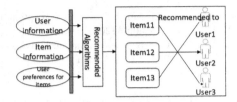

Fig. 1. Schematic diagram of the recommender system

The data modules are the basis of the recommender system. It can store users' basic information, such as items' preferences and other information; The algorithm modules use the recommendation algorithm to predict the preferences of unknown things; And the recommended modules recommend items for users with the recommended algorithm.

Hybrid recommendation algorithm is a new concept to improve the precision of various recommendation algorithms in order to meet various application requirements. The below Fig. 2 shows that the framework of the entire recommender system. Hybrid recommendation systems can be classified from the perspective of data source, algorithms and technologies:

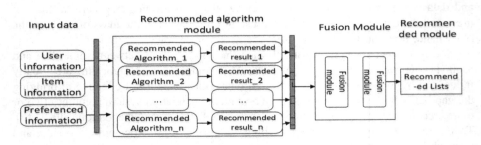

Fig. 2. Recommended system block diagram

(1) Mixed recommendation framework with multiple segments: it consists of three modules: offline modules, approximately online modules and online ones. Each module can meet the different needs of different users for response time, and the users select the recommendation result from the corresponding module as required.

(2) Hierarchical mixed recommendation system: The recommendation algorithm is divided by different precision, selecting high precision algorithms adapt to different application scenarios to select high precision algorithms. This recommender system uses a more sophisticated hybrid technology combining several indicators.

(3) Weighted mixed recommendation system: The recommendation algorithm is used to predict the score, the weighted value of each algorithm's prediction score is calculated by using the weight of the algorithm.

(4) Cross-harmonic recommender system: The system is to mix the results of various recommendation algorithms in proportion to generate mixed recommendation results, which have both diversity and better interpretability.

2.2   Recommended Algorithm

There are three recommended algorithms: content-based recommendation algorithm, collaborative filtering recommendation algorithm and model-based recommendation algorithm.

(1) Collaborative Filtering, CF: This algorithm was originally used to process message filtering in mail [4], and now it is widely used in e-commerce system. Collaborative filtering algorithm is mainly based on the idea of object clustering, that is, object - like clustering. For example, if u and v have the same interest in goods, they think that u and v are similar users. The algorithm execution process is shown in Fig. 3 below.

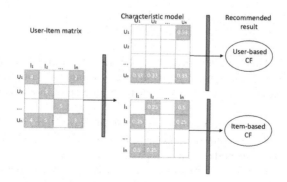

Fig. 3. Collaborative filtering algorithm process

(2) Content-based recommendation algorithm, CB, it is a commonly used algorithm in recommendation system. It mainly uses the similarity of the configuration file to recommend the items to the user [5].

(3) Model-based recommendation algorithm, MB, this algorithm trains the user implicit feature model and the object implicit feature model by using the scoring matrix, and predict unknown data with the two models.

2.3 Spark Technology

Spark is an ecosystem that provides solutions such as flow operation, iteration operation and graph calculation, as the Fig. 4 shown below.

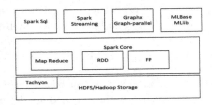

Fig. 4. Spark ecosystem diagram

Spark SQL: It conduct the big data query analysis [6]. By the SQL expression processing data query on Spark. To improve the query efficiency user-defined functions can also be called to combine query results with analysis results.

Sparking Streaming: It is a flow processing system, also can operate real-time data on mapping, reducing and joining. And the result are saved to the external file system [7].

GraphX: It is the graph operation API on Spark, it provides the concept and operation of elastic distributed attribute graph, and implement graph operation by the framework [8].

MLBase/Mllib: This component provides common machine learning algorithms and utilities, includes classification, regression, clustering and bottom optimization.

Tachyon: It is a distributed system with high efficiency, high fault tolerance and high reliability.

Spark: It is the core computing framework of the ecosystem, which can run either alone or on a cluster [9]. Cluster operation requires the help of the management system to distribute tasks to each node to run.

In short, the Spark system is based on RDD, it is a large data platform for parallel computing of memory computing with Spark framework as the core.

Different products in the system can be used to meet the computing needs of different systems.

3 Cross-Harmonic Recommender System Framework Based on Spark

There are four modules in the cross-harmonic recommender system based on Spark [10]. It includes the storage modules, Algorithm modules, Recommended modules [11] (Fig. 5).

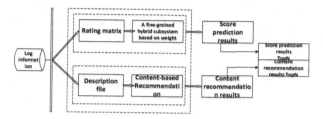

Fig. 5. The frame diagram of cross-harmonic and recommendation system based on Spark

(1) Storage modules: This module collects and cleanses the log data and stores it in distributed storage.

(2) A fine-grained hybrid subsystem module based on weight: The system module builds a user-item scoring matrix [12], it contains user-CF, item-CF and LFM. Using Fine-grained Weight Calculation Method to Calculate the weight vector of each recommendation algorithm [13], and make predictive recommendations for unknown score data.

(3) Algorithm modules: This module is to implement the distributed recommendation algorithm based on content. First, Creating feature properties files for users and items, then making predictions about user preferences. The formatting data file as the input of the recommendation algorithm module, Training feature model of recommendation algorithm is used for processing. Finally, the preference prediction based on the feature model is realized.

(4) Recommended modules: This module is the recommendation system to provide users with the recommendation list information. The results of each recommendation algorithm are combined with cross-harmonic technology to generate a personalized recommendation result for users.

4 Design of the Cross-Harmonic Recommendation System Module

4.1 Design of Data Storage Module

User preference data is the basis of recommendation system. The recommendation algorithm finds valuable information from the preference data to know about the characteristics of each use. Therefore, data storage module is the basic of Spark-based cross-harmonic recommendation system. The main function of data storage module is to collect log data to extract data features and store data:

(1) Collecting datas: The data storage module mainly collects two types of log data. The first is the common user behavior log, which can be converted into a scoring matrix; The second type is the description file of user items, which contains the description information of user items and is often converted into the feature vector of user items.

(2) Extracting feature data: After the log file is collected, the data storage module cleans the outliers and null values of the missing values, and the data is converted to a specific data structure as the input to other modules.

(3) Data structure: After extracting the data features, the grading data format is converted to userFactor, itemFactor, Event, Rank and Time. The user and the object are identified by the user and object feature vectors respectively. Its data structure is like the below table (Table 1).

Table 1. Grading data structure

userFactor	itemFactor	Event	Rank	Time
<uf1, uf2, ..., ufp>	<if1, if2, ..., ifr>	4	4	978300760
<uf2, uf4, ..., ufq>	<if3, if5, ..., ifs>	6	1	978301260
<uf3, uf8, ..., ufo>	<if6, if9, ..., ift>	5	5	978302240

(4) Data storage: The data storage module stores the collected logs and formatted data in a distributed file system to ensure the reliability of data storage. Common distributed file systems include HDFS and Tachyon.

4.2   Fine-Grained Weight Hybrid Subsystem

The fine-grained weight hybrid subsystem is an important part of the cross-harmonic re-commendation system. The input data of this subsystem is user-item rating data. After the calculation of the weight hybrid subsystem, the mixed prediction score of user-item is output to complete the process of rating prediction.

4.3   Design of the Recommended Modules

Recommendation module is the module that the system interacts with users. The main function of this module is to generate personalized recommendation list for users. The recommendation module of the cross-harmonization recommendation system based on Spark adopts the recommendation method of cross-harmonization to generate personalized recommendation list for users. The cross-harmonic recommendation means that the system performs multiple recommendation algorithms, each of them compute a list of recommendation. Finally, the system selects a part of the result combination from each recommendation list and generates the recommendation list displayed by users.

5 Distributed Recommendation Algorithm

Recommendation algorithm is the basis of the system to predict user preference, and also the core content of the recommendation system, which directly affects the performance of the system. The cross-harmonic recommendation system based on Spark introduces content-based recommendation algorithm to improve the diversity of recommendation results and alleviate the problem of data sparseness.

5.1 Content Recommendation Algorithm Implementation Based on Spark

Content-based recommendation algorithm (CB) is one of the first recommendation algorithms to be applied in practice. This algorithm is good at information retrieval and other fields because of its simple idea and strong interpretability of recommendation results. The basic idea of CB algorithm is to recommend similar items to users according to their favorite items.

The recommendation algorithm flow based on content is shown in the Fig. 6, According to the flow chart, the algorithm consists of three steps:

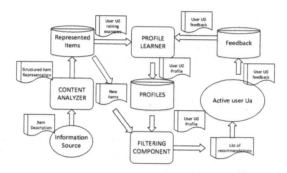

Fig. 6. Content recommendation algorithm processing based on Spark

(1) Character description: The content-based recommendation algorithm first extracts multiple keywords corresponding to users or items according to their description files, and these key words are used to form the feature vector of user items.

(2) Training preference model: This algorithm trains the user's preference model and generates the user preference configuration file according to the product feature vector that users like. Or training the feature model of the item according to the user feature vector of the item you like.

(3) Generating recommendation list: The content-based recommendation algorithm recommends the most relevant items to users by comparing the similarity between the user preference profile and the item feature vector; Or compare the user feature vector with the item feature profile and recommend the item to the relevant use. According to different recommendation objects, CB algorithm is divided into user-CB and item-CB.

5.2   User Recommendation Algorithm Implementation Based on Spark

User-CB algorithm trains the preferences configuration file according to the user fea-ture vector. By comparing the correlation between other user feature vectors and the preferences profile of the item, this algorithm recommends the item to the most relevant multiple users. Therefore, the user-CB is implemented based on spark as the Fig. 7 shows, which contains three steps:

```
User_CB Algorithm Pseudo-code for distributed implementations
based on Spark
01:Input :the description file of user and item
02:Output:the similarity between user and item profile
03:
04:user_factor=readMatrix.Split( '' )
05:for user in user_factor:
06: for item in description file:
07:    if user like item:
08:       map{case(f1,f2,···,fn)=>item_profile}
09:    end if
10: end for
11:end for
12:
13: calculate similarity between user factor and item
profile
14:
15:  for user in similarity:
16:     for item in similarity[u]:
17:        recommend item to other users
18:     end for
19:  end for
```

Fig. 7. User_CB Algorithm Pseudo-code

(1) Constructing the eigenvector: It is similar to the rating prediction recommendation algorithm to construct the user-item rating matrix, the recommendation algorithm based on user content first constructs the user's feature vector according to the description file, as the data base of system training. Content-based recommen-dation algorithms usually extract several keywords from a series of description files to constitute the user's eigenvector. So the format of the eigenvector is (userFactor_1, userFactor_2, ..., userFactor_n), each userFactor means a char-acteristic keyword. User_CB this algorithm uses the textFile interface to read the user feature Vector file from the distributed file system and stores each user feature Vector in Vector format. By specifying that the parameter of the persist interface is MEMORY_AND_DISK, the user feature vector is stored in memory and disk to complete the construction of the feature vector;

(2) Training preference model: According to the user feature vector of the favorite item, the user_CB algorithm trains the preference configuration file of the item. First, use the filter operation to match users who like the item and get a collection of users. Then, the user's feature vector is mapped to the item preference vector by the map operation. Finally, the same characteristics are merged by the redu-ceByKey operation to obtain the preferences profile;

(3) Recommendation list: The user_CB algorithm compares the correlation between user feature vector and item preference configuration, which recommends items to relevant users. The algorithm uses the look-operation to find the matching features. The more matches there are, the more relevant they are.

5.3 Item Recommendation Algorithm Implementation Based on Spark

Item_CB algorithm is similar to the idea of user-CB. According to the product feature vector training user preference configuration file, compare the relationship between the user profile and the product feature vector, and recommend related items for the user. Therefore, the item-CB is implemented based on spark as the Fig. 8 shows, which contains three steps:

```
Item_CB Algorithm Pseudo-code for distributed implementations based on
                                  Spark
01:Input :the description file of user and item
02:Output:the similarity between user and item profile
03:
04:item_factor=readMatrix.Split(  ''  ).Map
05:for item in item_factor:
06:  for user in description file:
07:     if user like item:
08:           map{case(f1,f2,···,fn)=>user_profile}
09:     end if
10:  end for
11:end for
12:
13: calculate similarity between user factor and item profile
```

Fig. 8. Item_CB algorithm Pseudo-code

(1) Constructing the eigenvector;
(2) Training preference model;
(3) Recommendation list.

6 Analysis of Experimental Results

6.1 Content-Based Recommendation Algorithm Efficiency Test

As the cross-harmonic system implements the distributed recommendation algorithm based on content, which ensures the diversity of data types. Therefore, this experiment tests the efficiency of distributed content-based recommendation algorithm. The experimental process is as follows:

(1) Data Sets: The experiment USES movie-tags data set to compose test data of different scales, with data scale ranging from 100K to 1M. Each data set is divided into a training set and a test set.

(2) Recommendation Algorithm: The content - based recommendation algorithm is adopted in this experiment.

(3) Experiment parameter: N = 30, That is, the recommendation results are sorted according to the item correlation, and the first 30 items are selected to generate the recommendation list.

(4) Evaluation index: The execution time of distributed content-based recommendation algorithm

In this experiment, the article profile is constructed by using CB algorithm, the correlation between the user profile and the article profile is calculated, and the recommendation list is generated. The experimental results are shown in the Fig. 9.

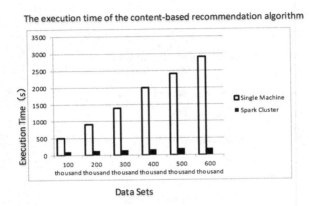

Fig. 9. Execution time of the content-based recommendation algorithm

(1) At the same data scale, the execution time of distributed content-based recommendation algorithm is better than that of single machine algorithm.

(2) The execution time of distributed content-based recommendation algorithm increases slightly with the increase of data scale, but it is always better than single-machine algorithm.

(3) The execution time of distributed content-based recommendation algorithm is less affected by data size. That is, compared with single-machine algorithm, distributed content-based recommendation algorithm is not sensitive to changes in data scale.

The introduction of CB algorithm cross-harmonic recommendation system based on Spark enables the system to handle more diverse data types, such as rating data with label information. And this algorithm has good execution efficiency.

6.2   Efficiency Test of the System

The cross-harmonic system based on Spark include fine-grained weight hybrid sub-systems and distributed content-based recommendation algorithms, Therefore, the execution time experiment process of this experiment test based on Spark cross - harmonic system is as follows:

(1) Data sets: The experiment uses movie-tags data set to compose test data of different scales, with data scale ranging from 100K to 1M. Each data set is divided into a training set and a test set;

(2) Recommendation algorithm: user collaborative filtering, Latent factor model, Content-based Recommendation.

(3) Experiment parameter: N = 30, That is, the recommendation results are sorted according to the item correlation, and the first 30 items are selected to generate the recommendation list.

(4) Evaluation indicator: system execution time.

In this experiment system, the user collaborative filtering cryptography model and the combination of user collaborative filtering and cryptic model and the recommendation algorithm based on content are implemented to test system execution time. The experimental results are shown in Fig. 10.

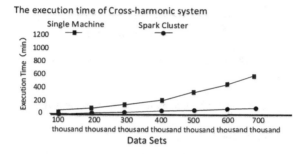

Fig. 10. The execution time of Cross-harmonic system

(1) At the same data scale, the execution time of distributed system is always better than that of single machine system. With the increase of data scale, the execution time of distributed system increases slightly, while the execution time of single machine system increases significantly. Therefore, Distributed systems are not sensitive to changes in data size.

(2) After implementing distributed content-based recommendation algorithm, the system efficiency is stable. The effectiveness of the algorithm is verified.

(3) The largest scale of single-machine system is 900,000 pieces of data, while distributed system can effectively process larger scale data and has stronger practical application value.

Scalability test of the system

In this section, by changing the number of nodes in the cluster, the scalability test scheme of hybrid recommendation system based on Spark. The steps are as follows:

(1) Data sets: MovieLens-100K, MovieLens-1M and BookCrossin. To meet the computing capacity of different Numbers of nodes, 100,000 scoring data were randomly selected from BookCrossing to form a BookCrossing-100K subset.
(2) Recommendation Algorithm: user-CF and item-CF.
(3) Evaluation index: the running time of the system is in minutes (min).

In this experiment, by changing the number of nodes in the cluster, the test system specifies the running time of the system on different scale clusters when the user-cf algorithm and item-cf algorithm are specified. The experimental results are shown in Figs. 11 and 12.

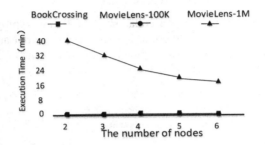

Fig. 11. The scalability of distributed user_CF algorithms

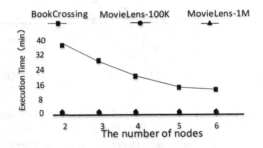

Fig. 12. The scalability of distributed item_CF algorithms

The experimental results show that:

(1) As the number of cluster nodes increases, the training time of both user-CF and item-CF algorithm in the system decreases.
(2) The larger the size of the data set, the faster the training time of the proposed algorithm decreases with the increase of the number of nodes. For example. When training movielens-im data, its training time decreases with the increase of the number of nodes.
(3) When the number of nodes increases to more than 6, the decrease speed of the training time of the proposed algorithm slows down. This is because the

communication cost between nodes will increase with the increase of the number of nodes, so the number of nodes in the cluster is not the more the better, it needs to take into account multiple factors such as the complexity of data size algorithm.

6.3   Spark SQL Performance Test

This article stores the recommendation results in memory as an RDD table, and users query the recommendation results interactively with Spark SQL. Therefore, this section tests the data query performance of Spark SQL and compares it with the performance of MySQL data query. The experimental process is:

(1) Data sets: Recommended list of size 100K, 1M and 10M;
(2) Evaluation indicators: Data query time in milliseconds (ms).

First, the movieLens-10M data set's recommended list of 72,000 users is copied to 0.12 million, 1.2 million and 12 million. Then, the three recommendation lists were randomly divided into six, in each experiment, 5 copies of the user recommendation list with a scale of 0.1, 1, 10 million were selected. Repeat the experiment 5 times and take the average. Spark SQL and MySQL Query the recommended list of 100 users separately to test the time to get the query results. Experimental results are shown in the Fig. 13 below:

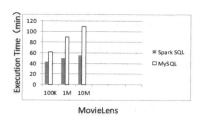

Fig. 13. Data query time of Spark SQL and MySQL

(1) Spark SQL Query the RDD table in memory, and MySQL uses SQL statements to get the results after writing the query results to the database. Therefore, the data query time of Spark SQL is shorter than that of MySQL.
(2) Because the Spark SQL data query engine assigns query tasks to multiple nodes to execute in parallel, Therefore, as the data size increases, MySQL query time increases significantly, while SparkSQL query time increases slowly.

In this section, a series of experiments are conducted to test the accuracy efficiency and scalability of the hybrid recommendation system based on Spark, and the performance bottleneck of the system and the cause of the bottleneck are further analyzed according to the experimental results. The final experimental results show that the hybrid recommendation system based on Spark has good performance in terms of precision efficiency and scalability.

7 Conclusion

Based on Spark, a distributed data processing platform, the hybrid recommendation system with high precision, high efficiency, diversity and extensibility is designed and implemented in this paper, which improves the accuracy and diversity of the recommendation results and reduces the training time of the model.

References

1. Shvachko, K., Kuang, H., Radia, S., et al.: The hadoop distributed file system. In: 2014 IEEE 26th Symposium on IEEE Mass Storage Systems and Technologies (MSST), pp. 1–20 (2014)
2. Zaharia, M., Das, T., Li, H., et al.: Discretized streams: an efficient and fault-tolerant model for stream processing on large cluster. HotCloud 12, 34–56 (2015)
3. Meng, X., Bradley, J., Yavuz, B., et al.: Mllib: machine learning in apache spark. J. Mach. Learn. Res. 12(34), 23–34 (2017)
4. Wang, Z., Sun, L., Zhu, W., et al.: Joint social and content recommendation for user-generated videos in online social network. IEEE Trans. Multimed. 15(3), 698–709 (2017)
5. Koren, Y.: The bellkor solution to the netfix grand prize. Netflix Prize Doc. 34, 32–45 (2016)
6. Zaharia, M., Chowdbury, M., Franklin, M.J., et al.: Spark: cluster computing with working sets. HotCloud 10(11), 80–98 (2015)
7. Li, H., Ghodsi, A., Zaharia, M., et al.: Tachyon: reliable, memory speed storage for cluster computing frameworks. In: Proceedings of the ACM Symposium on Cloud Computing, pp. 13–25. ACM (2016)
8. Engle, C., Lupher, A., Xin, R., et al.: Shark: first data analysis using coarse-grained distributed memory. In: Proceeding of the 2012 ACM SIGMOD International Conference on Management of Data (2012)
9. Armbrust, M., Xin, R.S., Lian, C., et al.: Spark SQL: relational data processing in spark. In: Proceedings of the 2015 ACM SIGMOD International Conference on Management of Data, pp. 1383–1394. ACM (2015)
10. Deshpande, M., Karypis, G.: Item-based top-N recommendation algorithms. ACM Trans. Inf. Syst. 22(1), 143–177 (2014)
11. Yang, R., Hu, W., Qu, Y.: Using semantic technology to improve recommender systems based on slope one. In: Li, J., Qi, G., Zhao, D., Nejdl, W., Zheng, H.T. (eds.) Semantic Web and Web Science, pp. 11–23. Springer, New York (2013). https://doi.org/10.1007/978-1-4614-6880-6_2
12. Takács, G., Pilászy, I., Németh, B., Tikk, D.: Major components of the gravity recommendation system. ACM SIGKDD Explor. Newsl. 9(2), 80–83 (2014)
13. Nightingale, E.B., Chen, P.M., Flinn, J.: Speculative execution in a distributed file system. ACM (2010)

Author Index

Printed in the United States
By Bookmasters